50 GREAT FAMILY VACATIONS

Eastern North America

50 GREAT FAMILY VACATIONS

Eastern North America

Candyce H. Stapen

A Voyager Book

The Globe Pequot Press

Old Saybrook, Connecticut

Library of Congress Cataloging-in-Publication Data
Stapen, Candyce H.
   50 great family vacations : Eastern North America / Candyce H. Stapen. — 1st ed.
      p.   cm.
   "A Voyager Book."
   Includes index.
   ISBN 1-56440-169-3
   1. East (U.S.)—Tours. 2. Canada, Eastern—Tours. I. Title. II. Title: 50 great family vacations.
E158.S775 1993   93-24255
973—dc20   CIP

Manufactured in the United States of America
First Edition/First Printing

To my favorite traveling companions
Alissa, Matt, and David

CONTENTS

MIDWEST

CANADA

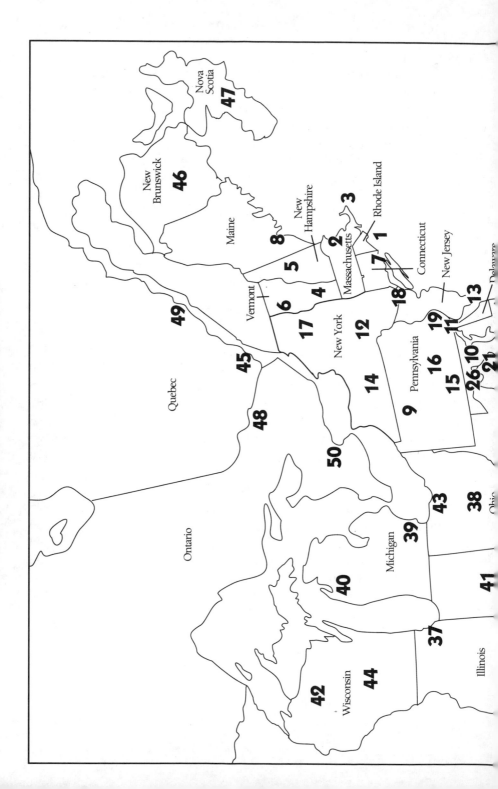

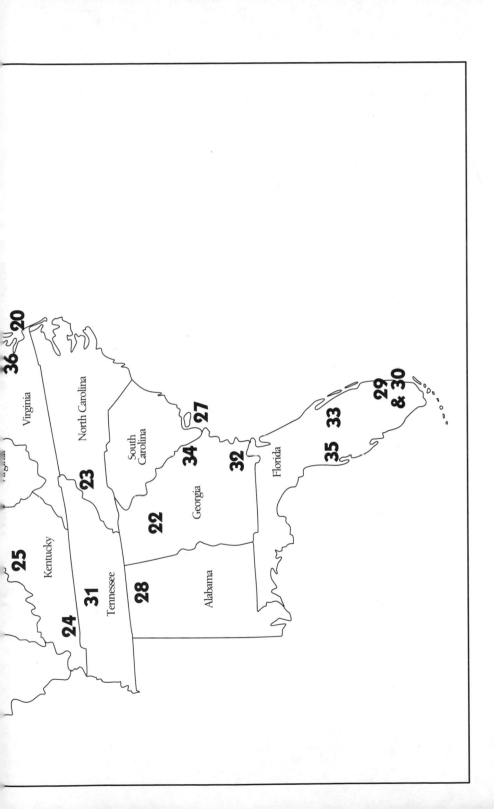

Virginia

Kentucky

Tennessee

North Carolina

South Carolina

Georgia

Alabama

Florida

25

24

31

28

22

23

36 20

27

34

32

35

33

29
& 30

ACKNOWLEDGMENTS

I want to thank my editors, Mace Lewis and Mike Urban, for their patience and assistance and my agent Carol Mann for her support. Special thanks goes to Carol Eannarino, whose fine writing contributed much to this book, and to my editorial assistants, Neil Weston, Ann LaVigne, and Kerry Sheridan, who worked diligently to help me with the research and drafts. As a family travel writer, I want to acknowledge Dorothy Jordon, of Travel With Your Children, New York City, New York, for her pioneering leadership in the field.

INTRODUCTION

There is a Chinese proverb that says the wise parent gives a child roots and wings. By traveling with your children you can bestow many gifts upon them: a strong sense of family bonds, memories that last a lifetime, and a joyful vision of the world.

Traveling with your children offers many bonuses for you and your family. These days no parent or child has an excessive amount of free time. Whether you work in the home or outside of it, your days are filled with meetings, deadlines, household errands, and carpool commitments. Your child most likely keeps equally busy with scouts, soccer, music lessons, computer clinics, basketball, and/or ballet. When your family stays home, your time together is likely to be limited to sharing quick dinners and overseeing homework. If there's a teen in your house, an age known for endless hours spent with friends, your encounters often shrink to swapping phone messages and car keys.

But take your child on the road with you, and both of you have plenty of time to talk and be together. Traveling together gives your family the luxury of becoming as expansive as the scenery. Over donuts in an airport lounge or dinner in a new hotel, you suddenly hear about that special science project or how it really felt to come in third in the swim meet. By sharing a drive along a country road or a visit to a city museum, your children get the space to view you as a person and not just as a parent.

Additionally, both you and your kids gain new perspectives on life. Children who spend time in a different locale, whether it's a national forest or a city new to them, expand their awareness. For you as a parent, traveling with your kids brings the added bonus of enabling you to see again with a child's eye. When you show a six-year-old a reconstructed Colonial village or share the stars in a Tennessee mountain night sky with a thirteen-year-old, you feel the world twinkle with as much possibility as when you first encountered these sites long ago.

Part of this excitement is a result of the exuberance kids bring, and part is from the instant friendships kids establish. Street vendors save their best deals for pre-schoolers, and, even on a crowded rush hour bus, a child by your side turns a fellow commuter from a stranger into a friend. Before your stop comes, you'll often be advised of the best toy shop in town and directed to a local cafe with a kid-pleasing menu at prices guaranteed to put a smile on your face.

New perspectives also come from the activities you participate in with your children. Most of these activities you would probably pass up when shuttling solo. Whether it's finding all the dogs in the paintings at the Metropolitan Museum of Art, going for a sleigh ride at a ski resort, or trying cross-country skiing in a park, you always learn more when you take your kids.

Surprisingly, traveling with your kids can also be cost-effective and practical. By combining or by extending a work-related trip into a vacation, you save money since your company picks up a good part of your expenses. Because tag-along-tots on business trips are an increasing trend, several hotel chains have responded with a range of family-friendly amenities including children's programs, child-safe rooms, and milk and cookies at bedtime.

For all these reasons, traveling with your children presents many wonderful opportunities. It is a great adventure to be a parent, and it is made more wondrous when you travel with your children. You will not only take pleasure in each other's company, but you will return home with memories to savor for a lifetime.

FAMILY TRAVEL TIPS

Great family vacations require careful planning and the cooperation of all family members. Before you go you need to think about such essentials as how to keep sibling fights to a minimum and how to be prepared for medical emergencies. While en route you want to be sure to make road trips and plane rides fun, even with a toddler. You want to be certain that the room that is awaiting your family is safe and that your family makes the most of being together. When visiting relatives, you want to eliminate friction by following the house rules. These tips, gathered from a host of families, go a long way toward making your trips good ones.

General Rules

1. Meet the needs of the youngest family member. Your raft trip won't be fun if you're constantly worried about your three-year-old being bumped overboard by the whitewater the tour operator failed to mention or if your first-grader gets bored with the day's itinerary of art museums.
2. Underplan. Your city adventure will dissolve in tears—yours and your toddler's—if you've scheduled too many sites and not enough time for the serendipitous. If your child delights in playing with the robots at the science museum, linger there and skip the afternoon's proposed visit to the history center.
3. Go for the green spaces. Seek out an area's parks. Pack a picnic lunch and take time to throw a frisbee, play catch, or simply enjoy relaxing in the sun and people watching.
4. Enlist the cooperation of your kids by including them in the decision making. While family vacation voting is not quite a democracy, con-

sider your kids' needs. Is there a way to combine your teen's desire to be near "the action" with your spouse's request for seclusion? Perhaps book a self-contained resort on a quiet beach that also features a nightspot.

5. Understand your rhythms of the road. Some families like traveling at night so that the kids sleep in the car or on the plane. Others avoid traveling during the evening cranky hours and prefer to leave early in the morning.

6. Plan to spend time alone with each of your children as well as with your spouse. Take a walk, write in a journal together, play ball, share ice-cream in the snack shop, etc. Even the simplest of things done together create valuable family memories.

Don't Leave Home Without

1. *Emergency medical kit.* The first thing we always pack is the emergency medical kit, a bag I keep ready to go with all those things that suddenly become important at 3:00 A.M. This is no hour to be searching the streets for baby aspirin or Band-Aids. Make sure your kit includes items suitable for adults as well as children. Be sure to bring:
   - aspirin or an aspirin substitute
   - a thermometer
   - cough syrup
   - a decongestant
   - medication to relieve diarrhea
   - bandages and Band-Aids
   - gauze pads
   - antibiotic ointment
   - a motion-sickness remedy
   - sunscreen
   - insect repellant
   - ointments or spray to soothe sunburn, rashes, and poison ivy
   - something to soothe insect stings
   - any medications needed on a regular basis
   - tweezers and a sterile needle to remove splinters

Keep this kit with you in your carry-on luggage or on the front seat of your car.

2. *Snack food.* As soon as we land somewhere or pull up to a museum for a visit, my eleven-year-old daughter wants food. Instead of arguing or wasting time and money on snacks, I carry granola bars with me. She munches on these reasonably nutritious snacks while we continue on schedule.

3. *Inflatable pillow and travel products.* Whether on the road or in a plane, these inflatable wonders help me and the kids sleep. For travel pillows plus an excellent variety of light yet durable travel products

including hair dryers, luggage straps, alarms, adaptor plugs for electrical outlets, and clothing organizers, call Magellan's (800–962–4943). TravelSmith (800–950–1600) carries these items as well as clothing, mostly for teens and adults.

4. *Travel toys.* Kids don't have to be bored en route to your destination. Pack books, coloring games, and quiet toys. Some kids love story tapes on their personal cassette players. For innovative, custom-tailored travel kits full of magic pencil games, puzzles, and crafts for children three and a half or older, call Sealed With A Kiss (800–888–SWAK). The packages cost about $30. Surprise your kids with this once you are on the road. They'll be happy and so will you.

Flying with Tots

1. Book early for the seat you like. Whether you prefer the aisle, window, or bulkhead for extra legroom, reserve your seat well in advance of your departure date.

2. Call the airlines at least forty-eight hours ahead to order meals that you know your kids will eat: children's dinners, hamburger platters, salads, etc.

3. Bring food on board that you know your kids like even if you've ordered a special meal. If your kids won't eat what's served at meal time, at least they won't be hungry if they munch on nutritious snacks.

4. Be sure to explain each step of the plane ride to little kids so that they will understand that the airplane's noises and shaking do not mean that a crash is imminent.

5. Stuff your carry-on with everything you might need (including medications, extra kids' clothes, diapers, baby food, formula, and bottles) to get you through a long flight and a delay of several hours . . . just in case.

6. Bring a child safety seat (a car seat) on board. Although presently the law allows children under two to fly free if they sit on a parent's lap, the Federal Aviation Administration and the Air Transport Association support legislation that would require all kids to be in child safety seats. In order to get a seat on board, the seat must have a visible label stating approval for air travel, and you must purchase a ticket for that seat. Without a ticket, you are not guaranteed a place to put this child safety seat in case the plane is full.

7. With a toddler or young child, wrap little surprises to give as "presents" throughout the flight. These work wonderfully well to keep a wee one's interest.

8. Before boarding, let your kids work off energy by walking around the airport lounge. Never let your child nap just before take-off—save the sleepy moments for the plane.

9. If you're traveling with a lot of luggage, check it curbside before park-

ing your car. This eliminates the awkward trip from long-term parking loaded down with kids, luggage, car-seats, and strollers.

Road Rules

1. Use this time together to talk with your children. Tell them anecdotes about your childhood or create stories for the road together.
2. Put toys for each child in his or her own mesh bag. This way the toys are easily located and visible instead of being strewn all over the car.
3. Avoid long rides. Break the trip up by stopping every two or three hours for a snack or to find a restroom. This lets kids stretch their legs.
4. When driving for several days, plan to arrive at your destination each day by 4:00 or 5:00 P.M., so that the kids can enjoy a swim at the hotel/motel. This turns long hauls into easily realized goals that are fun.

At the Destination

1. When traveling with young children, do a safety check of the hotel room and the premises as soon as you arrive. Put matches, glasses, ashtrays, and small items out of reach. Note if stair and balcony railings are widely spaced or easily climbed by eager tots. Find out where the possible dangers are, and always keep track of your kids.
2. Schedule sightseeing for the morning, but plan to be back at the resort or hotel by early afternoon so that your child can enjoy the pool, the beach, miniature golf, or other kid-friendly facilities.
3. Plan to spend some time alone with each of your children every day. With pre-teens and teens, keep active by playing tennis or basketball, jogging, or doing something else to burn energy.
4. Establish an amount of money that your child can spend on souvenirs. Stick to this limit, but let your child decide what he or she wants to buy.

With Relatives

1. Find out the rules of your relatives' house before you arrive, and inform your kids of them. Let them know, for example, that food is allowed only in the kitchen or dining room so that they won't bring sandwiches into the guest bedroom or den.
2. Tell your relatives about your kids' eating preferences. Let the person doing the cooking know that fried chicken is fine, but that your kids won't touch liver even if it is prepared with the famous family recipe.
3. To lessen the extra work and expense for relatives and to help eliminate friction, bring along or offer to shop and pay for those special items that only your kids eat—a favorite brand of cereal, juice, frozen pizza, or microwave kids' meal.

4. Discuss meal hours. If you know, for example, that grandma and grandpa always dine at 7:00 P.M. but that your pre-schooler and first-grader can't wait that long, feed your kids earlier at their usual time, and enjoy an adult dinner with your relatives later.

5. Find something suitable for each generation that your kids and relatives will enjoy doing together. Look over old family albums, have teens tape record oral family histories, and have grade-schoolers take instant snapshots of the clan.

6. Find some way that your kids can help with the work of visiting. Even a nursery-school age child feels good about helping to clear a table or sweep the kitchen floor.

Family Travel Planners

These specialists can help you assess your family's needs and find the vacation that's best for you.

- *Family Travel Times.* This monthly newsletter (ten issues per year) offers the latest information on hotels, resorts, city attractions, cruises, airlines, tours, and destinations. $55 for ten issues from Travel With Your Children, 45 West Eighteenth Street, New York, NY 10011. For information call (212) 206–0688.

- **Rascals in Paradise.** Specializing in family and small-group tours to the Caribbean, Mexico, and the South Pacific, Rascals' tours usually include nannies for each family and an escort to organize activities for the kids. Call (800) U–RASCAL for more information.

- **Grandtravel.** This company offers a variety of trips for grandparents and grandchildren 7 through 17. Domestic trips include visits to New York, New England, and the Grand Canyon. Foreign destinations include safaris to Kenya. Call (800) 247–7651 for more information.

- **Grandvistas.** Grandparents can take their grandkids on a variety of trips including tours of Mount Rushmore, Custer State Park, and Yellowstone National Park. Call (800) 647–0800 for more information.

- **Families Welcome!** This agency offers travel packages for families in London, Paris, and New York. Soon the company will expand their services to include Venice, Rome, and Florence. With their packages, you can choose to stay at a hotel or an apartment. Their "Welcome Kit" includes tips on sightseeing, restaurants, and museums. Call (800) 326–0724 for more information.

The prices and rates listed in this guidebook were confirmed at press time. We recommend, however, that you call establishments before traveling to obtain current information.

NEW ENGLAND

1
BLOCK ISLAND
Rhode Island

Block Island, about 7 miles long and 3 miles wide, is for beach lovers. While not perfect—it can be crowded and noisy near the Old Harbor— the island still has all the ingredients necessary for an old-fashioned beach vacation. These include great stretches of sand, windswept dunes, and such picturesque touches as a lighthouse and 200-foot-high bluffs. Other bonuses include nature trails, birds, and white-tail deer. Many of the Victorian-era grand hotels, turreted homes, and cottages have been renovated and turned into bed and breakfast accommodations. Their silhouettes lend an old-world graciousness to the streets. Stroll or bike along the roads in-season, and you smell the honeysuckle, bayberries, and blackberries. Devotees swear Block Island is less expensive and less pretentious than other New England beach areas.

GETTING THERE

Block Island, located in Block Island Sound, about 9 miles south of the Rhode Island mainland, and 13 miles east of Montauk, New York, on Long Island, is most easily reached by ferry. If the waves are friendly, this is a fun trip and an exciting start, especially for young kids who may not have spent much time on a boat. Bring some bread to throw to the sea gulls who hover nearby. Then listen to your kids' giggles as these gulls dive for the treats.

Ferries run fairly frequently from mid-June to mid-September, and less frequently in the off-season. Only ferries from Galilee State Pier, Point Judith, Rhode Island, to the Old Harbor area, the quickest run, operate year-round. The first rule about ferries, though, is to make reservations well in advance, especially if you want to bring your car. Interstate Navigation (401–783–4613), which takes both cars and people, operates the run from Point Judith to Block Island.

Nelseco Navigation (203–442–7891) operates a summertime ferry from New London, Connecticut. The *Jigger III* (516–668–2214) totes people and bikes only for the two-hour ride from Montauk, New York, available mid-June to mid-September. Viking Ferry Lines (516–668–5700 or 800–MONTAUK) on Block Island provides the quickest ride (beach goers and bikes only) from Montauk: one hour and fifteen minutes. In summer a ferry also makes the two-hour trip from Newport. For general ferry information, call (401) 789–3502 or (401) 421–4050.

Those with their own boats are welcome to dock at public harbors and private marinas. Since New Harbor has more public moorings than Old Harbor, it has become the place for private boats. Call the dockmaster at (401) 466–3235 for more information.

You also can arrive by plane, landing at Block Island State Airport; (401) 466–5511. Commercial airlines access the island via New England Airlines, Westerly State Airport, Westerly, Rhode Island; (401) 596–2460 or (800) 243–2460. Action Air, Groton/New London Airport (203–448–1646 or 800–243–8623), also provides air flights from Groton, Connecticut.

For a special treat, try a personal aerial view of Rhode Island Sound by chartering an airplane. Capital Airlines, Waterbury/Oxford Airport, Connecticut (203–264–3727 or 800–255–3727), provides service from the Northeast and Canada.

GETTING AROUND

The best way to explore this 10-square-mile island is by bicycle or on foot. If your accommodations are near the harbor, you'll have no need for a car at all since the Old and New Harbors are less than a mile apart, and within walking distance to the beaches. While you might be tempted to book your car aboard the ferry, don't. Instead park in the long-term lots, and start your vacation free from automobile hassles, and open to the slower holiday pace of strolling or pedaling.

If you must have a car, rentals are available from Block Island Bike & Car Rental, (401) 466–2297; Boat Basin Rentals, (401) 466–2631, Ext. 14; Coastline Rental & Leasing, (401) 596–3441; and Old Harbor Bike Shop, (401) 466–2029.

You will probably want to rent bicycles, which come in all shapes and sizes for different island uses. Mountain bikes or beach cruisers with thick treads are best equipped to handle the dirt roads. The *Travel Planner* brochure available through the Block Island Chamber of Commerce

(401–466–2982) has a full listing of several rental shops on the island. Mopeds are also available, but are restricted to paved roads only. For bicycles, check ahead to be sure the shop has the right size equipment (as well as helmets) for your child. Ask if you can reserve bikes and mopeds ahead of time. Other shops you might call in addition to the ones listed above are Cyr's Cycles (401–466–2147) and the Moped Man (401–466–5011).

WHAT TO SEE AND DO

Since the island is so small, most locations are pinpointed by street names alone, not addresses.

Beaches
The island's best beaches are on the east side, running from Old Harbor up to Jerry's Point, in a strip called **Crescent Beach**. **State Beach** (401–466–2611) is a bustling place, equipped with public bathrooms, lifeguards, and refreshments. It's also one of the most crowded beaches. If you're looking to browse the shops in town, but your older kids and teens can't get enough of the sand, drop them off at **Ballards Beach**, adjacent to Ballard's Inn at the Old Harbor. The beach has a lifeguard and is open to the public, even those not dining at Ballards.

Quieter choices include **Mansion Beach**, which is just north of the Great Salt Pond. You should bring a picnic (drinks included) and act as your own lifeguard. Your family will enjoy the waves, the sandy bottom, and searching for "points," small arrowheads left by the Manissean Indians. Another quiet choice is **Charleston Beach** near Harbor Neck.

Nature Exploration and Bicycle Trips
With 25 percent of Block Island's land designated as protected open space, getting off the beaten path is fun, and easy. One way to become acquainted with the island's wildlife is to book a ninety-minute hike with **The Nature Conservancy**, Ocean Avenue; (401) 466–2129. These guided nature walks are available mid-June through Labor Day. The *Block Island Times* lists some of the departures, but feel free to call and schedule your own tour, a special treat because guides are glad to tailor your walk and their commentary to any age group. Bring along binoculars to help you spot some of the hundreds of bird and insect species. In autumn some 150 species of migratory birds stop for their own island vacation on their way south.

After you are oriented, explore on your own. Bicycles come in handy here. Trip number one should be to the **Clayhead Nature Trail**, on the northeast side of the island off Corn Neck Road. Here you'll find 11 miles

The scenic Mohegan Bluffs area is just one of the beautiful places you can visit on Block Island. (Courtesy Rhode Island Tourism Division)

of grass trails winding through a 192-acre preserve. Start along the water-side cliffs and work your way north to **Settler's Rock** on the edge of Sachem Pond. This is where sixteen men from Boston, in search of religious freedom, landed in 1661. Read their names engraved on a plaque and try to imagine their first thoughts as they gazed out over Sachem Pond. Just off of the Clayhead Trail, you'll find **Lapham's Bluestone** bird sanctuary, a.k.a., "The Maze." This puzzle of trails cuts through thick trees and brush and leads to unexpected ocean vistas.

Now continue on the dirt road to the **North Lighthouse**, on Sandy Point, the island's northernmost point. Check out the new **Maritime Museum,** and watch the sunset shimmering off the waves.

Visiting **Rodman's Hollow,** on the southwestern part of the island, offers another good bike trip. Once you've arrived you'll want to explore this ancient formation on foot. Created by a prehistoric glacier, the ravine is actually below sea level. A pond never formed here, however, since the sandy soil wouldn't hold water. One of the island's five wildlife refuges, the Hollow is a good place for bird watching.

After exploring here take one of the winding paths down to **Mohegan Bluffs** on the island's southern shore. The bluffs are named after fifty Mohegan Indians who invaded the island only to be tossed from these heights by the island's native Manissean tribe. From the bluffs, some of which are 200 feet high, it's a long fall to the rocks below! The view here of the ocean to the south and off the island's rocky southern shoreline is exceptional. On a clear day you can see all the way to Montauk Point in New York. **Southeast Lighthouse,** off South East Light Road

(401–466–5009), is not far away. Constructed in 1875 this Gothic revival building with peaked gables has a beam that travels 35 miles out to sea. What's more impressive is that the lighthouse has recently been moved, piece by piece, from a dangerous perch just feet from the eroding cliff, to its current location.

Sports

Fishing is a favorite pastime here, and the Block Island Sound is known for striped bass, bluefish, cod, and flounder. Charter the *G. Willie Makit,* Old Harbor (401–466–5151), for a half or full-day ocean adventure. Captain Bill Gould and his crew provide fishing equipment and instruction from April through October. More independent anglers can captain their own rowboat. **Twin Maples,** Beach Avenue by New Harbor (401–466–5547), rents rowboats, fishing equipment, tackle, and even sells bait. If you're a landlubber, walk to the end of Coast Guard Road and cast off the beach on the Great Salt Pond.

Little kids can ride the waves with a boogie board rented from **Island Sport Shop,** 995 Weldon's Way; (401) 466–5001. Surfboards and sailboards are also available here and at other sports shops.

The **Block Island Club,** Corn Neck Road (401–466–5939), a resort club that offers weekly memberships to island visitors, is a great idea for families too energetic to just sunbathe. Besides a lifeguarded beach, the club, located on the island's Great Salt Pond, offers tennis, sailboarding, and sailing. Since the tide is gentle, the waves are manageable.

For horseback riding, saddle up at **Rustic Rides,** West Side Road (401–466–5060), for a guided tour of the rocky west coast. Let your horse do the work as you ramble from trail-to-road to the west coast beach.

Performing Arts

Oceanwest Theater, Champlin's Marina, New Harbor (401–466–2971), presents first-run movies nightly as well as rainy-day matinees from late May to mid-September. If you've already seen the movie, check out the **Summerstock Theatre** running Tuesday through Saturday nights for fun family comedies. The **New Summer Theater,** at Champlin's Resort (401–466–2641), also features first-run movies as well as live off-Broadway performances.

The **Historical Society,** Old Town Road, Old Harbor (401–466–2481), is a good rainy-day activity. Two permanent exhibitions focus on the Manisseans, the Native Americans who lived here for centuries, and the mounted birds of Elizabeth Dickens, an island legend.

Special Tours

For an overview of the island and the low-down on its lore, legends, and local happenings, take a guided tour of the island from O.J.'s Taxi, (401) 782–5826 or (401) 466–2872. This is a particularly good trip if you have little tots too young to bike, or if you don't enjoy pedaling in the sun. A seasoned islander himself, O.J. gives you the inside scoop from the Indian skirmish at Mohegan Bluffs to the island's present-day fight against commercialization. He'll even tell you how Cow Cove got its name when white settlers made their cows swim ashore to test the depth of the water.

Other historic tours may be available through the Chamber of Commerce. Call them at (401) 466–2982 for more information.

More Local Family Fun

Playground fanatics will want to climb through the tunnels and ride the swings on the island grammar school's new wooden jungle gym on High Street. Or how about an island baseball game? Everyone is welcome to join in the evening youth games listed in the *Block Island Times*. If it's too windy to stay on the beach, and sailing is not your family forte, head over to the **Block Island Kite Company** on Corn Neck Road; (401) 466–2033. After a kite-flying demonstration, launch your own colors into the breeze.

SPECIAL EVENTS

Festivals

Listed below are festivals and special events for **Block Island** and **Newport**. For more information, call the Block Island Chamber of Commerce (401–466–2982) and the **Newport County Convention and Visitors Bureau** (800–326–6030 or 401–849–8098).

May: Bed and Breakfast Open House, Block Island.

June: Annual "Taste of Block Island" Seafood Festival and Chowder Cook-off, with live music, arts and crafts, and kids' games. Block Island Race Week, sponsored by *Yachting* Magazine. New Harbor Circus, Samuel Peckham Inn.

July: July Fourth Celebration. Block Island Arts and Crafts Guild Fair. Annual Barbershop Quartet Concert. Newport Music Festival. Classical Music at the Mansions, Newport.

August: Block Island Triathalon. Annual Block Island House and Garden Tour. Nature Conservancy Annual Conservation Event. Ben & Jerry's Newport Folk Festival. Newport JVC Jazz Festival.

September: Annual Block Island Pasta Cook-off. Block Island Gardeners' "Edibles from the Fall Harvest."

October: National Audubon Birdwatching Weekend. Annual Harvest and Cider Festival.

November: Annual Block Island Christmas Shopping Stroll. Block Island Arts and Crafts Guild Fair.

WHERE TO STAY

Surf Hotel, Dodge Street (401 466 2241 or 401–466–2240), is one of the grand Victorian inns still standing on the island. Situated on the beach in the center of town, the Surf Hotel tempts with hearty breakfasts, grills for barbecuing on the porch, a playground and basketball hoop, and a parrot in the lobby! If you want to be where the action is, this is the place. But remember, it can be noisy, and most rooms have only a sink, and no private bathroom. There's a six-night minimum stay in July and August.

The **Atlantic Inn,** High Street (401–466–5883), a short walk from the Old Harbor, offers twenty-one rooms, many with good views. Amenities include a croquet court, two tennis courts, and a playhouse replica of the inn just for kids. Children under twelve stay free. Three-night stay minimum during summer weekends.

The **New Shoreham House Inn,** Water Street (401–466–2651 or 800–272–2601), in the historic downtown district, overlooks the Old Harbor. This lodging offers special family packages in July and at various times during the late spring and fall, and family fun suggestions all of the time. Kids under twelve stay free, and cots and cribs are available on request. If you can visit for a week, an apartment provides more flexibility.

The **Bellevue House** on High Street (401–466–5268 or 401–466–2912) has two-bedroom apartments and three-bedroom cottages for rent.

The **Gothic Inn,** Dodge Street (401–466–2918), perched on the beach, features two-bedroom efficiencies and a country cottage.

Most inns request a deposit. For a complete listing of accommodations, call the Block Island Chamber of Commerce at (401) 466–2982. Open-air camping is allowed for Boy Scouts and Girl Scouts only, at a designated campsite.

WHERE TO EAT

Seafood entrées are the forte here, but atmosphere counts as well. Take a leisurely breakfast in the sun at **Ernie's,** Old Harbor (401–466–2473), and watch the ferries pull in with new arrivals from the mainland. Later you can fill up on what some say is the best seafood on the island at **Dead Eye Dick's,** Payne's Dock, New Harbor (401–466–2654). Get goofy with the natives at sing-alongs with Jim Kelley at **Ballards Inn** (401–466–2231), a long-time island fish house.

If you're fished out, go to **Aldo's** (401–466–5871), for Italian food for the whole family and a video arcade for the kids. For pizza, **Capizzano's**, Old Harbor (401–466–2829), has all kinds from pies to calzones to plain old pizza with almost any topping you want. If you want burgers, visit **The Beachhead**, Corn Neck Road (401–466–2249). Parents, older kids, and teens appreciate dining at **Manisses** on Spring Street (401–466–2421). Reserve ahead for the deck, or a view from indoor tables, and enjoy the seafood and pasta specialties.

DAY TRIPS

On your way back from Block Island, take one of the ferries to **Newport, Rhode Island**. Tour the nineteenth-century European-style mansions cliff side along Bellevue Avenue, then stroll through Colonial Newport's brick-paved streets harborside. Music lovers should time their visit with the summertime classical, jazz, or folk festivals. (See SPECIAL EVENTS for more information.)

Call the Newport County Convention and Visitors Bureau, 23 America's Cup Avenue, Newport (401–849–8098 or 800–326–6030), for a free travel planner with attraction, event, and accommodation information.

FOR MORE INFORMATION

Block Island Chamber of Commerce, Water Street, Old Harbor (401–466–2982), is a friendly and helpful source of tourist information. Their *Travel Planner* brochure is a comprehensive reference to the island's attractions and resources. South County Tourism Council, 4808 Tower Hill Road, Wakefield, Rhode Island (410–789–4422 or 800–548–4662) has visitor brochures and tourist information on Block Island. Pick up a copy of the weekly *Block Island Times*, which has a map of the island and a list of community activities.

Emergency Numbers
Ambulance, fire, and police: 911
Block Island Medical Center, P.O. Box 919, Payne Road; (401) 466–2974
Block Island Pharmacy, P.O. Box 1179, High Street; (401) 466–5825
Block Island Police: (401) 466-3220
Coast Guard: 1-789–0444
Poison Hotline: (401) 277–5727
Public Health Nurse, Mary Donnelly: (401) 466–2332

2
BOSTON
Massachusetts

Ever since a group of Revolutionaries dumped tea in the Boston harbor, the city has held a special fascination. Despite the busy, big-city ambiance, Boston is eminently family friendly, offering an uncommon mix of history, museums, and fun. Don't miss the opportunity to visit here with your kids, whether you tour on a family getaway or take the kids with you as part of a business trip.

GETTING THERE

Most major domestic and international airlines, as well as several regional carriers, provide service to Logan International Airport, about 3 miles from downtown Boston.

Traffic in the morning and evening rush hours can significantly lengthen the time it takes to reach town from the airport, thus increasing taxi fares. For taxi information call MASSPORT at (617) 561–1769. One way to beat the traffic is to take the Airport Water Shuttle. The seven-minute trip—kids will love the ferry ride—departs from the airport to Rowes Wharf, downtown, and from downtown to the airport, every fifteen minutes Monday through Friday, from 6:00 A.M. to 8:00 P.M. and Sundays every thirty minutes from noon to 8:00 P.M. No service is available on Saturdays and holidays. Call (800) 23–LOGAN for more information.

If you're traveling light, consider taking the subway. The MBTA (Massachusetts Bay Transit Authority) Blue Line stops at the airport. Call (800) 23–LOGAN for schedule information. This same number gives you information on bicycle access to the airport, parking, and schedules for airport shuttle buses to Braintree, Framingham, and other locations. This 800 line operates twenty-four hours, Monday to Friday from 9:00 A.M. to 5:00 P.M. and is staffed by information specialists (real people).

Amtrak trains (800–USA–RAIL) service Boston arriving at South Station, on the Red "T" line, and Back Bay Station, on the Orange "T" line. Commuter trains link Boston with the suburbs. For information on the MBTA Commuter Rail, call (617) 722–3200.

Another airport note: When awaiting departures be sure to stop by the airport's Kidport, a free play space for kids with climbing equipment for wee ones and several computer terminals for older kids.

GETTING AROUND

The only time your kids will be bored in Boston is when you're stuck in traffic. Take to the streets, not as the early Revolutionaries did to protest taxes, but to avoid the often clogged roads and to savor the city. Whenever possible, walk, or take the subway, known as the "T." Reasonably safe during the day—as in any city, be vigilant and use common sense—the "T" gets you around quickly and inexpensively. Divided into Red, Green, Orange, and Blue lines, the fares depend on the number of zones traveled. The Visitor Passport gives you unlimited travel within Boston for three days for $9.00, or seven days for $18.00. Obtain these at the Visitor Information Centers (see FOR MORE INFORMATION), or call the T Customer Service Center at (617) 722–3200.

WHAT TO SEE AND DO

Museums

Forget about dry-as-dust exhibit halls with a look-but-don't-touch rigidity. Boston's museums offer lots of family fun. At **Children's Museum**, 300 Congress Street (617–426–8855), there's something for every family member from preschoolers to teens. Ask at the information desk for the booklet about exploring the museum with kids under five.

Toddlers dress up as circus performers in Backstage at the Big Top; in Playspace, kids four years and under climb in cars, build with blocks, and enjoy a variety of other activities. At Science Playground such simple acts as spinning tops and plates teach kids about scientific principles. This museum also engages preteens and teens. While Studio 10-15 is more a safe hangout for locals than an exhibit area, Teen Tokyo introduces American teens to their Japanese peers. Learn about the life of a Japanese student by stepping into a subway car and standing on the footprints that show you just how packed the place gets. You can push a mannequin of a sumo wrestler from his ring to learn about this sport, browse through *manga* (popular comic books), listen to Japanese rock 'n roll, and compare fashions.

Computer Museum, 300 Congress Street; (617) 426–2800. Don't skip this place. The museum proves that computers aren't just for "nerds." The easy-to-follow programs let you and your kids enjoy such instant creativity as designing a sailboat, composing music, drawing a dinosaur, planning a car, and recording and editing your own television commercial. While kids love the place, parents, especially those from the precomputer generation, may have even more fun gaining familiarity with the programs and possibilities through play. Your children may have to tear you away from the terminals.

Museum of Science, Science Park; (617) 723–2500. Easily accessible via the "T," this museum gets mixed reviews. Skip the anemic rain forest and the deadly dioramas of marshes complete with mounted birds looking as bored as the viewers. Go directly to the must-see galleries. These include the egg hatchery, a giant incubator that allows you to watch chicks peck their way into the world, and the Discovery Space, which features three-dimensional puzzles of the human body that you piece together by placing the liver, lungs, ribs, and all the organs in the right spots. One of the liveliest spaces is Seeing the Unseen, which renders the world of fleas, termites, tadpoles, shrimp, and other tiny critters visible through high-powered microscopes.

The Theater of Electricity will snap, crackle, and pop you into attention. Here the world's largest Van de Graaff generator produces bolts of lightning as the guide explains the phenomenon. Instructive with a flash of Frankenstein eeriness, the show is loud and flamboyant. Small children may be frightened, but older ones will be fascinated. Since the museum also features an Omni Theater plus a planetarium with both laser and sky shows, plan to spend several hours on site.

The New England Aquarium, Central Wharf; (617) 973–5200. Fishy and fine, the New England Aquarium, while not large, opens a window on some watery wonders. You'll love watching the lazy sea turtles float, the sharks swim swiftly, and the schools of fish wriggle by in the big, central tank. Feeding time is especially interesting.

Be sure to visit the sea lions in the *Discovery,* the ship next door. Guthrie, a 650-pound performer, puts on quite an educational show as he swims, dives, "talks," and teaches kids about recycling.

The Sports Museum of New England, CambridgeSide Galleria, 100 CambridgeSide Place, Cambridge; (617) 787–7678. This museum has three theaters offering films and facts on great moments in New England sports history from high school through professional sports.

Markets, Historical Markers, Parks

From the aquarium it's an easy walk to **Faneuil Hall Marketplace.** The ranger talk about the historic liberty speeches delivered here isn't likely to rouse your children, but the rows upon rows of shops, stalls, and eateries in the nearby markets will. This place offers cheap eats for lunch and limitless possibilities for parting with some allowance money for souvenirs.

From Faneuil Hall follow the red path that details some of the best parts of the **Freedom Trail,** including Paul Revere's house and the Old North Church. There's something about Paul Revere's house that renders this famous personage real. Looking at the furnishings and rooms helps round out the life of this Revolutionary as father, provider, and silversmith. The 3-mile Freedom Trail, which passes by sixteen historic sites from the Colonial and Revolutionary eras, starts at the Boston Common.

Across from the Common is the **Public Garden,** a great take-a-break place. The ponds, swans, and brass ducklings kept shiny by so many little bottoms saddling them offer a pleasing city oasis. Plan to picnic or at least play awhile here.

The Bull & Finch Pub, 84 Beacon Street; (617) 227–9600. Television history was made here. The outside of this pub served as the model for "Cheers." While Norm and Sam are nowhere to be seen, parents can have a beer and buy their kids a T-shirt with the Cheers logo. Upstairs, there's a more formal restaurant. While kids are welcome, the prices may be high for some family budgets.

Special Tours

Whale Watching. From April–October get ready to yell "there she blows" when you spot one of these magnificent leviathans breaching the waves. Two places that book whale-watching tours in the city are A.C. Cruise Line, 28 Northern Avenue, Boston (617–426–8419 or 800–973–5281), and the New England Aquarium, Central Wharf (off Atlantic Avenue) (617–973–5277 or 800–973–5281).

Black History. Grab a Black Heritage Trail brochure for a self-guided tour of fourteen Beacon Hill historic sites including the memorial to the 54th Regiment. Guided tours are available by appointment (617–742–5415).

Walking tours. Boston By Foot (617–367–2345) offers walking tours spring through fall. Boston By Little Feet has walking tours for children eight to twelve and their parents.

Performing Arts

In addition to the Boston Ballet, the Boston Symphony, the Boston Pops, and several theaters, check the schedule for the Boston Children's Theatre, the New England Hall, 225 Clarendon Street; (617) 277–3277. The engaging performances are by children for children.

A ride on the swan boats in Boston's Public Garden will delight every member of the family. (Courtesy Greater Boston Convention and Visitors Bureau, Inc.)

More Useful Numbers

BOSTIX Ticket Booth, Faneuil Hall (617–423–4454), Fax (617) 423–2131), offers tickets to entertainment and cultural events. Open Tuesday–Saturday 11:00–6:00, Sunday 11:00–4:00. BOSTIX also sells half-price tickets for same-day performances.

SPECIAL EVENTS

Boston is not only a town that loves its sports, but a place that knows how to celebrate. When phone numbers are not listed, for detailed information on festivals and celebrations, contact the Greater Boston Convention and Visitors Bureau at (617) 536–4100. Here are some happy highlights.

Sporting Events

The Boston Garden, 150 Causeway Street (617–277–3200), hosts the city's hockey team, the Bruins, from October through March, and the basketball team, the Celtics, from October through May. The Red Sox, the American League baseball team, play at Fenway Park, 4 Yawkey Way, April–October. For ticket information, call (617) 267–8661; to charge tickets (617) 267–1700. For TDD (617) 236–6644. Football fans wanting to root for the New England Patriots, Foxboro Stadium, Route 1, Foxboro, should call (800) 543–1776 or (800) 828–7080.

For three days during the World Cross-Country Championship Weekend in March, star athletes compete in track-and-field events. In April the world-famous 26-mile Boston Marathon takes joggers from Hopkinton to Copley Square, Boston. Grab some oranges and water, and enjoy cheering on the runners with your kids, (617) 236–1652. In October line the shores of the Charles River for the renowned rowing event, Head of the Charles Regatta, (617) 536–4100.

Festivals

February: At the Children's Museum Chinese New Year celebration, have your name written in Chinese, make lanterns, and learn about Chinese customs. At the museum's Japan Day, try Kabuki face painting, origami lessons, and rice cakes. The Boston Festival, a city-wide winter celebration, takes place on five consecutive weekends from Valentine's Day to St. Patrick's Day. Festivities include a laser light show, food festival, baked beans and Boston cream pie contests, and often ice dancers and dog-sled races. The Museum of Science Vacation Week helps kids combat the winter blues with special programming and events.

March: Bloom into spring with the New England Spring Flower Show.

April: Ducklings Day, honoring Robert McCloskey's classic children's tale, *Make Way For Ducklings,* celebrates the city, children, and spring. Don't miss the parade of ducklings from the State House to the Public Garden.

Celebrate freedom's legends with the Reenactment of the Battle of Lexington and Concord, and the Reenactment of Paul Revere's Ride.

May: Watch thousands of kites soar at the Annual Kite Festival, Franklin Park. Street Performers Festival, Faneuil Hall Marketplace, lightens the pace with mimes, jugglers, magicians.

June: Annual Teddy Bear Picnic and Sing-Along.

July: Celebrate America's Independence with Boston Harborfest, more than one hundred waterside events, including the annual Boston Chowderfest, fireworks, special cruises, and also a Boston Pops annual Fourth of July concert.

August: Boston Seaport Festival, Charlestown Navy Yard, features boat tours and a regatta.

September: Boston Arts and Music Festival offers a variety of cultural events.

December: Holiday events include the lighting of a Christmas tree on the Boston Common and a reenactment of the Boston Tea Party, with a rally and a parade to the Tea Party Ship.

The city takes to the streets on New Year's Eve with First Night, a citywide celebration featuring music, mime, dance, theater, and film. Go with your kids, as the festival kicks off December 31st around 1:00 P.M. with a children's festival. The festival ends with a bang as fireworks light up the sky.

WHERE TO STAY

The easiest way to see the city with kids is to stay close-in at a well-located hotel near a "T" stop in a good walking neighborhood. Call the Boston CVB for accommodation brochures and information on the latest family packages available. Remember that hotels always have lower rates on weekends; ask for these. Several hotels offer kids' amenities. Some possibilities:

The Boston Marriott Long Wharf has a package that includes tickets to the Aquarium, Computer Museum, or Children's Museum; (800) 228–9290. **The Copley Plaza Hotel's** Kids Love Boston package features free parking, a superior guest room, stuffed lion gift, and a roll-away bed. Call (800) 8–COPLEY. **The Copley Square Hotel** has a family suite package of two connecting rooms, and a welcome gift for kids; (617) 536–9000. **The Four Seasons Boston** offers a Weekend With the Kids package that includes a free VCR, children's movies, and an executive suite with sitting area. Child-friendly amenities include kid-size bathrobes, turn-down service of milk and cookies, and box games and toys to borrow; (800) 332–3442. **Guest Quarters Suite Hotel** gives you a suite and breakfast; (617) 783–0090. **The Ritz-Carlton** can't be beat for sheer grandeur, although this comes at a cost. The hotel's Children's Presidential Suite comes with books and toys, Nintendo, and children's play areas.

Boston has several **Bed and Breakfast** registries. Try the **Bed and Breakfast Agency of Boston** (617–720–3540 or 800–CITY–BNB for town houses, studios, and condominiums). **Host Homes of Boston** (617–244–1308) offers guest rooms in town homes and houses in Boston and its nearby suburbs. Make sure, however, that the property really is family friendly before booking.

WHERE TO EAT

It's not just baked beans, chowder, and Boston cream pies—though these can be very good here. Boston has lots of good restaurants. **Faneuil Hall Marketplace** offers many spots for quick and cheap eats. Nearby, **Ye Olde Union Oyster House**, 41 Union Street (617–227–2750), open since 1862, is well known for its seafood and pastas. The crowds at **No-Name Restaurant**, 15½ Fish Pier (617–338–7539), attest to the popularity of this inexpensive seafood place. **Boodle's**, 40 Dalton Street (617–266–3537), in the Back Bay area has burgers, salads, and sandwiches. Adventurous kids might like **Casablanca**, 40 Brattle Street (617–876–0999), for its crab cakes, chili, and couscous. **Bnu**, 123 Stuart Street (617–367–8405), offers inexpensive pizza, pasta, and salads. For a wider Italian menu, try **Ristorante Lucia**, 415 Hanover Street (617–523–9148), in the North End.

The Official Guidebook of the Greater Boston Convention and Visitors Bureau lists many area restaurants.

DAY TRIPS

Boston can serve as the hub of a great family foray. **Lexington** and **Concord** offer more Revolutionary history, and in **Salem** the Salem Witch Museum and the Witch House will intrigue kids. Farther north try the beaches at **Parker River Refuge**, Newbury; **Plum Island**; **Newburytown**; and **Good Harbor Beach**, Gloucester.

FOR MORE INFORMATION

The Greater Boston Convention and Visitors Bureau offers many free maps, brochures, seasonal travel planners, and accommodation guides. The GBCVB also produces *Kids Love Boston,* $3.95, a big-type guide with pleasing illustrations aimed at elementary-school kids. Get one of these ahead of time so your child can help plan your visit, a good way to ensure cooperation. For more information, including a guide to accommodations, call the bureau: (617) 536–4100.

Visitor information centers: Boston Common Information Center, 146 Tremont Street (617–536–4100), is open Monday–Saturday from 8:30 A.M. to 5:00 P.M. and Sunday from 9:00 A.M. to 5:00 P.M. Prudential Information Center, Prudential Plaza, 800 Boylston Street (617–536–4100), is open Monday–Saturday from 9:00 A.M. to 6:00 P.M. National Park Service, 15 State Street (617–242–5642), is open daily from 9:00 A.M. to 5:00 P.M. Cambridge Discovery, Harvard Square, Cambridge (627–497–1630), is open Monday–Saturday from 9:00 A.M. to 6:00 P.M. and Sunday from 1:00 to 5:00 P.M.

The Boston Parents Paper, P.O. Box 1777, Boston 02130; (617) 522–1515. This monthly publication lists special events and resources for families and children. Browse the advertisers for kid-oriented shops and services.

Persons with disabilities can get referrals and information from **The Information Center for Individuals with Disabilities,** Fort Point Place, 27-43 Wormwood Street, Boston 02210; (617) 727–5540.

For Boston Parks & Recreation, call (617) 725–4505. You can reach the National Historical Park Visitor Center at (617) 242–5642.

Emergency Numbers
Ambulance, fire, and police: 911
Boston Police: (617) 247–4200
Children's Hospital Emergency Room: (617) 735–6611
Poison Hotline: (617) 232–2120
Twenty-four hour pharmacy: Phillips Drug Store, 155 Charles Street, Boston; (617) 523–1028 or (617) 523–4372

3
CAPE COD
Massachusetts

Cape Cod, a 70-mile stretch of land separated from the Massachusetts mainland by the Cape Cod Canal, is an idyllic seaside getaway. The Cape is divided into two diverse sections: the Upper Cape is closer to the mainland and highly developed; the Lower Cape, with Provincetown at its tip, is quieter and includes much of the Cape Cod National Seashore, established to protect the area from commercialism. Cape Cod consists of fifteen towns plus a number of villages. Those who want to be close to nature may consider a cottage or camping in the more isolated Wellfleet–Truro–Eastham area of the Lower Cape. Families who want nearby conveniences and attractions—and great beaches—however, prefer the Upper Cape. The West Yarmouth–West Dennis area, for instance, at the Cape's geographical center, has the best family beaches and is close to the shopping and conveniences of Hyannis. Heading west it's just one hour to the recreational area surrounding the Cape Cod Canal; on the east an hour's drive leads to the beautiful National Seashore.

GETTING THERE

Barnstable County Airport, near Hyannis (508–775–2020), is served by Delta Connection to Boston and by a commuter line, Colgan Air, to Newark.

Bonanza (800–556–3815) runs frequent buses from Boston and Logan Airport to Bourne, Falmouth, and Wood's Hole, plus daily service from New York, Danbury, Hartford, Albany, Springfield, and Providence to Hyannis and Wood's Hole. Plymouth & Brockton Company buses travel to and from Boston, Logan Airport, Plymouth, Provincetown, and towns in between. Call (508) 775–5524/(800) 328–9997 (Massachusetts) for schedules.

Amtrak (800–USA–RAIL) runs limited service between New York and

Hyannis on summer weekends. Otherwise, you'll have to take a train to Boston's South Station and link up with the nearby Bonanza Bus Line.

By car the Cape can be accessed from two main highways, I–495, which leads to the Bourne Bridge, or Route 3, to the Sagamore Bridge. It's about a two-hour drive (less if the traffic is light) from Boston to the bridges.

Bay State Cruises (617–723–7800) runs passenger vessels between Boston and Provincetown in the summer.

GETTING AROUND

Driving, sometimes a slow process, is the main form of transportation. There are three highways: Mid-Cape Highway (Route 6) is the fastest but has no water view; Route 28 goes along the south shore and is slow and highly trafficked; Route 6A provides scenic views of the north shore.

Public transportation: RTA (Regional Transit Authority) runs buses from the commuter parking lots at the Sagamore Bridge to Wood's Hole. Call (508) 385–8311 for schedules. Provincetown has a public shuttle bus (508–487–3353) that serves Provincetown and Herring Cove Beach from late June to early September.

Ferry service includes Hy-Line (508–778–2602) during summers, from Hyannis to Martha's Vineyard and Nantucket. Steamship Authority (508–540–2022) operates year-round from Wood's Hole to Martha's Vineyard (the shortest route on the Cape, it takes 45 minutes) and from Hyannis to Nantucket. In the summer these ferries also run from the Vineyard to Nantucket, returning to Hyannis. Island Commuter (508–548–4800) heads to the Vineyard from Falmouth Harbor.

Cape Cod Canal's service roads are great for biking, walking, and jogging. You'll also find three bicycle trails within the Cape Cod National Seashore. See the Cape Cod Visitor's Guide for trail details and bike rental companies.

WHAT TO SEE AND DO

Museums and Attractions

While the Cape isn't teeming with museums with kid appeal, there are a number of kid-friendly attractions. The museums are generally low-key and best for rainy days, or as part of a general sight-seeing tour.

Bourne. **Aptucket Trading Post Museum,** Aptucket Road; (508) 759–9487. If you're near the Bourne Bridge, stop by the Pilgrim trading post, one of the first in North America. Its claim to fame: It was reconstructed in 1930 on the original site with original materials. President

Grover Cleveland's private railroad is also on the premises, as are a windmill, herb gardens, and picnic area.

Brewster. Located mid-Cape on the bay side, Brewster has charming nineteenth-century homes built by sea captains, antique shops, art galleries, a summer day camp for ages seven to seventeen (508–896–3451), and the following attractions:

Bassett Wild Animal Farm, Tubman Road; (508) 896-3224. Take the kids on hayrides and pony rides, and see a variety of birds and wildlife in natural surroundings. There's a picnic area, too.

Cape Cod Aquarium/Atlantic Education Center, 281 Main Street; (508) 385–9252. Call to find out when they give daily presentations featuring rescued seals and sea lions; it's educational and appealing. Colorful fish swim in giant tanks, and there are daily educational workshops, plus a picnic area. Open year-round.

Cape Cod Museum of Natural History, Route 6A; (508) 896–3867. While not huge, there are two floors of indoor exhibits, plus nature walks and family programs.

New England Fire and History Museum, Route 6A; (508) 896–5711. This large collection of antique fire-fighting equipment and memorabilia includes eye-catching exhibits: a Victorian apothecary shop, blacksmith shop, and an interesting diorama of the Great Chicago Fire of 1871. The museum is open late May through Columbus Day.

Stoney Brook Mill, Stoney Brook Road, grinds corn Thursday, Friday, and Saturday afternoons during July and August. Small kids will be intrigued, and they should like the small museum upstairs.

Falmouth. This picturesque town on Route 28 on the Cape's southwestern tip is the home of the new **Cape Cod's Children's Museum,** which opened in temporary quarters in late 1992 with hands-on activities for ages one to ten. There are plans to move the year-round museum to a permanent space in 1994 and to construct a Native American exhibit and a miniature Cape Cod village—including child-size houses, grocery, and fire station. Give them a call at (508) 457–4667 before you go.

Hyannis. Yes, it's congested and suburbanized, but it's also a transportation and shopping hub, and boasts **Cape Cod Potato Chips,** Breed's Hill Road in Independence Park; (508) 775–7253. This probably will make a bigger impression on your kids than most museums. On weekdays, watch the hand-cooking process that results in these tasty tidbits. Then visit the gift store to sample some chips and, of course, buy a bag or two.

Provincetown. "P-town," the tip at the end of the Lower Cape, has beautiful beaches, sand dunes, shops, galleries, and a lively, openly gay crowd. This colorful artistic colony also is the site of the first Pilgrim landing and boasts the Cape's most visited attraction: **Pilgrim Monument and Provincetown Museum,** off SR 6 on High Pole Hill; (508) 487–1310.

If your kids are energetic, climb the stairs and ramps to the top of the 252-foot tower honoring the Mayflower Pilgrims, which provides splendid views of the town and harbor. You won't be disappointed by the museum, which contains lots of intriguing things: Mayflower memorabilia, ship models, items taken from nearby shipwrecks, old toys, scrimshaw, figureheads, and an old fire engine made by an apprentice of Paul Revere.

Sandwich. Located on the bay in the Upper Cape, charming Sandwich, the oldest town on the Cape, was the site of one of the country's largest glass factories during the nineteenth century. **The Sandwich Glass Museum** at 129 Main Street (508–888–0251) displays this beautiful vintage glass, but most kids will be ready to bolt in under five minutes. (Instead, they may prefer seeing the glassblowing demonstrations at **Pairpont Crystal** near the Sagamore Bridge; (508) 888–2344/(800) 899–0953.)

One attraction that will appeal: **Heritage Plantation**, Grove and Pine streets, (508) 888-3300. Pack a lunch (there are picnic grounds, plus a windmill, outside) and plan to spend some time here. Take a ride on the restored carousel, then see the antique and classic cars in the Round Stone Barn. The antique miniatures at the military museum are appealing. There's also an art museum, although the large Currier & Ives exhibit will leave most kids bored. The seventy-six acres of trails and gardens offer a nice respite. If you came foodless, The Daniel Webster Inn serves three meals.

Another Sandwich attraction: **Yesteryears Doll Museum**, at the corner of Main and River streets; (508) 888–1711. If there's a doll lover in the family, stop to see the lovely vintage dolls, dollhouses, and miniatures. In East Sandwich, don't miss **Green Briar Nature Center**, 1 Discovery Road; (508) 888–6870. Besides the natural history exhibits inside, there are two reasons to stop at the center: The lovely fifty-seven-acre Briar Patch Conservation Area's nature trails and the Green Briar Jam Kitchen, where you can tour an old-fashioned kitchen to see jams, jellies, and preserves made in the traditional way. In the summer the demonstrators use an unusual sun-cooking method. Call for days when the kitchen is in operation.

West Yarmouth: Aqua Circus of Cape Cod on Route 28 (508–775–8883) has winning sea lion and dolphin shows. There is also a zoo with llamas, ponies, monkeys, and a petting zoo.

Beaches

Every town on the Cape has saltwater beaches; some also offer sandy beaches on lakes or ponds. Towns charge parking fees, and some require beach stickers. The visitor's guide from the Chamber of Commerce lists all public beaches and fees.

Some families with young children prefer the bay beaches because the lack of waves makes swimming and wading easier for little ones. On calm days, however, the ocean beaches are irresistible. Chances are you'll sample both during your stay. Particularly good ocean beaches for families include those in the West Yarmouth area, which have playgrounds and frequently organize activities for kids. The West Dennis Beach has a huge parking lot close to the beach and attracts tons of kids—instant playmates for your youngsters. An outstanding bay beach? Try Sandy Neck, West Barnstable, off Route A on Sandy Neck Road.

Cape Cod National Seashore, a breathtaking natural wonder, encompasses a good deal of the Lower Cape from Chatham to Provincetown. It includes 30 miles of bay and ocean beaches, dunes, glacial cliffs, nature trails, and green forests that are protected by law from commercial development. Swimming is permitted on six beaches, where there are lifeguards. If the crowds are too intense (arrive as early as possible), head to the warm waters of Gull freshwater pond in Wellfleet, which connects by channels to several others where you won't find a mob scene. The town is also home to Wellfleet Bay Wildlife Sanctuary, off U.S. 6; call (508) 349–2615. Daily organized programs, which might include a bird walk or canoe trip, often are suitable for youngsters. The sanctuary's mile-long Goose Pond Trail has plants and birds that kids can help identify, with the assistance of an inexpensive guide sold here.

The Seashore has a total of nine nature trails, all a mile long (except for the 8-mile Great Island trail in Wellfleet). The **National Visitors Center** at Salt Pond, off U.S. 6 in Eastham (508–255–3421), has information on the entire seashore, films, a free museum, plus a mile-long trail to the pond, where flocks of shorebirds congregate for "lunch." There's also a visitor's center some 25 miles away at Provincetown: **Province Lands Visitor's Center**, Race Point Road, off U.S. 6.

Special Tours

If your kids are seaworthy, take them on a fascinating whale-watching tour. (The trips often last several hours, so they're best with older kids. Just in case, check with your pediatrician ahead of time about possible seasickness preventatives and remedies.) A number of tours are listed in the Cape Cod Resort Directory from the Chamber of Commerce. Two examples: From Provincetown the **Portuguese Princess** has day and sunset trips, food, and guarantees sightings. Call (508) 487–2651/(800) 442–3188—Massachusetts, for information and reservations. The four-hour narrated **Hyannis Whale Watcher Cruise** departs from Millway Marina in Barnstable Harbor. Call (508) 362–6088/(800) 287–0374—Massachusetts.

The **Cape Cod Scenic Railroad**, consisting of first-class parlor cars and restored coaches, travels between Hyannis, Sandwich, and Sagamore. Ride past cranberry bogs, Cape Cod Bay, Cape Cod Canal, and other sights. Younger kids may get restless on the one-and-three-quarter-hour trip, but fortunately food is available. There are also three-hour dinner trips. Call (508) 771–3778 for information.

Shopping

You'll find antique shops, galleries, and country stores throughout the Cape. If you need some basics, stop at Falmouth Mall, Route 28, open seven days. It has major stores, such as Bradlees, specialty shops, and a cinema. Bargain shop at Cape Cod Factory Outlet Mall, off exit 1, Route 6, Sagamore. Kids' stores include Toy Liquidators and Carter's Childrenswear.

Performing Arts

Melody Tent, 21 West Main Street, Hyannis, has nightly theater-in-the-round musical comedy concerts, with kids' shows on Thursday mornings. Call (508) 775–5630 for schedules. Summer theater is also performed at Falmouth Playhouse, Theatre Drive, Hatchville; (508) 563–5922. Contact the Chamber of Commerce for other summer playhouses and for the date in mid-August when the Boston Pops plays its annual performance on the Village Green in Hyannis.

SPECIAL EVENTS

Check with the Cape Cod Chamber of Commerce for details on these annual fairs and festivals and obtain the calendar of events.

April: Brewster in Bloom, daffodil festival.

July: Barnstable County Fair, with rides, exhibits, and food.

September: Harwich Cranberry Festival, week-long event with food tastings, band concerts, parade, craft show and sale, and more.

Thanksgiving through New Year's Eve: Christmas in Cape Cod, series of events including choirs, orchestras, caroling on the green, town-green lightings, and more.

WHERE TO STAY

The Cape Cod Chamber of Commerce has a comprehensive resort directory that includes campgrounds. Don't be disappointed: make reservations very early. If you're stuck, the information booths located throughout the Cape can also help with accommodations. The following, all on the Upper Cape, represent the variety of accommodations available for families.

The Breakers, 61 Chase Avenue, Dennisport, has newly renovated rooms, including minisuites and two-bedroom two-bath efficiencies. The

The breaching of a whale off Cape Cod will thrill family members of all ages.
(Courtesy Cape Cod Chamber of Commerce)

heated pool faces the ocean, and there's a private beach. Lower rates mid-week; (508) 398–6905.

Gull Wing Suites, 822 Main Street, South Yarmouth, is an all-suite motor inn that offers refrigerators, two pools, and family and weekend packages. Call (508) 394–9300/(800) 541–3480.

Lighthouse Inn, West Dennis, has cottages on seven oceanfront acres, a restaurant, plus tennis, pool, miniature golf, a private beach, and supervised activities for ages two and up in July and August. Call (508) 398–2244.

New Seabury Resort and Conference Center, midway between Falmouth and Hyannis, features 160 villas spread out over 2,000 oceanfront acres, with pool, golf, and tennis. A summer program keeps ages four and up busy, and there's a center for teens. Call (508) 477–9111/(800) 752–9700/(800) 222–2044.

WHERE TO EAT

What would a visit to Cape Cod be without a lobster dinner? Consult *The Cape Cod Times,* the local daily paper, for restaurant listings. On the

Lower Cape, the self-service **Bayside Lobster Hutt,** Commercial Street, Wellfleet Center, is in an old oyster shack and offers inexpensive, fresh Cape seafood. Upper Cape locals love **Joe Mac's,** Taunton Avenue, Dennis. It's not fancy, but families feel at home (there's a game room for kids), and the menu includes everything from pizza to lobsters. **Hearth 'n Kettle Family Restaurant** chain serves affordable, traditional food at locations in Plymouth, Orleans, South Yarmouth, Hyannis, and Falmouth. These restaurants are accessible for patrons in wheelchairs.

DAY TRIPS

American history comes alive in Plymouth, about halfway between the Cape and Boston. **Plimouth Plantation,** a 1627 village, is a fascinating place where costumed residents reenact daily life in New Plymouth. Adjoining the village is **Hobbamock's Homesite,** which features the Wampanoag Indians of southeastern New England and their culture. Step aboard *Mayflower II,* a reproduction of the ship that brought the Pilgrims to Plymouth in 1620. For more information call (508) 746–1622. Stop by to see **Plymouth Rock,** Water Street (which, with its portico protection, is not very imposing). Another day, take a passenger ferry to explore the splendid beaches and picturesque towns of **Martha's Vineyard,** only forty-five minutes from Wood's Hole. (See GETTING AROUND.)

FOR MORE INFORMATION

Cape Cod Chamber of Commerce, junction of Routes 6 and 132, Hyannis 02601 (508–362–3225), has helpful brochures and guides, including a resort guide that lists which lodgings are wheelchair accessible. In addition to their main location, the Chamber of Commerce operates several information booths: a large center on Route 3, exit 5; at the Bourne traffic circle in Buzzards Bay; and at the Sagamore rotary.

For a complete Massachusetts vacation kit, which includes Cape Cod, call the Massachusetts Office of Travel and Tourism: (617) 727–3201/ (800) 447–MASS Great Dates in the Bay State is a recorded list of statewide events, updated biweekly. Call (800) 227–MASS (Northeast only).

Emergency Numbers

The Cape is not tied into the 911 system. Each town has its own emergency numbers for ambulance, fire, and police prominently displayed in color on the front page of every phone book.

Hospitals: Cape Cod Hospital, 27 Park Street, Hyannis, well marked from all exits; (508) 771–1800. A smaller facility is Falmouth Hospital, 100

TerHeun Drive, Falmouth; (508) 457–3524. The twenty-four-hour emergency rooms at these two hospitals are jammed in the summer. If you have a smaller emergency, you may get faster service at one of the many walk-in clinics scattered throughout the Cape that are listed in the phone directory. Most keep standard office hours.

Poison Control: (800) 682–9211 from the Cape.

There are no twenty-four-hour pharmacies. Stop 'n Shop pharmacy, 65 Independence Drive, Hyannis (508–790–2149), is open from 8:00 A.M. to 8:00 P.M. Monday through Saturday and 12:00 P.M. to 9:00 P.M. on Sunday.

4
GREEN MOUNTAINS:
Manchester and southern Vermont

A southern Vermont vacation offers the best of both worlds: postcard perfect towns and villages, lush scenic beauty—and the choice of back-to-nature basics in the woods or pampered luxury at a resort. For rustic recreation head to the southern half of the Green Mountain National Forest, which starts at the Massachusetts border and extends north to the town of Wallingford. As for civilized pleasures southern Vermont boasts comfortable lodgings, terrific restaurants, and, if you like, structured activities at Stratton Mountain, a destination resort. The area around the village of Manchester is a good place to hang your family's collective hat while you explore surrounding mountains, trails, and man-made pleasures. Manchester has charming elm-lined streets and gracious white homes, and the adjacent town of Manchester Center is a shopping outlet haven.

GETTING THERE

The closest major airport to Manchester is Albany (New York) County Airport (518–592–1105), about ninety minutes away. Bradley International in Windsor Locks (Hartford), Connecticut, (203–627–3000) is about a two-hour drive away; it's convenient for those staying in the Stratton area. Car rentals are available at both airports. Two taxi services and a limousine company provide service to all major airports and train stations.

The Amtrak Montrealer from New York stops at several Vermont towns. The closest is Bellows Falls about 40 miles away, convenient to the Stratton area. The closest Amtrak station from Manchester is Albany-Rensselaer, New York. Call (800) USA-RAIL.

Vermont Transit buses arrive and depart in front of Rite-Aid Drug

Store, Route 7A, Main Street, in Manchester Center. Buy tickets at the dry cleaner behind the Wild World Science and Nature Store.

Manchester Center is at the junction of routes 11–30 and 7A. The two-lane State Route 7 leads to Manchester from Bennington in the south and from East Dorset in the north.

GETTING AROUND

The traffic entering Manchester Center during peak tourist season looks something like midtown Manhattan at rush hour—particularly at the main intersection of routes 7A and 11–30, where there's only a caution light to control traffic. The locals have dubbed the intersection "Malfunction Junction." But once you get beyond this, you'll find fairly smooth going on the area's highways and byways—except during "leaf peeping" season. Visitors heading directly to Bromley or Stratton can bypass "Malfunction Junction" by taking the new Route 7 from the north and south and exiting onto Route 11–30, then heading north. In the summer, an open-air trolley transports passengers from parking lots to various shopping areas.

WHAT TO SEE AND DO

Parks, Forests, and Mountains

A four-season destination, Manchester offers the recreation of its surrounding mountains, forests, and lakes.

Green Mountain National Forest has a District Office in Manchester, Route 11–30 (802–362–2307), that provides information on recreational opportunities, including wilderness areas, hiking trails, campgrounds with brooks and ponds, picnic areas, and winter ski trails and snowmobiling.

If you're here during the famous **Vermont foliage**, some of the best viewing is in the Manchester District along Forest Road 10, which crosses the Green Mountains between Peru and Danby. South of town in the Arlington/West Wardsboro area, the Kelley Stand Road reaches an altitude of 2,726 feet, revealing breathtaking foliage. Along the way look for beaver ponds and deer. Closed in the winter this road serves as a great self-guided nature trail for families.

Another spectacular view is from Mt. Equinox, on Route 7A south of Manchester. Drive the steep 5½-mile toll road that goes up to the 3,816-foot summit which affords views of New York, New Hampshire, Massachusetts, and Quebec. Be sure your car's transmission, brakes, and radiator are in good shape before setting out.

There are many **cross-country skiing** trails in the Manchester District of the Forest. For families rangers recommend the more moderate terrain around Grout Pond and Peru. For groomed trails, however, opt for Hildene and Stratton (see the following listings) or the Viking Ski Touring Center in Londonderry, past Bromley Mountain, with over 40 kilometers of groomed trails through open fields and woodlands. Call (802) 824–3933 for information.

Developed **campgrounds** are located at several sites in this district. One of the nicest is Hapgood Pond in Peru, northeast of town, with a beach where local families swim.

The **Appalachian and Long hiking trails**, which share the same route in the Manchester District, extend along the ridge line of the Green Mountains from Massachusetts to Canada, crossing the Green Mountain National Forest. The trail is identified by white painted blazes on trees and rocks. It's possible to take a pleasant summer or fall day hike on the trail, which crosses Route 11 between Manchester Center and Peru. Park at the trail head and either cross the road and hike south to Spruce Peak or follow the trail north for ⅖ mile to Bromley Brook. If your kids are good hikers (the last half mile is steep), continue 2 miles to the summit of Bromley Mountain (elevation 3,260 feet). Round trip this hike should take about three and one half hours. Note: There are no toilet facilities on the trails. On autumn hikes anywhere in the forest, be aware of changeable trail conditions, weather (call 802–773–7500), and hunting seasons (during deer season in November, the Forest allows hunting with rifles; especially avoid hiking in the forest in November).

Merck Forest and Farmland Center, northwest of Manchester off Route 315 in Rupert; (802) 394–7836. Operated by a private, nonprofit organization to provide outdoor educational and recreational opportunities, Merck Forest spreads over 2,802 acres. The facility is open to the public throughout the year. Activities include swimming in Birch Pond (there are no lifeguards), fishing, camping, hiking, and skiing. This is a great place for kids, particularly younger ones who like the small nature museum, farm animals, and the self-guided 1½-mile nature trail.

In addition, 26 miles of hiking and skiing trails wind throughout the forest, and there's primitive camping at eleven overnight shelters. The lodge, used as a warming hut for skiers, is headquarters for special programs such as winter wildlife studies. Seasonal events include a winter solstice celebration where visitors hear solstice stories and traditions and participate in outdoor activities. Register at the gate and pick up a map. Although there is no admission fee, contributions are welcome. Note: Hunters are permitted during legal hunting seasons.

Emerald Lake State Park, East Dorset (802–362–1655), is just a short drive north of Manchester. Residents and visitors come for the sandy beach, boat rentals, picnic area, and campsites. The other attraction is the easy-to-moderate hiking trails, which take you along the shoreline through hemlock forests to an old beaver meadow. Another trail follows old town roads, passing by former homesteads. The surrounding mountains and crystal clear water make this a quiet, scenic place to spend an afternoon.

Manchester Center's town recreation center, not far from Main Street on Route 30, has a nice pool and small playground. Nonresidents may use the facilities (although for a higher fee than residents).

Museums and Historic Sites

American Museum of Flyfishing, Route 7A, Manchester; (802) 362–3300. The subject may not sound thrilling, but this museum, located inside the Orvis flagship retail store, is quite interesting, and it's free. You'll see rods, reels, flies, art, literature, photos, manuscripts, and other memorabilia relating to fly fishing. Some belonged to such avid sportsmen as Dwight Eisenhower, Daniel Webster, Herbert Hoover, Ernest Hemingway, Bing Crosby, and others. Orvis is well known for its fly-fishing gear and also sells classic men's and women's country clothes, so you can browse around the museum and shop in one swoop.

Hildene, Route 7A, Manchester Village; (802) 362–1788. Abe's eldest son, Robert Todd Lincoln, lived in this twenty-four-room Georgian Revival mansion, and his descendants stayed until 1975. The home, with original furniture and family memorabilia, includes a 1908 Aeolian pipe organ that is sure to grab your kids' attention. Stroll in the formal gardens and enjoy the panoramic views. If you're here right after Christmas, Hildene offers candlelight tours that start with a sleigh ride to the main house and include hot cider and cookies. There's a visitor's center in the carriage barn with exhibits and an audiovisual presentation. Cross-country ski on the property's 412 acres; group ski lessons are given daily.

Attractions

Bromley Alpine Slide and Scenic Chairlift, on Bromley Mountain, 6 miles east on Route 11; (802) 824–5522. Coast down a winding, mile-long slope on passenger-controlled sleds (there's room for two). Or ride the chairlift to the midstation and back for views of surrounding states. At the base, you eat lunch on the deck of the outdoor café.

In the winter, Bromley is a downhill skiing area with a loyal following. One of the oldest in Vermont (it opened in 1936), and the closest to Manchester, the area doesn't have the glitz and glamour of nearby Stratton. But fans come for its down-to-earth charm, southern exposure, 35 varied trails, and its family orientation: there are comprehensive kids' programs and a state-accredited nursery.

Stratton Mountain, Stratton, about thirty-five minutes northwest of Manchester, off Route 30; (802) 297–2200/(800) THE–MTNS, is southern Vermont's highest peak. Stratton Mountain Village, on twenty-two acres with shops, restaurants, and lodgings, is truly a destination in itself.

A tour of Hildene, a Georgian Revival mansion that Abraham Lincoln's eldest son lived in, provides a pleasant outing. (Courtesy Vermont Travel Division)

You may decide to stay there as lodging includes a 91-room condominium hotel, plus villas and town houses. Day trippers, however, can take advantage of many of the resort's facilities.

In the summer the Starship XII gondola affords 360-degree views across four states. Take a ride just for the scenery, or to reach hiking trails (maps available at the gondola) or mountain bike trails. Your family can join a two-hour guided mountain bike tour or go out on your own. Tennis and golf are big at Stratton, and a number of tournaments are held here. Tennis or golf-school packages are available with or without lodging. Stratton Junior Day Camp for ages seven to eleven and twelve to seventeen includes at least four-and-one-half hours of daily tennis instruction. Daily or weekly rates are available. Other summer pleasures: escorted horseback trail rides and pony rides (call Stratton Stables at 802–297–2200), and swimming and windsurfing on Stratton Lake (instruction through the New England Sailboard Academy). On weekdays kids can attend Camp Manicknung on a daily, weekly, or monthly basis: Little Bears is for ages three to five; Big Bears, ages six to twelve. Baby Bears under three have fully licensed day-care in the new child-care center in the base lodge.

In the winter, skiing is the main attraction. Stratton has over ninety-two trails covering 476 acres, more skiing on a single peak than any other area in the East. There's a full ski school program for Big Cubs, ages seven to twelve, and a SKIwee-affiliated Little Cub program for ages four to six. Child-care for ages six weeks to five years is in the base lodge child-care center. Sun Bowl Ski Touring Center offers 20 kilometers of groomed trails and 50 kilometers of backcountry skiing, along with instruction and rentals. Sleigh rides are offered every day but Monday. Stratton's Sports Center—with indoor tennis, pool, racquetball, aerobics, and a fitness center—is open to resort guests.

Performing Arts

Dorset Theatre, Cheney Road, Dorset, northwest of Manchester, puts on performances year-round, with local players in the winter and a professional troupe in the summer. Call (802) 867–5777. Manchester's Southern Vermont Art Center, West Road, has summer concerts, films, and art classes; (802) 362–1405. Stratton Mountain hosts a summer-long series of concerts featuring top performers. Acts range from classical and jazz to pop, country, rock, and comedy. They also sponsor an annual arts festival in late September to mid-October that includes visual and performing artists. Call (802) 297–2200 for more information. The Mark Skinner Library, Route 7A, Manchester Village, has weekly films, children's authors, storytellers, and events for kids; stop by for a schedule. Check the weekly *Vermont News Guide* for listings of other events.

Shopping

Manchester is outlet heaven: discount stores include Anne Klein, Donna Karan, Esprit, Calvin Klein, Brooks Brothers, Benetton, Boston Traders Kids, Liz Claiborne, Polly Flinders—you name it, it's here! Other notable area stores: The Enchanted Doll House, 2½ miles north on Route 7A, has twelve delightful rooms of play and collector dolls, dollhouses, stuffed animals, miniatures, and books. Call (802) 362–1327.

Shopping at the Jelly Mill and Friends, in town on Route 7A, is great fun: four floors include everything from toys to kitchenware, unusual collectibles, gourmet foods, candy, and the Buttery Restaurant (802–362–3494). Northshire Bookstore, Main Street in Manchester Center, has an excellent assortment of books, including a great children's section (802–362–2200). South of town on Route 7A, Basketville has hundreds of homemade baskets and other products; (802) 387–5509.

Vermont Country Store, Route 100, Weston, is old-fashioned, with penny candy, practical clothing, regional foods, and home and kitchen supplies; (802) 824–3184. Weston, about forty minutes northeast of Manchester, has several other interesting shops, including the Weston Bowl Mill, also on Route 100, where they make and sell more than two hundred wooden items for the home; (802) 824–6219.

SPECIAL EVENTS

Sporting Events

A number of ski and snow-board events, including national championship-level tournaments, are held at Bromley and Stratton, which also hosts championship golf and tennis tournaments. Check with resorts for schedules.

Fairs and Festivals

Many small towns around Manchester have fairs, festivals, and church suppers throughout the year. Check the weekly calendar in the *Vermont News Guide*. Here are some highlights.

January: Manchester Winter Carnival, with adult, family, and children's winter sports. Boy Scouts Annual Race, Bromley.

Easter: Egg Hunt and Parade, sponsored by Mother Myrick's.

August: Bondville Fair, Bondville Fairgrounds (near Stratton), Vermont's oldest fair has games, entertainment, food, and tractor and horse pull competitions. Manchester Crafts Fair.

WHERE TO STAY

Call the **Area Lodging Service** at (802) 824–6915/(800) 677–7829. **Bromley Lodging Services** (802–824–5458) can make summer and winter reservations for fully equipped condominiums. Another choice for families is **The Equinox**, Historic Route 7A, Manchester Village, which has been in this area since 1769. If you like New England atmosphere with modern amenities, this is for you. Fully restored, the Equinox has rooms and suites plus town houses with kitchens and porches, an eighteen-hole golf course, health club, tennis, and heated pools. Call (802) 362–4700/ (800) 362–4747.

Basin Harbor Club, Basin Road, Vergennes, 25 miles south of Burlington, is directly on Lake Champlain's eastern shore. Everything here is well-manicured: the lovely grounds, the staff, and the guests. Boys and men are required to wear coats and ties in the public area after 6:00 P.M. The playground offers supervised activities for ages three to ten in the summer from 9:00 A.M. to noon. Kids eat dinner together, too. Afternoons bring craft activities suitable for all ages. Older children can avail themselves of the resort's superb recreation: golf, tennis, swimming, softball, and lots of water sports on the lake or poolside. If there are enough teens on the property, evening activities are planned. The resort is open from June through mid-October. Call (802) 475–2311/(800) 622–4000.

Johnny Seesaw's, Route 11, Peru, on top of Bromley Mountain, has suites and cabins with fireplaces. The game room, tennis court, and swimming pool will keep everybody happy. Rates include breakfast. Call (802) 824–5533/(800) 424–CSAW.

Kandahar, Junction of routes 11 and 30, Bromley Mountain, is a family resort motel featuring a trout pond, heated pool, game room, canoes and rowboats, and hiking and cross-country trails. A family restaurant serves dinner. Call (802) 824–5531/(800) 879–STAY.

Manchester View Motel, Route 7A, is set on nine acres and offers lovely mountain views. There are one- and two-bedroom suites, fireplaces, refrigerators, jacuzzis, an outdoor pool, and golf and tennis privileges at Manchester Country Club. Call (802) 363–2739.

WHERE TO EAT

The Manchester and the Mountain Area Guide, available from the Chamber of Commerce, lists restaurants. Also check in the weekly *Vermont News Guide,* which is free and available all over town.

Here are some choices for families: **The Quality Restaurant,** right on Main Street in Manchester Center, has been dishing out hearty home-style breakfast, lunch, and dinner since 1920. (Children's menus are available.) This was the setting for Norman Rockwell's famous War News painting; there's a copy on the wall over the counter. Rockwell used locals for a number of his paintings. Call (802) 362–9839 for menu information. **The Sirloin Saloon** is a popular steak house right in the heart of Manchester Center on Route 11–30. There's a big salad bar and a kid's menu. Call (802) 362–2600. Heavenly homemade muffins, freshly squeezed juice, Irish scones, buttermilk pancakes: you'll find them at **Up For Breakfast** on Main Street. Call (802) 362–4204. For dessert, head straight to **Mother Myrick's Confectionery and Ice Cream Parlor** on Route 7A, where you'll find sinfully delicious chocolate desserts and other delicacies; (802) 362–1560.

DAY TRIPS

Bennington, about 20 miles south, has some worthwhile sights. The town was the site of a successful 1777 battle, which some called a turning point of the American Revolution. At 306 feet the **Bennington Battle Monument,** a half mile west of the junction of SR 9 and U.S. 7, is the tallest structure in Vermont. There's a diorama of the battle and an exhibit area in the base. Take the elevator to the upper lookout chamber for panoramic views. Call (802) 447–0550.

Stop by the **Bennington Museum,** West Main Street, which houses the famous 1776 Bennington Stars and Stripes as well as Civil and Revolutionary War uniforms and artifacts, plus old toys and other interesting objects. The Grandma Moses Schoolhouse, donated by her family, houses memorabilia and the charming, primitive paintings of this beloved artist. Call (802) 447–1571.

Your kids might also like to walk or drive through the town's three covered bridges. The Silk Road and the Papermill bridges are near SR 67A. You'll find the Bert Henry Bridge on Murphy Road.

On historic Route 7A, heading back to Manchester, stop in Arlington, where Norman Rockwell lived from 1939 to 1953. The **Norman Rockwell Exhibition**, SR 7A, Main Street, contains hundreds of *Saturday Evening Post* covers and printed work housed in a historic 1800s church; (802) 375–6423.

FOR MORE INFORMATION

Manchester and the Mountains Chamber of Commerce has an office on Adams Park Green, Route 7, Manchester Center, 05255; (802) 362–2100. Vermont summer and winter guides contain information and lodging on the Manchester area; pick one up at the Vermont Travel Division, 134 State Street, Montpelier 05602; (802) 828–3236.

Emergency Numbers
Ambulance, fire, and police in Manchester: 911 (If you are staying in outlying areas, check the front of the phone book.)
Poison Control: (802) 658–3456
Rite-Aid Pharmacy, Route 7A, Main Street, Manchester Center, is open 9:00 A.M. to 9:00 P.M., Monday through Saturday, and 9:00 A.M. to 5:00 P.M. on Sunday.
Twenty-four-hour emergency rooms are located in Bennington, 20 miles south, or Rutland, 25 miles north, at the Southwestern Vermont Medical Center, Dewey Street, Bennington (802–442–6361); and Rutland Regional Medical Center, 160 Allen Street, Rutland (802–775–7111).

5
JACKSON AND THE MOUNT WASHINGTON VALLEY
New Hampshire

Jackson and the Mount Washington Valley, in the heart of the White Mountains, offer a splendid array of outdoor family activities. In the winter Jackson comes alive; it's a noted cross-country ski area. Gliding through a snowy forest is great fun, and the slow pace, perfect for admiring icicles and looking for deer tracks, allows for easy conversation with your kids, one of the prime reasons for going away together in the first place. From Jackson it's an easy drive to several downhill ski areas that feature quality children's programs. And in fall the woods fill with brilliant reds, oranges, and yellows.

In summer the mountains offer miles of trails for horseback riding and hiking, and clear streams for fishing and wading. One cautionary note: Avoid the region during black fly season. While the time period and the intensity of the infestation vary with the weather, generally these insects invade for three weeks from late May to mid-June. For anglers, the black flies bring some of the season's best fishing, but most visitors will want to avoid the woods during this time. (Some seasoned campers swear that Avon's Skin So Soft, in addition to its other attributes, also repels these pests.) So before booking in late May to mid-June, check with the locals first about conditions.

GETTING THERE

Portland Jetport (207–774–3941), about ninety minutes southwest of Jackson in Portland, Maine, is the closest major airport and is serviced by most major domestic airlines. Other airports include Manchester, New Hampshire's Airport (603–624–6556), about 100 miles southeast of the region; Boston's Logan Airport (617–561–1800), 140 miles to the south, and the Eastern Slope Regional Airport in Fryeburg, Maine (207–935–2800), about twenty-five minutes from North Conway.

By bus, Concord Trailways (800–639–3317) runs a daily route from Boston, arriving in Jackson about 9:00 P.M.

For those traveling by car, Jackson and the surrounding towns are easy to locate off I–93. From Boston it's a three-hour drive into Jackson, taking I–95 to Portsmouth, New Hampshire, then Spaulding Turnpike and Route 16 to North Conway, and into town. Avoid the North Conway traffic, which can be formidable, by taking West Side Road at the first light in Conway to River Road, and then taking Route 16 or Route 32.

GETTING AROUND

A car is an absolute necessity, although families should bring their bicycles as well. Car rentals are available at regional airports in Conway, which is just south of Jackson.

WHAT TO SEE AND DO

Since most area attractions use post office boxes and route numbers instead of numbered street addresses, route numbers are listed here. Call the attractions if you need more specific directions.

Mountains Magic: Summer Outdoor Recreation

Hiking. With more than 250 trails in the White Mountain National Forest's 750,000 acres, there's a great variety of paths for all ability levels. City kids especially appreciate the feathery green and cool woods.

For some easy adventure with younger kids, try these under-one-hour round-trip trails. Wear your bathing suits on the ⅖-mile hike to Gibbs Falls on the Crawford Path, which starts 13⁹⁄₁₀ miles west of Silver Springs Country Store and Campground, Bartlett. The road ascends slightly and then there's a steep descent to the falls. Another easy hike, the Diana's Bath trail, ⅖ mile, takes you along a babbling brook to a series of small cascades and shallow pools.

Other popular hikes include the **Crystal Cascade/Tuckerman's Ravine**, Mount Washington. The ¾-mile round-trip hike starts from the AMC Pinkham Notch Camp, Route 16, north of Jackson, and leads to the waterfall. If you continue on to Tuckerman Ravine, 4⅘ miles, three hours round trip, you'll see splendid views of Mt. Washington. The trail to **Arethusa Falls,** Crawford Notch State Park, Bartlett (603–374–2272), begins from the parking lot on the west side of Route 302, Crawford Notch. Follow the north bank of Bemis Brook to the falls, the highest in the state, cascading from 200 feet. From the south side of Hurricane Mountain Road, North Conway, take the **Black Cap Mountain** trail for 1½ miles, one hour round trip. Rewards include an exceptional view of the valley.

For hiking that's a bit more challenging, good for hearty elementary school kids and teens, try this two-hour round-trip hike. **Winniweta Falls** is a 2⅒-mile relatively easy hike that begins 3⅒ miles north of Jackson's Covered Bridge. The trail crosses Ellis River, meadows blooming with wild flowers, and ascends for the last fifteen minutes as you near the 40-foot falls.

Obtain hiking information from the Mt. Washington Valley Information Center and the Jackson Resort Association (See FOR MORE INFORMATION). The Silver Springs Country Store and Campground, Route 302, Bartlett, New Hampshire 03812 (603–374–2221), sells a tip sheet of "Twenty of the Most Rewarding Hikes in the White Mountains" for a nominal fee.

The Appalachian Mountain Club (AMC), another reliable source of information, has its main headquarters at Pinkham Notch, Mt. Washington. Call (603) 466–2721 or (603) 466–2725 for trail information, and (603) 466–2727 for workshop and family vacation package information. The AMC offers quality trail maps and advice, plus lectures and workshops for children and adults. Learn about flora and fauna, bushwhacking, bug and birding, and wild edibles. Many workshops include an overnight stay in one of the AMC area huts. Families new to hiking might consider a beginner backpacking and camping weekend workshop. If that's too long, try an AMC Family Discovery day hike for 4 miles of fun. AMC activities operate year-round. In the fall follow a waterfall tour, in the winter sample snowshoeing, and in the early spring go maple sugaring.

For those who want to enjoy Mt. Washington but only want a limited amount of walking, sign on for an AMC Alpine Garden Tour. Guides drive you to the top of Mt. Washington then lead you on a hike through the Alpine Garden and back up to the summit for your van ride back down. Call (603) 466–2727.

Eastern Mountain Sports (EMS), Main Street, North Conway (603–356–5433), also organizes guided hikes on weekend mornings from June through September.

Llama Trekking in the White Mountains. Even a tenderfoot can see Maine's valleys and the purple ridges of New Hampshire's peaks from a scenic lookout high in the White Mountains. With a llama trek from Telemark Inn, Bethel, Maine, you get to these heights the easy way—the llamas carry all your equipment. While the inn is located in Bethel, the hikes actually explore nearby New Hampshire's White Mountains. You and your kids (as young as 4) enjoy the challenge of leading the llamas, intelligent and furry beasts of burden, to your backwoods camp. These trips appeal to families with young kids, and to parents and grandparents who want to share the wilderness and the wildlife with their clan without the work or responsibility of setting up camp. The guides pitch the tents, cook dinner, and wake you up in the morning with hot towels, hot coffee, or hot chocolate.

The owner, Steve Crone, who has a great affinity for both kids and llamas, also offers a variety of family-pleasing day trips. These include one-day llama treks, guided hikes, and canoe trips. Crone also leads a seven-day combination llama trek and canoe trip. For information, contact the Telemark Inn Llama Treks, RFD #2, Box 800, Bethel, Maine 04217; (207) 836–2703.

Canoeing/Kayaking/Whitewater Rafting. Canoe outfitters Saco Bound, Route 302, Center Conway (603–447–3801), make it easy to enjoy a lazy paddle on the Saco River, combining sunning, swimming, and picnicking. Follow the current for 43 miles if you go the distance, or take a shorter trip. Saco Bound provides equipment and instructions. They even provide a guide for a day-long trip on Tuesdays and Thursdays in July and August. Call ahead. For a more exciting ride, try springtime white-water rafting. Most excursions include a steak barbecue lunch and time to swim and explore the river and surroundings.

The Appalachian Mountain Club (AMC) organizes a two-day canoe and camping trip to Lake Umbagog. Call (603) 466–2727 for more information.

Biking. For older children and adults, mountain biking offers a challenge along with some spectacular views. The North Conway Athletic Club (603–356–5774) organizes mountain bike outings and suggests good routes. Bike rentals are available at the Joe Jones Shop (603–356–9411) and the Sports Outlet (603–356–3133), both in North Conway.

If you want a guide, Off Road Cycling Adventures, North Conway (603–356–2080), operates one-to-five-day custom-tailored tours of the White Mountains that include a bike, helmet, and a box lunch. Children must be eleven years or older.

Parks. **Echo Lake State Park**, Route 302, North Conway (603–356–2672), is a good family day trip as the park has a swimming area for children, picnic tables and grills for lunch or a barbecue, and a trail that circles the lake. You can even rent a boat. The park is open June through Labor Day.

Fishing. With forty-five lakes and ponds as well as 650 miles of streams in the region, Mt. Washington Valley is an angler's delight. Good spots include the Wild and Saco rivers as well as Basin Reservoir and Russell Pond. A state license is required for nonresidents over twelve, and certain restrictions apply. Call the New Hampshire Fish and Game Department at (603) 271–3421 for more information.

Tennis. New England Tennis and Hiking Holidays, Mt. Cranmore Recreation Center, North Conway (603–356–9696 or 800–869–0949), organizes hiking and tennis vacations, including meals and lodging at local inns or at condominiums. While not catering to families, their programs are suitable for parents and teens.

Golfing. Appreciate the beauty of the mountains from the valley golf courses. Duffers have their choice of three public eighteen-hole courses in the area: North Conway Country Club (603–356–9700), Hale's Location Country Club (603–356–6377), and the Wentworth Resort Golf Club (603–383–9461).

Additional Summer Through Fall Attractions
Scenic Drives and Views
In summer and fall these mountain drives offer eye-popping vistas. The **Mount Washington Auto Road**, Route 16, Pinkham Notch, Gorham (603–466–3988), is famous. Take your car 8 winding miles to Mount Washington's summit; at 6,288 feet, it's the highest in the northeastern United States. The drive is worth the views, but only if you're comfortable with steep, windy roads as the grades average 12 percent. If the sky is clear, you can see six states; if not, you can still see the Sherman Adams Summit museum with its slide show, *Home of the World's Worst Weather.* The locals are not kidding either. Be sure to dress warmly, for this hour-long trip to the top of Mt. Washington is known for its winds and quickly changing weather. To access the auto road take Route 16 about 8 miles south of Gorham to Glenn House, which is open mid-May to mid-October.

Another well-known scenic route is the **Kancamagus Highway**, Route 112, which runs 35 miles from Conway to Lincoln. Stop for a picnic at Lower Falls (6⁷⁄₁₀ miles from Conway) and an easy hike through the Rocky Gorge 8⅖ miles from Conway. The short walk from the parking lot at Sabbaday Falls, 14⁹⁄₁₀ miles from Conway, leads you by cascading falls. With any luck you'll spot some moose taking a splash at Lily Pond (18¹⁄₁₀ miles from Conway). Cool off at the Wilderness Trail, 28⅖ miles from Conway. The trail from the parking area leads you along a suspension bridge to a spot with good river swimming.

But you can still enjoy the views even if you don't want to hike or drive. Kids love the **Conway Scenic Railroad**, Main Street, North Conway; (603) 356–5251 or (800) 232–5251. This one-hour ride in an antique coach pulled by a steam- or diesel-powered engine departs from an 1874 railway station and chugs along 11 miles of tracks. In warm weather spend some time in the open-air car. Reserve in advance during the fall foliage season. The railroad is open from May through October. For a more extensive and impressive train ride, climb Mt. Washington on the second steepest railway track in the world. At the **Mount Washington Cog Railway**, Route 302, Bretton Woods (603–846–5404 or 800–922–8825, ext. 7), an 1869 steam-powered train takes you to the top on a three-hour trip over rough and rugged terrain. Early risers save money on a discounted 8:00 A.M. train ride. Reservations are recommended; it's open May through October.

The **Wildcat Mountain Gondola**, Route 16, Pinkham Notch (603–466–3326), provides yet another way to climb the White Mountains without hiking boots. This fifteen-minute ride brings you to the top of the 4,100-foot Wildcat Mountain for a sweeping view. Bring a bag lunch for a summit picnic, explore the surrounding trails, then ride back down. The gondola is open mid-May through mid-October. Call for scheduled hours.

Other Fall Attractions. In fall, bite your way into some of the areas edible wonders: crisp apples. Pick your own bushels at several area orchards, including Hatch Orchard in Center Conway; (603) 447–5687.

Additional Attractions. **Story Land**, Route 16, Glen; (603) 383–4293. This is a must-see if you have preschool children or young grade-schoolers. They will love the come-to-life Mother Goose settings complete with child-size buildings and recognizable characters. Humpty Dumpty—sitting on a wall, of course—greets you. Rest on a bench, and Little Miss Muffet's spider comes and sits down beside you. Walk into Peter, Peter, Pumpkin Eater's house, and visit the Old Woman in the Shoe. Drift by the castle on a swan boat, get sprayed by a gentle raft ride, or sit in a Polar Coaster, where the seats resemble walruses. Story Land is great low-tech fun for little kids. It's open from June through October.

Next door, operated mid-May to mid-October by the same company, is **Heritage New Hampshire**, Route 16, Glen; (603) 383–9776. Explore local history here, beginning with a 1634 English village from which the ship *Reliance* sailed to Portland. Visitors "see" President George Washington, the effects of the Industrial Revolution in New Hampshire, and come back to the present on a simulated train ride through Crawford Notch at peak foliage.

Less educational, but also fun, is the **Attitash Alpine Slide and Outdoor Amusements**, Route 302, Bartlett; (603) 374–2368. Choose the fast track or a slower one. The park also offers a scenic chair lift ride to the top of the mountain and plenty of space for a countryside picnic. It's open from May through October. Another play park, the **Fun Factory Amusement Park**, Route 16, North Conway (603–356–6541), features minigolf and a water slide that twists and turns before dropping you into a pool.

Adventures abound in the majestic White Mountains. (Courtesy Mt. Washington Valley Visitors Bureau)

Somewhat hokey, but also fun, especially for young kids, are Santa's Village and Six Gun City. **Santa's Village**, Route 2, Jefferson (603–586–4445), is Santa's summer home. Tots delight in their visit with Santa's helpers and with the big guy himself. Christmas-theme attractions include a kiddie roller coaster, a Yule Log water flume, animals to pet, and two shows—the Jingle Jamboree and the Live Tropical Bird Show. At **Six Gun City**, Route 2, Jefferson (603–586–4592), see the Wild West of the White Mountains complete with a frontier village, a bank robbery, and a sheriff and outlaw shoot-em-up. Kids may even earn a deputy's badge. At the Frontier Show, hear stories of this hard-knock life; at the Miniature Diamond B Ranch, pet miniature goats, burros, and horses. Amusements include a miniature golf course, water slide, and boat rides. It's open from mid-June to Labor Day.

Winter Fun

Horse Logic Hay and Sleigh Rides, Route 116, Jackson (603–383–9876), bundles you into its cozy carriage and takes you through Jackson's scenic winter wonderland.

Downhill Skiing. Mt. Washington Valley is home to several family-friendly ski areas. It's a great place to learn how to ski, (ask about Learn to Ski packages). **Attitash**, in Bartlett (603–374–0946), has something for all ages beginning with an Attitots ski program for ages one to three, and continuing up to an Attiteens racing program. Lift tickets for kids cost less with a pay-what-you-ride system and a Sunday kids-pay-their-age deal. **Black Mountain**, in Jackson (603–383–4490 or 800–698–4490 in New Hampshire), offers Midweek Madness, which makes weekday skiing low budget. A Family Passport allows two kids (ages five to fifteen) to ski free when two adults purchase tickets.

Waterville Valley, New Hampshire, offers comprehensive ski programs for kids, child care for wee ones, a family-friendly atmosphere, and a variety of packages. Often kids ski free midweek, so ask. Choose to stay in condos, bed and breakfasts, or lodges. In summer the ski area offers attractively priced family packages and lots of activities. For information call (800) 468–2553. (See WHERE TO STAY.)

Consult the Official Guide to Mt. Washington Valley for a full description of ski area offerings.

Cross-Country Skiing. New Hampshire's White Mountains offer a classic ski getaway not only for downhill (Alpine) but for cross-country (Nordic) skiers as well. Besides 600 kilometers of groomed trails, the area frequently offers a special reduced-rate bed and breakfast ski package midweek. As you glide from inn to inn, the trails take you near covered bridges, over snowy fields, and along creeks. Several of the lodgings welcome children. For package information call Country Inns in the White Mountains, P.O. Box 2025, North Conway 03860; (800) 562–1300.

Jackson has been rated one of the four best places in the world to cross-country ski because of the abundance, quality, and variety of trails. The paths around the village through meadows and woods are particularly scenic. Ski up to a country inn for lunch or tea. The Jackson Ski Touring Foundation, Jackson (603–383–9355), makes sure that more than 90 miles of trails in the village of Jackson and throughout the White Mountain National Forest are groomed. Trails are marked by ability, and maps are available from the center. Ski rentals and lessons are available at the Jack Frost Nordic Shop.

The **Mt. Washington Valley (MWV) Ski Touring**, Intervale (603–356–9920), is a similar organization that offers 65 kilometers of groomed trails. Special events include a Holiday Cookie Fest when skiers go from inn to inn tasting holiday cookies. The **Appalachian Mountain Club**, Route 16, Pinkham Notch (603–466–2727), offers its hiking trails for cross-country skiing. The **Intervale Nordic Center**, off Route 16A, Intervale, North Conway (603–356–5541), features 40 kilometers of trails and has snowshoe rentals to boot.

Ice Skating. When you tire of the snow, take to the ice at public rinks in Jackson Village as well as in Conway and North Conway Villages. If you didn't bring your own skates, rent them at Joe Jones' Ski and Sports Shop, North Conway (603–356–9411).

Shopping. With more than 200 factory outlet stores and no sales tax in New Hampshire, shopping in North Conway is worthwhile despite the frequent crowds. Scores of people come here seasonally to outfit the whole clan. With Levi's, Dexter Shoe, OshKosh B'Gosh, Benetton 012, Calvin Klein, Liz Claiborne, Donna Karan, Bugle Boy, Danskin, London Fog, L.L. Bean, and lots more, families pack their cars with bargains. Check the Official Guide to Mt. Washington Valley, available at the visitor information centers, for a full listing of outlet stores.

Performing Arts. The **Eastern Slope Playhouse**, Main Street, North Conway (603–356–5776), offers Broadway run musicals performed by the Mount Washington Valley Theater Company. Call in June for schedules and tickets. The **Arts Jubilee**, Settler's Green at Routes 16 and 302, North Conway (603–356–9393), is a fine arts festival featuring a weekly family series in the summer. Often you're treated to magicians, acrobats, country music, and even barbershop quartets.

SPECIAL EVENTS

For more information on events listed, call the Mt. Washington Valley Chamber of Commerce at (603) 356–3171.

January: Jackson Skiing Legends, Black Mountain, features a vintage attire ski race and a classic film festival.

February: Family Frolics Week at Mt. Cranmore, North Conway. Wildcat Silly Slaloms and kid's special events week, Wildcat Mountain. Winter Carnival, King Pine Ski Area, with races, barbecues, and fireworks.

March: Canada Month in Mt. Washington Valley, with special packages for the northern neighbors. Spring Carnival, Mt. Cranmore, North Conway. March Madness at King Pine Ski Area, family fun for all ages.

April: Easter Parade, North Conway.

May: Wildquack River Race Festival, Jackson Village. Race your duck in the stream or join in the Quackers Parade.

June: Annual Mt. Washington Valley Old Car Show, Grand Manor Antique Car Museum, Glen. Conway Village Festival, a weekend of fun featuring a parade, children's games, a pet show, and live entertainment. Mt. Washington Auto Road Climb to the Clouds, road race and celebration.

July: New Hampshire State Parks Week features special family activities. Fourth of July Carnival, North Conway, has face painting, fried dough, and rides galore. Independence Day Parade, North Conway. Jackson Family Day in the Park has special children's July fourth celebration.

July/August: Sunday night outdoor band concerts in North Conway.

August: Attitash Equine Festival, Attitash Mountain, Bartlett, is a world-class riding show that also includes a children's playground, pony rides, and food fest. Later in the month the Attitash Double R Rodeo comes to town with bronco riding, steer wrestling, and country music. Blueberry Festival, Attitash Mountain, Bartlett, has a kid's Blueberry Olympics.

September: Railfans' Day, Conway Scenic Railroad, celebrates old trains. New Hampshire Jazz Festival, Attitash Mountain, Bartlett, has mountains of jazz.

October: Fryeburg Fair, Fryeburg, Maine; more than a century-long tradition, this country fair is the real thing. Sandwich Fair, Sandwich, New Hampshire, bustles with farm animal activity, a parade, and kid's fun.

WHERE TO STAY

After a day full of mountain air and activity, come home to a cozy New England inn. Here are some that are family friendly, and have hiking and cross-country skiing trails just out the back door. Be sure to ask about weekend or other family packages.

Attitash Mountain, Route 302 in Bartlett; (800) 862–1600, offers ski packages, family passes, and a variety of kids' programs for skiers and non-skiers alike. The Children's Center offers day care for infants and toddlers as well as a variety of full-day, learn-to-ski programs for Attitots, Attiteens, and Attidudes. Ask about weekend, mid-week, and vacation lodging packages. **Attitash Mountain Village,** across from the slopes, has one-, two-, and three-bedroom units, some of which have kitchenettes. For reservations call the **Attitash Travel and Lodging Bureau;** (800) 223–SNOW, which will provide you with information on bed and breakfasts, hotels, and inns. The service also arranges ski school lessons, rentals, lift tickets, and day care.

Ellis River House, P.O. Box 656, Jackson (603–383–9339 or 800–233–8309), is a turn-of-the-century farmhouse overlooking the Ellis River. The country breakfast includes homemade bread and fresh eggs. **Christmas Farm Inn,** Route 16B above the village, Jackson (603–383–4313 or 800–HI–ELVES), is a guaranteed hit for the younger ones with a game room, sauna, and outdoor pool. A small sitting room off the main parlor features a child-size rocking chair, as well as puzzles, games, and a television.

The **Eagle Mountain Resort,** Carter Notch Road, Jackson (603–383–9111), has a nine-hole golf course that becomes a cross-country ski area in winter. Other features include a health club, outdoor pool, and tennis courts. The **Wentworth Resort Hotel,** Route 16A at Carter Notch Road, Jackson; (603) 383–9700 or (800) 637–0013, is right in the heart of Jackson and offers sixty-two rooms. The cross-country ski trails start nearby, and the property features an outdoor ice rink in winter and an outdoor pool in summer. In warm weather try your skill at the eighteen-hole golf course, and on the tennis courts. At the **Sheraton White Mountain Inn,** Route 16 at Settlers' Green, North Conway (603–356–9300 or 800–648–4397), kids under twelve stay and eat for free.

The **Mount Washington Hotel & Resort,** Bretton Woods, New Hampshire 03575 (603–278–1000 or 800–258–0330), is a grande dame hotel built in 1902 that keeps to its early century pace. The hotel features 177 rooms, wrap-around porches, great views, and a golf course. The property also has the Bretton Woods Motor Inn and town homes complete with kitchens.

The **Nordic Village Vacation Resort,** Route 16, Jackson (603–383–9101 or 800–472–5207), offers one- and two-bedroom rental condominiums. The Mt. Washington Valley offers a reservation service. Call (800) 367–3364 for more information.

In winter **Waterville Valley,** New Hampshire, has comprehensive ski programs, and child care; in summer the area offers boating, tennis, horseback riding, a sports center, and a daily activity program for kids ages three to five, six to eight, and nine to twelve. Family activity packages get the gang going with daily tennis clinics, hikes, aerobic classes, as well as mountain biking, roller blading, and boating. Choose to stay at a variety of inns, lodges, or condominiums. For information call (800) 468–2553.

WHERE TO EAT

Try a smoked chicken and tortilla salad or a plain hearty New York Sirloin at **The Christmas Farm Inn,** Black Mountain Road, Jackson; (603) 383–4313. Taste a Reuben Express or a Turkey Trolley at **Glen Junction,** Route 302 in Glen (603–383–9660), where a toy train chugs around the room on a track on the wall. For seafood, **Snug Harbor,** Route 16, North Conway (603–356–3000), is the place with fried and baked regional fish and a little pirates kid's menu. **Elvio's,** Main Street, North Conway Village (603–356–3307), has the best pizza in town featuring thin-crust, thick-crust, and/or white varieties. **I Cugini,** Route 302, Bartlett (603–374–1977), has particularly good soup, pasta entrées, and a menu tailored to children's appetites.

The **Appalachian Mountain Club,** Route 16, Pinkham Notch, Gorham (603–466–2721), offers dinner get-togethers after a long day's hike. Dinner begins at 6:00 and don't be late. The menu changes daily. Call in advance for reservations.

After a trip on the Cog Railway, stop at **Fabyans Station,** next door, Route 302, Bretton Woods (603–846–2222), in the old railroad depot.

They offer hearty burgers and sandwiches. For dessert, out-of-towners will find a sweet surprise at **Ben & Jerry's Scoop Shop**, Norcross Place, North Conway; (603) 356–7720.

DAY TRIPS

There is no shortage of day trips from the Jackson area. **Portland, Maine,** is ninety minutes southeast, and **Boston** is two-and-a-half-hours south. (See the Boston and Portland chapters.)

Portsmouth offers **Strawbery Banke**, P.O. Box 300, Portsmouth, New Hampshire 03802; (603) 433–1100. This house museum includes more than forty houses that trace the development of the area from 1630 through the 1950s. Kids love the Colonial and Federal furniture and artifacts. The museum is open May through October, and weekends in December for a candlelight stroll. Portsmouth also features **The Children's Museum**, 280 Marcy Street, 03801 (603–436–3853), where there's hands-on fun for little ones.

FOR MORE INFORMATION

Jackson Resort Association, P.O. Box 304, Jackson (603–383–9356 from New Hampshire and Canada, 800–866–3334 from elsewhere), publishes a free visitor's travel guide and will book reservations for you. Mount Washington Valley Visitors Bureau, Box 2300, North Conway (603–356–3171), publishes the *Official Guide to Mt. Washington Valley.* For information on recreational facilities, including biking and hiking trails, contact the White Mountain National Forest at P.O. Box 638, Laconia, New Hampshire 03246; (603) 528–8721. Also check with the Trails Bureau, New Hampshire Division of Parks, and Recreation, P.O. Box 856, Concord, New Hampshire 03301; (603) 271–3556 (parks) or (603) 271–3627 (recreation services).

Tourist information booths are located in Jackson Village as well as North Conway and Conway villages. For specific locations, call the visitor's numbers listed above.

Check out the local happenings with *The Mountain Ear* (603–447–6336), Mt. Washington Valley's weekly newspaper. For twenty-four-hour weather-line call (603) 447–5252.

Emergency Numbers
Ambulance, fire, and police in Conway and North Conway: 911
Ambulance and fire in all other towns: 1–539–6119
Health-Net information line: (800) 499–4171

Memorial Hospital emergency room, Route 16, North Conway; (603) 356–5461

Poison Control: (800) 562–8236

Police in Bartlett: 1–539–2234

Police in Jackson and Glen: (800) 552–8960

There is no twenty-four-hour pharmacy. A convenient pharmacy is CVS Pharmacy, Shaw's/North Way Plaza, Route 16, North Conway; (603) 356–6916.

6
LAKE CHAMPLAIN AND BURLINGTON
Vermont

After the Great Lakes, Lake Champlain is the next largest inland lake in the United States. Extending southward from Canada, the 120-mile-long lake lies between New York State and Vermont, whose boundaries claim two-thirds of the lake. The sparkling blue water, beautiful bays, islands, and miles of Vermont shoreland are havens for swimming, sailing, boating, fishing, windsurfing, waterskiing—and just relaxing. (Keep an eye out for Champ, the sea monster who has allegedly been spotted several times over the years.) Burlington, Vermont's largest city, sits on the terraced eastern slopes of Lake Champlain and is the headquarters for navigation around the lake. It's also an important business and educational center, home to the University of Vermont. Burlington has a charming downtown, and some noteworthy attractions are nearby. Once you've explored the area, see what other pleasures the Champlain Valley holds.

GETTING THERE

Burlington International Airport, (802) 863–2874, is New England's third busiest. Car rentals are available at the airport.

Vermont Transit, 133 Saint Paul Street at Main, (802) 864–6811/ (800) 642–3133—Vermont/(800) 451–3292—New England. Buses go to and from other Vermont towns as well as Boston, Albany, and Montreal, with connections made with Greyhound.

Amtrak is at 29 Railroad Avenue, Essex Junction (5 miles east of Burlington); (802) 879–7298/(800) USA–RAIL. Trains run to and from New York and Montreal. A bus leaves hourly for downtown Burlington.

Auto/passenger ferries link Vermont and New York at three northern crossings: Burlington to Port Kent, New York (one-hour trip); Charlotte, Vermont, to Essex, New York (eighteen minutes); and Grand Isle, Vermont, to Plattsburgh, New York (twelve minutes). All are operated by Lake Champlain Transportation Company, King Street Dock; (802) 864–9804.

Burlington is at the end of the scenic portion of highways I–89 and SR 116.

GETTING AROUND

Public CCTA (Chittendon County Transit Authority) buses operate Monday through Saturday throughout the city and to outlying areas, including Shelburne, from the CCTA hub on Cherry and Church streets.

WHAT TO SEE AND DO

Museums and Historical Sites

We're starting with the biggest and the best: **Shelburne Museum**, U.S. 7, Shelburne; (802) 985–3344. The heritage of New England is celebrated here with impressive eighteenth- and nineteenth-century folk art, artifacts, and architecture. But this collection of Americana—among the best in the country—isn't presented in a boring, dry-as-dust museum manner. Instead, the history and artifacts are incorporated into a small village of buildings, most transported from various places in Vermont: a covered bridge, 1800s homes and shops—even a private, furnished 1890 railroad car and a vintage railroad station. Discover the life and art of another era in a vital, living history setting.

Kids especially like the 1830 one-room schoolhouse; the 1890 jail featuring cells, stocks, and pillory; and the old-time general store with barbershop, tap room, and post office. A big hit with all ages, the circus building houses carvings of a miniature circus parade, big-tent wonders, vintage carousel animals, and circus wagons.

Don't miss the *Ticonderoga*, the last vertical beam sidewheel steamboat intact in the United States, which was built in Shelburne Harbor in 1906. A film on board shows the ingenious way the ship was moved to the museum. The Toy Shop will delight with penny banks, mechanical toys, dolls, and animals; for more dolls, and dollhouses, see the Variety Unit. Also eye-catching: the big red round barn and the white lighthouse. Steer kids in the direction of paintings by masters such as Rembrandt, Degas, Manet, and Monet.

The Family Activity Center at Owl Cottage features a reading area, costume play, and art projects. From late October through late May,

You and your family can learn what life was like in another era at the Shelburne Museum, which features, among other things, an authentic print shop. (Courtesy Shelburne Museum)

theme tours for children ages five and older (with adults along) are given twice on Saturdays. One theme might be searching the museum for "cats" then picking a favorite for an art activity. (Reservations are required.) In July and August, the museum offers a weekly series of children's workshops. These fill quickly; to register in advance, call the Educational Department at (802) 985-3346, ext. 395, weekdays.

Try to time your visit to coincide with one of the special events weekends. In late May, the Museum celebrates the opening of its warm weather season with Lilac Sunday, nineteenth-century entertainment and leisure activities that include a Victorian picnic, croquet, carriage rides, music—and lots of fun. July Fourth is celebrated with Old Time Farm Day, featuring horse-drawn wagon rides, farm animals, traditional folk music, dances, games, crafts, and storytelling. There's an old-time baseball game, too, and the chance for your family to milk a cow, churn butter, make ice cream, and shuck peas.

Plan on spending at least three hours, though you could easily spend much more; there's a "second day free" admission policy. A snack bar and cafeteria are on site, and a jitney service helps with touring the museum's forty-five acres. Baby strollers and carriers aren't permitted in some of the buildings because of the narrow hallways or fragile exhibits. A physical accessibility guide and wheelchairs are available at the McClure Visitor Center.

If you have more time in the area, the following sites offer kid-pleasing diversions.

Discovery Museum, 51 Park Street, Route 2A, Essex Junction; (802) 878–8687. This small hands-on museum, located in a historic home, gears its exhibits and programs to kids up to age twelve. Attractions include a Science Center area with a 727 cockpit, fossil table, freshwater fish tank, rocks and minerals, and—everyone's favorite—bubble experiments. Call for information about weekly and monthly programs.

Ethan Allen Homestead, off Route 127; (802) 865–4556. School-age children may like a visit to this restored 1787 timber farmhouse belonging to Revolutionist Allen, leader of the famous Green Mountain Boys. Guided tours are given, and there's a multimedia show on this local hero who helped establish the state of Vermont. When you're through, enjoy a respite at the 258-acre Winooski Valley Park, with hiking trails, that surrounds the homestead.

Parks and Beaches

North Beach, reached by following North Avenue to Institute Road, is Burlington's most popular place to swim, bike, walk, rollerblade (rentals available), and picnic (grills are provided). This is also the site of seasonal festivals and special events.

Catamount Family Center, near the airport (802–879–6001), offers 500 acres for mountain biking (rentals and lessons available), orienteering, walking, and winter cross-country skiing.

Downtown, you'll find a scenic oasis in **Battery Street Park**, the scene of an 1812 skirmish between American land batteries and British vessels on Lake Champlain. Sit back and enjoy the now peaceful view of the lake and, beyond, the Adirondack Mountains. In the summer, free concerts add to the appeal.

Shelburne Farms, off Route 7, Shelburne; (802) 985–8686. Enjoy the best of the countryside at this 1,000-acre historic site with spectacular lake/mountain views. There's a restored inn and restaurant on the property, cheesemaking and tasting, plus daily tours that feature the lovely formal gardens.

Vermont Wildflower Farm, U.S. 7, Charlotte, 5 miles south of the Shelburne Museum; (802) 425–3500. Even the youngest tot will be in heaven strolling pathways leading through open fields and forests with acres of wild flowers. Each flower is identified, and facts about its history and characteristics are provided. In July and August, in an air-conditioned theater, there's a short but striking film. Seeds are for sale—and just try to leave without a gift. Kids will undoubtedly want the coloring book.

Special Tours

The **Spirit of Ethan Allen** excursion boat leaves Perkins Pier for shoreline cruises that include Captain's Dinner Cruises. Call (802) 862–9685. Tell the kids to keep their eyes peeled for Champ. In 1984, seventy passengers made the largest mass sighting of the elusive sea serpent, according to the cruise line. Numerous charters and boat rentals are available around the lake.

Performing Arts

Flynn Theatre for the Performing Arts, 153 Main Street, offers excellent dance, music, and theater performances. Call (802) 88–FLYNN, for ticket information. **Saint Michael's College**, Route 15, Winooski Park, puts on professional summer theater performances from late June to mid-August. Call (802) 655–0122 for schedules. A number of cultural festivals are held annually (see SPECIAL EVENTS).

Shopping

The traffic-free downtown **Church Street Marketplace** is a pleasant place to shop and eat, with street musicians and sidewalk cafés adding to the festive atmosphere. **The Vermont Teddy Bear Company**, 2031 Shelburne Road, Shelburne, invites visitors on a guided tour to see how these cuddly, handmade bears are created. This is a winner. Call (802) 985–3001/(800) 829–BEAR.

SPECIAL EVENTS

Culture—and fun—is the theme of many of Burlington's fairs and festivals. Contact the Lake Champlain Regional Chamber of Commerce for more information on the following events.

June: Discover Jazz Festival. Lake Champlain Balloon Festival, Champlain Valley Fairgrounds, Essex Junction, includes children's petting zoo and amusement rides, entertainment, exhibits, and more.

July: Champlain Shakespeare Festival.

July–early August: Vermont Mozart Festival.

August: A Taste of Stowe and For Art's Sake, Stowe.

September: Harvest Festival, Shelburne Farms, entertainment, crafts, and hayrides.

WHERE TO STAY

Families have a wide choice of accommodations in the area, but first decide if you want to stay in town, on the lake, or at one of the full-service, year-round resorts not far from Burlington. (Actually, you might want to do all three.) *Vermont Traveler's Guidebook* lists lodgings throughout the state. Here are a few with family appeal.

Burlington

Radisson Hotel Burlington, 60 Battery Street, has 255 rooms, many overlooking the lake and the Adirondack Mountains. Features you'll like: indoor heated swimming pool, restaurants (including a casual café), complimentary airport shuttle, and free covered parking. Adjacent is the Burlington Square Mall and Church Street Marketplace. Call (802) 658–6500/(800) 333–3333.

Lake Champlain

Basin Harbor Club, Basin Road, Vergennes, 25 miles south of Burlington, is directly on Lake Champlain's eastern shore. Everything here is well-manicured: the lovely grounds, the staff, and the guests. Boys and men are required to wear coats and ties in the public area after 6:00 P.M. The playground offers supervised activities for ages three to ten in the summer from 9:00 A.M. to noon. Kids eat dinner together, too. Afternoons bring craft activities suitable for all ages. Older children can avail themselves of the resort's superb recreation: golf, tennis, swimming, softball, and lots of water sports on the lake or poolside. If there are enough teens on the property, evening activities are planned. The resort is open from June through mid-October. Call (802) 475–2311/(800) 622–4000.

Tyler Place Inn and Cottages on Lake Champlain, Highgate Springs. If you're looking for less formality, but lots of fun, this family favorite may be just the ticket. Located on a mile of private lakeshore, the casual resort offers twenty-seven fireplace cottages or family suites, all with separate parents' bedroom. Programs are held for toddlers to teens, with sports, activities, early dining, and mother's helpers for younger kids. Ask about special May, June, and September rates. Meals are included. Reserve early: This place is popular; (802) 868–4291/868–3301.

All-Season Resorts

Two popular family resorts near Lake Champlain are Bolton Valley and Smuggler's Notch.

Bolton Valley Resort, Bolton, 19 miles from Burlington, offers hotel rooms (some with kitchens) or modern, trailside condominiums (all with kitchens) in a splendid mountain setting. The resort's nature center has daily summer activities, rotated during the week, that might include nature photography, a moose watch, or mountain biking classes, plus guided nature walks. Camp Bear Paw occupies the days of ages six to twelve, and there's a nursery for ages three months to six years. In the winter, the nursery is open, and there are pre-ski and child-care programs for ages four and five, plus full-day skiing sessions for ages five to fifteen (divided by ages). Call (802) 434–2131/(800) 451–3220—hotel reservation/(800) 451–5025—condos.

Smugglers' Notch, Route 108, 30 miles northeast of Burlington International Airport, consistently ranks among the top family ski resorts in North America. Much has to do with what it does for kids and parents. Alice's Wonderland child-care for ages six weeks and older, with indoor and outdoor play, is open in summer and winter seasons. In winter the resort has ski camps for ages three to six and seven to twelve and a teen program that includes sports and evening dance parties. Ski Week packages feature family game nights and sledding parties, while the five-day FamilyFest includes camp and one free Parent's Night Out—selected supervised evenings for ages three to twelve. Summer brings day camps and programs for ages three to seventeen. When the kids aren't in camp, they head to the three water slides or two pools (there are toddler wading pools, too). Mountainside lodgings, from motel units to five-bedroom condos, are in the walkabout village where you'll also find a miniature golf course, horseback riding stables and hayrides, restaurants, convenience store, and deli, indoor and outdoor tennis—even a post office. Call (802) 644–8851/(800) 451–8752—United States/(800) 356–8679—Canada).

WHERE TO EAT

Vermont Traveler's Guidebook lists area restaurants—or consult the Burlington *Free Press*. Here are some possibilities.

Get a tasty, inexpensive bite and hobnob with the locals at **Henry's Diner**, 155 Bank Street, which has been at this site for years. If your kids are adventurous eaters, don't miss the **Five Spice Cafe**, 175 Church Street, with a variety of Asian dishes including Shanghai Noodles, Hunan Chicken with Leeks, Vietnamese Calamari, Thai Red Snapper, and dim sum on Sunday. At **Poppy's Prime Factor**, Main Street in Winooski, enjoy a river view and menu that includes prime ribs, chicken, and soup and salad bar. Kids can eat for a nickel times their weight. Out on Route 2A to Williston, **Espresso** serves fresh pasta, pizza, and homemade desserts; they offer a kid's menu.

DAY TRIPS

Head to the lovely village of **Stowe** by taking I–89 to Route 100N. On the way, stop at **Waterbury** for a **Ben & Jerry Ice Cream Factory Tour** offered seven days (although there's no ice cream production on Sundays and holidays). The tours are thirty minutes long and include a slide show on the colorful, socially conscious founders plus a bird's-eye view of the production room. Best of all, you'll get a free sample of what many consider Vermont's (and the world's) finest ice cream. There's a small fee for the tour, and it's worth it. For information, call (802) 244–TOUR.

A popular winter ski resort, the Stowe area is more peaceful in the summer, when it offers a wealth of recreational possibilities. At the **Stowe Mountain Resort**, take a gondola ride on Mount Mansfield, the highest peak in Vermont, and enjoy spectacular vistas. There's also an alpine slide ride (adults can accompany younger kids). On Sunday evenings, concerts are held at the Trapp Family Concert Meadow (yes, the Sound of Music family offspring operate a lodge in town). Biking, swimming, hiking, golfing, tennis, and loads of special events are all at your fingertips. Call (802) 253–3000/(800) 24–STOWE for information and central reservations.

FOR MORE INFORMATION

Summer and winter editions of the *Vermont Traveler's Guidebook* including the Burlington area, and other literature, can be obtained from **Vermont Travel Division**, 134 State Street, Montpelier 05602; (802) 828–3236. Contact **Lake Champlain Regional Chamber of Commerce** for their *Vermont Area Guide* to the region: P.O. Box 453, 209 Battery Street, Burlington 05402; (802) 863–3489. Or stop by the **Information Center** at the Church Street Marketplace, corner of Church and Bank, mid-May through mid-October. Call (802) 828–3239 for fall foliage reports.

Emergency Numbers
Ambulance, fire, and police: 911
Poison Control: (802) 658–3456
Twenty-four-hour care for minor or major emergencies: Medical Center Hospital of Vermont, 111 Colchester Avenue; (802) 656–2345
Twenty-four-hour pharmacy: Price Chopper, 555 Shelburne Road (U.S. 7, 2 miles south of downtown); (802) 864–8505

7
MYSTIC, GROTON, and NEW LONDON
Connecticut

The area surrounding the old shipping and whaling port of Mystic offers enough family-pleasing diversions to warrant spending several days. The town of Mystic is divided by the Mystic River. On the east bank is the aquarium, and the area's best-known attraction, Mystic Seaport Museum. Family-pleasing attractions can also be found in the neighboring towns of Groton and New London. Mystic is also superbly located on Connecticut's Long Island Sound, near the Rhode Island border, a scenic spot.

GETTING THERE

Major carriers fly into Bradley International Airport, Windsor Locks (203–627–3000), about 1–1½ hour's drive from Mystic. T.F. Green Airport, Warwick, Rhode Island (401–737–4000), about a one-hour drive from Groton's New London Airport, is served by commuter lines.

Greyhound bus lines arrive and depart from New London. Call (203) 447–3841. Amtrak (800–USA–RAIL) serves Mystic daily on a limited schedule and nearby New London on a more regular basis.

Several ferries serve the area. The Block Island Ferry goes to New London (seasonally); call (203) 442–9553/442–7891. The Cross Sound Ferry serves New London–Orient Point, Long Island; (203) 443–5281. The Montauk Passenger Ferry provides New London–Montauk, Long Island service, May through October; (516) 668–5709/(800) MONTAUK.

To reach Mystic by car, take Connecticut Route 27 approximately one mile south of I–95, exit 90.

GETTING AROUND

SEAT (Southeastern Area Transit, 203–886–2631) has buses that serve Mystic on a limited basis.

Yellow Cab Company, 64 Brainard Street, New London (203–536–8888), provides twenty-four-hour service within Mystic as well as to Mystic and to the airport.

WHAT TO SEE AND DO

Museums

Mystic Seaport Museum, 50 Greenmanville Avenue; (203) 572–5317. Your family will love this indoor/outdoor, nonprofit, educational maritime museum, which is a nineteenth-century coastal village on seventeen waterfront acres. Visitors often help out during the frequent demonstrations throughout the village—so you and the kids may find yourselves setting type at the printing press or giving the barrelmaker a hand. The more than 130 programs and special events held throughout the year (including some wonderful Christmas programs) add another dimension to a visit here. Check the schedules at the visitor's center near the main entrance.

Many of the twenty-two historic buildings—including homes, shops, and workplaces—were brought from other New England locations, while several remain on their original sites. Board the three major historic ships, and explore the shipyard, where old vessels are rehabilitated. Nineteenth-century sailors navigated by the stars. Learn about the skies at the daily planetarium shows.

If you're blessed by good weather, you'll find yourself spending most of the time outdoors. If not you'll find much to see and do indoors, even in the off-season. Plan on spending the entire day. If you only have a few hours, though, head to **Chubb's Wharf** where you can board the seaport's prize: the *Charles W. Morgan,* the last of America's wooden fishing fleet. During its eighty years the ship was home to more than 1,000 whalers. At least five of the ship's twenty-one captains brought their wives and children along, a fact that never fails to impress the youngsters who step on board. Try to be here for the fascinating whaling demonstration. You'll also want to visit the 1921 *L.A. Dunton,* a Gloucester fishing schooner, and the *Joseph Conrad,* an 1882 training ship.

Kids ages two to eight shouldn't miss the **Children's Museum**, located in the circa-1885 Edmondson House. The recently redesigned facility includes several activity spaces that show how sailors and their families lived on sea and shore. On the deck kids listen to music, dance, draw,

At the children's museum at the Mystic Seaport, kids can play with nineteenth-century toys and games. (Photo by Judy Beisler/courtesy Mystic Seaport)

and tie sailor's knots. On the outdoor rigging kids climb for the fun of it. Inside, a museum teacher answers questions, and kids play with replicas of nineteenth-century toys and games, read books, and try on replicas of nineteenth-century clothes. In the winter, spring, and fall, a Morning Fun for Kids program (parents included) is held in the Children's Museum. Tuesdays are for ages two and three, and Thursdays are for ages four and five. Call (203) 572–5322 for a schedule.

Older kids and adults marvel at the ship's models, paintings, and scrimshaw in the the **Stillmen Building**, the colorful figureheads and ship's carvings in the Wendell Building, and the beautifully restored small craft in the North Boat Shed.

During the summer when the Seaport is open from 9:00 A.M. to 8:00 P.M., attend the free drop-in activities on the **Village Green**. These let kids duplicate what nineteenth-century children did for fun—before television and videos. Games might include a tug-of-war, stilt walking, or rolling hoops. During the week after Christmas, special one-hour tours (called "Plum Pudding Voyages") give children ages six to eleven a behind-the-scenes tour and feature storytelling and crafts.

At the seaport several "tours" are available for extra fees. These include a horse-and-carriage ride through the village, which leaves from

Chubb's Wharf. Sail on the catboat *Breck Marshall*, which leaves from the Boathouse on Lighthouse Point. Take a daily river tour, downriver excursion, or, on Sunday, board the *S.S. Sabino*, the last coal-fired passenger steamer in operation in the United States, for a Dixieland cruise.

The Galley, near the Visitor's Services building, is an informal, self-service place for sandwiches or burgers. The Seamen's Inne, near the North Entrance, serves lunch and dinner; reservations are suggested, (203) 536–9649.

If your kids like it here (and they will), they may want to return some day for the six- and nine-day youth sailing programs for ages twelve to sixteen, and ages fifteen to nineteen. If you're staying in town for awhile, consider the Seaport's Summer Day Camp, which offers one-week sessions for ages seven and eight, and two-week sessions for ages nine to eleven.

Mystic Marinelife Aquarium, 55 Coogan Boulevard, exit 90 off I–95; (203) 536–3323. More people visit here than any other admission-based attraction in Connecticut, according to the aquarium. With 6,000 marine creatures displayed in fifty exhibits, there's plenty to see. The outdoor Seal Island complex on two-and-a-half acres recreates New England, Alaskan, and California habitats and features four species of seals and sea lions. School-age kids enjoy watching sharks swim in a 30,000-gallon tank behind a sixteen-window display, the largest fish exhibit at the aquarium. Even the tiniest tot will delight in the daily dolphin, whale, and sea lion demonstrations in the Aquarium's Marine Theater. And everybody loves the penguins; view their antics above and below water in their outdoor pavilion. *The Deep Frontier,* shown on a large screen in the Aquarium's main building, explores marine life 2,700 feet below the ocean's surface, using footage provided by scientists in a submersible.

Parks, Preserves, and Beaches

Denison Pequotsepos Nature Center, Pequotsepos Road, Mystic; (203) 536–1216. About 2 miles from the Seaport museum is this 125-acre wooded wildlife sanctuary with 7 miles of hiking trails that traverse ponds and meadows. There's a small natural history museum, too. Bring a picnic lunch and stay awhile.

In downtown Norwich, about forty minutes from Mystic, **Chelsea Harbor Park and the Marina at American Wharf** is beautifully landscaped, with flower beds and green lawns. The marina has promenades and walkways, and there are outdoor grills, benches, and, in the winter, an ice-skating rink. In the summer, bring your bathing suits as you can swim in Mohegan Pond. Phone (203) 886–2381/889–6516—weekends. While you're in Norwich, see if there's a performance of the **Gazebo Summer Music Series** at Howard T. Brown Memorial Park. The series, which runs from May through July, includes everything from jazz to sea chanteys. Call (203) 886–2381.

For ocean swimming, locals head to **Watch Hill**, Rhode Island, a good family beach about 13 miles east of Mystic. The sandy **Ocean Beach Park** on Ocean Avenue in New London has gentle surf and also offers a fresh-water pool, water slide, miniature golf, game arcade, and picnic area. **Esker Point** in Noank, 3 miles southwest of Mystic, is a local beach on the Sound.

Special Tours

Whale Watch Sunbeam Fleet, Captain John's Sport Fishing Center, 15 First Street, Waterford. Spend a day watching for whales with a naturalist and research teams from Mystic Marinelife Aquarium. From late June through Labor Day, the tours head out toward the waters of Montauk Point on Sunday and Thursday. For these tours the boat departs from Captain John's Dock, near Niantic River Bridge, Route 156, Waterford.

From February to early March, Sunday excursions look for bald eagles along the Connecticut River. The boat departs from the Dock and Dine Restaurant, Old Saybrook, about 15 miles west of Waterford. Other nature tours are also available. From mid-March to May there are three-hour Sunday excursions to Fisher's Island, south of Mystic, to visit harbor seals. This trip departs from the Waterford dock. Always call ahead for the latest information; (203) 443–7259.

Performing Arts

Garde Arts Center and Vangarde Gallery, 329 State Street, New London, is a professional performing arts center that features family theater, Broadway shows, and comedies. Call the box office at (203) 444–7373. **Summer Music at Harkness Park,** Route 213, Waterford, offers Saturday evening concerts ranging from jazz to classical; (203) 442–9199. Summer children's theater is held on Friday or Saturday at the **Ivoryton Playhouse,** 103 Main Street, Ivoryton, near Essex; (203) 767–8348.

Shopping

Olde Mistick Village, Route 27 at I-95, Mystic, is a colonial-style shopping center with more than sixty shops, restaurants, and a theater. There are free weekend concerts June through October. Call (203) 536–4941. Across the way, bargain shop for clothes, toys, crafts, and more at **Mystic Factory Outlets,** Coogan Boulevard; (203) 443–4788.

Mystic's nearby neighboring towns offer these attractions:

Groton

Groton is about 5 miles west of Mystic.

USS *Nautilus* **Memorial/Submarine Force Library and Museum,** U.S.

Sub Base; (203) 449–3174/(800) 343–0079. The self-conducted tour aboard the world's first nuclear-powered ship is free. *The Nautilus* was built in Groton by General Dynamics and launched in 1954. You see the torpedo room, officers' and crews' living and dining areas, and the attack center. The museum has submarine memorabilia, including a model of Captain Nemo's *Nautilus* from Jules Verne's *20,000 Leagues Under the Sea*. There are also working periscopes, and a fascinating display of submarines dating from the Revolutionary War and midget submarines from World War II. The library, however, is only open to researchers.

Project Oceanology, Avery Point; (203) 445–9007. Your family will learn a good deal during your two-and-one-half-hour trip aboard this 55-foot research vessel run by a nonprofit marine education association. Marine scientists teach you how to measure lobsters, identify fish, test sea water, and perform other seaworthy chores. The cruises depart daily at 10:00 A.M. and 1:00 P.M. during the summer; reservations are recommended.

New London
New London is about 9 miles west of Mystic.

The whaling industry once thrived here, and you can relive some of the glory by strolling through the downtown historic district, comprised of **Whale Oil Row**, an area of Greek revival homes, and surrounding areas. **Nathan Hale Schoolhouse**, Union Plaza (203–443–8331), is where this Connecticut hero taught before he enlisted in Washington's Army.

Lyman Allyn Art Museum, 625 Williams Street; (203) 443–2545. The kids gravitate toward the extensive collection of dolls, dollhouses, and antique toys. There are regularly changing exhibits by contemporary artists as well as American, European, and Oriental fine and decorative arts. The museum is free, though a donation is requested.

Thames Science Center, Gallows Lane; (203) 442–0391. This museum focuses on the land, life, and technology of eastern Connecticut. A marine touch-tank, beehive, salt marsh diorama, slide show, plus changing exhibits and kids' programs make this an interesting stop for younger school-age kids. Free admission. Guided tours are available of the nearby nature trails, part of a lovely arboretum on the campus of Connecticut College. Your family can explore the 434 acres on your own, too; open from dawn to dusk.

U.S. Coast Guard Academy, just off I–95 on SR 32, Mohegan Avenue; (203) 444–8270. If you're driving by, this is worth a stop, especially when the cadet corps pass in review (most Friday afternoons at 4:00 P.M. during the spring and fall). There's a visitor's pavilion on Tampa Street with a multimedia show on life at the academy. Board the training ship when it's in port.

SPECIAL EVENTS

Fairs and Festivals

In addition to listing the many seasonal events held at Mystic Seaport, the *Mystic Guide* from the Chamber of Commerce has a complete calendar of events. Here are some annual festivities.

June: Mystic/Noank Library Fair includes a plant, food, and book sale. Blessing of the Fleet, Stonington Borough, includes Saturday night lobster feast and band, and Sunday parade.

July: Sailfest, New London, international food, music, arts and crafts.

August: Mystic Outdoor Art Festival, downtown.

WHERE TO STAY

You'll find a listing of lodgings in the Chamber's *Mystic Guide*. Be sure to reserve in advance. The area has a mixture of guest houses and motels; some of the inns have age restrictions. **Covered Bridge Bed and Breakfast Reservation Service** (203–542–5944) offers a wide range of selections in the area. **Nutmeg Bed and Breakfast Agency** (203–236–6698) has 170 listings throughout the state.

Large motels with outdoor pools include the **Comfort Inn** (800–228–5150 or 203–572–8531), and the **Days Inn** (800–325–2525 or 203–572–0574) in Mystic. Other possibilities for families include the following.

Randall's Ordinary, Route 2, Stonington. This country inn, a registered landmark, is on twenty-seven acres and is less than a mile from Mystic. Fifteen guest rooms and suites are furnished with four-poster canopied beds and other antiques. The rooms in the Jacob Terpenning Barn come with televisions. The farm setting appeals to families, and children are welcome. Call (203) 599–4540.

Sandy Shore Motel and Apartments, 149 Atlantic Avenue, Misquamicut, Rhode Island. Stay right on the ocean in rooms with refrigerators or one- and two-bedroom apartments with kitchens. There's a kids' amusement area nearby. Call (401) 596–5616.

Taber Inn and Townhouses, 29 Williams Avenue, Route 1, Mystic. Two-bedroom townhouses have jacuzzis and water views. Modern motel rooms are available, too. Call (203) 536–4904.

WHERE TO EAT

The Chamber's *Mystic Guide* details a number of area restaurants. These are some good choices for families.

Kitchen Little, Route 27, Mystic (and Kitchen Little in the Village in Stonington) is the place to go if your family loves breakfast. You'll probably have to wait in line for the creative egg dishes and pancakes. Light lunches served, too; (203) 536–2122. Where to get locally caught lobster and other seafood specialties? Follow the crowds to Abbot's Lobster in the Rough, 117 Pearl Street, Noank (ten minutes south of Mystic). If it's nice, sit outside at picnic tables that overlook the Sound; (203) 536–7719. Two Sisters Deli, 4 Pearl Street, Mystic, serves tasty sandwiches with catchy names (such as Big Sister's Midnight Snack) and delicious desserts; (203) 536–1244. And, yes, there is such a place as Mystic Pizza—in fact, there are two: one is on West Main Street in Mystic (203–536–3700); the other is in North Stonington (203–599–3111).

DAY TRIPS

The town of Essex, northwest of Mystic, with sea captain's homes lining Main Street, looks much the way it did in the early 1800s. The Valley Railroad, Railway Avenue, Route 9, exit 3, offers passengers an old-fashioned, 12-mile steam-train ride through the Connecticut River Valley to Deep River. There you can connect with an optional riverboat cruise, or return to Essex. The round-trip train ride takes just under an hour. The combination train and boat trip takes two hours, ten minutes. The regular season is May through October. Fall foliage trips go through late October, and a North Pole Express ride with Santa on board operates in December. Call (203) 767–0103 for schedules.

If you're heading to New York from Mystic, take a break and stop by the Barnum Museum, 820 Main Street, Bridgeport. (Take I–95, exit 27 in Bridgeport.) This lively place is housed in the newly restored original building provided by showman and circus impresario Phineas Taylor (P.T.) Barnum in 1893 as a home to local historical and scientific societies. Barnum was a local boy, born in Bethel, Connecticut. Among the highlights: a hand-carved scale model of Barnum's "Greatest Show on Earth", a recreated library from Barnum's first Bridgeport mansion, a simulation of Tom Thumb's Bridgeport home, a Punch and Judy Show (Barnum was the first to introduce the puppets to American audiences), plus an exhibit devoted to clowning. One section of the building houses temporary exhibits. Call (203) 331–1104 for information.

FOR MORE INFORMATION

Mystic Chamber of Commerce and Convention and Visitors Bureau, P.O. Box 143, Railroad Depot, Mystic 06355 (203–572–9578), provides information and literature. You may also stop by the Mystic and Shoreline Visitor Information Center, Olde Mistick Village; (203) 536–1641. A map and guide of Mystic coast and country is available from Southeastern Connecticut Tourism District, P.O. Box 89, 27 Masonic Street, New London 06320; (800) 222–6783.

Emergency Numbers

Ambulance, fire, and police: 911

Mystic Pharmacy, 17 East Main Street (203–536–8615), is open from 8:00 A.M. to 8:00 P.M. weekdays and 8:00 A.M. to 6:00 P.M. weekends.

Poison Control: (800) 343–2722

Twenty-four-hour emergency room: Lawrence and Memorial Hospital, 365 Montauk Avenue, New London, about 9 miles from Mystic; (203) 442–0711

8
PORTLAND
Maine

In the harbor city of Portland, Maine, seagulls' cries float above the downtown office buildings and boats take you out to look for whales, to admire the lighthouse, and to sigh at views of the coastline. Portland is a family-friendly harbor town that your kids will like. Combine a maritime seaside tour with a day trip to nearby Freeport or Kittery for discounted clothes at the scores of outlet shops.

GETTING THERE

Portland is accessible by land, sea, and air. The Portland International Jetport (207–774–7301) is just ten minutes from downtown and has direct flights from most major cities on the East Coast. A Metro City bus (207–774–0351) will take you from the airport to downtown.

By land arrive via Greyhound bus (207–772–6587), although most bus routes are lengthened by frequent stops. A car is the more convenient option since Portland is just off I–95. For Maine Turnpike travel conditions, call (207) 871–7771.

To spice things up Canadians might want to try taking the *M.S. Scotia Prince* ferry from Nova Scotia. Call (800) 482–0955 in Maine or (800) 341–7540 out of state. Those with their own boats are welcome to stay in private marinas; the harbor master can be reached at (207) 772–8121.

GETTING AROUND

Portland's old town can and should be explored on foot. To reach points out of walking distance in the greater Portland area, Metro bus services (207–774–0451) and taxis are available. Town Taxi runs twenty-four hours a day; (207) 773–1711. If you want to explore greater Portland by

car, several rental agencies are located near the airport, including Avis
(800–331–1212) and Hertz (800–654–3131).

WHAT TO SEE AND DO

Museums and Historical Sites

One of the best things to do in Portland is to meander around Old
Port, exploring the harbor by foot and boarding one of the tour boats.
(See Shopping and Special Tours.)

Downtown Portland also features several historical buildings that are
open to the public. Most are only open seasonally from June to October,
so be sure to call in advance.

Portland Museum of Art, 7 Congress Square, Portland; (207)
775–6148. Come here to view artists' renditions of the surrounding sea
and landscapes. Maine's largest art museum, it features works by
Winslow Homer, Edward Hopper, and Andrew Wyeth.

The Portland Head Light, 1000 Shore Road, Cape Elizabeth; (207)
799–5251. The oldest lighthouse in the state towers over a classic Maine
scene: a windswept rocky coast with waves breaking into sprays of
whitecaps. This impressive structure, located just outside Portland in
Cape Elizabeth, is the most photographed of Maine's attractions. The
lighthouse, which George Washington ordered to be lit in 1791, has a
new museum that opened in July of 1993. Located in the former keeper's
house, the museum at Portland Head Light details the history of this
lighthouse as well as that of Fort Williams, the adjacent park that was
once home to the Coast Artillery Core.

Kids will like listening to the boom of the fog horn and browsing the
small exhibit to uncover such secrets as the details of famous wrecks,
how the lenses magnified the light, and what life as a keeper was like in
the nineteenth century when Joshua Freeman Strout and his family
tended the beacon. According to newspaper reports of the day, keeper
Strout gave visitors "as fine a glass of wine as ever was pored down the
neck of an alderman."

Other finds: Fresnel lenses, photographs of storms, and a series of—
what else—lights illustrate the location of other Maine lighthouses.
Allow time for the gift shop with its kid-pleasing array of stickers and
magnets. Be sure to bring a picnic lunch to take advantage of the adjacent park with its sea views and acres for romping.

The Lightship #112 Nantucket, 58 Fore Street, Portland; (207)
775–1181. In town at the Coast Guard Moorings on Commercial Street,
the Lightship Nantucket offers more nautical lore. Board this vessel for a
firsthand look at the lightship stationed at sea to serve as a beacon where
a lighthouse was needed but impossible to build because of shallows and

A trip to Portland Head Light is a treat for the whole family. (Courtesy Portland Conventions and Visitors Bureau)

rocks. For ships arriving from Europe, the red and white Nantucket #112 provided the first sighting of the U. S. flag.

The tour takes you through the radio room, the galley, the ship's quarters, and lets you peek at the engine room and the anchor. Kids see what life was like on board for the old salts who rode out the storms and learned to talk to each other in twenty-four-second intervals to beat the fog horn that blared for six seconds out of every thirty. Ask about the tales of near collisions with ocean liners, and just how to weather a hurricane.

Portland Observatory, 138 Congress Street, Portland; (207) 774–5561. This signal tower built in 1807 for merchants and ship owners offers a great view of the city, bay, and the White Mountains. It is open from June to October.

Children's Museum of Maine, 746 Stevens Avenue, Portland; (207) 797–5483. It features hands-on art and science exhibits.

Tate House, 1270 Westbrook Street, Portland (207–774–9781), provides another glimpse into Portland's maritime history. Take a tour of this Georgian house constructed in 1755 by George Tate for an inside view of a Colonial merchant's home.

The Victoria Mansion, 109 Danforth Street (207–772–4841), is also known as the Morse-Libby House. With its stone towers it reminds some kids of the manse in "the Addams Family." Built 1858–1860 this Italianate home with its elaborate staircase and furnishings will interest your kids if they go wide-eyed at the sight of mansions.

Wadsworth-Longfellow House, 485 Congress Street, Portland; (207) 774–1822. Poetry enthusiasts might want to visit the childhood home of poet Henry Wadsworth Longfellow. Built in 1785 by his grandfather, the home still includes family furniture.

Performing Arts

Add some culture to your visit. The Portland Concert Association, 262 Cumberland Avenue, Portland (207–772–8630 or 800–639–2707), offers dance, opera, theater, and music presentations. Theater buffs should check out Portland Stage Company, 25A Forest Avenue; (207) 774–0465. The Portland Symphony Orchestra performs at 30 Myrtle Street; (207) 773–8191, or (800) 639–2309.

Special Tours

Harbor Cruise. What's a Maine vacation without some time on the sea? Seasonally—from about June through Columbus Day—several ships offer either scenic or whale-watching cruises. Check out the kiosks along Commercial Street for a line and a time that suits your schedule. Bay View Cruises, 184 Commercial Street (207–761–0496), adds a nice touch to their scenic tours by bringing bread on board for the kids to feed to the seagulls who swoop down, catching the pieces in mid-air to the giggles of all. Casco Bay Lines, P.O. Box 4656 DTS, Portland (207–774–7871), is another option. Scenic autumn foliage cruises (dress warmly) let you admire the coast as our Founding Fathers did—from the deck of a ship.

A cruise is a wise option for the afternoon, a time when kids are often tired and cranky. Instead of dragging them off to yet another museum, lounge on deck by the rail, listen to the ninety-minute narrated tour, and admire the scenery, including the ruins of the old forts and the panoramic sea view of the Portland Head Light. Along the way look for seals and admire the shoreline.

Shopping

Old Port. Be sure to meander through Old Port, an area of boutiques, interesting shops, and restaurants just across Commercial Street from the harbor. This is the place to let your kids spend their allowance on inexpensive pleasures. Stroll along Exchange Street to Something Fishy, 22 Exchange Street (207–774–7726), for a fine selection of T-shirts. Try Abacus American Crafts, 44 Exchange Street (207–772–4880), for unusual and affordable pins, platters, boxes, and other crafty pleasures.

Stein's Glass Gallery, 20 Milk Street (207–772–9072), sports an eye-catching array of swirled and rainbow-colored goblets, bowls, and sculpture. **The Maine Potters' Market** at Fore and Moulton streets (207–774–1633) is a cooperative shop representing people from around the state. They sell a wide selection of mugs, dishes, candle holders, and lots more. For a Maine souvenir visit **Just ME.,** 490 Congress Street (207–775–4860), where everything is "Maine-made."

SPECIAL EVENTS

Fairs and Festivals

When the long Maine winter finally comes to a close, Maine is ready to celebrate. Festivals abound in the summertime, and the visitor's guide has a complete calendar.

June: The Old Port Festival features crafts, food, and entertainment for the family. Explore Maine's rich maritime heritage at the Waterfront Festival.

July: The Rotary Club Crafts Festival and the Yarmouth Clam Festival, often a classy affair, offer clams galore and quality entertainment. The Maine Lobster Festival in Rockland between July and August is for lobster lovers.

August: The Maine Festival of the Arts includes demonstrations and live music. Six-Alive's Sidewalk Arts Festival features artists from around the country. Spring Point Festival includes a mock Civil War encampment. There's also the Italian Street Festival, and Art in the Park, which brings together artists from the Eastern Seaboard.

Other summer activities include weeknight activities in Deering Oaks, Portland. Tuesday Evening Concerts at the Oaks are presented most Tuesday nights and Thursday Children's Performance at the Oaks are held on most Thursday nights. Call (207) 874–8793 to verify.

September: Fall brings the Thomas Point Beach Bluegrass Festival in Brunswick (207–725–6009); call for a listing of performers. Country fairs abound, including the Common Ground Country Fair in Windsor and the Cumberland Fair.

October: American Indian Dance is held at the Portland City Hall. Maine Audobon Society's Apple Cider Day offers a taste of autumn.

November: Try the United Maine Craft Shows for holiday shopping.

December: The holiday season puts Portland back in a festive mode. Tree-lighting ceremonies in most towns, Portland Symphony Orchestra Christmas Concerts, and Christmas at the Victoria Mansion. If you're in town for the new year go to New Year's Portland downtown for a nonalcoholic celebration for the whole family.

WHERE TO STAY

Portland offers a variety of accommodations. The **Portland Regency**, 20 Mile Street, Portland (207–774–4200 or 800–727–3436) is in the heart of Old Port. It offers family-friendly lodging in a renovated century-old armory. Another possibility is the **Sonesta Portland Hotel**, 157 High Street (207–775–5411 or 800–777–6242). Recently renovated it offers a harbor view. The **Hotel Everett**, 51A Oak Street, Portland (207–773–7882), has both personality and low rates.

Many major chain hotels are in Portland including the **Holiday Inn by the Bay** (207–775–2311 or 800–HOLIDAY), **Sheraton Inn** (207–775–6161), **Marriott** (207–871–8000), and **Howard Johnson's** (207–774–5861).

Bed and breakfast lodgings are available too. Try the **Inn on Carleton**, 46 Carleton Street (207–775–1910), and **Keller's B & B**, Island Avenue (207–766–2441). Both welcome children. For more information on places to stay, call the Maine Publicity Bureau at (207) 289–2423.

If you're roughing it, the Maine State Parks has campground reservations; call (207) 289–3824 or (800) 332–1501 in Maine. The Maine Campground Owners Association can be reached at (207) 782–5874.

WHERE TO EAT

Hungry? **DeMillo's**, on Long Wharf (207–772–2216), is a floating, somewhat touristy restaurant, but it offers a dockside array of reasonably priced sandwiches and soups. Your kids may like the novelty of eating on deck. At **Carbur's Restaurant**, 123 Middle Street (207–772–7794), grab a moderately priced hamburger and some Victorian ambiance in this renovated 1877 commercial building. Other recommended Portland restaurants include **The Olive Garden Restaurant**, 200 Gorham Road (207–874–9005), for Italian food, soups, and salads, and **Village Cafe**, 112 Newbury Street (207–772–5320), for steaks and seafood at reasonable prices.

Try the **Muddy Rudder** on U.S. 1, Yarmouth (207–846–3082), for scenery and seafood on the Cousins River. **Two Lights Lobster Shack**, 225 Two Lights Road, Cape Elizabeth (207–799–1677), offers lobster stew and fried seafood.

A more extensive listing of area restaurants can be found in the Greater Portland, Maine Convention & Visitor's Bureau visitor's guide.

DAY TRIPS

Portland is an excellent base for day trips to quaint old villages dotting the shoreline as well as to the mountains of Maine and New Hampshire.

Freeport, Maine. Freeport is outlet heaven. About twenty minutes north of Portland, you can get discounts on almost everything. Some back-to-school bests include the Gap, J. Crew, a Down Outlet, a Nike store, and Benetton. Parents will find such fashion staples as Calvin Klein, Coach, and Polo-Ralph Lauren. And if you've spent time all these years browsing the catalogues and imagining yourself a stalwart Mainelander, be sure to visit L.L. Bean; (207) 865–4761 or (800) 341–4341, which is open twenty-four hours a day, 365 days a year. For a Freeport map call the Freeport Merchants Association at (207) 865–1212.

Kittery, a little farther than Freeport, is about an hour south of Portland on routes 95 and 1. It offers more discount stores for the die-hard outlet shopper.

Kennebunkport, a household word after George Bush's presidency, is only about thirty minutes away. This nineteenth-century village created by merchants and seamen boasts authentic Victorian mansions. Stroll around Dock Square stocked with shops, art galleries, and restaurants.

Ogunquit, forty-five minutes away on routes 95 and 1, is a village option for art enthusiasts. An artists' colony today, there is also a beach, so don't forget your bathing suit.

Maine Maritime Museum, 243 Washington Street, Bath; (207) 443–1316. About a forty-minute drive this museum is worth a stop. Located on ten acres along the Kennebec River on the site of a former shipyard, the museum offers both wildlife cruises and lobster bakes in-season, along with several buildings of nautical lore. Some of the buildings intrigue such as the exhibit on lobstermen. The boats, traps, buoys, and the video tell the story of this Maine folk staple. Other buildings may disappoint with static displays and cursory explanations, but your kids will learn something by browsing the Mill and Joiner's Shop, which tells how a keel was built and what riggers' tools were needed.

The Maritime History Building has an eclectic collection that includes ship models, art, and several early navigational devices. Be sure to find the World Trade Game, a kid-friendly way to learn about nineteenth-century sea trade. Spin the pointer and your trade ship may face such perils as desertion, mutiny, or man overboard.

The Calendar Islands, scattered throughout Casco Bay, once numbered 365, bringing about their name. These tiny worlds can be toured with the Casco Bay Lines ferry, call (207) 774–7871.

Western Mountains and Lakes Region. It takes less than an hour on Route 302 to reach the White Mountains. Take a hike in the summer or fall for a new perspective of the Atlantic Ocean and wash the salt off your body in the freshwater lakes. For more information call Maine State Parks at (207) 289–3824 or (800) 332–1501 in Maine; and also the Department of Inland Fisheries and Wildlife at (207) 289–2871.

Bethel, Maine. Steve Crone, proprietor of the **Telemark Inn,** RFD #2, Box 800, Bethel, Maine 04217 (207–836–2703) offers wonderful outings for families. In summer he has three–day llama trek trips, which take families through nearby New Hampshire's White Mountains. Encouraged by Crone, even four-year-olds enjoy leading their own llama. The comforts in camp—guides pitch your tents, cook your food, and even awaken you with hot coffee and warm towels—make the backcountry accessible to a wide range of ages from kindergartners to octogenarians. Crone also combines a llama trek with a canoe expedition. In winter at his plain, but comfortable inn, he offers cross-country skiing.

FOR MORE INFORMATION

Be sure to obtain a visitor's guide from the Convention & Visitors Bureau of Greater Portland, 305 Commercial Street, Portland (207–772–5800). The guide includes a map and a calendar of events. Other sources of information are Portland Recreation (207–874–8793), the Greater Portland Chamber of Commerce, 145 Middle Street, Portland (207–772–2811), the Maine Office of Tourism (207–289–5710), and the Maine Publicity Bureau (800–533–9595), which provides information on state events including foliage and ski condition reports. You can reach AAA at (207) 774–6377.

Local newspapers give a glimpse of less touristy events. The *Portland Press Herald* lists daily city events, and the *Maine Sunday Telegram* has a comprehensive weekly listing.

Emergency Numbers

Ambulance, fire, and police: 911
Maine Medical Center, 22 Bramhall Street, Portland; (207) 871–0111
Mercy Hospital, 144 State Street, Portland; (207) 879–3000
Poison Hotline: (800) 442–6305
Portland Police: (207) 874–8300
Rite Aid Discount Pharmacy (open until 9:00 P.M.), 713 Congress Street, Portland; (207) 774–8456

9
ALLEGHENY NATIONAL FOREST
Pennsylvania and New York

The Allegheny National Forest offers families fresh air, recreation, and beautiful natural surroundings. Comprised of more than 500,000 acres that stretch across the rugged plateaus of northwestern Pennsylvania's Elk, McKean, Forest, and Warren counties, the Allegheny National Forest has another bonus. Since this area isn't highly promoted, you'll find fewer crowds here than in the Poconos. To explore the forest choose between camping in one of its seventeen campgrounds or staying in one of the small communities on the fringes.

GETTING THERE

The forest's northern borders are just 40 miles south of the New York–Pennsylvania line. It's within easy driving distance from Buffalo to the north, Pittsburgh to the south, Erie to the northwest, and the Youngstown–Akron–Cleveland areas to the west. The following are considered gateways—areas where you can find food, lodging, and services.

Western gateway: the town of Warren, in Warren County, a major stop for visitors touring along U.S. 6, called "the Grand Army of the Republic Highway," or GAR, and considered one of the most scenic routes in the United States. The transcontinental highway, U.S. 6, is the second longest highway and stretches from Provincetown, Cape Cod, to Bishop, California.

Eastern gateway: Ridgway, in Elk County.
Northern gateway: Bradford, in McKean County.

Southern gateway: Tionesta, in Forest County (twenty minutes from I–80).

Commuter flights from Pittsburgh arrive at Bradford Regional Airport, Mount Alton, McKean County (814) 368–4928. Rental cars and taxis are available at the airport. There is no Amtrak service to this area.

GETTING AROUND

Within the forest, cars have access to more than 500 miles of roads. In addition, there are ATV trails, groomed snowmobile trails, hiking trails, and six boat launches. Note: Be particularly careful during rainy weather since about half of the forest region is served by dirt roads.

ATA (Area Transportation Authority, 800–822–3232—Pennsylvania or 814–965–3211) provides public transportation in Elk and McKean counties.

WHAT TO SEE AND DO

The Forest

First, get your bearings. The main forest office is at 222 Liberty Street, downtown Warren; (814) 723–5150. Four ranger stations dispense maps and information about activities and facilities within their region:

Southwest: Marienville Ranger District, Highway 66; (814) 927–6628.

Northwest: Sheffield District, Kane Road, U.S. 6; (814) 968–3232.

Northeast: Bradford District, Kinzua Heights, Highway 59 and 321; (814) 362–4613.

Southeast: Ridgway District, Montmorenci Road, State Highway 94B; (814) 776–6172.

In addition, the U.S. Corps of Engineers, which operates the Kinzua Dam, run an information center at Kinzua Point (814–729–1291), on Route 59, at the junction of Route 262. This center is open from Memorial Day to Labor Day.

Swimming, Boating, Fishing

The 27-mile Allegheny Reservoir on the upper Allegheny River stretches over the border to New York's Allegany State Park. The Reservoir is the hub of summer recreation in the forest: Kinzua and Kiasutha, two of the forest's four beaches, are located here. (The other beaches are at Loleta and Twin Lakes.) No, you won't be alone. In the summer this area is extremely popular with tourists, especially those who love boating and fishing. Some of the state's record fish were caught in reservoir waters. First, however, obtain a state fishing license.

An 85-mile stretch of the Allegheny River, from the Kinzua Dam to Oil City, is a recreational waterway, attracting pleasure and fishing boats.

More than 170 miles of forest trails wind through the forest, meadow, and glens that comprise the Allegheny National Forest. (Courtesy Pennsylvania Bureau of Travel Marketing)

A number of boat launches within the forest provide access to the reservoir's waters. Major sections of this stretch, including seven uninhabited islands perfect for picnics and wildlife viewing, are serviced by **Allegheny Outfitters** (814–723–1203), a Warren canoe rental outfit. The company suggests three itineraries that range from 6⁷⁄₁₀ to 15⁷⁄₁₀ miles, or they'll be glad to plan a route that suits your needs. The 17-foot canoes accommodate two adults and two children.

The **Kinzua-Wolf Run Marina**, 11 miles east of Warren on Route 59 (814–726–1650), rents canoes, rowboats, and motorboats, and also offers forty-five-minute, scenic, narrated tours of the reservoir aboard a twenty-passenger paddlewheeler, the *Kinzua Queen.*

The reservoir beaches are unsupervised, and parents are urged to keep a vigilant watch on their children because Kinzua's shorelines have steep, sudden drop-offs. In addition, because of fluctuating water levels, swimmers may encounter such hazards as submerged stumps, logs, and rocks, especially near the shoreline.

Families with young children are better off using the beach at **Chapman State Park**; (814) 723–5030. Although it's in the heart of the forest, the 805-acre park near Warren, off Route 6, is a separate entity, so none of its facilities appear on the forest's maps and brochures. Chapman has a sixty-eight-acre lake on the west branch of Tionesta Creek. Its beach, which is free, is the only one within the forest region with lifeguards. Chapman also has facilities for the physically challenged. There are two fishing docks for the handicapped at opposite ends of Lake Chapman. In the swimming area on the southeast side of the lake is a handicapped swimming pier, which can be accessed without a wheelchair. The carpeted deck and hand rails allow a handicapped person to slide down into the shallow water. The kid's area is 1 foot deep, and the adult area is 3 feet deep.

On busy days the park holds four designated sites with electric hook-ups for the handicapped until late in the day. Those with a state handicapped sticker can use all of the service roads to drive up to activity areas. Stickers are available at the park's entrance. Several picnic sites have handicapped accessible picnic tables. Naturalists also tailor programs for the handicapped.

In addition, Chapman hosts a variety of Junior Naturalist programs for kids and activities for families. Check the weekly newsletter for details.

Hiking

There are about 170 miles of forest trails that wind through dense forest, meadow, and glens. You're sure to spot some wildlife along the way, perhaps a muskrat, raccoon, or birds (even bald eagles have been spotted at Kinzua Dam).

White tail deer, black bears, and wild turkeys also live here, and this is a popular spot for hunting from late October to early January. This is a good time to avoid hiking in the woods. In addition, there may be some type of bird or game hunting throughout most of the year. May, for example, is spring gobbler season. Campsites have "safety zones," but exercise extreme caution. Before setting off for a hike, ask the park rangers about safety precautions and hunting seasons. For more information on hunting, contact the Pennsylvania Game Commission, 2001 Elmerton Avenue, Harrisburg 17110-9797; (717) 787–4250.

The North Country National Scenic Trail, 86⅔ miles, wends through the forest's rich landscapes and is part of a 3,200-mile National Scenic Trail which, when completed, will extend from Crown Point, New York, to Lake Sakawea, North Dakota. The trail is divided into ten segments that range from 2³⁄₁₀ to 13⁷⁄₁₀ miles. A map listing services and toilet facilities is available from the forest's headquarters. Young children—or anyone who prefers shorter, "tamer" walks—will enjoy the interpretive trails at many of the campgrounds.

Scenic Overlooks

The forest is beautiful to explore all year-round, particularly during the brilliant fall foliage season (but not during hunting season), and in June when the fragrant laurel blossoms, Pennsylvania's state flower. Both Jakes Rocks and Rimrock scenic overlooks, above the Kinzua Dam east of Warren, offer fabulous views of the Allegheny Reservoir, Kinzua Dam, and the forest. Both have walking trails, rest rooms, and picnic facilities.

Camping

The Forest Service operates seventeen campgrounds. Of the ten located along the Allegheny River shoreline, six can be accessed only by boat. You can reserve sites in most campgrounds by calling the national MISTIX Reservation Service at (800) 283–CAMP. Some campgrounds, however, are on a first-come basis. Reservations for family sites can be made ten to 120 days in advance. Obtain local campground information by calling the Kinzua Point Information Center at (814) 726–1291. The Kiasutha Recreation Area is particularly popular, with ninety-two sites, flush toilets, showers, a play area, swimming beach, and interpretative trails. Some facilities remain open before and after the regular summer season (Memorial Day to Labor Day weekends) but with limited service. A hostess is assigned to each site and can summon emergency assistance.

Some families prefer camping in Chapman State Park (see above) since no alcoholic beverages are allowed, creating what some feel is a more wholesome family atmosphere.

Winter Sports

Treat the kids to a sleigh ride in the forest's Tidioute area every January and February weekend, snow permitting. Call (814) 484–3441 or

484–7484 to reserve. For downhill sledding and tobogganing, Chapman State Park keeps a hill lit until 10:00 P.M. nightly. Snowmobiling is permitted on designated routes within the forest from December 20 to April 1. A trail connects to New York's Allegany State Park. There are numerous cross-country ski trails, such as those in Forest County, where the **Buzzard Swamp Cross-Country Ski Area** offers 7⅔ miles of ungroomed beginner's trails in a forest studded with ponds. To get here take the road in the center of Marienville, the road between the Uni-Mart and the Bucktail Hotel. This is Forest Road 130. Follow this for 3 miles and turn onto Forest Road 376.

Performing Arts

The Library Theatre Summer Playhouse, 102 Third Avenue, West Warren, is a professional troupe that performs musicals and dramas from late June to late July. Call (814) 723–7231.

Shopping

It's great fun browsing around **America's First Christmas Store**, Main Street, Route 6, Smethport (McKean County). What started as a pharmacy in 1932 turned into a Christmas display business which, at its peak, shipped outdoor displays to every state in the U.S.A. Four rooms feature decorated trees, dolls, bears, stained-glass scenes, and other holiday delights. Call (814) 887–5792.

SPECIAL EVENTS

Contact the individual county tourist associations listed below for more information on activities in their area. Here's a sampling.

June: Forest Fest, activities centered in and around the Allegheny National Forest. Free camping and swimming the first weekend, picnicking, fishing contests, nature hikes, boat rides, interpretative walks.

July: Elk "Hunt," Benezette, Elk County. Twelve elk silhouettes are hidden in the forest. The hunt starts at dawn until midafternoon; successful "hunters" receive prizes. Black Cherry Festival, Kane, McKean County, parade, family and children's activities, entertainment.

August: Elk County Fair, Fairgrounds, Kersey, includes magic shows, music, rides, games, food, and more. Warren County Fair, Pittsfield, large agricultural fair includes tractor and horse pulls.

WHERE TO STAY

If camping isn't your family's forte, visit the forest by day and stay at night in comfortable lodgings in nearby towns. There are several lodg-

ings on the forest's borders—ranging from national chains to cozy bed
and breakfasts that welcome kids.

McKean County

Blackberry Inn Bed & Breakfast, 820 West Main Street, Junction
U.S. 6 and PA 59, Smethport, is a restored Victorian home with five guest
rooms that share two full bathrooms. There's a parlor with TV, two large
porches, and a yard where the kids can romp. Full breakfasts are included. Call (814) 887–7777.

Kane Manor Country Inn, 230 Clay Street, welcomes families to their
1897 inn with ten guest rooms. The gathering room has a grand piano,
loads of books, and great views of the mountains and the Kinzua Valley.
On weekdays a continental breakfast is served while on weekends there's
a full breakfast, including teddy bear pancakes for the kids. Hiking and
cross-country trails are nearby. Call (814) 837–6522.

Warren County

Holiday Inn, Route 6 & 62, Warren, has an indoor pool, restaurant,
and a nightclub; (814) 726–3000.

WHERE TO EAT

You'll find a selection of eateries in all gateway areas. In Kane (McKean
County), **Papa Nick's Family Restaurant**, 316 Chase Street, offers casual
Italian American meals, plus a kid's menu. Call (814) 837–6652. At Ridgway, 25 miles from I–80 (exit 16) at the southeastern corner, grab a
burger, fries, or submarine sandwich at **The Original Italian Pizza**, 161
Main Street; (814) 772–7576. There's a jukebox, too. **The Jefferson
House and Pub**, 119 Market Street, U.S. 62, Warren, serves mainly
mesquite grilled food in a restored 1890 home. There's a kid's menu. Call
(814) 723–2288.

In Elk County, the **Bavarian Inn**, which is also a motel, 33 St. Mary's
Street, St. Mary's (814–834–2167), serves German food. In Bradford,
McKean County, **Shady Point Family Restaurant**, North Farley Street,
Route 6, offers daily specials, homemade soups, and pies. The only draw-
back is the sometimes slow service. Call (814) 837–7361.

DAY TRIPS

Knox, Kane, Kinzua Railroad operates June through October. This
steam-and-diesel train travels through the peaks and valleys of the Allegheny National Forest and across the historic Kinzua Bridge. Built in

1892, this bridge is one of the world's highest railroad bridges. If you leave from Marienville in Forest County, the round trip is 96 miles; from Kane in McKean County, the round trip is 32 miles, a better option with young kids. You can order a box lunch for a small additional fee.

The train stops before crossing the bridge so that those passengers afraid of heights may disembark. Then the train turns around and picks those passengers up.

Evergreen Enchanted Playground, Evergreen Park, Chestnut Street, in the town of Kane (McKean County), is delightfully creative. Your kids will love the dragon, wolf den, tire net, tree fort, pirate ship with gangplank, suspension bridge, and several mazes, slides, swings, and ramps.

FOR MORE INFORMATION

For National Forest information and literature, contact: Forest Service, USDA, P.O. Box 847, Warren, Pennsylvania 16365; (814) 723–5150. For information on Chapman State Park, located within the forest, contact RD #1, Box 1610, Clarendon, Pennsylvaina 16313-9607; (814) 723–8030.

The tourist associations in gateway areas provide information on lodging, restaurants, and local attractions.

Elk County Recreation & Tourist Council, P.O. Box 35, Ridgway, Pennsylania 15853; (814) 772–5502.

Seneca Highlands Association (McKean) Box 698, Mt. Jewett, Pennsylvania 16740; (814) 778–9944.

Forest County Tourist Promotion Agency, P.O. Box 608, Tionesta, Pennsylvania 16353; (814) 927–8818/(800) 222–1706 in Pennsylvania only.

Travel Northern Alleghenies (Warren County), 315 Second Avenue, P.O. Box 804, Warren, Pennsylvania 16365; (814) 726–1222/(800) 624–7802.

Emergency Numbers

As some of these areas may be switching to 911 numbers, consult the front pages of the phone book in the area where you are staying for the most up-to-date information on ambulance, fire and police.

Elk County Police: (814) 776–6136

Elk County fire and ambulance: (814) 772–0000

Emergency Rescue Squad: (814) 723–4220

Forest County Police: (814) 755–3565

Forest County fire and ambulance: (814) 755–3200

McKean County Police: (814) 778–5555. Most, but not all of McKean County is tied into the 911 system for fire and ambulance. Check the front of the phone book.

Warren County Police: (814) 723–8880

Warren County fire: (814) 723–4200

If you are in a National Forest campsite, the site's host or hostess can summon emergency help. Area hospitals with a twenty-four-hour emergency room include:

Elk County: Andrew Kaul Memorial Hospital, 763 Johnsonburg Road, St. Marys; (814) 781–7500; Elk County General Hospital, Ridgway; (814) 776–6111

McKean County: Bradford Regional Medical Center, 115 I–Parkway, Bradford; (814) 368–4143

Warren County: Warren General Hospital, Two Crescent Park, Warren; (814) 723–3300

Poison Control: (412) 681–6669 (Pittsburgh)

There are no twenty-four-hour pharmacies in the area, although several have after-hour emergency numbers. Ott & McHenry, 102 Main Street, Bradford (McKean County), is open weekdays from 8:30 A.M. to 8:00 P.M., closing at 6:00 P.M. on Saturday. Sunday hours are 10 A.M. to 1:00 P.M. Call (814) 362–3827. After-hours emergency number: (814) 368–7361.

10
BALTIMORE
Maryland

Baltimore, nicknamed "Charm City," has lots to recommend it, including personality. With its dazzling inner harbor, brand-new old-style baseball stadium, top-notch art museums, the windy waterfront of Fells Point, and lots of ethnic neighborhoods, Baltimore is very different—but no less alluring—than its neighbor, Washington, D.C, less than one hour away. Instead of a planned, grand design for the ages, Baltimore exudes a down-to-earth hominess that adds, what else, charm to the historic sites, children's attractions, and educational museums.

GETTING THERE

The Baltimore/Washington International Airport (410–859–7100) is a fifteen-minute drive from downtown Baltimore. The BWI Airport Van Shuttle (410–859–7545) escorts visitors to many Inner Harbor hotels for reasonable rates. Taxis are also available.

Amtrak trains stop at Baltimore's Penn Central Railroad Station, North Charles Street, between Oliver and Lanvale streets. Call (800) 872–7245. For day trips to points between Washington, D.C., and Baltimore during the week, including Camden Yards and Penn Station, the MARC commuter train (800–325–RAIL) offers inexpensive service and frequent departures.

Bus travelers arrive at the Greyhound/Trailway terminals, 210 West Lafayette Street, and the Baltimore Travel Plaza. For information, call (410) 744–9311.

By car Baltimore is easily reached by I–95 from the north or south, and I–70 and U.S. 40 from the west.

GETTING AROUND

Much of Baltimore, including the newly renovated waterfront and Fells Point, can be reached on foot. For cold days and weary feet, however, there are several transportation possibilities. To avoid the challenge of navigating the many one-way streets in Baltimore by car, visitors should consider the Metro, a limited subway system that runs until midnight, or the Mass Transit Administration (MTA) bus lines which run twenty-four hours. MTA offers a one-day Tourist Passport for unlimited travel downtown. For fare and route information, call (410) 539–5000.

The Water Taxi (410–547–0090 or 800–658–8947) is an enjoyable way to reach points along Baltimore's Inner Harbor, including Fells Point, Little Italy, and the Aquarium. Inexpensive all-day passes are available for adults and children. Another entertaining possibility for children is the trolley servicing the downtown region. Call (410) 752–2015 for more information.

A car is also handy. Driving around Baltimore is easy, as street signs are easy to read, and routes are marked. The trick to remember is that many of Baltimore's main streets are one-way.

WHAT TO SEE AND DO

Inner Harbor Attractions

If you have limited time in the city, head for the Inner Harbor where many of the family attractions are located. Park the car, as you can walk to everything. You will easily find a day's worth of attractions here, if not more.

National Aquarium in Baltimore, Pier 3, 501 East Pratt Street; (410) 576–3800. This world-class aquarium alone merits a trip to Baltimore's Inner Harbor. The several stories of exhibits in this aquarium offer everything from shark tanks to a rain forest, and the facility houses more than 5,000 specimens.

Discover the world's aquatic life at the twelve major displays. Highlights include Wings Under Water, the largest ray exhibit in the nation, featuring cow-nose rays and blunt-nose rays among others. The Open Ocean exhibit, a.k.a. the Shark Tank, is home to sand tigers, nurses, and sandbar sharks; the kids will love this one for its easy-but-safe access to the ferocious-looking fish. The Atlantic Coral Reef, a coral reef recreated in fiberglass, features colorful tropical fish, and the South American rainforest demonstrates a wealth of plant and animal life with more than 600 species of tropical plants, plus parrots, sloths, and a fish tank that includes piranha. Maryland: Mountains to the Sea displays such local critters as bullfrogs, softshell turtles, flounders, and blue crabs.

Three of the friends you will meet at the National Aquarium in Baltimore. (Photo by George Grall/courtesy National Aquarium in Baltimore)

Be sure to take in an enlightening dolphin show at the Marine Mammal Pavilion's 1.2 million–gallon pool, where you'll learn about the behavior of beluga whales and bottle-nose dolphins.

Maryland Science Center, 601 Light Street (410–685–5225), entertains all ages with its hands-on exhibits. At the exhibit on Maryland's Chesapeake Bay, look at tiny baby crayfish under a microscope, and find out about the life of a blue crab. The Hubble Space Telescope opens kids eyes to the skies while Energy Place lets them use their bodies to generate electricity.

Take young children, ages two to seven, to K.I.D.S, a room with blocks, play areas, and appropriate hands-on items. The Davis Planetarium's sky show will leave your kids starry-eyed, and any of the educational, but usually entertaining, movies at the IMAX Theater are a big hit since the screen is 5-stories tall. The programs at both the planetarium and the IMAX theater are included in the price of admission.

What's an Inner Harbor without some maritime lore and actual ships? Baltimore has three noteworthy vessels that the curious can board. The **Baltimore Maritime Museum,** Pier 3, Pratt Street (410–396–3854), is a floating museum that consists of two ships: a 1940s submarine, *U.S.S. Torsk,* and the *Lightship Chesapeake.* Both are open for self-guided tours.

The Torsk submarine is distinguished for sinking the last Japanese warship in World War II. A walk through these narrow corridors lets kids know just how cramped life under the sea can be. The Chesapeake's beacon lantern served as a floating lighthouse in areas where rocks or shoals made the construction of a stationary lighthouse impossible. Quarters were tight here too, and talk was often punctuated by the blast of foghorns.

Aboard the *U.S. Frigate Constellation,* Inner Harbor Constellation Dock (410–539–1797), learn about nineteenth-century sea life. This National Historic Landmark was the first commissioned ship of the U.S. Navy. Launched in 1797, the warship participated in the War of 1812, the Civil War, and in World War II, after which she was permanently docked.

Because of the steep ladders used to get from deck to deck, this attraction is suitable only for children comfortable, and careful, about climbing. But come aboard, matey, and discover the berthing deck, the battle stations, and officer's quarters. During summer and on holidays, costumed interpreters take you back to 1861, loading cannon balls, and recounting life aboard ship. Kids keep enthralled with details about dinner—salt pork and biscuits—and facts about crew members as young as ten.

For a literal overview of Baltimore, check out the view 27 stories up at the **Top of the World** in the World Trade Center, 401 East Pratt Street; (410) 837-4515. The museum features exhibits on the port, the city's history, and economic development. Top of the World often holds special events geared to kids, especially around holidays. Activities include puppet shows, storytelling, and face painting. Call ahead to check out the schedule.

Now that you've seen the top, try a bottoms-up view at the **Baltimore Public Works Museum and Streetscape,** 751 Eastern Avenue at Fallsway; (410) 396–5565. Housed in the Eastern Avenue Pumping Station, a plant that originally processed the city's sewage, the museum demonstrates the city's public utility services from street lighting to trash removal to plumbing. The brightly colored outdoor Streetscape gives an insider's glimpse of the workings beneath the city streets. Children enjoy picking out the underground phone lines, water, and gas pipes by color. An activity center for ages three to ten, Construction Site, is open on weekends and by request.

Isaac Myers Shipyard, Inner Harbor. Baltimore's first black-owned and -controlled shipyard was established after the Civil War by Isaac Myers. Visit the historic beginnings of the man who went on to establish the National Labor Union for blacks in 1869.

Slated to open in December of 1994, the **Christopher Columbus Center of Marine Research and Exploration,** located on piers 5 and 6, will add another major attraction to the Inner Harbor. In this facility de-

voted to marine biotechnology and nautical archaeology, a computerized "brain" will customize tours according to the special interests of visitors.

Museums and Historic Baltimore Sites

In addition to the prosperity brought to Baltimore by its port, Baltimore grew because of its railroad. With the laying of the Baltimore and Ohio tracks at the Mount Clare station in 1827, the city solidified its importance as a commercial distribution center.

Often overlooked is the **B & O Railroad Museum**, 901 West Pratt Street (410–752–2490), located at the site of the former Mount Clare Station. It's worth a stop, especially if toy trains, tracks, and thoughts of steaming around the countryside in a locomotive keep your child, or the child within you, happy.

Upstairs this museum displays a priceless collection of model trains, including a Lionel freight set from the 1920s, and some rare locomotives. Enjoy the elaborate display of tracks that wind through a replica of a 1940s city and of Maryland's mountains. Downstairs—save that for last—is the real thing, restored trains in an authentic roundhouse. As you listen to the taped sounds of whistles, chugs, and clanking, climb on and ogle such railroad darlings as a mail car, a caboose, and a big "mountain hauler."

After you explore the museum's three buildings, take a train ride to the nearby Mount Clare Mansion. Dating back to about 1756, this Georgian estate was home to Charles Carroll, founder of the Baltimore and Ohio Railroad.

For more city history, visit the **Baltimore City Life Museums**, 800 East Lombard Street; (410) 396–3524 or (410) 396–4545. This conglomeration of six museums gives a rounded view of Baltimore history. Four of the museums—the Carroll Mansion, the Center for Urban Archaeology, the Courtyard Exhibition Center, and the 1840 House—are located on Museum Row with a single entrance at the above address. The other two are located in other areas.

Start at the **Carroll Mansion** (410–396–3523) where Charles Carroll, the last surviving signer of the Declaration of Independence, resided at the end of his life. The **Center for Urban Archaeology** (410–396–3156) entertains older children and adults with its Archaeologists as Detectives exhibit in which history's puzzles are solved like a classic mystery. The center also features a working laboratory and a life-size excavation pit. The **Courtyard Exhibition Center** (410–396–3524) illustrates Baltimore's historic revitalization from the 1930s to the present.

The **1840 House** (410–396–3279), a reconstructed row house recreates nineteenth-century life in Baltimore with its living-history theater performances and weekend tours. The 1840 House also features three unique programs for the entire family. For children ages five to twelve, the 1840 House staff conducts a ninety-minute 1840 Birthday program with historical games, craft activities, and baking in the open hearth. Ages ten through adult are invited to join the staff for An Evening in 1840. Guests prepare an authentic meal at the hearth, dine in the upstairs parlor, then join in parlor games. The Overnighter is the most comprehensive program. Escape the twentieth century by delving into the nineteenth. This begins with a tour, then you prepare dinner 1840s style, eat, and enjoy parlor games before bedding down for the night. In the morning you fix your own breakfast and help out with the 1840s household chores. Reserve these programs ahead. Call (410) 396–3279 for more information.

Star-Spangled Banner Flag House and Museum, 844 East Pratt Street at Howard Street (410–837–1793), is the home of Mary Pickersgill, the woman who sewed the flag that flew over Fort McHenry, inspiring Francis Scott Key to compose "The Star Spangled Banner." Pickersgill, a widow, paid nearly $200 of her own money to purchase the 400 yards of material for the 30-by-42-foot flag, the largest in the world at the time. Working more than 1,000 hours, she received $405.90 for sewing this flag and another, smaller version. The receipt is showcased in the museum.

Fort McHenry, Fort Avenue; (410) 962–4299. The American flag flying here after a long night of British attack in 1814 inspired Francis Scott Key to write "The Star Spangled Banner." Visitors can explore the fort restored to its pre–Civil war appearance, walk o'er the ramparts, and see where the British invaded. From Memorial Day through Labor Day, there's shuttle boat service to the fort from Baltimore's Inner Harbor.

An industrial city, Baltimore's laborers—garment workers, oyster canners, printers, and others—come to life in **the Baltimore Museum of Industry,** 1415 Key Highway; (410) 727–4808. Housed in a former 1870 cannery, the hands-on exhibits teach kids about the labor in these laborers' days. Kids feel the muscle it took to operate a printing press, sample a foot-operated sewing machine, and—against a sweatshop display—see a photo of the real women who worked cramped together at their machines. At Children's Motorworks kids join a scaled-down assembly line, learning firsthand about the benefits, and boredom; at the Cannery they take part in shucking and canning oysters in a simulated 1883 factory.

Several famous people associated with Baltimore have historic sites in the city. Budding journalists may want to breeze through the **H.L. Mencken House,** 1524 Hollins Street (410–396–1149), home to the outspoken journalist Henry Louis Mencken, "The Sage of Baltimore." This nineteenth-century row house is furnished with Mencken's belongings and presents a short film on his life and works.

Westminster Hall and Burying Ground, West Fayette and Greene streets (410– 328–7228), is where Edgar Allan Poe and his wife, first-cousin Virginia Clemm, are buried. Many other notable Marylanders rest here as well. Tours are conducted the first and third Friday evening and Saturday morning each month with prior reservations. The **Edgar Allan Poe House**, 203 North Amity Street (410–396–7932), where Poe lived from 1831–1835, is open with abbreviated hours.

The **Eubie Blake National Museum and Cultural Center**, 409 North Charles Street (410–396–1300), honors the Baltimore-native, jazz musician Eubie Blake. It also displays national and local African-American artwork. **Babe Ruth Birthplace and Baseball Center**, 216 Emory Street (410–727–1539), features a permanent exhibit on George Herman "Babe" Ruth, as well as famous Baltimore Orioles. At the new Baseball Center slated to open in the fall of 1994, computer and laser technology will enable you to try your skill batting at a pro's best curve or fastball.

Art Museums

Baltimore Museum of Art, Art Museum Drive between Charles and 31st streets (410–396–7101), is the city's premier art museum featuring the Cone Collection, with outstanding works by Matisse, Picasso, and Cézanne. Besides these paintings—and the gift shop—kids seem to enjoy the Arts of Africa—specifically the masks—and the Cheney Miniature rooms, whose scaled-down furnishings depict life-styles from the seventeenth to the nineteenth century and are guaranteed to elicit an "ooh" from anyone who appreciates miniatures.

Besides its permanent collection the museum is noted for its frequent, top-quality shows. Call and see what's being featured, and inquire about their children's classes, often scheduled on weekends.

The **Walters Art Gallery**, 600 North Charles Street (410–547–9000), boasts more than 30,000 items in its collection that spans 5,000 years. Some kid-pleasing highlights include Byzantine silver and jewelry, an extensive arms and armor collection, jewelry by Faberge, and an extensive Asian arts wing, Hackerman House, 1 West Mount Vernon Place. Some children love the delicate swirls, patterns, and colors of these works in porcelain and lacquer.

Two more art museums include the **National Museum of Ceramic Art**, 250 West Pratt Street (410–837–2529), which presents temporary exhibitions of a wide variety of ceramic arts. The gift shop is a good place to browse and buy. **The Black American Museum**, 1765–69 Carswell Street (410–243–9600), presents changing exhibitions of contemporary black Americans and Third World artists.

Zoos

The **Baltimore Zoo**, Druid Hill Park (410–366–5466), boasts a large colony of African black-footed penguins, an elephant compound, and a nice children's zoo. Take the kids for a lesson on Maryland's Wilderness at the Children's Zoo, which features replicas of five Maryland ecosystems.

Performing Arts

Baltimore has an abundant selection of theaters. Among the choices are the **Theatre Project**, 45 West Preston Street (410–752–8558), featuring national touring groups; the **Morris A. Mechanic Theatre**, Hopkins Plaza, Baltimore and Charles streets (410–625–1400), which presents Broadway hits, and **Center Stage**, 700 North Calvert Street (410–332–0033), home of the state theater of Maryland, which hosts repertory and original shows. Go to the **Fell's Point Cafe**, 723 South Broadway Street (410–327–8800), for audience participation theater, which may include improvisation or mystery theater. **The Arena Players**, 801 McCulloh Street (410–728–6500), feature mainly African-American productions, and the **Children's Theater Association**, in the Walter's Art Gallery, 600 North Charles Street (410–225–0052), hosts children's productions.

The Baltimore Opera Company performs at the Lyric Opera House, 140 West Mount Royal Avenue; (410) 685–0693. The Baltimore Museum of Art is home to the Maryland Ballet, Art Museum Drive; (410) 467–8495. The Baltimore Symphony Orchestra plays at Joseph Meyerhoff Symphony Hall, 1212 Cathedral Street; (410) 783–8000. The Chamber Music Society of Baltimore presents monthly concerts at Meyerhoff Auditorium, at the Baltimore Museum of Art, Art Museum Drive; (301) 486–1140.

Shopping

At **Lexington Market**, 400 West Lexington Street (410–685–6169), grab some lunch. This is the country's oldest continuously operating market where 140 merchants offer fresh seafood, including Maryland crabcakes, meats, cheeses, wines, and anything else you can imagine. **Harborplace**, at the corner of Light and Pratt streets, offers more than 130 shops, eateries, and restaurants in two pavilions. When you tire of browsing, enjoy the water view from the terraces.

Tours

Several creative tours in Baltimore are worth a try. The **Insomniac Tour** run by Baltimore Rent-A-Tour (410–653–2998) is a fun tour of the city at night for adults and teens. **Trolley Tours** of downtown Baltimore run daily. Call Baltimore Trolley Tours (410–752–2015) or Tres Bon Trolley at (410) 252–7001.

Available harbor and boat tours include the **Baltimore Patriot I and II** (410–685–4288), the **Clipper City/Baltimore's Tall Ship** (410–539–6277), and **Harbor Cruises and Showboats** (410–727–3113), for dinner, dancing, and musical revues.

SPECIAL EVENTS

Sporting Events

Oriole Park at Camden Yards, 333 Camden Street (410–685–9800), is open from April to October for Baltimore Oriole baseball games. Built in 1992, the park mixes an old-stadium feel with modern amenities. Be sure to purchase tickets in advance for this popular summer activity. The Preakness, one jewel in racing's Triple Crown, is run in May, Pimlico Race Course, Baltimore.

Festivals

January: First Day Celebration at Harborplace.

February: Celebrate Black History Month at city sites. Call the Visitors Center at (410) 836–4636 for a calendar of events.

March: Annual Street Performers Auditions, Inner Harbor. Public Works Museum Open House for Archeology Week.

April: Mayor's Easter Egg Hunt, Druid Hill Park.

May: Preakness Stakes horse race at Pimlico Race Course with a week-long celebration throughout the city, including a parade.

June: National Flag Day Celebration at Fort McHenry.

July: July Fourth Celebration at the waterfront. Major League Baseball's All-Star Fanfest. Major League Baseball All-Star Game, Camden Yards. ARTSCAPE (410–396–4575) annual arts festival.

September: Baltimore City Fair. Harborplace Street Performers Festival. Kunta Kinte Heritage Festival, St. John's College, Waterfront, Annapolis, Maryland.

October: Baltimore on the Bay, the annual family festival of the city's maritime heritage. Annual Fell's Point Fun Festival. Kids on the Bay, a waterside children's festival.

November: Baltimore's Thanksgiving Parade from downtown to the Inner Harbor.

December: Noontime Christmas concerts all month long, except on Sundays, at Lexington Market. Parade of Lighted Boats at the Inner Harbor. Christmas at Harborplace. Baltimore's New Year's Eve Extravaganza, a nonalcoholic celebration geared toward the entire family and ending with fireworks over the harbor.

WHERE TO STAY

The Inner Harbor is a practical area to stay in since much of Baltimore can be visited on foot from here. Among accommodation possibilities are the Holiday Inn-Inner Harbor, 301 West Lombard Street (410–685–3500); Baltimore Marriott Inner Harbor, 110 South Eutaw Street (410–962–0202). Ask about the Marriott's Two for Breakfast package. Try the Clarion Hotel Inner Harbor, 711 Eastern Avenue; (410) 783–5553. The Harbor Court Hotel, 550 Light Street (410–234–0550), on the harbor, offers a Baltimore on Ice wintertime package where children stay free. The Hyatt Regency at the Inner Harbor, 300 Light Street (410–528–1234), has easy access to Harborplace and the Convention Center, plus special packages for families. The Stouffer Harborplace Hotel, 202 East Pratt Street (410–547–1200), is a convenient lodging. The Omni Inner Harbor, 101 West Fayette Street (410–752–1100), offers seasonal family packages often with discounted attraction tickets and $1.99 children's menus. The Sheraton Inner Harbor, 300 South Charles Street (410–962–8300), also features seasonal packages.

The Brookshire Inner Harbor Suite Hotel, 120 East Lombard Street; (410–625–1300), is an all-suite hotel. The Comfort Inn at Baltimore's Mt. Vernon, 24 West Franklin Street (410–727–2000), is located near the Walters Art Gallery.

For reservations on bed and breakfasts that welcome children, call Amanda's Bed and Breakfast Reservation Service, 1428 Park Avenue (410–225–0001). The Shirley-Madison Inn, 205 West Madison Street (410–728–6550), is a Victorian B&B in the Mount Vernon historic district.

WHERE TO EAT

Baltimore is a great place to taste the Chesapeake Bay region's seafood specialties, among them crab cakes, steamed crabs, steamed shrimp, and fresh oysters. Suggestions for family-friendly restaurants include Phillips, 301 Light Street (410–685–6600 or 410–327–5561), for seafood near the Inner Harbor. If you're looking for lunch at the Inner Harbor, the fast-food eateries at Harborplace, Pratt and Light streets (410–332–4191), offer enough choices to please any picky eater. An amphitheatre within the glass pavilions often provides free entertainment while you munch. Nearby, Freddie's of Water Street, 106 Water Street (410–752–5757), is a coffeehouse with a selection of sandwiches and salads.

Little Italy, 6 blocks east of the Inner Harbor, is the place to be for authentic Italian food in one of the oldest neighborhoods in the city. Try out Velleggia's, 829 East Pratt Street (410–685–2620); or Sabatino's, 901 Fawn Street (410–727–9414). For seafood in Fells Point, locals like the Fishery, 1717 Eastern Avenue; (410) 327–9340. If you're downtown and just want a sandwich, get one at Lenny's Deli of Lombard Street, 1150 East Lombard Street; (410) 327–1177.

Baltimore's *Guest Quick Guide* offers a comprehensive list of restaurants.

DAY TRIPS

Annapolis

About an hour away from Baltimore, Annapolis, at the picturesque junction of Chesapeake Bay and the Severn River, is a worthy day trip. Settled in 1649 much of the city has been designated a National Historic Landmark District. Stroll along its narrow streets, admiring the architecture and the shops, and grab a bite to eat. A kid-pleaser is a tour of the bay. Several are available from the forty-minute harbor tour aboard the *Harbor Queen,* to the seven-and-a-half tour aboard the *Bay Cruise,* which passes the city landmarks en route to the Eastern Shore town of St. Michaels. For tour information, contact **Chesapeake Maritime Tours,** city dock at Main Street; (410) 268–7600.

Be sure to tour the **U.S. Naval Academy,** bordered by King George and Randall streets; (301) 263–6933. Established in 1845 the Academy's museum in Preble Hall exhibits flags, ship models, and war relics. In warm weather watch the cadets muster in front of Bancroft Hall at noon. Older children may like visiting the historic houses such as the eighteenth-century **Hammond-Harwood House,** 19 Maryland Avenue, with its period pieces.

Before leaving the city take some time to romp at the **Neuman Street Playground,** an eclectic collection of climbing apparatus surrounded by green spaces for running.

Greenbelt

This Washington, D.C. suburb has **NASA's Goddard Visitor Center,** Greenbelt, Maryland (301–286–8981), where you can educate the family about space exploration at interactive exhibits created for children. Highlights include a Manned Maneuvering Unit in which kids capture satellites in space and a reproduction Gemini capsule with a mock take-off recording. Rockets are launched on the first and third Sundays of each month and weekly grounds tours run every Thursday afternoon.

For additional day trips to points along the Eastern Shore, see the chapter on Washington D.C. For a free Maryland Travel Kit, call (800) 543–1036.

FOR MORE INFORMATION

Visitor Information Centers

The Baltimore Area Convention and Visitors Center, 300 West Pratt Street; (410) 837–4636 or (800) 282–6632. Chamber of Commerce; (410) 269–0642. The Department of Recreation and Parks; (410) 396–7900.

Senior citizens will find the Waxter Center for Senior Citizens help-

94   MID-ATLANTIC

ful. Call (410) 396–1341. Persons with disabilities can get referrals and information from the **Handicapped Services Coordinator** at the Mayor's Office (410–396–1915), or from the **Disabilities Information and Assistance Line**; (410) 752–DIAL. The Easter Seal Society of Central Maryland has published a Baltimore guide for travelers with disabilities, *Bright Lights, Harbor Breezes*. For a copy call (410) 335–0100.

Emergency Numbers

Ambulance, fire, and police: 911

Block's Pharmacy, Baltimore Street at Linwood Avenue, is open from 9:30 A.M. to 9:00 P.M. Monday–Saturday and from 10:00 A.M. to 2:00 P.M. on Sundays; (410) 276–2312.

Johns Hopkins Hospital Emergency Room: (410) 955–5000

Maryland Poison Center: (410) 528–7701

11
BRANDYWINE VALLEY AREA
Pennsylvania and Delaware

For more than 300 years—from the time of William Penn—people have sought refuge and renewal in the Brandywine Valley. This bucolic landscape on either side of the Brandywine River in Pennsylvania and Delaware offers the weekend sojourner an American sampler. Here, where southeastern Pennsylvania meets northern Delaware, you find extravagant country estates and simple farmhouses, fine art and nineteenth-century factories, Revolutionary War history, Colonial craft fairs, and pastoral back country roads.

GETTING THERE

Philadelphia International Airport (215–937–1930), the one closest to Brandywine Valley, serves most major airlines and has car rental agencies.

By car from the north, take Route 202 into the area. From the south I–95 north leads to Route 202. To visit by train take Amtrak (800–USA-RAIL or 302–429–6530) to the Wilmington, Delaware, station at the intersection of Martin Luther King Jr. Boulevard and French Street. The Wilmington station has car rental agencies.

GETTING AROUND

The best way to travel and tour the Brandywine area is by car. The Delaware Administration for Regional Transit (DART) provides transit service within northern New Castle County and the Greater Wilmington area. Call the DARTline at (302) 655–3381.

WHAT TO SEE AND DO

Parks and Green Spaces

Brandywine Battlefield Park, on Park Drive between the Augustine and Market Street bridges (302–571–7747), is a historic site. On September 11, 1777, when the morning mist rose over these Pennsylvania meadows and apple orchards, one of the most significant battles of the Revolutionary War began. By day's end 25,000 British and Revolutionary soldiers lay dead in the fields. Despite General George Washington's defeat by British General William Howe, the nascent Revolutionary forces scored an important psychological victory: Washington prevented Howe from capturing the iron forges that supplied ammunition and muskets for the soldiers, and Washington proved his forces were capable of sustaining a difficult attack by the skilled British. This helped Washington obtain official support from the French the following spring.

September is an especially good time to visit. During **Brandywine Battlefield Days** the park stages a reenactment of this battle, complete with cannon, cavalry, a horse unit, 300 soldiers in period dress, and camp followers. At night, enjoy the troops' encampment featuring demonstrations of eighteenth-century tenting, cooking, and wound dressing.

For more Revolutionary spirit during fall, board the shuttle bus for the quick ride to Chadds Ford for a Colonial crafts festival, called **Chadds Ford Days.** Stroll the grounds and watch as blacksmiths, broom makers, weavers, potters, quilters, toy makers, and other costumed craftspeople demonstrate these essential eighteenth-century skills.

Longwood Gardens is at the junction of U.S. 1 and Route 52 near Kennett Square, Pennsylvania; (215) 388–6741. The gardens transport you from the rustic, rugged history of the Revolution to the tranquil, mannered society of the du Ponts, Brandywine's nineteenth- and twentieth-century industrial heroes. The former summer estate of Pierre du Pont, the onetime board chair of General Motors, Longwood features more than 1,000 acres of outdoor gardens, woodlands, and meadows, plus twenty indoor conservatories, several ponds, three acres of fountains, even an open-air water theater.

Walk among rows of trees, sit on a stone whispering bench, or stroll through conservatories bursting with orchids, roses, and blooming cacti. In summer watch a dazzling dance of colored fountains choreographed to classical music, capped by fireworks. Touring Longwood can take all day, but allow at least three hours. After an introductory slide show at the visitor's center, start your walking tour of the outdoor gardens under the towering beeches and ginkgoes planted by the original Quaker settlers in 1730. Walking tour highlights, depending upon the season, include tulips and rose gardens or fall gardens bright with red, yellow, and gold chrysanthemums. Throughout the gardens, especially along the woodland walk, enjoy the sunlight streaming through the sugar maples, beeches, and poplars.

For an *Alice in Wonderland* maze of outlandish shapes, tour the topiary gardens. Surrounded by a sundial that took du Pont and his engineers five years to build, the carefully clipped yews assume unlikely geometric and animal shapes. The topiary garden even has a rabbit—reputedly created in tribute to Bunny du Pont, a relative of Pierre.

Be sure to allow time for a tour of the conservatories. These nurseries, with Palladian windows, house everything from bonsai, cacti, and palms to medicinal plants and rare orchids. The East Conservatory, where concerts are held, contains a 10,010-pipe organ. The Main Conservatory, an elegant pillared structure, provided shelter for du Pont's garden parties. Pink bougainvillea drape the archways around the original dance floor.

Afterward, enjoy the water displays mid-June through August. Legend has it that as a child du Pont would open the bathroom faucets to watch the water run—despite the reprimands of his parents. At Longwood du Pont gave free reign to his water fantasies. Start with the Italian water garden, lined with linden trees, and based on the fountains of an Italian villa du Pont loved. Four large fountains delicately frame a tranquil scene. Du Pont devilishly inaugurated the cascading staircase fountain: he positioned his nieces and nephews on the marble stairs, dressed in their Sunday best, then drenched them with water.

Check the schedule of events as Longwood often features such family activities as Fabulous Fun Days for Children. Enliven a dreary winter day with a plant hunt amid acres of blooming plants in an indoor conservatory. Events are held periodically for the Wiggle Club, ages three to five, and Kool Kids, ages six to ten.

Museums

Nearby **Winterthur**, 6 miles northwest of Wilmington, Delaware (302–888–4600 or 800–448–3883), also features hundreds of acres of gardens and woodlands. From mid-April through October sign up for the tram tour, which is a great way to see the blooms, beeches, maples, and oaks, and save your feet.

The estate belonged to Pierre du Pont's cousin Henry Francis du Pont. Henry's passion was American furniture, and the furnishings at Winterthur will bedazzle you and older kids, especially preteens in love with historical mansions. The 196 rooms of this magnificent country estate hold more than 60,000 antiques. From the William-and-Mary carved wardrobes to the eighteenth-century Pennsylvania blanket chests to the fine examples of Chippendale styling, Winterthur houses an astonishing collection of furniture, textiles, and other objects made or used in America between 1650 and 1850.

The galleries opened October 1992 with a permanent exhibit, Perspectives on Decorative Arts in Early America. This is a good place to begin your tour with kids. They can choose one of six perspectives from which to look at objects. For example Change Over Time shows how fashions changed in certain periods. Change Over Place shows how design and craftsmanship differed from one city to another. The Henry S. McNeil Gallery, opened June 1993, intrigues future furniture builders with its tools, exhibits on the evolution of design styles, and lessons about furniture study. A gallery for changing exhibits opens in 1994.

You can't see all of Winterthur in one visit. A popular overall tour is the Winterthur Experience, which includes a forty-five-minute tour of about twenty rooms, plus a short tour of the gardens. Special tours focus on specific topics such as textiles, craftsmanship, folk art, or Queen Anne furniture. It's best to reserve these ahead of time.

Highlights of the museum include the elegant Port Royal parlor, with its matched Chippendale highboys and lavender-and-yellow color scheme; the Chinese parlor, noted for its vivid green Oriental wallpaper; the Baltimore drawing room, with its woodwork salvaged from a Baltimore mansion; and the Montmorenci stairway, a graceful curved staircase rescued from a North Carolina home built in 1822.

The Brandywine River Museum, U.S. Route 1, Chadds Ford; (215) 388–7601. This intimate museum on the banks of the Brandywine River is housed in a converted nineteenth-century gristmill. The pastoral setting and unpretentious galleries provide a low-key way for kids to enjoy art. This is an especially good place to introduce kids to American illustrators.

In the museum the American countryside comes to life. Those who have been captured by three generations of Wyeth paintings—by patriarch N.C. Wyeth, son Andrew Wyeth, and grandson Jamie Wyeth— will especially enjoy these special exhibits.

View Andrew Wyeth's paintings: the wistful *Christina's World*, the weathered barns of *Night Sleeper,* the country boy by the roadside in *Roasted Chestnuts.* Enjoy Jamie Wyeth's whimsical *Portrait of Den Den,* a likeness of his pig. You also can see such American illustrations as N.C. Wyeth's drawings for *Kidnapped* and *Treasure Island,* Howard Pyle's Brandywine settings, William Smedley's New York scenes, and Harrison Cady's lion drawings.

After your tour take a Wordsworthian turn through the grounds to experience firsthand the countryside you've viewed in the museum. Follow the trail along the banks of the winding Brandywine River where lush birches and maples grow near fields of wild flowers. Pack a picnic lunch or buy one from the museum's café, where you may dine overlooking the Brandywine. In fall the museum's cobbled courtyard comes alive with a crafts festival and harvest market each weekend from mid-September to mid-October.

The Hagley Museum and Library is off State Route 141, in Wilmington; (302) 658–2400. The du Pont fortune that nourished Longwood and Winterthur began at the Hagley in Greenville, Delaware, 3 miles north of Wilmington. The Hagley is strung along the banks of the Brandywine River on 230 acres. Here nineteenth-century industrial history is set against a sweep of centuries-old trees, including such unusual ones as blue atlas cedars transplanted from Africa and Chinese empress trees from the Orient. After all, in 1799 when E. I. du Pont emigrated to America, he listed his occupation as "Botaniste." The careful cultivation of these grounds was his lifelong interest.

To the rustle of the river and the wind, this mostly outdoor museum tells the story of nineteenth-century America's booming need for explosives, and the birth of the Du Pont Company. The new nation demanded black powder not only to fight the War of 1812, but to blast its way west—clearing farmland, developing mines, and building railroads. Here along the Brandywine River, Irénée du Pont built gunpowder mills in 1802 to supply the United States Army.

With prosperity came the mansion and the workers' village, blacksmith's shop, machine shop, and schoolhouse. All are restored and open to the public. This industrial park displays the stark contrasts of wealth and poverty that characterized nineteenth-century industrial life.

Start with the exhibits in the Henry Clay Mill. Once a cotton-spinning mill, it was converted by the Du Pont Company to barrel manufacturing and is now a museum. The exhibits offer an overview of eighteenth- and nineteenth-century Brandywine Valley industry and include explanations of tanning, water turbines, and an interesting model of Oliver Evans's 1819 automatic flour mill. This Rube Goldberg–looking device of conveyors, descenders, and elevators greatly increased a mill's efficiency.

At the mill purchase a ticket for the five-minute jitney ride to Eleutherian Mills, du Pont's first property. With borrowed money E. I. du Pont began the family's American fortune. The house, completed in 1803 and later enlarged, was home to du Ponts for nearly one hundred years. A tour reveals the tasteful antiques of the last occupant, E.I.'s great granddaughter, Louisa Evelina du Pont Crowninshield, who received the house as a wedding gift from her father in 1923.

But the drawings lining the ground floor hallway and the view from the veranda reveal the most. Instead of the terraced garden that now sweeps down the hill, the pictures depict rows of billowing smokestacks. E. I. du Pont built his home in the European tradition of close proximity to the factory. This pastoral landscape once bustled with workers, smelled rancidly of sulphur, and rang with frequent blasts from the mills just below.

Before heading to the heart of the museum—the Hagley Yard—tour the original office, and visit the barn, with its cooper shop, cars, carriages, and a Conestoga wagon. Reboard the jitney to visit the engine house where, upon request, volunteers demonstrate the 1870 slide-valve, box-bed steam engine used to power the pack house where the finished powder was packaged. Take the quarter-mile walk along the tree-lined river bank to the sixteen-foot wooden waterwheel, which was used prior to the 1840s when the family switched to water turbines.

At the Millwright Shop in Hagley Yard, an interpreter explains the manufacture of black powder. Displays show how saltpeter imported from India and sulphur from Sicily were heated, purified, and blended with local charcoal to create the volatile substance. Stamp mills were originally used to mix these materials, but by 1822 more efficient roll mills replaced them. A roll mill ground the mixture between its two eight-ton cast-iron wheels for three to eight hours, depending on the consistency required.

The roll mills are the paired, granite curiosities lining the river banks. Several stand tall, and some are just foundations covered by plants. With 3-foot-thick walls, a thin roof, and a gaping opening, these buildings were designed to channel the force of any explosion toward the water. Just one roll mill, originally built in 1839 and rebuilt in 1886, survives intact. The others sacrificed their iron wheels for World War II.

Still powered by a water turbine, this one mill operates at selected intervals. A guide explains how du Pont used the mill race, a man-made canal, to harness the natural power of the seventeen-foot drop in water level. Then the guide opens the sluice gate to set the force in motion.

But the roll mill was just one step in the production process. Before the powder could be sold, the mixture still needed to be compressed in the pressing house, broken into chunks and ground in the graining mill, polished in the glazing mill, dried in the dry house, and screened and packed in the pack house.

Take time to stroll along the mill race and to follow the river path to the creek banks. With its contrast of stone, water, and rows of trees, this area is among the nicest spots at the Hagley. Stop by the machine shop as well. Inside, hear the slap and leathery hum of belts that drive nineteenth-century lathes, planers, and presses used in repairs.

Blacksmith's hill and other areas hold periodic demonstrations, including living history interpretations. Check the schedule. Spring and summer are beautiful at the Hagley, but autumn is a special gift as the grounds fill with brilliant foliage.

Delaware Art Museum, 2301 Kentmere Parkway, Wilmington; (302) 571–9590. This respected museum is known both for the works of Howard Pyle and his disciples, and for its Pre-Raphaelite collection, the largest collection on permanent view in the United States. As an intriguing aid in your tour, pick up *Take Apart Art*, a booklet with fill-in blanks that helps kids and parents talk about such components of art as color,

Kids can create their own works of art at the Children's Participatory Gallery in the Delaware Museum of Art. (Courtesy Delaware Tourism Office)

line, shape, and texture. The booklet makes the illustrations and paintings more accessible to kids. Pyle, born in Wilmington in 1853, is an important American illustrator credited with training such soon-to-be-famous students as N.C. Wyeth and Maxfield Parrish, whose works are also here. Most kids respond to the techniques, colors, and subject matter of these noted American illustrators.

Take younger children to the Pegafoamasaurus, otherwise known as the Children's Participatory Gallery. Kids create their own art work from foam pieces of various shapes and colors. January features the annual Children's Event, a festive affair that in the past has included tea parties and teddy bear picnics. Summer offers "Jazz-On-Tap" in the early evenings.

The **Delaware Museum of Natural History**, on Kennett Pike, Route 52 (302–658–9111), is 5 miles northwest of Wilmington. Must-sees here include the 500-pound clam shell; the world's largest bird's egg; and the recreated natural habitats, such as an African watering hole and the Great Barrier Reef. For some hands-on exploration, take younger children to the Discovery Room, open to the public weekday afternoons and weekends.

Ask about the museum's special event Children's Weeks in spring and winter, usually coinciding with holiday school breaks.

Rockwood, 610 Shipley Road, Wilmington (302–571–7776), is an 1851 Gothic-style country estate, on seventy acres. The period furnishings here will probably appeal only to older children with an interest in antiques, but the landscaped grounds offer a pleasing place for a family romp, especially during the mid-July Old Fashioned Ice Cream Festival when Victorian bicyclists, jugglers, clowns, and interpreters in period dress take over.

SPECIAL EVENTS

May: Winterthur Point-to-Point Races, an equestrian event with tailgate picnics and a parade.

July: Rockwood Museum sponsors its annual **Ice Cream Festival** on the first weekend following the Fourth of July. The **Philadelphia Eagles** host their summer camp in the Brandywine Area from mid-July through August at West Chester University's football stadium.

September: Revolutionary Times at Brandywine Battlefield Park features a battle reenactment.

October: Chadds Ford Pumpkin Carve, at the Chadds Ford Historical Society Fairgrounds, features professional carvers showing their skill at carving jack-o-lanterns, plus food and drink for the public.

November–December: A Brandywine Christmas is an areawide celebration with concerts, and decorated house and museum tours.

December: Christmas at Hagley festive decorations.

WHERE TO STAY

A nice way to experience the bucolic Brandywine Valley is by staying at a bed and breakfast inn. **Bed and Breakfast of Philadelphia** (800–220–1917) offers several places that welcome families with children of all ages. Among the finds:

Lenape Springs Farm (call 800–220–1917 for reservation information), located on thirty-two acres along the Brandywine Creek in Pocopson, is an 1850 three-story farmhouse. Kids love seeing the horses and cows in the pasture, and parents like the hot tub. The carriage house offers two rooms that share a bath, and the farmhouse has a family suite with two rooms and a hall bath. Children of all ages are welcome.

Pheasant Hollow Farm (800–220–1917) is in Thorndale, about a half-hour's drive from Longwood Gardens and the Chadds Ford area. This colonial home is furnished with country antiques. The grounds have a pond, stream, and gardens.

Wilmington offers a range of accommodations, from the posh **Hotel** du Pont at Eleventh and Market streets (302–594–3100), to the **Sheraton Inn** at 4727 Concord Pike (302–658–8511) to the **Days Inn** at 1102 West Street (302–429–7600 or 800–325–2525). The **Best Western Brandywine Valley Inn,** 1807 Concord Pike, Wilmington (800–537–7772), frequently offers sampler packages that include lodging and admission to several area attractions. Brandywine Valley packages are also available from the **Holiday Inn,** 4000 Concord Pike, Wilmington; (302) 478–2222 or (800) HOLIDAY.

Summerfield Suites Malvern-Great Valley, 20 Morehall Road; (215) 296–4343 or (800) 833–4353. This chain offers one- or two-bedroom suites with kitchen facilities and a daily continental plus breakfast buffet. There are also children's videos to rent (the two-bedroom units have three televisions plus a VCR) and a twenty-four-hour convenience store on site. Ask about special weekend rates.

For bed and breakfast accommodations in Delaware, contact **Bed and Breakfast of Delaware** at (302) 479–9500 or (800) 233–4689. Many of their properties are best suited to families with older children and teens.

WHERE TO EAT

The **Chadds Ford Inn,** Routes 1 and 100, Chadds Ford, Pennsylvania; (215) 388–7361. This Wyeth family favorite is just up the street from the Brandywine River Museum. Established in 1763 for travelers fording the Brandywine River, the restaurant offers Continental and American fare and is a good choice for families with older children and teens.

Buckley's Tavern, 5812 Kennett Pike, Centreville; (302) 656–9776. Housed in a 160-year-old building in the historic town of Centreville, near Winterthur, Longwood, and the Brandywine River Museum, the tavern has everything from burgers for the kids to grilled salmon for their parents.

For seafood servings head to **Dinardo's Restaurant,** 405 North Lincoln Street, Wilmington; (302) 652–9503. Try their hard-shelled crabs, lobster tails, or fisherman stew. **Arthur's Family Restaurant,** 215 North Dupont Highway, New Castle (302–322–3279), offers good seafood and homemade pastries.

DAY TRIPS

Easy day trips include Philadelphia and Valley Forge (see the chapter on Philadelphia), and the Amish areas near Lancaster and Hersheypark (see the chapter Hershey and the Pennsylvania Dutch Country).

Bird lovers and nature lovers should visit the **Bombay Hook National Wildlife Refuge,** RD 1, Box 147, Smyrna, Delaware; (302) 653–9345.

The refuge includes 15,122 acres, three-quarters of which are tidal salt marsh. In fall and spring thousands of migratory birds fill the skies over the refuge. In October and November look up to see peak populations of snow geese, Canada geese, and ducks. Shorebirds arrive in quantity in May and June. Obtain a map for a driving tour—kids enjoy the comfort—and a trail guide. Some trails are easily conquered by young kids.

FOR MORE INFORMATION

For more information on the Brandywine Valley area, visit the Brandywine Valley Tourist Information Center at Longwood Gardens or write to them at P.O. Box 910, Dept. VG, Route 1, Kennett Square, Pennsylvania 19348; (215) 388–2900 or (800) 228–9933. For information about Delaware attractions, contact the Greater Wilmington Convention and Visitor's Bureau, 1300 Market Street, Suite 504, Wilmington, Delaware 19801; (302) 652–4088 or (800) 422–1181.

Emergency Numbers
Ambulance, fire, and police: 911
Medical attention in Delaware: Medical Center of Delaware, 4755 Ogletown Stanton Road; nonemergency (302) 733–1000, emergency (302) 733–1601
Medical attention in Pennsylvania: Crozer-Chester Medical Center, 1 Medical Center Boulevard, Upland; (215) 447–2000
Poison Control in Delaware: (302) 655–3389
Poison Control in Pennsylvania: (215) 386–2100
Pharmacy in Delaware: Brandywine Drug Center, 4605 Market, Wilmington (302–762–6940), open Monday to Saturday from 9:00 A.M. to 8:00 P.M. and Sunday from 9:00 A.M. to 4:00 P.M.; Eckerd Drugs, 2005 Concord Pike, Wilmington (302–655–8866), open daily from 8:00 A.M. to 10:00 P.M.
Twenty-four-hour pharmacy in Pennsylvania: CVS Pharmacy, 246 Concord Road, Aston; (215) 497–2225

12
CATSKILL MOUNTAINS
New York

Mention the word "Catskills," and many people envision the large hotels in Sullivan County where families from New York City once flocked by the carload. While a number of these resorts exist today (most have modernized their images along with their facilities), there's much more to this area than stereotypes. The Catskill Mountains cut across four counties, each with its own personality: Ulster in the east, Sullivan in the south, Delaware in the west, and Greene in the north. The 386,000 acres of unspoiled state-owned Catskill Forest Preserve and the 705,000 acres of privately- and state-owned Catskill Park offer a variety of simple, natural pleasures: miles of hiking and skiing trails, plus creeks and streams for fishing, canoeing, and tubing. Much of this pristine area is in western Ulster and southwestern Greene counties, although Sullivan and Delaware counties have their share of natural places as well.

Whether your lodging choice is simple, fancy, or in-between—and there's a wide selection of each—the Catskills afford your family a wonderful opportunity to get in touch with the outdoors any time of year. The WHAT TO SEE AND DO section includes some attractions in Ulster, Sullivan, and Greene counties—in addition to just hiking and enjoying the scenery—that you might enjoy during a stay in the area. Delaware County, largely rural, also provides beautiful scenery, particularly during fall.

GETTING THERE

The area is served by a number of commuter and regional airlines, with limousine service to Albany International, New York City's JFK and LaGuardia airports, and Stewart Airport in Newburgh. Commuter flights are available from Stewart Airport to Sullivan County International Airport in White Lake; (914) 583–6600.

Amtrak currently doesn't serve the Catskills. Closest stops: Rhinecliff and Hudson, New York; (800) USA-RAIL. Adirondack Trailways, Trailways, Short Line, and Mountain View serve various areas of the Catskills. By car, the Catskills are accessed via exits 16 through 21B of I–87, the New York State Thruway. The Route 17 "Quickway," beginning at exit 16, stretches westward to Lake Erie, passing through Sullivan and lower Delaware counties.

GETTING AROUND

Some Catskill cities have their own local bus service, although vacationers invariably rely on their cars to get around.

WHAT TO SEE AND DO

Ulster County

More than one-third of northwestern Ulster County lies within the Catskill Forest Preserve, which starts just west of the city of Kingston. The southern part of the county is in the Shawangunk Mountains, officially not a part of the Catskill mountains. But since this is also a popular vacation destination, attractions and lodging in the Shawangunk area are included here. The Hudson River runs along Ulster's eastern boundaries.

Northern Ulster County

Tubing is a great way for older kids and adults to enjoy the **Esopus Creek,** located within the preserve. **Town Tinker Tube Rental** has a substation at the Mt. Pleasant Lodge, 3 miles before Phoenicia, where kids ages twelve and older can rent tubes and equipment. (Head protection and life vests are required for everyone under fourteen.) The novice section of the creek is about 2½ miles, or about a two-hour trip, and features one set of fast-moving rapids at the beginning. After that, enjoy a slow, winding ride through gorgeous scenery. Call (914) 688–5553.

Opus 40 and the Quarryman's Museum, High Woods, Saugerties; (914) 246–3400. Opus 40 is an environmental sculpture made of tons of finely fitted bluestone and constructed over thirty-seven years by sculptor Harvey Fite. The creation spreads over more than six acres. You and the kids can walk through, around, and over it, past pools and fountains, and up to the monolith that is the summit of the work. Summer concerts of jazz, folk, and classical music are held on selected evenings. Fite's collection of tools (many hand-forged) and furnishings from a quarryman's household (stove, cupboard, and handmade dominoes) are housed in the museum. It's open from Memorial Day to November 1, but call first; some Saturdays are reserved for special events.

Visit the **Village of Saugerties'** sandy public beach on Esopus Creek, at the bottom of Hill Street. A lifeguard is on duty from July 4th weekend through Labor Day; (914) 246–2321.

Woodstock, just west of Saugerties, is at the foot of Ohayo and Overlook Mountains in the Catskill range. A brochure of area attractions, including hiking trails, is available from the Chamber of Commerce, P.O. Box 36, Woodstock 12498; (914) 679–6234. Stores that sell area hiking maps include the **Golden Notebook,** 29 Tinker Street (914–679–8000), which also has a children's book and cassette annex.

Woodstock is known for the 1960s music festival, although that didn't take place here. The festival was already named when the original deal fell through, and the site was relocated to Sullivan County. Woodstock—a community of writers, musicians, artists, and craftspeople—is worth a stop. Browse in the shops on and around Tinker Street. Don't miss **Tinker Toys of Woodstock,** 5 Mill Hill Road. Then take the kids for a romp in the **Woodstock Wonderworks,** a community-built playground on the grounds of the elementary school, Route 375. The complex is open to the public when school isn't in session, and it features tunnels and mazes, a dragon slide, Viking ship, a guitar car, and picnic tables. Just outside of Woodstock, you'll find **Kenneth L. Wilson State Park,** Wittenberg Mountain Road, Mount Tremper; (914) 679–7020. A sandy beach on the park's shallow lake is perfect for tots. Nearby, marked trails wind through the woods. There are rest rooms, a picnic area, and overnight campsites by reservation.

Southeast of Woodstock the city of **Kingston,** along the Hudson River, was a leading nineteenth-century maritime center. At the Historic Rondout area—a revitalized nineteenth-century waterfront community with shops and restaurants—those days are relived. See the **Hudson River Maritime Museum,** 1 Rondout Plaza (at the end of Broadway); (914) 338–0071. The small museum tells the story of the Hudson through models, artifacts, photographs, and paintings. Exhibits change yearly. In the outdoor area, antique vessels are displayed. Visiting vessels, such as the sloop *Clearwater,* are often tied up on the museum's bulkhead. The *Indie II* excursion boat leaves for a ten-minute cruise to the Rondout II Lighthouse where you can climb to the top for river views. The museum, open from May to October, has a number of special events, including the Shad Festival each May. Shad and shad roe are served along with music, puppet shows, and boat rides. The September Harvest Festival features crafts, harvest food, music, and boats.

Across the street is the **Trolley Museum,** 89 East Strand; (914) 331–3399. The big draw is the excursion ride that runs 1½ miles along the tracks of the old Ulster & Delaware Railroad to picnic grounds on the Hudson shores. The museum displays trolley, subway, and rapid transit cars. It's open Memorial to Labor Day.

Rondout Landing is the departure point for Hudson River cruises aboard the excursion ship *Rip Van Winkle* from May through October. Two-hour sight-seeing tours of river estates and lighthouses are included, as are all-day sojourns down to West Point Military Academy in Orange County. The West Point round trip takes seven hours and doesn't stop, except to let off one-way passengers, so unless your kids love cruising, opt for the shorter tours. The boat has a snack bar on board. Reservations are suggested for evening music cruises, which feature local country and western or rock 'n' roll bands. Call (914) 255–6515/(800) 843–7472.

Shawangunk Area

Widmark Honey Farms, Route 44–55, 2 miles west of Gardiner (914–255–6400), has been producing honey on this working farm for more than one hundred years. Along with honeybees and livestock, the farm has three American black bears that wrestle and perform in ninety-minute shows from May to October, on Saturday, Sunday, and holidays at 3:00 P.M. The farm and apiaries are open all year. There's free honey tasting and goats, calves, and lambs to pet and feed. Picnicking is allowed.

Ice Cave Mountain, Route 52, Ellenville; (914) 647–7989. This national landmark can be seen via a self-guided driving and walking tour that includes well-marked nature trails, rugged rock formations, canyons, and mountaintop vistas of five states. The walkways slope gently, making this an easy hike for kids. (The paths are too narrow for baby strollers.) There's a snack bar, rest rooms, and a gift shop. It's open mid-August through November.

Winter pleasures include **Belleayre Mountain Ski Center**, NY–28, Highmount (914–254–5600), the county's largest downhill area. It's open Thanksgiving weekend to the end of March. The lower mountain is for beginners and novices. A nursery caters to ages eight weeks to twelve years (reservations suggested), and SkiWee lessons for ages four to twelve are available on weekends and holidays. Anyone purchasing a ticket gets a free lesson. Some 6.2 kms of ungroomed cross-country trails are free. Lessons are available. At presstime, Belleayre planned to stay open in the summer, offering tennis, hiking, volleyball, and a swimming beach on their snow-making lake for a nominal entrance fee.

Sullivan County

This southwestern Catskill county, bordered on the west by Pennsylvania, has many of the big hotels and resorts long associated with these mountains. There are also more simple lodgings and plenty of family-friendly activities. The *Sullivan County Travel Guide* suggests several different driving tours; one includes the county's famous covered bridges.

This county was the site of the Woodstock Festival, held in **Bethel**. If

Consider a taking canoe trip on the Delaware River when you visit the Castskills. (Copyright © 1993 New York State Department of Economic Development)

your teens consider this a historic site, then drive by for a look. The farm is located off Route 17B on Hurd Road. You'll be close to the 1,409-acre **Lake Superior State Park** in Bethel, on Duggan Road, between Route 17B and 55. This lake has a nice, sandy beach, lifeguards, rowboat rentals, and allows fishing and picnicking. Call (914) 583–7908, ext. 5002.

With older kids, consider a canoe trip on the **Delaware River**, located on Sullivan County's western border. The *Sullivan County Travel Guide* lists outfitters who plan day or overnight trips.

In the northern half of the county is **Apple Pond Farming Center**, Hahn Road, Calicoon Center; (914) 482–4764. Call for reservations. This is a working farm; all equipment is pulled by horses. On the horse-drawn wagon tour, you meet sheep, goats, lambs, and several breeds of horses. As you ride through the fields, you hear about farming in the olden days. The farm is open year-round, so depending on when you visit, you may see wool spinning, beekeeping, or maple syrup–making.

There are hayrides in the summer and sleigh rides in the winter. There's a picnic area. A guest house is available by the weekend or week; reserve in advance. Since this tour involves walking through fields, strollers aren't appropriate.

In the southern half of the county, stop at the **Fort Delaware Museum of Colonial History**, Route 97, Narrowsburg; (914) 252–6660. This is a no-frills (but interesting) recreation of the first settlement in the upper Delaware River Valley in 1754. Costumed interpreters explain how these wilderness dwellers survived. The stockaded settlement is comprised of log dwellings, a blacksmith's shop, a weaver's shed, armory, pens for animals, and the fort. Demonstrations of spinning, candle dipping, and musket and cannon firing are held frequently. Open from Memorial Day weekend through Labor Day, there are a variety of special events in July and August.

Lucky Penny Riding Stables, Fosterdale, 20 miles west of Monticello on Route 17B; (914) 932–8348. At the free barnyard zoo, kids pet and feed baby goats, calves, lambs, ducks, pigs, geese, chickens, and rabbits. There are pony rides for younger kids and horseback trail riding for ages six and up. It's open May 1 to October 30.

Minisink Battlefield, Minisink Ford (SR–97 west to Route 168); (914) 794–3000, ext. 5002 (State Government offices). This is the site of the 1779 battle in which American militiamen were massacred by Tories and Mohawk Indians sympathetic to the British. Three flat interpretive nature trails wind through woodlands. Across from the entrance is the 1848 Roebling's Suspension Bridge, the oldest in America, created by John Roebling of Brooklyn Bridge fame.

Downhill ski from December to March at **Davos Ski Resort** (formerly Big Vanilla), Woodbridge, New York (exit 109 off Route 17 at Rock Hill); (914) 434–1000. The twelve trails on the main mountain offer a good place for novices and some more advanced slopes, too. SkiWee is offered for ages four to eight.

Cross-country ski at **Morningside Park**, in the town of Fallsburg, Brickman Road, Route 52; (914) 434–5877. The park offers 2½ miles of marked, groomed trails and is open dawn to dusk.

Greene County

This northern Catskill county offers a variety of ethnic and music festivals, scenic trails, one hundred waterfalls (many with natural pools for swimming), and appealing family attractions. The city of **Catskill**, just off the New York State Thruway in the eastern central part of the county, has several of particular interest.

Carson City and Indian Village, Route 32; (518) 678–5518. At this large "western" village, expect lots of gunfights, bank robberies, and other high jinks performed by "bad" and "good" guys. Cancan, magic and Native American shows, stagecoach and train rides, and a wagon museum with horse-drawn vehicles and sleighs add to the fun. Eat at their Chuckwagon, or bring your own picnic lunch. Open Memorial through Labor Day.

Catskill Game Farm, off Route 32; (518) 678–9595. Families have been coming here for generations, and the appeal is obvious: 2,000 animals, including bears, tigers, lions, and performing acts such as monkeys who juggle and elephants who dance. Buy crackers to feed deer and llamas at the petting zoo, or bottle feed small baby pigs and lambs. A train heads from the petting zoo to the birdhouse. Have lunch either at the snack bars or the picnic area, and stay the day. It's open Memorial to Labor Day.

Clyde Peeling's Reptiland, Route 32; (518) 678–3557. Your kids will either be totally fascinated or completely repelled by the approximately one hundred reptiles ranging from little garden snakes to big king cobras. Reptiland is open Memorial to Labor Day.

Elsewhere in the county, you'll find **Zoom Flume Waterpark**, Shady Glen Road, East Durham, northwest of Catskill; (518) 239–4559. This is the Catskill's largest, with giant water slides, bumper boats, waterfalls, and a dry area with a moon walk and coasters that glide down a track on the mountain. It's open Memorial to Labor Day.

North-South Lake Public Campgrounds, Cty. Route 18, Haines Falls, southwest of Catskill; (518) 382–0680. This New York State–run recreation area has two sandy beaches on either end of the lake, plus boat rentals and fishing. Hike in the surrounding woods; one trail leads to the scenic Kaaterskill Falls. Call (800) 456–CAMP in advance for campground reservations, from Memorial Day to early December.

Winter pleasures include **Hunter Mountain**, NY 23A, Hunter; (518) 263–4223/(800) FOR–SNOW—taped ski report. This three-mountain complex covers forty-six slopes and trails. Machine-made snow keeps the place open from November through April. A Peewee program for infants up to age five combines child-sitting with skiing for the older tots. At SkiWee Frostyland ages five to twelve learn to ski on weekends and holidays from 9:30 A.M. to 3:30 P.M. (Reserve.) From July 1 to Labor Day, the mountain has ethnic and music festivals and a Sky Ride, with views of the Northeast from the Catskill's longest and highest chair lift.

There's also **Ski Windham**, Route 23 West, Windham; (518) 734–4300/(800) 729–SKIW/(800)729–4SNO—taped snow reports. Ski on twin mountain peaks with thirty-three trails. The Children's Ski School offers half- or full-day programs that include activities for non-skiers ages one to seven; for pre-skiers age three; for ages four to seven at Mini-Mogul Skiers, and two- or five-hour sessions on weekends and holidays for Mogul Master Skiers ages eight to thirteen. Reservations with full payment required. Area lodging can be reserved through their Lodging Service, (800) 729–SKIW.

Performing Arts

In Ulster County, Kingston's **Ulster Performing Arts Center**, 601 Broadway (914–339–6088), features Broadway plays suitable for families, concerts ranging from symphony to rock, and second-run movies for reasonable prices. **Shadowland Theatre**, Ellenville (914–647–5511), has a professional company in residence performing Broadway-style productions, musicals, and children's plays from June to October. In Sullivan County, **Catskill Actors Theatre**, County Road 47, Highland Lake (914–557–6523), has professional theater in a historic church, July through September, including original kid's theater. In Greene County, **Bond Street Theatre**, Interarts Colony, Woodstock Avenue, Palenville (914–678–3332), offers original children's programs from June to September.

SPECIAL EVENTS

Fairs and Festivals

Contact individual tourist offices for more information on festivals in their area.

May: Woodstock–New Paltz Arts and Crafts Fair, New Paltz, Ulster County; Shad Festival, Maritime Museum, Kingston, Ulster County.

July: Fourth of July celebrations in Village of Ellenville, City of Kingston, New Paltz, and Saugerties in Ulster County. St. Joseph's Italian Festival, New Paltz, Ulster County.

August: Ulster County Fair, New Paltz. Antique and Classic Boat Show, Rondout Landing, Kingston, Ulster County.

September: Woodstock–New Paltz Arts and Crafts Fair.

July–October: A variety of ethnic and music festivals at Hunter Mountain, Greene County, with food, crafts, and entertainment.

August: Delaware County Fair, Walton. Old Franklin Day, Franklin, Delaware County, features crafts, flea markets, and activities.

October: Annual Apple Festival, Hensonville, Greene County.

WHERE TO STAY

Fancy resorts, simple motels, bed and breakfast inns, cabins in the woods: the Catskills have them all. Each county tourist office can supply a listing of lodgings. Here are a few to give you an idea of what's available for families.

Ulster County: Catskill

Frost Valley YMCA, Frost Valley Road, Claryville; (914) 985–2291.

This splendid place is closed in late June (except Father's Day weekend) and in July and August, when it becomes a summer camp, but the facility is open the rest of the year to the public. Accommodations include some grand rooms in the "Castle," once the home of the industrialist who owned this property, where you share the house (and baths) with other guests. Lodges, much like motel accommodations, and basic cabins are also available. Everyone eats family-style in the main dining hall. When you check in, obtain a schedule of events, which include Junior Naturalist programs, crafts, group hikes, and orienteering. There's supervised swimming in a pond, rowboats, hayrides, bikes, evening entertainment (such as square dancing and sing-a-longs), even cross-country skiing and sledding during the winter.

Shawangunk Mountains

Mohonk Mountain House, Lake Mohonk, New Paltz; (914) 255–1000 or (800) 772–6646—from area codes 212, 516, or 718. This historic, Victorian resort situated on 7,000 acres of nature preserve offers specialty, themed weekends fall through spring. During January's What's in the Winter Woods, you and your kids learn about forest animals and winter night skies; during the March Family Festival, listen to storytellers and join in sing-alongs.

When not busy with events, hike the woods; if it's cold enough, skate on the frozen lake or the pond. When it snows there's cross-country skiing as well. On weekends a modified kid's program operates for ages three to twelve. From Memorial Day to Labor Day, there are programs for kids age two to seventeen. Baby-sitting is available at an extra charge. The rates include three meals a day. The rooms, remember, are not "hotel modern." Rather than glitz, you have lots of Victorian oak and many fireplaces.

Pinegrove Resort Ranch, Lower Chestertown Road, Kerhonkson, NY 12446; (800) 346–4626 or (914) 626–7345. This year-round dude ranch caters to families by offering day-long activities at an all-inclusive price. Located on 500 acres between the Shawangunk mountains and the Catskill range, this ranch runs instructional horseback rides eight times a day. From 10:00 A.M. to 5:00 P.M. every day, a nursery cares for kids up to two years old, and a day camp keeps kids ages three and up happily busy feeding llamas, singing on hay rides, and riding ponies. Children under age seven learn to ride in the corral, and kids over seven go on trail rides with adults. Evening entertainment includes square dancing, scavenger hunts, and family games. The price includes three meals a day, an all-day snack bar, rides, and entertainment. Rates are half-price for children four through sixteen, and kids under four stay for free.

Sullivan County

Concord Resort Hotel, Kiamesha Lake; (800) 431–3850. This place is representative of the big, Catskill hotels: nightly entertainment, twenty-four outdoor and sixteen indoor tennis courts, indoor and outdoor pools, a health club, forty-five-hole golf, downhill and cross-country skiing, and day camps. Opt for the meal plan or go European. Food is an activity in itself here. Waiters bring you platefuls of things to try. While this bustling resort is not for everyone, some doubting Thomases come home with surprisingly fond memories.

Greene County

Kutscher's Country Club, near Monticello, is another of the old-style resorts that has been trying to woo a new generation by promoting its kids' programs. These include a nursery for young ones, programs for ages three to five and six to nine, plus some activities for preteens and teens. With 450 rooms and more than 1,200 acres, Kutscher's is big. This Catskill's fixture offers tennis, golf, ice skating, and nightly entertainment. Call (800) 431–1273, (914) 794–6000.

Balsam Shade Farm, Route 32, Greenville; (518) 966–5315. This casual, country, family lodging has pool, tennis, hiking, and lovely mountain views. There's nightly entertainment and three meals served daily with their own farm-grown vegetables.

Villagio, Route 23A, Haines Falls; (800) 843–4348. This year-round resort is set on 300 acres and has an Italian theme in food and entertainment. You'll find indoor and outdoor pools, movies, tennis, and 5 miles of cross-country trails. Note: Greene County has "pockets" of resorts with ethnic ambience: Italian in Haines Falls/Tannersville area, Irish in East Durham, and Austrian-German in Round Top.

WHERE TO EAT

Each county's travel guide offers dining listings. If you have young kids, don't miss **Dinosaur Dave's**, 608 Ulster Avenue, Kingston, with a jump-in Ping-Pong ball area and loads of video games that operate with tokens. Pizza, burgers, and hot dogs are on the menu; (914) 338–9332. In Greene County **Alla Conca D'Ora**, 440 Main Street, Catskill, serves delicious Northern Italian food; (518) 953–3549. **Red's**, Route 9W, West Coxsackie, is known far and wide for its fresh seafood; (914) 731–8151.

DAY TRIPS

Wherever you stay, take a day trip to explore adjacent Catskill counties (Greene County, for instance, is about forty-five minutes north of Kingston). From Delaware County, drive north to Cooperstown in adjoining Otsego County to the National Baseball Hall of Fame; (607) 547–9988. Parts of Ulster and Sullivan counties are less than ninety minutes from New York City.

FOR MORE INFORMATION

Tourist Information in Greene County, Thruway exit 21, Catskill (518–943–3223), is open seven days a week, or call (800) 542–2414. For Ulster County information, write to Public Information Office, P.O. Box 1800, Kingston, NY 12401; (800) DIAL–UCO. Sullivan County has two Information Center Cabooses. The first, on Broad Street, Roscoe, is also a mini railroad museum, open Memorial Day to mid-October. The Livingston Manor Caboose, exit 96 off Route 17, is open July and August on Friday, Saturday, and Sunday from 11:00 A.M. to 4:00 P.M. You can also call (914) 794–5000, ext. 5010 or (800) 882–CATS. Delaware County Chamber of Commerce, 97 Main Street, Delhi, New York 13753; (607) 746–2281 or (800) 642–4443.

Emergency Numbers

Since we're covering a wide area, we've listed county sheriff numbers. Much of the area will be tied into 911 in the near future. Consult the front of your area's phone directory for the latest information.

Greene County
Sheriff: (518) 943–3300
Catskill Community Care Clinic, 159 Jefferson Heights, Catskill: (518) 943–6334

Ulster County
Sheriff: (914) 338–0939
Kingston City Hospital, 396 Broadway: (914) 331–3131

Sullivan County
Sheriff: (914) 794–7100
Community General Hospital has two branches: one on Bushville Road, Harris, in the center of the county (914–794–3300), and one in Callicoon, in the west, Route 97 (914–887–5530).
Poison Control: (914) 353–1000/(800) 336–6997 (from 518 and 914 area codes)
There are no twenty-four-hour pharmacies in the area. A number are open seven days a week, such as CVS, Route 9W, King's Mall, Kingston (914–336–5955), 9:00 A.M. to 9:00 P.M., Monday through Saturday, closing at 6:00 P.M. on Sunday. Some pharmacies post emergency numbers on their front doors for after-hours assistance.

13
CAPE MAY
New Jersey

Cape May, New Jersey, a born-again beach town, boasts a historic district
with colorfully restored Victorian homes. Turreted, gabled, bay-windowed,
and laced with gingerbread, these houses are a treat to the eye. How the
town came to be is an interesting story.

The rich and the famous flocked to Cape May in its nineteenth-
century heyday. Arriving by steamboat and railroad from Philadelphia,
Baltimore, and Washington, political leaders such as Millard Fillmore,
Franklin Pierce, Abraham Lincoln, and Ulysses S. Grant shook off the
rigors of politics for sand and surf on Cape May's shores. Along these
once-wide beaches, Louis Chevrolet and Henry Ford raced their automo-
biles. John Philip Sousa played at Congress Hall, one of the grande-dame
hotels, and Wallis Simpson, the future Duchess of Windsor, debuted at
the Colonial Hotel on Ocean Avenue. In 1891, Benjamin Harrison took
over Congress Hall, making it his summer White House.

Spurred by such high-society tourism, entrepreneurs built hotels like
the Mount Vernon which, though it burned just before its official opening, offered 2,000 rooms and stretched for blocks along the Atlantic. In
1878, a disastrous fire destroyed many of these grand hotels, particularly
in the West End. The locals, hurriedly rebuilding for the coming summer
season, eschewed costly and difficult-to-build large hotels for three-story
Victorian "cottages" with plenty of spare rooms for summer guests.
These now grace the streets of Cape May, still offering bed and breakfast
in rooms filled with Victorian antiques, and polite conversation in elabo-
rately draped parlors where afternoon tea is almost always served.

At the turn of the century, Atlantic City's modern accommodations
had stolen Cape May's place in the sun, and the town experienced a grad-
ual decline. But in the 1960s when urban renewal planners began tearing
these old Victorian dwellings down to make way for modern motels,
preservationists rallied. After a protracted fight in the early seventies,
Cape May was designated a historical district. Restoration then began in

earnest, and cottages formerly partitioned into boarding houses and apartments were born again as elegant guest homes.

GETTING THERE

Traveling by land take either of two routes to Cape May: I–95 over the Delaware Memorial Bridge to Route 49 south, to Route 55 south, to Route 47 south, to U.S. 9 into Cape May; or, travel I–295 to U.S. 322 south, to Route 55 south, to Route 47 south, to U.S. 9 into Cape May.

The Cape May–Lewes Ferry runs daily between Cape May and Lewes, Delaware. Kids really enjoy this boat ride because it offers a welcome break from being cooped up in a car. The ferry terminal is on U.S. 9, 3 miles west of the southern terminus of the Garden State Parkway. For schedule information call (302) 645–6313 or (609) 886–2718.

GETTING AROUND

The best ways to see Cape May are by foot or by bicycle. Self-guided tour maps outlining walking tours of Cape May are available at the Washington Street Mall's information booths. **Surrey Bicycles**, a four-seated bike with a canopy-hood—perfect for the family—can be rented at Victorian Village Plaza's **Victorian Village Bikes**, Ocean and Washington streets; (609) 884–8500. Carriage, trolley, and guided walking tours also originate at the Washington Street Mall. Call (609) 884–5404.

WHAT TO SEE AND DO

Nature: Beaches and Birds

Miles of **beach** lure summer crowds. The beach along Beach Avenue offers families the typical delights of sun and sand. Come early as these shores get really crowded. Pick a spot and bring or rent a beach umbrella. Collect starfish, great cream-colored whelks, giant horseshoe crab shells, and driftwood. A time-honored tradition is strolling the boardwalk and munching such beach delights as pizza and fries.

Fall, with smaller crowds, quieter beaches, and water temperatures still warm enough for swimming, may be the best time to enjoy this historic beach town. Additional autumn attractions include a Victorian festival, and a great migration of birds. Each fall the birds come by the tens of thousands to Cape May, funneling through here for food and rest before crossing the Delaware Bay and continuing south. The beaches afford a perfect vantage point for such spectacular sights as a phalanx of Canada geese in precise formation above the gray-blue surf, or thousands of hawks gliding on warm air currents before swooping down on their prey.

Besides the beachfront near the heart of town, three areas offer less crowded beaches, and in fall, the best spots for birding: **Cape May Point State Park**; the **Cape May Migratory Bird Refuge**, a stretch of beach and dunes along Sunset Boulevard; and **Higbee's Beach**.

Cape May Point State Park—take Sunset Boulevard to Lighthouse Drive—has 195 acres of nature trails, wooded areas, and a half-mile of beachfront. Check out the station headquarters for a modest display of birds and shells and for the schedule of beginner bird walks and demonstrations of hawk banding.

Walk the boardwalk trails (wide enough for wheelchair access and strollers) through clusters of red cedars and shrubs to ponds where, especially in fall, snowy egrets hover like angels, and herons seem to walk on water. A special fall treat is the sight of thousands of hawks. A hawk-watch platform adjacent to the parking lot provides a good observation point for those with small children too weary to wander, or climb the abandoned World War II concrete bunker that juts out into the ocean. This, incidentally, is a good place to glimpse the falcons gliding on an updraft.

Higbee's Beach, a wildlife area, is more isolated and features clusters of trees that lead to the water. Higbee's also provides a quiet space for birding and solitary strolls, where you can often hear the cries of laughing gulls. To get here take Route 7, called Bayshore Road, and continue for about 2 miles almost to the dead end sign, then turn left. (It's New England Road, but there's often no sign.)

For more information on birding, contact the **Cape May Bird Observatory**, New Jersey Audubon Society, 705 East Lake Drive, P.O. Box 3, Cape May Point 08212; (609) 884–2736 or (609) 884–2626 (the hotline) for the latest information.

Nearby Nature

Don't miss **Leaming's Run Gardens and Colonial Farm**, 1845 Route 9 North, Cape May Courthouse, New Jersey 08210, about 14 miles north of Cape May; (609) 465–5871. Open mid-May to mid-October, this garden offers thirty acres of beautifully sculpted, tranquil gardens and fern-carpeted woods.

Allow at least ninety minutes, preferably longer, to follow the winding path through each of twenty-five gardens, carefully planted with colorful annuals and graced with lily ponds, gazebos, and benches shaded by tall trees. By June the roses are best, and in October it's still warm but the leaves are turning. The gardens, set above a forest bed of soft cinnamon ferns, each illustrate a color theme, or solve such common gardening problems as hillsides and too much shade.

This kind of "education" is easy on the eyes. The English cottage gar-

You and your family can climb the 199 steps to the top of the Cape May Point Lighthouse . . . the view will not disappoint. (Courtesy Cape May Department of Tourism and Economic Development)

den pops into color with 140 varieties of flowers; the Serpentine Garden (demonstrating how to plant in a long narrow area) winds its way to the lake in a burst of red salvias; the Knoll Garden, with its wild flowers, illustrates planting at different levels; and the reflecting pond laced with water lilies demonstrates how to use water to mirror flowers.

As owner Jack Aprill intended, this is a garden for relaxing and sharing a pleasant moment. Just to be sure, Aprill has placed signs urging you to PLEASE LOOK BACK, RELAX HERE and WATCH FOR HUMMINGBIRDS.

Another surprise is the occasional sound of roosters. Aprill has planted a Colonial farm that recreates the world of Thomas Leaming, the whaler who originally settled this farm in 1706. There's a one-room log cabin, a barn with roosters, and a dooryard garden planted with such typical Colonial crops as cotton, tobacco, peanuts, okra, pumpkin, and squash. The gardens end at the Cooperage, one of the largest dried-flower shops in the East—and Aprill's main business. With artifice that would have been much admired by the Victorians, Aprill has masterfully blended art and nature.

Victorian Architecture

If you're a fan of whimsical architecture and the plutocratic life-style, be sure to stroll along Columbia Avenue, Hughes Street, Perry Street, and Ocean Avenue past some gaily painted structural dowager queens. Sit on the serpentine porches of the surviving grand hotels—the Chalfonte, Congress Hall, and the Colonial—or rest in a wicker rocker on the back veranda of an elegant inn and take in a view from the past.

The **Emlen Physick House**, 1048 Washington Street, is open for tours. Built in 1879 this home has the elaborate furnishings of its eccentric and wealthy resident, Dr. Emlen Physick. Sometimes, from Memorial Day to mid-June, *The Doctor is In* takes place in the evenings. Among the heavy drapes and rococo Victoriana, you'll find the good doctor himself, talking politics and town gossip.

Look for the Mid-Atlantic Center for the Arts' (MAC) weekly flyer *This Week in Cape May*, which highlights Cape May's upcoming attractions and events. For more information contact the Chamber of Commerce of Greater Cape May at (609) 884–5508 or MAC. Trolleys offer a wide variety of historic, architectural, and seasonal tours of Cape May throughout the year. Generally, there are special guided tours and open houses in May and during Victorian week celebrations.

SPECIAL EVENTS

Festivals, Theater, and Cultural Events

April: Tour Cape May's Tulip Festival. The trolleys offer a great vantage point that's easy on little feet.

May: Cape May Music Festival, a six-week-long festival which show-cases the talents of noted soloists and musicians. Almost all of the festi-val's numerous concerts are held at Congress Hall, Beach Drive at Perry Street.

July–August: The **Cape May Kid's Playhouse** and the **Vintage Film Festival** offer entertainment for both young and old.

October: During Victorian Week, this town throws a Victorian fete filled with vaudeville, a fashion show, an antiques fair, walking tours, and old-house restoration workshops.

November: During Victorian Holmes Weekend Cape May is the set-ting for amateur sleuths to solve Sir Arthur Conan Doyle's Sherlock Holmes mysteries.

December: Christmas Lights Trolleys tour the decorated streets.

WHERE TO STAY

Some of the best bets for family lodging in Cape May are motels and the handful of bed and breakfast inns that welcome families. Book as far in advance as possible as Cape May is a very popular summer spot. And please be advised that most of the charming bed and breakfast inns do not really welcome children. In addition, many of these inns, in keeping with the period, either don't have air-conditioned bedrooms, or only have one or two at most. Don't believe that stuff about cross-breezes and fans. Without this modern convenience in summer, you will be either hot or very hot. If this matters, ask ahead of time and find a lodging that accom-modates your needs. Also, many of the inns close for the season in fall. A few like the Queen Victoria are open year-round.

The **Camelot Motel**, 103 Howard Street (609–884–1500) only 50 yards from the beach, has two-bedroom efficiencies complete with kitch-enette. Another near-the-beach motel is the **Atlas Motor Inn**, 1035 Beach Drive (609–884–7000), which has a pool and restaurant, as well as effi-ciency apartments. **The Dormer House International**, 800 Columbia Av-enue (609–884–7446), 3 blocks from the beach, rents one- and two-bedroom apartments with kitchens.

Featuring 1885 Victorian guest quarters, **Goodman House**, 118 De-catur Street (609–884–6371), is ½ block from the beach and also offers rental apartments with kitchens.

If you're traveling to Cape May with young children, a good bet is the **Chalfonte Hotel**, Box 475, 301 Howard Street; (609) 884–8409. The Chalfonte has special two-bedroom apartments and separate dining facil-ities for kids six years old and under. Parents can enjoy a romantic din-ner while their kids eat and then play with new-found friends supervised by college-age counselors.

The Queen Victoria, 102 Ocean Street (609–884–8702), a nicely appointed bed and breakfast with Edwardian antiques, welcomes children and offers cot rentals for the little ones, but has a limited number of rooms for families. According to the owners this bed and breakfast offers comfortable and functional antique furniture "sturdy enough to plunk down in, relax, and put your feet up on." Congress Hall, Beach Avenue and Perry Street (609–884–8421), is one of Cape May's grand old hotels. Built in 1879 Congress Hall offers real variety in its 112 rooms—some with antique brass bed and ocean views, and others with a more motel-like feel.

The Virginia Hotel, P.O. Box 557, 25 Jackson Street (609–884–5700 or 800–732–4236), is an upscale Victorian inn, restored to its late nineteenth-century grace. Families can feel comfortable in rooms that come with oversize beds, down comforters, a television, and VCR. Children under ten stay for free, while kids over ten are charged a nominal fee per night. There's a free continental breakfast.

WHERE TO EAT

In high season—summer, and during fall's Victorian Week—book your dinner reservations ahead. Otherwise, the lines and the wait can be long.

For affordable and casual family meals, try the Filling Station, 615 Lafayette Street; (609) 884–2111. It's open only for dinner. One local innkeeper says this place serves "the best hamburgers, steaks, and salads in town." For an Italian dinner try God Mothers, 413 Broadway; (609) 884–4543.

Dillons Restaurant, 524 Washington Street (609–884–5225), is open for breakfast, lunch, and dinner, and serves light, café-style fare. The Ocean View Restaurant, Beach Drive and Grant Avenue (609–884–3772), is open for breakfast, lunch, and dinner; they serve diner fare. McGlade's, 722 Beach Drive (609–884–2614), offers seafood and American cuisine.

For fine dining those with older children should try The Ebbitt Room, in the Virginia Hotel, 25 Jackson Street; (609) 884–5700. Dishes combine French, Latin, and Euro-Asian touches. While at the Ebbitt Room, stop by the Ebbitt Lounge, a piano bar that offers nightly entertainment.

DAY TRIPS

Board the Cape May–Lewes ferry for a trip to Lewes, Delaware, another beach town. Within several hours of Cape May, you can be in Philadelphia or the Brandywine Valley, Pennsylvania. (See the appropriate chapters.)

FOR MORE INFORMATION

For more information on Cape May, New Jersey, contact the **Greater Cape May Chamber of Commerce**, P.O. Box 554, Cape May, New Jersey 09204; (609) 884–5508. For information concerning upcoming Cape May activities and cultural events, contact the **Mid-Atlantic Center for the Arts (MAC)**, P.O. Box 340, 1048 Washington Street, Cape May, New Jersey 06204; (609) 884–5404.

Emergency Numbers
Ambulance, fire, and police: 911.
Poison Control: 911
Twenty-four-hour pharmacy and around-the-clock medical attention: Burdette Tomlin Hospital, Cape May Courthouse, exit 10 off U.S. Route 9; (609) 403–2000

14
FINGER LAKES and ITHACA
New York

The Finger Lakes region of West Central New York State makes for an idyllic family getaway. Here you find rolling hills, crystal blue lakes, lush green forests, glacier-carved gorges, cascading falls, and unlimited recreation, highlighted by boating and swimming. Indian legend says that God created the Finger Lakes by reaching down to bless the area, leaving an imprint of His hand behind. There are six major lakes—Canandaigua, Keuka, Seneca, Cayuga, Owasco, and Skaneateles—plus many smaller ones, spread over a number of counties, from south of Syracuse west to south of Rochester. **Ithaca** is at the southern tip of Cayuga Lake—one of the largest. Ithaca is an educational center and a city of outstanding beauty, an ideal spot to stop, stay, and—if you can tear yourself away—use as a base for exploring the surrounding region.

GETTING THERE

Tompkins County Airport, 5 miles north on Route 13 (607–257–0456) is served by USAir, Continental, and TWA. Car rentals are available at the airport. Airport Limousine Service provides van service to town; (607) 273–3030. Other major airports serving various areas of the Finger Lakes include Rochester, Syracuse, and Elmira/Corning.

Greyhound, Short Line, and Trailway buses stop at Ithaca Bus Terminal, West State and North Fulton streets; (607) 272–7930.

The closest Amtrak trains (800–USA–RAIL) arrive in Syracuse, 57 miles away.

Ithaca is located at the junction of routes 13, 79, 96, 96B, and 89. Interstates 81 and 90 (the New York State Thruway) have exits leading to these highways.

GETTING AROUND

The best way to tour the Finger Lakes is by car. Ithaca Transit buses (607–273–7348) serve the immediate area, while TomTran buses (607–274–5370) extend throughout Tompkins County.

WHAT TO SEE AND DO

Museums and Learning Centers

Most people don't come to Ithaca to museum hop, but if you have the time, here's where to go.

Cayuga Nature Center, Taughannock Boulevard; (607) 273–6260. This outdoor education center, 6½ miles north on Route 89, is on 128 acres of nature preserve. Along with hiking trails, it offers an occasional Sunday Family Nature Series. If you're staying a while, check into their Pee Wee Naturalist Series for kids, held in six sessions and reserved in advance.

DeWitt Historical Society Museum, 116 North Cayuga Street; (607) 273–8284. It's free—and might contain something of interest for school-age kids, depending on when you visit. Changing exhibits reflect local history, focusing on arts, industry, and ethnic groups. That sounds dry, but recent displays have ranged from Italian immigrants to Finnish American saunas, hardly colorless subjects. Call to see what's up when you're in town.

Herbert F. Johnson Museum of Art, Cornell University; (607) 255–6464. Designed by architect I.M. Pei, this distinctive building houses an excellent collection of art spanning thirty centuries. While there's nothing specifically for kids, there's lots to catch a youngster's eye, particularly in two of the museum's strongest collections: Asian and contemporary art. The fifth floor, where the Asian Art galleries are located, also offers superb views of the campus, town, and Cayuga Lake. Workshops, films, and concerts are held regularly; call for a schedule.

Parks and Beaches

The outdoors is what draws families. The Ithaca area has some wonderful state parks. For camping reservations in any New York State park, call (800) 456–CAMP. If you only have time for one, head 8 miles north of town to **Trumansburg**, where you'll find:

Taughannock Falls State Park; (607) 387–6739. The 215-foot falls that gives the park its name is visually striking, plunging down a mile-long rock amphitheater with sides rising from 350 to 400 feet. Many consider this sight one of the most scenic in the Northeast. Hiking and

The swimming at Robert H. Treman State Park can be enjoyed by everyone. (Copyright © 1993 New York State Department of Economic Development)

nature trails wind around the edge of the gorge. Plan to spend an idyllic day here: There are picnic areas, a swimming beach, playgrounds, camping, fishing, and, in the winter, ice skating, sledding, and some cross-country skiing.

Hopefully, you'll have time to visit these other noteworthy state parks right in Ithaca.

Buttermilk Falls, Route 13; (607) 273–5761. This pleasant park with ten waterfalls and twelve glens is highlighted by Buttermilk Creek, which descends more than 500 feet in a series of rapids and cascades. At the base of Buttermilk Falls, a natural pool with a "swimming hole" feel is popular with swimmers. Picnic areas, hiking trails, a playground, and fishing round out the fun.

Robert H. Treman State Park, Route 327; (607) 273–3440. Lovely Enfield Glen, along with the park's craggy gorges, winding trails, and twelve cascades (including 115–foot Lucifer Falls) create the scenic focus of this park. Swim in a supervised stream-fed pool at the park's lower end; there's a shallow end for tots. You'll also find playgrounds and picnic areas. Stop by the one-hundred-year-old mill in the upper park for a look at the antique milling machinery.

City parks are worth a stop. The first is **Cass Park,** 701 Taughannock Boulevard, which can be reached by car, bike, or foot along a waterside path. Splash in the Olympic-size pool or children's wading pool and take advantage of picnic facilities, tennis courts, a fishing area, and fitness trail. In the evening, summer soccer and softball games take place on lighted playing fields; (607) 273–9211.

The other noteworthy city park is **Stewart Park,** routes 13 and 34, on Cayuga Lake ½ mile north of Meadow Street, where families come to unwind, picnic, and take a ride on the restored carousel. Other features: playing fields, tennis courts, and a playground. A stroll along the walkways offers superb lake views, particularly at sunset; (607) 272–8535.

Cornell University owns the following family-appealing facilities, which are free.

Sapsucker Woods, 3 miles northeast of Cornell's main campus at 159 Sapsucker Woods Road; (607) 254–BIRD. You've got to love the name of these woods, home to the Cornell Laboratory of Ornithology. There's no charge to walk along the 4 miles of trails that travel through swamps and woodlands, where you'll spot nesting and migrating birds. (The trails are open twenty-four hours a day, so if your gang rises early, this is a great morning activity.) At the Lyman K. Stuart Observatory, take an intriguing look through the picture window at the bird-feeding garden and ten-acre pond.

Cornell Plantations, 2½ miles north on SR 79 and 366 at One Plantation Road; (607) 255–3020. Commune with nature (you can picnic too) at this splendid facility containing botanical gardens with cut flowers, herbs, vegetables, international crops and weeds, peonies, and a variety of plants native to the Cayuga Lake Basin. There's also a pleasant arboretum. Trails, streams, ponds, woodlands, and a lake will make your family want to linger. It's open from dawn to dusk.

Education Vacation

How about spending a family vacation on campus "high above Cayuga's waters," as the college song goes? **Cornell Adult University** (**CAU**) offers families—from tots to grandparents—a unique opportunity to do just that. The Summer CAU program hosts 300 people a week; 65 percent are couples, half with youngsters. They come to learn, relax, and enjoy the natural beauty of the area. Adults choose from stimulating seminars and workshops, which recently ranged from the cerebral ("Shakespeare's Greece and Rome") to the physical ("Pedal-Power Paleobiology"—a bicycle touring program). When studies finish in midafternoon, adults can take advantage of campus athletic facilities, lectures, and area recreation. Each day a special culinary event—such as a barbecue, faculty roast, or graduation party—is held.

Meanwhile, kids from potty-trained pre-kindergarteners to age twelve are subdivided into age groups and participate in morning, afternoon, and evening sessions that include learning activities, outings, games, crafts, and cookouts. When possible, kids are paired with roommates from their own age group and housed in rooms adjacent to their parents, with whom they have breakfast and dinner. Teens from thirteen through sixteen live and dine in separate quarters and take part in morning courses, field trips, sports parties, and other activities selected by the group, plus a one-day wilderness skills course. There's no formal program for infants and toddlers under three, but CAU can arrange part- or full-time and evening babysitting. This is a popular program, so plan well in advance. Contact CAU, 626 Thurston Avenue, Ithaca 14850–2490; (607) 255–6260.

Special Tours: Enjoy dinner—and lakeside views—on a cruise aboard the *M.V. Manhattan,* which sails daily from May to October from Old Port Harbor Restaurant. (The three-hour cruise may prove too long for younger children, however.) Call (607) 272–4868.

Performing Arts

The Hangar Theatre, a professional regional summer troupe, performs five productions that range from drama to comedy to musicals. They also offer KIDSTUFF, a children's theater, as well as one-act plays and musical cabarets. Call the box office at (607) 273–4497 to see what's playing. If you're here during fall, winter, or spring, you'll find lots more to choose from: check with the Convention and Visitors Bureau for information or buy a daily Ithaca *Journal.*

Shopping: Stop by the colorful Ithaca Farmer's Market at Steamboat Landing or DeWitt Park for an assortment of ethnic food, fresh produce, flowers, plants, clothing, and crafts. Call (607) 564–9246 for a schedule. Ithaca Commons, 108 East Green Street, is a downtown pedestrian marketplace with more than one hundred specialty shops set amidst fountains, benches, trees, and flowers. Sit down and absorb the international atmosphere: You may see a street performer or cultural event going on.

SPECIAL EVENTS

Sporting Events

Baseball addicts may want to travel to Elmira (between Ithaca and Watkins Glen) to see the Elmira Pioneers Red Sox, a minor league professional team affiliated with the Boston Red Sox. Call (607) 734–1811. If you're here during school season, root for an Ithaca College or Cornell team. Tickets for both sporting and cultural events can be purchased at Dewitt Mall ticket center, downtown Ithaca, on the corner of Buffalo and Cayuga streets; (800) 724–0999. For big-time teams travel to Syracuse to see the Orangemen play at the Carrier Dome. Auto races frequently take place on weekends at the Watkins Glen International Racing Circuit.

Fairs and Festivals

The Finger Lakes has an abundance of county and state fairs, arts festivals, and agricultural fairs. Obtain the latest, complete calendar of events from the Finger Lakes Association. (See FOR MORE INFORMATION.) In Ithaca you can count on a good time at these two annual shindigs.

June: Ithaca Festival, downtown, with children's activities and parade, crafts, entertainment, theater, and food.

October: Apple Festival offers entertainment, crafts, and food.

WHERE TO STAY

Finger Lakes Central Reservations can help with accommodations, including cottage rentals, and arrange escorted and self-drive packages as well as airport transfers or rental cars. Call (800) 828–3088. In addition to such tried-and-true chains as Holiday Inn, Howard Johnson, Sheraton, Ramada, Econo Lodge, and Super 8 Motel, Ithaca has some modest local lodgings that stand out for families.

Austin Manor B & B, 210 Old Peruville Road, Groton, is fifteen minutes from Ithaca in a peaceful country setting. This large and comfortable Victorian home welcomes children and serves a full breakfast. Call (607) 898–5786.

Hillside Inn, 518 Stewart Avenue, is in a residential area near the Cornell campus and offers inexpensive family suites with bath and free continental breakfast. Call (607) 272–9507/(800) 427–6864.

Margaret Thacher's Spruce Haven B & B, Route 13N, Dryden, will charm your family—particularly the kids, who are quite welcome here and will love staying in a real log cabin. The comfortable home is surrounded by spruce trees on a quiet side street in this village near Ithaca. A full breakfast is served. Call (607) 844–8052.

Spring Water Motel, Route 366, has a quiet country setting not far from town. Some rooms have kitchenettes. Call (607) 272–3721/(800) 548–1890—New York state.

Whitetail Crossing Cottages, 21 Belvedere Drive, rents new lakefront two- and three-bedroom cottages. Call (607) 257–3946

WHERE TO EAT

The Ithaca/Tompkins County Convention and Visitor's Bureau has a helpful dining guide to area restaurants. Don't forget dessert: Ithaca claims to be the birthplace of the ice cream sundae. Here are a few family selections.

Treat the kids to an unforgettable dinner in a restored railroad station or aboard a plush railroad car. **The Station**, West Buffalo and Taughannock Boulevard, serves American cuisine and has special dinners for children. Call (607) 272–2609. **Joe's Italian Restaurant** has been around since 1932, so you can assume it's doing something right. This casual place has an art deco decor, friendly service, and tasty food; veal is a specialty. College students flock here during the school year. Call (607) 273–2693.

DAY TRIPS

Emerson Park, routes 38 and 38A, 2 miles south of Auburn on Owasco Lake Shore, offers loads of things to do: playgrounds, kids' amusement rides, miniature golf, two natural sand swimming beaches, picnic facilities and fireplaces, boat rentals, an agricultural museum, and professional summer stock theater. Call (315) 253–5611.

Watkins Glen, a short drive away (and site of the auto racing circuit), has a stunning gorge with nineteen waterfalls, plus cascades, grottoes, and amphitheaters. The state park above the gorge has a large pool, picnic facilities, and fabulous Finger Lakes view. If you're here at night, catch Timespell, a sound and laser light show within the gorge.

From Watkins Glen, it's a short drive southwest to Corning, home of the **Corning Glass Center** (607–974–8271), where you can join the crowds touring the Museum of Glass, Hall of Science and Industry, and Steuben Glass Factory. Kids will gaze wide-eyed as glass animals and other objects are created in front of them. English double-decker buses transport visitors between the Center and other Corning attractions.

Halfway up Cayuga Lake's western shore in Romulus, **Misty Meadow Farm** (607–869–9243) offers guided tours of their working farm which produces 1,200 pigs a year. Guests can hold piglets, feed larger pigs, and learn about farming. There's a lunch restaurant on the premises and a farm store.

While you're driving about, consider taking an informative winery tour at one of the area's many vineyards. In the Cayuga Lake region, a number are located along the Cayuga Wine Trail (routes 79 and 89). In Hammondsport, about thirty minutes north of Corning, the **Taylor/Great Western/Gold Seal** winery (607–569–2111) offers a detailed tour.

FOR MORE INFORMATION

For Ithaca tourist literature, contact: Ithaca/Tompkins County Convention and Visitors Bureau, 904 East Shore Drive, Ithaca, New York 14850; (607) 272–1313/(800) 284–8422. Request the comprehensive *I Love New York Finger Lakes Guide* from the Finger Lakes Association, 309 Lake Street, Penn Yan, New York 14527, or call (800) KIT–4–FUN. It includes handicap access information.

Emergency Numbers
Ambulance and fire: (607) 273–8000
Ithaca City Police: (607) 272–3245
Poison Control Center: (607) 274–4111
Tompkins Community Hospital Emergency Room, 101 Dates Drive; (607) 274–4011
There are six pharmacies in Ithaca, none of which are open twenty-four-hours. Fay's Drugs has two branches, both open from 9:00 A.M. to 9:30 P.M. daily and to 6:00 P.M. Sunday and holidays: Cayuga Mall, Route 13 (607–257–3035) and 710 South Meadow Street (607–272–1955).

15
GETTYSBURG
Pennyslvania

Take your family back to July of 1863 when Confederate General Robert
E. Lee's army met the greater forces of the Northern army in a historic
battle and turning point of the Civil War. The Gettysburg National Military Park, encompassing some 1,000 monuments and cannons, commemorates this important, national event. Add a bonus to your visit by
timing it to coincide with one of Gettysburg's popular festivals, such as
the apple festival in May or the bluegrass music festival in May and September. A special time to visit is during the **Gettysburg Civil War Heritage Days**, the end of June through July Fourth, when battle
reenactments and special events will add excitement to your visit. Besides visiting the battlefield, take time to enjoy driving and picnicking in
the rolling countryside dotted with apple orchards.

GETTING THERE

One bus a day leaves from York, Pennsylvania, to Gettysburg. It's best to
drive to Gettysburg. Several roads lead to the battlefield park, including
U.S. 30 and 15, as well as state routes 134 and 116.

GETTING AROUND

There is no public transportation in Gettysburg. A car is a necessity.

WHAT TO SEE AND DO

Civil War History
    Gettysburg National Military Park; (717) 334–1124. Begin your tour

Adults and children alike can learn what Civil War life was like at Gettysburg National Military Park. (Courtesy Gettysburg Travel Council)

at the **Visitor's Center.** Brush up on your history by reviewing the 750-square-foot electric map that illustrates the famous battle and is accompanied by a taped narration. Books and souvenirs are also available, some aimed at children.

From here there are three options for a comprehensive tour of the 25-square-mile battlefield. Obtain a park service tour pamphlet, and try a self-guided drive which takes you past the designated landmarks. Another option is to rent a narrated tape produced by a private company. The **CCInc. Auto Tape Tours** add voice, music, and sound effects to enliven your self-guided driving tour. The rental tapes are available for about $11 from the National Civil War Wax Museum, 297 Steinwehr Avenue (717–334–6754), or the tape can be ordered for about $14, including postage, by writing, CCInc, P.O. Box 631, Goldens Bridge, New York 10526.

The best way, we think, is to hire a national park guide to accompany you in your car. A real guide makes dramatic history of what might be dubbed "boring stones and markers" by some kids. Guides, who cost approximately $20 per car for families of up to five, add the vivid narrative and background necessary to turn these grassy slopes into important history. Ask and the guides will also tailor a tour to meet your family's interests. Ask where your state's unit or a distant relative's unit was positioned, and the guide will take you to the spot and tell you a more specific story.

Some guides cater to children, commanding them to disembark from their vehicle and assume the positions of an artillery crew in order to explain how a cannon was fired. Another kid-favorite place that a guide can easily lead you to is the monument for Sally the War Dog, who saw her share of battle.

But try to get out of your car for even a little bit. Walking along one of the several marked trails not only gives you a different perspective on the battle; it also enables your kids to see the monuments and cannons up close. Trails vary in length from about 1 to 9 miles. Bring along a picnic lunch and break for food at one of the various picnicking sites. Maps of the trails and picnic areas can be obtained at the Visitor's Center. A favorite path is the mile-long **High Water Mark Trail** that begins at the Cyclorama Center and takes you by regimental monuments, Union soldier territory, and General Meade's headquarters. Boy Scouts should ask about hiking the Johnny Reb and the Billy Yank Trails, which when completed can lead to a Gettysburg Merit Badge.

Bicycling or horseback riding through the park adds fun to your visit as well. Biking trails wind through parts of the park, and an 8-mile horseback bridle trail meanders through the second- and third-day battle areas. Bicycle and horse rentals are available at the **Artillery Ridge Campground**, 610 Taneytown Road (717–334–1288) from April 1st through October 30th.

The best time to visit the outdoor park is when the weather is good. Your kids will feel freer to roam outside, and from mid-June to mid-August the National Park Service presents a living history program in which costumed interpreters act out Civil War roles. A nineteenth-century civilian carefully explains what it was like for him when the battle rolled into his home town, and a soldier sitting next to him relates a different story of woe and worry.

The Cyclorama Center, also on the grounds of the national park, presents the *Gettysburg Cyclorama,* Paul Philippoteaux's painting of Pickett's charge which is accompanied by an entertaining sound-and-light presentation. The center also displays exhibits and a ten-minute film.

Be sure to climb the **National Tower,** an observation tower, across from the National Park Visitor Center, but not officially part of the park. The 307-foot tower affords a panoramic view of the battlefield. There's also a twelve-minute tape that details the battle.

If your kids aren't scared of graveyards, don't miss the **Gettysburg National Cemetery,** which encompasses twenty-one acres and contains nearly 4,000 graves of Civil War soldiers. It was at the dedication of this cemetery on November 19, 1863, that President Abraham Lincoln delivered his two-minute speech. Since then Lincoln's Gettysburg Address has been immortalized as inspired rhetoric and a moving speech about the sacrifices of war.

Additional Attractions

Adjacent to Gettysburg Park is the **Eisenhower National Historic Site**; (717) 334–1124. This tour may interest older children who have some knowledge of former-president Eisenhower. A one-hour narrated tour takes visitors through the decorated rooms of the retirement home of Dwight and Mamie Eisenhower. Tours of the home are conducted from the Visitor's Center only. Be sure to get your tickets first thing, as there is a limited number of tours per day.

The following museums are not part of the National Park Service, but are privately run, and expound on aspects of the famous battle and surrounding history. Some families like these, others find them not worth the trouble. If you plan to visit a number of these attractions, look into a package plan which includes a two-hour bus tour and admission costs to either four or eight of the participating attractions. Package plans are available from the Gettysburg Travel Council; (717) 334–6274.

Jennie Wade House & Olde Town, Baltimore Pike; (717) 334–4100. This museum strikes a chord with children who can easily identify with the story of Jennie Wade, the only civilian killed in the battle of Gettysburg. Across the street in Olde Town, you'll find a gathering of old-fashioned crafts and merchant shops.

The National Civil War Wax Museum, Steinwehr Avenue (717–334–6245), is another favorite for kids. They can watch and listen to a full presentation where two hundred life-size wax figures recreate the Battle of Gettysburg and Lincoln's Gettysburg Address.

Battle Theatre, Steinwehr Avenue (717–334–6100), presents a general overview of the battle as well as a multimedia reenactment on a 50-foot diorama screen. Visit **General Lee's Headquarters and Museum**, Route 30 West, eight blocks west of Lincoln Square. In this old stone building, now displaying Civil War relics, General Lee and his advisors planned for the Battle of Gettysburg. **The Lincoln Room Museum**, Wills House, Lincoln Square (717–334–8188), is the former home of David Wills, where Lincoln revised his famous Gettysburg Address in November of 1863.

Lincoln Train Museum, Steinwehr Avenue; (717) 334–5678. Younger children and train enthusiasts will be drawn to this quaint museum where visitors take an imaginary ride from Washington to Gettysburg and eavesdrop on reporters and other distinguished guests. There are model trains to see as well. The **Hall of Presidents and First Ladies** (717–334–5717) offers more wax figures, this time presidents and first ladies, relating their visions of America. The kids might like the first ladies' inaugural dresses. The **Confederate States Armory & Museum**, 529 Baltimore Street (717–337–2340), displays rare and original Confederate edged weapons and small arms. The **Soldier's National Museum,** Baltimore Pike (717–334–4890), displays dioramas and exhibits of the Civil War from 1861 as well as the Charley Weaver Collection, miniature carved figures from ten major battles of the Civil War. **The State Museum of Pennsylvania,** Harrisburg, Pennsylvania; (717) 787–1974, located about 35 miles north of Gettysburg, documents the history of the state and presents The Keystone of the Union, an exhibit on Gettysburg and the Civil War.

Gettysburg Land of Little Horses, Off Route 30 West, follow signs; (717) 334–7259. Here's a good rainy day activity. Watch these three-foot tall horses race, jump, and perform in the indoor arena. Call in advance for performance times.

Special Tours

Downtown Historic District Tour of the more than one hundred recently restored buildings will give visitors a feel of the town that gave the battlefield its name. The walking starts at the Gettysburg Travel Council Office and includes the Wills House where President Lincoln composed his Gettysburg Address, and Samuel Gettys' Tavern, originally owned by James Gettys, the town's founder. Tour brochures are available at the Gettysburg Travel Council; (717) 334–6274.

The **Adams County Scenic Valley Tour** is a self-paced driving tour covering 36 miles south, west, and north of Gettysburg. The estimated driving time is two hours. Tour brochures are available at the Gettysburg Travel Council (717–334–6274), and posted signs mark the route. Highlights of the tour, which covers some of the famous orchards in Pennsylvania, include the Civil War site "Cashtown Pass," the 1790 Lower Marsh Creek Presbyterian Church, and Biglerville, the "Apple Capital."

The **Historic Conewago Tour** is a 40-mile driving tour, about two hours, which weaves around the Conewago Creek on the eastern side of the county. Tour highlights include the East Cavalry Battlefield, the historic towns of New Oxford and East Berlin, and country farms, churches, and the Adams County countryside. Tour brochures are available at the Gettysburg Travel Council; (717) 334–6274.

Gettysburg Battlefield Bus Tours (717–334–6296) presents various battlefield tours including a sunset tour on a double-decker bus. Tours are conducted by a cast of actors who use sound effects to act out the drama of the battlefield.

SPECIAL EVENTS

Antique Shows

There are several large antique shows in and around the Gettysburg area. For more information call the Gettysburg Travel Council at (717) 334–6274.

Festivals

May: Gettysburg Spring Bluegrass Festival the first full weekend in May. Join in the Apple Blossom Festival for a fuller appreciation of Adams County's outstanding apple orchards and enjoy magic shows, apple-bobbing contests, music, and dancing. Gettysburg Square-Dance Round-up is the real thing, featuring nationally recognized square-dance callers. Memorial Day Parade.

June/July: Civil War Heritage Days is a nine-day event including a two-day historically accurate reenactment of the Battle of Gettysburg. Festivities include band concerts and lectures by America's foremost historians. A fairly new addition is the Living History Camp where soldiers set up a realistic Civil War camp on the premises and demonstrate Civil War tactics, infantry drills, loading their weapons, and other pastimes. Children will love the realism of this event and are welcome to ask the soldiers questions.

Younger children will be entertained at the Gettysburg Firemen's Festival, a week-long evening celebration at the same time as the Heritage Days including games, rides, and a July Fourth fireworks display.

In conjunction with the Civil War Heritage Days, a Civil War Book Fair is held on the first weekend in July with book dealers selling new, used, and out-of-print Civil War–related documents. The Annual Gettysburg Civil War Collectors' Show features some 250 dealers displaying their Civil War memorabilia.

In order to have a choice of accommodations during Heritage Days and other events, especially during the most popular anniversary days July 1–3, families should make reservation at least three to four months in advance. Group packages are available. For more information call (717) 334–6274; for ticket reservations call (717) 334–6246.

August: South Mountain Fair. Enjoy one last hurrah at this country fair before school starts.

September: East Berlin Colonial Days is an eighteenth-century crafts and cultural fair. Gettysburg Fall Bluegrass Festival is for those who didn't get enough of the country sounds in May.

October: National Apple Harvest Festival, Biglerville, Pennsylvania. These two weekends are full of country music, crafts, rides, and, of course, apples. The festival is organized with kids in mind.

November: Anniversary of Lincoln's Gettysburg Address and Remembrance Day.

December: Yuletide Festival is a three-day festival of Christmas music, crafts, food, and religion, including tours of historical homes and crafts. Ask about special children's events.

WHERE TO STAY

Colonial Motel at 157 Carlisle Street (717–334–3126 or 800–336–3126) is just north of Center Square. It is centrally located and offers family rates. Kids stay free at the **Criterion Motor Lodge**, 337 Carlisle Street; (717) 334–6268. Other family-friendly hotels where children stay for free are the **Quality Inn-Gettysburg Motor Lodge**, 380 Steinwehr Avenue (717–334–1103 or 800–221–2222) and the **Howard Johnson Lodge**, 301 Steinwehr Avenue; (717) 334–1188 or (800) 654–2000. Teens stay free at the **Holiday Inn Battlefield**, Routes 97 and 15 (717–334–6211), which also offers discount meals.

Be sure to ask your hotel about special battlefield tour arrangements.

The Gettysburg region is well stocked with country inns and bed and breakfasts, however most prefer children ages twelve and older. An exception is the **Keystone Inn**, 231 Hanover Street; (717) 337–3888. They welcome children older than infants at this late-Victorian Inn. The **Doubleday Inn**, 104 Doubleday Avenue (717–334–9119) is located on the Battlefield. It's decorated with war artifacts and period furniture and offers free Civil War lectures. Children over the age of ten are welcome here.

The following inns prefer children twelve and older: The **Old Appleford Inn**, 218 Carlisle Street (717–337–1711) is a historic Victorian Inn downtown which dates back to 1867 and is filled with antiques. The **Baladerry Inn**, 40 Hospital Road (717–337–1342) was the site of a Civil War hospital. The **Homestead Guest Home**, 785 Baltimore Street (717–334–2037) is the Historic Dormitory of Civil War Soldier's Orphanage, and it offers family rates.

Campgrounds are another option. Try the **Drummer Boy Campground**, 1300 Hanover Road, Gettysburg (800–336–DBOY) or call the Travel Council (717–334–6274) for a longer listing.

For a full listing of area accommodations, call the Gettysburg Travel Council at (717) 334–6274 for a visitor's guide.

WHERE TO EAT

Dobbin House Tavern, 89 Steinwehr Avenue (717–334–2100) combines history and food for the whole family. This 1776 tavern includes a country store, bakery, and underground railroad hideout that guests can tour. The **Herr Tavern Publick House**, 900 Chambersburg Road (717–334–4332) was standing as the Confederate troops attacked in 1863, and it offers good food. The **Farnsworth House Inn**, 410 Baltimore Street (717–334–8838) is open for dinner only and has children's menus.

Among its Civil War food offerings are pie, peanut soup, spoon bread, and pumpkin fritters. **General Pickett's Buffets**, 571 Steinwehr Avenue (717–334–7580) is a good spot for lunch as it has all-you-can-eat buffets, children's menus and a **Dinner Theater** (717–334–6100) with 8:00 P.M. performances Monday through Saturday, Sundays at 6:30. **Hickory Bridge Farm**, west of Gettysburg in the Orrtanna orchard area (717–642–5261) features farm-style dinners. Be sure to make reservations. For non–Civil War family dining, **Hoffa's**, 1140 York Street (717–337–2961) is a casual family restaurant with reasonable prices.

DAY TRIPS

Hersheypark, a little over 50 miles from Gettysburg, has a full day's chocolatey adventure for every sweet tooth in your family, including roller coasters and live entertainment. (See the chapter on Hershey for more information.)

FOR MORE INFORMATION

The local newspaper, the *Gettys Times*, is published Monday through Saturday mornings and is a good source of information about local events.

Visitor Information Centers
Gettysburg Travel Council, 35 Carlisle Street (717–334–6274) has free tour brochures and maps available to the public.
Gettysburg National Military Park Visitor's Center: (717) 334–1124.

Emergency Numbers
Ambulance, fire, and police: 911
Gettysburg Hospital, 147 Getty Street; (717) 334–2121
Poison Hotline: (800) 521–6110
Rite Aid Pharmacy, 236 West Street (717–334–6447), is open Monday through Saturday from 9:00 A.M. to 9:00 P.M., Sundays from 10:00 A.M. to 4:00 P.M.
Twenty-four-hour emergencies: (717) 337–HELP

16
HERSHEY and the PENNSYLVANIA DUTCH REGION

On a visit to Hershey, combine the thrills of a theme park with the sweet excesses of chocolate and enjoy a tour of the Pennsylvania Dutch countryside with its simple life-style and scenic back roads. Easy day trips take you into Adamstown, the antiques capital of the state, to browse for treasures or to Reading, the self-proclaimed "Outlet Capital of the World," to search for bargains on clothing and housewares.

GETTING THERE

Twelve airlines offer more than ninety nonstop departures to Harrisburg International Airport. Amtrak trains and Greyhound/Trailways buses arrive at the Harrisburg Transportation Center, 411 Market Street (800–872–7245 or 717–232–4251). If you're staying at the Hotel Hershey or the Hershey Lodge, there's a complimentary shuttle from the airport and from the Amtrak and Greyhound/Trailways stations in Harrisburg.

Hershey is easy to reach by car as many highways lead into town. From the north and east, take I–81 and I–78. From the south take I–83, and from the east and west take the Pennsylvania Turnpike (I–76).

GETTING AROUND

During the summer months Hershey provides a free shuttle service throughout the park, Hotel Hershey, the Hershey Lodge, Campground, and ZooAmerica.

WHAT TO SEE AND DO

Hersheypark, 100 West Hersheypark Drive; (800) HERSHEY. With more than fifty attractions on eighty-seven-acres, the park offers a sweet day's outing for kids of all ages. The daring will want to ride some of the four roller coasters, including the self-explanatory SooperDooperLooper and the Sidewinder that twists and turns upside down. Beat the heat with the Canyon River Rapids white-water rafting ride and the Coal Cracker flume ride. For a slower pace, go to Carousel Circle to sit astride one of the sixty-six hand-carved wooden horses which adorn this 1919 carousel. Preschoolers like this attraction as well as the Tiny Timbers ride.

Especially if you have young kids, book the Breakfast in the Park package (See WHERE TO STAY). This special deal lets your kids cuddle with such Hershey characters as Mr. Hershey Bar and Ms. Reeses Peanut Butter Cup before the park's official morning opening. Another bonus: This package gets you beyond the turnstiles before the crowds so your children have first crack at the kiddie rides.

For a respite from lines and rides, sit and enjoy the live entertainment that often includes a barbershop quartet, dolphin shows, a Dixieland music band, and strolling performers.

The park is open from May to September. Part of the park reopens in mid-November through December for Christmas Candylane, a wonderland of 300,000 lights that puts holiday stars in your child's eyes. At Dinner with Dickens you dine with Scrooge and Tiny Tim who recite key parts from the Dickens classic.

Chocolate World Visitors Center, Park Boulevard; (717) 534–4900. On this twelve-minute tour, trace the creation of a candy bar from the harvesting of a cocoa bean to the wrapping in tinfoil. Follow up with lunch at the Hershey Cafe inside an enclosed tropical garden. Of course if it's past lunchtime, go straight to the Chocolate Fantasy dessert counter for a milk shake, hot-fudge sundae, or delectable cookies.

The Hershey Museum, 170 West Hersheypark Drive, Hershey (717–534–3439), gives you the scoop on the man behind this chocolatey world. Trace the history of Milton Hershey from his beginnings as a farm boy to the sweet success of his dreams, and explore the Hershey's collection of Pennsylvania German and Native American objects, including furnishings and folk art.

Founders Hall, south of Hersheypark, is the center of the Milton Hershey School. Founded in 1909 by Milton and Catherine Hershey as a school for orphaned or abandoned boys, it's now a coed facility for disadvantaged children. Pick up a brochure and take a self-guided tour of the school beginning with a twenty-minute video, *The Vision,* on the Hershey's mission to provide top-notch education to disadvantaged children.

The Hershey's Chocolate costumed characters greet guests with a chocolately wave or hug. (Courtesy Capital Region Chamber of Commerce)

Hershey Trolley Works Tours (717–533–3000) escorts visitors on a forty-five-minute tour through "the sweetest place on earth" where even the streetlights look like chocolate kisses. Costumed players are on board to entertain with historic anecdotes as you ride by the gardens, Hershey's childhood home, and the chocolate factory. A separate ticket is necessary for these tours which depart from Chocolate World mid-May through Labor Day, and again in November through December. During Christmas Candylane the trolley has special rides with Santa.

Hershey Gardens, Hotel Road, Hershey; (717) 534–3492. Stroll through twenty-three landscaped acres, including a Japanese garden and an area of dwarf conifers. Spring brings forsythia, magnolias, and 25,000 tulips. Take time to smell the award-winning roses, at their best in June. ZooAmerica, 100 West Hersheypark Drive (717–534–3860) is open year-round and free with admission to Hersheypark. This eleven-acre wildlife park includes plants and animals from five North American regions in natural settings. Kids see wild turkeys, skunks, hawks, porcupines, prairie dogs, alligators, bobcats, peregrine falcons, black bear, bison, and elk.

SPECIAL EVENTS

Performing Arts

Hersheypark Arena and Stadium regularly hosts the Ice Capades (which were founded at the Hotel Hershey), Disney on Ice, Sesame Street Live, and the circus, plus musicians and comedians. Call the Arena Box Office at (717) 534–3911 for information.

Hershey Theatre, a classic and classy old cinema, has clouds that literally float across its star-studded ceiling. The theater regularly hosts touring Broadway shows, dance performances, classical music recitals, and, most appropriately, vintage films. Call (717) 534–3411 for general information and (717) 534–3405 for tickets.

Sports

Hersheypark Arena hosts the Hershey Bears hockey team most Wednesday and Saturday nights from October through March. For tickets and game schedules, call (717) 534–3911.

Festivals

Make your visit to the Hershey area extra fun by arriving for a special themed weekend. For more information on all Hershey events, call (800) HERSHEY. For Lancaster and Pennsylvania Dutch area events, call the Pennsylvania Dutch Convention and Visitors Bureau at (800) 735–2629.

January: Winter Fantasy at Chocolate World, when kids learn to ski indoors on a 32-foot-long skiing deck, then ice skate, and break for a hot chocolate.

February: At Chocolate Lover's Extravaganza, Hotel Hershey, sample chocolate, learn to create chocolate desserts, and play chocolate games with your valentine. Pennsylvania Dutch Food Festival, Lancaster.

March: Great American Chocolate Week, featuring kid's games, live entertainment, and—of course—scrumptious desserts. Murder Mystery Weekend, Hotel Hershey. Annual Quilters' Heritage Celebration, Lancaster. Berks Jazz Fest, VF Factory Outlet, Reading.

April: Family Easter in the Country, Hotel Hershey and the Hershey Lodge. Easter Bunny Express, Blue Mountain & Reading Railroad; (215) 562–2102 or (215) 562–4083.

May: Hersheypark opens up for the season with live entertainment.

June/July: The Kutztown Folk Festival celebrates the Pennsylvania Dutch way of life with old-time art, hand-woven coverlet displays, and food.

July: All American Ragtime Festival and Contest, Strasburg. Scenic River Days, Reading, with music, arts, and children's events.

July–October: Pennsylvania Renaissance Faire, Cornwall.

October: Antique Auto Show, Hershey. Balloon Classic, Hershey. Take a hot air balloon ride or stay on ground for arts, crafts, and entertainment. Oktoberfest, Blue Mountain & Reading Railroad; (215) 562–2102 or (215) 562–4083.

December: Christmas Candylane in Hersheypark.

WHERE TO STAY

Hershey

Hotel Hershey, Hotel Road, Hershey, Pennsylvania; (800) 533–3131 or (717) 533–2171. If you're looking to travel in style, Hotel Hershey, a four-diamond resort, offers several family packages including admission and shuttle service to the park and ZooAmerica. A Breakfast in the Park package allows little ones to breakfast with the Hershey cast of characters and enter the park before the crowds.

Although Hersheypark is closed from late September to early May, the fun continues at the Hotel Hershey with a host of themed weekends. Besides the month-long Christmas Candylane for the holidays, just after New Year's the Teddy Bear Jubilee—have your children dress up their favorite fuzzy for the parade—is a "beary" good pageant. Kids are Special Weekend in mid-February jam packs two days of fun with cupcake decorating, T-shirt designing, pony races, and storytelling. In April try a Family Easter in the Country featuring a springtime trolley ride, a country fair, and—of course—the Easter Bunny.

Spring through Labor Day there is a Kids' Kiss Kamp on Saturday mornings from 9:30 A.M. to 11:00 A.M. with lots of crafts, sing-alongs, and games. For a complete listing of packages and reservations, call (800) 533–3131.

Hershey Lodge, West Chocolate Avenue and University Drive, Hershey (800–533–3131), is more casual than the hotel, but features such family-friendly amenities as indoor and outdoor pools, tennis courts, a nine-hole pitch-and-putt golf course, and nightly movies in the Lodge Cinema. Family packages are available, including admission and transportation to Hersheypark and ZooAmerica. Go on a chocolate egg hunt on Easter or breakfast with Santa on Christmas. For a full listing of packages, call (800) 533–3131.

Hershey Highmeadow Campground, Hershey; (717) 566–0902. When the weather turns warm, families that love to camp should consider this campground with 296 sites on fifty-five acres. Roughing it is easy when there's a country store, playgrounds, a game room, picnic tables, grills, and two outdoor swimming pools. Bring an RV, a tent, or stay in a cabin that comes with laundry service. Call (717) 566–0902 for reservations.

Lancaster County

The Village Inn of Bird-in-Hand, 2695 Old Philadelphia Pike, Bird-in-Hand; (717) 293–8369. This nineteenth-century Victorian Inn just east of Lancaster welcomes families. Be sure to take advantage of the complimentary tour of the close-by Pennsylvania Dutch country.

At **the Historic Smithton Inn,** 900 West Main Street, Ephrata (717–733–6094), you'll sleep soundly under Pennsylvania Dutch quilts in beds hand-crafted by co-owner Allen Smith. Then wake up to homemade waffles at this cozy bed and breakfast in the heart of Pennsylvania Dutch country. Kids are welcome, especially in the self-contained two-level South Wing suite that includes a kitchenette, a living area, a pull-out couch, and an upstairs bedroom with a sleeping nook for wee ones.

The **Swiss Woods Bed & Breakfast,** 500 Blantz Road, Lititz; (717) 627–3358 or (800) 594–8018. This inn is tucked in the woods about 10 miles north of Lancaster, and guests stay in chalet-style rooms by a stream. Outdoor enthusiasts and families are welcome to hike the surrounding countryside.

To learn even more about the Pennsylvania Dutch Country, allow the Mennonites to be your hosts. Both **Mennonite Farm** and **Sunny Acres** in Atglen are working farms that welcome families. Help feed Henny Penny the hen at the Mennonite farm, milk the cows on a tour of the grounds, and get insider tips on the local Amish and Mennonite craft stores. For information and reservations contact Bed and Breakfast of Philadelphia at (215) 735–1917 or (800) 220–1917.

For more lodging information and seasonal package deals, request a *Map and Visitors Guide* from the Pennsylvania Dutch Convention and Visitors Bureau; (800) 735–2629.

Reading

The **Inn at Reading**, 1040 Park Road, Wyomissing (215–372–7811 or 800–345–4023), and the **Sheraton Berkshire**, Route 422 West, Paper Mill Road Exit, Reading (215–376–3811), both offer special weekend rates in the off-seasons.

For recommendations and reservations to bed and breakfasts near Reading, call **Bed & Breakfast of Southeast Pennsylvania** at (800) 992–2632. Be sure to ask if children are welcome, if the guest rooms are comfortable, and whether the bathrooms are shared or private.

WHERE TO EAT

Lancaster County

Fill up on homemade breads, mashed potatoes, and fresh pies at the region's family-style and buffet restaurants.

The Family Style Restaurant, Route 30, four miles east of Lancaster (717–393–2323), features all-you-can-eat buffets, and kids pay according to their weight. It's open daily April through November, weekends only in the off-season. At **The Amish Barn Restaurant**, Route 340 between Bird-in-Hand and Intercourse (717–768–8886), taste the apple dumplings and other Pennsylvania Dutch specialties.

Reading

Visit one of Reading's oldest neighborhoods for outstanding wild mushroom dishes at **Joe's Restaurant**, 450 South Seventh Street; (215) 373–6794. If the kids say "yuck" to mushrooms, then try **The Peanut Bar**, 332 Penn Street (215–376–8500); tykes can toss their peanut shells onto the floor while waiting for their burgers.

DAY TRIPS

Pennsylvania Dutch Country; (800) 735–2629. Lancaster County, about forty-five minutes from Hershey, is the heart of the Pennsylvania Amish and Mennonite locales. In addition to its religious past, the region made history as a station for both the underground and the above-ground railroad. Be sure to explore the region's famous covered bridges.

To decide which tourist attractions will interest your family, start at the **Pennsylvania Dutch Convention and Visitor's Bureau**, 501 Green-field Road, Lancaster; (717) 299–8901. Here you will find information on attractions, accommodations, and restaurants. You'll also want to take in an introductory film *There is a Season* on the region's cultural history. The movie is presented daily from April to November. Call in advance for film times.

The town of Lancaster is rich with history and home to Franklin and Marshall College, the country's fourteenth oldest. A 1½-mile **Historic Lancaster Walking Tour** stops at the town's major community structures. Guides well-stocked with historic tidbits leave daily from the **Lancaster Information Center,** 100 South Queen Street (717–392–1776), April through October, and by prior reservation from November through March. If visiting on a Tuesday, Friday, or Saturday, stop by the **Central Market** on Penn's Square. It is open from 6:00 A.M. to 2:00 P.M. Laying claim to be the nation's oldest continually operating farmer's market, it offers truly farm-fresh vegetables, meats, and cheeses. This is a good place to buy those famous Pennsylvania baked goods from whoopie pies (cakes with filling), to shoo-fly pies (has gooey-but-good molasses and brown sugar). On the Square as well is the **Heritage Center of Lancaster County,** 13 West King Street; (717) 299–6440. It showcases such Pennsylvania Dutch arts and items as grandfather clocks and quilts. The **Landis Valley Museum,** 2451 Kissel Hill Drive, Lancaster (717–569–0401), is the largest outdoor museum that depicts Pennsylvania German life. Families enjoy the craft demonstrations and the Harvest Days festival in October.

In Northern Lancaster County, the **Ephrata Cloister,** 632 Main Street, Ephrata; (717–733–6600), is the restored cloister established in 1732 by Conrad Beissel. Imagine yourself a part of this religious commune on a guided tour of the twenty historic buildings. For an entertaining living history of the cloister, families shouldn't miss the musical pageant, *Vorspiel,* presented at the cloister's outdoor amphitheater on Saturday nights from July to August. Call (717) 733–4811 for performance information.

At the **Sturgis Pretzel Company,** 215 East Main Street, Lititz (717–626–4345), kids eat up the demonstrations of pretzel making. If you're interested in the history of this charming old Moravian village, stop by the Lititz Historical Foundation at the **Johannes Mueller House,** 137–39 East Main Street (717–626–7958), for a brochure and a walking tour. It's open from Memorial Day to October 31st.

At the **Strasburg Railroad,** PA 741, just east of Strasburg (717–687–7522), come aboard for a steam train ride on one of the oldest operating train lines in the country. It's open daily from May through October and some weekends in the off-season. There are also special holiday theme rides.

But don't just go along for the ride, learn about the history of the railroad at the nearby **Railroad Museum of Pennsylvania,** PA 741; (717) 687–8628. Here train lovers find train cars from sleepers to diners. There's also a railroading film shown in the station.

If toy trains are more your speed, take a quick look at the **Toy Train Museum,** Paradise Lane off PA 741; (717) 687–8976. Kids are enthralled by five toy train displays and a video presentation. The museum is open daily May through October and on limited weekends in the off-season.

Travel down the Route 30 Corridor in Eastern Lancaster County for an education on Amish and Mennonite culture. Begin at the **Mennonite Information Center**, 2209 Millstream Road, between Smoketown and Strasburg; (717) 299–0954. As a quick introduction to the religion and culture, watch the twenty-two minute movie, *Morning Song,* which begins on the half-hour. The center provides information on Mennonite and Amish attractions as well as books. An exceptional way to learn about these hard-working people is with a two-or-more-hour **Farm Country Tour**. With prior reservations a Mennonite guide will hop in your car and narrate the region's rich history, answering any questions you may have along the way.

At the **Amish Homestead**, 2034 Lincoln Highway, southeast of Smoketown (717–392–0832), take a fifty-minute guided tour of a working Amish farm, and go back in history to a simpler time before machine plows and threshers. Walk through an Old Order Amish-decorated home and imagine what life is like for those who choose to live without telephones, televisions, or Nintendo. Another Amish experience can be had at **Amish Farm and House**, 2395 Lincoln Highway East, south of Smoketown (717–393–3679), which includes a blacksmith shop with crafts. **The Amish Village**, PA 896, between Smoketown and Strasburg (717–687–8511), features a guided tour of an 1840 farmhouse and a self-guided tour of a working smokehouse, windmill, waterwheel, and schoolhouse.

If the little ones are in need of more entertainment, try **The People's Place and Quilt Museum**, P.O. Box 419, on PA 340, west of Route 30 in the tiny town of Intercourse; (717) 768–7171. Come here for movie action with the 25-minute *Who are the Amish?* film. For older kids try the hour-and-forty-five-minute *Hazel's People,* a fictional documentary on the Mennonites. You'll also find arts and crafts, a bookstore, and Amish World, an exhibit area that gives kids an up-close view of the clothes, books, and objects of daily Amish life.

Food lovers should plan their visit to Lancaster County around the Dutch Food Festival in mid-February, a week-long Amish taste-fest where you sample such regional specialties as whoopie pies, grape mush, and banana pickles. In March, quilters patch together their own schedule of workshops and tour the Dutch country at the Annual Quilters' Heritage Celebration. Call (800) 735–2629 for more information.

Outlet Shopping in Reading

Reading, about an hour away from Hershey, is the outlet capital of the world. Here a bargain hunter has to smile while tracking the red-brick paths around the minimalls. Refurbished former factory mills now harbor more than 200 stores promising 20 to 70 percent off retail prices.

Begin the adventure at the **Vanity Fair Factory Outlet**, Hill Avenue and Park Road, across the river in Wyomissing; (215) 378–0408. Start here because you may not wend your way out of this huge complex—900,000 square feet and nine factory buildings—until nightfall. Stay here if your nerves can take only one outlet complex per trip. In a slightly prettier part of town than Reading's urban milltown heart, the VF stores offer easy parking, clear signs, a McDonald's for junkies, and more floor space for goods. VF also has such kid-friendly names as Health-tex, Lee, and Wrangler.

If you can still stand, stop by the **Reading Outlet Center**, 801 North Ninth Street, Reading; (800) 5–OUTLET or (215) 373–5495. In this tired-looking former factory, sixty stores are tucked away in labyrinths of dead-end halls and narrow staircases. Finds include Izod/Lacoste, Liz Claiborne, and J. Crew.

Not sated yet? Then buzz over to **Hiesters Lane**, 755 Hiesters Lane, Reading (215–921–9394), on the edge of town. The Flemington Fashion Outlet here sports a reasonable selection of Saville, Evan Picone, and Kasper women's suits at 25 percent or more off. **Big Mill Outlet Center**, Eighth and Olney streets, Reading (215–378–9100), is also worth some time.

Outlets are pure Americana. Busloads of purchasers come seeking the promise of cut-rate goodies. Who shops here? The tourists, the penny-wise, and, increasingly, the trendy. Some of your best friends probably met their Adolfo, Evan Picone, or Ralph Lauren suits in Reading's shops. While you may be shopped out, with any luck you'll come home saving lots of money on clothes for the whole family.

Manufacturers Outlet Mall, exit 22, Pennsylvania Turnpike, Morgantown; (215) 286–2000. Affectionately called MOM, this outlet is 12 miles, about 20 minutes, south of Reading. It features more than seventy stores, including Flemington Plus—a larger-size women's dress store—and Marlene Fashion Outlet, which sells some designer labels such as Adolfo. Discounts range from 25 to 75 percent.

Contact Berks County Visitor's Information Association at (215) 375–4085 or (800) 443–6610 for a full listing of outlet stores. Be sure to call the malls in advance to find out the hours and which shops, if any, take credit cards. Many accept only cash and personal checks, so be prepared.

Antiquing in Adamstown

If Reading is the outlet capital, then Adamstown, in the east of Pennsylvania's Dutch Country, is the state's antique capital. You will find 1,000 antique dealers within a two-mile strip along U.S. 272 and U.S. 222. Head here to find antiques and collectibles ranging from scanty twenties satin camisoles to nineteenth-century pocket watches, oak rolltop desks, and even fifties Hop-A-Long Cassidy mugs.

Bring along some quiet entertainment for the kids while you browse the bargains, often 10 to 30 percent lower than in the city. Begin at **Ed Stoudt's Black Angus Restaurant and Antiques Mall**, U.S. 272, a mile north of Pennsylvania Turnpike, exit 21; (215) 484–4385. Among the

200 neatly displayed dealers' stalls, you'll find jewelry, linens, china, and furniture. All this within a pink fantasy Bavarian building filled with a wafting aroma of sauerkraut and lager from the adjoining cafeteria. **Renninger's** (215–267–2177), almost next door, is a single-story sprawl of gray cinder blocks packed with 400 booths. The kids can snack on pretzels and popcorn while you browse through cluttered aisles filled with quirky collectibles: dinner plates with Richard Nixon smiling demonically or Howdy Doody dolls. **Adams Antiques and Collectibles**, just down the strip (215–267–8444), features an array of 150 shops. Besides such small dealer staples as thirties music scores and old tins, browse Adams for fifties furniture and a good selection of oak.

Take in some Civil War history at **Gettysburg**, a forty-five-minute drive from Hershey. (See the chapter on Gettysburg.)

FOR MORE INFORMATION

For Hershey information and reservations, call (717) 534–3090 or (800) HERSHEY. Request a *Vacation Guide*, which describes the various family packages available, park schedules, and event information. Harrisburg–Hershey–Carlisle Tourism and Convention Bureau, 114 Walnut Street, Harrisburg (717–232–1377 or 800–995–0969), offers a free visitor's guide.

The Pennsylvania Dutch Convention and Visitors Bureau, 501 Greenfield Road, Lancaster (717–299–8901 or 800–735–2629), publishes a comprehensive map and visitor's guide with information on attractions, events, accommodations, and dining. Stop by the downtown Visitors Information Center, South Queen and Vine streets, Lancaster.

The Berks County Visitors Information Association, VF Factory Outlet Complex, Reading (215–375–4085 or 800–443–6610), publishes a visitor's guide listing the area's outlet shops, plus local restaurants and hotels.

Emergency Numbers

Ambulance, fire, and police: 911

Medical emergencies: In Hershey, contact the Hershey Medical Center, 500 University Drive; (717) 531–8521. The facility also operates a twenty-four-hour pharmacy. In Lancaster, contact the Lancaster General Hospital, 555 North Duke Street, Lancaster; (717) 299–5511. In Reading, call the St. Joseph's Hospital, Twelfth and Walnut streets, Reading; (215) 378–2000.

17
LAKE GEORGE
New York

Much different than bustling New York City in ambience, Adirondack Park encompasses about two-thirds of upstate New York, including some six million acres of private and state-owned land, approximately 60 percent of which is wilderness. Forty-two mountains plus thousands of miles of lakes, ponds, brooks, and streams make this a recreational paradise.

Lake George stands out among the developed areas as the Adirondack's most complete family vacation destination. Summer is a prime season to visit. The 32-mile lake, ringed by green mountains, is truly striking and, although commercialism abounds downtown, just a short drive north are quiet lakeside villages and mountain retreats. The area is also a winter playground and fall foliage hotspot that caters to families.

GETTING THERE

The closest airport to Lake George is Albany County (518–792–1195), some 50 miles away. Car rentals are available at the airport.

Adirondack Trailways (800–225–6815), runs buses to Lake George, Glens Falls, Tupper Lake, and Lake Placid from Albany, with connections to New York City. In Lake George the bus stops at the Mobil Station, 320 Canada Street; (518) 668–9511. Greyhound travels from New York to Glens Falls, 10 miles away, stopping at All Points Diner, 21 South Street; (518) 793–5052. To reach Lake George, passengers must hook up with an Adirondacks Trailways bus, which leaves from the Rainbow Cafe on Hudson and Elm; (518) 793–5525.

Amtrak's Montrealer train stops at nearby Fort Edward; however, this small town provides no transportation to Lake George.

The village of Lake George is located off the Northway, I–87, near the junction of U.S. 9 and SR 9N, which travels north along the lake's western shore.

GETTING AROUND

A car is a must as there's no public transportation within the Lake George area. Boat rental facilities are located at various points along the lake (see the Chamber of Commerce guide for specific locations).

WHAT TO SEE AND DO

Museums and Historical Sights

Most people are so busy having fun in Lake George that they don't seem to notice the scarcity of museums. (We don't consider the House of Frankenstein Wax Museum on Canada Street a "museum" in the true sense of the word.) Many museums are small ones dedicated to local history and not terribly interesting to kids. One area attraction does fill the bill, however.

Fort William Henry Museum, Beach Road and Route 9 entrances; (528) 668–5471. If your kids have seen or read James Fennimore Cooper's *The Last of the Mohicans*, they'll especially appreciate this restored Colonial fortress which played an integral role in the French and Indian War. Costumed guide-historians conduct tours during July and August. The musket and cannon firings and demonstrations of musketball molding and grenadier bomb–tossing appeal to school-age kids and teens, though younger ages may wince at the noise from the firings. For some reason the dungeons and stockades are always the most popular exhibits with kids. During the late spring and early fall, audiovisual displays take the place of the guides.

Parks and Beaches

Whatever type of trail you and your kids want to try—nature or hiking, easy or strenuous—you'll find it in or near Lake George. The Adirondack Mountain Club (518–668–4447), publishes *An Adirondack Sampler* in two volumes, with easy to moderately difficult hikes and backpacking trips of Warren County and Adirondack Park.

Easy nature trails through pines and hardwoods are just part of the attraction of **Crandall Park International Trail System**, south of Glens Falls city border on Route 9. Bring a picnic, frisbee, and fishing poles and spend the afternoon: there's also a fishing pond, tennis and basketball courts, baseball field, and playground. A Fit-Trail has wooden exercise stations. Let the kids join in on some.

Prospect Mountain's entrance to its splendid hiking trail is on Montcalm Street, Lake George. Ages eight and up should be game for the moderate climb to the 2,100-foot summit for splendid views of the Adirondacks, Vermont's Green Mountains, and New Hampshire's White Mountains. If that's too strenuous, take the free trams that leave from the parking lot.

A listing of area beaches appears in the *Warren County 4-Season Travel Guide*. **Million Dollar Beach**, on the southern shore, east of U.S. 9 on Beach Road (518–668–3352), is the town's largest and best suited to families, with a lifeguard, bathhouse, picnic facilities, and volleyball courts. There's a small admission and parking fee.

Boaters can explore the lake's many islands, some with sandy beaches.

Other Attractions

Aqua Adventure Water Slide, Route 9, Queensbury; (518) 792–8989. Slide, splash, loop, curve—this water park is fun! There's a kiddie pool play area, too.

Great Escape Theme Park, Route 9; (518) 792–3500. When your family wants to have fun, the state's largest amusement park is the place. Enjoy one hundred rides, shows, and attractions, such as Noah's Sprayground Water Area, Raging River Raft Ride, and Corkscrew Loop Coaster.

Lake George Zoo, Route 9, Queensbury; (518) 793–3303. The kids can feed llamas and goats, then watch the captivating chimp show and live animal presentations.

Magic Forest, Route 9; (518) 793–3393. Younger kids may prefer this smaller, calmer park to Great Escape. With twenty rides, a Fairy Tale area, and Santa's Hideaway, this small park is just right for tots.

Rodeos are held at three area ranches weekly in the summer: **Painted Pony Rodeo**, Lake Luzerne, (518) 696–2421; **1000 Acres Ranch and Rodeo**, Stony Creek, (518) 696–2444; and **Ridin Hy Ranch and Rodeo** (see WHERE TO STAY). For a list of area stables, consult the *Warren County 4-Season Guide*.

Special Tours

A guided horse-and-carriage ride is a fun way to see Lake George Village; (518) 668–9665. **Lake George Steamboat Cruises** (518–668–5777/ 800–553–BOAT) has narrated trips that range from one to four-and-one-half hours.

Shopping

Bargains abound in Warren County's more than eighty factory outlets, most located in what's known as the "**Million Dollar Half-Mile**" Factory Outlet Strip (take I–87 exit 20, then north on Route 9). **Aviation Mall**, I–87, exit 19, in Queensbury, is the area's largest mall and rents strollers.

A narrated cruise around Lake George aboard the Minne-Ha-Ha *is a great way to take in the scenery.* (Copyright © 1993 New York State Department of Economic Development)

Performing Arts

Lake George Dinner Theater, Holiday Inn Turf at Lake George, features Broadway show performances by professional equity theaters. Call (518) 668–5781 for program information. Renowned artists perform at **Luzerne Chamber Music Festival;** (518) 696–3892.

Thirty miles away, the **Saragota Performing Arts Center** has top-named artists, such as the New York City Ballet, and popular entertainers. Call (518) 587–3330 for schedules.

SPECIAL EVENTS

Sporting Events

Adirondack Red Wings Hockey team plays at the Glens Falls Civic Center, Route 9 (Glen Street); (518) 798–0202.

Fairs and Festivals

February: Warren County comes alive with winter carnivals. Lake George usually celebrates on weekends with a variety of races, including one in which participants pull full-size outhouses (yes, outhouses). For the kids: Olympic games, clowns, contests, and Georgie the Snowman. The village of Hague's carnival is family oriented, with children's games and prizes, fishing contests, clowns, snow sculpture contests, and more. Lake Luzerne's one-day carnival has horse-drawn sleigh rides, clowns, arts and crafts, and other delights. Gore Mountain in North Creek, the area's largest downhill ski area, adds children's programs to their carnival's events. The Warren County Chamber of Commerce can provide specific dates, and sites and listings of cross-country ski centers. Ask for details on these other seasonal events.

July–August: Family movies at Shepard Park, Lake George, Thursday nights.

August: Warrensburg Country Fair. Family Festival Week, Shepard Park, Lake George, with entertainers, crafts, games, and more.

September: Hot Air Balloon Festival, Glens Falls–Queensbury.

October: Gore Mountain's Octoberfest, with music, food, parade, and entertainment for kids.

WHERE TO STAY

If your family likes being in the middle of the action, the commercial strip of wall-to-wall motels on Route 9 will do. To appreciate the true beauty of the area, however, venture somewhat beyond. A complete chart of accommodations, ranging from rustic cabins to luxurious resorts, is included in the *Warren County Travel Guide* available from the Chamber of Commerce. Family-friendly possibilities include the following.

Cresthaven Resort Motel, Lake Shore Drive, Route 9N, is spread out on thirteen acres, with its own 300-foot sandy beach. Choose from log cabins, cottages, or efficiencies. A kiddie pool, game room, playgrounds, grills, and picnic tables are tailor-made for families. Call (518) 668–3332.

Roaring Brook Ranch and Tennis Resort, 2½ miles south on Route 9N, has one indoor and two outdoor pools, horseback riding, five tennis courts, and a playground, plus a children's counselor in July and August. Families appreciate the coin laundry on premises. Call (518) 668–5767.

Ridin Hy Ranch Resort is on 800 acres on Sherman Lake, Warrensburg. This year-round resort offers all-inclusive vacation plans. There's an indoor pool, beach, and playground area, and rodeos are held throughout the summer. Call (518) 494–2742.

Sagamore Resort sits on its own private island in Lake George, just ½ mile from the village of Bolton Landing. This luxury resort has efficiencies and hotel rooms, including junior suites, some with lake views. Although pricey (ask about packages), the resort has good facilities, including an indoor pool, spa, beach, tennis, golf, racquetball, and supervised kids' activities. Restaurants range from casual to gourmet. In the summer the resort's wooden touring boat offers dinner and sight-seeing cruises. Call (518) 644–9400/(800) 358–3585.

Treasure Cove, Diamond Point, 4 miles north of town, is directly on the lake, with its own private sandy beach. Stay in two- or three-bedroom cottages, some with fireplaces. Two pools, a playground, lawn games, and row and motor boats add to the appeal. Call (518) 668–5334.

WHERE TO EAT

With more than 275 restaurants in the area, your family need never go hungry. For restaurant listings check out the *Lake George Guide*, a weekly tourist paper available around town. When your taste for fast food begins to fade, try **Log Jam**, 4½ miles south on U.S. 9 at the junction of 149. This casual place has a rustic, log cabin feeling and serves solid American fare, with a children's menu available. **Mario's Restaurant**, ¼ mile north on U.S. 9 and SR 9N, dishes out large portions of chicken, beef, seafood, and veal. They also feature a children's menu and valet parking. For older kids with sophisticated palates, or for a parent's night out, try the nouvelle American cuisine at **The Trillium** in the Sagamore Resort, Bolton Landing. This highly rated restaurant doesn't come cheap, but it's truly a fine dining experience.

DAY TRIPS

The touring possibilities in the Lake George area are numerous. The Warren County guidebook offers some appealing possibilities.

Adirondack Park

If you decide to head northwest and explore the more remote parts of Adirondack Park, keep in mind that many mountain highways can be slow going, albeit scenic, so don't plan too much for one day. Two interpretive visitor centers offer indoor and outdoor exhibits and year-round programs about Adirondack Park. One is in Paul Smiths, New York, northwest of Lake Placid on SR 30, 1 mile north of SR 86 (518–327–3000); the other is in Newcomb on SR 28N, 14 miles east of Long Lake; (518) 582–2000. Blue Mountain Lake, northwest of Lake George, is home to the Adirondack Museum on SR 28N/30; it's worth a stop. The indoor and outdoor exhibits reveal area history and culture in an interesting way and include Adirondack guide boats, log hotel, black-smith shop, and posh private railroad car. Open summer to mid-October, this is a splendid trip during the peak foliage period. Call (518) 352–7311/7312 for hours.

Lake Placid

You'll see some of the best scenery on the way to Lake Placid (I–87 north to exit 30, follow Route 73 west). The village, on the shores of Mirror Lake and Lake Placid, hosted the 1932 and 1980 Winter Olympics, and the game sites and facilities are open to visitors. Depending on the ages and stamina of your kids, you can either visit individual sites or purchase a complete self-guided auto tour package. Included are chair-lift rides to the summit of Whiteface Mountain (site of the 1980 Alpine events), a trolley ride to the mile-long bobsled and luge runs; and visits to the Olympic Center ice complex and the Olympic Jumping Complex, where U.S. Ski Team freestyle aerialists polish their techniques in summer by jumping off ramps into a pool of water. For information call the Olympic Regional Development Authority at (518) 523–1655/(800) 858–7782—Eastern Canada/(800) 462–6236—United States.

In winter Lake Placid is a haven, and heaven, for snow enthusiasts. **Whiteface Mountain** offers the greatest vertical drop in the East, varied terrain, plus a play and ski program for ages three to six and a ski school for ages seven to twelve. In addition there's a nursery for tots one to six.

The **Mt. Van Hoevenberg Cross-Country Center**, a ten-minute drive from Lake Placid village, features 50 kilometers of groomed trails, including novice, intermediate, and expert loops. Next door to the center, try the bobsled and luge runs. The bobsled ride is generally offered Tuesdays through Sundays 1:00 to 3:00 P.M. Sign up for the luge ride Saturdays and Sundays from 1:00 to 3:00 P.M. In addition the **Jackrabbit Trail** offers nearly 25 miles of cross-country skiing that links the towns of Keene, Lake Placid, Saranac Lake, and the High Peaks region. Obtain a map from the Adirondack Ski Touring Council, P.O. Box 843, Lake Placid, New York 12946; (518) 523–1365.

For more thrills visit **Mirror Lake** where Eric Heiden claimed five gold medals in 1980. Skate indoors at the Olympic Center or outdoors at the Olympic Oval. For something different try tobogganing and dogsledding across the lake.

For a schedule of winter events and ski conditions, call (518) 523–1655, or (800) 462–6236 in the United States, or (800) 858–7782 in eastern Canada. For Lake Placid lodging reservations, call (800) 44–PLACID, (800) 447–5224, or (518) 523–2445.

Wilmington

Santa's Workshop in Wilmington will delight preschoolers. Families have been coming to this nonglitzy attraction for generations to meet Santa at his home and workshop, pet his live reindeer, go on the rides (including a miniature railroad), and see puppet shows. For a taped message of the park schedule, call (518) 946–7838.

FOR MORE INFORMATION

Warren County Tourism Department, 2750 Municipal Center, Lake George 12845–9795; (518) 761–6366/(800) 365–1050. Drop by their office or phone for a *Warren County 4-Season Travel Guide* and other helpful information. Information on Adirondack Park can be obtained from Department of Conservation, 50 Wolf Road, Albany, New York 12233; (518) 457–3521. For the entire Adirondack Region, call (800) ITS–MTNS. If you're heading to Lake Placid, lodging and sight-seeing information can be obtained from **Lake Placid/Essex County Visitor's Bureau,** Olympic Center, Lake Placid 12946; (518) 523–2445/(800) 44–PLACID.

Emergency Numbers
Ambulance, fire, and police: 911
Glens Falls Hospital, 100 Park Street, Glens Falls: (518) 792–3151 (it has
    a twenty-four-hour emergency room).
Poison Control: (518) 761–5261
There are no twenty-four-hour pharmacies open to the public, although
    Pharmacy Associates in Glens Falls (518–792–1195) has a service
    that responds to a doctor's emergency calls after hours.

18
NEW YORK CITY
New York: Manhattan

If your family loves the energy and excitement of a big city vacation, there's no place like New York. Like many other cities, this one's not all polish and shine. But, with proper planning, a trip to the Big Apple can be one of your family's most memorable. If possible, come in spring, fall, or at Christmas, when the city is at its finest. But even sizzling summer comes with merits: many New Yorkers head for the hills on the weekends, leaving behind a less crowded city.

GETTING THERE

New York is served by three airports: John F. Kennedy International (JFK) about 15 miles from mid-Manhattan; LaGuardia, about 8 miles; and Newark (NJ) International, about 16 miles. Buses, limousines, and taxis are available at all three. Yellow medallion metered taxis are the most convenient mode into Manhattan if you're arriving with kids and baggage. Fares range from $20–$35 to midtown, plus bridges, tolls, and tip; there's an extra $10 charge to Newark. Avoid the limousine drivers who appear near the baggage areas soliciting fares. Instead, arrange service through Ground Transportation.

Amtrak (800–USA–RAIL) and a number of commuter trains arrive at either Grand Central Terminal, Forty-second Street and Park Avenue, or Penn Station, between Thirty-first and Thirty-third streets and Seventh and Eighth avenues. Taxi stands and public transportation are available at both.

Greyhound, Trailways, and other long-distance and commuter buses use the Port Authority Bus Terminal, between Fortieth and Forty-second streets and Eighth Avenue. Taxis line up at the front entrance.

Manhattan is an island entered via bridges, tunnels, parkways, and expressways. The New York Thruway (Routes 287 and 87) leads to Manhattan's East and West sides. The New England Thruway (I–95) leads, via connecting roads, to all five boroughs: Queens, Manhattan, Bronx, Brooklyn, and Staten Island. The western entry is accessed by I–80 (Bergen Passaic Expressway), while the south is served by the New Jersey Turnpike (I–95), which leads to the Holland Tunnel in Lower Manhattan or George Washington Bridge in Upper Manhattan.

GETTING AROUND

The streets in midtown Manhattan, where most hotels are located (Thirtieth and Sixtieth streets from the East River to the Hudson River), are arranged in a grid, with streets running east to west and avenues north and south. Fifth Avenue separates the east from the west side. Once you figure out the avenues, New York is a surprisingly easy city to navigate; however, Lower Manhattan (with Greenwich Village, Chinatown, Little Italy, and the Financial District) doesn't adhere to this system. In midtown, walking is often the best way to get around, particularly at rush hour. At night, exercise common sense and stay away from streets that aren't well lit or well trafficked.

Public buses require exact fare in change or a token, sold mostly in subway stations. Request a transfer upon boarding. This entitles you to a free ride on a connecting line. Some buses have maps in a receptacle near the driver. Maps may also be obtained near the entrance of some major library branches.

The subway system is fast and extensive, but not aesthetically pleasing. Avoid it after dark. Tokens are sold by clerks near turnstiles. Request a map. Information for both the subway and buses is available from 6:00 A.M. to 9:00 P.M. by calling (718) 330–1234.

WHAT TO SEE AND DO

Museums and Historic Sites

New York has some of the best museums in the world. Since you could literally spend days—even weeks—exploring them, the following list includes only those with special kid appeal.

American Museum of Natural History, Central Park West at Seventy-ninth to Eighty-first streets; (212) 769–5100. This museum—the biggest of its kind—is tops with kids. Yes, everyone loves the dinosaurs, but there's lots more to delight: the gems and mineral gallery with one of the largest pieces of crystallized gold ever found; the largest meteorite ever retrieved (which you can touch), a herd of wild (mounted) elephants, a 1,300-year-old giant sequoia, and lots more. At the Natural Science Center, kids can touch and explore fossils, shells, and other natural objects. The Naturemax Theatre boasts a 4-story screen for interesting educational films.

Use the lower level museum exit to connect to the adjacent **Hayden Planetarium**, Central Park West and Seventy-ninth Street; (212) 769–5920. This facility has two floors of exhibits, plus interesting sky shows, and evening laser light shows on the weekend. Kids love the scales where they can see how much they would weigh on other planets.

Children's Museum of Manhattan, 212 West Eighty-third Street; (212) 721–1234. While this doesn't rank with, say, Boston's Children's Museum, it has enough changing and permanent exhibits to keep kids of all ages busy. Older kids will head straight upstairs to the Media Center where they can work a TV camera or sit behind the mike and read the news. The outdoor urban environment area encourages kids to think seriously about recycling. For younger kids, the family learning center has a grocery store, building blocks, and frequent supervised art activities. Special events and activities are constantly going on; call for a schedule. It's open on Monday when many other museums aren't. The museum closes on Tuesdays.

Intrepid Sea-Air-Space Museum, Pier 86, West Forty-sixth Street and Twelfth Avenue; (212) 245–0072. This 900-foot aircraft carrier is best appreciated by school-age kids, who will love the freedom to roam about and explore. The carrier was used in World War II, during the Vietnam War, and as a space program recovery ship. Along with peering through a periscope and exploring the deck, kids can see the cockpit of the world's fastest jet, historic aircraft, an Army armor tank display, and the world's only nuclear missile submarine open to the public (guided tours available). Call about Saturday afternoon workshops and hours. Multimedia presentations are offered Wednesday through Sunday.

Jewish Museum, 1109 Fifth Avenue at Ninety-second Street; (212) 423–3200. By the time you read this, the museum will be back in its permanent quarters after more than a year of renovations. Four floors of exhibits with frequently changing themes, family workshops, and special events make this a worthwhile place to visit.

Liberty Science Center, Liberty State Park, New Jersey; (201) 200–1000. This new hands-on science and technology museum across the river from Lower Manhattan, is easily accessible by ferry. Particularly pleased are Manhattanites who find the excellent **New York Hall of Science** in Flushing Meadows, Queens (718–699–1341), less convenient. At the Liberty Science Center three floors of exhibits center around the body. Kids love the pitch-black touch tunnel and an illusion labyrinth with mirrors and optical illusions. The environmental area includes a Bug Zoo and touch pool with horseshoe crabs. There's also a huge OMNIMAX theater, the largest in the country. An added plus: a fabulous view of Manhattan and the Statue of Liberty.

A ferry leaves from three points in Manhattan; call (201) 902–8736/ (800) 53–FERRY for information. People movers pick up passengers at the dock. Call the museum for other transportation options.

Lower East Side Tenement Museum, 97 Orchard Street; (212) 431–0233. This fascinating living-history museum is dedicated to immigrants and their experience on the Lower East Side. It offers walking tours, dramatizations, and special exhibitions. Orchard Street, with its bargain shops—some schlock, some name brands at hefty discounts—is an experience in itself. There's lots of local color in this area, and you're a short cab ride away from Chinatown and Little Italy.

Metropolitan Museum of Art, Fifth Avenue and Eighty-second Street; (212) 535–7710. As one of the world's greatest museums, the facility's enormity can overpower young ones, particularly during the crowded weekends. The key: arrive early and focus on areas of particular appeal. Most kids are fascinated by the extensive Egyptian exhibits; wend your way toward the Temple of Dendur, housed in its own glass-enclosed wing. Nearby is the American Wing Garden Court, a peaceful place to sit and enjoy the stained glass (some of it by Tiffany), potted trees, and fountain. Off the court is the arms and armor area. In the second-floor Chinese Garden Court, watch fish swimming in pools and absorb the serenity of this magical place. In nice weather proceed to the pleasant rooftop sculpture gallery (it has its own elevator) with views of Central Park and the city. Weekend family programs are free with admission and include short films and lectures; call for information.

Museum of the City of New York, Fifth Avenue at 103rd Street; (212) 534–1672. You can combine a visit to the Jewish Museum with one here; it's just 11 blocks north, a nice walk on a pleasant day. The kids will be especially attracted to the toys and dollhouses, and the costumes and accessories of another era. Half of the museum is devoted to changing exhibits, and there are frequent family workshops tied to these exhibits, plus seasonal walking tours of the five boroughs. Families who like to walk are cordially invited.

The museum is directly across from the beautiful **Conservatory Gardens** in Central Park, called "The Secret Garden" by some. Stop in for a peek—but note that this part of the park is a bit more desolate than the lower part below Eighty-sixth Street, so don't stray off the main pathways.

Museum of Modern Art, 11 West Fifty-third Street; (212) 708–9480. This museum bucks the trend and opens Mondays, closing instead on Wednesdays. Some kids enjoy the art here, others will be bored. Aim for a Saturday visit when guides host special tours to introduce families with kids ages five to ten to the important aspects of the museum's collections. On Saturdays there are also workshops with games and activities, and a Family Films program that presents classic shorts. The museum is directly across from the New York Public Library's Donnell branch, which has one of the best children's rooms in the city (second floor) as well as frequent activities and performances for kids. Stop by for a schedule.

Museum of Television and Radio, 25 West Fifty-second Street; (212) 621–6600. An extensive collection of 20,000 radio and television program tapes is listed in a computerized file; select one and watch or listen to it in a console booth. Because of reruns and cable TV, kids think they've seen it all, but there are some gems they'll never catch on "Nick at Nite." Recreating Radio workshops for ages eight to thirteen are held on Saturdays during the school year. Kids read scripts and make sound effects to create their own classic show. Call (212) 621–6000 to reserve.

South Street Seaport Museum, Visitor's Center, 12 Fulton Street; (212) 669–9400. This isn't just a museum, it's a 12-block historic district in lower Manhattan where your family can easily spend most of the day. Stop by the Visitor's Center for information on what's going on, as special events are scheduled frequently. At the children's center, kids interact with special exhibits and take part in weekend workshops. A number of historic ships anchored here can be boarded. Kids also enjoy strolling the traffic-free, cobblestone streets lined with shops, restaurants, and inexpensive eateries.

Parks

Smack in the middle of the city, the green oasis called **Central Park** extends north to south from Central Park South (Fifty-ninth Street) to 110th Street and from Fifth Avenue to Central Park West. This is where the city comes to walk, jog, bike, play, rollerskate, and just have fun. Some places not to miss: the nice and fairly new **Zoo** at Sixty-fourth Street (212–988–0286), with wildlife in natural surroundings. The penguins and sea lions are always popular. Nearby, a visitor's kiosk has maps and special activity information. Close by, the **Wollman Rink** has ice skating in winter and miniature golf and roller skating in summer. The **Dairy,** a restored building that serves as a visitor's center, hosts weekend children's activities. From here it's a short walk to the wonderful **carousel.** Then head south to the **Hecksher Playground,** which has a wooden bridge, sandbox, slides, seesaws, and swings.

On the West Side, the **Belvedere Castle** (near Seventy-ninth Street) is a learning center with nature exhibits and children's programs. Rent a rowboat at **The Boathouse** on East Seventy-second Street; then walk over to see the **Alice in Wonderland** statue, a favorite for climbing. Note: Stick to the main walkways during the day, and you will be safe. The park has a deserved reputation for being dangerous at night.

Attractions

So it's not the world's tallest building: could you come to New York without seeing the **Empire State Building,** Thirty-fourth Street and Fifth

Avenue (212–736–3100)? The view from promenades on the Eighty-sixth or 102d floor on a clear day is exhilarating.

Further up Fifth Avenue, **Rockefeller Center** (Forty-seventh–Fifty-second streets) has a sunken plaza where your family can ice skate in winter. **The benches at the Channel Gardens** on the Fifth Avenue side, with their always changing flower and plant arrangements, offer a pleasant place to sit and people watch.

The **United Nations**, First Avenue at Forty-sixth Street, may be exciting for older kids (those under age five aren't allowed on tours). Free tickets to General Assembly and Security Council meetings are available on a first-come, first-served basis. Call (212) 963–7713. Downtown, the distinctive towers of the **World Trade Center** offer an Observation Deck; (212) 435–4170. Next door, the **World Financial Center** has shops and restaurants and a pleasing waterfront walkway, with a playground nearby.

"The Lady in the Harbor," the **Statue of Liberty National Monument**, is reached via Circle Line Ferry from Battery Park in Lower Manhattan. There's an American Museum of Immigration in the base. Call (212) 269–5755 for ferry information; (212) 363–3200 for Statue information. Summer crowds are endless; arrive early and expect lines. Likewise for the nearby **Ellis Island Immigration Museum**, where the Great Hall has been restored to its 1918–1924 appearance and houses galleries filled with memorabilia, an oral history recording studio, two theaters, and a wall honoring immigrants who passed through. Ellis Island is also reached via Circle Line ferry; a shuttle service runs between the two attractions.

Performing Arts

What could be more exciting than a Broadway play? It can be an expensive proposition; however, half-price tickets are available on the day of the performance for many (but not all) on- and off-Broadway plays at the Times Square Theatre Centers at Broadway and Forty-seventh and 2 World Trade Center. New York has many kids-only presentations and theater groups, such as the Paper Bag Players, TADA!, The Triplex, and Theatreworks U.S.A.: Consult the Children's listings in the weekly *New York Magazine* for current performances. If you're here for the holidays, don't miss the Easter or Christmas show at Radio City Music Hall, featuring the famous Rockettes. Call (212) 247–4777.

Lincoln Center for the Performing Arts, 70 Lincoln Center Plaza (Columbus Avenue at Sixty-fourth Street) is considered the Cultural Capital of the World. The complex frequently features musical performances for kids, such as the Little Orchestra Society and Young People's concerts, and the Metropolitan Opera's Growing Up With Opera program for kids five to fourteen and their parents. Other performances with kid-appeal are held throughout the year and, of course, *The Nutcracker* ballet is a perennial Christmas sellout. If you come to see Lincoln Center during the day, the public library branch at the east end of the complex has a nice kid's reading room on the second floor. For more information call (212) 875–5350.

SPECIAL EVENTS

There's never a dull moment in the Big Apple. Check the Other Events listings in *New York Magazine* and the Friday Weekend section in the *New York Times* for the latest happenings. Here's a sampling of what you'll find.

January: Chinese New Year celebrations. Ice Capades, Madison Square Garden.

February: Westminster Kennel Club Dog Show, Madison Square Garden.

March: International Cat Show, Madison Square Garden.

March–April: Ringling Brothers Circus. Easter Show, Radio City Music Hall. Spring Flower Show, New York Botanical Garden.

Easter: Easter Parade, Fifth Avenue.

May: Ninth Avenue International Food Festival. Salute to Israel Parade. Ukrainian Festival, Lower East Side

June–August: Central Park SummerStage.

July: Fourth of July Festivities with Harbor Festival and fireworks over Central Park and the East River.

July–August: Free Shakespeare in Central Park. Free Summergarden Concerts, The Museum of Modern Art. Free Summer Pier Concerts, South Street Seaport.

August: Lincoln Center Out-of-Doors.

September: Feast of San Gennaro, streets of Little Italy. Third Avenue Street Fair. New York is Book Country fair on Fifth Avenue. Atlantic Antic, Brooklyn Street Festival. Columbus Avenue Festival, Manhattan.

Thanksgiving: Macy's Thanksgiving Day Parade.

December: Lighting of giant tree, Rockefeller Center. Origami Christmas Tree, American Museum of Natural History.

WHERE TO STAY

Located in the theater district **Embassy Suites**, Forty-seventh Street and Seventh Avenue (212–719–1600; 800–362–2779) offers family-friendly floors. Rooms here have covers on electric outlets and plastic on furniture edges. If needed, the staff brings you diapers or other necessities. The child care center looks after kids from tots to twelve-year-olds daily, year-round. This is a boon when you have those business meetings but want to take your kids along. Also in the theater district, the **Hotel Macklowe and Conference Center,** 145 West Forty-fourth Street (212–768–4400) offers upscale amenities. Ask about their lower weekend rates.

Journey's End Hotels, 3 East Fortieth Street (212–447–1500; 800–668–4200) offers limited services at lower than typical big-city rates. Other less expensive choices include the **Days Inn,** 440 West Fifty-seventh Street (212–581–8100; 800–231–0405) where kids under seventeen stay free, and those under twelve eat free as long as adults dine with them. The **Southgate Tower Suite Hotel,** 371 7th Avenue (212–563–1800), offers studios as well as and one- and two-bedroom units with kitchens.

Don't forget to inquire about weekend deals at some of the upscale properties. Depending on the season, you could be pleasantly surprised with a posh room at a good price.

WHERE TO EAT

New York has some of the finest restaurants in the world. *The Zagat Restaurant Survey,* available at all bookstores, is a handy, objective guide to New York eateries, with special headings for those appealing to kids and teens.

It seems all kids ten and up somehow gravitate to West Fifty-seventh Street, where they have a choice of the **Hard Rock Café** at #221 (212–459–9230), or **Planet Hollywood** at #140 (212–333–7827). Both have incredibly long lines during peak vacation times; arrive early to avoid the crunch. Also on West Fifty-seventh Street, between Fifth and Sixth avenues, is a high-tech **McDonald's** that's eye catching—and convenient after a trek to F.A.O. Schwarz or Central Park. In the same neighborhood, **Mickey Mantle's,** 42 Central Park South (212–688–7777), is a big hit with baseball fans, and Mickey is frequently around to sign autographs. There's sports memorabilia, ten television monitors, and a kid's menu.

Serendipity 3, 225 East Sixtieth Street (212–838–3531), close to Bloomingdale's, is a favorite for ice cream concoctions. The place also has a funky gift/toy store. On Seventh Avenue the overstuffed sandwiches at the **Carnegie Deli,** at 854 (212–757–2245), and the **Stage Deli,** at 834 (212–245–7850), could feed an army. Both are good; the jury is still out on which has the best pastrami and corned beef.

Consider a trip to Chinatown for local color and good, inexpensive food. Try **20 Mott Street,** the name of the restaurant as well as the address; (212) 964–0380. They have superb dim sum and daily specialties.

A day trip to the Bronx Zoo will be a day well spent. (Copyright © 1993 New York State Department of Economic Development)

Next door, stop in the arcade to play ticktacktoe with a chicken (that's right, a chicken). Later, cross over Canal Street to Little Italy for a pastry at **Ferrara's**, 195 Grand Street; (212) 226–6150.

DAY TRIPS

Most people find so much to do in Manhattan that they hardly consider leaving it for a day. But if you're so inclined—or are on your second or third trip to New York— head straight to the **International Wildlife Conservation Park,** formerly called the **Bronx Zoo,** the largest urban zoo in the United States and home to more than 4,000 animals. Explore 265 acres of green parklands and naturalistic habitats. The Bengali Express monorail travels over 2 miles of tracks through the forests and meadows of Wild Asia, where you'll see rhinos, elephants, and Siberian Tigers roaming about. At the Children's Zoo, kids imitate what animals do:

crawl through a prairie dog tunnel or climb a spider's web, for instance. Perhaps the most impressive exhibit is JungleWorld, an indoor rain forest with tropical Asian plants and animals. You can easily spend a complete day at the zoo. Although this zoo is open all year, the zoo shuttle, camel rides, and Skyfari aerial tramway close during winter. Baby strollers can be rented at the entrance. Call (212) 367–1010 for information. Liberty Lines runs express bus service between mid-Manhattan and the Bronxdale entrance to the zoo. Call (212) 652–8400 for schedules.

Don't leave New York without catching a glimpse of the magnificent Brooklyn Bridge, which you can see from Manhattan's Seaport area. You can cross over to Brooklyn Heights, a pleasant residential area, where the esplanade provides a great view of Manhattan. Brooklyn's Coney Island area, once the city's fun spot, has seen better days. Home to the **New York Aquarium,** as well as an amusement park and beach, the area is sadly run down, but the Aquarium is modern and pleasant, and has its own parking lot.

If it's sizzling hot and your family is in dire need of a beach, head to the Rockaways in the borough of Queens, where you'll find **Jacob Riis Park** (IRT #2 subway to Flatbush Avenue, then bus Q35). Manhattan area beaches are not world famous, but this one, part of **Gateway National Park,** has a nice sandy stretch. Note that the western portion is almost exclusively gay. Call (718) 318–4300. If you have a car, head out to the **Hamptons,** on Long Island, a much more scenic option, though the traffic on weekends is horrendous. The Hampton Jitney (516–283–4600) has express motorcoach service from New York City. At the easternmost tip of the island, the town of **Montauk** has a beautiful, clean public beach, a scenic lighthouse, and two large oceanside state parks. Passenger ferries leave daily for Block Island and Newport. Call the Montauk Chamber of Commerce at (516) 668–2428 for more information.

From New York, you're also a day trip away from the sights in Mystic, Connecticut. (See the Mystic chapter.)

FOR MORE INFORMATION

New York Convention and Visitors Bureau, Inc. is at 2 Columbus Circle (Fifty-ninth Street between Broadway and Eighth Avenue), New York 10019; (212) 484–1200. They have helpful literature and advice, and an information center that is open 365 days a year. Another helpful resource are the All Around Town listings in the front of the Yellow Pages phone directory, containing loads of basic information and phone numbers.

The Big Apple Parent's Paper (212–533–2277) and *New York Family* (914–381–7474) are publications that feature news and events of interest to families.

Emergency Numbers

Ambulance, fire, and police: 911

Poison Control Center: (212) 764–7667 or 340–4494

Twenty-four-hour pharmacy: Kaufman Pharmacy, Lexington Avenue and Fiftieth Street; (212) 755–2266

If your child has a middle-of-the-night ear infection, go to the twenty-four-hour emergency room at Manhattan Eye, Ear and Throat Hospital, 210 East Sixty-fourth Street: (212) 838–9200. For other emergencies head to one of the city's respected hospitals, which include Emergency Pavilion at New York Hospital Cornell Medical Center, 510 East Seventieth Street: (212) 746–5050.

19
PHILADELPHIA
Pennsylvania

Philadelphia, the site of America's first capital, is rich in history. Your kids will love seeing the sites they've read about from the Liberty Bell to Independence Hall. After exploring the birth of American democracy, families can discover their personal heritage at the city's ethnic museums. There is more fun at the waterfront, which, in warm weather, hosts several cultural festivals featuring music, food, dance, and entertainment.

GETTING THERE

Philadelphia International Airport (215–492–3181 or 492–3000), 8 miles south of central Philadelphia, services all major domestic airlines and several international lines. The Southeastern Pennsylvania Transportation Authority (SEPTA) railway system is a good way to get downtown from the airport.

Amtrak train lines (800–USA–RAIL) run out of Penn Station on Thirtieth Street (215–824–1600), just across the Schuylkill River from downtown. Philadelphia is a regular stop on the northeast corridor line for the high-speed Metroliner that runs between New York and Washington. Train lines also connect the city to Atlantic City and Harrisburg. For more luxurious accommodations try the American-European Express (800–677–4233), a deluxe overnight train servicing Chicago, Indianapolis, and several eastern locations.

The bus connecting Philadelphia with New England, Chicago, St. Louis, and the rest of the country is another option. Intercity buses stop at the Greyhound Terminal, Tenth and Filbert streets (215–931–4000). Bus travel is a cheap alternative for short trips.

GETTING AROUND

You can tour the city by bus, trolley, or subway. For specific information call SEPTA at (215) 580–4000. Dial-A-Schedule (215–574–7777) will mail you a schedule in advance.

The commuter rail system circulates throughout the Center City and connects downtown with the airport, the Amtrak station, and the suburbs. The Port Authority Transit Corporation (PATCO) is an inexpensive way to travel to southern New Jersey. For more information call (215) 922–4600 or (609) 772–6900 in New Jersey.

SEPTA offers a day pass to all buses and trains, including a one-way trip on the airport line. Passes can be obtained at the visitor's center on Sixteenth Street and John F. Kennedy Boulevard (215–636–1666).

For information on parking within the city, call the Philadelphia Parking Authority at (215) 563–7670 or (215) 977–7275.

WHAT TO SEE AND DO

Historic Sites

Independence National Historical Park, with forty buildings on thirty-seven acres, is a must-see in Philadelphia. Stop off first at the Visitor's Center, Third and Chestnut streets (215–597–8974 voice, 215–597–1785 TDD), to get a map and to watch the short film *Independence*. Then choose the historic sites that interest you most. The Declaration of Independence was adopted and the Constitutional Convention was held at Independence Hall, which offers daily tours. The Liberty Bell Pavilion, on Chestnut Street between Fifth and Sixth streets, hosts talks on the nation's symbol of independence. Carpenters' Hall at 320 Chestnut Street (215–597–8974) is the site of the first Continental Congress. Other attractions include an Army-Navy Museum, Chestnut Street between Third and Fourth, which details the development of these military branches; Congress Hall, Sixth and Chestnut streets, where the U.S. Congress met from 1790–1800, and Declaration House, Seventh and Market streets, where Thomas Jefferson drafted the Declaration of Independence in rented rooms.

Other sites of interest on the historic square mile include Franklin Court, Market Street between Third and Fourth streets (215–592–1289), with its museum, theater, and printing and binding exhibit all dedicated to Benjamin Franklin, and the Old City Hall, Fifth and Chestnut streets, where the U.S. Supreme Court met from 1791–1800.

It won't take long to tour the Betsy Ross House, 239 Arch Street (215–627–5343), the restored Colonial home of the woman credited with the creation of the first American flag. The Edgar Allan Poe Na-

The Liberty Bell is just one of the many historical attractions in Philadelphia kids can see first-hand. (Courtesy Philadelphia Convention and Visitors Bureau)

tional Historic Site, 532 North Seventh Street (215–597–8780), is for Poe buffs. Here the author probably wrote "The Tell-Tale Heart" and "The Black Cat." Attractions include a reading room and slide show.

Art Museums

When you tire of history, enjoy the city's art. Turn this into a treasure hunt by asking your kids to find the great works in these galleries.

The Philadelphia Museum of Art, 251 South Eighteenth Street (215–763–8100), is the nation's third largest art museum with works varying from paintings to furniture to period rooms. Some of many highlights include works by Renaissance masters and by the nineteenth-century Philadelphia artist, Thomas Eakins. Kids also like to browse the collection of arms and armor. Among the delights at the **Rodin Museum,** Twenty-second Street and Benjamin Franklin Parkway (210–763–8100), is the *Thinker,* and a cast of the *Burghers of Calais.* This museum boasts the largest collection outside Paris of the famous sculptor's works.

An American favorite, the **Norman Rockwell Museum** at 601 Walnut Street (215–922–4345) features the artist's familiar illustrations plus a video presentation. All Rockwell's cover illustrations for the *Saturday Evening Post* are here. For more art the **Institute of Contemporary Art,** Thirty-sixth and Sansom streets (215–898–7108), presents temporary exhibitions in all mediums including performance art. **The Pennsylvania Academy of Fine Arts,** 118 North Broad Street (215–972–7600), displays a wide variety of both older and contemporary artwork.

More Family-Friendly Attractions

Take a self-guided tour of the U.S. Mint, Fifth and Arch streets; (215) 597–7350. You will get an inside view of the money-making process. Watch as molten metal is cooled and rolled into thin sheets, blank coins are punched out, and coin designs are impressed. In summer the museum is open on Saturdays and during the week.

The **Franklin Institute Science Museum and Futures Center,** Twentieth Street and Benjamin Franklin Parkway (215–448–1200), has a host of hands-on science fun and merits a full day. Benjamin Franklin would be proud of the scientific achievements and exhibits displayed here, including a heart you can walk through, a 350-ton locomotive, a rooftop observatory, and an astronomy exhibit. The Futures Center includes eight permanent exhibits on technology in the twenty-first century, along with an Omniverse movie theater. The Fels Planetarium features fun-filled lessons in astronomy as well as less scientific laser shows, and Jazz Under the Stars concerts every other Thursday. **The Academy of Natural Sciences,** Nineteenth and Benjamin Franklin Parkway (215–299–1000), is for dinosaur lovers. Here the kids and you get to finger replicas of bones and eggs. Check out the temporary shows which are often designed for children. The **Philadelphia Maritime Museum** at 321 Chestnut Street, Philadelphia (215–925–5439), presents various exhibitions including one on the history of Philadelphia's seaport. Those interested in boat building should check out the floating Workshop on the Water exhibition at the Boat Basin at Penn's Landing; (215) 925–7589.

Just for kids, the **Please Touch Museum,** 210 North Twenty-first Street (215–963–0667), offers interactive exhibitions for ages seven and under, including a Nature's Nursery for those under two years. These playful exhibits include lessons on the muscles of the body, the origin of the food we eat, and works of art. Children can design their own theater sets at the new Puppet Land theater.

Ethnic Philadelphia

The city of brotherly love offers a good place for you and your kids to explore your ethnic heritage. Begin at the **Balch Institute of Ethnic Studies,** 18 South Seventh Street (215–925–8090), with the Do Your Own Heritage computer. Visitors input one of nineteen ethnic groups; the computer responds with a printout of that ethnic group's history and influence in the United States. The institute also presents regular educational programs on ethnicity. The Do Your Own Heritage computer program is found at four other sites as well. Call (215) 636–1666 for more information.

The **Afro-American Historical and Cultural Museum,** Seventh and Arch streets (215–574–0380), traces the history of African-American culture, displays African-American artwork, and talks about people who have made contributions to sports, theater, music, and the sciences. There's also a moving depiction of slavery in the United States. The **National Museum of American Jewish History** at 55 North Fifth Street (215–923–3811) traces the Jewish experience in America since 1654. Other ethnic museums include the **American Swedish Historical Museum,** 1900 Pattison Avenue (215–389–1776), and the **Polish American Cultural Center Museum,** 308 Walnut Street (215–922–1700).

To learn about an interesting group that has no ethnic identity, visit the **Mummers Museum** at Second Street and Washington Avenue (215–336–3050). You'll find out there's more to them than their parade.

Waterfront Attractions

Take a walk down to **Penn's Landing** along the Delaware River to visit the historic ships in port. Among them are the *Cruiser Olympia* and World War II submarine *U.S.S. Becuna,* at Christopher Columbus Boulevard and Spruce Street; (215) 922–1898. In the Basin check to see if *Gazela of Philadelphia* is in dock; this masted sailboat is more than one hundred years old. If not, the *Lightship Barnegat,* dating back to 1903, is sure to be there. Call the Basin at (215) 923–9030 for visiting hours.

For a glimpse of the art of wooden boatbuilding, visit the Philadelphia Maritime Museum's floating **Workshop on the Water,** at the Boat Basin; (215) 925–7589.

Parks and Zoos

The **Philadelphia Zoo,** 3400 West Girard Avenue, Philadelphia; (215) 243–1100. You can't avoid history in this city. Their zoo, established in 1874, was the nation's first. It now encompasses more than forty acres. Be sure to visit the Carnivore Kingdom where animals wander around in simulated natural habitats; the Reptile House, for slithery snakes and slow-moving tortoises; the Jungle Bird Walk, where you stroll through an aviary where birds fly free. The Children's Zoo is great for little kids who love riding the camels, petting and feeding the goats, and exploring the Treehouse with exhibits to climb through and touch.

The zoo is located in **Fairmount Park** (215–685–0000). This park, covering nearly 9,000 acres at the north end of the Benjamin Franklin Parkway, is the world's biggest landscaped city park. Besides the zoo other highlights include the **Japanese House and Gardens** at North Horticultural Drive off Belmont Avenue (215–685–0104), a replica of a seventeenth-century home; and **Strawberry Mansion** at Strawberry Mansion Drive (215–228–8364), a Federal and Greek Revival mansion that houses some fine period furnishings and an antique toy exhibit. At

Boathouse Row (214–686–2176) enjoy seeing for yourself this frequently painted and photographed image of Philadelphia. The kids might enjoy catching one of the rowing clubs at practice. Also, be sure to take a break from the city to hike or bike miles of trails.

Smith Memorial Playground, Reservoir Drive by Thirty-third Street, Philadelphia (215–765–4325), is fun for children of all ages and features an outdoor swimming pool and sliding board.

Performing Arts

Philadelphia offers several theater options. Check out the Annenberg Center at 3680 Walnut Street (215–898–6791) for international productions and a children's theater series. The Freedom Theatre, 1346 North Broad Street (215–765–2793), established in 1966, has been rated one of the top six theaters in the country. It's located in the historic Heritage House. Other options are the Merriam Theater, 250 Broad Street (215–732–5446), the Philadelphia Theatre Company, 1714 Delancey Street (215–592–8333), and Society Hill Playhouse, 507 South Eighth Street (215–923–0210) for off-Broadway plays.

Children will delight in the Philadelphia Marionette Theater; (215) 879–1213. Or drop by the free live taping of Bill Cosby's "You Bet Your Life." Tickets at (215) 574–3314; contestant interviews, (215) 574–3301.

If music is more your style, you can listen to the Philadelphia Orchestra. Call (215) 893–1999 for performance information, including children's productions. For the city's Bach Festival, call (215) 247–BACH; for the Mozart Orchestra, call (215) 284–0174. The Curtis Institute of Music, 1726 Locust Street (215–893–7902), presents free student performances.

The Pennsylvania Ballet performs at the Academy of Music, Broad and Locust streets (215–551–7000), along with the Opera Company of Philadelphia, (215–981–1454).

Sports

Philly is a town for sports lovers as well. In the summer check out the Phillies baseball team at Veterans Stadium, Broad Street and Pattison Avenue; tickets and information, (215) 336–3600. In autumn the Eagles football team takes over Veterans Stadium. Call (215) 463–2500 for tickets and information. The 76ers basketball team plays at the Spectrum, Broad Street and Pattison Avenue, Philadelphia. For tickets and information call (215) 339–7600. Hockey fans can watch the Flyers in season at the Spectrum. Tickets and information are available at (215) 465–4500.

More Useful Numbers

For general entertainment and sports tickets, there are a few ticket sales bureaus: Central City Ticket Office, 1312 Sansom Street; (215) 735–1350 or 735–1351. Upstages, Sixteenth Street and John F. Kennedy

Boulevard; (215) 567–0670. Wanamaker's Ticket Office, Thirteenth and Chestnut streets; (215) 568–7100. Call (215) 646–3566 for "The City Perks" coupon book offering discounts at Philadelphia area attractions.

Special Tours

Conduct your own walking tour of African-American history in Philadelphia with the *African-American Historical and Cultural Guide* published by the Philadelphia Convention and Visitor's Bureau; (215) 636–1666. Worthwhile sites include the Mother Bethel African Methodist Episcopal Church founded in 1794 and considered to be the oldest piece of property continually owned by blacks in the country, and Heritage House, the oldest black cultural center. This helpful guide includes information on restaurants, shopping, and nightlife as well.

A guided walking tour of historic Philadelphia begins at Barry Statue, Sixth and Walnut streets. Call (215) 592–1971 for more information. If you prefer to go at your own pace, try Audio Walk & Tour, Sixth and Sansom streets (215–925–1234), for a cassette guided tour. Candlelight Tours (215–735–3123) offers a candlelight stroll with costumed guides on selected evenings.

If you're looking to get off your feet, old trolley tours of the historic district leave from the Visitor Center, John F. Kennedy Boulevard and Sixteenth Street; (215) 333–0320. For a trolley tour of Penn's Landing, call (215) 627–0807.

Horse and Buggy. The even more old-fashioned enjoy horse-drawn carriage rides available at Fifth and Markets streets and South Street at Headhouse Square.

SPECIAL EVENTS

Festivals

The Visitors Center publishes a calendar of events and has a twenty-four-hour event hotline; (215) 337–7777, ext. 2540.

January: Start off the new year with the Mummers Parade on New Year's Day. This world famous event features 30,000 mummers. Later in the month, enjoy Valley Forge Day and the Chinese New Year Celebration

February: Presidential Jazz Weekend offers three days jam-packed with jazz for the whole family.

March: The Philadelphia Flower Show, the largest flower show on the East Coast. In March or April, The Book and the Cook, celebration of cookbook authors and fine food is featured at many area restaurants.

Summer/Fall: Penn's Landing Summer Season sponsors more than sixty free concerts on the waterfront. Mann Music Center Summer Concerts are staged in Fairmount Park.

May: USAir sponsors a Jambalaya Jam, a festival of food and music on Memorial Day weekend. Other festivals include Africamericas Festival, Italian Market Festival, and International Choral Music Festival. Philadelphia International Theatre Festival for Children at the **Annenberg Center** features juggling workshops and an international atmosphere.

June: The Odunde Festival of the African New Year, Twenty-third and South streets, features live performances. Rittenhouse Square Fine Arts Annual Festival and Mellon Jazz Festival also are highlights.

July: Freedom Festival celebrates America's birthday. Philadelphia International Film Festival (Philafilm) and Annual Riverblues Music festival draw big crowds.

August: Polish Festival at Penn's Landing, Great Gospel Picnic Weekend in Fairmount Park, and African American Extravaganza.

September: South Street Seven Arts Festival. Annual Pepsi Penn's Landing Jazz Fest.

October: Freedom Fest sponsored by the Freedom Theatre.

November: Thanksgiving Day Parade.

December: There is no lack of holiday events. Among the more exceptional are the Flashlight Symphony at the Franklin Science Institute. Bring your flashlight and your singing voice for holiday carols. Attend the Presence of Kwanzaa, and bring in the New Year with First Night Philadelphia and fireworks on the waterfront.

WHERE TO STAY

Hotels

Philadelphia has a wide range of accommodations. Some upscale choices include the **Rittenhouse,** 210 West Rittenhouse Square; (215) 546–9000. Situated on historic Rittenhouse Square, it offers large rooms and luxurious bathrooms. **The Four Seasons,** One Logan Square (215–963–1500 or 800–332–3442), is a full-service luxury hotel including complimentary town-car service within the city. **The Ritz-Carlton** (215–563–1600) at Liberty Place in the business district features luxury accommodations, including a fitness center and three restaurants. Investigate their weekend getaway packages.

Less expensive choices, especially with weekend packages, include the **Sheraton Society Hill** at 1 Dock Street (215–238–6000) near Independence National Historical Park; it offers quality accommodations and weekend packages. The **Holiday Inn Independence Mall** at Fourth and Arch streets (215–923–8660) is close to the Liberty Bell. The **Holiday Inn Center City,** Eighteenth and Market streets (215–561–7500), centrally situated, offers a practical base for tourists. The **Comfort Inn at Penn's Landing,** 100 North Delaware Avenue (215–627–7900), is on the waterfront and has relatively inexpensive weekend rates.

Near the airport there are two all-suite choices. **Embassy Suites**, 9000 Bartram Avenue (215–364–4500), has five floors of suites and weekend packages. **Guest Quarters Suite Hotel**, 1 Gateway Center (215–365–6600), also near the airport, offers suite space.

Bed and Breakfast Accommodations

Bed and Breakfast homes offer an especially nice alternative for families in Philadelphia because many are located in historic districts. **Bed and Breakfast of Philadelphia**, 1530 Locust Street, Suite K (800–220–1917 or 215–735–1917), has several possibilities for families. **Rittenhouse Comfort** and **Rodman Renaissance** are both historic town houses. **Spruce Street Seclusion**, in Center City, offers a suite with two bedrooms and two baths, perfect for families.

Another bed and breakfast registry to check out is **Bed and Breakfast Connections**, P.O. Box 21, Devon (215–687–3565 or 800–448–3619). **All About Town-Bed and Breakfast**, P.O. Box 562, Valley Forge (800–344–0123 or 215–783–7838), has listings for the Valley Forge region, in town, and in other suburbs.

WHERE TO EAT

You've got to have an authentic hoagie or steak sandwich while staying in Philadelphia. Two good suppliers are **Jim's Steaks**, 400 South Street (215–928–1911) or **Pat's King of the Steaks**, 1237 East Passyunk Avenue (215–468–1546). **Tacconelli's**, Somerset Street and Aramingo Avenue (215–425–4983), has some of the best pizza in town.

A fun place to stop for a quick bite, coffee, or dessert is **Reading Terminal Market**, Twelfth and Arch streets, just off Market Street. Here you can put together a lunch mixing fresh produce, deli meats, and cheeses available from a bustling array of individual food service booths. Or get some chicken pot pie from the Amish vendors who come to the market on Wednesdays and Saturdays.

When your stomach is growling in Independence Park, the **Food Court at Liberty Place** is not far away on the second floor of Liberty Place between Chestnut and Market streets in Center City. It's well stocked with fast food spots.

If you're in the mood for Chinese food, Chinatown's the place with a lineup of restaurants stretching from Ninth to Eleventh streets. Good picks are the **Imperial Inn**, 142 North Tenth Street (215–627–5588) and the **Harmony Vegetarian Restaurant**, 135 North Ninth Street (215–627–4520).

For fine dining with older kids and teens, **Le Bec-Fin**, 1523 Walnut Street, in Center City (215–567–1000), has excellent French cuisine. In the Historic District try **The Dickens Inn**, 421 South Twenty-second Street; (215) 928–9307. Housed in a Federal-style town house with British owners, the restaurant is decorated with Dickens paraphernalia. For Italian cuisine and a waterfront view, go to **Ristorante Panorama** on Front and Market streets; (215) 922–7600.

DAY TRIPS

The **New Jersey State Aquarium**, Riverside Drive and Delaware River, Camden, New Jersey; (609) 365–3000. Take the *Delawhale Ferry* (800–634–4027), from Penn's Landing to the Camden Waterfront, right next to the Aquarium. If you prefer to be on land, take the PATCO train line, which connects downtown Philadelphia to the Aquarium by way of the scenic Ben Franklin Bridge. The relatively new Aquarium features a huge open-ocean tank with fish species ranging from sharks to minnows.

The **Valley Forge National Historic Park**, Route 23 and North Gulph Road, Valley Forge (215–783–1077), is thirty minutes outside the city, and worth the trip. In 1993 the area celebrated its one hundredth anniversary, and there's always something to celebrate at this Revolutionary War site where George Washington and 12,000 soldiers barricaded the British for six months. Take a self-guided tour of the reconstructed huts, headquarters, and fortifications of the encampments. Other attractions in the area include the 1770 **Isaac Potts House**, the **Washington Memorial Chapel**, a 1903 Gothic chapel with Sunday concerts, and the **Valley Forge Historical Society Museum**; (215) 783–0535.

Germantown, a historic Philadelphia district occupied since the 1680s, offers enough sight-seeing to justify a day's trip. Stop off at the **Visitors Center**, Sixteenth Street and John F. Kennedy Boulevard (215–636–1666), where you can obtain a map. The main sites are historic residences including the **Clivedon**, 6401 Germantown Avenue (215–848–1777), an old Georgian mansion; the **Ebenezer Maxwell Mansion**, 200 West Tulpehocken Street at Green Street (215–438–1861), a Victorian mansion; and **Stenton**, Eighteenth Street and Windrim Avenue; (215) 329–7312.

Bucks County, about an hour by car from Philadelphia, is well stocked with historic estates, antiques stores, and country inns. Call **Bucks County Tourist Commission**, 152 Swamp Road, Doylestown (215–345–4552), for more information.

A great place for families in Bucks County is **Sesame Place**, Oxford Valley Road, Langhorne, Pennsylvania; (215) 757–1100 for recorded information, or (215) 752–7070. This theme park, aimed at kids ages three and older, delights with characters from Sesame Street and lots of climbing and water activities.

The **Pearl S. Buck House** at Green Hills, 520 Dublin Road, Perkasie (215–249–0100), also in Buck's County, is a good place for a picnic. Relax at this sixty-acre farm, a National Historic Landmark and home of the Nobel and Pulitzer prize winner.

The **Pennsylvania Renaissance Faire,** on the grounds of Mount Hope Estate and Winery in Cornwall, Pennsylvania (717–665–7021), simulates a 1599 English country faire for fifteen weekends throughout the summer and fall beginning in late June or July. Activities in this thirty-acre spread include crafts, sporting events, music, and food. Many, including a petting zoo and marionette shows, are expressly for children. The faire runs Saturday through Monday during early September, and weekends only from then until October. Summer hours are 11:30 A.M. to 7:00 P.M.; fall hours are 10:30 A.M. to 6:00 P.M.

The **Brandywine Valley,** about an hour's drive from Philadelphia, mixes scenery and history. (See the chapter on the Brandywine Valley.)

FOR MORE INFORMATION

The Visitor's Center of Philadelphia, Sixteenth Street and John F. Kennedy Boulevard, Philadelphia: (215) 636–1666 or 800–537–7676

Twenty-four hour event hotline: (215) 337–7777, ext. 2540

The Philadelphia Convention and Visitors Bureau, 1515 Market Street, Philadelphia: (215) 636–3300

International Visitors Center: (215) 823–7261

Philly Fun Line: (215) 568–7255

Travelers Aid Society: (215) 546–0571 or 386–0845, for travel problems, lost luggage, etc.

The Philadelphia *Inquirer* puts out a Weekend section of entertainment events on Fridays. The *Daily News*, a paper with heavier local coverage, also lists events.

Persons with disabilities can get referrals and information from the **Mayor's Office for the Handicapped,** Room 143, City Hall, Philadelphia; (215) 686–2798.

Emergency Numbers
Ambulance, fire, and police: 911
Children's Hospital of Philadelphia: (215) 590–1000
Health Hotline: (800) 692–7254
Philadelphia Police: (215) 231–3131
Poison Control Center: (215) 386–2100
Twenty-four-hour pharmacy: CVS, 6501 Harbison Avenue; (215) 333–4300

20
VIRGINIA BEACH, NORFOLK, NEWPORT NEWS, AND HAMPTON
Virginia

It was in the Tidewater and the Hampton Roads area of Virginia that the bright promise of the New World first lured the curious and the adventuresome to our shores. These waters along the Atlantic, the Chesapeake Bay, and the James River still beckon the curious and the fun-loving. There are miles of sandy beaches, plus museums provide off-the-beach fun.

GETTING THERE

Two airports provide service. The Norfolk International Airport (804–857–3351) has more than 200 flights daily and is about a twenty-minute drive from the ocean. The Newport News/Williamsburg International Airport (804–877–0221) offers nonstop, jet, and hub service; it's about a forty-five-minute drive from the ocean.

Several major highways lead to the area. From the west take I–64, U.S. 460, or U.S. 58. From the north or south: I–85, I–95, U.S. 13, or U.S. 17. These routes connect with the Virginia Beach–Norfolk Expressway, Route 44, which leads directly to the visitor information center and the oceanfront area.

Amtrak trains stop in Newport News; call (800) USA–RAIL. From the train station a bus goes to Virginia Beach, about forty minutes away without rush hour traffic. The Greyhound/Trailways Bus station is at 1017 Thirty-first Street; (804) 422–2998.

GETTING AROUND

Take a tour on one of the local trolleys, popular with tourists for transportation, sight-seeing, and visiting historical attractions. The Boardwalk Trolley operates in the summertime from 6:00 P.M. to midnight and covers Sixth to Thirty-sixth streets, and the North Seashore Park Trolley operates year-round from the Civic Center Dome to Sixty-eighth Street. Area bus transportation is provided by Tidewater Regional Transit (TRT); call (804) 499–3300. Pick-ups near the oceanfront are on Nineteenth and Pacific streets.

Rent bicycles (or bring your own) and use the bicycle paths near the oceanfront. And, of course, strolling the boardwalk is a time-honored sport.

WHAT TO SEE AND DO

Beaches, Refuges, and Parks

Virginia Beach lives up to its motto of "good, clean fun." It offers 28 miles of sandy, though often crowded, ocean beaches. The shore and the surf bring out the kid in even the most work-weary city dweller. The highest concentration of boom box, bikini, and college crowds are usually found in the resort area. Although Virginia Beach is bustling in summer, there are some relatively quiet spots for families. These include the strip of sand along the North End, from Forty-third Street north toward Fort Story. The southern end of town, the Sandbridge area, has lifeguards and a quieter pace than the hubbub in the heart of town. For something different try the beach at Fort Story, the army base, which is open to the public.

Whatever stretch of sand you pick, you can enjoy swimming, sunning, and bodysurfing. Here you can look up from your sand castle to sight dolphins breaching the sea. Ever swish along on roller blades? Here's your chance. Rent some at Beach Blades, Thirty-first and Atlantic, where you can skate in the rink, or glide down the boardwalk with the sea breeze blowing in your hair.

Come in July and visit Art in the Park at Twenty-fourth Street and the boardwalk. Local artists sell their creations every Sunday afternoon from 2:00 to 8:00 P.M. In August the park features a different type of live music every night from jazz to country to rock 'n' roll.

But near Virginia Beach's see-and-be-seen strip of sand, you can still view the New World as America's first settlers saw it. Stop at **Back Bay National Wildlife Refuge**, P.O. Box 6286, 4005 Sandpiper Road (804–721–2412) and **False Cape State Park**, just 5 miles south of the Back Bay refuge at 4001 Sandpiper Road. Leave behind the tourists and boom boxes for 10 miles of unspoiled beach, thousands of acres of marshlands, and woods filled with songbirds. For camping and other information, call (804) 426–7128.

Located at the southeastern end of Virginia Beach, Back Bay and False Cape share similar topography, but serve different functions. Back Bay's more than 4,000 acres are a managed area created as a waterfowl refuge, while False Cape offers the changing interplay of beach, dune, and forest. Both are havens for nature lovers. Access is primarily by foot, bicycle, or private boat. When here, think about the unspoiled beaches of False Cape and how this section of what became Virginia Beach lured the New World dreamers.

To enjoy False Cape you must first hike 5 miles through Back Bay. Be sure to bring your own water, and lots of it. The trek is worth the trouble; the solitude seduces. In Back Bay along the 9 miles of dikes built to separate the man-made freshwater impoundments from the saltwater Chesapeake Bay, egrets and herons dance on the water, and turtles dive into pools. The sounds of geese and ducks echo through these gentle stretches of water. For a quick tour try the 1-mile boardwalk beach loop past dune barriers to the Atlantic, or the 4-mile dike loop through marshlands. At both Back Bay and False Cape, you can surf-fish for flounder or site the herds of whitetail deer that dart through the thickets.

The hearty who hike to False Cape get a gift from nature: 6 miles of beautiful shoreline graced by dunes, gulls, and sandpipers, but inhabited by only a handful of people. At the height of the beach season, birds far outnumber bathers, and the unspoiled arc of surf and sand stretches for miles. Other delights include walks through loblolly pine forests rising above tiers of blueberry patches, marshes speckled with white hibiscus, and sprays of gold asters. Along the Barbour Hill trail, 2⅗ miles, stop to crab at the boat docks (bring your own gear) or dangle your feet into the cool water as you look across at Cedar Island, a 400-acre heron rookery.

Seashore State Park and Natural Area, U.S. 60 at Cape Henry (804–481–2131), offers a pleasant respite. Walk along 19 miles of hiking trails past lagoons and large cypress trees, or enjoy the scenery and a picnic by bringing your bicycles.

Museums

If it's raining or you need a break from the sun, try these off-the-beach attractions. At the **Virginia Marine Science Museum**, 717 General Booth Boulevard (804–425–FISH), touch a horseshoe crab and come face-to-face with a 75-pound red drum fish. Learn about the local turtles, flounders, sharks, and other critters by observing them in the 50,000-gallon Chesapeake Bay tank.

The museum has lots of hands-on fun. Use a computer to "build" a fish, look at water from a salt marsh through a microscope, and "tong" for oysters just like a bay waterman. Kids also like the weather forecast-

Getting up close and personal with a horseshoe crab at the Virginia Marine Science Museum. (Courtesy Virginia Beach Visitor Information Center)

ing room and the outdoor boardwalk which leads through a salt marsh. In winter sign on for the whale-watching trips (804–437–4949) sponsored by the museum. From January through mid-March look for real humpback whales as museum staff tell you about these leviathans.

The **Life-Saving Museum of Virginia**, Twenty-fourth Street and Atlantic Avenue; (804) 422–1587. Learn about life-saving techniques from the early days of shipwrecks through submarine-mined waters during both world wars.

Other Attractions

Virginia Beach offers the usual array of amusements and T-shirt shops. **Ocean Breeze Festival Park**, 849 General Booth Boulevard (804–422–4444), offers four off-the-beach attractions: a water park with wave pools, water slides, log flume rides, plus Rocky Springs, a just-for-adults activity pool with slides. (Why should kids have all the fun?) Dry off by playing 36 holes of miniature Shipwreck Golf, test your racing at Motorworld by zooming along a track in ¾-scale Grand Prix cars, or play slugger by batting home runs at the Strike Zone. There's also bungee jumping, but we wouldn't recommend it. Watch if you must as thrill seekers dive into the air near Rudee Inlet and First Street.

Dive into the world of parapsychology and psychical research at the **Association for Research and Enlightenment**, Sixty-seventh Street and

Atlantic Avenue; (804) 428–3588. Turn-of-the-century seer Edgar Cayce obeyed instructions he received in a trance to move to Virginia Beach in 1925 to establish a hospital. Cayce, frequently called the "sleeping prophet," garnered his information from higher states of consciousness and gave "readings" in which he diagnosed people's illnesses and pre-scribed cures, skills he never possessed in his waking state.

On a tour you can "test" your extrasensory perception or browse the library containing Cayce's transcribed readings. At the bookstore find tomes on holistic health, numerology, dream interpretation, meditation, and channeling to expand your beach reading.

SPECIAL EVENTS

Festivals

Late January–February: Wildfowl Festival in Virginia Beach features decoys, carvers, and photography. Kids also get a chance to paint their own decoys.

April: Cycling Classic race in Virginia Beach. International Azalea Festival in Norfolk includes parades, exhibits, and an air show.

May: Enjoy Memorial Day Weekend fireworks festival, wine festival, and Chalk-the-Boardwalk Art Show. Catch a wave—at least vicariously—at the East Coast Surfing Championships. All in Virginia Beach. Country Comebacks at Bluebird Gap Farm in Hampton, features hayrides and sheep shearing.

June: Jazz Festival attracts national headliners to Hampton.

July: July Fourth with fireworks in Virginia Beach. Mid-July brings a two-week Can-Am festival.

August: Great American Family Day at Mount Trashmore Park in Virginia Beach honors the U.S. military for their contributions. See the Hampton Cup International Championships, the largest inboard hydroplane race in the United States.

September: Hampton Bay Days is a tribute featuring Chesapeake Bay seafood, lots of children's entertainment, and fireworks.

WHERE TO STAY

The Visitor Information Center of Virginia Beach (800–VA–BEACH) provides a list of up-to-date vacancies, but does not make reservations. To reserve rooms at many, but not all, of the area accommodations, call (800) ROOMS–VB, a private reservation service. The Virginia Beach Convention and Visitors Bureau offers an accommodations guide; call (800) VA–BEACH.

Here are some family-friendly suggestions:

The Halifax Hotel, on the boardwalk at Twenty-sixth Street (804–428–3044), offers families a choice of a bed and breakfast or modified American plan with breakfast and dinner included. **The Holiday Inn On The Ocean**, Twenty-first and Oceanfront (804–428–1711 or 800–94–BEACH), has an outdoor pool and some organized activities for the kids in season. **The Friendship Inn**, 1112 Pacific Avenue, offers motel rooms, one-room efficiencies, and two-bedroom suites; (804) 425–0650 or (800) 372–4900. The **Barclay Towers**, 809 Atlantic Avenue (804–491–2700 or 800–344–4473), is an all-suite property whose rooms have kitchenettes. Five- and seven-night package plans are available. **The Days Inn Oceanfront** at Thirty-second Street is right on the beach and has an indoor pool; (804) 428–7233 or (800) 325–2525. **The Belvedere Motel**, Oceanfront at Thirty-sixth Street, caters to families and has motel rooms and efficiencies; (804) 425–0612. The **Cavalier Hotel**, Forty-second Street and Oceanfront (804– 425–8555 or 800–446–8199), has two locations—one on the beach and one nearby. Both have balconies and children under eighteen stay free. **The Hilton Resort**, Oceanfront at Eighth Street (804–428–8935 or 800–HILTONS), has refrigerators in every room, a heated indoor and outdoor pool, and children under twelve stay free.

Visitors planning on a longer stay may consider real estate rentals. Several companies are available. **Affordable Properties** (804–428–0432) has a wide range of listings. **Siebert Realty—Sandbridge Beach** (804–426–6200 or 800–231–3037) offers weekly rentals of more than 380 furnished beach homes.

Norfolk has a toll-free hotel reservations system; call (800) 843–8030.

WHERE TO EAT

Virginia Beach offers the usual array of cheap eats plus some good restaurants. Some good picks: **Pasta e Pani**, 1065 Laskin Road (804–428–2299), where the bread is legendary, the pasta and pizza fine; try the **Lucky Star**, 1608 Pleasure House Road (804–363–8410), where the imaginative entrées may include mahi-mahi with sautéed bananas and rum. **Aldo's Ristorante**, 1860 Laskin Road (804–491–1111), has good pasta and chicken. Try **The Big Tomato**, Second Street and Atlantic Avenue on the boardwalk, for nouvelle American; (804) 437–0155. **Coastal Grill**, 1427 North Great Neck Road (804–496–3348), is another nouvelle American restaurant offering good seafood and tasty black bean soup.

Treat your family to the homemade crab cakes and dinner buffet at the **Duck-In**, Route 60 at Lynnhaven Inlet Bridge; (804) 481–0201. Looking for the best cheesecake in town and some good seafood too? Stop by and sample the freshness at **King of the Sea**, Twenty-seventh

Street and Atlantic Avenue; (804) 428–7983. Seafood and chicken plus the house specialty—She-Crab Soup—can be had at the **Lighthouse Oceanfront**, First Street and Atlantic Avenue. There's a kid's menu.

Hampton

Besides such chain restaurants as **Bennigan's**, 2029 Coliseum Drive (804–838–9261), and **Chi-Chi's Mexican Restaurante**, 1119 West Mercury Boulevard (804–838–4155), try **Cap. George's Seafood Restaurant**, 2710 West Mercury Boulevard (804–826–1435), for its seafood buffet. **Grandy's**, 1044 West Mercury Boulevard (804–827–1886), offers steaks, catfish, and southern fried chicken. The **Golden Corral Family Steak House**, 4801 West Mercury Boulevard (804–838–2648), offers steaks, a salad bar, and a kid's menu.

DAY TRIPS

Hampton, Norfolk, and Newport News are easy and enjoyable day trips from Virginia Beach, each about thirty to forty-five minutes away by car.

Hampton

Across the Chesapeake Bay, **Hampton** sparkles with a $30 million **Virginia Air and Space Center**, opened in April 1992. The facility at 600 Settlers Landing Road (804–727–0800 or 800–296–0800) also contains the **Hampton Roads History Center**.

Highlights include the Apollo 12 command module, IMAX movie theater, and interactive exhibits that allow you to "launch" your own rocket and view the heavens close up. With Glimpses into the Future, ponder the airplane of the future, possibly a craft geared for air flight and space travel. At the IMAX theater whose screen is ten times bigger than the one in your local movie house, your kids enjoy the sensation of flight as they learn about space exploration and aviation.

The **Hampton Roads History Center** takes you back to the Colonial past then forward to the 1960s, the days of the Mercury astronauts. Kids can ogle a pirate skeleton and a reproduction of the *USS Monitor.* In Hampton get out in the water yourself on the *Miss Hampton II.* Cruise away from the visitor's center, for a watery look at the naval base (you don't dock there), to Fort Wool, a Civil War fortress. At the waterfront don't miss the nearby **Hampton Carousel**, a restored 1920s merry-go-round with forty-eight prancing steeds. Even if your video-age kids find riding this a bit tame, a spin will probably bring back great memories from your own childhood. **Bluebird Gap Farm**, Pine Chapel Road between I–64 and Queen Street, appeals to very young children who enjoy petting the resident pigs, horses, cows, and goats. Call (804) 727–6347.

Newport News

Nearby Newport News has the **Mariners' Museum**, 100 Museum Drive; (804) 595–0368. Both nautical and nice this is a must-visit for sea lovers. The museum chronicles 3,000 years of maritime history. Kids delight in the size, shape, and look of things here. Discover the remarkable craftsmanship of the Crabtree collection of miniature ships. In other galleries you'll find figureheads, paintings, and the workaday wonders of a real sampan, canoe, and gondola in the small craft collection.

Other highlights include the Age of Exploration Gallery, which chronicles the changes in navigation, and shipbuilding through charts, maps, and rare books from as early as the fifteenth century. Early representation of the world and the seas will amaze kids. The maritime paintings and decorative arts offer glimpses of seascapes and ships in port.

Be sure to allow time to walk the **Noland Trail**. This 5-mile path that crosses fourteen bridges is a good place to enjoy a picnic lunch.

Explore more wildlife at the **Virginia Living Museum**, 524 J. Clyde Morris Boulevard (804–595–1900), which presents both the wildlife and the region as it existed before high rises and office buildings. Small, but interesting, this facility presents wildlife in its natural habitat. Eye a native red fox rustling through the underbrush, watch wood ducks quack by, and see egrets swoop above the water in the museum's outdoor wetland aviary.

Norfolk

In Norfolk visit the **Chrysler Art Museum**, Olney Road and Virginia Beach Boulevard; (804) 622–1211. Originally the Norfolk Museum of Arts and Sciences, it was renamed in 1971 after Walter Chrysler donated much of his personal collection. The facility features displays ranging from Chinese bronzes and European masters to modern stars such as Lichtenstein, Warhol, and Stella. The French nineteenth-century paintings by Manet and Renoir and the roomful of Tiffany lamps and vases are great.

For more dazzling colors, stroll through the 175 acres of the **Norfolk Botanical Garden** (804–441–5381), rated one of the top ten display gardens. Paths lead you by profusions of roses, and a canal boat ride floats along banks terraced with daffodils and tiers of multi-colored tulips. Don't pass this one by, as it's located right next to the municipal airport.

For battleships blooming all in a row, visit the **Norfolk Naval Base** (804–444–7955), the world's largest. Situated on over 5,000 acres, it's home to one hundred ships of the Second Fleet. At the Naval Tour Office, south of Gate 5, board a bus for an escorted tour—visitors are not allowed to stroll the base on their own. Frigates, oilers, floating drydocks, and destroyers look formidable with their radar screens and antennae tuned to the seas. What you see depends on what's in port, but even as you drive by, these grey behemoths bellied up to the docks are impressive.

In Norfolk try your sea legs by taking a harbor tour on either a tall ship, sails flying in the breeze; a mock paddle wheel boat; or a dinner-and-dance excursion.

Norfolk is also home to **the Virginia Zoological Park**, 3500 Granby Street; (804) 624–9937. The more than 300 animals here include the diamondback terrapin; the two-toed sloth; and the interesting Baird's Tapir, which resembles a miniature elephant. Don't forget to see the clouded leopard or the white rhinoceros. The zoo is open every day.

For more history visit Colonial America at the **Jamestown Settlement** and **Colonial Williamsburg**. (See the chapter Williamsburg, Virginia.)

FOR MORE INFORMATION

Virginia Beach
In Virginia Beach contact the visitor information center at (804) 437–4888 or (800) VA–BEACH.

Hampton
Hampton Conventions and Tourism is at 2 Eaton Street; (804) 722–1222 or (800) 487–8778.

Norfolk
The Norfolk Convention and Visitors Bureau, 236 East Plume Street; (804) 441–5266. The toll-free hotel reservations number is (800) 368–3097. For a visitor's guide or information, call (800) 368–3097.

Newport News
The Virginia Peninsula Tourism and Conference Bureau, 8 San Jose Drive, Newport News (804–873–0092 or 800–333–7787), offers information about Hampton, Newport News, and Yorktown, and will reserve area accommodations.

Emergency Numbers
Ambulance, fire, and police: 911
Municipal Police: (804) 427–4377
Oceanfront Police: (804) 428–9133
Poison Control Center: (804) 480–5288
Sentara Bayside Hospital: (804) 460–8000
Sentara Hampton General Hospital, 3120 Victoria Boulevard; (804) 727–7000
Twenty-four-hour pharmacy: Revco Drug Store at Wards Corner; (804) 583–0515 or (804) 588–4501
Virginia Beach General Hospital: (804) 481–8000

21
WASHINGTON, D.C.

In Washington, D.C., prepare to have fun and to feel proud as our nation's capital is a city that belongs to all Americans. Even after more than 200 years, the city of Washington still sparkles. Pierre L'Enfant, the French architect who planned this city of wide avenues and open spaces, paved the way for a city of heroic proportions.

Spring is an especially good time to visit the nation's capital, for the city blooms with tulips and azaleas, and with any luck, you might catch the famous cherry blossoms. An autumn stroll through Rock Creek Park serves as a wonderful respite to life in the fast lane. Winter in Washington is lots of fun, too. After touring many of the museums' special exhibits, take the whole family ice skating on the mall.

GETTING THERE

Air travelers touch down at one of three airports in and around the District of Columbia. **Washington National Airport** is the closest to downtown, about 4.5 miles or fifteen minutes away. Metrorail, Metrobus, and taxi service are available from the airport. **Washington Dulles International Airport,** approximately 26 miles from downtown, is a forty-minute drive, although during rush hour, the time and charges can increase significantly. From downtown Washington, Flyer vans leave 1517 K Street NW for the airport every half-hour. Children under 6 ride for free. Call (703) 685–1400 (tape) or (703) 892–6800 for more information.

Baltimore/Washington International Airport (BWI), approximately 28 miles to downtown Washington, D.C., is about a fifty-minute drive in non-rush hour traffic. AMTRAK trains (800–USA–RAIL) and the Maryland Commuter train line (MARC) (800–325–7254) run frequently from BWI to Union Station in Washington.

For those traveling from major east coast cities including Boston, New York, Philadelphia, and Baltimore, taking Amtrak is a convenient way to access Washington. Amtrak is stationed at the beautifully restored

Union Station, which has many boutiques, restaurants, and movie theaters. First Street and Massachusetts Avenue, NE. Call (202) 383–3067
for information or (800) USA–RAIL for reservations.

GETTING AROUND

An exciting town, Washington remains a manageable destination. Since
the mall acts as the tourist hub, the must-see sites can be navigated more
easily than in most cities. In pleasant weather and with a solid pair of
sneakers, you can see the sights by walking from Capitol Hill, along the
mall with its museums, to the memorials.

To get to other parts of the city, Washington Metropolitan Area Transit Authority's (WMATA) **Metrorail**, the city's amazingly clean and safe
subway, is your best bet. It's easy to navigate with five color-coded subway lines—Orange, Red, Blue, Yellow, and Green—that cover much of
the city and surrounding suburbs. Obtain Metro maps at the Visitors
Center, 1455 Pennsylvania Avenue, or at any Metro station. Call (202)
637–7000 or TTD (202) 638–3780 for more information.

Up to two children ages five and under may ride free with a paying
passenger. If you're darting all over the city, on any day except holidays, a
One Day Pass allows unlimited travel after 9:30 A.M. WMATA also operates an extensive bus system. Call (202) 637–7000 for route and fare information.

The district's cab companies include **Diamond Cab** (202–387–6200),
Yellow Cab Company (202–544–1212), and **Capitol Cab**
(202–546–2400). Fares are based on a zone-system, and the charge is
generally $2.50 per zone passed, per person, plus added charges for bag-
gage, number of passengers, and time of day.

Since public parking is scarce and parking lots fill up quickly, avoid
driving downtown. You'll wind up frustrated. A popular and easy way to
get around is to climb aboard either the **Old Town Trolley** or the **Tourmobile.** (See Special Tours.)

WHAT TO SEE AND DO

Museums

The largest and arguably most popular museum complex in the
world, the Smithsonian Institution, is in Washington, D.C. Begun in
1846 with a $500,000 donation from British scientist James Smithson,
the Smithsonian complex today consists of fifteen museums, fourteen of
which are in Washington, plus the **Cooper-Hewitt Museum** in New York
City.

The Smithsonian Institution Building, 1000 Jefferson Drive, SW; (202) 357–2700, the first to be completed in 1855, is affectionately called "the Castle" because of its architecture. Besides housing administrative offices, the building serves as the Smithsonian Information Center. Come here first to get oriented, find out about special exhibits, and plan your museum visits.

It's not likely that you'll be able to visit every one of the Smithsonian Museums, and if by some chance you did, you surely wouldn't spend enough time to do them justice. Your best bet is to choose a few that most interest you. The Smithsonian complex includes: **The Arts and Industries Building**, 900 Jefferson Drive, SW; **The National Museum of American History**, Constitution Avenue between Twelfth and Fourteenth streets, NW; **The Museum of Natural History**, on Constitution Avenue at Tenth Street, NW; **The Freer Gallery** (Asian Art), Twelfth Street and Jefferson Drive, SW; **The Arthur M. Sackler Art Gallery** (Asian Art), 1050 Independence Avenue, SW; **The National Museum of African Art**, 950 Independence Avenue, SW; **The Hirshhorn Museum and Sculpture Garden**, Independence Avenue at Seventh Street, SW; **The National Air and Space Museum**, Seventh Street and Independence Avenue, SW; **The Renwick Gallery** (American Crafts), Seventeenth Street and Pennsylvania Avenue, NW; **The National Museum of American Art**, Ninth and G streets, NW; **The National Portrait Gallery**, Eighth and F streets, NW; the **Anacostia Museum**, 1901 Fort Place, SE; the **National Zoo**, 3001 Connecticut Avenue, NW; and the newest addition to the Smithsonian, **The National Postal Museum**, 2 Massachusetts Avenue, NE, which, at press time, was scheduled to open July 1993. All can be reached by telephone at (202) 357–1300 or (202) 357–2020 for a recording of daily events and (202) 357–2700 for general information.

The Arts and Industries Building, 900 Jefferson Drive, SW; (202) 357–2700, was completed in 1881. Kids love the elaborate carousel out in front and will demand 75 cents to ride it. Inside you'll take a walk through American Victoriana, and in the southern area of the building, you can see how curators decide on display set-ups in the Experimental Gallery.

The **National Postal Museum**, 2 Massachusetts Avenue, NE, the Smithsonian's newest museum, is dedicated to the history and development of the United States mail. Here you can trace the route of the Pony Express, decide whether it's best to route a letter by land, rail, or sea; climb aboard a stagecoach; create your own greeting card; and watch stamps being printed. While stamp lovers will delight in the Smithsonian's philatelic collection, this museum offers a lot more, including actual mail artifacts. Gape at the 1920 air mail planes suspended in the atrium, and climb aboard a stage coach. In one exhibit read actual letters sent by soldiers in wars from the Civil War to Desert Storm.

The Museum of Natural History, Constitution Avenue at Tenth Street, NW, presents wonders of another kind. In the Fossil Hall, the 80-foot-long skeleton of Diplodocus, the largest land animal to have existed, renders kids as well as adults wide-eyed. Peruse the bony remains of such fear-inspiring beasts as the Stegosaurus, and in the Ice Age Hall, the Wooly Mammoth. A gigantic African bush elephant is your host at the front door, and check out the 45.5 carat Hope diamond. Visit the Insect Zoo where glass tanks buzz, chirp, and whir filled with beetles, bees, and scorpions. Watch centipedes wriggle, and if you time it right, help feed the friendly tarantula—he professes a fondness for crickets.

At the National Museum of American History, Constitution Avenue between Twelfth and Fourteenth streets, be sure to see "Land of Promise/Land of Paradox," displaying the experiences of African Americans, Cherokee Indians, and Central and Eastern European Jews in nineteenth-century America. Another favorite is "First Ladies: Political Role and Public Image," which includes much more than the First Ladies' inaugural ball gowns. Kids like the Railroad Hall with its locomotives, the exhibit on the machines that sparked the Industrial Revolution, and the coin collection in Money and Medals. This is a good place to let your kids browse for hours, stopping briefly at whatever catches their fancy. Allow time to shop at the extensive gift and bookstore on the lower level, among the best of all the mall museums' shops.

The National Gallery of Art, 600 Constitution Avenue, NW; (202) 737-4215, is a gift to the eye. This museum consists of two buildings: the classically inspired West Wing designed by John Russell Pope, and the East Wing, a dramatic asymmetrical trapezoid designed by I.M. Pei. The museum houses a world-class collection of paintings, sculpture, and graphic arts from the Middle Ages to contemporary times. The huge Calder mobile suspended above the lobby of the East building especially charms children as does the bold colors and lines of post-modern art. To turn the museum into an exciting treasure hunt for your kids, ask them to select several favorite postcards of paintings from the gift shop, and then set out in search of the originals as you meander through the galleries. Master works in the West wing include paintings by Leonardo da Vinci, Rembrandt, and Van Gogh.

The most popular museum of them all is the National Air and Space Museum, Seventh Street and Independence Avenue, SW. Chronicling the story of flight, the museum presents a galactic lineup of aircraft, including such stars as the Wright Brothers' *Kitty Hawk Flyer*, Charles Lindbergh's *Spirit of St. Louis*, John Glenn's *Friendship 7*, and the *Apollo 11* Command Module. Walk through the Skylab Orbital Workshop to see just how little room astronauts have in space. Allow time for the museum's famed, 40-minute movies, and stop in the gift shop for some astronaut ice cream on the way out.

The recently renovated **Freer Gallery of Art,** Twelfth Street and Jefferson Drive, SW, houses a renowned collection of Asian art as well as an often overlooked wonder—the Peacock Room, the only interior design scheme by noted artist James McNeil Whistler. Walk in here and you and your kids will be delighted by the intricate peacock-like swirls. The museum has a children's guide both to this room and to its Asian collection. Don't skip this museum as the swirls, patterns, and colors of this type of art delight kids.

One of D.C.'s newest addition is the **United States Holocaust Memorial Museum,** 100 Raoul Wallenberg Place, SW, between Fourteenth and Fifteenth streets near Independence Avenue; (202) 488–0400. Opened in April, 1993, this major addition to Washington's museums tells the story of the Holocaust through a series of moving exhibits composed of actual artifacts.

Each visitor receives an identity card that matches him or her with someone of about the same sex and age who experienced the Holocaust. You find out what happened to "your person"—if they survived, escaped, worked in a camp, or perished. Because the main exhibits are likely to elicit strong emotions, these are recommended for kids ages eleven and older.

For ages eight and above, visit "Remember the Children Daniel's Story," an exhibit dedicated to the 1.5 million children who died in the Holocaust. This exhibit, told from a child's point of view and using interactive exhibits, traces Daniel's experience of the Holocaust from a happy childhood to a concentration camp survivor.

Government Buildings

The Capitol, First Street between Independence and Constitution avenues; (202) 225–6827, sitting majestically atop the mall's gentle rise, lends a commanding presence to the city. Inside, the building reveals a richness of intricate decoration complete with elaborate frescoes, murals, paintings, and mosaic tiles. Tours, which depart every five minutes from 9:00 A.M.–3:45 P.M., start at the Rotunda.

In the main complex, check out **Statuary Hall,** the old meeting chamber of the House of Representatives, which is lined with bronze and marble statues of two of each state's notable personages (some have spilled over into adjacent hallways). Children not only love finding their state's designee but also giggle at discovering the secret of the whisper. Because of an architectural anomaly, discussions on one side of the room could be overheard across the floor at the spot where John Quincy Adams sat at his desk. Legend has it that Adams owes much of his political acumen to this eavesdropping.

When the House or Senate is not in session, line up before or after your tour for a peek at these august rooms. To view these chambers when elected officials hold sway, *obtain a pass ahead of time from your congressperson or senator.*

In the Jefferson Building, across the street from the Capitol, at First and East Capitol Street, SE; (202) 707–5458, the **Library of Congress** reigns. Comprising three entire buildings, it is reputed to be the world's largest library containing over 90 million items, 30 million of which are books.

Some architectural critics deem the Reading Room, now completely renovated, to be one of the nation's best interior spaces. The reading room, open to any researcher eighteen years and older, is a sweep of mahogany desks set off by cream and red-hued marble pillars and archways, all topped with a grand decorated dome.

At the **White House**, 1600 Pennsylvania Avenue, NW; (202) 755–7798, more of the official rooms that dominate the public images of power come into view. As you walk through these carefully-decorated spaces, you can imagine the pomp and flourishes of formal Washington. *A VIP pass from your representative* (ask as far in advance as possible) gains you entrance into one of the less crowded and more informative guided tours that depart at 8:00 and 10:00 A.M. Tuesday through Saturday. But the regular tours (10:00 A.M. to noon Tuesday through Saturday) take you through the same rooms, although the crowds are continuous and the information from the guides less detailed.

From May through Labor Day, generally, you need to line up at the Ellipse ticket booth (Fifteenth Street and Constitution Avenue, NW) before it opens at 8:00 A.M. Call: (202) 456–7041 to check whether a state function has closed the building. Each family member older than eight must stand in line to receive his or her own ticket, a rule that prevents tour companies from gobbling up the daily allotments. Then, enjoy breakfast or window shopping before you come back at the time specified on your ticket.

To stir interest, especially for the kids, and to pick your favorite items to gaze at, purchase *The White House An Historic Guide* before your tour. This informative book, published by the White House Historical Association, features color photographs and lots of details about furniture, paintings, and china. (Available at bookstores or by mail from the White House Historical Association, 740 Jackson Place, NW, Washington, D.C. 20506; (202) 737– 8292.)

Historic Sites, Monuments, and Memorials

Visit **Cedar Hill**, 318 A Street, NE; (202) 543–5579, Frederick Douglass's Washington home. This often overlooked National Historic property conveys the personal side of this powerful and important leader. Sit on this leader's front porch and you can literally look out over the capital as he did.

A 70-second elevator ride will take you and your family to the top of the Washington Monument. (Courtesy of the Washington, D.C., Convention and Visitors Association)

Monuments and memorials adorn the city, part of the nation's homage to its heroes. **The Washington Monument,** Constitution Avenue at Fifteenth Street, NW; (202) 426–6840, a marble obelisk rising 555 feet and ⅛ inches, dominates the city's skyline. While the panoramic view from the top is among the best in town, the wait to board the elevator can stretch to hours. To beat the crowds, try lining up before 8:00 A.M.

The Jefferson Memorial, just off Fifteenth Street, NW, in West Potomac Park; (202) 426–6821, adorns the south bank of the Tidal Basin. In spring, you may find yourself surrounded by a sea of pink flowers if you are lucky enough to catch the famous cherry trees in blossom. The graceful, domed building reflects the architectural shape Jefferson used in designing Monticello, his Virginia home. Inside the columned rotunda, a nineteen-foot bronze statue of the statesman captures your attention. Passages from his writings, including quotes from the Declaration of Independence and the Virginia Statute of Religious Freedom, are engraved on the walls.

Like the Jefferson Memorial, the **Lincoln Memorial,** Independence and Constitution avenues, SW; (202) 426–6895, reminds the visitor of the leader's commitment to liberty. See sculptor Daniel Chester French's masterpiece at night, highlighted by the moonshine and subtle beams surrounding the monument. Seated, pensive, and brooding over the concerns of the Civil War, this Lincoln depicts a man burdened. Carved on the memorial's walls are Lincoln's stirring Gettysburg Address and his second inaugural speech.

The Vietnam Memorial, Twenty-first Street and Constitution Avenue, NW; (202) 634–1568, is perhaps the most moving monument in the city. As people walk along the path in front of the black granite monument set into the ground, they become quiet and contemplative, moved by the thousands upon thousands of names of that era's dead. Sometimes a mother or a child the soldier never knew leaves flowers, a flag, or a note next to their loved one's name. Few people walk away from this simple monument unmoved.

The 612-acre **Arlington National Cemetery,** in Fort Meyer across the Memorial Bridge in Virginia; (703) 692–0931, honors more than 200,000 of our war dead as well as several national heroes. Sites not to be missed include the changing of the guard every half-hour (every hour from October through March) at the Tomb of the Unknown Soldier, where the remains of soldiers from both world wars, the Korean War, and the Vietnam War are interred; Arlington House, the residence of General Robert E. Lee restored to its Civil War appearance, and the gravesites of John Fitzgerald and Robert F. Kennedy.

A new monument downtown scheduled to be installed in July of 1993 is the **Korean War Veterans Memorial,** between Independence Avenue, SW and the Lincoln Memorial; (202) 208–3561. The statues of nineteen soldiers marching toward Old Glory will be standing alongside a reflecting pool and granite wall.

Green Spaces, Zoo, and Recreation

Be sure to see Amazonia, an indoor recreation of a tropical rain forest, at the Smithsonian-affiliated **National Zoological Park,** 3001 Connecticut Avenue, NW; (202) 673–4800 or (202) 673–4717. The elaborate exhibit includes waterfalls, 300 species of plants, and an adjacent gallery with hands-on exhibits for kids who want to learn more about rain forests. Visit with Hsing-Hsing, the male panda (Ling-Ling died), then go over to the renovated Reptile Discovery Center where you'll see the crocodiles, poison elf frogs, and Komodo dragons, and learn about the scent trail of snakes. Kids are fascinated by the interactive exhibits explaining how reptiles get by in daily life. Peek in on the cheetahs at the Cheetah Conservation Center where experts research these oversized cats.

A winter visit to the city wouldn't be complete without an ice skating session on the mall, an often overlooked capital splendor. Glide in tune to your own political promises with the National Archives as your backdrop at the **rink on the Mall,** Seventh Street and Constitution Avenue, NW, or at **Pershing Park,** Fourteenth Street and Pennsylvania Avenue, NW, where you can easily escape into the grand Willard Hotel for warmth. And if the weather is cold enough, take to the ice on the Mall's **reflecting pool**. Framed by the Lincoln Memorial and the Washington Monument, this rink exudes a special glory on a starry winter night.

In summer, take time to golf at **East Potomac Park Golf Course**, in the East Potomac Park, Ohio Drive at Haines Point 20011; (202) 863–9007. Near the Jefferson Memorial, this facility has an 18-hole course, a driving range, and a miniature golf course. For information on miniature golf, call (202) 488–8087.

When it's spring in Washington, enjoy the outdoors by foot, by bike, and by boat. Take the time to smell the flowers, literally, at the **U.S. Botanic Garden**, First Street, SW, near the Capitol; (202) 225–7099. Enjoy the greenhouses where kids love the fossil-filled dinosaur garden. Also walk through the greenhouses to the open courtyards blooming with seasonal delights. Cross the street to the iron **Bartholdi Fountain**, Independence Avenue and First Street, NW; (202) 224–3121, surrounded by a variety of small gardens, which kids are encouraged to enjoy.

Dumbarton Oaks Park, Dumbarton Oaks, Thirty-first and R streets; (202) 338–8278, is located in Upper Georgetown and is part of a chain of parks. Donated by the Robert Wilson Bliss Estate to the National Park Service in 1920, Dumbarton Oaks Park has retained its woodsy feel by forgoing formal landscaping. Dumbarton Oaks' beauty attracts many people to its 27 acres of woods.

Take a stroll through one of the largest urban parks in the country, **Rock Creek Park**, a wonderful oasis encompassing northwest Washington. Contact the Rock Creek Park Office of the Superintendent, 5000 Glover Road, NW; (202) 426–6832. The park's miles of wooded trails and paths for horseback riding and bicycling run from the Potomac River by the Kennedy Center all the way north to the D.C.–Maryland border. On Saturdays and Sundays the long stretch of Beach Drive that hugs the creek from Broad Branch Road to Military Road, NW, is closed to traffic from 7:00 A.M. to 7:00 P.M. Join the locals who roller skate, bike, and stroll along this scenic stretch. Horse lovers can saddle-up and take scenic trail rides at the Rock Creek Park Horse Centre, 5100 Glover Road, NW in Rock Creek Park; (202) 362–0117. The one-hour trail rides cost $17. Riders must be twelve years of age.

For those who like to bike, the **C&O Canal** is popular. The C&O Canal and its tow path stretch for 184.5 miles from Georgetown in the District to Cumberland, Maryland. If you don't want to bike, try a mule-drawn barge trip narrated by costumed interpreters. These operate from mid-April to mid-October. The 1½ hour trips originate at Georgetown; (202) 653–5844, and at the Visitors Center in the park at Great Falls, Maryland; (301) 299–3613. The falls, not high but powerful, draw crowds, but the biking trails that are farther away from the park's Visitor Center are peaceful. A snackbar offers light fare for the hungry traveler.

Contact the National Park Service's Office of Public Affairs of the National Capitol Region, 1100 Ohio Drive, SW; (202) 619–7222, for detailed information about the district's many parks. Those who would like to venture to a park outside of D.C., contact the National Park Service at 1849 C Street, NW, Room #1013; (202) 208–4747.

Special Tours

D.C. has two fun options that take the weariness out of walking for small children. Buy a ticket for the Old Town Trolley Tours or the **Tourmobile**. Along its two-hour narrated tour, **The Old Town Trolley**, 5225 Kilmer Place, Hyattsville, Maryland; (310) 985–3020, makes stops throughout Washington, including at some hotels, a bonus that many parents enjoy. After leaving the trolley, visitors can reboard for another stop along the route. The trolley runs every thirty minutes seven days a week from 9:00 A.M. to 4:00 P.M.

The **Tourmobile**, 1000 Ohio Drive, NW; (202) 554–7950, offers a year-round narrated tour that stops at eighteen sites including the White House, Washington Monument, Smithsonian Museums, Arlington National Cemetery, and Mt. Vernon. Riders are allowed to reboard and ride to another stop on their route.

Scandal Tours of Washington serves up an irreverent look at the sites of D.C.'s past and current scandals, which are especially appreciated by parents and teens. This 90-minute bus ride presented by the local comedy group, Gross National Product, careens past such infamous sites as the Vista Hotel, where former D.C. mayor Marion Barry was arrested, and the Tidal Basin, where former congressman Wilbur Mills splashed with "exotic dancer" Fanne Fox. On board, the Gross National Product actors bring the satire to life. Tours depart on Saturdays outside the Washington Hilton Hotel, 1919 Connecticut Avenue, NW. Call ahead for reservations; (202) 783–7212.

The Black History National Recreation Trail is a self-guided walking tour highlighting several black history sites throughout Washington, D.C., including the Metropolitan A.M.E. Church, Frederick Douglass's home, Howard University, and more. Informational pamphlets are distributed at each of the trail's sites. For a pamphlet and more information call the National Park Service at (202) 619–7222.

Theater, Music, and the Arts

The **John F. Kennedy Center for the Performing Arts**, New Hampshire Avenue, NW near D Street; (202) 416–8341, (800) 444–1324, offers a schedule of cultural, theatrical, and dance performances. Ticket prices vary per event, and the box office is open from 10:00 A.M. till 9:00 P.M. Monday through Saturday, Sunday noon to 6:00 P.M.

In March and April the Kennedy Center hosts "The Imagination Celebration," where the best of children's theaters across the country put on a variety of plays, dances, and inspired puppet shows for pre-schoolers through pre-teens.

The **Shakespeare Theatre**, 450 Seventh Street, NW; (202) 547–3230, shows Shakespeare's finest. Contact the box office for the latest production at (202) 393–2700. This relatively small theater is the place to introduce your pre-teen to an English classic. Children under five are not admitted.

Ford's Theatre, 511 Tenth Street, NW; (202) 638–2941, is a family-oriented theater, featuring plays and musicals most of the year. They are known for their annual Christmas showing of Charles Dickens' "A Christmas Carol." Shows normally take place every Tuesday through Sunday evening, with Thursday and Sunday matinees.

SPECIAL EVENTS

Festivals
January: Martin Luther King's Birthday. Every four years, enjoy the Inauguration Celebration.

February: Black History Month.

March: Smithsonian's Annual Kite Festival on the grounds of the Washington Monument.

March/April: National Cherry Blossom Festival. Don your Sunday best for the White House Easter Egg Roll, where children ten and under can roll eggs on the White House lawn. Imagination Celebration at the Kennedy Center.

May: Festival of the Building Arts, National Building Museum.

June: The Festival of American Folklife on the Mall.

July: The best, brightest 4th of July. Celebrate independence with fireworks and the sounds of the National Symphony Orchestra near the Capitol.

August: The Lollipop Concert at the Jefferson Memorial features Navy-sponsored music and favorites from the world of Disney.

September: The International Children's Festival in Vienna, Virginia, with plays, dances, and puppet shows for the kids. Toss a disc around at the National Frisbee Festival.

October: Explore the Rose Garden and the South Lawn of the White House on the Garden Tour.

November: Veteran's Day remembrances at Arlington National Cemetery.

December: The President lights the National Christmas Tree at the Pageant of Peace.

WHERE TO STAY

Washington, D.C., offers a wide range of accommodations for a variety of budgets. Visitors can choose from a wide range of lodgings from luxury hotels to more moderate accommodations. Some of the District's best lodging buys are weekend hotel packages. These special room rates re duce prices as much as 30 to 50 percent.

Near necessities for a family vacation hotel are a metro stop within walking distance and an indoor pool for cooling off and re-energizing after a day full of walking.

Hotels that frequently run weekend packages include **Hyatt Regency Washington-Capitol Hill**, 400 New Jersey Avenue, NW; (800) 233–1234 or (202) 737–1234, **Loews L'Enfant Plaza**, 480 L'Enfant Plaza, SW; (202) 484–1000, **Hotel Washington**, Fifteenth Street and Pennsylvania Avenue, NW; (202) 638–5900, (just one block from the White House), **Washington Hilton**, 1919 Connecticut Avenue, NW; (800) HILTONS or (202) 483–3000, and the **Four Seasons Hotel**, 2800 Pennsylvania Avenue, NW; (202) 342–0444.

For reduced rates every night of the week, call **Capitol Reservations**, 1201 K Street, NW; (800) VISIT–DC, (800) 847–4832 or in D.C. call (202) 842–4187. This reservation service advertises discounts of approximately 30 percent at 70 area hotels, all in safe neighborhoods.

For all suite properties that offer more space and a kitchenette, consider **Embassy Suites Hotel-Downtown**, 1250 Twenty-second Street, NW; (202) 857–3388, **Embassy Square Suites**, 2000 North Street, NW; (202) 659–9000, **Carlyle Suites**, 1731 New Hampshire Avenue, NW; (202) 234–3200, **Capitol Hill Suites**, 200 C. Street, SE; (202) 543–6000, and **Guest Quarters Suite Hotel** at two locations: 801 New Hampshire Avenue, NW; (202) 785–2000 and near Georgetown at 2500 Pennsylvania Avenue, NW; (202) 333–8060.

If you don't mind a bit of a commute (about a half-hour drive in non-rush hour or a fifteen-minute drive to the Vienna Metro subway stop), try **Summerfield Suites Dulles Airport**, 13700 Coppermine Road, Herndon, Virginia; (703–713–6800 or 800–833–4353). This lodging chain offers one- or two-bedroom suites with kitchen facilities and a daily continental plus breakfast buffet. There are also children's videos to rent (the two-bedroom units have three televisions plus a VCR) and a twenty-four-hour convenience store on site. Ask about special weekend rates.

WHERE TO EAT

Washington hosts a number of good American restaurants located in all sections of town. **Union Station**, 50 Massachusetts Avenue, NE; (202)

371–9441, just north of the Capitol, offers a vast food court on the lower level where even the pickiest eater will be satisfied. The **Old Post Office Pavilion**, Pennsylvania Avenue and Twelfth Street; (202) 289–4224, features an open air food court in its renovated central courtyard. Here you combine history and good eats, and there's often live music. Go for lunch or stop in for a homemade ice cream cone at **Scoops Homemade Cones.**

American Cafe, (202) 682–0937, located in Union Station, Georgetown, and downtown, offers fresh sandwiches and salads. For inexpensive Tex-Mex, check out the **Austin Grill**, 2404 Wisconsin Avenue; (202) 337–8080. Pizza lovers will find a creative twist and a tasty crust at **Pizzeria Paradiso**, 2029 P. Street; (202) 223–1245. For cheap spaghetti under the moonlight, the **Spaghetti Garden**, 2317 Eighteenth Street; (202) 265–6665, hits the spot.

Down by the Mall it gets a bit tricky to find a good lunch spot outside of the museum cafés and cafeterias. These are most crowded during the peak lunch hours, so eat early or snack on some popcorn and wait until two o'clock or so. The *Sunday Magazine, the Washington Post,* and the *Washingtonian* frequently review restaurants.

DAY TRIPS

Monticello

From D.C. it's easy to visit Thomas Jefferson's **Monticello**; (804) 295–8181, 125 miles away, and just three miles southeast of Charlottesville, VA. See for yourself how the house reflects Jefferson's passions, architectural genius, his inventions, and love of gardening. Step outside to the eighteen acres of gardens, recreated from Jefferson's personal records. There are horticultural exhibits and plant sales at the Thomas Jefferson Center for Historic Plants, and on Saturdays in the summer, you can take a wildflower walk or a planting workshop for which you pre-register.

Show yourself around Mulberry Row, the work place of the laborers and the site of woodworking shops, slaughterhouses, and smokeshops.

Mount Vernon, Virginia

The home of our nation's very first president, George Washington's **Mount Vernon** is just 16 miles outside of Washington; (703) 780–2000. The property is accessible by car or by Metrobus; (202) 637–2437. You may even get there by boat in the summertime by calling Spirit of Mount Vernon at (202) 554–8000. Get to know Mr. Washington, the farmer, as you learn of his cultivation of tobacco and wheat. Inside the mansion, see Martha's porcelain tea service, the grandiose, two-story-high dining room, and paintings of Washington area landscapes as interpreted by eighteenth-century artists. Meander through the gardens, and enjoy a respite while admiring the trees that George Washington himself so adored.

Old Town Alexandria

With its centuries of history, its legendary tales, and its sophisticated restaurants and shops, Old Town Alexandria makes for an enjoyable outing that is hardly out of the city, merely across the Potomac River. First, stop by the visitor's center at the **Ramsay House**, 221 King Street, and stock up on brochures about Alexandria's boutiques and history.

Wear your sneakers because the best way to explore Old Town is by walking. Stroll along King, Cameron, Queen, and Duke streets, names that harken back to the town's colonial past.

Visit **Gadsby's Tavern**, in the Old City Tavern and Hotel, 138 North Royal Street; (703) 548–1288, the gentleman's pub often frequented by the Marquis de Lafayette, James Madison, and Thomas Jefferson, and take the tavern museum tour. Drop by **Robert E. Lee's** boyhood home, 607 Oronoco Street; (703) 548–8454, a stately Federal house. See one of the gathering places of the merchants, the **Carlyle House**, 121 North Fairfax Street; (703) 549–2997, a sandstone manor dating to 1753. If you plan on touring many properties, consider purchasing a block ticket.

Also of interest is the **Alexandria Black History Resource Center**, 638 North Alfred Street; (703) 838–4356. Follow their walking brochure to black historic sites, which include streets where the first free blacks lived.

Stop by the waterfront **Torpedo Factory Art Center**, 105 North Union Street; (703) 838–4565, the 1918 manufacturing site of World War II torpedo shell cases where 160 professional artists not only work at their craft but display their wares.

For a river view, board the **Admiral Tilp**, 205 The Strand; (703) 548–9000, for a 40-minute narrated tour.

Additional day trips worth a stop are **Baltimore**, **Annapolis** (see Baltimore chapter), and **Philadelphia** (see Philadelphia chapter).

FOR MORE INFORMATION

Contact the **Washington, D.C., Convention and Visitors Association**, 1212 New York Avenue, NW; (202) 789–7000, which has many pamphlets for tourists that are distributed by the **Visitor Information Center**, 1455 Pennsylvania Avenue, NW, open Monday through Saturday, 9:00 A.M. to 5:00 P.M.; (202) 789–7038.

Several free periodicals serve as good references for current exhibits and special happenings for families. "Potomac Children," a newspaper published ten times a year, P.O. Box 151544, Chevy Chase, MD 20815 (301–656–2133), has a calendar of events. "Washington Parent" appears six times a year and focuses on happenings around town and informative articles, although much of this information may be more useful to residents than visitors. Contact the Parent Connection, 5606 Knollwood Road, Bethesda, MD 20816; (301) 320–2321.

The handy **1993 Washington Weekends Brochure** not only lists hotels but also offers a variety of useful phone numbers, including museums and Metro information. For a free brochure, call (800) 422–8644 or contact the D.C. Committee to Promote Washington, 1212 New York Avenue, NW 20005; (202) 724–4091.

Emergency Numbers

Ambulance, fire, and police: 911

Children's National Medical Center, 111 Michigan Avenue, NW; (202) 745–5000

George Washington University Medical Center Emergency Room, 901 Twenty-third Street, NW; (202) 994–3211

Metropolitan Police: (202) 727–1010, TDD Users (202) 727–9334

Poison Control Center: (202) 625–3333

Twenty-four-hour pharmacies: People's Drug at 6–7 Dupont Circle, NW; (202) 785–1466; People's Drug at 1121 Vermont Circle, NW; (202) 628–0720

22
ATLANTA
Georgia

Atlanta, the site of the 1996 Summer Olympics, is bustling with renovations and activity. This family-friendly city offers lots of hands-on educational fun for kids. If you have a business trip to Atlanta, consider taking your child as there's much to see and do. Atlanta is rich in African-American heritage and Civil War attractions, and for pure fun, head for the nearby theme parks.

GETTING THERE

The Hartsfield International Airport (404–765–1300), just south of the city, is Atlanta's main airport and is serviced by several national and international airlines. MARTA (Metropolitan Atlanta Rapid Transit Authority), Atlanta's rapid rail system, provides an inexpensive fifteen-minute connection to the airport. Call (404) 848–3454 for more information. Several bus lines, including AAA Airport Express Inc. (404–934–8003) and Atlanta Airport Shuttle (404–524–3400), also provide service to and from the airport.

Southern Railways/Amtrak on Deering Road, NW (800–872–7245) is nearby in midtown. The Greyhound Bus terminal is at 81 International Boulevard, NW; (404) 522–6300. Several major highways, including I–85/75 and U.S. 78, intersect with roads leading into the city.

GETTING AROUND

You need a car to get to several of the attractions in the Atlanta metro region; however, for your downtown adventures simplify life and take

MARTA, 2424 Piedmont Road, NE; (404) 848–5000. MARTA is visitor friendly and a snap to decode. Five Points is the central station; all other stations are identified by a name, the direction, and the number of stops away from Five Points. For example, Midtown N4 means four stops north. For schedules and handicapped services, call (404) 848–4711.

Car rentals are available at the Atlanta airport.

WHAT TO SEE AND DO

Museums

Fernbank Museum of Natural History, 767 Clifton Road, NE; (404) 378–0127. New in 1992 this hands-on museum is not to be missed. The permanent exhibit, A Walk Through Time in Georgia, dazzles visitors with fifteen galleries leading from a high definition video of the Big Bang to a spectacular hall overrun with seven life-size dinosaurs to an Oke-fenokee Swamp display filled with sounds and sights.

Kids are catered to with special discovery rooms. In the Fantasy Forest, three- to-five-year-olds learn about nature by doing and "bee"ing. Guided by four fantasy creatures, kids put on bee gloves, collect pollen balls, and pollinate crayola-colored flowers. In a hide-and-see maze, kids discover how nature protects plants and animals by donning a camouflage smock and finding the environment in which they blend in best. Georgia Adventure, for six- to ten-year-olds, is a "state of adventure" with five theme areas. After picking up a map at the ranger station, kids are on their way to Jekyll Island to drag for shellfish off a shrimp boat, to Cohutta Cave to learn about hibernation, and to Atlanta to construct their own cityscape.

If that's not enough, try the Spectrum of the Senses, with seventy-four interactive exhibits that literally illuminate the physical laws of sight and sound. Computer-age kids won't be bored by these galleries filled with lights, videos, and lasers. There's even an IMAX theater with a five-story screen, and a puppet theater where plants and animals come alive.

The **Fernbank Science Center**, 156 Heaton Park Drive, NE (404–378–4311), features an exhibition hall, a planetarium, an observatory, a greenhouse, and sixty-five acres of forest. Be sure to catch a creative show at the planetarium, evenings from Tuesday through Friday. Get an up-close perspective of the night sky and learn to spot star clusters and galaxies. If you're lucky, there might even be a meteor shower in store. Children under five aren't allowed into the nightly shows, so there's a program just for them. Changing holiday programs have included the adventures of Marvin the Martian who leaves Mars to discover the winter sky, and Santa and the Tales of the Big Dipper. Call in advance for a schedule.

On Thursday and Friday evenings, weather permitting, the largest telescope in the world dedicated to public education is open to the pub-

The wonders of science and technology come to life at Atlanta's SciTrek Museum.
(Photo by Diane Kirkland/courtesy Georgia Department of Industry Trade and Tourism Division)

lic. Come hear a seasoned astronomer speak, and take a peek through the massive telescope.

Nature lovers will enjoy the 2½-mile walk through Fernbank Forest. Pick up a seasonal guide sheet and search for the Georgian flora and fauna in this nature reserve. It's open Friday through Sunday only.

For more flowers visit the **Botanical Garden and Greenhouse** at 765 Clifton Road, which is open to the public on Sunday afternoons. Adults appreciate the guided tour of the extensive herb and rose garden while kids get a kick out of potting their own plants to take home.

The **SciTrek Museum**, 395 Piedmont Avenue, NE (404–522–5500), is Atlanta's Science and Technology Museum. Opened in 1988 this colorful neon-lit facility features five theme halls filled with more than one hundred hands-on exhibits. Alter your image without plastic surgery in the Hall of Light and Perception, or learn a lesson when you drink and drive in Impact!. The littlest ones will want to get their hands wet in Kidspace, a water playground with dams and waterfalls.

For an extended museum adventure, children between the ages of eight and twelve can participate in the SciTrek Overnight Program in the spring and fall. They explore the museum, take a workshop, wind down with a bed-time video, then wake to breakfast and a science demonstration. Call (404) 522–5500, ext. 11 for more information.

The **World of Coca-Cola** is at 55 Martin Luther King, Jr. Drive (adjacent to Atlanta Underground); (404) 676–5151. Trace the history of Coca-Cola from its birth in Atlanta in 1886 to the present day with interactive exhibits, videos, and enough commercials to leave visions of Coke bottles dancing in your head. You get a view of the bottling process in the imaginative Bottle Fantasy kinetic sculpture, witness a "soda jerk" prepare a soft drink at an 1930s soda fountain, and finally quench your thirst at the spectacular soda fountain featuring neon lights and sound effects.

The self-guided tour takes about one hour. Reservations are strongly recommended.

Atlanta's major visual arts museum is the **High Museum of Art**, 1280 Peachtree Street, NE (404–892–3600 or 404–892–HIGH for twenty-four-hour recorded information). This museum has something for everyone with displays ranging from decorative and contemporary art to folk and photography. Children ages two to ten should check out Spectacles, a hands-on exhibit where they can create their own art designs by sticking colored velcro blocks on carpeted walls.

At the **Jimmy Carter Library and Museum,** One Copenhill Avenue, NE (404–331–3942), trace Jimmy Carter's life and actions at the White House, see the Oval Office replica, and review modern day issues and events in display stalls. Highlights include a town hall where visitors can pose questions to the president including, "What did Amy do all day at the White House?"

Black Heritage

Sweet Auburn, known as the birthplace and home of the young Martin Luther King, Jr., has been preserved as a historic district, symbolizing African-American achievement in America after the Civil War. Walk through history in this neighborhood of businesses, churches, community organizations, and private homes. The **Freedom Walk**, a self-guided tour of the Sweet Auburn district, begins at the information center, Underground Atlanta, Peachtree and Alabama streets; (404) 523–2311. Pick up this colorful, illustrated map and follow it through 16 blocks (1.2 miles) of civil rights history. Highlights include the *Atlanta Daily World* building, site of the first black-owned newspaper, and the Top Hat/Royal Peacock nightclub, plus the major sites described next.

The **Martin Luther King, Jr. National Historic Site**, within the Sweet Auburn District, encompasses Martin Luther King, Jr.'s restored Birth Home and his grave site, the Martin Luther King, Jr. Center for Non-Violent Social Change, and the Ebenezer Baptist Church. The National Park Service provides information and free tours of these historically important sites at the Interpretation and Visitor Services Office, 443 Edgewood Avenue.

The **APEX Museum** is at 135 Auburn Avenue, NE; (404) 521–2739.

(APEX stands for African American Panoramic Experience.) The museum portrays the story of African Americans in Atlanta in a seventeen-minute video. There's a replica of the first black-owned drugstore, and a vintage trolley. Sankofa!, an African artwork exhibit, is accompanied by African music and photography. The museum also presents changing American art shows.

Herndon Home, 587 University Place, NW (404–581–9813), is the historic home of Alonzo Herndon, a field slave who went on to found the profitable Atlanta Life Insurance Company. Free tours run Tuesday through Saturday. At Hammonds House, 503 Peeples Street, SW (404–752–8215), get a broad view of African-American art and artists from the nineteenth century to the present in this gallery and national research center. Tours are available with prior reservations. It's open Tuesday through Sunday.

Other Family Attractions

Center for Puppetry Arts is at 1404 Spring Street at Eighteenth; call (404) 873–3089 for recorded information or (404) 873–3391 for tickets. Call ahead and get tickets for a Family Series presentation. In the past they've done *Winnie the Pooh* and *Hansel and Gretel*, but each year brings new adaptations of classic stories.

Tots four and up can try their hand at creating their own puppets in Create a Puppet workshops, Monday through Saturday, while older children learn how to manipulate puppets in scheduled Saturday workshops. Advance reservations are necessary.

At the center's museum you soon discover that puppets aren't only the Muppets, and Punch and Judy (although they're here, too). Take a free guided tour and discover how puppets are used in entertainment, rituals, and sociopolitical satire across the globe. Three temporary exhibitions focus on a specific artist or cultural use. Kids flock to Puppetworks, the "please touch" exhibit where imaginations run wild with puppets and props. Check out the daily performances at the minitheater.

In summer a six-week International Summer Festival presents six different productions from regional and international theaters. Call for schedules and reservations. Open Monday through Saturday from 9:00 A.M. to 4:00 P.M., the museum offers free admission with a performance or workshop.

The cable generation will appreciate a CNN Studio Tour, 100 Techwood Avenue, SW; (404) 827–2300. Get a behind-the-scenes look at the production of CNN and Headline News. By walking along an elevated glass tour route, visitors watch technicians, writers, and on-air journalists in the act. The fifty-minute tour also includes a glimpse of Turner Broadcasting interests, including Cartoon Network, Atlanta Braves, and a World Championship Wrestling exhibit.

Tours begin on the half hour, Monday through Saturday. Get your tickets an hour or two in advance since tours sell out quickly. Tickets are only valid on the day of purchase.

Sixteen miles east of the city, the sports-oriented family will be tempted by **Stone Mountain Memorial Park,** Highway 78, Stone Mountain; (404) 498–5600. Its 3,200 acres offer swimming, fishing, tennis, and golf, a sky lift to the top of the mountain, a scenic railroad tour, and a paddle wheel riverboat adventure. Tiny tots enjoy the intricate playground and their own petting zoo. Don't miss the nightly laser show, spring through fall, on the north face of the mountain.

If that's not enough, the mountain's monumental granite carving of southern heros President Jefferson Davis, General Robert E. Lee, and General "Stonewall" Jackson is sure to impress.

Several restaurants and two hotels are also located here. Attraction hours vary according to season, so be sure to call in advance.

Wren's Nest, 1050 R.D. Abernathy Boulevard, SW (404–753–8535), is the home of Joel Chandler Harris, creator of the Uncle Remus characters including Br'er Rabbit and Fox. Take a trip to Atlanta's oldest neighborhood to tour this 1870s house decorated with authentic furniture, photos, and family artifacts. There's a slide show of the author's life and works. The best time to come with children is Tuesdays through Thursdays in the summer when a storyteller enacts one of Harris's classic stories three times a day.

Green Spaces

Zoo Atlanta, Grant Park, 800 Cherokee Avenue, SE; (404) 624–5678 or (404) 624–5600. Recently renovated to simulate natural habitats, the zoo highlights include orangutan antics in Ketambe, black rhinos and zebras in the tall grasses of the East African Masai Mara, and wildcats in the forest glades of the Sheba Sumatran Tiger Forest. Don't forget to say hello to Willie B. the gorilla, the mayor's namesake and the zoo's most popular resident. Take little ones for a ride on the zoo train and to pet and feed the animals at the OK-to-Touch Corral, which is open daily.

The **Atlanta Botanical Garden,** Piedmont Avenue at the Prado; (404) 876–5858 for recorded information or (404) 876–5859 for the offices. Immerse yourself in flowers and plants just 3 miles from downtown Atlanta. Situated on thirty acres of preserved land in midtown Piedmont Park, the Botanical Garden features a variety of gardens including rock, rose, Japanese, and herb. There's a desert house with exotic plants from Madagascar and a tropical forest in the Dorothy Chapman Fuqua Conservatory. If you're looking to beat the heat, stroll among the hardwood trees in the fifteen-acre Storza Woods. It's open Tuesday through Sunday.

At the **Chattahoochee Nature Center,** 9135 Willeo Road, Roswell (404–992–2055), go on a guided nature hike to discover native Georgian plants and animals. This environmental education center features exhibits on nature and one-hour learning programs, including talks on forest and river ecology. Afternoon sessions are geared toward children: call for more information.

The **Yellow River Game Ranch**, 4525 Highway 78, Liburn (404–972–6643), is situated 2½ miles past Stone Mountain (about thirty minutes from Atlanta). This unique place is a must-see for animal-loving kids and parents. Far surpassing any petting zoo, Yellow River allows visitors to get "up close and personal" with animals they once knew only from books and television, including ferrets, deer, black bears, even cougars.

What you do is stock up on animal food that the ranch supplies, then follow a mile-long path to befriend the beasts. Wait until you see your child's face light up when deer come to nuzzle and eat out of your hands. Yellow River has more than 600 animals, most indigenous to Georgia, including a hundred white-tail deer and the area's only buffalo herd. Be sure to bring a camera to capture this educational "touching experience."

Plan your outing to coincide with the springtime weather prediction from General Lee the groundhog on Groundhog Day, February second. Or, join in on Sheep Shearing Saturday in mid-May when everyone can help clip and snip. Springtime means baby animals, in the fall there are hayrides and hot-dog roasts, and all year-round there's a Birthday Cabin for that special celebration.

Strollers and picnic tables are available at the ranch. Yellow River is open seven days a week from 9:30 A.M. to 6:00 P.M. (or dusk during the summer).

Civil War and Other Historic Attractions

The **Atlanta Cyclorama**, Grant Park, Georgia and Cherokee avenues, SE (404–658–7625), starts off with a short movie, *The Atlanta Campaign*, which relates background, then depicts the warfare. The Cyclorama, a century-old oil painting, has lights that depict The Battle of Atlanta in 1864. Afterward, take a look at a Palmetto Pistol and learn the story of the great locomotive chase involving *Texas*, a steam locomotive, in the museum. Hour-long tours—including the movie, Cyclorama, and a visit to the museum—depart every thirty minutes.

At the **Atlanta History Center**, 3101 Andrew Drive, NW (404–814–4000), find out what happened to Atlanta in the aftermath of the Civil War. Learn how the city rebuilt itself from rubble at the Atlanta Resurgence exhibit. Other historic displays include an extensive Civil War show; photo shots from *Gone with the Wind*; and displays from the Tullie Smith Farm, a plantation. Take time to stroll through the gardens of this thirty-two-acre spread, and explore the 1928 Swan House mansion. The **Atlanta History Museum**, the newest addition to the History

Center, is scheduled to open in October 1993. It examines Georgia's past and present, including exhibits on the Herndon family and Atlanta's black upper class and the function of folk crafts in southern life.

The **Big Shanty Museum**, 2829 Cherokee Street, Kennesaw (404–427–2117), houses *The General*, Atlanta's famous Civil War locomotive stolen by Union forces in 1862 and recaptured in a dramatic train chase. Train buffs will enjoy a tour of the locomotive and a slide show on the historic incident. The museum is open Monday through Saturday.

At **Kennesaw Mountain National Battlefield Park**, Old Highway 41 and Stilesboro Road, Marietta (404–427–4686), relive the 1864 Battle of Kennesaw Mountain where Sherman's 100,000 Union troops faced the lesser 65,000 Confederate troops at this three-thousand-acre preserved park and battlefield. Walk through 17 miles of trails, and stop for a picnic. Living history programs on Sunday afternoons in the summer bring the Civil War to life for the whole family.

Historic Air Tours, P.O. Box 88423 (404–457–5217), offers a narrated fifty-minute aerial view of the major Civil War sites in the Atlanta region, including Kennesaw Mountain, the historic town of Roswell, and Stone Mountain Park. Or follow the Battle of Atlanta from the first gunshots at Pickett's Mill preserved battlefield to the siege and torching of Atlanta. Other plane tours focus on the city of Atlanta, its antebellum homes, and modern-day attractions, including the CNN Center and the Georgia Dome. Guests are welcome to mix and match tours. For the most flexibility make reservations a few days in advance. Check the minimum ages for children.

Amusement Parks

Six Flags Over Georgia, 7561 Six Flags Road, SW, at I–20 West in Mableton (404–948–9290 or 404–739–3440), is 12 miles west of Atlanta. Here tour-weary kids find plenty of fun. They can meet their favorite cartoon characters in a Bugs Bunny Party Show, take a twisted ride on the Ninja, and cool off in the Ragin' River. This amusement park includes restaurants, a Looney Tunes shop, live performances, and a nightly Batman Fireworks and Laser Show. Recent additions include a Dennis the Menace Screen Test, where the audience members take the stage and star in a video, and a Batman Stunt Show. Six Flags Over Georgia is open from March to October. Be sure to call ahead for hours of operation since these vary.

White Water, 250 North Marietta Parkway, Marietta (404–424–WAVE), offers wicked water shutes or lazy river rafting. This thirty-five-acre water park's recent addition, Captain Kid's Cove, is a wet-and-wild jungle gym just for the preschool crowd. Parents can sunbathe in peace since Red Cross–certified lifeguards are on duty. The park also includes six restaurants and shopping. It's open from May through August. Call in advance for hours of operation.

American Adventures, 250 North Cobb Parkway (404–424–9283), next door to White Water, caters to the little ones. Here there's an easier-paced Ridgeline Roller Coaster and a Timber Line Truckers convoy for toddlers. Grammar school children will be entertained by two miniature golf courses, bumper cars, and a Formula K racetrack for speed demons.

If you plan to visit White Water too, look into a money-saving joint ticket to both parks. American Adventures is open year-round.

Performing Arts

Ticketmaster (404–249–6400) sells tickets to most arts and sports events. **Woodruff Arts Center** at 1280 Peachtree Street, NE (404–892–3600), is Atlanta's major arts center housing the Atlanta Symphony Orchestra, Alliance Theatre Company, Studio Theatre, the Atlanta Children's Theatre, and the High Museum of Art. For performance and ticket information, call (404) 892–2414.

The Alliance Children's Theatre at Woodruff Arts Center (404–898–1128) presents classics and new children's productions throughout the year. Special workshops and study guides make this entertaining experience educational as well. Enjoy the great acoustics at **Fox Theatre**, 660 Peachtree Street, NE; (404) 881–2100, or (404) 249–6400 for tickets. Built in 1929, this Byzantine-style theater stands as one of Atlanta's landmarks. The Fox's summertime program features a film festival.

SPECIAL EVENTS

Sports

Atlanta's best-known team, the Braves, play ball at the Atlanta-Fulton County Stadium, 521 Capitol Avenue, SW; (404) 249–6400 or (800) 326–4000. In football season the Atlanta Falcons take the field at the brand-new Georgia Dome. Call (404) 261–5400 for ticket information. Other professional sports include the Atlanta Hawks basketball team (404–827–3800) and the Atlanta Attack soccer team (404–431–6111). Both play at the Omni Coliseum at the CNN Center.

Festivals

Unless otherwise stated, further event information can be obtained from the Atlanta Convention & Visitors Bureau by calling (404) 222–6688.

January: During Martin Luther King, Jr., Week, special events all over the city celebrate the civil rights leader. In January of 1994 Atlanta hosts the Super Bowl.

February: Super Fair, Georgia Dome. Mardi Gras Atlanta, parade and celebration. Southside Black Arts Festival. Atlanta Flower Show, featuring landscaped gardens and free seminars.

March: St. Patrick's Day Parade. Antebellum Jubilee, Georgia's Stone Mountain Park.

April: Atlanta Dogwood Festival, Piedmont Park, features a parade and a hot-air balloon race. Sheep to Shawl, Atlanta History Center, includes sheep shearing and open-hearth cooking. Spring Break Out at Six Flags.

May: Storytelling festival, Atlanta History Center.

June–August: Georgia Shakespeare Festival, Oglethorpe University, Atlanta.

July: KidsFest, Six Flags. Civil War Encampment, Atlanta History Center.

July/August: In 1996 Atlanta hosts the Summer Olympics. Call the Atlanta Committee for the Olympic Games at (404) 224–1996 for more information.

August: Legends from Las Vegas Show, Six Flags, stars Dolly Parton and Elvis Presley impersonators.

September: Arts Festival of Atlanta, Piedmont Park, presents arts, puppet shows, music, and children's workshops. Country Star Jamboree at Six Flags features arts and crafts, food, and fun. Chattahoochee Mountain Fair, Cornelia, has a horse show, petting zoo, and live entertainment.

October: At Fright Fest, Six Flags, spookiness prevails in a haunted park. The rides and attendants are all decked out for horror.

November: Folklife Festival, Atlanta History Center. Steeplechase at Calloway Gardens.

December: Santa's Zoo Review, at the zoo. Celebrate the holiday with Santa and his team of wild animals, plus music and conservation education.

WHERE TO STAY

Kids under seventeen stay free, and those under twelve eat for free at three Days Inn locations in Atlanta. While you're at it, ask about their "Atlanta Now" package. **Days Inn—Atlanta/Downtown,** 300 Spring Street; (404) 523–1144 or (900) 942–PKGE. Other major hotel chains that organize family packages and special children's services include the **Hyatt Regency Atlanta,** located downtown (404–577–1234); the **Ritz-Carlton,** 181 Peachtree Street, NE (404–659–0400); and the **Omni Hotel at CNN Center,** 100 CNN Center (404–659–0000). **Marriott** (800–922–7849) offers discounts to families visiting Six Flags Over Georgia.

Summerfield Suites Atlanta-Buckhead, 505 Pharr Road; (404) 262–7880 or (800) 833–4353, about ten minutes from downtown. This chain offers one- or two-bedroom suites with kitchen facilities and a daily continental plus breakfast buffet. There are also children's videos to rent (the two-bedroom units have three televisions plus a VCR) and a twenty-four-hour convenience store on site. Ask about special weekend rates.

For a homey feel try a bed and breakfast. **Atlanta International Bed & Breakfast Reservation Service**, 223 Ponce de Leon Avenue (404–875–1209 or 800–473–9449), or **Bed & Breakfast Atlanta**, 1801 Piedmont Avenue, Suite 208; (404) 875–0525, will help you find a place to suit your family. Be sure to ask if children are welcome.

Atlanta also offers a free travel service that will book reservations for your stay. Call (800) ATL–TOUR.

WHERE TO EAT

Underground Atlanta, Peachtree at Alabama Street; (404) 523–2311. With twenty restaurants, this restored market in the heart of downtown has something to appeal to everyone's taste. Open Monday through Saturday from 10:00 A.M. to 9:30 P.M., Sundays from noon to 6:00 P.M.

Eat on the go aboard a dinner train at the **New Georgia Railroad**, One Martin Luther King, Jr., Drive, SW; (404) 656–0768. Excursions run around the city and to Stone Mountain Village. Reservations are required.

Other family favorites include **Jagger's**, 1577 North Decatur Road (404–377–8888); the pizzas win awards and the burgers aren't bad either. **Lettuce Surprise You** is a healthy choice, featuring a cafeteria-style salad bar including soups, baked potatoes, and exceptional muffins. For breakfast try **Thumbs Up**, 254 West Ponce de Leon Avenue, Decatur; (404) 377–5623. You can eat your stack of pancakes at the counter and watch the home fries sizzle on the grill. **The Old Spaghetti Factory**, 249 Ponce de Leon Avenue, NE (404–872–2841), is a good dinner spot with inexpensive eats and a fun atmosphere. **Johnny Rockets**, 6510 Roswell Road, NW (404–257–0677), brings you back to the 1950s with a burger, fries, and a cold shake.

DAY TRIPS

Where do Cabbage Patch dolls come from? Find out at **Babyland General Hospital**, 19 Underwood Street, Cleveland; (404) 865–2171. About ninety minutes north of Atlanta, discover the doctors and nurses who deliver Cabbage Patch Kids.

Strike it rich in **Dahlonega**, where gold rushing took place in Georgia long before 1849. Pan for gold in the area mines and visit the Gold Museum. While you're at it, tour the nearby Chattahoochee National Forest. For more information call the Chamber of Commerce at (404) 864–3711.

An hour east of Atlanta, tour the antebellum mansions of **Madison** and get a glimpse of the pre–Civil War South. Call the Chamber of Commerce at (404) 342–4454 for more information. To see the largest glass-enclosed butterfly conservatory in North America or explore more than 3,000 acres of woodlands, visit **Calloway Gardens,** ninety minutes southwest of Atlanta. Call (404) 663–5080 for more information. **Warm Springs,** the home of President Franklin D. Roosevelt, is an hour and forty-five minutes southwest of Atlanta. For information on a house and museum tour, call (404) 655–3511.

FOR MORE INFORMATION

Atlanta Convention & Visitors Bureau (ACVB), 233 Peachtree Street, Suite 2000, Atlanta (404–521–6600), publishes *Atlanta Now,* a free bimonthly visitor's guide. ACVB Visitor Information Centers are located at the Peachtree Mall, 231 Peachtree Street; Underground Atlanta, 65 Upper Alabama Street; and Lenox Square, 3393 Peachtree Road. Call (404) 222–6688 with any questions. You can reach the Atlanta Chamber of Commerce at (404) 880–9000.

Emergency Numbers
Ambulance, fire, and police: 911
Atlanta Police: (404) 658–6600
Piedmont Hospital: (404) 605–5000
Poison Hotline: (404) 589–4400
Twenty-four-hour pharmacy: Big B's Drugs, 1061 Ponce de Leon Avenue;
    (404) 876–0381

23
GREAT SMOKY MOUNTAINS NATIONAL PARK and JACKSON COUNTY
North Carolina

Vistas from the overlooks of the Great Smoky Mountains offer a gift to the eye—a series of craggy peaks and soft ridges that roll, seemingly endlessly, into the soft, blue, smoky mist from which the chain takes its name. For 70 miles these dramatic mountains straddle the border of Tennessee and northwestern North Carolina.

The Great Smoky Mountains National Park, with more than a half million acres, offers myriad recreational opportunities. For families with young children, there are scenic drives and easy hikes. Older kids and teens appreciate the more challenging trails. The natural beauty of the waterfalls, gorges, and the mountains, plus the history of stalwart pioneers, and the culture of the Cherokee Indians combine to make the Great Smoky Mountains interesting, educational, and scenic.

While the Great Smoky Mountains National Park claims to be the most-visited national park in the U.S, Jackson County, bordered by the Great Smoky Mountains, the Balsam Mountains, and the Blue Ridge Mountains, may be North Carolina's best-kept secret. Centered around Sylva, some 35 miles west of Asheville, the 491-acre county encompasses lush mountains, valleys, and crystal-blue lakes. Combine a trip to the park with a stay in Jackson County.

GETTING THERE

Asheville Regional Airport (704–684–2226, –9784, –1422; 800–428–4322) about 50 miles east of the Great Smoky Mountains, is serviced by USAir and Delta as well as several regional airlines. Car rentals are available at the airport. From Asheville travel along I–40 west to U.S. 19 to Cherokee, North Carolina, a mile from the park entrance at the Oconaluftee Visitors Center. From Gatlinburg, Tennessee, drive 2 miles south to the Sugarlands Visitor Center.

If driving from Virginia or northern North Carolina, try a route that includes the scenic Blue Ridge Parkway, which winds its way for 470 miles from Shenandoah National Park in Virginia to Great Smoky Mountains National Park in North Carolina. Take a leisurely drive, stopping for picnics, short hikes, and photographs. The visitor's center has a map. The Northwest Trading Post, Milepost (MP) 258.6, features crafts by artisans from eleven counties in North Carolina. Trails from E. B. Jeffress Park, MP 272, lead to an old frontier cabin and a church. At Moses Cone Park, MP 292 to 295, there are more crafts and demonstrations of weaving and woodworking at the Southern Highland Handicraft Guild Shop, as well as scenic trails. For a sample of the area's mining heritage, visit the Museum of North Carolina, Spruce Pine, near MP 331. Visit a mine in Emerald Village near MP 334. The Blue Ridge Parkway intersects Route 441. Follow Route 441 north to the park's entrance at the Oconaluftee Visitors Center.

Asheville is accessible by Trailways bus. The station is at 2 Tunnel Road, Asheville; (704) 253–5353.

GETTING AROUND

A car is a must. If arriving by plane, rent a car at the Asheville Airport.

WHAT TO SEE AND DO

Near Great Smoky Mountains National Park
Great Smoky Mountains National Park has three gateways. The two visitor's centers in Tennessee are Sugarlands Visitors Center, which is the park's headquarters, 2 miles south of Gatlinburg (615–436–1200), and the Cades Cove Visitor Center, Cable Mill, Tennessee.

For your North Carolina journey, start at the visitor's center in Oconaluftee, 150 Highway 441 North, about a mile north of Cherokee (704–497–9146). Be sure to obtain maps of driving tours and hiking trails, and a schedule of special park activities. Have your kids ages eight to twelve get a sheet of activities required to obtain a Junior Ranger badge, a particularly nice memento of their trip.

Near the Oconaluftee entrance is the **Pioneer Homestead** (704–497–9146). Tour these fifteen turn-of-the-century buildings—including an apple house, blacksmith's shop, hog pen, meat house, and chicken coop—and come away with a sense of the stalwart nature of the mountain people. A half mile north at the water-powered Mingus Mill are frequent demonstrations of corn and wheat being ground the old-fashioned way.

A nice thing about this park is the ease of combining a tour by car and by foot. Don't just see these mountains by zipping through in your car. Get out to enjoy the trails, especially since a number are easy, including the twenty-one Quiet Walkways, quarter- and half-mile trails just off the main roads. Hiking these gives even young kids a sense of accomplishment and an appreciation of the park's natural beauty. Check out the self-guided nature trails as well; many are relatively easy to walk and conveniently located off U.S. 441. Some favorite and easily accessible trails from the Oconaluftee area are the 4-mile Mt. Noble trail, the 3½-mile Boundary River trail, the ½-mile Collins Creek trail, and the 4-mile Kephart Prong trail. With over 900 miles of hiking trails from easy to difficult back country treks, there are paths for every ability and interest.

If you only have time for a quick tour, drive the **Newfound Gap Road** that bisects the park, connecting the entrance in Cherokee, North Carolina, with the one in Gatlinburg, Tennessee. When not crowded, viewing this winding road dotted with spectacular lookouts takes about ninety minutes. For a panoramic view drive the **Clingmans Dome Road** and hike the Spruce-Fir nature trail to the observation tower situated atop the park's highest peak at 6,643 feet. The truly spectacular 360-degree view of the park is worth the climb.

In the western portion of the park located in Tennessee, **Cades Cove Valley** is surrounded by an 11-mile loop road which winds around a historic pioneer community that includes a blacksmith shop, a barn, and a smokehouse. Kids can peruse these nineteenth-century buildings and easily imagine pioneer life. During the summer living history is enacted by costumed interpreters at Cable Mill, which has a functioning water-powered gristmill. The Cades Cove Visitor Center, open from March to Thanksgiving, has a small store for supplies.

There are many other auto routes and hiking trails. To dip your feet in the chilly waters of some of the Smokies' famous waterfalls, set out on one of three popular trails on the North Carolina side. Branching off of Deep Creek Road, the trail to **Indian Creek Falls** is a mile long, the path to **Juneywhank Falls** is 1½ miles, and the trail to **Toms Branch Falls** is an easy quarter-mile hike.

If the kids become tired of walking and driving, consider a horseback ride through the park, or a fishing expedition. Stables, usually closed during the winter months, are located at several points. These include the Cades Cove Riding Stables, Cades Cove (615–448–6286); the Cosby Riding Stables, the Cosby Campground (615–623–6981); and the Smokemount Riding Stables, near the Smokemount Campground

(704–497–2327). Anglers enjoy fishing for brown and rainbow trout. A North Carolina or Tennessee permit is required.

Park rangers offer several programs to the public. Some teach how to tie a fly, spot a fox squirrel, or distinguish between some of the park's hundreds of varieties of trees. Check the schedules at the visitor's centers, ranger stations, or campgrounds.

The most beautiful and most popular time to visit the park is when the leaves turn in autumn. Mid-October is considered the peak, but from late summer throughout the fall, visitors wanting to avoid crowds should not visit on weekends when the roads are jammed with cars.

Cherokee Indian Reservation, Qualla Boundary, Great Smoky Mountains. Cherokee Visitors Center, U.S. 19, and Business 441 in downtown Cherokee; (704) 497–9195 or (800) 438–1601. Once inhabiting all of the Great Smoky Mountains, the Cherokee Indians now lay claim to a 56,000-acre reservation within the mountains. Open to the public, the reservation offers campgrounds, crafts, Cherokee historical and cultural attractions, and some exceptional trout fishing. If you don't have a license but want to catch some rainbow trout, try Cherokee Trout Farms (704–497–9227).

Unto These Hills, Cherokee Indian Reservation, Cherokee; (704) 497–2111. This summertime outdoor drama depicts the history of the eastern band of Cherokee Indians from the arrival of the Spanish explorers in 1540 to the near extinction of the tribe on the forced march, the Trail of Tears. This visual history lesson in the Mountainside Theater is worth watching; some one hundred actors in authentic dress, dance, sing, and act out their past. Performances are nightly, except Sundays, from mid-June through August.

Oconaluftee Indian Village, U.S. 441 North, Cherokee; (704) 497–2315 or (704) 497–2111. Set against the pines and peaks of the Great Smokies, Oconaluftee recreates a 1750 Cherokee reservation. Cherokee men wearing bear-claw necklaces demonstrate such survival skills as hunting with a blowgun, chipping flint into arrowheads, and fashioning a dugout canoe. Women in long skirts and beaded necklaces weave baskets from river cane and white oak saplings, cook bean bread, and mold coiled ropes of clay into pottery. A tribe elder in the seven-sided council house talks of the traditional customs and dances.

Then take time to smell such seasonal flowers as Indian paintbrush, Indian pipe, and sunflowers, along the trails of the adjacent **Cherokee Botanical Gardens**; (704) 497–2315. At the **Museum of the Cherokee Indian**, U.S. 441 at Drama Road, Cherokee (704–497–3481), hear the Cherokee language spoken, listen to tapes that tell the ancient legends of the origins of fire and the formation of the mountains, and learn about the Trail of Tears, the 1830s forced march of the Cherokee from this area to Oklahoma.

Oconaluftee Indian Village, home of the Eastern Band of the Cherokee Indians, is an authentic recreation of an eighteenth-century Indian community. (Photo by Clay Nolen/ courtesy North Carolina Division of Travel and Tourism)

There's more Indian lore and legends at **Kituwah,** the annual **American Indian National Exposition of Arts and Education,** sponsored by the High Country Art and Craft Guild, 46 Haywood Street, Asheville 28801; (704) 252–3880. Usually held in September at the Asheville Civic Center, Asheville, this gathering brings together scores of Native American tribes.

You and your kids will enjoy browsing the arts and crafts, watching the dance demonstrations, and listening to elders at the wisdom-keeper sessions discuss customs.

Jackson County

Besides more hiking and horseback riding, nearby Jackson County offers such family fun as river rafting and scenic train rides.

Hiking. The Jackson County Chamber of Commerce, 18 North Central Street, Sylva (704–586–2155 or 800–962–1911), is a good source of hiking-trail information. The *Hiker's Guide to Five of the Best Trails in Jackson County*, available at the bureau, gives directions to several family-friendly hikes and to waterfalls. Among those listed is a short, but somewhat steep, 1¼-mile trek to Waterrock Knob, known for its spectacular views. There's also an easy 3-mile walk to Wet Camp Gap, a mile-high meadow.

White-water Rafting. Enjoy a ride on one of the county's three rivers, the Tuckaseegee, Oconaluftee, and Nantahala, where the trips range from a mellow float trip on Class I waters to an exhilarating Class III white-water journey. **Blue Ridge Outing Company**, U.S. 74–441 between Dillsboro and Cherokee (800–572–3510), offers a white-water rafting trip specifically for families with children twelve and under, plus flat-water rafting and tubing trips. **Tuckaseegee Outfitters**, U.S. 74–441 near Dillsboro (704–586–5050), will equip you for all sorts of river adventures, including rafting, tubing, and canoeing. Bring old sneakers, towels, and a change of clothes.

Horseback Riding. Check out the terrain by horse with **Arrowmont Stable**, Cullowhee Mountain Road, Cullowhee; (704) 743–2762. A forty-minute drive from Sylva, Arrowmont offers 6 miles of trails. Take a day trip and ride up to Trout Lake for fishing, swimming, and an evening campfire.

Skiing. **Fairfield Sapphire Valley Resort**, Cashiers; (704) 743–5022 or (800) 533–8368 (for the rental management company). Snow-making makes this cozy mountain with four slopes and a vertical drop of 425 feet a fine winter destination. A great beginner's mountain, the resort offers kids' programs and lessons. (See WHERE TO STAY.)

Museums. **Mountain Heritage Center**, Western Carolina University, off Highway 107 between Sylva and Cashiers, North Carolina in Cullowhee; (704) 227–7129. Appreciate the history of Appalachian mountain life through exhibits on the Scotch-Irish migration to the region. On the last Saturday of September, the center celebrates Mountain Heritage Day with music, food, and crafts.

Special Tours

Great Smoky Mountains Railway, Dillsboro Depot, Dillsboro; (704)

586–8811 or (800) 872–4681. Take an enchanted ride through tunnels, river gorges, and across mountains aboard a brightly colored 1942 train. The Great Smoky Mountains Railway offers several excursions in an open or enclosed car. The Tuckaseegee River Excursion follows the river on a three-hour-and-thirty-minute route from Dillsboro to Bryson City, with a layover in Bryson City. You'll travel through an 836-foot tunnel and see for yourself whether or not it's haunted by the nineteen convict laborers who died while digging it with a pickax. The Nantahala Gorge excursion leaves from Bryson City for a four-and-one-half-hour trip along Fontana Lake that allows for an hour's stop in the gorge. The all-day "raft and rail" package travels to the gorge where you join a raft trip down the Nantahala River. Several trips, but not all, are offered daily from June to October and on weekends only November through May. Call ahead for reservations.

SPECIAL EVENTS

Festivals

April: Carolina Mountains Arabian Horse Festival, Asheville. Annual Chimney Rock Park Easter Sunrise Service, celebrate Easter high above Lake Lure in a setting used in the film *Last of the Mohicans*. Spring Pioneer Living Day and educational living history celebration.

April/May: Biltmore Estate Festival of Flowers, Biltmore. Come see the annuals blossom in a month-long celebration, including an Easter Egg Hunt and a Mother's Day celebration at George Vanderbilt's French Renaissance chateau. Memorial Day Pow Wow, Ceremonial Grounds of the Cherokee Indian Reservation.

May: Wildflower and Bird Pilgrimage, Botanical Gardens, Asheville. Black Mountain Herb Festival, Black Mountain, features herb crafts, seminars, and all the herbs you'll ever want.

June: Dillsboro Heritage Food & Craft Festival, Dillsboro, featuring fiddling and clogging to the local music.

July: July Fourth Fireworks, Ceremonial Grounds, Cherokee Indian Reservation.

August: Mountain Dance and Folk Festival, Asheville Civic Center.

September: Mountain Life Festival, Pioneer Homestead, Great Smoky Mountains National Park, includes a cooking demonstration and taste of sorghum molasses and apple butter. Mountain Heritage Day, Mountain Heritage Center, Cullowhee. Kituwah, the annual American Indian National Exposition of Arts and Education, is generally held in Asheville.

October: Cherokee Fall Festival, Cherokee Ceremonial Grounds, Cherokee. Celebrate with the Cherokees with Indian dancing, gospel singing, and carnival rides.

WHERE TO STAY

Great Smoky Mountains National Park

There are only two public lodges within the park. The **LeConte Lodge**, P.O. Box 350, Gatlinburg, Tennessee 37738 (615–429–5704), is accessible only by an all-day hike. **Wonderland Hotel**, Route 2, Gatlinburg, Tennessee 37738 (615–436–5490), offers rustic rooms 7 miles from the Gatlinburg, Tennessee, entrance.

Ten campgrounds with varying facilities are scattered throughout the park. Three developed campgrounds with water, but no showers or trailer hook-ups, are **Cades Cove**, **Elkmont**, and **Smokemont**; all are open year-round and operate on a first-come basis from November through mid-May. Reservations, however, are required from mid-May through mid-October. Call or write Ticketron, P.O. Box 2715, San Francisco, California 94126; (900) 370–5566.

Jackson County

Balsam Mountain Inn, Box 40, Balsam, North Carolina 28707; (704) 456–9498. This inviting turn-of-the-century mansion with a two-tier porch rests at the foot of the Smoky Mountains. Curl up in the rockers with a book or watch as the Great Smoky Railroad chugs by through the Balsam Mountains. After a restful night and a hearty country breakfast, head out for such mountain treasures as Yellow Face, Licklog Gap, and Waterrock Knob. Children are welcome.

Dillsboro Inn, 2 River Road, P.O. Box 490, Dillsboro, North Carolina 28725; (704) 586–3898. This family-friendly inn near the Tuckaseegee River overlooks a waterfall. Frolic on the waterfront, and enjoy canoeing and rafting. Both the Great Smoky Mountain Railroad and the shops in Dillsboro are easily accessible, and children are welcome.

Fairfield Sapphire Valley Resort, 4000 Highway 64 West, Cashiers; (704) 743–3441, (800) 222–1057 in North Carolina, or (800) 438–3421 outside North Carolina. Situated on 5,700 acres in Cashiers Valley, this resort offers cabins (with or without kitchens) or deluxe condominium suites complete with kitchen and fireplace.

Adults and older children will enjoy a full eighteen-hole golf course carved into the valley's thick forest, and younger tots can practice their swings on the miniature golf course. There are tennis courts, outdoor and indoor pools, a beach, and a health club. Try horseback riding, or pack a picnic lunch for a long canoe or paddleboat ride on Fairfield Lake. The little ones will be entertained by the Sunburst Kids Program, a half-day or full-day camp running June to August.

For a complete accommodations guide, including camping information, call Jackson County Chamber of Commerce at (704) 586–2155 or (800) 962–1911.

Asheville

Grove Park Inn, 290 Macon Avenue, Asheville; (704) 252–2711 or (800) 438–5800. An hour-and-a-half's drive from Cherokee, surrounded by Blue Ridge peaks, this 140-acre mountain resort combines a grand-old-hotel tradition with southern hospitality. Built of granite boulders, it features massive stone fireplaces and arts-and-crafts period furnishings. In Asheville it's warm enough to play golf year-round; you can share nine holes with your budding golfer, then splash in the indoor pool, or move on to tennis. Kids ages three to eleven enjoy crafts, volleyball, and sing-alongs from 9:00 A.M. to 4:30 P.M. on Saturdays and holidays, and daily in summer. Nearby attractions include the lavish Biltmore Estate and the scenic Blue Ridge Parkway.

Fontana Dam

Fontana Dam and Village Resort, Fontana Dam, in the far west of the Smoky Mountains; (800) 849–2258. Once you settle in here, you'll want to stay a few days. This low-key family-oriented resort was created from the community where 1940s workers lived while the Fontana Dam was under construction. Situated on the southwestern edge of the Great Smokies, bordering the man-made 10,000-acre Fontana Lake, the environment provides entertainment enough. Ask at the check-in office for hiking maps for the Great Smokies, and discover which of the 1,300 varieties of wild flowers and plants are in season. Gaze upon trees older than our nation in the Joyce Kilmer Memorial Forest, and climb along the nearby Appalachian Trail up to Lookout Rock to view the immense misty mountains. Then cool off at the lake where the bass fishing is exceptional, or go for a boat ride and swim. Smaller children are entertained year-round by the resort's organized activities, including horseback riding, badminton, archery, and craft classes. If that's not enough, there's a playground and even a miniature golf course.

WHERE TO EAT

Jackson County

Balsam Mountain Inn Restaurant, Balsam (704–456–9498), has a hearty meal to take care of your fresh-air appetite. The menu features southern dishes, and house specialties include roasted leg of lamb and homemade bread. For dessert treat yourself to the hot-fudge-brownie cheesecake. Reservations are recommended.

A good lunch spot is Bradley's General Store, in Dillsboro; (704) 586–3891. Try the homemade soups, sandwiches, and salads, or take an afternoon break with an ice cream soda or a fresh-squeezed lemonade at the store's old-fashioned soda fountain. Lunch is served from April through December.

Dillsboro Smokehouse in downtown Dillsboro (704–586–9556) is for the barbecue-loving family. Try some finger-licking hickory-smoked ribs marinated in a secret sauce or a smoked turkey sandwich. There's fresh fruit cobbler with vanilla ice cream for dessert.

Start off your day of outdoor adventure with a big breakfast at **Grandma's Barn** in Sylva; (704) 586–6532. Country ham, pancakes, grits, and hash browns will keep you going all day long. Lunchtime here means thick and juicy hamburgers or hot ham-and-cheese sandwiches, and dinner features the local favorites, barbecue, flounder, and mesquite chicken.

Meatball's, in Sylva (704–586–9808), is the place to go for Italian food. There's homemade pizza and calzones for lunch and pasta and seafood for dinner. The atmosphere is relaxed and casual, and weather permitting, there's outdoor dining.

The Well House, among the Riverwood Shops in Dillsboro (704–586–8588), is in the town's first home. Children can peer into the enclosed well at the front of the restaurant and imagine what it was like to live without a tap. Hot deli sandwiches are the specialty of the house.

Take a leisurely drive through the Blue Ridge Mountains to the **Fairfield Sapphire Valley Resort** in Cashiers (704–743–3441) for a taste of Chicken Raspberry or Grilled Salmon at **Mica's** restaurant.

Asheville

For German cuisine go to the **Black Forest Restaurant,** 2155 Hendersonville Highway (704–684–8160). Children will enjoy this Hansel-and-Gretel–style building hung with cuckoo clocks. At **Bill Stanley's Barbecue & Bluegrass,** 20 South Spruce Street (704–253–4871), sample hickory-smoked ribs or fried catfish while bluegrass music plays and cloggers stomp up a storm. This family-friendly restaurant has long dining hall tables and a buffet option. Call in advance to make sure the band's playing.

DAY TRIPS

Asheville

Situated in a valley surrounded by peaks, Asheville has a natural beauty. The number-one attraction here is the **Biltmore Estate,** off Biltmore Avenue, Asheville; (704) 255–1700 or (800) 543–2961. Built in 1895 by George W. Vanderbilt, this private home was modeled after a sixteenth-century French chateau. If the astounding architecture of this 250-room mansion isn't enough, the formal gardens, designed by Frederick Law Olmstead of New York Central Park fame, are sure to impress. Visitors are encouraged to take a two-hour self-guided tour around the lagoon and grounds, then into the mansion's interior which includes an immense dining room hung with elk and moose heads, a gymnasium, and a bowling alley.

The **Thomas Wolfe Memorial** at 48 Spruce Street (704–253–8304) is the childhood home and boardinghouse this novelist described in *Look Homeward, Angel*. Take a guided tour and view the authentic 1920s furnishings, including many of Wolfe's personal belongings. On October third celebrate the author's birthday with an open house and readings.

The **Botanical Gardens at Asheville**, 151 W.T. Weaver Boulevard; (704) 252–5190. Take a Sunday stroll through the ten acres planted with trees, flowers, and plants native to the Appalachian Mountains.

Museums in Asheville include the **Asheville Art Museum** at 87 Haywood Street (704–253–3227), showcasing contemporary Appalachian artistry; the **Colburn Mineral Museum** in the Asheville Civic Center (704–254–7162), displaying the area's gems; and the **Estes-Winn Memorial Antique Automobile Museum** on Grovewood Road, exhibiting classic cars.

Near Charlotte

Paramount Theme Park, Paramount's Carowinds, 10 miles south of Charlotte; (704) 588–2600 or (800) 888–4FUN. This theme park is packed with eighty-three acres of rides, shows, shops, and water recreation. Be sure to call ahead since its days of operation change with the seasons.

FOR MORE INFORMATION

Great Smoky Mountains Region

For park information write to Great Smoky Mountain National Park, Gatlinburg, Tennessee 37738; (615) 436–1200. The Oconaluftee Visitor Center is at the North Carolina entrance to the park, 150 Highway 441 North, Cherokee, North Carolina 28719; (704) 497–9146. The *Smokies Guide*, the park's official newspaper, is available at park visitor centers and includes good seasonal information.

Cherokee Visitor Center, P.O. Box 460, Cherokee, North Carolina 28719; (800–438–1601 or 704–497–9195), has information on Cherokee reservation attractions and events. Ask for an official visitor's guide and directory to the reservation.

Jackson County

Jackson County Chamber of Commerce, 18 North Central Street,

Sylva; (704) 586–2155 or (800) 962–1911. The Sylva *Herald* is published every Thursday.

Asheville

Asheville Travel and Tourism, P.O. Box 1010, Asheville, North Carolina; (704) 258–6111 or (800) 257–1300. They have information on special events, attractions, and accommodations. Contact the Visitors Center, 151 Haywood Street; (704) 258–3858. The evening paper, the Ashevillle *Times* publishes a useful weekend entertainment guide on Fridays.

Persons with disabilities can obtain the *Access North Carolina* travel guide free of charge from the North Carolina Division of Travel and Tourism, 430 North Salisbury Street, Raleigh; (800) VISIT–NC or (919) 733–4171.

Emergency Numbers

Ambulance, fire, and police: 911. In the Great Smoky Mountains National Park, call Smoky Mountains National Park Headquarters at (615) 436–1230.

C.J. Ham's Hospital, Sylva: (704) 586–7000. Prescriptions can be filled twenty-four-hours a day at C.J. Ham's Hospital as well.

Jackson County Police: (704) 586–2916

Poison Hotline: (800) 672–1697

24
LAND BETWEEN
THE LAKES
Kentucky and Tennessee

Low-cost, low-key, and lots of fun, Land Between the Lakes (LBL), in western Kentucky and Tennessee, lures those who like to camp, fish, and hike on the more than 200 miles of trails, and enjoy the 220,000 acres of lakes. Besides boaters, windsurfers abound as the region's best breezes blow here. Land Between the Lakes is an inland peninsula bordered by Lake Barkley and Kentucky Lake, which were originally part of the Tennessee River and the Cumberland River before damming projects in the 1940s and 1960s impounded their flow. This 170,000-acre tract of land serves as a national outdoor recreation and environmental education area managed by the Tennessee Valley Authority.

In this region, once known as the moonshine capital, the three interpretive centers present a nineteenth-century living-history farm, endangered wildlife, and star shows. A destination in itself, LBL is also a pleasant place to stop on your way elsewhere. During hunting season, which stretches from mid-August through February, be extremely cautious when walking in the woods. Wear blaze (hunter's orange) and attach a small bell to your packs, clothing, or bicycles; better yet, don't visit during hunting season. Enjoy LBL at other times of the year.

GETTING THERE

By car take U.S. 24 west to exit 31, follow Route 453 to the Trace, then follow signs to Land Between the Lakes.

Amtrak does not offer train service to the area. The Blue Grass Airport (606–254–9336) in Lexington, Kentucky, is about 200 miles from Land Between the Lakes and serves Delta Airlines, Comair, Trans World Express, USAir, American Eagle, and Northwest Airlines. Call the airport for more information on rental cars. Greyhound/Trailways (606–299–8804) offers daily bus service from Cincinnati, Ohio, to Paducah, Kentucky, which is about 20 miles from LBL's North Welcome Station.

GETTING AROUND

The Trace is LBL's own 40–mile north-south artery. The Trace connects to secondary roads leading to campsites, boat accesses, attractions, and the three visitor's centers: the North Welcome Center, the South Welcome Center, and the Golden Pond Visitors Center. Obtain a map of the Trace at the entrances, attractions, or visitor's centers, or contact **TVA's Land Between the Lakes**, 100 Van Morgan Drive, Golden Pond, Kentucky 42211–9001; (502) 924–5602. Once inside LBL, besides going by foot, opt to get around by biking (including riding off-road vehicles), by horseback riding, and by boating. LBL allows motorized off-road vehicles such as trail bikes and all-terrain vehicles in the Turkey Bay ORV Area during daylight hours. All ORV riders must wear helmets.

Equestrians like the 23 miles of horse trails near Wranglers Campground, a horseback riders' campsite complete with a barn and thirty stables, plus full RV hook-ups, showers, picnic tables, and grills. There's one catch: You must supply the horse, as LBL does not rent horses. Riding isn't permitted on the hiking trails.

Boating is another favored way to get around and a fine way to try your luck fishing. For those sixteen and older, fishing licenses are required. Since LBL has no commercial stores, be sure to stock all supplies and obtain the necessary fishing licenses before arriving.

WHAT TO SEE AND DO

Trails

Teens, parents, and hearty hikers enjoy stepping along the **North-South Trail**, which stretches for 65 miles from the North Welcome Station. Follow the **North-South Trail's** white blaze metal strips which lead you along old logging roads to valleys where moonshine reigned, to historic homesteads, and alongside lakeshores and stream beds. Metal open-air shelters placed about every 15 miles offer a resting place for backpackers. Scenic and varied, this trail is strenuous.

You can customize a trip along the **Fort Henry Trail**, the 26-mile trail that traces the route General Ulysses S. Grant's troops took through the region. Begin at Boswell Landing where parking is available. Ask the guides at the visitor's center to assist you in mapping out a portion of this criss-crossing and looping trail that appeals to you. While hiking here look for soldiers' graves and artillery dating back to the Civil War.

The **Canal Loop Trail**, which includes the 9-mile Barkley Trail, plus connecting paths, offers easier terrain and scenic lake views. Hiking around the **Woodlands Nature Center** is also a good choice, particularly with younger children. The center's on-site naturalists give interpretive information on the **Center Furnace Trail**, an informative trail outlining the history of the Iron Industry. While at the center ask about guided trail hikes. The nearby **Hematite Trail**, 2⅕ miles, and **Honker Trail**, 4½ miles, offer good opportunities for seeing beaver, eagles, and wild turkey. Look for flocks of Canada geese on Honker Lake. Many other trails wind throughout LBL; pick up a trail map before hiking off into the wilderness.

Boating and Fishing

LBL is dubbed the "crappie fishing capital of the world." Besides going after these fish, anglers seek small and large mouth bass, catfish, and bluegill. Anyone sixteen or older must obtain a fishing license. These cannot be purchased inside LBL; obtain a license at nearby stores.

Besides taking to the water with windsurfing, you can sample LBL's lakes, which cover more than 220,000 acres, by sailing, powerboating, or jetskiing. Ask at the welcome centers about boat rentals. Lake Barkley State Park (502–924–9954) has a marina and boat rentals. Several marinas in the area rent boats, including Green Turtle Bay, Lake Barkley at the dam (502–362–8364), which also rents houseboats; and Prizer Point Marina and Resort, Hurricane Creek, Lake Barkley (502–522–3762).

Attractions

Each of LBL's attraction sites charge admission, except for children ages six and younger.

At the **Homeplace 1850**, a nineteenth-century living-history museum, located off the Trace in LBL's southern section, interpreters in period dress work a typical farm. Be sure to see the seven-minute film at the Interpretive Center before starting on your self-guided tour. Then watch the hands ploughing the fields with oxen, shearing sheep, feeding the chickens and pigs, churning butter, cooking, and dyeing and weaving. The sixteen log cabin structures, collected from the LBL area, lend authenticity to the farm. Join in an old-fashioned Fourth of July celebration or, in October (call ahead for the date), be a guest at a local wedding.

After touring the Homeplace, visit the **Buffalo Range**, a 200-acre tract of grazing land directly across the Trace. This privately owned herd, numbering about seventy-five, is the largest east of the Mississippi. Watch these big animals and imagine what life was like when these herds roamed freely, but don't jump the fence or attempt to get close to these buffalo as they are big and can be dangerous.

The Homeplace 1850, a nineteenth-century living-history farm, offers families a glimpse of the past. (Photo by Denise Schmittou/courtesy Tennessee Valley Authority)

The **Woodlands Nature Center,** on the northeast side of LBL off of Silver Trail Road, gives visitors the chance to see endangered species up close. The center cares for a bald eagle, golden eagle, a pair of red wolves, a vulture, owls, deer, and many other animals. Nature interpreters give daily talks on topics such as local wildlife and bird watching. Informed, head off to Silo Overlook, a nearby observation area, to scan for Canada Geese, hawks, and eagles.

The **Golden Pond Planetarium and Visitors Center,** centrally located, offers multimedia presentations, films, and planetarium shows. Kids love Bear Tales and Other Starry Stories, which uses Native American folklore to explain the constellations. From March through November presentations on the area and its wildlife are shown on the hour. Kids also like browsing the handmade crafts in the gift shop.

Golf

Get out of the rough and visit the area's golf courses which include **Kenlake State Resort Park Golf Course,** Highway 94, east of Murray, in Aurora, Kentucky (502–474–2211); **Kentucky Dam State Resort Park Golf Course,** U.S. 62 and 641, Gilbertsville, Kentucky (800–325–0146 or

502–362–4271); **Lake Barkley State Resort Park Golf Course**, Lake Barkley State Resort, Cadiz, Kentucky (502–924–1131, ext. 533).

SPECIAL EVENTS

Festivals

For more information on special events, call (502) 924–1243.

January and February: the Woodlands Nature Center offers guided eagle-watching tours.

June: The Four Rivers Folk Festival, Homeplace 1850, has bluegrass and folk music, storytelling, and nineteenth-century crafts.

September: On Public Lands Day volunteers help clean LBL's shoreline.

October: The Homeplace 1850 Apple Festival has apple cider, demonstrations of apple-butter making, wagon rides, and storytelling.

WHERE TO STAY

Camping

Camping keeps you close to the outdoors, and is inexpensive, but before heading off to one of LBL's developed campsites, call ahead to make sure that all of the site's utilities have been turned on for the season. If you plan to camp in the wilderness, inform LBL's rangers of your plans and of the trails you intend to use. You can contact rangers at any of the visitor's centers and welcome stations, or call (502) 924–5602.

In addition to Wrangler's Campground, **Hillman Ferry, Piney**, and **Energy Lake Campgrounds**, which are all lakefront, offer electrical hookups for RVs, water, showers and toilets, grills, and picnic tables. Energy Lake is the only site that takes reservations. All other camping is on a first-come basis.

Energy Lake, on the east side of LBL, offers campers a swimming beach, rental paddleboats, and canoes. Hillman Ferry, on the western side south of the North Welcome Station, is currently under renovation that is scheduled to be completed in 1994. Piney, accessed via the Fort Henry Road on the peninsula's southwest side, is known for its prime fishing pier. Piney has 382 sites, 322 of which have electrical hook-ups.

A visit to LBL doesn't have to mean roughing it as the surrounding area offers a range of lodging facilities.

One family-friendly resort is the **Palisades Resort**, Route 1, Box 359, Eddyville, Kentucky 42038; (502) 388–7667. Situated on Lake Barkley, this lodging offers one-, two-, and three-bedroom chalets, and there's a recreation room for kids. The **Shawnee Bay Resort**, Route 4, Box 408, Benton, Kentucky 42025 (502–354–8360), offers cottages and boat rentals. The **Ken-Bar Inn Resort & Club**, Highway 641, P.O. Box 66, Gilbertsville, Kentucky 42044 (502–362–8852); has rooms, cottages, saunas, and an indoor and outdoor pool. The **Big Bear Resort**, Route 4, Box 143, Benton, Kentucky 42025 (800–922–2327), offers cottages, villas, and condominiums as well as lakeside camping sites and boat rentals. The **Hickory Hill Resort**, Route 5, in Fairdealing, Kentucky (502–354–8207 or 800–264–8207), has lake-front cottages, boat rentals, a playground, and sandy beaches.

The **Cedar Lane Motel**, Route 1, Highway 68, Aurora, Kentucky (502–474–8042), a quarter-mile from Kentucky Lake, has rooms and efficiencies with kitchenettes. The **Ramada Inn Resort**, exit 27 off of I–24, Gilbertsville, Kentucky (502–362–4278 or 800–628–6538), has an indoor and outdoor pool, and miniature golf.

For more information on where to stay in the LBL area, consult *A Guide to Land Between the Lakes,* available at all Welcome Centers, or call (502) 924–1243.

WHERE TO EAT

There are no restaurants or grocery stores in LBL (and no gas stations either). But food and gas are nearby. The Barkley and Kentucky Lake State Parks, on the shores surrounding LBL, serve food, as do restaurants in the nearby towns. Sample some mountain cuisine at **Patty's**, 100 Main Street, Grand Rivers, Kentucky (502–362–8844). They serve 2-inch-thick pork chops and homemade pies. Country cooking at the **Iron Kettle** (502–362–8396), 3 miles from LBL, features homemade breads, ham, and sandwiches. (From I–24 take exit 31 to Highway 453 South into downtown Grand Rivers, Kentucky.) The **Brass Lantern**, Highway 68, Aurora, Kentucky (502–474–2773), offers lobster tails, prime rib, and fresh fish specials.

For more information on places to eat, consult *A Guide to Land Between the Lakes*, available at all LBL Welcome Centers, or call (502) 924–1243.

DAY TRIPS

Nashville, Tennessee, is about 70 miles from the LBL's south entrance and offers more than a day's worth of attractions. (See the Nashville chapter.)

Is there a boy scout in your bunch? Take him to the **National Scouting Museum**, Sixteenth and Calloway Avenue, Murray, Kentucky (502–762–3383). Less than 30 miles from LBL's western entrance, on Murray State University's campus, the museum offers an obstacle course for kids to romp on, storytelling by professional "spinners," plenty of scouting memorabilia, interactive video and computer exhibits and displays, plus the world's second largest collection of Norman Rockwell paintings.

For more background on another American pastime, visit the **Museum of the American Quilting Society,** located 20 miles from LBL at 215 Jefferson Street, Paducah, Kentucky (502–442–8856). The museum displays 200 quilts of various styles from antique to contemporary, traditional to innovative. The museum is open Tuesday through Saturday, 10:00 A.M.–5:00 P.M.

Fort Donaldson National Battlefield, off U.S. 79 about 30 miles east of Clarksville (615–232–5706), is a museum and National Historic Park dedicated to the Civil War battle fought here in 1862. A 6-mile driving tour includes markers that explain the battle. Originally a Confederate Fort, Fort Donaldson fell to the growing Union forces led by U.S. Grant. Grant gained the nickname "Unconditional Surrender Grant" after issuing his staunch ultimatum, "no terms except unconditional and immediate surrender," to Fort Donaldson's Confederate forces. The Union victory marked the fall of much of the Confederate's strongholds; soon after Fort Donaldson fell, the Confederates surrendered Bowling Green, Kentucky, and most of western and central Tennessee, including Nashville. Today the national battlefield contains the Dover Hotel, where the rebels surrendered to Grant, a national cemetery, and 554 acres of parkland. In summer costumed National Park Service staff turn the battlefield into a living-history museum, complete with demonstrations and exhibits highlighting the Civil War soldiers' daily activities.

FOR MORE INFORMATION

For additional information contact the Land Between the Lakes, Golden Pond, Kentucky 42231; (502) 924–5602. Also try the Northwest Tennessee Tourist Promotion Council, Box 963, Martin, Tennessee 38327; (901) 587–4213.

Emergency Numbers

Clarksville Memorial Hospital (nearest to LBL's South Welcome Center), 1771 Madison Street, Clarksville, Tennessee; (615) 552–6622

Lourdes Hospital (near LBL's North Welcome Center), 1530 Lone Oak Road at I–24, Paducah, Kentucky; (502) 444–2111

Murray/Calloway County Hospital (closest to the Golden Pond Visitor Center), 803 Poplar Street, Murray, Kentucky; (502) 762–1100

Poison Control: (800) 722–5725

Twenty-four-hour pharmacy: Western Baptist Hospital, 2501 Kentucky Avenue, Paducah, Kentucky; (502) 575–2100

Twenty-four-hour Public Safety Headquarters (near Highway 68): (502) 924–5602

25
LEXINGTON
Kentucky

Lexington, Kentucky's second largest city, is set in the heart of Bluegrass horse country. If your kids get starry-eyed watching a thoroughbred go through his paces, enjoy taking riding lessons at camp, or just like to imagine themselves astride the perfect steed, Lexington is a good place to be. Besides all that, the countryside with its white-planked fences, rolling pasturelands, and tobacco farms is picture-perfect for a Sunday drive. Added attractions include historic buildings, a thriving arts and crafts scene, several golf courses, and some interesting museums.

GETTING THERE

Delta Air Lines, Comair, Trans World Express, USAir, American Eagle, and Northwest Airlines serve the Blue Grass Airport; (606) 254–9336.

Amtrak (800–USA–RAIL) does not run direct service to Lexington, Kentucky. You could take the train to Cincinnati, where Greyhound/ Trailways (606–299–8804) bus service has daily routes between Cincinnati and Lexington. Flying or driving here, though, is preferable to the combined bus and train route. Lexington is easily accessible as three highways, I–64, U.S. 60, and U.S. 68, lead to this city.

GETTING AROUND

Route 4 circles the area surrounding the city and serves as a beltway. Lexington's public bus line, LexTran and Trolley (606–252–4936), serves the downtown area. For taxi service, dial (606) 231–8294.

Rental car companies include Agency Rent-A-Car (606–259–1296), Dollar Rent-A-Car (606–269–4177), and Snappy Rent-A-Car (606–293–6260), all of which provide car-leasing services. WHEELS offers transportation for the physically challenged. Call (606) 233–3433, 7:00 A.M.–8:00 P.M., for transportation arrangements twenty-four hours in advance.

WHAT TO SEE AND DO

Horse Country Attractions

Kentucky Horse Park, 4089 Iron Works Pike, exit 120 off I–75; (606) 233–4303 or (800) 678–8813 TDD. It claims to be "the only park in the world that is dedicated to horses exclusively." The showcase of Kentucky's proud horse tradition, Kentucky Horse Park is set on more than 1,000 acres and offers an extensive look at the horse, its history, its breeding, and its importance to humans. Plan your day by starting at the visitor information center, where you can book some options, including a horse-drawn carriage ride (sleigh ride in the winter months), pony ride or horseback trail ride across the sweeping acres of bluegrass. Either of two films shown regularly should delight older children. *Thou Shalt Fly Without Wings* describes the relationship between humans and horses, and *All the Kings Horses* describes the development of the Budweiser Clydesdales.

Allow time to browse the **International Museum of the Horse,** which documents the evolution of human/equine relations from pre-historic times to today. Kids like discovering that the earliest ancestor of the horse, the Eohippus, was no bigger than a fox. They also are tickled to learn that in ancient Rome up to one hundred chariot races were staged daily with results delivered to bettors by carrier pigeons. There's also an eye-catching collection of thirty horse-drawn vehicles featuring carriages, racing rigs, and commercial wagons such as an ornate hearse.

On the **Walking Farm tour,** you can review a day in the life of a race horse and his handlers. Visit the farrier's (blacksmith's) shop, the harness maker's shop, the training track, and the horse cemetery. At the **Hall of Champions** take a look at some of the elite racers of yesteryear who live at the park. Among the stars are John Henry, the first horse ever to win $3 million, $5 million, and $6.5 million, and Kentucky Derby Winner Bold Forbes.

Don't miss the **Parade of Breeds** or the **American Saddle Horse Museum.** The narrated parade, available April through October, presents thirty breeds, some with costumed riders. At the **American Saddle Horse Museum,** 4093 Iron Works Pike; (606) 259–2746, (separate admission), discover more facts, such as what a saddlebred is (Mr. Ed, TV's talking horse, was a saddlebred). The museum dedicates itself to the history and heritage of the American saddlebred horse, Kentucky's only native breed. *Saddlebred for America,* a multi-image presentation, is a vivid portrait of the history and racing records of these stately steeds. A touch-screen video scrapbook highlights past world-champion horses.

Throughout the year the park hosts many championship equestrian events. Plan ahead to see if you can obtain tickets to the Rolex Kentucky Three-Day Event (the United States Equestrian Team's spring event) and the polo matches, which are held each Sunday from June through October.

A visit to Lexington wouldn't be complete without spending some time observing horses close-up at a track. At **Keeneland Race Course,** U.S. 60 west, 4201 Versailles Road (606–254–3412 or 800–456–3412), about 13 miles from Lexington, you can be railside from spring through fall while watching some of racing's best. The catch: you should arrive by 6:00 A.M. to watch these horses go through their paces until about 9:30 A.M. Afterward, tour the course grounds and training facilities. Keeneland races generally occur in April and October, but call ahead for a schedule. Among the notable runs is the spring Blue Grass Stakes, the last of the major prep races for the Kentucky Derby. The **Red Mile Harness Track,** South Broadway and Red Mile Road (606–255–0752 or 800–354–9092), offers harness racing and welcomes the public at morning workouts. But phone ahead for rules about admitting children to facilities where betting occurs.

Historic Sites

There's more to Lexington than just horses. While in town, tour **Ashland,** the Henry Clay Estate, Richmond Road at Sycamore Road; (606) 266–8581. It's closed during January. Henry Clay, "The Great Compromiser," served as Secretary of State, Speaker of the House of Representatives, and United States Senator. This National Historic Landmark features twenty acres of woodland and is furnished with nineteenth-century antiques.

Another famous American is remembered at the **Mary Todd Lincoln House,** 578 West Main Street (606–233–9999); open April to mid-December. Built in 1803 the home was restored and opened to the public in 1977, when it became the first shrine to a first lady in America. In 1832 the Todds purchased this home where Mary Todd Lincoln spent her girlhood years before she met Abraham Lincoln.

If you and your older children are still in the mood for more homes, visit **Hopemont,** the Hunt-Morgan House, 201 North Mill Street; (606) 253–0362 or 233–3290. Open March to mid-December. Located in Gratz Park, the county's oldest historic district, this well-appointed Federal style town house holds an impressive collection of porcelain and nineteenth-century Kentucky furniture. **The Waveland State Historic Site,** 225 Higbee Mill Road (606–272–3611), is an 1847 Greek Revival house built by Joseph Bryan, a grandnephew of Daniel Boone. Kids like peeking into the brick servants' quarters, the ice house, and the smokehouse.

Museums

Lexington Children's Museum, 401 West Main Street, Victorian Square; (606) 258–3253. While not as large as some big city museums, this could prove an entertaining respite for younger kids. The museum, with seven galleries of interactive exhibits, appeals to toddlers and preteens. Preschoolers head for the toys and educational games at the Beginnings Gallery. Older kids enjoy the Physics and Space Gallery, while the curious enjoy discovering "treasures" from the late 1800s to the 1960s at the History and Time Gallery.

Green Spaces

Lexington's many playgrounds and community parks have trained supervisors who plan and direct activities. The playgrounds are open Monday through Friday, 11:30 A.M.–8:30 P.M., June through August. Activities include movie nights, horseback riding, sports, and nature hikes. Call the Lexington Parks and Recreation Department (606–288–2900) for specific program information.

Jacobson Park, on Richmond Road, offers 216 acres, a stocked lake for fishing (permit required), paddleboat rental, and picnic shelters. **Masterson Station Park**, Leestown Road, covers 732 acres, and has football and soccer fields, jogging, and walking trails. The **Raven Run Nature Sanctuary**, Jacks Creek Pike (call 606–272–6105 or 606–288–2900 for directions), features 7 miles of hiking trails that lead visitors along streams and into meadows and woodlands. The park is open Wednesday through Sunday year-round.

Woodland Park, off High Street on Woodland, hosts Shakespeare in the Park, Woodland Arts Festival, Dance festival and Ballet Under the Stars during the summer months. The park also has a swimming pool, playground, and volleyball and tennis courts.

Tours

Maps for self-guided walking and driving tours of downtown Lexington and the horse farms are available from the Greater Lexington Convention and Visitors Bureau, Suite 363, 430 West Vine Street, Lexington, Kentucky 40507; (606) 233–1221 or (800) 84LEX–KY.

For a scenic tour of downtown, call **Carriage Rides** (606–259–0000); they will take you around in a horse-drawn buggy.

Shopping

Lexington offers several shopping areas, including the following.

Clay Avenue Shops, Clay Avenue off East Main, features an eclectic group of stores in a turn-of-the-century neighborhood. Specialty stores include children's fashions, custom stationery, yarn and needlework, furniture, jewelry, antiques, collectibles, and more. The **Festival Market**,

Lexington showcases many forms of art including exciting museums, unique art exhibits, and various performing arts groups that appeal to all ages and tastes. (Courtesy Greater Lexington Convention and Visitors Bureau)

325 West Main Street (606–254–9888), offers three floors of unique boutiques, shops, and eateries. Take a break from the shopping scene and ride Festival Market's carousel or sit back and watch the entertainers on the center stage. **Victorian Square**, 401 West Main Street (606–252–7575), is a block of renovated Victorian-era buildings whose shops include Laura Ashley, Talbots, Benetton, and Churchill Weavers.

Performing Arts
The **ArtsPlace**, 161 North Mill Street (606–255–2951), hosts numerous cultural events, including the Lexington Ballet, Lexington Philharmonic, Lexington Children's Theatre, the Opera of Central Kentucky, and Lexington Musical Theatre. The **Opera House**, 401 West Short Street (606–233–4567, ext. 236), hosts musicals, plays, ballet, and opera.

Golf
For a complete listing of Lexington's public golf courses, call the Lexington Parks and Recreation Department at (606) 288– 2900. Some public courses on which to enjoy the bluegrass are **Cabin Brook Golf Course**, Versailles Road (606–873–8404); **Campbell House Golf Club**

(606–254–3939); **Kearney Hill Links**, 3403 Kearny Road (606–253–1981). There's also **Marriott's Griffin Gate Golf Club**, 1800 Newtown Pike (606–254–4101) and **Shady Brook Golf** on Hutchinson Road (606–987–1544).

SPECIAL EVENTS

Festivals

For more information about these events, contact The Greater Lexington Convention and Visitors Bureau at (606) 233–1221 or (800) 845–3959.

January: Bluegrass Wheelchair Basketball Tournament, University of Kentucky, Seaton Building.

April: Rolex Kentucky Three-Day Event and the High Hope Steeplechase, both at Kentucky Horse Park.

May: Spring Premier Saddlebred Show, Kentucky Horse Park. Air Show, Blue Grass Airport.

June: Polo at the Park, Kentucky Horse Park. Annual Egyptian Event (features the Egyptian Arabian horse), Kentucky Horse Park. Festival of the Bluegrass, Kentucky Horse Park Campgrounds.

July: Shakespeare in the Park, Woodland Park. Mid-America Miniature Horse Show, Kentucky Horse Park. Festival of Appalachian Humor, Berea College Campus, call (800) 598–2563.

August: Big Hill Mountain Bluegrass Festival (VanWinkle Farm, 7 miles from Berea, 800–598–2563).

September: Senior Golf Classic, Kearny Hill Links. The Belgian Horse Classic and the $40,000 Lexington Grand Prix, Kentucky Horse Park. Grand Circle Meet at the Red Mile, the final leg of racing's triple crown, is held at Red Mile in late September or October.

October: Fall Classic Saddlebred Show, Kentucky Horse Park. Equifestival of Kentucky (various locations).

WHERE TO STAY

Kentucky Horse Park Campground, Kentucky Horse Park, 4089 Iron Works Pike, Lexington, Kentucky 40511; (606) 233–4303, ext. 257. This facility has 260 sites, each with electrical and water hookups, and picnic tables. The resort-like amenities also include a swimming pool, tennis and basketball courts, plus a recreation center, playground, grocery, and laundromat. This facility is open year-round.

Rooms at the **Best Western Regency Lexington**, 2241 Elkhorn Road, Lexington (606–293–2202 or 800–528–1234), include free continental breakfast. The **Campbell House Inn Suites and Golf Club**, 1375 Harrods-burg Road, Lexington (606–255–4281), is a 300-room hotel with seventy suites, tennis courts, and golf facilities. The **Radisson Plaza Lexington,** 369 West Vine Street, Lexington (606–231–9000 or 800–333–3333), has an indoor pool and a restaurant.

WHERE TO EAT

For family dining and American cuisine Kentucky-style—including lamb chops, veal cutlets, salmon coquettes, and country ham—head to **Rogers Restaurant** at 808 South Broadway; (606) 254–1077. The daily specials at **Ramsey's Diner**, 496 East High Street (606–259–2708), sometimes include cajun catfish and chicken dishes. For leg of lamb and country ham, try **Merrick Inn**, 3380 Tates Creek Road; (606) 269–5417.

DAY TRIPS

Toyota Plant Tours, 1001 Cherry Blossom Way, Georgetown; (502) 868–3027. What's a car assembly line really like? Travel 12 miles north of Lexington on I–75 to the Toyota Factory, and you'll find out. The tour, restricted to those eight years and older *with reservations*, features a thirty-five-minute tram tour of the factory, a fifteen-minute introductory film, and the opportunity to witness the behind-the-scenes construction of a Kentucky Camry. Admission is free. Tours are available year-round: Tuesday—8:30 A.M., 10:00 A.M., and noon; Thursday—8:30 A.M., 10:00 A.M., noon, and 2:00 P.M.

   Churchill Weavers, Box 30, Lorraine Court, Berea; (606) 986–3126 or (606) 986–3127. About 38 miles south of Lexington, Berea, a small community of artisans, bears the official designation "Folk Art and Craft Commonwealth of Kentucky." Churchill Weavers, founded by Carrol and Eleanor Churchill in 1922, is an interesting stop. One of the top handweaving studios in the United States, it dedicates itself to quality hand-made goods. Enjoy the daily tours of the loomhouse, and allow time to shop for blankets, scarves, and table linens in the gift shop.

   For more information concerning the **Berea crafts area**, including a map and directory, contact the Berea Welcome Center, 201 North Broad-way (606–986–2540), in the Old L and N Train Depot. Artisans at work here include potters, chair makers, stained glass artists, leather workers, jewelers, and wood workers.

   The **Nostalgia Station Toy Train Museum and Train Shop**, 279 Depot Street, Versailles (606–873–2497), is about 13 miles from Lexing-ton. Train buffs will appreciate such items as a Lionel girl's stove, and a

Lionel O gauge dealer display, as well as a gift shop crammed with books and train accessories.

Fort Boonesborough State Park, 4375 Boonesborough Road, Richmond (606–527–3131), is 26 miles outside Lexington and was the site of Kentucky's first fortified settlement in 1775. Part of Fort Boonesborough State Park features a reconstructed fort containing a variety of cabins, each with a craftsperson demonstrating a particular Colonial skill. Featured techniques include weaving, spinning, quilting, wood working, soap-making, candle-making, doll-making, and potting.

An orientation film, shown in the block house, introduces visitors to the frontier life of 200 years ago. In the park's museum, peruse a collection of Daniel Boone's possessions. Daniel Boone's original settlement was near Fort Boonesborough.

Save some time to hike the Boonesborough Historic Walking Trail, which passes fourteen sites detailing stories of early Kentucky settlers' rocky relations with local Indian tribes. One site recalls the capture of three young girls, including Daniel Boone's daughter, by a local Indian tribe. Find out the details of how Boone rescued his daughter.

The park has year-round camping, in-season miniature golf, and an outdoor pool.

Shaker Village of Pleasant Hill, 3500 Lexington Road, Harrodsburg; (606) 734–5411. Located 25 miles from Lexington, this landmark is a 2,700-acre preserve with thirty-three buildings from the original Shaker settlement begun in 1805. This outdoor living-history museum is believed to be the largest of its kind in the United States.

The structures, some dating back to 1809, reflect the Shaker credo of simplicity of function. Inside this compound costumed historians demonstrate and describe different aspects of Shaker life, including weaving and broom-making. The flat broom, the wooden clothespin, and the circular saw are all unique Shaker inventions. While you're there, take a good look at Shaker period furniture in the Centre Family House.

If you get hungry try the **Trustee's Office,** which serves breakfast and lunch as well as a family-style dinner and is noted for its cakes and pies. Reservations are a good idea.

For a change of pace, catch the *Dixie Belle,* a sternwheel riverboat at Shaker Landing. Available May through September, the one-hour trip along the Kentucky River provides an enjoyable respite and some scenic views of limestone cliffs and green shoreline.

The village is open daily from 9:30 A.M.–6:00 P.M. from April through late November; otherwise, hours vary. It's closed Christmas Eve and Christmas. For a special treat, stay on site. Overnight lodging is provided in fifteen of the restored buildings. Although each room keeps to its original Shaker simplicity, telephones, televisions, and private baths help modernize your quarters.

Wild Turkey Distillery, 1525 Tyrone Road, Lawrenceburg; (502) 839–4544. Here, 23 miles from Lexington, Kentucky's best bourbon has been distilled and aged for a century. Tours are offered Monday through Friday.

FOR MORE INFORMATION

Contact the **Greater Lexington Convention and Visitors Bureau**, Suite 363, 430 West Vine Street, Lexington (606–233–1221 or 800–84–LEXKY), for more information on Lexington, Kentucky.

Emergency Numbers
Ambulance, fire, and police: 911
Police department (nonemergency): (606) 258–3600
Fire department (nonemergency): (606) 254–1120
Emergency medical information, poison control, and twenty-four-hour pharmacy: Central Baptist Hospital, 1794 South Limestone (606–275–6100); and University of Kentucky Albert B. Chandler Medical Center, 800 Rose Street (606–233–5000)
Health care information, symptom assistance, and medical referral by registered nurses: Saint Joseph's free Ask-A-Nurse program; (606) 278–3444 or (800) 866–3444

26
HARPERS FERRY
West Virginia

On the night of October 16, 1859, John Brown led his band of twenty-one men on an abolitionist-inspired raid of Harpers Ferry. Brown's gang targeted the armory and several key strategic points throughout Harpers Ferry. Hoping to gain access to the munitions, Brown's gang envisioned their raid as the event that would spark a nationwide abolitionist movement. Although John Brown and the surviving members of his band were captured by Robert E. Lee, convicted of murder, treason, and conspiracy, and hanged, this small group's actions had an impact and are remembered in Harpers Ferry, a town of 308 residents. The Brown gang's abolitionist efforts, and their trial and punishment by their countrymen, foreshadowed the bloodiest years in the history of the United States. Sixteen months after John Brown's arrest and execution, the Civil War broke out. For its historical significance the lower part of town has been preserved as a living-history park, the Harpers Ferry National Historical Park.

The area surrounding the town, at the confluence of the Potomac and the Shenandoah rivers, affords scenic countryside and miles of hiking, including some paths along the Appalachian trail. A visit to Harpers Ferry puts you near a Civil War battle site, natural springs, and enjoyable white-water rafting rides.

GETTING THERE

By car take Interstate 81 to exit 12 and follow Route 340 to Harpers Ferry. The green and white signs lead to downtown Harpers Ferry where limited parking is available. It's often easier to follow the brown and white signs to the main entrance of Harpers Ferry National Historical Park Visitors Center, where there is a parking lot. A shuttle service operates between here and town. The park remains open every day of the year except Christmas and New Year's.

Amtrak (304–535–6346 or 800–USA–RAIL) stops in Harpers Ferry. An afternoon train leaves Washington, D.C., at about 4:15 P.M. MARC (Maryland Area Rail Commuter) (304–535–2578) is a commuter train line to Harpers Ferry. Both rail services use the Harpers Ferry train station on Potomac Street.

GETTING AROUND

Walking is the best way to see Harpers Ferry National Historical Park. Since the park occupies the lower portion of Harpers Ferry, which has only a few main streets, directions are easy to follow. The shuttle stop for the parking and visitors' center and the information center/bookstore is outside the Stagecoach Inn on Shenandoah Street. Two of the town's other important streets, High and Potomac, run perpendicular to Shenandoah Street. As street addresses are not easily visible, and not frequently used, find your way around town with a map obtained from the visitors' center, the information office on Shenandoah Street, or by writing to Harpers Ferry National Historical Park, P.O. Box 65, Harpers Ferry, West Virginia 25425.

Physically challenged travellers will find limited accessibility to some of the buildings and exhibits. Also, note that many of Harpers Ferry's sidewalks and steps are fashioned from cobblestone and brick; the uneven nature of these surfaces could pose a problem for some visitors and can prove to be a difficult obstacle for a baby stroller or wheelchair. For information on physically challenged accessibility, call the Harpers Ferry National Historical Park at (304) 535–6223.

WHAT TO SEE AND DO

Harpers Ferry National Historical Park, Harpers Ferry, West Virginia; (304) 258–6223. Encompassing all of Harpers Ferry's lower, downtown district, the National Historical Park has restored some buildings and tried to keep facades of others as they appeared in the town's most famous year, 1859, when John Brown and his group attempted their raid. With some imagination a visit to this pre–Civil War village captures the Harpers Ferry of John Brown and his contemporaries. Imagination is necessary because while the park exhibits convey the era, many of the town's stores have been turned into souvenir and craft shops. Some are interesting, and some are kitschy. You have to get beyond the commercialism to envision the nineteenth century, the era of slavery, and John Brown's bold attempt.

To help transport you back to the nineteenth century, the park has some rangers dressed in period costumes taking part in living-history

John Brown's Fort is one of the many nineteenth-century buildings you can tour in Harpers Ferry National Historical Park. (Photo by David Fattaleh/courtesy West Virginia Division of Tourism and Parks and the State of West Virginia)

demonstrations. More of these occur in the summer than at other times. Depending upon the availability of park rangers, interpreters may be in the dry goods store, the blacksmith's shop, the tavern, the confectionery, and the marshal/provost office. Historical tours and guided walks of the nature trails in the 2,300 acres are available throughout the summer, and sometimes during other seasons. Call ahead.

Among the most interesting exhibits and museums in town are the **John Brown Museum, John Brown's Fort**, the **Master Armorer's House**, the **Civil War Museums**, and **Black Voices from Harpers Ferry**.

After visiting the Information Center, the Shenandoah Inn, start at the **John Brown Museum**, at the opposite end of Shenandoah Street. The exhibits set the stage by explaining the complexity of the economic, cultural, and political issues of the era, and by displaying an 1859 map of the town.

Nearby is the **Master Armorer's House**, Shenandoah Street. Built in 1858 for the chief smith of the armory, it details the history of gun production. The armory that John Brown and his men seized was destroyed in 1861 to prevent its falling into Confederate hands. **John Brown's Fort**, Old Arsenal Square, at the intersection of Shenandoah and Potomac streets, is actually the firehouse where John Brown and his men barricaded themselves from the authorities. Col. Robert E. Lee and Lt. J.E.B. Stuart captured Brown and his "army of liberation" here on the morning of October 18th.

Civil War Museums, High Street, documents life in Harpers Ferry during the Civil War years. Exhibits emphasize the small, quiet town's transition to a war-torn village. Some of the documents, letters, and photographs of Harpers Ferry's citizens are moving testaments to the disruption of war.

Black Voices from Harpers Ferry, High Street, chronicles 250 years of African-American heritage through the diaries and letters of Harpers Ferry's African-American community. Many exhibits feature audio stations, which hold kids' interest. Also visit the grounds and buildings of the former **Storer College,** along Fillmore Street in upper Harpers Ferry. Established in 1867 this was the first institution of higher education for African Americans in this area. The college closed in 1955.

Along the footpath of the **Appalachian Trail,** which extends behind the **Black Voices from Harpers Ferry** museum, explore **St. Peter's Catholic Church,** built in the 1830s and still in use today. Don't miss the oldest structure in Harpers Ferry, **Harper House.** Built in 1782, it houses nineteenth-century furniture. Continue along the path away from town to the ruins of **St. John's Episcopal Church,** before reaching historic **Jefferson Point.** Stand where, in 1783, the former president proclaimed the view "stupendous." The **Harper Cemetery** has some good views, and old gravestones, which might interest older kids who won't be spooked.

John Brown Wax Museum, Shenandoah Street; (304) 535–6342. Depending upon how you feel about wax museums, this one can add to your understanding of John Brown and his importance. Through slides and other exhibits, the museum helps capture the spirit of John Brown's raid. The museum is open daily mid-March to December and on weekends during February and March.

Green Spaces

The famed **Appalachian Trail** that extends for more than 2,100 miles from Maine to Georgia splits and makes two passes through Harpers Ferry and over Maryland Heights creating 25 miles of scenic hiking trails. The **Appalachian Trail Conference Visitors Center** is in town at the corner of Washington and Jackson streets; (304) 535–6331. If you and your children are hardy hikers, don't leave town without setting foot on a bit of this historic trail.

Pick up the **Appalachian Trail** at the **Stone Steps** located just off High Street behind the **Black Voices from Harpers Ferry** museum. The trail cuts through the lower town and extends across the pedestrian footbridge which runs alongside the B & O Railroad tracks. Watch for signs leading to the Maryland Heights trail.

The Overlook Trail runs from Jefferson County, West Virginia, to Loudon County, Virginia. It includes Jefferson Point—named after the former president's 1783 visit, during which he remarked the site was "worth a voyage across the Atlantic." The Stone Fort Trail traverses Peters Mountain from Monroe county, West Virginia, to Giles County, Virginia, and passes by the ruins of a Civil War fortification.

Special Tours

Call **Ghost Tours** at (304) 725–8019 and stalk the streets looking for one of Harpers Ferry's many ghosts with a local guide. The guides for this privately operated tour prefer customers at least eighteen years old, but call and discuss the issue if you think your slightly younger teen would be interested.

Winding through town this one-hour tour has you looking for the ghost of Dangerfield Newby, a fellow raider and the first man killed in the botched John Brown Raid. Newby's body was mutilated by townsfolk, then left in an alley (Hogs Alley) where hogs feasted upon his corpse. Other ghosts who are presumed to haunt the town, though in a friendly manner, are the departed spirits of spies, soldiers, and a priest. Some date back to the Revolutionary era.

If interested, meet at the Back Street Cafe, Potomac Street, at 8:00 P.M. on Saturday nights in April, and at 8:00 P.M. on Friday, Saturday, and Sunday nights from May through November. Reservations required for large groups only.

For more history in your ear, try an **audio-cassette** tour, available from the Harpers Ferry National Historical Park at (304) 535–6298.

Shopping

Harpers Ferry has lots of shops from quaint to kitschy. The bookstore at the Information Center offers some of the best buys—good reads and picture books on the era, especially helpful for children. But the shop-til-you-drop set can take heart; the surrounding area has lots of possibilities. (See DAY TRIPS.)

SPECIAL EVENTS

Participant Sports

River rafting, tubing, canoeing, and kayaking are all popular diversions in the Harpers Ferry area. Always ask about safety precautions before riding the white-water, and match a run to your own capability. Here are some area white-water rafting companies and outfitters.

Blue Ridge Outfitters, P.O. Box 750, Harpers Ferry, West Virginia 25425; (304) 725–3444. Rivers: Potomac, Shenandoah. **River & Trail**

Outfitters, 604 Valley Road, Knoxville, Maryland 21758; (301) 695–5177. Rivers: Shenandoah, Potomac. **River Riders Outfitters Inc.**, Route 3, P.O. Box 1260, Harpers Ferry, West Virginia 25425; (304) 535–2663. Rivers: Shenandoah, Potomac, Tygart, Greenbrier.

Festivals and Seasonal Highlights

The following includes events for Harpers Ferry and the surrounding towns. The most popular festivals in Harpers Ferry are the October 1860 Election Celebration, where visitors interact with interpreters who stump nineteenth-century style, and the December Old Tyme Christmas celebration which features street carollers and nineteenth-century entertainers in period dress. For specific information on these events, contact the various towns' convention and visitors' bureaus.

January–February: Winter Festival of the Water, with a host of events highlighting Berkeley Springs and its history as a spa.

February: Mountain Lore Weekend and Toast to the Tap, an International Water Tasting and Competition in Berkeley Springs.

March–April: Murder Mystery Weekend at local inns in Berkeley Springs.

May: Potomac Eagle Scenic Rail Excursions begin and continue through fall in Romney.

June: Charles Town Spring Mountain Heritage Arts & Crafts Festival.

September: Charles Town Farmer's Market and Fall Mountain Heritage Arts and Crafts Festival. Bavarian Inn's Octoberfest in Shepherdstown.

October: Harpers Ferry hosts Election of 1860 Celebration.

November: Jefferson and Berkeley counties hold Over the Mountain Studio Tour of artists' craft studios.

December: Harpers Ferry Old Tyme Christmas celebration.

WHERE TO STAY

Harpers Ferry, West Virginia

Cliffside Inn, U.S 340 West, Harpers Ferry; (304) 535–6302. This hotel has an indoor and an outdoor pool, tennis courts, and a restaurant. The **Comfort Inn**, U.S 340 and Union Street, Harpers Ferry (800–221–2222 or 304–535–6391), offers free continental breakfast, a convenient location, and affordable prices. The **Hilltop House**, 400 Ridge Street, Harpers Ferry (304–535–2132) is a century-old restaurant and hotel with a casual atmosphere.

Berkeley Springs, West Virginia

The **Country Inn** offers rooms in the historic hotel, which are appointed with antiques, or updated motel-style rooms. Call (800)

822–6630 or (304) 258–2210. The facility has a restaurant, but the food is sometimes mundane. The **Cacapon Resort State Park** has 6,000 acres and a fifty-room stone lodge, where the accommodations are serviceable and inexpensive. There's a restaurant as well. Call (800) CALL–WVA or (304) 258–1022.

Coolfont Resort and Conference Center, not far from the town of Berkeley Springs, offers 1,200 acres of woods. The A-frame chalets are especially nice for families. They include kitchen facilities, and often two bedrooms. Guests enjoy the lake and the lap pool, but mostly come here to walk in the woods. Call (800) 888–8758 or (304) 258–4500.

Sharpsburg, Maryland

The **Inn at Antietam**, 220 East Main Street, P.O. Box 119, Sharpsburg, Maryland 21782 (301–432–6601), offers friendly hosts and a charming inn with comfortable Victorian pieces. On weekdays, it is suitable to bring children over the age of ten. On weekends, however, the inn caters to adults only. This former farmhouse is surrounded by the Antietam battlefield.

Shepherdstown, West Virginia

Bavarian Inn and Lodge, Route 1, Shepherdstown; (304) 876–2551. Shepherdstown is about 12 miles outside of Harpers Ferry. Set along the banks of the Potomac, the Bavarian Inn offers forty-two rooms overlooking the Potomac, each with a television. The Bavarian Inn's restaurant emphasizes German cuisine. Each fall the inn hosts Octoberfest.

WHERE TO EAT

Harpers Ferry

Try the **Mountain House Cafe**, High Street, Harpers Ferry; (304) 535–2339. The Mountain House offers sandwiches and salads. Across High Street from the Mountain House Cafe stands the **Garden of Food Restaurant**, High Street, Harpers Ferry; (304) 535–2202. They serve home-cooked specialties and sandwiches. **The Anvil Restaurant**, 1270 Washington Street (304–535–2142), offers American fare and a children's menu. It's located within the historic area.

Berkeley Springs

Maria's Garden Restaurant (304–258–2021) offers good, basic Italian fare.

Shepherdstown

Try the **Yellow Brick Bank Restaurant**, West German Street

(304–876–2208), where the interesting cuisine mixes American and Continental touches. Nancy Reagan liked to lunch here on a fine spring day when she was First Lady.

DAY TRIPS

Sharpsburg, Maryland

Antietam National Battlefield, Sharpsburg, Maryland; (301) 432–5124. This 960-acre park, about 18 miles from Harpers Ferry, is one of the best-preserved, least commercial, and most moving of all the Civil War battlefields. The September 17, 1862, battle fought here, an important Union victory, took the lives of more than 22,000 Americans; it was known as one of the most bloody battles of the war. Robert E. Lee led the Confederates against the Union's George McClellan who sent 87,000 Union soldiers into combat. On certain weekends from June to October, costumed interpreters talk about life for the Civil War soldier. Maps, markers, and self-guided tours are available. Also visit the **Antietam National Cemetery**, established in 1865. The Antietam Visitors Center, a mile north of Sharpsburg on I–65, has murals depicting the battle scene, a movie, and information about the park.

Berkeley Springs, West Virginia

Berkeley Springs is about 45 miles from Harpers Ferry. At the **Berkeley Springs State Park**, visit the site where George Washington bathed as a young surveyor. The springs also served as the hallowed waters of local Native American Indian tribes. Founded in 1776, Berkeley Springs calls itself the "country's first spa." Today the area is known for its affordable "tub and rub"—a soak in the mineral waters and a massage—available from the state park facility at the town square. You can enjoy the same mineral waters in more upscale surroundings at the **Renaissance Spa and Boutique** behind the **Country Inn** (800–822–6630 or 304–258–2210).

Each winter, starting in January, the town hosts a Festival of Waters and in February adds an international water-tasting competition. For information on the area, call (800) 447–8797 or (304) 258–9147. Golf, horseback riding, tennis, and golf are nearby at **Cacapon State Park** (304–258–1022 or 800–CALL–WVA).

Blue Ridge Outlet Center, I–81, exit 13, 315 West Stephen Street, Martinsburg; (304) 263–7467 or (800) 445–3993. Housed in a former woolen mill, this outlet center, while not huge, offers discounted prices on such name brands as **Carter's Childrens Wear, Dansk, Bass Shoe, Benetton, Donna Karan, Jones New York, London Fog, J. Crew, Anne**

Klein, and others. When you need to take a break, try the sandwiches at the **American Deli** or the hamburgers at the **Grill**. Nearby the **Pottery Outlet**, I–81, exit 13, 615 West King Street, Martinsburg (304–267–7500), offers discounted pottery.

Charles Town, West Virginia

For horse racing, venture to **Charles Town Races**, U.S 340; (304) 725–7001 or (304) 737–2323. It's in Charles Town just 5 miles from Harpers Ferry. Post time is 1:00 Wednesdays and Sundays, 7:00 P.M. Mondays, Fridays, and Saturdays, but call ahead.

Shenandoah National Park

From Harpers Ferry, follow U.S 340 south 60 miles to the Shenandoah National Park's closest entrance, Skyline Drive in Front Royal, Virginia. This park rides along the Blue Ridge Mountains and extends from Front Royal in the north 80 miles to Waynesboro in the south. Drawing from its Indian name, "Daughter of the Stars," the Shenandoah reaches a variety of different peaks from 600 feet at the north entrance to 4,050 feet at the summit of Hawksbill Peak. Outdoor families enjoy the horseback riding, the scenic views, and the hiking trails. A 94-mile stretch of the Appalachian trail crosses the park as well. Trail maps are available at park headquarters, visitor centers, and concession stands. Horses are available from May through October at Skyland. Check with the rangers for the free guided hikes, nature walks, and slide presentations. The Harry F. Byrd, Sr. Visitor Center (mile 51) at Big Meadows is open daily with a reduced schedule in January and February. The Dickey Ridge Visitor Center (mile 4.6) is open April through mid-November. Write to Shenandoah National Park, Route 4, P.O. Box 348, Luray, Virginia 22835; (703) 999–2229.

Shepherdstown, West Virginia

Shepherdstown, West Virginia, about 12 miles from Harpers Ferry, is one of the oldest towns in West Virginia. Originally settled by German and English farmers around 1730, Thomas Shepherd purchased the town in 1732. The steamboat had its first successful run here thanks to inventor James Rumsey. A monument stands along the Potomac commemorating the 1787 event. A stroll through town offers a look (from the outside mostly, except for commercial shops) of well-preserved late eighteenth- and early nineteenth-century buildings. Shepherd College has a lovely campus and may offer some activities for visitors. For more information on Shepherdstown, contact the Welcome Center, King Street (304–876–3325) or call the West Virginia Division of Tourism and Parks (800–CALL–WVA).

FOR MORE INFORMATION

For more information on the Harpers Ferry area, contact the Jefferson County Visitor and Convention Bureau, P.O. Box A, Harpers Ferry, West Virginia 25425; (800) 848–TOUR. Also contact the West Virginia Division of Tourism and Parks, State Capital, Building 6, Room 564 B, Charleston, West Virginia 25305; (800) CALL–WVA. Harpers Ferry National Historical Park, P.O. Box 65, Harpers Ferry, West Virginia 25425; (304) 535–6223 or 535–6029.

Emergency Numbers
Ambulance, fire, and police: 911
Jefferson County State Police (nonemergency): (304) 267–0000
Jefferson Memorial Hospital, 300 South Preston Street, Ranson, West Virginia; (304) 725–3411
Twenty-four-hour pharmaceutical needs and poison control: City Hospital, Dry Run and Tavern roads, Martinsburg, West Virginia; (304) 264–1000

27
HILTON HEAD
South Carolina

The well-heeled, well-connected, and just, plain choosey have been traveling to Hilton Head for years. Why? This island off the southern coast of South Carolina does a good job of balancing beach and wildlife areas with development. The result is 12 miles of white sand barrier beach, plus twenty-three golf courses, more than 300 tennis courts, fifty racquet clubs, and numerous resorts, all of which create a treasure trove of family delights.

GETTING THERE

If you choose to fly to Hilton Head, Savannah International Airport (912–964–0514), 45 miles south of Hilton Head Island, is the nearest major airport. American, Delta, USAir, and United offer daily flights to Savannah. USAir Express and American Eagle offer daily commuter flights from Charlotte and Raleigh direct to the Hilton Head Airport.

Amtrak (800–USA–RAIL or 912–234–2611) offers train service to Savannah (forty-five minutes from Hilton Head). Amtrak lines stop at the Savannah terminal, 2611 Seaboard Coastline Drive, six times daily. Trains originate from New York, Jacksonville, Miami, and St. Petersburg.

Traveling by car to Hilton Head Island, take I–95. Hilton Head Island is 40 miles east of I–95. Highway 278 leads to the island.

GETTING AROUND

Hilton Head Island is divided into plantation and village areas, both public and private. Destination areas are often labeled according to these plantation and village boundaries.

The best way to get around the island is by car. There are major rental

Hilton Head Island holds something special in store for every member of the family.
(Courtesy Hilton Head Island Chamber of Commerce)

car companies at the Savannah International Airport. In addition, among the car rental companies on the island are Ace Rent-A-Car (803–785–8545), Avis Rent-A-Car (803–681–4216), and Budget (803–689–4040).

Biking offers a practical and fun way to travel around Hilton Head. Also the island's hard, sand-packed beaches make biking suitable along the shoreline. Call the following establishments for bicycle rentals: The Beach Factory (803–686–6565), Cycle Center Rentals (803–686–2288), Fish Creek Landing (803–785–2021), Peddling Pelican (803–785–5470), and Sea Pines Bicycle (803–671–5839).

For taxi service, call Taxi World (803–681–TAXI).

WHAT TO SEE AND DO

As an island resort, Hilton Head offers the best of surf and turf. Families with kids will find it hard to exhaust Hilton Head's possibilities. From sand to sun, court sports to greens sports, there's something for everyone.

Beaches and Beach Activities

Hilton Head's 12 miles of beach offer white sand, swimming, sailboarding lessons, parasailing, jetskiing, and beaches for resort guests, There are also thirty-five public beach entrances with two main parking areas at Coligny Circle and Folly Field Road. **Sea Pines** allows visitors to enjoy its facilities for the day for a nominal charge.

Aside from swimming, beach diversions include a variety of water craft rentals. For powerboat rentals contact **Breakwater Adventures** (803–689–6800) and **Island Watersports of Hilton Head** (803–671–7007). **Fishcreek Rentals** offers canoe and rowboat rentals. For windsurfing fun, call **Windsurfing Hilton Head Island** (803–686–6996. They also rent kayaks and rollerblades. Breakwater Adventures and Island Watersports both rent waterskiing equipment, jetskis, and parasailing equipment.

For a day of fishing on the high seas, contact **Drifter Excursions** (803–842–9320), **Outdoor Resort-RV Resort and Yacht Club** (803–681–3256), and **South Beach Marina** (803–671–3060). To simply enjoy a sailing day on the ocean, call **Advanced Sail, Inc.** (803–686–2990). Advanced Sail offers private, daily, and sunset catamaran and sailboat charters. **Hilton Head Yachts, Ltd.** (803–686–6860) and **Island Watersports** (803–671–7007) also offer sailboat charters.

But don't forget the beaches and the simple pleasures. You can practice your "porpoise" stroke by swimming alongside real pods of friendly bottle-nosed dolphins who arch through the waves close to the Atlantic shore. Enjoy kite flying, crabbing, sand castle building, or simply relaxing in the sun to the sound of the surf.

For more information on Hilton Head Island's beaches, refer to the Hilton Head Island Visitor and Convention Bureau's *Hilton Head Island Vacation Planner*.

Golf

Ranked as one of the top golf and tennis destinations in the United States, Hilton Head lures avid sports enthusiasts who want quality facilities and pleasing views. Duffers should try the relatively new, and markedly novel **Robert Cupp Golf Course** at the **Palmetto Dunes Resort**, P.O. Box 5649; (803) 689–4100. Opened in the spring of 1991, this course puts a new angle on the game with geometrical designs, including angular sand traps and square greens. Among the places island regulars practice their swings is on the **Harbour Town Golf Links**, Sea Pines Plantation (803–671–2446), site of the annual, April PGA tour event, the MCI Heritage Classic.

Other courses include the two eighteen-hole **Arthur Hills** courses— one at Palmetto Dunes (803–785–1140), and the other at Palmetto Hall (803–689–4100). **Rose Hill Country Club**, Rose Hill Plantation (803–842–3740), and **Shipyard**, Shipyard Plantation (803–686–8802), both have twenty-seven holes of quality golf.

For miniature golf excitement head to **Legendary Golf** (803–686–3399) and **Pirate's Island Adventure Golf** (803–686–4001).

For reservations at all eighteen of Hilton Head's golf courses, call Tee Times (800–562–5532). For a complete listing of Hilton Head Island's eighteen golf courses, refer to the Hilton Head Island Visitor and Convention Bureau's *Hilton Head Island Vacation Planner.*

Tennis

To learn to lob and serve with the best, try the clinics and the private lessons at the island's posh tennis clubs. Four that made *Tennis Magazine's* 1991 list of the top 50 tennis clubs are **Port Royal Racquet Club,** Port Royal Resort (803–681–3322); **Sea Pines Racquet Club,** Sea Pines Plantation (803–842–8484); **Palmetto Dunes Tennis Center,** Palmetto Dunes Resort (803–785–1152); and the **Shipyard Racquet Club,** Shipyard Plantation (803–785–2313).

For some intensive instruction for you and your children, sign on for the Tennis University at the **Van Der Meer Tennis Center,** DeAllyon Avenue; (803) 785–8388 or (800) 845–6135. Besides lessons for adults, the center offers daily and weekly programs for ages three to five, six to eight, plus clinics and advanced programs for ages nine to sixteen.

For more information on Hilton Head's tennis facilities, refer to the Hilton Head Island Visitor and Convention Bureau's *Hilton Head Island Vacation Planner.*

Wildlife and Waters

When you want a break from such man-made pleasures as tennis and golf, sample the art of nature at Hilton Head. See deer, or possibly an alligator, as you walk along 7 miles of trails at the **Sea Pine Forest Preserve,** Sea Pines Plantation; (803) 671–3333. The forest preserve offers visitors a taste of South Carolinia wilderness. Bring along a picnic lunch. The preserve's two trails, the Indian Shell Ring Loop and the Waterfowl Pond Loop, are both self-guided nature walks, although during summer months an on-site naturalist is available to lead walks. With the help of informational signs, the trails transform a woodsy stroll into an educational tour. Check out the hayride tours on Tuesday and Wednesday afternoons, and the horseback rides. For reservations call (803) 671–2586.

A must-see stop in the park includes the Heritage Farm and its two functional old-style mills: the mule-powered cane mill, which grinds cane; and a windmill used for water pumping. The residents of the farm also demonstrate their organic farming techniques. Learn how these farmers grow peanuts, table greens, watermelons, and potatoes completely free of artificial substances. Cars and bicycles are not allowed inside the preserve.

For more information on the **Sea Pines Plantation Forest Preserve,** write or call Sea Pines, P.O. Box 7000, Hilton Head Island, South Carolina 29938; (803) 785–3333.

Be sure you see the plants and birds along the paths of the **Audubon-Newhall Preserve**, Palmetto Bay Road (803–785–3670), while touring its 50 acres of woods and wetlands. Walk through areas of saw palmetto, sapling live oak, thickets of bracken ferns, and fetterbush. Along the nature trail look for raccoon and deer prints, and mole tunnels. Although the Audubon-Newhall was designed as a self-touring refuge (self-guiding brochures are available inside the park), free guided tours of Audubon-Newhall are available on Saturdays during March and April at 10:00 A.M. and 11:00 A.M.

Look for snowy egrets, blue herons, the endangered wood stork, and white ibis, as well as raccoons and deer at the **Pinckney Island Wildlife Preserve**, entrance on U.S. 278, a half-mile west of Hilton Head Island (912–652–4415 or 803–842–9197). It's the largest refuge island in the South Carolina-Georgia area. Bring your own drinking water to Pinckney as there's none available on the island. Covering more than 4,000 acres of saltmarsh, forestland, brushland, and freshwater ponds, Pinckney is located between the island and the South Carolinian mainland. Cars are not allowed, so bring your bikes, as the 14 miles of trails make scenic bicycling and hiking paths. Pinckney Island is named after Charles Cotesworth Pinckney, who received the island from his father and lived there until 1824. C.C. Pinckney was a soldier in the Revolutionary War, a presidential candidate in 1804, and a signer of the U.S. Constitution.

Theater

On the island of Hilton Head, call **Hilton Head Playhouse**, on Dunnigans Alley (803–785–4878), and **The Island Theatre**, at Coligny Plaza (803–785–4468), for a current listing of stage productions. Call **Main Street Cinemas**, on Main Street near Hilton Head Plantation (803–681–8778), and **Park Plaza Cinemas**, at Park Plaza near Sea Pines Resorts (803–785–5001), for movie listings and times.

WHERE TO STAY

Hilton Head Island has a variety of lodgings, ranging from elegant resorts to more affordable home and villa rentals. The brand new **Crystal Sands**, Shipyard Plantation (803–842–2400 or 800–HOLIDAY), the first Holiday Inn Crowne Plaza resort in the continental United States, opened in March 1993. It combines the familiarity of the Holiday Inn chain with such family-friendly amenities as Camp Castaways for kids, and upscale touches including a spa and health club, twenty tennis courts, and twenty-seven holes of golf. Crystal Sands offers daily child care programs for ages three to twelve from Memorial Day through Labor Day, plus a modified program at other times. Call and ask to be sure. Supervised activities include arts and crafts, beach outings, nature walks, and teen scavenger hunts. For more information call (803) 842–2400.

The tried-and-true standard for luxury is the **Westin Resort**, Port Royal Plantation (803–681–4000 or 800–228–3000), the island's only five-diamond property. Pamper your family by booking one of the two- and three-bedroom villas, or rooms in the **Royal Beach Club** Concierge Wing which come with attentive service and a special lounge. In summer, the Westin offers Camp Wackatoo for ages four to twelve.

Sea Pines Plantation, 32 Greenwood Drive (800–845–6131), is a villa resort complex with its own nature preserve, plus golf and tennis facilities. In addition to junior tennis, golf, and sailing clinics, Sea Pines offers a full-day children's program complete with hayrides, miniature golf, fishing, and other outdoor activities for three to eleven year-olds from Memorial Day to Labor Day. During the off season, the children's program has limited hours. Call ahead.

On a moderate budget? Try the **Holiday Inn Oceanfront**, Pope Avenue at Coligny Circle, 1 South Forest Beach Drive, Oceanfront; (803) 785–5126 or (800) 456–4329. This hotel has one- and two-bedroom units on the beach, a pool, and golf and tennis packages. **Sea Crest Oceanside Inn** (803–785–2121 or 800–845–7014) is a ninety-one-room beachfront inn that offers conventional rooms, plus two-bedroom units with kitchen, and other efficiencies.

Villa rentals provide families with more space for less money, especially when these homes are shared with another family. For rental information, call **Adventure Inn Villa Rentals** (803–785–5151 or 800–845–9500), **Great Southern Vacations** (803–686–3375 or 800–542–5535), **Hilton Head Holidays** (803–689–5205 or 800–442–3442), **Vacation Villa Rentals of Hilton Head** (803–686–6226 or 800–654–7101).

For more information on Hilton Head's child care services, contact the Hilton Head Island Visitor and Convention Bureau at (803) 785–3673.

WHERE TO EAT

For a romantic, candlelit tete-a-tete without the kids, dine at the Westin's four-diamond **Barony Grill**; (803) 681–4000.

There are lots of places where it's fun to take the whole family, especially if your kids are older ones. The **Tavern-on-the Creek**, William Hilton Parkway on the island's north end (803–681–4591), draws crowds for its smoked fish, ribs, and steamed shrimp. This popular new spot is managed by the same team responsible for the success of another island favorite—the **Old Fort Pub**, 51 Skull Creek Drive; (803) 681–2386. (It's known for its low country cuisine, especially its oyster pies.) For casual dining with a marina view, try award-winning island chef Geoff Fennessey's new seafood restaurant, the **Kingfisher**, Shelter Cove Harbour; (803) 785–4442. Also try **Crazy Crab**, Harbour Town (803–363–2722), for reasonably priced seafood and a marina view. A special treat is Crazy Crab's low country *Crazy Crab Boil* (Alaskan crab legs boiled with sausage and sweet corn served with a baked potato).

The Hilton Head Island Visitor and Convention Bureau's *Hilton Head Island Vacation Planner* has an extensive listing of the island's many restaurants.

DAY TRIPS

Day trips from Hilton Head include **Savannah** (see the Savannah chapter), and a chain of islands called the **Golden Isles of Georgia**. These include **Jekyll Island, St. Simons Island, Sea Island, Sapelo, Blackbeard, St. Catherines, Cumberland**, and **Little St. Simons**. Each has a different personality. Jekyll Island, with 10 miles of beach plus golf and tennis courts, is a true resort area. Contact the Jekyll Island Welcome Center, 901 Jekyll Island Causeway (912–635–3636), for more information. St. Simons, which was a base for English ships as early as 1736, now offers visitors golf, fishing, and biking trails. Cumberland, accessible by ferry from Saint Mary's, Georgia (912–882–4335), was once the exclusive retreat of wealthy families. Now along with a few remaining private estates, and bed and breakfast inns, the island has more than 8,000 acres of wilderness available for day visits and camping. Kids love hiking the trails, admiring the dunes and forests, searching for wild horses, and from April to August, seeking the loggerhead turtles who lay their eggs along the beach. For more information contact the Cumberland Island National Seashore, P.O. Box 806, Saint Mary's, Georgia 31558; (919) 882–4335.

A good way to enjoy an extended exploration of some of these and other Georgia barrier islands is with **Wilderness Southeast**, 711 Sandtown Road, Savannah, Georgia 31410 (912–897–5108), a nonprofit group that emphasizes both education and fun. Among the trips are sea kayak expeditions to Little Tybee Island (minimum age sixteen) and, on Cumberland, a sea turtle watch and a hiking/camping trip (for both trips the minimum age is twelve).

Not part of the Golden Isles, **Dafuskie**, an island 4 miles south of Hilton Head and accessible by ferry from Hilton Head (call 803–681–7335), provides another interesting day trip. This is the island about which Pat Conroy wrote *The Water is Wide*. His book depicts the rural life-style of this isolated island where many inhabitants still speak

Gullah, a dialect combining Creole and English. Nonetheless, the resorts are arriving, including golf clubs at Melrose and Haig's Point, and soon, too, there will be beach homes and cottages. For now you can still take a walk and imagine life here in plantation days and at the turn of the century.

FOR MORE INFORMATION

A handy reference is the *Hilton Head Island Vacation Planner,* available from the Hilton Head Island Chamber of Commerce, P.O. Box 5647, Hilton Head Island, South Carolina 29938; (803) 785–3673.

Emergency Numbers
Ambulance, fire, and police: 911
Hilton Head Hospital, 35 Bill Fries Drive; (803) 681–6122
Although Hilton Head Island does not have a twenty-four-hour pharmacy, the Hilton Head Hospital's pharmacy remains open until 7:00 P.M.
Twenty-four-hour poison control: Palmetto Poison Center; (800) 922–1117

28
HUNTSVILLE
Alabama

Ever want to send your kids to the moon and back? Then come to Huntsville, where space exploration is a way of life. This small, friendly southern town has been making a name for itself as America's space capital since 1950 when Dr. Wernher von Braun and 117 German scientists arrived to develop rockets for the United States Army. The 16,000-person cotton town that von Braun joined has blossomed into a city of 180,000. The major family attractions here are the Space and Rocket Center and the living history museum Constitution Hall Village. Combine these educational activities with a hike or picnic at one of the beautiful surrounding parks.

GETTING THERE

Huntsville International Airport (205–772–9395) is 12 miles from downtown and services several national airlines with direct flights to Chicago, Washington, Dallas, and Atlanta. The most frequent flights are to Atlanta. Most major hotels offer a free shuttle service downtown.

Hunstville is easily reached by several highways. Take Highway 72 east from Memphis, Tennessee; or Highway 72 west from Chattanooga, Tennessee, to arrive at Huntsville, Alabama. I–65 south leads to Huntsville from Nashville, and I–65 north leads to Huntsville from Montgomery and Birmingham, Alabama. The Greyhound/Trailways downtown bus terminal is on the corner of Monroe and Holmes streets, one block from the Von Braun Civic Center and the Chamber of Commerce. Huntsville does not have Amtrak train service. The nearest Amtrak train (800–USA–RAIL) arrives in Birmingham, which is about one hour and forty-five minutes away by car.

GETTING AROUND

Most major car rental companies are represented at desks inside the airport. Driving is the easiest way to get around town. The Depot Trolley, 320 Church Street (205–539–1860), offers a thirty-minute trolley ride through downtown Huntsville. You can get off and reboard for free.

WHAT TO SEE AND DO

Space Attractions

U.S. Space and Rocket Center, 1 Tranquility Base; (205) 837–3400. The center is open daily 9:00 A.M.–6:00 P.M., summers 8:00 A.M.–7:00 P.M.; closed Christmas Day. Dubbed the showplace of America's space program, the U.S. Space and Rocket Center is Huntsville's biggest attraction. "Awesome" is what your kids will call this vast park, which offers real-life space thrills and features more than sixty hands-on exhibits. The facility houses the NASA Visitors Center, the Space Museum, the Shuttle and Rocket Park, the U.S. Space Camp Training Center and its Space Camp Habitat, an OMNIMAX movie theater, plus two gift shops, a cafeteria, and picnic grounds. This place offers a day or more of family fun. Begin by obtaining a map and brochure at the NASA Visitors Center at the entrance so you can plan your day's activities.

The Space Museum, behind the Visitors Center, takes you on a history trip through the progress of space technology. The highlight here is a full-scale, 43-foot Hubble Space Telescope originally constructed as NASA's major exhibit for the 1989 Paris Air Show. One side of the lengthy telescope is cut away to reveal circular lines of neon light that mark the path light travels from the telescope back to earth. Other favorites are the *Gemini* and *Apollo* spacecraft. Kids enjoy climbing in and playing astronaut.

Outside at the Rocket Park, be awed by the most comprehensive collection of rocketry in the world. You can't help but see the 363-foot-tall *Saturn V* rocket that launched twenty-seven men to the moon. This park centerpiece has been declared a National Historic Landmark. Visit the simulated moonscape adjacent to the *Saturn V* to peer at the craters and look at the lunar module.

The grounds also bloom with high-tech military equipment developed by the U.S. Army Missile Command. Gawk at the Pershing II and Hawk missiles and the Patriot missile used to destroy Iraqi SCUDs in the Persian Gulf War. The United States Air Force's sleek *SR-71 Blackbird* draws a crowd as well. Take a walk around this 99-foot-long jet, and imagine it screeching through the atmosphere at more than three times the speed of sound.

More than sixty hands-on exhibits will keep your kids busy at the U.S. Space and Rocket Center. (Courtesy Alabama Bureau of Tourism and Travel)

The **Centrifuge** exhibit, a family favorite, offers an introduction to astronaut training as it prepares you for the "G" forces of launch and reentry, three times the force of the earth's gravity. Stars and planets surround you while you experience the same training as some high-performance jet pilots. For more space forces, observe the **Neutral Buoyancy Simulator,** a 40-foot-deep tank where astronauts experience weightlessness.

There's more space technology at the **Shuttle Park,** which displays the only full-scale Space Shuttle exhibit in the U.S.A., one formerly used to test procedures for the launching of the first shuttle from Florida. At the adjacent **Shuttle Liner Simulator,** sit down and get ready to enact a space voyage that has you docking with an orbiting space station.

Blast off to the movies at the **Spacedome Theater** whose 67-foot domed screen and OMNIMAX films make you feel you're floating in space. Be sure to warn younger kids about the sensations created by the huge screen, and remind them to simply close their eyes if they feel scared or queasy. A nice bonus for families: movie tickets are included in the price of admission.

NASA Bus Tour. Older children will appreciate this ninety-minute tour, included in your admission ticket, which departs from the Space Museum and travels to **Redstone Arsenal** and then to the **Marshall Flight Center** laboratories to see NASA engineers at work.

Redstone Arsenal, south of the Space and Rocket Center, is the birth-place of many of the Space Center's displays. This vast military post on the site of former cotton fields houses NASA's Marshall Space Flight Center and the Army Missile Command, which is currently conducting research on such projects as a "Star Wars" missile defense system. The Patriot missile, hero of the Persian Gulf War, was created here, as was the Redstone, America's first rocket, used to launch the *Explorer I* satellite into the Earth's orbit in 1959.

Marshall Space Flight Center, at Redstone Arsenal, is NASA's rocket base where Wernher von Braun and his team of German scientists constructed the *Saturn V* rocket that launched three men to the moon in 1969. The tour includes a close-up view of actual NASA engineers at work on the future Space Station.

Established in 1982 to encourage children to pursue careers in the space-related sciences, the **U.S. Space Camp,** Space Habitat, U.S. Space and Rocket Center (800–63–SPACE), has been expanding ever since. The facility features programs for all ages, including a family space camp and a new Aviation Challenge program on jet flight. Preregister for these overnight camps.

The space programs, which offer varying levels of astronaut training, culminate in a simulated space shuttle mission. Feel like an astronaut on a space walk when you strap on the Five Degrees of Freedom simulator which floats you above the ground, or discover the bounce of a real moon walk with the Microgravity Training chair that springs you forward.

U.S. Space Camp, for fourth to sixth graders, is a five-day introduction to space science and exploration. U.S. Space Academy, Level I, for grades seven through nine, offers a five-day intensive astronaut and mission training session. U.S. Space Academy, Level II, for grades ten through twelve, is an eight-day program featuring an extended duration simulated shuttle and space station mission. With Aviation Challenge, future jet pilots in grades seven–nine train for land and water survival and enact a simulated jet mission based on the Navy's "Top Gun" training.

But the fun is not for kids only. With Aviation Challenge adults can let the little kid in them take over as they work the controls of a big jet. Parent and Child Space Camp, featured on selected weekends May through early September, lets parents and children ages seven to eleven enjoy a space adventure together. Sign on and your kids will never again think of you as dull.

Two space camp programs are for adults only. The Adult Space Academy, for ages nineteen and older, is a three- or eight-day program, and the Space Academy for Educators is a five-day program that can culminate in graduate credits.

Call (800) 63–SPACE for information and applications.

Historic Museums and Sites

Constitution Hall Village, 400 Madison Street; (205) 535–6565 or (800) 678–1819. Go from high-tech space back to 1819 when Alabama became the twenty-second state to join the Union.

Costumed interpreters dressed in nineteenth-century garb guide you on a ninety-minute tour of several authentically decorated Federal period buildings. Children will find more to look at than antiques. There's a whole village bustling with the activities of the season. An old-fashioned carpenter constructs furniture in Constitution Hall while a pressman generates copies of the 1819 declaration of statehood. In the nineteenth-century kitchen visitors watch food being prepared the old-fashioned way while outside by the vegetable garden a villager washes clothes in an iron pot.

Call the village at (800) 678–1819 for a list of changing seasonal events and special children's activities. Spring events often include a Mother Goose tea party, a fleece-preparing demonstration, and an herbal cooking and healing workshop that shows you how to handle these nineteenth-century spices of life.

For another touch of the nineteenth century, peruse **Harrison Brothers Hardware Store**, Courthouse Square (205–536–3631), whose shelves simulate their 1897 look. Kids appreciate the hodgepodge array of hardware and goods, including local arts and crafts.

Huntsville Depot Museum, 320 Church Street; (205) 539–1860. At this train depot built in 1860, you discover the industrial history of Huntsville. Highlights include a robotic stationmaster, telegrapher, and engineer, and graffiti that dates to the Civil War.

Older children interested in furniture might like the **Weeden House Museum**, 300 Gates Avenue; (205) 536–7718. This restored Federal house was home to Maria Howard Weeden, a nineteenth-century artist and poet. Constructed in 1819 it is the only home in the Twickenham Historic district open as a museum.

Burritt Museum and Park, U.S. 431 East; (205) 536–2882. Obtain a fuller perspective of Huntsville from the heights of Monte Sano, where a prominent physician constructed this fourteen-room mansion. Inside, museum displays include local Indian artifacts and early medical instruments. Outdoors, the park offers 167 acres of trails to explore, some of which lead to a blacksmith shop, a smokehouse, a log cabin, and a picnic area.

Parks and Gardens

Take time out when you're downtown for a stroll through **Big Spring International Park**, between the courthouse square and the Von Braun Civic Center. Kids especially like the red Oriental bridge that spans the lagoon.

For more of the art of nature, instead of high-tech or historical happenings, walk along the grassy trails of the **Botanical Garden**, 4747 Bob Wallace Avenue; (205) 830–4447. This thirty-five-acre park offers a profusion of roses, day lilies, and dogwoods in season. **Ditto Landing Marina,** U.S. 231 South at the Tennessee River (800–552–8769), is a 253-acre park south of the city with picnic tables, campgrounds, and boat docks for public use.

Performing Arts

The **Von Braun Civic Center,** Clinton and Monroe streets, is the hub of Huntsville's entertainment and houses a sports arena, concert hall, and playhouse. For information regarding the center's events, call (205) 533–1953. For information on Huntsville's cultural activities, call the Arts Council at (205) 533–6565.

Huntsville Museum of Art, Von Braun Civic Center, Clinton Avenue (205–535–4350), features temporary and permanent exhibitions of paintings, prints, and sculpture.

Tours

Historic Huntsville Walking Tour. Pick up a guide to this do-it-yourself tour from the Huntsville Convention and Visitors Bureau; (800) SPACE–4U. The comprehensive tour of the Twickenham district takes you past one of the largest concentrations of antebellum houses in the South, while the somewhat newer Old Town district features mainly Victorian-era architecture. More than fifty sites are detailed in the tour, including the Weeden House Museum, the Harrison Brothers Hardware Store, and many private residences.

Alistair Vineyards Tours, Hurricane Valley; (205) 379–3527. For a pleasant Saturday outing, tour this wine vineyard 15 miles north of Huntsville. It's open Saturdays only.

SPECIAL EVENTS

Unless otherwise specified, call the Convention and Visitors Bureau (800–SPACE–4U) for additional information.

March: Finnegan's Parade celebrating St. Patrick's Day.

April: Huntsville Pilgrimage when a selection of the city's historic nineteenth-century homes are open for tours.

May: Panoply at Big Spring Park, a performing and visual arts fair featuring Huntsville-area artists and such guest performers as African-American dance ensembles, musicians, and actors.

Summer Series: Monday night big-band Gazebo Concerts in Big Spring Park.

July: Fireworks Celebration at the Milton Frank Stadium.

September: At the Hurricane Valley Harvest Festival, stomp the native grapes at this celebration of food and wine. On Old Fashioned Trade Day, downtown Huntsville goes back half a century to the time when merchants set up booths at the town square. The third Friday and Saturday listen to the tunes of the best pickers at the State Fiddling and Bluegrass Convention. On the third Sunday delight in the Mountain Dulcimer Festival at the Burritt Museum.

October: At the Indian Heritage Festival, members of five native tribes demonstrate crafts and dances.

December: Holiday Parade of Lights on the Tennessee River. Holiday Homes Tour in the Twickenham Historic District.

WHERE TO STAY

The **Huntsville Hilton,** 401 Williams Avenue (205–533–1400 or 800–544–3197), located downtown near the train depot, offers special packages. The **Huntsville Marriott,** 5 Tranquility Base, with slightly higher rates, is located on the grounds of the Space and Rocket Center. Call (205) 830–2222 or (800) 228–9290.

Other possibilities are the **Holiday Inn—Research Park,** 5903 University Drive (205–830–0600 or 800–465–7275), or the **Hampton Inn Huntsville,** 4815 University Drive (205–830–9400 or 800–HAMPTON). Smaller hotels centrally located between downtown and the space center include the **Brooks Motel,** 3800 Governors Drive (205–539–6562) and the **Parkway Motel,** 2101 South Memorial Parkway (205–536–8511).

The U.S. Space and Rocket Center has an on-site RV campground. Call (205) 837–3400 for more information. For a complete listing of area accommodations, call the Convention and Visitors Bureau at (800) SPACE–4U.

WHERE TO EAT

Among the recommended eateries in downtown Huntsville is **Eunice's Country Kitchen** (205–534–9550), specializing in southern country ham with biscuits and gravy. The **Village Inn On the Square** (205–533–9123) features home-cooked soups, plus salads and sandwiches. **Lofton's Huntsville Hilton** (205–533–1400) is a good dinner spot for seafood and steaks.

The **Cafe Berlin** (205–880–9920), a little farther out, serves German specialties. **Greenbrier Restaurant** (205–351–1800 or 205–351–9779) features barbecued fare, plus catfish and other seafood.

DAY TRIPS

Along Alabama's **Black Heritage Trail**, the landscape comes alive with a tale of tears and triumphs. This self-guided tour, available through a brochure from the Alabama Bureau of Tourism and Travel (800–ALA–BAMA), takes you on a drive throughout the state, pointing out scenes of historic importance.

Take a long weekend to trace African-American history from Selma to Montgomery to Tuskegee. In Selma travel the route the freedom marchers took on March 7, 1965, to the Edmund Pettus Bridge, where armed police confronted them. Go back a century in struggle to the Old Live Oak Cemetery, where ex-slaves are buried.

In Montgomery, visit the moving Civil Rights Memorial which lists the names of approximately forty people who died in the 1955–1968 struggle for racial equality. Then head to the Dexter Avenue King Memorial Baptist Church, the first pulpit for Dr. Martin Luther King, Jr., and imagine the future that Dr. King envisioned from this altar.

In Tuskegee, tour The Oaks, Booker T. Washington's home; the George Washington Carver Museum, which features the laboratory where Carver experimented with uses for peanuts; and the grounds of Tuskegee University, a formidable institution begun by ex-slave Booker T. Washington as a single school for thirty students.

The brochure highlights many other statewide sites, including scenes of struggle in Birmingham, black Civil War soldiers buried in Mobile, and the black infantry battles of 1864 at the Fort Morgan Historic Site in Gulf Shores.

FOR MORE INFORMATION

Visitor Information Centers

Huntsville/Madison County Convention and Visitors Bureau Tourist Information Center, 700 Monroe Street: (800) SPACE–4U.

Huntsville Parks and Recreation: (205) 535–6400.

Emergency Numbers

Ambulance, fire, and police: 911

Huntsville Fire Department (general information): (205) 532–7401

Huntsville Hospital: (205) 533–8020; twenty-four-hour Emergency Room: (205) 533–5600

Huntsville Police: (205) 532–7210

Poison Control Hotline: (800) 462–0800

Twenty-four-hour pharmacy: Huntsville Humana Hospital; (205) 532–5710

29 & 30
DOUBLE DELIGHTS: MIAMI, KEY BISCAYNE, FORT LAUDERDALE, AND THE EVERGLADES,
Florida

Visitors to Miami frequently stop in nearby Key Biscayne (both are in Dade County) before going just 30 miles north to Fort Lauderdale, in Broward County. It makes sense to discuss these destinations as a package.

The beaches in Miami and Fort Lauderdale have been attracting families for decades. But even the most avid beachcomber needs a day in the shade. Inland, there's a southern Florida for families that features kid-pleasing science centers, colorful parrots, wide-grinning alligators, performing dolphins, and vibrant modern art. Whether you need a break from the sun, a rainy day lift, or just a follow-your-fancy day trip, here are some suggestions for indoor, off-the-shore, and "other" Florida family fun in Miami, Key Biscayne, and Fort Lauderdale.

GETTING THERE

Miami International Airport (305–876–7000), only 7 miles from downtown Miami, is served by many airlines. Supershuttle (305–871–2000) offers twenty-four-hour service to and from Miami International Airport. Find the customer relations representatives located outside the baggage claim area.

Greyhound serves five stations in the Greater Miami Area: North Miami Beach, Miami Beach, Downtown, Miami International Airport area, and Homestead. Call Greyhound Bus Line at (305) 374–7222 or (800) 531–5332.

Amtrak, Miami Station, 8303 NW Thirty-seventh Avenue; (305) 835–1205 or (800) USA–RAIL. Tri-Rail (in Florida dial 800–TRI–RAIL) offers commuter rail service from Miami to West Palm Beach and Fort Lauderdale. Tri-Rail connects with Metrorail for downtown and south Miami service. Kids under five ride for free.

The closest airport to Fort Lauderdale is the Fort Lauderdale/Hollywood International Airport, 1400 Lee Wagener Boulevard, Fort Lauderdale; (305) 359–6111.

GETTING AROUND

Visitors to Miami have several public transportation options, although renting a car may still be the easiest for families. All Miami's public transportation services offer discounts for the physically challenged, senior citizens, and students holding specified Metrorail, Metrobus, and Metromover permits. Metrorail is an elevated 21-mile rail system serving downtown Miami, Hialeah to the west, and Kendall to the south. Metrorail connects to Metromover, Metrobus, and Tri-Rail. Metromover's individual motorized cars loop downtown Miami. Service includes Bayside Marketplace, Miami Arena, the Cultural Center, and the Miami Convention Center. Metrobus operates daily and on weekends. Call (305) 638–6700, TDD 638–7266 (metrobus) for information on these public transportation services.

Check the newspapers before you leave for low rates on rental cars as companies frequently advertise specials. Because of demand, it's wise to book your rental car before you leave home.

Rental car companies include: Alamo Rent-A-Car, 3355 NW Twenty-second Street (305–633–6076 or 800–327–9633); Avis Rent-A-Car, 2330 NW Thirty-seventh Avenue (305–637–4900 or 800–331–1212; Budget Rent-A-Car, 3901 NW Twenty-eighth Street (305–871–3053 or 800–527–0700); Hertz Rent-A-Car, 3795 NW Twenty-first Street (305–871–0300 or 800–654–3131). There are several taxicab companies, including American Taxi/Key American Taxi (305–947–3333) and Metro Taxi in North Miami (305–888–8888).

Tri-Rail connects Fort Lauderdale with Miami and West Palm Beach (305–728–8512 or 800–874–7245). Amtrak (800–USA–RAIL) stops at Deerfield Beach, Fort Lauderdale, and Hollywood.

WHAT TO SEE AND DO

Some attractions are still recovering from the damaging effects of Hurricane Andrew, which hit the area in the fall of 1992. Although most have rebuilt, and reopened, phone ahead to determine which facilities are only partially operational, or closed.

Beaches and Key Biscayne

Miami. Miami's 10 miles of beach stretch from South Pointe Park and continue northward to Sunny Isles Beach at 192nd Street. For convenience, it's easiest to head for the beach nearest your lodging. Pack for the day, and don't underestimate the sun's power. Kids and parents need hats, cover-ups, and sunscreen. Ask the concierge at your hotel about renting a beach umbrella for shade, or check with the local concessions.

From May to September on Friday nights, **Friday Night Live** brings evening entertainment to South Pointe Park. The festivities include street performers, a mini petting zoo, live music, and carriage rides. Call (305) 673–7730.

For a change from the sand outside your hotel door, head for two family-friendly parks in Key Biscayne, a quieter stretch just over the Rickenbacker Causeway. **Bill Baggs/Cape Florida State Recreation Area,** 1200 South Crandon Boulevard, Key Biscayne (305–361–5811), a 400-acre park on the tip of Key Biscayne is famous for its Cape Florida Lighthouse built in 1825. With a tour, you can climb inside. But, beware, there are lots of stairs. The wide, long beach is inviting, and lifeguards are on duty. The grove of Australian pine trees offers shade.

This is a good place for quiet beach days, and biking—bring your own bikes. But take the occasional gate house warnings about mosquitoes seriously. Sometimes this place swarms with these pesky insects.

Crandon Park, 4000 Crandon Boulevard, Key Biscayne; (305) 361–5421. This public park has 3 miles of beach, a golf and tennis center, a picnic area shaded by sea grape trees, a baseball field, and lots of green spaces.

While you're in Key Biscayne, visit the **Miami Seaquarium,** 4400 Rickenbacker Causeway, Key Biscayne; (305) 361–5705. Come home to the tanks that trained everybody's favorite, 1950s television dolphin— Flipper. During shows at the Miami Seaquarium, his descendants still twist, dive, glide, and, of course, "dance" to "Surfin' USA." These performances are among the park's highlights. Be sure to check the schedule for times. Although the tanks are being repaired following Hurricane Andrew, brilliantly colored fish still dart through exotic coral formations as they swim through the Reef Aquarium. It's also fun to follow the feeding frenzy of the sharks at the Reef Tank.

Broward County. **Fort Lauderdale.** Along Fort Lauderdale's 7 miles of beaches, the spring break tradition took shape and became legendary for thousands of high school and college kids. While these sun hopefuls still come, their numbers are fewer because local officials have made a concerted effort to discourage students and attract families.

The beautiful beaches of Miami and Fort Lauderdale offer hours of family fun and relaxation. (Courtesy Greater Fort Lauderdale Convention and Visitors Bureau)

The **Hollywood** area, between Fort Lauderdale and Miami, offers a particularly nice 6-mile stretch of beach that includes a broadwalk, a paved walkway that extends for 2½ miles and features a bicycle lane. This is a great place for beach strolls and bicycling.

Dania. The **John U. Lloyd State Park**, 3 miles south of Fort Lauderdale, is a 244-acre park with sandy beaches, nature trails, and boat rentals. Another popular park is the **Hugh Taylor Birch State Recreation Area,** Sunrise Boulevard and A1A, which also has nature trails, beaches, and boating.

Miami Museums

In addition to communing with nature on Miami's beaches, you can visit interesting museums that reveal the nature of art and history.

Miami Museum of Science and Space Transit Planetarium, 3280 South Miami Avenue; (305) 854–4247. Fun at the Museum of Science includes such head-turning illusions as seeing your noggin served on a platter, your feet flying, and your shadow frozen. Then try to fix the perpetual faucet, or keep a straight face in the distorting mirrors. With more than one hundred hands-on exhibits, this museum truly makes science fun. Outside there is a small nature wildlife area. The Space Transit Planetarium also offers a variety of interesting shows for the star-struck.

Allow at least two hours, or longer if you plan to see a planetarium show. The Space Transit Planetarium also hosts laser and astronomy shows. For show times call the Cosmic Hotline: (305) 854–2222.

Historical Museum of Southern Florida, 101 West Flagler Street; (305) 375–1492. The Miami Dade Cultural Center houses the Historical Museum of Southern Florida. Here your kids learn about Miami before condos. At the Historical Museum the tropical dreams of Miami's days from Indians to the 1940s resort era come alive. Kids ride cannons, board trolleys, and dress up in fancy Henry Flagler-era gaiety. For a view of the city lazing down under a sunset, book ahead for a moonlight canoe dinner trip around Biscayne Bay. Ask for the brochure *Traditions: South Florida Folk Life,* which describes an ongoing program of demonstrations, workshops, and lectures on crafts, folk music, and architecture.

Check out the changing art exhibits at the **Center For the Fine Arts,** 101 West Flagler Street; (305) 375–3000. Major exhibits are showcased here.

The **Miami Youth Museum,** Bakery Center, 5701 Sunset Drive (305–661–ARTS), while small, really does live up to its label as a "hands-on cultural arts experience." Changing exhibits have included such kid-pleasers as *Buenos Días, Cuba,* a recreation of Cuba, circa 1902, complete with La Bodega (grocery store), a bohio (farmhouse), and Cuban craftsmen such as cigar rollers. KIDSCAPE, a permanent exhibit, lets children eighteen months to third grade crawl, climb, and pretend to be dentists and supermarket shoppers.

Vizcaya Museum and Gardens, 3251 South Miami Avenue; (305) 233–5197. Built in 1916 as James Deering's winter residence, this Italian Renaissance–style villa now showcases fifteenth- to nineteenth-century furnishings and decorative arts. The antique-filled rooms and the ten acres of formal gardens with fountains are likely to interest teens, not tots.

American Police Academy Hall of Fame, 3801 Biscayne Boulevard; (305) 573–0070. The facility displays more than 10,000 law enforcement items, including police vehicles and weapons. Visitors see what a jail cell and an electric chair really look like, and can take part in solving a crime.

Zoos, Parks, and Green Spaces

Again, since many outdoor installations were damaged by Hurricane Andrew, call ahead to be sure of the status of each attraction.

Miami Metrozoo, 12400 SW 152nd Street (Kendall Area); (305) 251–0400. Leapin' lizards, this is one of the top zoos in the United States. The facility is recovering from the devastation of Hurricane Andrew. The Metro Zoo features animals in natural environments, confined by moats and landscaping rather than barred cages. With more than one hundred animal species on display, there's a lot to see. Highlights include the fascinating white Bengal tiger, a family of gorillas, the Caribbean flamingo lake, the free-flight aviary with trees full of tropical birds, plus Asian River Life, an exhibit that recreates an exotic jungle setting complete with mist, drumbeats, bamboo, and a 6½-foot Malayan water monitor, one of the world's largest lizards.

At PAWS, the children's zoo, visit the petting area, see an elephant show, and climb aboard for an elephant ride. At Ecology Theatre, guides teach children about such critters as alligators, rats, and snakes. Use the monorail to minimize walking, and go early to stay out of the afternoon sun.

Biscayne National Underwater Park, P.O. Box 1369, Homestead, Florida; (305) 247–7275. While hit by Hurricane Andrew, this park has reopened. Here, just a forty-five-minute drive from downtown Miami, you'll find more than 20 miles of reefs. Biscayne National Underwater Park encompasses more than 180,000 acres, only 8,800 of which are land.

You can tour this park on your own, but taking a guided boat tour is much more fun. Captain Ed Davidson's four-hour glass bottom boat tour gives you time to snorkel the coral reefs, looking for striped, mottled, and brightly colored fish. Family forays are encouraged. With shallow waters, and wind-protected reefs, this is a good place for your pre-schooler's first snorkel. With parental guidance and a flotation vest, kids as young as four have grabbed their first peek at sea life. For these excursions, contact the Biscayne Aquatic Center, P.O. Box 1270, Homestead, Florida 33030; (305) 247–2400.

Parrot Jungle and Gardens, 11000 Southwest Fifty-seventh Avenue; (305) 666–7834. This facility also was hit by the hurricane, but it's back in business, and replanting. Take a walk on the wild side through these landscaped grounds filled with cages brimming with parrots. In this park, subtropical garden paths lead you through thirteen landscaped acres, where palm, date, and cypress trees create a jungle feel for the plumed, perky, and exotically colored parrots.

Appropriately, most of the cages are at easy eye level. The regularly scheduled animal shows provide interesting facts and colorful antics. Cockatoos ride tricycles, and macaws engage in chariot races. An animal show adds typical Miami wildlife—raccoons, reptiles, and flying squirrels. Be sure to stop at the posing area. Kids can't resist having their picture taken with gaily colored macaws perched atop their heads and arms. This is a great shot for the family album.

Monkey Jungle, 14805 Southwest 216th Street; (305) 235–1611. Within the safety of caged walkways, visitors view hundreds of primates roaming free in replicas of their tropical habitats. Monkey Jungle's three daily shows feature trained chimps and monkeys.

Fairchild Tropical Garden, 10901 Old Cutter Road; (305) 667–

1651. A stroll through this eighty-three-acre garden, landscaped with plants and trees from around the world, is peaceful. Kids can touch, and smell—but not pick—the plants. Wander through a rain forest, sunken garden, and a rare plant house. If you tire, try the narrated tram tour.

Special Tours

Art Deco Tour, Miami; (305) 672–2014. More than 800 buildings in South Beach boast 1930s and 1940s pastel colors, neon, porthole windows, and other Art Deco adornments. Start your self-guided walking or driving tour at Ocean Drive and Fifth Street, and continue on Ocean Drive to about Twenty-third Street. This bustling area features many renovated hotels, cafés, and trendy shops. The streets are filled with roller bladers, and passersby taking in the scene. Small kids might find this noisy and crowded while teens may love the "scene." A visitor's guide and walking tour are available from the Welcome Center.

Cruises. A number of family-oriented cruise lines embark from the Miami–Fort Lauderdale area, making it easy to explore the region before or after you sail. Some of the family-friendly cruise lines include Royal Caribbean Cruise Lines, Carnival, and NCL.

Shopping

In Miami, head for the **Bayside Marketplace**, 401 Biscayne Boulevard; (305) 577–3344. Located on sixteen waterfront acres, the mall offers everything from vendor stalls to boutiques, and classy shops to department stores, including Neiman Marcus and Saks Fifth Avenue. Sightseeing cruises can be arranged from Bayside's marina.

Sawgrass Mills, 12801 West Sunrise Boulevard, Sunrise; (305) 846–2300 or (800) FL–MILLS. Come to this megadiscount mall with 2½-million-square-feet just 12 miles north of Ft. Lauderdale. Some people dub this a shopping event. There are good buys on school clothes and plenty of stores for browsing.

Performing Arts

Miami offers many cultural attractions. Among the possibilities: Coconut Grove Playhouse, 3500 Main Highway (305–442–4000), offers innovative productions and two stages. The **Florida Shakespeare Company**, The Minorca Playhouse, 232 Minorca Avenue (305–446–1116), performs the Bard's works and also features a children's theater on Saturdays at 11:00 A.M. and 2:00 P.M. The **Greater Miami Broadway Series**, Jackie Gleason Theater, 1700 Washington Avenue (305–673–8300), hosts touring companies of Broadway shows.

The **Miami City Ballet**, Dade County Auditorium, 2901 West Flagler Street (305–532–4880), presents world-class ballet. The **Ballet Flamenco**

La Rosa, 1040 Lincoln Road (305–672–0552), presents flamenco dance as well as ballet. The **Ballet Theatre of Miami**, 1809 Ponce de Leon Boulevard (305–442–4840), offers professional ballet.

For opera, there's the **Greater Miami Opera**, Dade County Auditorium, 2901 West Flagler Street; (305) 854–1643. For classical music, buy tickets for the **New World Symphony**, Gusman Center for the Performing Arts, 174 East Flagler Street (downtown). Lincoln Theatre, 555 Lincoln Road (305–673–3331) offers concerts by gifted young musicians. The **Florida Philharmonic Orchestra** also performs at the Gusman (800–226–1812) and the Jackie Gleason Theater, 1700 Washington Avenue (305–673–7311). Ask about their concerts for children. Check with the **Concert Association of Florida**, 555 Seventeenth Street, Miami Beach (305–532–3941), for information concerning upcoming concert and performing arts events.

TicketMaster (305–358–5885) has tickets to major sporting, theatrical, and concert events. Call ahead for locations.

SPECIAL EVENTS

Spectator Sports

For basketball, watch the NBA's **Miami Heat**, Miami Arena, 721 Northwest First Avenue (305–577–HEAT); the **University of Miami Hurricanes** (University of Miami Ticket office at 305–284–2655 or sports marketing at 305–284–2400); and **Florida International University's Golden Panthers**, University Park, Southwest Eighth Street and 107th Avenue (305–FIU–GAME).

For football, the **Miami Dolphins**, an NFL team, hold forth at Joe Robbie Stadium, 2269 Northwest 199th Street; (305) 620–5000. The **University of Miami Hurricanes** play at the Orange Bowl Stadium. For tickets, contact the University of Miami Ticket office; (305) 284–2655, or sports marketing at (305) 284–2400.

Baseball fans can enjoy seeing one of the National League East's newest teams, the **Florida Marlins**. For a schedule or special baseball and hotel packages, contact the Greater Fort Lauderdale Convention and Visitors Bureau at (800) 22–SUNNY.

Participatory Sports

Fishing. **Deep sea and freshwater fishing** are year-round sports. For boat charter information, contact the Greater Miami Convention and Visitors Bureau (800–283–2707) and the Greater Fort Lauderdale Convention and Visitors Bureau (305–765–4466).

Golf and Tennis. This is the land of golf and tennis. Besides the courses and courts affiliated with your hotel or resort, Miami has several public golf and tennis facilities. Tee Time Services offers a twenty-four-hour reservation line for golf (305–669–9500). For information about public golf and tennis, contact the Metro-Dade County Parks and Recreation Department (305–579–2676) or the City of Miami Beach Parks and Recreation Department (305–673–7730).

Bicycling. Ask your hotel staff about the nearest shop that rents or lends bicycles. One in the Art Deco district is **Cycles on the Beach**, 713 Fifth Street; (305) 673–2055.

Festivals and Seasonal Highlights

January: Blockbuster Bowl (NCAA Football bowl game in Joe Robbie Stadium). Orange Bowl Football Classic (NCAA Football National Championship Game). Art Deco Weekend Festival. Taste of the Grove, in which Coconut Grove restaurants provide music and food. At the Beaux Arts Festival of the Arts, more than 240 artists present their wares. Enjoy dancing, floats, and music during the Martin Luther King, Jr., Parade and Festival. At the Annual Jewish Film Festival, watch a week's worth of noted movies.

February: Black Heritage Month Celebration features a month of special events at area museums. The Annual Homestead Championship Rodeo and Parade presents an old-fashioned rodeo. The annual Miami Film Festival is another chance to watch the best in film. The Miami Beach Festival of the Arts also offers plenty of family-friendly events.

March: Kick up your heels at the annual Southeast Florida Scottish Festival and Games. The Carnival Miami/Calle Ocho, the nation's largest Latin-American festival, features a 23-block street party. Tennis enthusiasts like the Lipton International Players Championships, the world's fifth largest tennis tournament. The Dade County Youth Fair and Exposition, which continues into early April, showcases award-winning student exhibits.

April: Dade Heritage Days celebrates the history and ethnicity of the region. The Annual Nicaraguan Music Festival highlights music and food. The Annual Japanese Spring Festival features Japanese and Asian food, music, and demonstrations.

May: At the International Hispanic Theater Festival, which continues into June, works by Hispanic playwrights are performed.

June: At the annual Miami/Bahamas Goombay Festival, the largest black heritage festival in the United States, enjoy live entertainment, dancing, sailing events, arts and crafts, and events celebrating Bahamian settlers in Miami.

July: Pops By the Bay gives you headline performers and the Florida Philharmonic Orchestra for three weekends.

August: Miami Reggae Festival features Caribbean music, culture, and food.

September: Festival Miami offers international music in more than twenty concerts. There's more music at the Taste of Jazz Festival which presents South Florida's best jazz artists. Chocolate lovers will like the Fontainebleau Hilton's Annual Chocolate Festival and Fair.

October: The month-long Hispanic Heritage Festival has folklore, dancing, food, and music. Cornucopia of the Arts showcases young talent in the arts, dance, and music; performers include the Miami Youth Orchestra. The Metrozoo hosts the Red Ribbon Halloween Festival and Haunted House.

November: The Junior Orange Bowl Festival has eight weeks of cultural and sporting events for kids and teens.

December: The Orange Bowl Festival, Miami's largest festival, runs until February and features sailing, tennis tournaments, and the Orange Bowl football classic.

WHERE TO STAY

The Miami area offers various accommodations, including motels, hotels, and resorts. Here are some picks with a range of prices.

Key Biscayne

The Sonesta Beach Hotel Key Biscayne, 350 Ocean Drive, Key Biscayne; (305) 361–2021 or (800) 343–7170. Just across the causeway from Miami, this hotel in Key Biscayne offered good facilities only a short drive from the city's bustle. Although the property was severely damaged by Hurricane Andrew, there are plans to renovate, rebuild, and reopen in December 1993. This is good news for families because this hotel is known for its comprehensive and innovative kids' program. The complimentary kids' program for ages five to thirteen runs from 10:00 A.M. to 10:00 P.M. year-round. Besides beach games, scavenger hunts, and arts and crafts, the program takes kids off to see such attractions as the zoo, parrot jungle, and science museum. The teens' program during holiday weeks features windsurfing and tennis clinics. Packages are available.

Miami Beach

Holiday Inn - Oceanside, 2201 Collins Avenue, Miami Beach; (305) 534–1151 or (800) 356–6902. This beachfront resort with tropical gardens is near the Art Deco district. Some families find the noise and bustle of the Art Deco district interesting, but they would rather visit than lodge here.

The Alexander All-Suite Luxury Hotel, 5225 Collins Avenue, Miami Beach (305–865–6500 or 800–327–6121), offers families suite space on the ocean. Another all-suite property is the Crystal Beach Club Hotel Suites, 6985 Collins Avenue, Miami Beach; (305) 865–9555 or (800) 423–8604.

The **Doral Ocean Beach Resort**, 4833 Collins Avenue, Miami Beach
(305–532–3600 or 800–22–DORAL), is a big, glitzy oceanfront resort,
with all the amenities. At times, there are children's programs, but call
first. The **Days Inn—Oceanside**, 4299 Collins Avenue, Miami Beach
(305–673–1513 or 800–356–3017), has an oceanfront location and reasonable rates.

Sunny Isles Beach

Farther north in the Sunny Isles Beach area, try the **Beacharbour Resort Hotel**, 18925 Collins Avenue; (305) 931–8900 or (800) 643–0807.
This oceanfront resort attracts families as does the **Marco Polo Resort
Hotel**, an oceanfront property, 19201 Collins Avenue, Sunny Isles Beach;
(305) 932–2233—Florida/(800) 432–3664—United States/(800)
327–6363.

Fort Lauderdale

One choice is **Guest Quarters Suite Hotel**, 2670 East Sunrise Boulevard; (305) 565–3800. Many of these suites have balconies overlooking
the intracoastal waterway. The **Howard Johnson Oceans Edge Resort**,
700 North Atlantic Boulevard (305–563–2451), is across the street from
the beach. **Marriott's Harbor Beach Resort**, 3030 Holiday Drive
(305–525–4000 or 800–222–6543), sits beachfront and offers in-season
children's programs.

For small lodgings obtain the brochure *Greater Fort Lauderdale Superior Small Lodgings*. Some of these efficiencies and rental apartments offer
refrigerators, kitchens, and more space for your money. Call the Convention and Visitors Bureau at (305) 765–4466.

WHERE TO EAT

Miami's cuisine rivals such cities as San Francisco, Chicago, and New
York. Caribbean and Latin American influences add spice to south
Floridian cuisine. The following is a partial list of inexpensive, family
oriented restaurants.

Fuddruckers serves up "the world's greatest hamburgers" along with
sandwiches, chicken, fish, hot dogs, and taco salads. You'll find them at
3444 Main Highway, Coconut Grove (305–442–8164); 7800 Southwest
104th Street, Kendall (305–274–1228); and 17985 Biscayne Boulevard,
Aventura (305–933–3572). Teens will love **Harry's Bar**, at the Ritz Plaza
Hotel, 1701 Collins Avenue in the Art Deco district; (305) 534–3500.
This 1950s-style diner has a soda fountain and Wurlitzer jukebox. **Uncle
Sam's Music Cafe**, 1141 Washington Avenue, Art Deco district
(305–532–0973), is in a record shop and features ribs, chicken wings, and

charbroiled burgers. **Sierra's Cafe**, 600 Brickell Avenue (305–374–2551), is a family-style restaurant downtown serving homemade Latin cuisine. For Cuban fare, try **Yuca Restaurant**, 177 Giralda Avenue, Coral Gables; (305) 444–4448. Baby back ribs in spicy guava sauce, and pan seared grouper fillet touched with cumin, pumpkin seeds, and orange sauce are two favorite dishes. **Wolfie's Gourmet Deli Restaurant**, 2038 Collins Avenue, Art Deco district (305–538–6626), has been serving pastrami and other deli delights since 1947; open twenty-four hours. **Cafe Tu Tu Tango,** CocoWalk, 3015 Grand Avenue, Coconut Grove (305–529–2222), is fashioned after an artist's loft and serves a wide variety of dishes, from pizza to lobster quesadilla and Jamaican spiced chicken wings.

For more dining and lodging options, obtain *Destination Miami and the Beaches,* from the Greater Miami Convention and Visitors Bureau, 701 Brickell Avenue, Suite 2700, Miami (800–955–3646 or 305–539–3063).

Fort Lauderdale

Fort Lauderdale has an array of restaurants. Besides the chain restaurants, here are some local favorites to try. **Fisherman's Wharf**, 222 Pompano Beach Boulevard, Pompano Beach (305–941–5522), offers seafood and grilled hamburgers served on the pier. **The Pelican Pub**, 2635 North Riverside Drive, Pompano Beach (305–785–8550), has a casual ambience and fresh fish.

Two places vie for the title of best barbecue in Fort Lauderdale. Some prefer **Ernie's Bar-B-Que**, 1843 South Federal Highway (305–523–8636), whose specialties include conch chowder and barbecue on Bimini bread. Others vote for **Hotz Bar-B-Que Shanty**, 4261 Griffin Road (305–581–9085).

A popular twenty-four-hour eatery is **Lester's Diner**, 250 State Road 84, Fort Lauderdale; (305) 525–5641. It's famed for its 14-ounce cup of coffee, which parents on a long drive might appreciate. **Shooter's Waterfront Cafe U.S.A.**, 3033 Northeast Thirty-second Avenue, Fort Lauderdale (305–566–2855), is a lively, noisy place, serving American fare with some Oriental and Mexican touches.

DAY TRIPS

Fort Lauderdale

With 7 miles of beaches, and lots of attractions, Fort Lauderdale, just 30 miles north of Miami, is worth a day trip, or a stay of its own. For a novel way of getting around, try **Water Taxis** (305–565–5507). The kids will love traveling on this eclectic collection of cabin cruisers and glass bottom boats that take visitors to attractions along the Intracoastal Waterway and the New River. Hotel pick-up can be arranged as well.

Here are some attraction highlights.

Butterfly World, Tradewinds Park, 3600 West Sample Road; (305) 977–4400. This three-acre park featuring more than 150 species of butterflies is the first of its kind in the United States. Look through the windows of the breeding laboratory to watch the butterfly life cycle. Kids stare wide-eyed when they catch a butterfly emerging from its cocoon. The Insectarium displays exotic bugs, including giant beatles and tarantulas. But the highlight is the Tropical Rain Forest. In the netted, main aviary, thousands of live species of delicate, brilliantly colored butterflies flit through the air. Allow extra time to sample the miniature golf course and petting zoo at Tradewinds Park.

Museum of Discovery and Science and Blockbuster IMAX Theater, 401 Southwest Second Street, Fort Lauderdale (305–467–MODS or for IMAX information 305–463–IMAX). This new—opened in November 1992—science museum has seven interactive exhibit areas. *Florida Ecoscapes,* a "bilevel ecology mountain," recreates such habitats as beach, living reef, underwater grotto, barrier island, mangrove estuary, and swamp. Each terrain features different fauna and animals indigenous to the particular surroundings. For children ages three to five, Kidscience offers interactive exhibits. A favorite is the climb up and the slide down the musical staircase.

In Sound, another exhibit area, children whisper, scream, sing, or shout to change colors and shapes. KaleidoVision is an innovative sound-sensitive, walk-in kaleidoscope. Choose Health makes kids aware of fitness, nutrition, and substance abuse. They may also find out about rockets and outer space in Space Base. Kids also love the MMU (Man Maneuvering Unit) space jet pack, which lets them step into a simulated antigravity environment and challenges them to perform simple tasks. With Moon Voyager kids control a mock spaceship. No Place Like Home informs visitors about responsible energy consumption and conservation here on planet Earth. You should also visit the Travelling Exhibit Hall to view the most recent interactive and educational exhibits on tour. The new Blockbuster IMAX Theater shows films on screens five stories tall.

Fort Lauderdale Museum of Art, One East Las Olas Boulevard, Fort Lauderdale; (305) 763–6464 (for recorded events) or (305) 525–5500 (for more information). Inside the Museum of Art, the colors of the CoBrA artists shine brilliantly. These canvases of a group of post–World War II painters from Copenhagen, Brussels, and Amsterdam splash the walls with vibrancy. But begin your tour at Art Amaze, a gallery geared to explaining the lines and language of twentieth-century art to children. These eye-popping works include a polka dot merry-go-round and Andy Warhol's Mick Jagger portrait. Check the monthly Children's Openings (Saturday, 10:00 A.M. to noon) for special hands-on introductions to shows.

Black Broward. Available from the Greater Fort Lauderdale Convention and Visitors Bureau (305–765–4466), the *Visitors Guide to Black Broward* is a brochure that lists several places of historic importance, along with special events, festivals, and a list of black-owned businesses.

Seminole Reservation, U.S. 441 at Stirling Road; (305) 961–4519. The Seminole Indians moved close to Hollywood in the eighteenth century. Now, at the Seminole Native Village in Hollywood see native displays of arts and crafts and learn about Indian culture and history. The Seminole Tribal Fair and Rodeo is held in January and comes complete with alligator wrestling, snake shows, and hand-made crafts.

Davie Rodeo Arena, 6591 Southwest Forty-fifth Street, Davie; (305) 797–1166, hosts a rope-'em and ride-'em rodeo every Wednesday at 7:00 P.M. Somehow the horse lovers settled in Davie, a town with good western wear and gear stores. At **Yankee Stadium,** 5301 Northwest Twelfth Avenue, Fort Lauderdale (305–620–5000), watch the Yankees warm up during spring training for the regular season.

Additional Day Trips

Everglades National Park, Everglades National Park Boat Tours, P.O. Box 119, Everglades City; (800) 445–7724 (in Florida), (800) 233–1821 (out of state). Everglades National Park, P.O. Box 279, Homestead; (305) 247–6211. Twenty miles from Miami you can experience the kind of unspoiled natural beauty that existed long before Florida's resort and condo development. These rivers of grass harbor alligators, crocodiles, and herons, all of which you can see if you hike, bike, canoe, drive, or board a guided tram or boat through these 1.4 million acres. They include fresh and saltwater areas, snaking rivers, wetlands, mangrove forests, and truly impressive expanses of tall grasses.

Bring binoculars to catch sight of osprey, herons, pelicans, eagles, and many other species of birds. Pick up a brochure at the Visitor's Center and use it as your guide to natural wonders, wildlife, and stimulating walking tours. And remember, it's hot here. Be sure to wear a hat, and use insect repellant, especially in summer when the mosquitoes are thick. Fortunately, guided boat trips do give you a breeze in addition to a water view.

FOR MORE INFORMATION

For more information, contact the Greater Miami Convention and Visitors Bureau, 701 Brickell Avenue, Suite 2700, Miami, Florida 33131; (800) 283–2707 or (305) 539–3063. The Activity Line by Van Dee (305–557–5600) features information on dining, special events, and attractions and is available twenty-four hours a day in English, Spanish, German, French, Swedish, and Portuguese. For Fort Lauderdale information, contact the Greater Fort Lauderdale Convention and Visitors Bureau, 200 East Las Olas Boulevard, Suite 1500, Fort Lauderdale, Florida 33301; (800) 22–SUNNY or (305) 765–4466.

Emergency Numbers

Ambulance, fire, and police: 911

Emergency medical care in Miami: Around The Clock Medical Center, 3097 Northeast 163rd Street, North Miami Beach; (305) 940–9000; Jackson Memorial Hospital, 1611 Northwest Twelfth Avenue; (305) 585–7304 or (305) 585–1111

Twenty-four-hour pharmacy in southern Miami: Walgreens, 5731 Bird Road; (305) 666–0757. In northern Miami: Walgreens, 12295 Biscayne Boulevard; (305) 893–6860.

Emergency medical care in Fort Lauderdale: North Broward General Hospital, 303 Southeast Seventeenth Street, Fort Lauderdale; (305) 355–4888.

Twenty-four-hour pharmacy in Ft. Lauderdale: Eckerds Pharmacy, 1711 South Andrews Avenue, Fort Lauderdale; (305) 462–8185.

Physician referral: Dade County Medical Association; (305) 324–8717

Poison Control: call the local hospital emergency rooms or Tampa Bay General Hospital; (800) 282–3171.

31
NASHVILLE
Tennessee

Nashville is known as the home of country music. Come for the singing, but stay for the other attractions such as the science museum, the toy museum, the botanical gardens, and the Cumberland River. Then head out of town for drives in the rolling hills, and visit Chattanooga for its top-rated aquarium.

GETTING THERE

Nashville Metropolitan Airport, about 8 miles from downtown (615–275–1675), serves American, American Eagle, Comair, Delta, Northwest, Southwest, TWA, United, and USAir. Downtown Airport Express (615–275–1180) offers shuttle service between the airport and downtown. Rental cars are available at the airport. Companies include Avis Rent-A-Car (615–361–1212) and Hertz Rent-A-Car (615–361–3131). Driving from the airport to downtown Nashville, take I-40W.

Amtrak does not offer service to the Nashville area. The Southern Greyhound Lines (615–256–6141) stops at their Nashville terminal, Eighth Avenue and McGavok Street.

Major roads into Nashville are I–65, which runs north-south into Kentucky and Alabama, and I–24, which runs northwest into Kentucky and Illinois and southeast into Georgia. I–40 runs east-west across the state and accesses Knoxville, Nashville, and Memphis.

For a different trip, cruise your way into the heart of Nashville on a riverboat cruise aboard a paddle wheeler. While the Delta Queen Steamboat Company (504–586–0631 or 800–543–1949) has no special programs for kids, older children and teens may like the river scenery and the shore stops.

GETTING AROUND

Nashville's public bus service, the Metropolitan Transit Authority (MTA—615-242-4433), operates buses throughout the county. For van transportation for the physically challenged, call (615) 351-RIDE. Try a downtown trolley ride with the Nashville Trolley Company; call (615) 242-4433.

Among the taxicabs available are Checker Cab (615-254-5031), Nashville Cab (615-242-7070), and Yellow Cab (615-256-0101).

WHAT TO SEE AND DO

Attractions

Nashville's answer to Disney World is **Opryland USA**, 2802 Opryland Drive; (615) 889-6611. This huge entertainment complex spreads over 120 acres. One of the most popular family attractions is the theme park **Opryland**. Aside from the typical water rides (try the Grizzly River Rampage) and roller coasters (hold on tight when you ride Chaos and the Screamin' Delta Demon), Opryland offers dozens of shops filled with country souvenirs, and restaurants serving finger-lickin' down-home Southern fried chicken and barbecued ribs.

Don't just take advantage of the rides, though your kids will love them; use this visit to introduce your children to country music, even if you remain a die-hard Beatles fan. Check the schedule of live performances as stars sing frequently. Be sure to see Country Music USA, a toe-tapping tribute that takes in country's roots as well as today's headliners. Other shows feature gospel, bluegrass, rock 'n' roll, and children's music. Opryland USA also hosts the **Grand Ole Opry**, the country's oldest radio program, which takes place daily in the Grand Ole Opry House.

Kids like the Opryland Kid's Club Show performed by entertainers ages nine to twelve. Magic delights when Professor U. B. Sharp does slight-of-hand tricks in his Magical Musical Marvel Mobile. Other just-for-kids' treats are the tubes, mazes, and slides near General Jackson's showboat, and the boat ride and playhouse at the Big G Kid Stuff.

For a change of pace, try a scenic day cruise on the Cumberland River aboard the *General Jackson Showboat,* or come on board for an evening dinner cruise. Sign on for a Grand Ole Opry Sight-seeing Tour and drive by Music Row, home of some of Nashville's country crooners, and go backstage at the Grand Ole Opry. You might see some country stars sing for free at a taping of one of the Nashville Network's (TNN) cable shows. Call TNN Information Services at (615) 883-7000.

If you still have energy and time after all the rides and foot-stomping

Country Music USA, a toe-tappin' tribute to country music of yesterday and today, is a show you won't want to miss. (Courtesy Nashville Convention and Visitors Bureau)

shows, visit one of the Opryland museums. **Minnie Pearl's Museum** tells the story of this performer's life, and the **Roy Acuff Musical Collection and Museum** has memorabilia of this country legend.

If you plan to stay in Nashville awhile, consider purchasing a three-day Opryland USA Passport, which can save you money.

Museums and Historical Sites

Nashville knows music, and visitors won't want to miss the city's tribute to country rhythms at the **Country Music Hall of Fame**, 4 Music Square East; (615) 255–5333. See everything from a film detailing the life of Patsy Cline, to Elvis Presley's solid gold Cadillac, to Garth Brook's stage outfits. Check out a real recording studio and admire the legends on the Walkway of the Stars.

But Nashville offers Southern history as well as country songs. Visit the **Belle Meade Plantation**, 110 Leake Avenue; (615) 356–0501. At the "Queen of Tennessee Plantations," kids often have their own specially guided tour while you meander through the 1790 log cabin, explore the smokehouse, and visit the thoroughbred stables. Be sure to bring a picnic lunch so you can enjoy the sun and the landscaped grounds.

Pay tribute to an American hero at **The Hermitage**, home of the seventh President of the United States, Andrew Jackson. It's at 4580 Rachel's Lane, Hermitage (615–889–2941), about 12 miles east of Nashville. Discover the family side of Old Hickory as you stroll the grounds of the mansion, and tour the house which has several original furnishings as well as period pieces. Peruse the Andrew Jackson Center which acquaints you with Jackson's life through a film and exhibits.

If past presidents bore your young kids, then visit the **Nashville Toy Museum**, 2613 McGavok Pike (615–883–8870), instead. You may grow nostalgic as you exclaim, "I had a doll just like that one." Don't worry, though, your kids will tolerate you as they will be busy ogling the toy trains, ship models, fuzzy bears, matchbox cars, and toy soldiers on parade. These are just some of the more than 1,000 antique and "old" playthings on view.

At the **Cumberland Science Museum**, 800 Ridley Boulevard (615–862–5177), children try on new clothing and new ideas. In the Japanese Room kids wear a kimono, at the Curiosity Corner they participate in science demonstrations, and at the planetarium they explore the stars.

At the **Tennessee State Museum**, Polk Cultural Center, 505 Deaderick Street (615–741–2692), legends come down to life-size through artifacts, and Tennessee pioneer history is portrayed. See Sam Houston's guitar, Davy Crockett's rifle, and Andrew Jackson's inaugural top hat along with a gristmill, covered wagons, and a log cabin.

Green Spaces and Parks

Embark on a city safari at the **Nashville Zoo**, 1710 Ridge Road Circle, Joelton; (615) 370–3333. Look at the Siberian tigers, discover Vietnamese pot-bellied pigs; and at the Children's Petting Zoo, feed a baby capuchin monkey and ride on an elephant. This zoo features more than 500 animals and such nice touches as a 14-foot observation tower at the African Savannah, which lets you get eyeball-to-eyeball with a giraffe.

The **Grassmere Wildlife Park**, 3777 Nolensville Road (615–833–1534), is the home of such native Tennesseans as the gray wolf, the black bear, and the bald eagle. As you walk the trails, enjoy the natural setting. Enjoy the art and the gardens at the **Tennessee Botanical Gardens and Museum of Art**, 1200 Forrest Park Drive; (615) 356–8000. (The place is also known as **Cheekwood**, the namesake of former owners of this estate.) Inside the mansion browse the collection of Worcester porcelains and examine authentic Oriental snuff bottles. Cheekwood hosts a variety of special exhibitions, which have included local quilters and Rodin sculpture. Call for an update.

Step outside the mansion and gaze on fifty-five acres of boxwood, nine gardens, deep emerald woodlands, and sparkling fountains. Seasonal delights vary from the flaming fall foliage to the spring and summer flowers, and winter's bark and berry plants.

In town, **Centennial Park**, West End and Twenty-fifth Avenue (615–862–8431), has an interesting oddity, a full-size reproduction of the ancient Greek Parthenon.

Performing Arts

The whole family can chuckle at the **Jim Ed Brown Family Theater,** 2620 Music Valley Drive; (615) 872–7528. They serve up live music and comedy every Tuesday through Sunday, plus snacks for the youngsters. Those who laugh at slapstick comedy may like the **Nashville Country Music Revue**, Celebrity Theatre; (615) 889–0800. **Chauffin's Barn—A Dinner Theater,** 8604 Highway 100 (615–646–9977), gives you a play with your food. **The Tennessee Performing Arts Center** at 505 Deaderick Street (615–741–7975) is a multitheatrical complex that includes the Tennessee Repertory Theatre (615–244–4878) and the **Nashville Symphony Orchestra** (615–329–3033).

Special Tours

With **Grand Ole Opry Tours** (615–889–9490), trek down Music Row and go backstage at the Opry. Take your pick of day or evening excursions on the **Belle Carol Riverboat** (615–244–3430), which travels the Cumberland River and serves a Southern buffet dinner. **American Sightseeing of Tennessee, Inc.** (615–256–1200), offers a wide range of trips from sunset tours to sights of Star Country. Kids under six are free and ages six to twelve are half-price.

SPECIAL EVENTS

Music City hosts a variety of festivals. For updated happenings, call the Nashville Convention and Visitors Bureau; (615) 259–4730.

January: The Nashville Boat and Sport Show at the Nashville Convention Center features fishing seminars, boats, and marine recreation displays.

February: The Annual Americana Spring Sampler Craft, Folk Art, and Antique Fair has exhibits, lectures, and antique dealers from thirty states. At the Heart of the Country Antiques Show near the end of the month, a variety of textiles, folk art, and furniture from the eighteenth to nineteenth century is on display.

Late March–early April: Gospel Music Week offers seminars, workshops, and concerts for professionals and fans.

April: Get a taste of Nashville at the World's Biggest Fish Fry, where more than 10,000 pounds of fish are fried in four days. Other attractions include a rodeo, a midway, arts and crafts, and a car show. This event is 100 miles west of downtown Nashville at the fairground in Paris. Don't miss the Opryland American Music Festival, a competition of high school bands and choruses from across the nation. Enjoy the Main Street Festival, with more than 200 of the South's best artisans, food, and children's activities, just south of downtown Nashville in Franklin.

May: See the oldest ongoing steeplechase at the annual Running of the Iroquois Steeplechase. The annual Tennessee Crafts Fair claims to be the largest of its kind and features live music, and contemporary and traditional crafts. Witness the top women golfers in the world at the Sara Lee LPGA Golf Tournament.

June: The four-day Summer Lights Festival features performers in music, art, and dance. The International Country Music Fan Fair includes autograph sessions with the stars, and the Grand Masters Fiddling Championship.

July: Check out the Old Time Fiddlers' Jamboree and Crafts Festival, Smithville. Get a head start on the Fourth of July with fireworks and flags at the four-day Independence Celebration at Opryland, or celebrate Independence at the Riverfront Park. Honor one of the pioneers of the Grand Ole Opry at the Uncle Dave Macon Days, Cannonsburg Village, a music festival with clogging and buck dancing, banjo competitions, historical attractions, and plenty of food.

August: Let the sweet sounds of jazz, Big Band, and Dixieland fill your ears as you stroll through downtown Franklin at the Franklin Jazz Festival. Go to the Annual Tennessee Walking Horse National Celebration, Shelbyville, and see the renowned high-stepping Tennessee Walking horses for yourself.

September: Get back to early nineteenth-century Tennessee at the Country Fair and Sunday Supper on the Grounds, Historic Travellers Rest. The Belle Meade Fall Fest has craft sales. Those interested in historical architecture will want to go on the Majestic Middle Tennessee Fall Tour in late September, covering about a dozen homes and churches listed in the Register of Historical Places.

October: Sing a birthday song along with over 20,000 Grand Ole Opry Fans at the Opryland's Birthday of the Grand Ole Opry. This three-day annual celebration features autograph-signing sessions, Opry performances and concerts, and country cuisine. Bring the kids to the yearly Pumpkin Fest.

November: See a professional rodeo in Nashville's Municipal Auditorium at the Longhorn World Championship Rodeo. Get into the Christmas spirit at the month-long festival, A Country Christmas, at the Opryland Hotel. Get a head start on shopping at the Tennessee State Fairgrounds' Christmas Village, featuring unique gift ideas from hundreds of craftsmen and merchants.

December: Every year, the Nashville Ballet performs The Nutcracker, Polk's Theater. See the Annual Tribute to Blacks who Fought in the Battle of Nashville.

WHERE TO STAY

Experience Southern hospitality Nashville style. Near the airport and Opryland is the **Holiday Inn—Briley Parkway**, 2200 Elm Hill Pike; (615) 883–9770. The **Wilson Inn**, 600 Ermac Drive (615–889–4466), offers a wide range of rooms, from singles to suites, and children under nineteen stay free with an adult. Other possibilities for a family stay include **Comfort Suites**, 2615 Elm Hill Pike (615–883–0114) or **Shoney's Inn of Music Valley**, 2420 Music Valley Drive (615–885–4030). Both are conveniently located near Opryland and offer free breakfasts. The **Residence Inn by Marriott**, 2300 Elm Hill Pike (800–331–3131), features kitchenette-equipped suites, health club passes for guests, and VCR and video rental on site. Indulge at the grandiose **Opryland Hotel**, 2800 Opryland Drive (615–889–1000), a luxury property located in Opryland.

Nashville has many **bed and breakfasts**, but not all accept children. The **Hancock House**, 2144 Nashville Pike (615–452–8431), accommodates babies and children over twelve. For assistance in finding a place, call **Bed and Breakfast—About Tennessee** at (615) 331–5244 or (800) 458–2421.

Get back to nature, or at least to basic prices, by camping at one of the Nashville area's many campgrounds. These include the **Holiday Nashville Travel Park**, 2572 Music Valley Drive (615–889–4225); the **Two Rivers Campground**, 2616 Music Valley Drive (615–883–8559); and **Nashville KOA North**, 708 North Dickerson Road, Goodlettsville (615–859–0075).

WHERE TO EAT

In addition to the Burger Kings, Chi Chi's, and Denny's, Nashville has family restaurants that serve Southern cuisine. The biscuits at the **Loveless Restaurant**, Route 5, Highway 100 (615–646–9700), are said to melt in your mouth, and the country ham is good, too. Try **Carolyn's Homestyle Kitchen**, 330 Charlotte Avenue (615–255–1008), for Southern cookin', cafeteria style. Finicky eaters are sure to find something to munch.

In the mood for a slab of Tennessee pork shoulder or some Texas smoked sausage? Go to **Jack's Barbecue**, 100 Broadway; (615) 254–5715. Put a quarter in the jukebox as you wait to dine on pork, brisket, and chicken. Your kids eat for half-price. For a casual meal in an antique-filled restaurant, try **Darryl's 1827 Restaurant and Bar**, 4319 Sidco Drive; (615) 832–1827. The **Nashville Bagel Company Bakery and Delicatessen**, 3009 West End Avenue (615–329–9599), offers fresh breads, deli sandwiches, and soups.

You may find yourself surrounded by real country music stars if you eat breakfast at the **Pancake Pantry**, 1724 Twenty-first Avenue South; (615) 383–9333. For a unique dining experience suitable for preteens and older children, try the **Broadway Dinner Train,** First Avenue South and Broadway; (615) 254–8000. As the train winds through downtown Nashville, you enjoy a four-course meal. The train offers no kid-priced meals or high chairs for young children.

DAY TRIPS

About 120 miles from Nashville, **Chattanooga** offers lots of family attractions. The **Tennessee Aquarium,** One Broad Street (615–265–0695), is a state-of-the-art aquarium, the first devoted to freshwater ecosystems. The clever exhibits trace a drop of water from the heights of the Great Smoky Mountains, down through the Tennessee River, and on to the Gulf of Mexico. This 12-story, 45-million-dollar project is one of the United States' largest aquariums and features more than forty habitats. Begin in the Appalachian Cove Forest among free-flying birds and frolicking otters, then move on to the Tennessee River Gallery, where you go nose-to-nose with a Spoonbill Paddlefish in the Nickajack Lake. Then get your hands wet in Discovery Falls, the interactive gallery where children and adults learn about the Stream and Cove Critters, including crayfish, frogs, and salamanders. Watch out—alligators have been sighted in the black water swamps of the Mississippi Delta, and there are sharks and stingrays in the clear blue waters of the Gulf of Mexico. Rivers of the World takes you to Zaire, Europe, and Asia for a look at red-bellied piranha and fire eels. After you've travelled through these five exhibits, you're ready for the 60-foot-high central canyon. Climb on ramps and bridges to the upper waters, experiencing the change in plant and animal life.

Take a river ride aboard the *Southern Belle* (615–266–4488), which cruises along the Tennessee River offering dinners and music. See **Ruby Falls** (615–821–2544), a ruby red waterfall atop Lookout Mountain. **Rock City Gardens,** on Lookout Mountain (706–820–2531), has a myriad of natural wonders including a Lover's Leap Ledge from which, if you stay sure-footed, you see seven states. Just-for-kids attractions are Fairyland Caverns and Mothergoose Village.

Another way to get to the top of Lookout Mountain is by riding the **Incline Railway,** billed as the world's steepest passenger railway. For more information contact the Chattanooga Area Convention and Visitors Bureau, 1001 Market Street, Chattanooga; (615) 756–8687 or (800) 322–3344.

FOR MORE INFORMATION

For more information on Nashville events, lodging, and restaurants, contact **Nashville Area Chamber of Commerce,** 161 Fourth Avenue North

(615–259–4702), open weekdays from 8:00 A.M. to 5:00 P.M. Also check with the **Tourist Information Center**, I–65 and James Robertson Parkway, exit 85 (615–259–4747), open daily from 8:00 A.M. to 5:00 P.M.

Emergency Numbers

Ambulance, fire, and police: 911

Baptist Hospital, 2000 Church Street; (615) 329–5555

Poison Control Center: (615) 322–6435

Twenty-four-hour pharmacy: Farmer's Market Pharmacy, 715 Jefferson Street; (615) 242–5501; or Walgreens at one of three locations: 517 Donelson Pike (615–883–5108), 5412 Charlotte Avenue (615–298–5594), and 2622 Gallatin Road (615–226–7591)

Vanderbilt University Medical Center, 1211 Twenty-Second Avenue South (615) 322–7311

32
OKEFENOKEE NATIONAL WILDLIFE REFUGE
Georgia

The Okefenokee National Wildlife Refuge, the largest national wildlife refuge in the eastern United States, occupies 396,000 acres and is one of America's great unspoiled places. This slow moving body of water, comprised of lakes, marsh-like prairies, and islands, is a land where alligators bask on logs, white ibis roost on Ogeechee lime trees, and turtles slide into the dark brown waters.

The Okefenokee was established as a refuge in 1937 to preserve the unique ecosystem of the swamp; in 1974, to further protect the area, 353,981 acres of the refuge's interior was designated a National Wilderness area. The Okefenokee serves as an important habitat for water fowl, wading birds, alligators, and river otters. In these headwaters of the Suwannee River, cypress trees rise up in thickets that float almost magically on dense beds of peat, called "houses." Walk on them, and the land quivers, a phenomenon that led the Indians to call this place Okefenokee, or "the land of the trembling earth."

A journey here feels like breaching a strange, but wonderful new world. Your kids can't help but come away with an appreciation of the land and the wildlife. Another plus, a trip here is low-budget. Cabin rentals and campsites are inexpensive and a guided trip is moderately priced. Although you can drive from Savannah or Jacksonville for a day trip, your time in the park will be limited without sleeping on-property, as all canoers must leave the water before dark. Folkston and Fargo, small towns closer to the swamp, offer motel accommodations. (See WHERE TO STAY.) On a cross-swamp canoe trip, camping on raised platforms where alligators grumble below you adds an unusual element of excitement, but do this by yourselves only if you are experienced.

I recommend staying overnight in one of the park cabins, which are modern, heated, and come with two bathrooms, two bedrooms, and a kitchen. This location offers you ample opportunity for paddling different trails; at night come back to the sure comforts of hot chocolate, hot food, and hot showers. Such civilized touches make it easy to take even first graders into this wilderness. Even if you're an experienced camper, consider going with a guide. There's less work and more learning, as the guides supply all the food, do all the cooking, and teach you such swamp lore as the difference between moss and old man's beard, Ogeechee limes and cypress, and how to tell a peat "house" from an island. (See Special Tours.)

GETTING THERE

Traveling to Okefenokee by airplane, you can fly to **Savannah International Airport**, Davidson Drive (912–964–0514), which serves numerous national and international airlines. The drive from Savannah to the swamp is approximately two hours. To access **Stephen C. Foster State Park** on the western side of the park, take Route I–95 from Savannah, exit onto Route 84, then follow Route 441 South to Georgia Highway 177, and follow the signs to the park.

Coming from Jacksonville International Airport (904–353–9736), it's an 80-mile drive to the Okefenokee National Wildlife Refuge's east entrance. Jacksonville International Airport also serves several national and international airlines daily. From Jacksonville follow I–95 North to the Kingsland exit, to Georgia State Highway 40 West, to Folkston. In Folkston take Georgia State Highway 23/121 southwest for 11 miles, following the brown-and-white signs to the Okefenokee National Wildlife Refuge's east entrance.

Rental cars are available at the Savannah and Jacksonville airports. Rental companies include Avis Rent-A-Car (800–331–1212), Budget Rent-A-Car (800–527–0700), Dollar Rent-A-Car (800–800–4000), Hertz Rent-A-Car (800–654–3131), and National Rent-A-Car (800–227–7368).

Don't be fooled by the north entrance, 8 miles south of Waycross, Georgia, off U.S. Highway 1. This entrance does not offer access to the Okefenokee National Wildlife Refuge itself, but to the Okefenokee Swamp Park (912–283–0583), a privately administered commercial park.

The refuge has two primary entrances. The more frequently used east entrance (912–496–7156), the Suwannee Canal Recreation Area, is 11 miles southwest of Folkston, Georgia, off Georgia State Highway 23/121. The more remote west entrance, which leads to the Stephen C. Foster State Park (912–637–5274), is 17 miles from Fargo, Georgia, along State Highway Spur 177. Both these entrances lead to visitor's centers which feature exhibits, guided boat tours, canoes, and boat rentals. The west entrance also has campgrounds and cabin rentals.

Additional access to the park is via Kingfisher Landing, off U.S. 1 between Waycross and Folkston, Georgia. This unstaffed entrance has public boat ramps and parking lots.

GETTING AROUND

The best and only way to see the Okefenokee up close is by boat. Bring your own canoe, or rent a canoe or small motorboat at the Okefenokee National Wildlife Refuge's Suwannee Canal Recreation Area's east entrance, Folkston; (912) 496–7156. You can also rent from the Stephen C. Foster State Park, on the west side; (912) 637–5274. The park also offers bicycle rentals at hourly rates for use within the Foster State Park only.

WHAT TO SEE AND DO

Okefenokee National Wildlife Refuge

The best time to visit the refuge is spring. Come March, April, and May, long stretches of white and yellow water lilies carpet the refuge waters. When the sun comes out, hundreds of slider turtles live up to their names, splashing from the shore into the water, and thousands of alligators bask on logs along the 107 miles of canoe trails. In spring, too, the swamp resounds with the bellowing of breeding gators and the exuberant trilling of frogs. By late-June the temperatures and the bugs could make a visit uncomfortable. Local experts also like to visit in the fall, when some of the foliage turns russet, and the swamp is less crowded, but the weather still pleasant. June through September brings the rainy season, humid temperatures, wet afternoons, and frequent thunder and lightning storms. Avoid visiting during these months.

The rules and regulations of the Okefenokee swamp vary somewhat depending on whether, and where, you stay overnight. The Stephen C. Foster State Park is a Georgia state park within the Okefenokee National Wildlife Refuge, hence the differing rules. Be sure to call ahead to find out which permits, if any, you need.

If your time is limited, book a cabin at Stephen C. Foster State Park and explore from this area. Anyone staying in the state park's cabins or campsites does not need a canoe trail permit within the park or the refuge.

Stephen C. Foster State Park

The Visitor's Center, at the **Stephen C. Foster State Park** (912–637–5274), has a building of not terribly exciting wildlife exhibits

You never know just what you will encounter when you explore the Okefenokee National Wildlife Refuge. (Courtesy Georgia Department of Industry, Trade, and Tourism)

and a store that sells basic groceries—some canned goods and microwave popcorn—and books, including a surprisingly good selection of children's wildlife educational materials, including mazes, dot games, and naturalist guides. Whether you're camping or lodging at a cabin, pack in your supplies. Although it's nice to know there's a store nearby, you'll be a lot happier bringing your own food.

At Stephen C. Foster State Park, 25 miles of canoe trails are open to the public, and park rangers lead ninety-minute guided tours on a pontoon boat. Day trippers here do not need a permit. Depending on your endurance, you can paddle to some of the swamp's most magical sites on a day trip. **Billy's Island** is the closest point, a 2-mile one-way trip (4 miles round trip) from your put-in spot, and **Minnie's Lake** is a 10-mile round trip that should take about five hours.

In the morning a slight fog often enhances the park's mystery. Looming above you as you paddle out into this watery world are gnarled tree branches which hook thick swaths of Spanish moss that move in the wind with a ghostly flutter. The lake has a smooth, dark surface. But when you look below, you see nothing, as the high concentration of tannic acid makes the water an impenetrable brown.

As soon as you paddle out of the channel from the dock, the spell of the Okefenokee takes over. How to calm your kids who may worry about being eaten by alligators? First of all, paddled correctly, canoes rarely tip, and if they did, the great splash you would make would most likely frighten away the alligators who look for something smaller than themselves to eat. Still, use common sense. Teach your kids to sit still in the canoe (this is actually easy since they will like the scenery and be busy paddling), and make sure they wear properly sized life jackets. Call ahead to find out if the rental facility has child-size jackets, or bring your own.

Once in the swamp you'll be on a photo hunt for the critters. Seeing your first gator up-close, on his turf, is dazzling. Sighting a half-submerged barklike snout and two bulging eyes peering at you from the reeds is unforgettable. Such a peaceful meeting is likely to give you a case of "swamp wonder." Paddling along on a warm day, you'll pass by hundreds of these creatures. Rows of gators, the color of the logs they rest against, all bony stretches of crooked mouths and tails, bask in the sun with their permanent toothy grins.

The sun transforms the swamp. Not only do the alligators appear, but so do the birds. You'll see hawks, herons, woodpeckers, and lots more. The sun's effect on the dark water is magical as well, creating perfect, mirror-like reflections that shoot into the depths. Suddenly the cypress trees grow trunk down, and you and your kids canoe bottoms-up. In sunlight the swamp seems like a fun house in which you cannot tell the real from the reflected world. In fall and February and March, there tend to be more river otters since the gators are less active. Look sharp at the shoreline to find a family of otters catching a fish dinner.

You won't be bored paddling for several days as the swamp offers diverse stretches and subtle differences. **Billy's Lake** leads you to **Billy's Island**, 15 miles into the heart of the swamp, and about 2 miles from the put-in site at Stephen C. Foster State Park. Come ashore here for a picnic lunch and to explore. Hike through the island's pine forest, where through the 1920s loggers attempted to tame the swamp. Now there is just a small, family graveyard, a rusty steam-train boiler, and the remains of a rail hand cart.

Another favorite canoe trail, **Minnie's Lake Run**, feels like a real-life Disney World river ride. On this curvy, narrow trail paddle by dense stands of cypress whose branches canopy above you. Maneuver around knobby cypress stumps, called "knees," as you delight in the peacefulness and your quiet teamwork.

On the **River Narrows** trail, a winding stretch of cypress trees gives way to a forest of Ogeechee limes, which have clusters of mistletoe growing in the crook of their trunks. The wispy lichen, aptly named old man's beard, dangles from their branches like tinsel, lending a green feathery quality. In March pass by a group of golden club, a spiky yellow flower, a harbinger of spring. In spring, the sky fills with scores of ibis, fluttering back to their roosts like hovering white angels.

Wherever your paddles take you, don't forget your fishing gear. **Anglers** are welcome year-round at Stephen C. Foster State Park, but those sixteen years or older must have a fishing license. Pick one up in the Trading Post, at the park's entrance.

Suwannee Canal Recreation Area

The **Visitor's Center**, at the Suwannee Canal Recreation Area (912–496–7156), has information on the area's attractions, a wildlife observation drive, hiking trails, and photo blinds. Concession stands offer guided boat tours, boat and bicycle rentals, snacks, and souvenirs, plus camping and fishing supplies.

Since the trails branching off from the Suwannee Canal are wildlife refuge property, strict rules apply. Overnight visitors may stay for no more than five days and must apply for a canoe trail permit. Make reservations for the canoe trails by calling (912) 496–3331; you can book no sooner than two months prior to your trip.

If visiting for the day, you do not need permits, but you are restricted to day trails that access only a small portion of the swamp. Even so you can head into the heart of the swamp, known for its vast open areas, called prairies, by way of the man-made Suwannee Canal. Of three routes the most popular is the Cedar Hammock trail. Paddle 2 miles up the canal, then cut off to the right near Mizell Prairie—stop awhile for the exceptional bird watching—then continue to Cedar Hammock and back again for a round trip of 12 miles. This trail offers a good view of the swamp. The only problem: no place to dock for lunch and stretch your legs. To picnic, travel 6 miles farther to Coffee Bay, where there's a platform to spread out on; but remember, 6 miles is a long way to go for lunch. Think about eating—carefully—in your canoe. The easiest route is to paddle 3 miles from the canal to Cooter Lake. To stomp on the spongy swamp grounds, getting a first-foot feel of the trembling earth, take a short hike from the Suwannee Canal. The Visitor's Center has trail maps. Nearby is an automobile road that leads to a half-mile boardwalk trail with an observation tower. Keep a lookout for the Florida sandhill crane, which makes its home here.

In order to protect the swamp and its wild inhabitants, a limited number of overnight visitors are allowed into the park at one time. Overnight guests are allowed to travel throughout the refuge's trails, but only with a trail reservation. Obtain a permit by calling the U.S. Fish and Wildlife Service, Okefenokee National Wildlife Refuge (912–496–3331), but reservations can be made no more than two months in advance.

Overnight canoe trips in this section of the refuge take you through the Suwannee Canal and into the swamp's Chesser, Grand, and Mizell prairies, vast open areas of land scattered with small lakes.

Special Tours

Wilderness Southeast (WSE), 711 Sandtown Road, Savannah 31410; (912) 897–5108. This private, nonprofit organization offers guided canoe tours through the Okefenokee, a no-hassle, no-worry way to see the heart of the swamp for families without canoe or camping experience. Trips include tours by canoe, equipment, food prepared by your leaders, and naturalist guides. The canoe/cabin trip features lodging in the Stephen C. Foster State Park cabins. Wilderness Southeast puts at least two guides on every trip and is sensitive and flexible to children's needs. When paddling has pooped you out, there's often a guide to accompany you back to your cabin. After preparing a home-cooked meal in the cabins, WSE shows slides of the refuge's eastern section, not included in the cabin tour. They explain the swamp's wildlife and ecology, including carnivorous plants. If you're lucky, you may even witness the "bone box" filled with skeletal heads of swamp critters—including an alligator—and learn how to identify them yourself. The minimum age for the Okefenokee Cabin/Canoe trip is eight. Four-day trips depart February through May, and October to early November.

WSE also offers a more rigorous five-day canoe/camping trip in the Okefenokee. Paddling varies between 5–12 miles per day, and the minimum age is fourteen. Trip departures are April through May, and October through November. For both trips, rates are moderate, and children under sixteen traveling with an adult receive a 15–20 percent discount.

The Okefenokee Swamp Park, 8 miles south of Waycross off U.S. 1; (912) 283–0583. The wildlife sanctuary is on the northern end of the Okefenokee Swamp. With the price of admission, you see displays on the flower and fauna of the park and take a 2-mile boat trip. Locals tell us that this park has worked hard lately to be less touristy and more educational, and the displays and the boat rides interest kids; still, it can't match extended time in the refuge.

SPECIAL EVENTS

February: Sandhill Awareness Week, Okefenokee National Wildlife Refuge.

April: National Wildlife Week, Okefenokee National Wildlife Refuge.

October: Okefenokee Festival, Okefenokee National Wildlife Refuge.

November: Okefenokee Birding and Man in the Swamp, Stephen C. Foster State Park.

December: Christmas Yule Log Celebration, Okefenokee National Wildlife Refuge.

WHERE TO STAY

At **Stephen C. Foster State Park** (912–496–3331), nestled within the western side of the refuge, you can rent one of nine comfortable and inexpensive two-bedroom two-bath cabins with a full kitchen, but you must stay at least two nights. Reserve well in advance, generally five to eleven months ahead of time; closer to eleven months if you plan to visit during March and April, the high season. **Wilderness Southeast** offers a cabin/canoe tour in which you stay in these cabins.

There are also sixty-six campsites with water, electrical hook-ups, picnic tables, and grills. Each area has a comfort station with hot showers, flush toilets, and laundry facilities. Strict regulations apply to all campers. Visitors may stay only one night at any designated site and must remain at the site from sunset until sunrise. Like the cabins, campsites fill up quickly. Reservations can be made up to ninety days before your stay. Call the Park Office at (912) 637–5274.

For those who missed out on cabin and campsite reservations or are stopping by on a day trip, motels are available in Folkston, 10 miles from the Suwannee Canal East Entrance, and in Fargo, 18 miles from the Stephen C. Foster State Park.

In **Folkston**, try the **Daystop Tahiti**, 1201 South Second Street off of U.S. 1, Folkston; (912) 496–2514 or the **Okefenokee Motel**, U.S. 1 North, Folkston (912–496–7380). The Folkston Chamber of Commerce (912–496–2536) can supply other possibilities. In **Fargo**, visitors can rest their heads at the **Gator Motel**; (912) 637–5264 or (912) 637–5445.

WHERE TO EAT

Although the convenience store at the Stephen C. Foster State Park has some basic groceries and soups, the selection is minimal and the price higher than outside the park. Overnighters should stock up on groceries before arriving. Bring vegetables, meats for grilling at the campsites, juice, milk, and anything else you want for the cabins. On a cabin trip **Wilderness Southeast** makes good use of the kitchen, serving up such fare as grilled chicken, linguine with clam sauce, and apple pie for dessert.

The **Suwannee Canal Recreation Area** (912–496–7156) will pack a box lunch for you of barbecued hotdogs or sausage, baked beans, and coleslaw. Call ahead to be sure, or bring along your own lunch and picnic on the grounds. Snacks and drinks are also available. If traveling to the Okefenokee from Savannah, stop in Folkston for some food. Besides some fast-food restaurants, there's the **Okefenokee Restaurant**, Second and Main streets; (912) 496–3263. They serve sandwiches, salads, and a buffet lunch. Don't expect gourmet food in Folkston.

DAY TRIPS

Spend some time before or after the Okefenokee in Savannah, a southern charmer of a city made for strolling. (See Savannah chapter.) Combine a trip to the swamp with some upscale beach vacationing at Hilton Head, South Carolina. (See the Hilton Head chapter.)

FOR MORE INFORMATION

Note: While spring is likely to bring warm weather and sunny skies, bring appropriate gear to keep you dry, including waterproof jackets, pants, and shoes (rubber boots are fine), just in case. Bring layers as well, including a sweatshirt in case it's cool, a hat for shade, and leather gloves to save your hands from callouses. Remember the bug spray. Mosquitoes are in the swamp after dark April through October. Be mindful as well of snakes, although WSE likes to use the phrase "you'll be lucky if you see them," as snakes tend to hide from people.

For more information on the Okefenokee Refuge, write to Refuge Manager, Okefenokee National Wildlife Refuge, Route 2, Box 338, Folkston, Georgia 31537; or call (912) 496–3331.

To get in touch with the Stephen C. Foster State Park, contact Stephen C. Foster State Park, Fargo, Georgia 31631; (912) 637–5274. Write or contact Okefenokee Swamp Park, Waycross, Georgia 31301 (912–283–0583), for more information. To contact the Suwannee Canal Recreation Area, the main headquarters of the refuge, write or call Refuge Manager, Okefenokee National Wildlife Refuge, Route 2, Box 338, Folkston, Georgia 31537; (912) 496–3331.

For more information on Georgia's parks, write to Georgia Department of Natural Resources, Communications Office, 205 Butler Street, SE, Suite 1352 East, Atlanta, Georgia 30334; or call (404) 656–3530.

Emergency Numbers

Remember, a pay telephone is located at the east and west entrances only. In case of an emergency, dial (912) 637–5323, (912) 637–5282, or (912) 637–5276 for park emergency staff and rangers.

Charlton County Sheriff: (912) 496–2281

Clinch County Sheriff: (912) 487–5315

Clinch Memorial Hospital, 524 Carswell Street, Homerville, Georgia; (912) 487–5211. (about a 55-mile drive up Highway 441 North)

For twenty-four-hour emergency and pharmacy service, use the South Georgia Medical Center, Pendleton Park, Valdosta, Georgia; (912) 333–1086 (pharmacy)/333–1110 (emergency). The Center is about 65 miles from the park

33
ORLANDO
Florida

Orlando is a dream come true for children of all ages (and that means grown-ups, too). Naturally, Walt Disney World is the reason most families head here, and it invariably lives up to (or surpasses) everybody's expectations. Families who have budgeted enough time and money will find that the area is full of other exceptional attractions as well. In fact, even without Disney World (heaven forbid), the Orlando area would be a worthy vacation destination, full of family fun.

GETTING THERE

Orlando International Airport (407–825–2001) is served by numerous domestic and international airlines. Car rentals, van and bus service, and taxis are available. Many hotels also operate shuttles.

Amtrak (800–USA–RAIL) serves Orlando with four daily trains originating in New York, Tampa, and Miami, with stops in Winter Park and Sanford. Greyhound buses arrive at the terminal at 555 Magruder Boulevard.

Orlando may be reached by major highways including I–75 from the Midwest connecting with the Florida Turnpike, I–95 from the Atlantic Coast states, and I–4 running east/west through Orlando and connecting Daytona and Tampa.

GETTING AROUND

A car is extremely helpful in Orlando. The many attractions are spread out and it's often easiest to reach them by car. If you stick to the major attractions, however, it is possible to rely on van transportation and hotel shuttles. Check with the concierge at your hotel. Mear's Transportation (407–423–5566), one of the major van services, provides efficient and reliable service. When using a taxi, always heed the advice of the Convention and Visitors Bureau: use only a metered cab and confirm the cost of the trip with the driver before departing.

WHAT TO SEE AND DO

Attractions

Walt Disney World Vacation Kingdom, situated on 28,000 acres in Lake Buena Vista, is the number one attraction. Walt Disney World is comprised of the Magic Kingdom; Epcot Center; M.G.M. Studios; two water theme parks, River Country and Typhoon Lagoon; plus theme resorts. A world unto itself, it deserves a guide book of its own, and several excellent ones are available at bookstores. For Walt Disney World reservations and information, call (407) W–DISNEY. There are, however, many attractions beyond Walt Disney World.

Sea World of Florida, 7007 Sea World Drive; (407) 351–3600. This popular marine park combines entertainment and recreation with education and conservation. Plan to spend at least a half-day here. The outstanding attractions and shows include Shamu and the famous killer whale family. (If it's hot, your kids may want to sit in the "wet zones" up front, spots guaranteed to get them splashed.)

Additional must-sees include the humorous sea lion show starring Clyde, Seamore, and their otter and walrus friends. Kids love the hands-on displays, especially the Stingray Lagoon, where they can touch these harmless creatures, and the dolphin and sea lion pools, where they can buy food to feed these critters. At the Penguin Encounter, penguins waddle and stare at visitors.

An outstanding exhibit: Terrors of the Deep, though it's not for very young kids. (Strollers, which can be rented at the entrance, are not allowed here.) This exhibit contains the world's largest collection of dangerous sea creatures; it amazes your kids with up-close looks at such fiercesome denizens of the deep as eels, barracudas, and sharks.

Allow time for Shamu's Happy Harbor, an exceptional play area with crawlable, climbable places for all ages, a water maze, plus a scaled down playground for toddlers. The new manatee and pinniped habitats are also winners.

Universal Studios, 1000 Universal Studios Plaza; (407) 363–8000. This huge film and television studio—the largest outside Hollywood—lets visitors experience some of their favorite movies through a series of clever and entertaining rides and shows. Two things to know as you plan your day: Some of the top rides such as Back To The Future, Earthquake, and King Kong, might scare little kids, but will surely delight most children ages eight and older; and some of Universal's rides may be unsettling to those with queasy stomachs.

If jostling nauseates you, consider skipping Back to the Future, where kids under 40" tall aren't allowed. But if being shaken up adds to your fun, come here and board your Delorean. Experience old-fashioned thrills while a clever high-tech video whizzes you on a time chase that propels you past ice-age glaciers, volcanoes, dinosaurs, and into the twenty-first century.

Those with flighty stomachs don't have to skip the Futuristic World of Hanna-Barbera, the park's most popular ride. Even little tykes and pregnant women can enjoy this go-round with Yogi and pals by sitting in the front row's stationary seats. Similarly, don't forego E.T., a tame and sweet fling; just opt for riding a spaceship, not a bike. Listen carefully to E.T.'s good-by; he wows kids by saying their name.

Nickelodeon's studios are a treat for your grade-schoolers. They can ogle the Slime Geyser as it erupts and taste gak. If they're very lucky, they might participate in a routine for such popular Nickelodeon cable network kid shows as "Think Fast" and "Super Sloppy Double Dare."

More Universal fun includes picking the takes, music, and sound effects for your own production of "Murder, She Wrote," and learning how to fashion such special effects as gorillas and brains at "The Horror Make-Up Show." The fabulous Fievel's Playland, near the E.T. ride, delights young kids; everything is oversize as it would be from a mouse's perspective. Tots giggle as they climb up the 30-foot spider web or bounce under a thousand-gallon cowboy hat.

For preteens and teens lunch at the Hard Rock Café, the world's largest, located just outside the Back Lot exit, is a must. Be prepared to wait at peak meal hours. The Beetlejuice Graveyard Revue, a live rock show starring classic Universal monsters, such as Dracula and Frankenstein and his bride, is great fun for all ages.

Gatorland, 14501 South Orange Blossom Trail (U.S. 441), between Orlando and Kissimmee; (407) 855–5496/(800) 393–JAWS. Chances are you may have visited here when you were a kid; it's been around since 1949. The renovated attraction is worth a new look. Visitors observe and feed the 5,000 alligators and crocodiles who live in this fifty-five-acre park along with monkeys, snakes, deer, goats, talking birds, and a bear. A 2,000-foot walkway leads through a cypress swamp showing what Florida looked like long before condominiums and development. The Gator Jumparoo Show has kids wide-eyed as the creatures jump 4 to 5 feet out the water to grab food from their trainer's hand. There's Gator Wrestlin' too, which is called "educational and entertaining," though the emphasis seems to be on the latter. To learn more try a stroll on the new ten-acre breeding marsh observation boardwalk, or board the express train which travels around the park and listen to a lecture on alligators.

After all this it seems a bit heartless to venture into Pearl's Smokehouse for some smoked gator ribs and gator nuggets, or to buy an alligator wallet at the Gatorland Boutique, though these options are available.

Terror on Church Street, 135 South Orange Avenue; (407) 649–1912 (FEAR). The phone number should give you a clue that this evening attraction is not for the timid. Clue number two: They won't let kids under ten in without an adult. Don't say I didn't warn you, but if your older kids love a good scare, this place will provide it. It's the first American installation of a popular Spanish attraction that translates to "Passage of Terror." A combination of live actors, microchip technology, cinematic special effects, theatrical sets, plus twenty-three different sound tracks create a bone-chilling experience. Visitors enter in groups of eight, but fewer may make it the whole way through thanks to a "chicken out" exit.

Water Parks

Aside from Disney's water parks, the Orlando area has two major parks with something special for kids:

Water Mania, 6073 West Irlo Bronson Memorial Highway (U.S. 192), Kissimmee; (407) 239–8448—Orlando/(407) 396–2626—Kissimmee/(800) 527–3092. Just for kids: The Rain Forest, with minislides, water guns, and jungle characters; and the Aqua Xpress, a giant train with slides, spouting water, and whistles. Teens may want to bodysurf or boogie board on the new and unique Wipe Out surfing wave simulator, or try Riptide, a wild white-water adventure. There's lots more here, including miniature golf, arcade games, and a picnic area.

Wet 'n Wild, 6200 International Drive; (407) 351–1800/(800) 992–WILD. This park recently introduced a $1.5 million Kids' Park playground for ages one to ten featuring miniature versions of popular adult attractions, such as a Miniature Raging Rapids, Children's Lazy River, and a one-of-a-kind Children's Wave Pool. There's even kid-size beach chairs and lounges, plus a food kiosk. (Adult-size seating encircles the area.)

For older kids, thrills and chills include the new Bubba Tub, a tripledip thrill ride which holds up to five (brave) family members at a time.

Museums

If you have the time and energy after visiting the above, the following museums are worth a browse.

Orlando Science Center, 810 East Rollins Street; (407) 896–7151. This facility is constantly coming up with new live programs to keep kids involved. In the Natureworks area, touch live snakes, frogs, and turtles during one of the Reptile and Amphibian shows; then experiment with water testing in the WaterLab. Younger kids, ages two to eight, love the Kidspace, a supervised area where they pilot a large rubber raft, float boats, and build dams in the Waterway, act out plays in the Water Life Puppet Theater, and feel and touch sponges, shells, and other objects in the Please Touch Discovery Center. The John Young Planetarium has

daily feature and Family Laser shows and weekly live star shows and
laser shows. Call (407) 896–7151.

Orlando Toy Train Station and Museum, 5253 International Drive;
(407) 363–9002. Outside you can hop aboard the Orange Blossom Express, pulled by a circa-1924, narrow-gauge, diesel-fired steam engine.
Then head inside to see a wonderful display of G-gauge model trains zipping about, plus an interesting assortment of train memorabilia. The museum is aiming to add a children's hands-on play area and garden.

Parks and Beaches

See DAY TRIPS for the closest ocean or gulf beaches. If you want a
break from Orlando's fantasy world attractions, head to **Turkey Lake
Park,** 3401 Hiawassee Road, southwest Orlando; (407) 299–5594. This
recreational haven has two beaches, a swimming pool, picnic tables, a 3-
mile bicycle trail, numerous hiking trails, canoe rentals, a fishing pier, a
petting zoo, and an "All Children's Playground" that accommodates
physically disabled kids.

Performing Arts

Feel a sudden need for cultural activities? Orlando doesn't disappoint.
There's lots of area theater—even a professional opera company, ballet
troupe, and symphony orchestra. The most thorough listing of cultural
events and other happenings is the Friday "Calendar" supplement of The
Orlando *Sentinel.*

Shopping

All the major theme parks have shops where you will undoubtedly
spend a sizeable portion of your money. If there's anything left, however,
you'll have fun strolling through **Church Street Station** in downtown
Orlando, an all-in-one shopping, entertainment, and dining complex.
Mercado Mediterranean Village, 8445 South International Drive, offers
sixty specialty shops, free nightly entertainment, a food court, bird
shows, and colorful continental atmosphere. Call (407) 345–9337.

SPECIAL EVENTS

Sports

The Orlando Magic NBA basketball team plays at the downtown Orlando arena, (407) 89–MAGIC. The arena is also home to the Orlando
Predators football team. Check with the Convention and Visitors Bureau
about baseball spring training teams and locations.

Fairs and Festivals

Many of Orlando's seasonal festivities revolve around the theme
parks. Consult the Friday "Calendar" supplement of the Orlando *Sentinel*

for a listing of what's happening. The Kissimmee–St. Cloud area, just south of Walt Disney World, has a number of low-key annual festivities that include the following.

February: Livestock Show and Osceola County Fair. Silver Spurs Rodeo.
December: Lighted Christmas Boat Parade.

WHERE TO STAY

The Kissimmee–St. Cloud area offers reasonably priced accommodations close to the area's major attractions; you can book many by calling (800) 333–KISS. Since Orlando is a family vacation destination, most hotels and resorts offer appealing features for kids. Here's a sampling of what you'll find.

Holiday Inn has two of its SunSpree Resorts, the chain's latest mid-price family-pleasing hotels, in the Orlando area. The **Holiday Inn Lake Buena Vista**, 13351 S.R. 535, P.O. Box 22184, Lake Buena Vista, 32830 (800–FON–MAXX), serves as the flagship of this line. The family-friendly amenities here include Camp Holiday, which is free, daily child care and activity programs for ages two to twelve from 8:00 A.M. to midnight, year-round. You can rent a beeper for a nominal fee so that while you're at a business meeting or strolling Disney World on your own, you can be reached "just in case." In addition, rooms have microwaves, refrigerators, and a table with four chairs. When parents eat in the restaurant, kids under twelve eat free in their own Kids Kottage restaurant. Room snacks are easy as the on-site "marketessan" serves snacks and sells microwave meals, baby food, and other essentials. Room child-proofing kits are available at check-in.

Under the same management, an older property, **Holiday Inn Main Gate East**, 5678 Irlo Bronson Memorial Highway (U.S. 192), Kissimmee (800–FON–KIDS), offers similar amenities and services, but the child care here is from ages three and up, the rooms are smaller, and the property has been adapted to the SunSpree concept rather than created for it.

Sonesta Villa Resort, 10,000 Turkey Lake Road, features villas tucked away in a lakefront setting near I–4. Each has a fully equipped kitchenette and living/dining area, plus one or two bedrooms. Organized activities for ages five to twelve, outdoor pool, playground areas, and water activities on the lake (including water and jet skiing) make this an appealing place for families. You can arrange to have Sonny the Seal, the Kids' Club mascot, come to your villa to tuck in your tot and bring a bedtime snack. Call (407) 352–8051/(800) SONESTA.

Summerfield Suites Hotels offers two properties in Orlando, each featuring suites with a living area plus two bedrooms. **Summerfield Suites Orlando-International Drive**, 8480 International Drive (407–352–2400 or

800–833–4353) is about fifteen minutes from Walt Disney World. **Summerfield Suites Lake Buena Vista,** 8751 Suiteside Drive (407–238–0777 or 800–833–4353), is scheduled to open in October of 1993. This chain offers kitchen facilities and a daily continental plus breakfast buffet. There are also children's videos to rent (the two-bedroom units have three televisions plus a VCR) and a twenty-four-hour convenience store on site. Ask about special weekend rates.

Stouffer Orlando Resort, 6677 Sea Harbor Drive, is directly across from Sea World and has 780 rooms, with sixty-four suites. The huge atrium lobby will delight the kids with pools filled with rare fish (there's food to feed them) plus a large aviary. Shamu's Playhouse offers supervised activities and off-property excursions for ages two to twelve from 8:00 A.M. to 11:00 P.M. daily. There's a large outdoor pool and playground and several excellent restaurants on the premises. Call (407) 351–5555/(800) HOTELS 1.

Delta Orlando Resort, 5715 Major Boulevard, is near the main gate of Universal Studios (free shuttle is available). Choose from a variety of accommodations in different price ranges. There are three outdoor pools, tennis, minigolf, and a playground and supervised activities at Wally's Kids Club for ages four to twelve. Kids six and under can eat free in the three restaurants. Call (407) 351–3340/(800) 877–1133.

WHERE TO EAT

Leave it to Orlando to make eating a fantasy adventure: theme dinner theaters make for a fun evening out. These don't come cheap, however, so choose carefully. A few with kid appeal:

At **Wild Bill's Wild West Dinner Show** (formerly Fort Liberty), 5260 West Irlo Bronson Memorial Highway West, in Kissimmee, you get the works: Native American Comanche performers, trick rope artists, storytellers, singers, and dancers, plus lots of food. Call (407) 351–5151/(800) 347–8181.

Medieval Times, 4156 West Irlo Bronson Memorial Highway West, can either be a kid's dream come true (you eat mediocre food with your hands) or a weird dream: It all depends on your taste. As you dine stadium-style, knights atop horses joust for a fair maiden, who is plucked from the audience. Call (407) 396–1518/(800) 327–4024. We prefer **King Henry's Feast,** 8984 International Drive, Orlando, which takes place in a "castle" where you dine family-style on a four-course meal, while Henry, his minstrels, and magicians put on an entertaining show involving some of the audience—including the kids; (407) 351–5151/(800) 347–8181.

For more conventional fare, check the dining guide in the weekend "Calendar" section of the Orlando *Sentinel.* They have objective, right-on-the mark summaries of area restaurants.

Dinner at Medieval Times in Orlando is an enjoyable experience for all.
(Courtesy Orlando/Orange County Convention and Visitors Bureau, Inc.)

DAY TRIPS

Orlando is convenient to both the Atlantic Ocean east coast or Gulf of Mexico west coast beaches. The closest beaches—Cocoa, New Smyrna, and Daytona Beach—are about an hour's drive to the east. If your kids are up to it, you could combine a trip to Cocoa Beach with a visit to Kennedy Space Center's Spaceport USA, on SR 405, North Merritt Island. This interesting place features a two-hour bus tour of the facility, including launching sites, an IMAX presentation on flight, and a Satellites and You audiovisual exhibit. The Spaceport may be a little tough on toddlers, although school-age and older kids will find it fascinating. Call (800) SHUTTLE, (407) 452–2121.

Cypress Gardens, in Winter Haven, is forty minutes from Disney. It has gorgeous botanical gardens; waterski, circus, and exotic bird shows; high divers; synchronized swimmers; and special events throughout the year. Call (800) 282–2123 in Florida or (800) 237–4826—elsewhere in the United States.

FOR MORE INFORMATION

Orlando/Orange County Convention and Visitors Bureau operates a Visitor Information Center at Mercado Mediterranean Shopping Village, 8445 International Drive, Orlando 32819; (407) 363–5871. Call or stop by for their *Visitors Guide,* with information about accommodations, attractions, restaurants, shopping, and transportation. Also ask about the Orlando Magicard that offers discounts on hotels, attractions, and restaurants.

Kissimmee–St. Cloud Convention and Visitors Bureau can provide maps, brochures, directions, and discount coupons: P.O. Box 42207, Kissimmee, Florida 34742–2007; (800) 327–9159. Accommodations reservations number: (800) 333–KISS.

Wheelchair Wagon Tours, 3845 Henry J. Avenue, St. Cloud, Florida 34772 (407–846–7175), offers tours of area attractions and rents handicapped-equipped vans with lifts.

Emergency Numbers
Ambulance, fire, and police: 911
Emergency room (twenty-four hour): Orlando Regional Medical Center, 1414 Kuhl Avenue; (407) 841–5898
Poison Control: (407) 841–5222
Twenty-four-hour pharmacy: Walgreen's, 1003 West Vine Street, Kissimmee; (407) 847–5252

34
SAVANNAH
Georgia

Savannah, with its shady streets and courtly squares, is a city made for walking. As you stroll from the waterfront to Forsyth Park, you walk through part of the 2½-square-mile downtown, one of the largest urban historic districts. Laid out by General James Oglethorpe in the eighteenth century, the city's orderly pattern of shady streets and landscaped squares lends itself to leisurely strolls.

This southern city, easy to navigate, friendly, and historic, will charm you and your kids. Saunter along the streets lined by venerable oaks draped with Spanish moss and pass the numerous graceful squares. Called "the most beautiful city in North America" by *Le Monde*, the Parisian newspaper, Savannah will host the 1996 Summer Olympic Yachting competitions, another good reason for visiting.

GETTING THERE

Located 11 miles from historic Savannah, Savannah International Airport (912–964–0514) serves numerous national and international airlines. Amtrak (800–USA–RAIL or 912–234–2611) stops at the Savannah terminal, 2611 Seaboard Coastline Drive, six times daily. Trains originate from New York, Jacksonville, Miami, and St. Petersburg. Greyhound-Trailways, 600 West Oglethorpe Avenue (912–233–7723), stops in Savannah as well. Located 17 miles inland from the Atlantic Ocean near the Georgia–South Carolina border, the city is accessible via I–95 north-south and I–16 east-west (via I–75 from Atlanta).

GETTING AROUND

The best way to see Savannah is by walking or bicycling. A bicycle rental facility is located in the Hyatt Regency, 2 West Bay Street; (912)

238–1234 or (800) 233–1234. CAT (Chatham Area Transit) public bus service offers routes for the downtown and south side area. For CAT schedules, call (912) 233–5767.

For car rental companies, contact Avis Rent-A-Car, 2215 Travis Field Road, Savannah (912–964–0234); Budget Rent-A-Car, Rural Route 5, Box 262 H, Garden City (912–964–9186); Enterprise, 5102 Augusta Road, Garden City (912–966–1177).

Phone Yellow Cab at (912) 236–1133 or Adam Cab at (912) 927–7466, for taxi service.

WHAT TO SEE AND DO

A good place to begin your tour is at the **Savannah History Museum/ Savannah Visitors Center**, 303 Martin Luther King, Jr., Boulevard; (912) 238–1779. This facility presents a short film on Savannah's history, from its founding in 1733 to the present day. The museum has a few exhibits on coastal life, a locomotive, and lots of brochures.

Riverfront Attractions

Ships of the Sea Maritime Museum, 503 East River Street and 504 East Bay Street; (912) 232–1511. This converted turn-of-the-century warehouse, besides affording a splendid view of the harbor, features an interesting array of scrimshaw and figureheads. Any child who has ever built a model will be astounded by the fifty intricately constructed model ships that range from minuscule to 8 feet in length. And if that doesn't enthrall them, kids can puzzle over the extensive ship-in-the-bottle collection and admire the nautical paraphernalia.

The **Waving Girl Statue** on River Street embodies more of Savannah's sea lore. It commemorates Florence Martus, a city native who, from 1887 to 1931, reputedly waved at every ship entering the harbor in hopes of greeting her husband who sailed away just after their marriage never to return. Be sure to stroll along nearby **Factor's Walk**. At this historic site eighteenth-century merchants perched on the iron catwalks to judge the price of goods paraded below. The nineteenth-century riverside buildings, which once functioned as offices, now offer excellent browsing and shopping opportunities. Plan to spend some time here looking for T-shirts and souvenirs. The **River Street Train Museum**, 315 West River Street (912–233–6404), is a fun stop on your riverside walk for the model train buff in your family. Tour the miniature village and an extensive collection of "O" gauge trains dating from 1930 to present day.

Historic Houses

Savannah's stately homes are a gift to the eye with their archways, pillars, and fanciful iron railings, balconies, and gates. There's no shortage of historic homes in this city, but a tour of one or two of these goes a long way with kids, so don't attempt to see them all.

Juliette Gordon Low Girl Scout Center, 142 Bull Street (912–233–4501), is a must-see for any girl scout, or even boy scout, in your family. Juliette Gordon Low, founder of the Girl Scouts, was born here on Halloween night 1860. Now the 1818 Regency-style home, restored to its 1870s appearance, serves as the national center for the Girl Scouts. Find out why the youngest troops of girl scouts are called daisies and why Low started the group. After visiting the home, buy a merit badge in the gift shop.

The **Owens Thomas House,** 124 Abercorn Street (912–233–9743), is among the important historic houses. From a balcony at this English Regency-style mansion designed by William Jay and built between 1817 and 1819, the Marquis de Lafayette addressed the townspeople in 1825. Inside fine antiques and *trompe l'oeil* decorations convey the ruffles and flourishes of gentrified life in this southern town.

The **Telfair Mansion,** 121 Barnard Street (912–232–1177), also designed by architect William Jay, makes for an interesting comparison to the Owens Thomas House. The restored 1819 period rooms in this mansion are filled with southern finery including Duncan Phyfe furniture and Savannah silver. The oldest public art museum in the South, the mansion also includes a collection of paintings by American and European Impressionists, as well as changing special exhibitions.

The Gothic-style **Green-Meldrim House,** 1 West Macon Street (912–233–3346), marks ties to the Civil War. This house became General Sherman's Savannah headquarters in 1864 after his trail of destruction through the South. Pick up a brochure detailing the house's sophisticated architectural features, including a three-part front door designed for light and ventilation.

Temple Mickve Israel, 20 East Gordon Street at Monterey Square, whose current building dates to 1878, traces its congregants to the second boatload of settlers to Georgia, landing in 1733 after General Oglethorpe's English settlers. According to the legend, these Jews fleeing the Spanish Inquisition were allowed to take refuge in Savannah because among them was a physician whose services Oglethorpe needed for his ailing colonists. The good doctor refused to land unless all his shipmates were permitted ashore as well. The temple includes a small museum with historical books, including letters from presidents Washington and Jefferson, as well as one of the oldest Torahs in the country.

The **Isaiah Davenport House,** 324 East State Street (912–236–8097), was built in 1820 by Rhode Island carpenter Isaiah Davenport after a careful study of traditional Federal architecture. Older children will appreciate a tour of the home's intricate ironwork, flowing staircase, and

A stroll (or skate) through Savannah's Forsyth Park is a relaxing way to spend an afternoon. (Courtesy Savannah Area Convention and Visitors Bureau)

authentic period pieces. Be sure to tour the garden afterward. The museum shop is a good place to pick out a Savannah souvenir.

At the **King-Tisdell Cottage,** 514 East Huntingdon Street (912–234–8000), an 1896 gingerbread cottage, learn about African-American history in Savannah and the Sea Islands. A tour of this quaint home reveals black life a century ago through furniture, artwork, and historical documents. The museum also sponsors a **Negro Heritage Trail,** 502 East Harris Street (912–234–8000), a tour of seventeen historic sites from the river docks where the first slaves arrived to the first Negro Baptist church.

Green Spaces

Besides romping in the twenty town squares, find time for **Forsyth Park,** twenty acres of greenery and fountains between Gaston Street and Park Avenue. This is a great place for a picnic or an impromptu game of tag. If you're lucky, you might witness a wedding in front of the elaborate fountain, a favorite backdrop for brides.

If your kids don't spook at the mere mention of cemeteries, the **Colonial Park Cemetery,** Abercorn between Oglethorpe and Perry, is an interesting stop. The weathered gravestones mark many of the Revolutionary War dead.

Forts

Fort Jackson, One Fort Jackson Road (912–232–3945), on the Savannah River, served as the headquarters of the Confederate defense during the Civil War. This fortress actually dates back to the Revolutionary War and is now the oldest existing fort in the state. There's a maritime museum to explore, and on summer afternoons you can witness the firing of the thirty-two-pound blackpowder cannon. **Fort McAllister State Historic Park,** Route 2, Richmond Hill (912–727–2339), offers a space for a leisurely afternoon and a history lesson on the banks of the Great Ogeechee River. Built for the Civil War, the fort was created to protect Savannah's "back door" and the riverside rice plantations. Now restored to its original state, the fort has been called the best preserved earthwork fortification of the Confederacy, which held up during seven Union attacks. Along with a museum of Civil War artifacts, there's a 1³⁄₁₀-mile hiking trail and a picnicking area.

Fort Pulaski National Monument (912–786–5787) is 14 miles east of Savannah on Tybee Island. This fort, also constructed to protect Savannah from a sea approach, impresses with massive walls, a wide drawbridge, and two moats. Explore the fort outworks and surrounding nature trails, then stop by the museum and bookstore. In the summertime the fort presents daily talks and demonstrations on the Civil War.

More Attractions

If you want to take a drive beyond Savannah's historic district, there are other interesting sites. The **Wormsloe State Historic Site,** 7601 Skidaway Road (912–352–2548), brings you back to Colonial times and the accomplishments of one of Georgia's first settlers—Noble Jones. Children enjoy a discovery romp through the ruins of this early estate and a nature trail that leads to a living-history demonstration of early Colonial life given by costumed actors.

The **Savannah Science Museum,** 4405 Paulsen Street (912–355–6705), is a small-scale, hands-on museum. Call in advance for a schedule of planetarium shows. **The Aquarium,** Skidaway Island (912–356–FISH), is a public education branch of the University of Georgia. If there's an aquarium in your town, you might skip this attraction, as it's small, but for marine life buffs a view of the more than 200 live animals here is free of charge.

At the **Laurel Hill Wildlife Drive/Savannah National Wildlife Refuge** (912–652–4415), Highway 17 in South Carolina, about 6 miles from Savannah, pick up a brochure at the Visitors Center then explore the wildlife refuge on a 4-mile drive. You pass dikes constructed in the late 1700s and early 1800s to retain the rice fields, and the wildlife. The refuge is home to many of the area's marsh and saltwater birds and ducks (at certain times of the year). If you keep your eyes peeled, you might even sight an alligator.

Special Tours

Relive antebellum Savannah on an hour-long historic **carriage tour,** departing daily from the visitor's center, City Market and Madison Square. Kids love these carriage rides. They're easy on the feet, and the slow pace of the Percherons is in tune with this town. Try an after-dinner twilight tour. The drivers will happily pick you up at the restaurant. Call **Carriage Tours of Savannah,** 117 West Perry Street (912–236–6756), for information and reservations.

Kids also like rolling on the river. Savannah Riverboat Tours, 222 East Factor's Walk (912–236–0407), features a cruise to Daufuskie Island with an on-land cookout.

There's a tour for almost every sensibility—from black heritage to anecdotal history—in this southern hospitality town. For a complete listing of tour companies, call the Savannah Convention and Visitors Bureau at (912) 944–0456.

Spectator Events

The **Savannah Cardinals,** the AAA farm team of the St. Louis Cardinals, play baseball in Grayson Stadium, 1401 East Victory Drive. For information about home games and tickets, call (912) 351–9150 during business hours.

Participatory Sports

Golf Courses. **Bacon Park Golf Course,** Shorty Cooper Drive (912–354–2625), is a twenty-seven-hole course with a driving range, putting green, and golf carts; it's located in the southside. **Mary Calder,** West Lathrop Avenue (912–238–7100), is a nine-hole course in West Chatham with carts, a driving range, and putting green. **Southbridge Golf Club,** 415 Southbridge Boulevard, West Chatham (912–651–5455), and **Sheraton Savannah Resort,** 612 Wilmington Island Road, Islands/Beach (912–897–1612), are both eighteen-hole courses with putting greens, carts, and driving range.

Tennis Courts. Located on Skidaway Road on the south side of Savannah, all of **Bacon Park's** fourteen courts are lit for public play; call (912) 351–3850. Also on the south side are **Lake Mayer,** Montgomery Crossroad and Sallie Mood (912–925–8706), and **Louis Scott Stell Park,** off of Bush Road (912–925–8694). Both sites have eight tennis courts each, all of **Lake Mayer's** courts are lit while only half of **Louis Scott Stell Park's** courts have lights. In the historic district, head to **Daffin Park,** 1500 East Victory Drive (912–351–3851), for play on nine courts, three of which are lit. **Forsyth Park,** at Drayton and Gaston streets (912–351–3852), offers four courts all suited for night play. For courts on the Islands, look to **Tybee Island Community Park's** two lighted courts on Butler Avenue (912–786–4698). **Wilmington Island Community Park,** at Lang Street and Walthour Road (no phone), also has a pair of lit tennis courts.

SPECIAL EVENTS

Savannah will host yachting events during the 1996 Atlanta Summer Olympics. Located 250 miles from Atlanta, Savannah's events will include ten classes of fleet-race yachting—within each of the ten classes, the same type of crafts race one another. Yachting enthusiasts should make accommodation reservations as soon as possible.

Festivals

The Savannah Waterfront Association (912–234–0295) sponsors the **First Saturday Festival** throughout the year. With the exception of January and December, the first Saturday of each month means a Historic Waterfront celebration complete with food, music, arts and crafts, clowns, and face painting all weekend long—a perfect family outing.

For a schedule of Savannah's cultural and historical events, call (912) 233–ARTS.

January: In celebration of Martin Luther King, Jr., Day, Savannah hosts Martin Luther King, Jr., Week; a celebration offering week-long activities such as Gospelfest, jobs fair, blood drive at YMCA, parade, and dance.

February: Celebrate the past at Georgia Heritage Celebration, including tours, art exhibits, and craft demonstrations.

March: New talent converges at the International Arts Festival, five days of musical performances featuring fifteen rising young stars. Irishfest and the St. Patrick's Day Parade bring out the Irish in all of us.

March/April: As the winter months come to an end, the Seafood Festival comes to the waterfront with music and arts and crafts.

May: Arts on the River Festival brings together all sorts of arts with food and entertainment.

June–August: There's a free two-hour lunchtime concert waiting for you every Wednesday and Friday in Johnson Square.

June: Open yourself up to the newest in beach beats and shag demonstrations at the Annual Beach Music Festival.

July: The Savannah Maritime Festival adds a waterfront fish fry, bands, and a laser show to the city sights. Great American Fourth of July is a weekend full of fireworks on the river, live entertainment, and lots to eat. All the locals come together for music, dance, drama, and more at the Forsyth Festival.

September: The Savannah Jazz Festival brings four days of local and national jazz musicians, as well as food and festivities, to various venues around town. Traditionally, the fourth day of the festival is dedicated to a children's jazz fest.

October: Oktoberfest in Savannah means a weekend of sauerkraut and sausage, music and dancing.

December: Christmas on the River hails a riverside parade, arts and crafts, music, food, caroling, entertainment, Christmas boat parade, and the annual lighting of Savannah's Christmas Tree at sunset. Winter Muster brings history to the present in a recreation of General Sherman's occupation of Fort McAllister, as well as other historic fort events.

For a more extensive and comprehensive listing of Savannah's events, call the **Savannah Waterfront Association** at (912) 234–0295, and **The Savannah Area Convention and Visitors Bureau** at (912) 944–0456 or (800) 444–2427.

WHERE TO STAY

Two finds for families are the Lion's Head Inn and the Olde Harbour Inn. **The Lion's Head Inn** (912–232–4580), an elegantly restored 1883 bed and breakfast in the heart of the historic district, lets you enjoy period furnishings, and gracious rooms—and the company of your children—because the owners welcome ages three and older. Besides televisions and private baths, this bed and breakfast has Jonathan, the owners' young son, who warmly welcomes young guests. **The Olde Harbour Inn,** 508 East Factor's Walk (912–234–4100 or 800–553–6533), right on the river, offers twenty-four suites, each with a kitchenette. Your kids will like the extra space, the easy snacking, and the scoop of ice cream at turn-down. Ask about special weekend rates.

The Mulberry, 601 East Bay Street (912–238–1200 or 800–HOLI-DAY), operated by Holiday Inn, has 119 rooms. The rooftop deck offers a great view of the river by moonlight. **Presidents' Quarters,** 225 East President Street (912–233–1600 or 800–233–1776), an 1855 inn located in the historic and business district, invites you to afternoon tea, and children under ten stay for free.

R.S.V.P. Georgia and Savannah Bed and Breakfast (912–232–7787 or 800–729–7787) provides a free reservation service for bed and breakfasts and guest houses in historic Savannah. Call for more information. **Savannah Historic Inns and Guest Houses Reservation Service,** 147 Bull Street (912–233–7666 or 800–262–4667), is a similar organization.

WHERE TO EAT

For an authentic Savannah tradition, be sure to line up early for lunch at **Mrs. Wilkes' Boarding House,** 107 West Jones Street, served 11:30 A.M. to 2:00 P.M. Her family-style fare, served ten guests to a table, includes fried chicken, stew, rice, beans, biscuits, collard greens, sweet potatoes, and three kinds of dessert. **Carey Hillard's,** with four locations including

3316 Skidaway Road and 8410 Waters Avenue, scores good marks with little kids. This family-style restaurant pampers children with crayons and a coloring place mat, plus a children's menu with chicken fingers, fries, and milkshakes.

A dinner cruise on the riverboat **Magnolia**, 504 East River Street (912–234–4011), makes for a special evening. This leisurely two-hour meal will delight older children. The younger ones will be entertained by a Sunday morning brunch on the water. Kids can get up and move about at this buffet-style meal including live entertainment on the **Savannah River Queen**, 9 East River Street; (912) 232–6404.

DAY TRIPS

Tybee Island, thirty minutes outside Savannah, is a great family day trip combining beach bathing, recreation, and maritime history. Before or after you hit the beach, check out the **Museum and Lighthouse**. Call the Tybee Island Visitors Center (800–868–BEACH or 912–786–5444) for more information.

Georgia's **Golden Isles** are approximately 70 miles south of Savannah or a little more than an hour away. Treat yourself to a day on the beach on one of these four barrier islands, featuring untouched beaches and resorts galore with golfing, tennis, fishing, sailing, and swimming.

They have history as well. **Sea Island** was once a renowned cotton plantation, and **St. Simons** is home to Fort Frederica, a costly colonial British fort built by General Oglethorpe. Millionaire American families, including the Rockefellers and the Morgans, made **Jekyll Island** their summer playground in the early part of the century.

For more information contact the Brunswick and Golden Isles Visitors Bureau, 4 Glynn Avenue, Brunswick; (912) 265–0620.

Other day trip possibilities include the **Okefenokee Swamp**, about 2 miles to the south. (See Okefenokee chapter for attractions.) Located near Savannah, Wilderness Southeast (912–897–5108), a nonprofit educational group, offers soft adventure tours of Okefenokee and several other coastal areas.

Atlanta is about four-and-a-half hours by car. (See Atlanta chapter for more information.)

FOR MORE INFORMATION

The Savannah Area Convention and Visitors Bureau, 222 West Oglethorpe Avenue, Suite 100, Savannah, Georgia 31401 (912–944–0456 or 800–444–2427), has informational brochures and visitor's guides.

Other good sources of local goings-ons are the *Savannah Tourist Guide* bi-monthly newspaper and the *Savannah Parent*, available at area stores and libraries, which lists special children's events.

Emergency Numbers

Ambulance, fire, and police: 911

Medical services: The Memorial Medical Center, 4700 Waters Avenue; (912) 356–8000

Poison Control: (912) 355–5228

Twenty-four-hour pharmacy: Revco Medical Arts Shopping Center, Waters Avenue and Sixty-third Street; (912) 355–7111

35
TAMPA
Florida

Tampa, which began as a Native American fishing village, has been luring adventurers for centuries. Ponce de León, the first recorded European visitor, came here in 1513 in search of gold. So did explorers Hernando de Soto in 1539, and Pedro Mendez in 1565. Situated on Florida's west coast, Tampa is on Hillsborough Bay, which opens into the Gulf of Mexico. Tampa served as a military post in 1824 when Fort Brooke was established to monitor the Seminole Indians. In 1885 Don Vincente Martinez Ybor developed a cigar manufacturing center here. But since 1891 when railroad and steamship magnate Henry Plant opened the Tampa Bay Hotel, now a landmark building, Tampa has been a tourist area.

Only a short drive from some fine west coast beaches, Tampa offers sophisticated city attractions such as interesting museums and kid-pleasing adventures such as Busch Gardens and Adventure Island. In addition Tampa's waterfront is rapidly developing into a tourist attraction. Scheduled to open in in 1995 are an aquarium and a pirate museum. When you've seen enough of Tampa, nearby St. Petersburg offers family fun as well.

GETTING THERE

Tampa International Airport (TIA) (813–870–8700) is just 7 miles from downtown Tampa and serves twenty airlines.

Among the car rental companies Alamo (800–327–9633), Avis (800–331–1212), Budget (800–527–0700), Dollar (800–421–6868), and Hertz (800–654–3131).

Amtrak arrives at Union Station, 601 North Nebraska Avenue, (800) 872–7245. The Greyhound Bus terminal is at 610 East Polk Street, (813) 229–1501. Among the major highways leading to Tampa, I–75 provides access from the north and south.

Several cruise lines take advantage of Tampa's port location, leaving from Tampa for Caribbean cruises. Among the ships are Holland America's *Nieuw Amsterdam* and Regency Cruises' *Regent Rainbow* and *Regent Sea*. For cruise information call the Tampa Port Authority at (800) 741–2297.

GETTING AROUND

With its streets laid out in a geometrical grid, Tampa is a fairly simple city to navigate. Most Tampa attractions are near I–275 or I–4. An expressway, with tolls, takes you across town. The HARTline is Tampa's public transportation bus system. Call (813) 243–HART for fare and route information.

A car, however, may still be the best way to get around, although several hotels offer shuttle service to Busch Gardens.

WHAT TO SEE AND DO

Theme Parks and Zoos

Busch Gardens, 3000 East Busch Boulevard; (813) 987–5082. Busch Gardens, the area's biggest family draw, is a 300-acre theme park with rides, live performances, shops, restaurants, and a top-notch eighty-acre African zoo. When you purchase your admission, consider a combined ticket for Busch Gardens and the nearby Adventure Island, a water theme park.

Busch Gardens is one of those places you could explore all day, or for several days, depending on your family's exuberance for rides and tolerance for lines. Come early, wear a bathing suit with shorts or a T-shirt for the water rides, and bring some travel toys for kids to play with while waiting in lines. (Water bottles help, too.) The wait can be long, and hot, depending on the season. One possible strategy for a summer visit: go on the water rides fairly early. Being wet helps keep you cool as you stand in line; by the time you leave the park, you're likely to be dry for the ride back to your hotel.

What's fun here? Most everything will interest somebody in your clan. Several roller coasters deliver thrills. Kumba, the newest one which debuted in spring 1993, is touted as the fastest steel coaster in the southeastern United States. How fast? Named after the African Congo–language word meaning "roar," Kumba screams around its turquoise tracks, turning riders upside down seven times and reaching speeds of over 60 mph. If you're brave enough to hop on, Kumba swirls you around three first-of-a-kinds for coasters: an innovative diving loop, a camelback featuring a 360-degree spiral, and the world's largest loop. Other of the park's noted coasters include the Scorpion and the Python, both known for their dizzying loops.

Questor is another not-to-miss ride. This combination of flight simulation and special effects gives you roller coaster thrills in a sci-fi fantasy theme ride. Tanganyika Tidal Wave, one of the reasons you brought your bathing suit, takes you on a water "safari" that ends with a dousing by a big wave. Other watery wonders include the Stanley Falls log flume and the Congo River Rapids raft ride.

To its credit Busch Gardens is more than just a place for cheap thrills. The park makes an effort to feature wildlife habitats. The TransVeldt Railway takes you through the "Serengeti Plain," an area loosely representing the African savannah. Young kids especially like this easy way to sit back and see giraffes, gazelles, flamingoes, and ostriches. While the plains aren't teeming, enough animals amble by your window to hold your interest.

The Myombe Reserve, opened in 1992, features gorillas and chimpanzees in a three-acre tropical rain forest habitat. Take your kids by the petting zoo, the elephant habitat, and the Nairobi Field Station, where you can admire some interesting newborns through the glass. On one visit we saw a two-week-old cockatoo, a brand-new scarlet macaw, and a three-month-old gazelle. The Bird Gardens display a mixed, but colorful, grouping that includes more than just birds. You'll find koalas as well as 2,000 winged creatures, including Caribbean flamingos, and cockatoos. The Dwarf Village, located in the Bird Gardens, offers preschoolers and kindergartners a place to play. Thoughtfully, the area is mostly shaded, and you can relax on benches while your kids enjoy the fairy-tale theme and equipment.

When you enter the park, obtain a schedule of the daily shows. The variety acts—juggling, dancing, and magic—may appeal more to little kids than older ones, but try one of these as a way to rest a bit between the hustle and bustle of the rides and the roller coasters.

Adventure Island, 4500 Bougainvillea Avenue (813–987–5600), open mid-March through Labor Day, is located just ¼ mile from Busch Gardens. Cool off at this all-play park replete with twenty-two acres of water rides and sunbathing areas. Come early, though, perhaps an hour before the park opens. The chaise lounges and picnic tables are grabbed on busy days by 10:30 A.M. Bring towels, and a picnic lunch if you like. "Water socks" are a good idea as well since you and your kids will be dashing across paved areas to jump in and out of the water.

The brand-new Aruba Tuba twists under, over, and around the park's other water slides. You probably won't notice the other slides, though, as you rush through light into dark in this alternately open and closed tube. Fabian's Funport, added in 1992, offers water thrills scaled for young children. There are kiddie slides, a maze of water jets, a wave pool with gentle, rolling surf, and a spring that blows bubbles, sure to elicit giggles from

The Tanganyika Tidal Wave is a good reason to get wet when you visit Busch Gardens in Tampa. (Copyright © 1992 Busch Gardens Tampa)

even the most timid tot. Sunbathe on the surrounding decks while you keep a watchful eye on your little one climbing, sliding, and splashing.

The park also features attractions that delight school-age kids and even those hard-to-please teens. The hardy can ride down a four-story tower on the Caribbean Corkscrew, careen down the Gulf Scream slide; splash into the Everglides, a 72-foot-high water sled ride; and twist down the Runaway Rapids, a 34-foot-high series of water flumes. Nobody will be bored at Adventure Island.

More Zoos

Lowry Park Zoo, 7530 North Boulevard (813–935–8552), features a variety of animals from birds to alligators in twenty-four-acres of natural habitats. Be sure to visit the Manatee and Aquatic Center. Here you gaze upon lumbering masses of manatees. In fact they're at the zoo for more than our viewing pleasure. Lowry Park rehabilitates and studies these sea animals frequently found injured along Florida's west coast. Learn about the plight of these beasts and watch as the scientists go about their research in a laboratory open to public view.

Other attractions include a Florida aquatic and wetland animal exhibit, which includes freshwater and saltwater fish, coral, lobster, river otters, and Florida's most famous inhabitant—the alligator. With young children visit the petting zoo.

Museums

Museum of Science and Industry (MOSI), 4801 East Fowler Avenue; (813) 985–5531. Mosey on down to MOSI for half a day. Don't miss this science museum with more than 300 hands-on exhibits for all ages. New highlights to hit include WaterCycles, an educational exhibit about water resources and conservation in Florida, and the Florida Fossil Gallery, featuring a walk-through cavern filled with crystal-lined fissures and fossil impressions that's sure to please.

Younger children will be enchanted by the Butterfly Encounter, a delicate garden filled with dozens of free-flying butterflies. Then take your little one to Kids-in-Charge, a discovery area for those five and under. Tykes build their own houses and gardens, dress up like cowboys, and journey into a forest filled with stuffed animals.

There's much more: a simulated Gulf Coast hurricane, where you get blown away by 75-mile-per-hour winds; Wizard's Workshop, a lab which presents scientific experiments to small groups in a classroom atmosphere; Electric Plaza, which offers hair-raising fun as your locks stand on end from static electricity; and Dr. Thunder, who explains thunder and lightning.

MOSI offers a wide variety of fun-filled educational programs that require prior registration but are worth the planning. The fourth Saturday of each month (these times may change) is special. On those days any-one—not just school groups— can work the GTE Challenger Learning Center. Established as a memorial to the seven *Challenger* astronauts who perished in 1986, the center simulates a space mission. For four hours space-station teams take charge of navigation, communication, life support, and mission coordination in real-looking control rooms; it's more fun than the flight deck of a *Star Trek* vehicle.

Those with shorter attention spans can try a thirty-minute flight. Even the littlest children, ages three to five are accommodated in a Little Explorers science program. Ask about these programs as well as the family "Camp-In," an overnight learning adventure. You must register at least three weeks in advance. For more information call (813) 985–5092 or (800) 283–MOSI.

MOSI is in the midst of a fifteen-year, $35 million expansion and plans to triple in size, adding an OMNIMAX theater and the first-ever public library in a museum.

Museum of African-American Art, 1308 Marion Street; (813) 272–2466. Allow time for this one. Opened in 1991 this museum houses the Barnett-Aden Collection, considered one of the outstanding collections of nineteenth- and twentieth-century African-American art in the United States. Highlights include art from the Work Progress Administration and the Harlem Renaissance Period. Temporary exhibitions of works from the nineteenth and twentieth centuries are also presented.

There's more art at the **Tampa Museum of Art**, 601 Doyle Carlton Drive; (813) 223–8130. This museum specializes in classical antiquities and twentieth-century American art. Kids will like browsing through the Egyptian, Greek, and Roman antiquities collection. The museum also features up to twenty temporary exhibitions per year in addition to its permanent collection of over 7,000 pieces.

The Henry B. Plant Museum, 401 West Kennedy Boulevard (813–254–1891), displays turn-of-the-century artwork, furniture, and fashion in the former Tampa Bay Hotel, which dates to 1891. This hotel/museum—which once housed a casino, two ballrooms, a grand salon, and a swimming pool—gives an inside glimpse of Tampa's history.

If there's time you may want to stop at the **Children's Museum of Tampa**, 7550 North Boulevard; (813) 935–8441. Although it's hard to compete with Busch Gardens, Adventure Island, and MOSI, young children may like the outdoor miniature village and the indoor hands-on exhibits.

At the **Ybor City State Museum**, 1818 Ninth Avenue (813–247–6323), learn about Tampa's Latin heritage. Housed in an old bakery in the city's Latin Quarter, this museum delves into the history of Old Ybor City. La Casita (The Little House) recaptures the living quarters and life-style of the cigar makers.

Performing Arts

The **Tampa Bay Performing Arts Center** is at 1010 North MacInnes Place; (813) 222–1000/ Box Office (813) 221–1045 or (800) 955–1045. This facility includes a concert hall, festival hall, playhouse, and the intimate Jaeb Theater. This is the largest performing arts center south of Washington, D.C.'s Kennedy Center.

Check out what's playing at the **Tampa Theatre**, 711 Franklin Street Mall; (813) 223–8981. This fanciful theater, an attraction in itself, is housed in a restored 1926 movie palace ornately decorated with colonnades, balconies, and replicas of Greek and Roman sculpture. For further arts information call the **Arts Council** at (813) 229–ARTS. For Ybor City arts and entertainment events, call (813) 248–1381.

Tours

Ybor City Walking Tour. Don't forget that Tampa was once the "Cigar Capital of the World," populated by thousands of immigrants working in cigar factories. Take a free, guided, ninety-minute walking tour of Ybor City, Tampa's historic Latin quarter where more than 1,300 cigar factories were once concentrated. The tour focuses on historic sites in the neighborhood now transformed into an artist's and commercial community filled with shops, restaurants, and night spots. Call the Convention and Visitors Bureau at (813) 223–1111 for more information.

Canoe Tour. For kids old enough to paddle, an afternoon or day-long canoe trip along the Hillsborough River and through the sixteen-acre state park is an enjoyable way to see Florida's natural environment. Call Canoe Escape, 9335 East Fowler Avenue (813–986–2067), for more information.

Hot Air Balloon Ride. For a different perspective on Tampa and the surrounding area, leave earth on a big red balloon as you float over the city and its surrounding waterways. Call Big Red Balloon/Fantasy Flights, 16302 East Course Drive (813–969–1518), for more information.

Future Attractions

Tampa is building to become even more of a family destination. The **Florida Aquarium**, scheduled to open in April 1995 on Tampa's waterfront, is envisioned as among the country's largest and most modern facilities. Its four major exhibit areas mark the path of a drop of water. Visitors begin in freshwater springs and limestone caves, move to the bay and beaches, past coral reefs, and into the Gulf Stream and open ocean. Also planned is the **Whydah Pirate Complex**, scheduled to open in February 1995. Aboard the full-scale replica of the 110-foot pirate ship will be costumed interpreters demonstrating their roguish life. Visitors will be able to experience their own shipwreck on a simulated ride, then watch a movie about the salvage of the Whydah. But it's not purely fun and games. Families will be able to observe historic conservation methods in a working laboratory where Whydah artifacts are being restored. Then there's a lesson on justice at a reenactment of the Whydah pirate's trial in Boston, a history lesson on slave trading, and a hands-on marine archaeology exhibit.

The **Garrison Seaport Center,** slated to open in 1994, will serve as the revitalized waterfront's entertainment center and will include a Music-Dome amphitheater, concerts, a cinema complex, restaurants, and shops.

SPECIAL EVENTS

Sporting Events

Tampa offers a wide variety of sports events. The **Tampa Bay Lightning National Hockey** team (813–229–8800), Tampa's newest professional team, competes in the Exposition Hall at the Florida State Fairgrounds from September to April. The **Tampa Bay Buccaneers** football team (813–879–BUCS) plays at the Tampa Stadium from August through December. College football fans like the **Hall of Fame Bowl** (813–874–BOWL), usually held on New Year's Day. Soccer fans can root for the **Tampa Bay Rowdies** (813–877–7800) from May through August. Fans of the **Cincinnati Reds** can watch their team warm up at spring training in nearby Plant City. Call (813) 752–REDS for more information. For a free baseball game, check out the **New York Yankees' Minor League** team which competes at the Yankee Complex next to Tampa Stadium. Call (813) 875–7753 for further information. Polo matches are held Sunday afternoons from January to May. Call **Tampa Bay Polo Club** (813–223–2200) or **Cheval Polo and Golf Club** (813–920–3873).

Festivals

Winter is festival time in Tampa Bay. The most exciting is the **Gasparilla Festival** in February, when the legendary pirate Jose Gaspar and his rowdy crew invade the city from a fully rigged pirate ship for month-long pirate antics. Help Tampa hold on to the fort as hundreds of costumed pirates debark and attack. Then join in the fun of a parade, music, food, and crafts. For a good view of the invasion and parade, it's best to call ahead for reservations; (813) 223–4141.

Other festivals to check out are the Winter Equestrian Festival, the Strawberry Festival, and the Florida State Fair. See the following listing for phone numbers.

January: Franklin Street Mall Arts Festival.

February: Gasparilla Pirate Street Fest. Children's Gasparilla Parade. Florida State Fair.

March: Florida Strawberry Festival, Plant City. USF Jazz Festival on Harbour Island. Gasparilla Sidewalk Arts Festival and Performing Arts

Center Open House. Spring Arts and Crafts Festival, Ybor Square. Tampa Greek Festival.

March–April: Winter Equestrian Festival.

April: Jazz Festival, Harbour Island. Riverview Country Jamboree, Riverview.

May: Tastes of Ybor, Ybor City.

June: Florida Dance Festival.

July: Fourth of July Celebration. Summer Arts and Crafts Festival, Ybor City.

August: Harbour Island Boat Show.

September: Books by the Bay Festival, Harbour Island. International Festival.

October: Fall Arts and Crafts Festival, Ybor City. Seafood Festival. Guavaween, Tampa's Halloween Celebration, Ybor City. Brandon Balloon Festival at the Florida State Fairgrounds.

November: Zoofari Food Festival, Lowry Park Zoo.

December: Christmas Arts and Crafts Festival, Ybor City. First Night Tampa Bay, New Year's Eve Celebration, Harbour Island.

For a more extensive calendar of events, call the Tampa/Hillsborough Convention and Visitors Association at (800) 44–TAMPA or (813) 223–1111, ext.44. For a listing of arts and cultural events, call the Arts Council at (813) 229–6547.

WHERE TO STAY

Since the majority of the area's attractions are not near each other, almost any hotel location within Tampa is acceptable. Be sure to ask hotels about family and weekend packages, and deals in conjunction with Busch Gardens. These often include complimentary shuttle service to the park.

A pool is a must for those traveling in the warmer months, although your kids will appreciate it any time of year. All of the following hotels have pools.

Several hotels are situated around Busch Gardens, including **Crown Sterling Suites Tampa/Busch Gardens,** 11310 North Thirtieth Street (813–971–7690 or 800–433–4600); and **Quality Suites Hotel USF,** 3001 University Center Drive (813–971–8930 or 800–786–7446).

Both the **Holiday Inn Tampa–Busch Gardens,** 2701 East Fowler Avenue (813–971–4710 or 800–99–BUSCH) and the **Ramada Resort–Busch Gardens,** 820 East Busch Boulevard (813–933–4011 or 800–288–4011), are moderately priced and sometimes offer child-care services. Inquire.

The Wyndham Harbour Island Hotel, 725 South Harbour Island Boulevard (813–229–5000 or 800–822–4200), features deluxe accommodations on the waterfront at Harbour Island. If you prefer to be in the heart of downtown, the **Hyatt Regency Tampa**, 2 Tampa City Center (813–225–1234 or 800–233–1234), sometimes has a children's program and child-friendly services. Other possibilities include the waterfront **Guest Quarters Suite Hotel**, 3050 North Rocky Point Drive West (813–888–8800 or 800–424–2900); and the **Hampton Inn**, 4817 West Laurel Street (813–287–0778 or 800–426–7866).

For a more complete listing of accommodations, call (800) 44–TAMPA or take advantage of Discover Tampa (800–284–0404), a vacation information and planning hotline visitors can use to book complete vacation packages to Tampa and Central Florida, including hotels, car rentals, and tickets to attractions.

WHERE TO EAT

Tampa has a wide range of cuisine from fresh seafood catches straight out of the Gulf of Mexico to authentic Spanish and Cuban dishes in the city's ethnic neighborhoods. Red snapper, grouper, and shrimp are some regional favorites. Florida lobster can be a tasty change, although don't expect it to be like New England's. The waterfront is the place to go for a large selection of seafood restaurants, Cajun and Creole cuisine and music, plus a bay view.

Wine lovers won't want to miss **Bern's Steak House**, 1208 South Howard Avenue (813–251–2421), with an astounding collection of over seven *thousand* wines. Kids will love it for the juicy steaks and hamburgers, but make sure they eat some of the locally grown organic vegetables as well.

For a taste of Tampa's Spanish heritage, try the **Columbia Restaurant**, 601 South Harbour Island Boulevard (813–248–4961); it's operated by the fourth generation of the family that founded it in 1905. Inside, kids are dazzled by the Spanish decor and the flamenco dancing. Adventurous children will want to try some of the classic Spanish dishes, including seafood with saffron rice, and black bean soup with crusty Cuban bread. **Cafe Pepe**, 2006 West Kennedy Boulevard (813–253–6501), is a good place to try Spanish dishes in a casual, family atmosphere.

Ybor Square Ltd, 1901 North Thirteenth Street (813–247–4497), is a fun place to stop for lunch on your tour of Ybor City. Choose from a variety of ethnic cuisines all under the roof of this old cigar factory, and imagine yourself a factory worker in the early part of the century. Or, pop into one of the Cuban luncheonettes or creative cafés in Ybor City for a healthy and hefty sandwich. Taste some seafood gumbo or Jambalaya at **Cafe Creole**, 1330 East Ninth Avenue (813–247–6283) in Ybor City where there's live jazz and New Orleans–style brunches on Sundays.

DAY TRIPS

St. Petersburg

A mere 18 miles to the west, St. Petersburg and Tampa could almost be considered twin cities. The kids won't mind this half-hour drive to a day full of discovery at the Salvador Dalí Museum and the hands-on exhibits at Great Explorations just across the street.

Start at the **Salvador Dalí Museum**, 1000 Third Street, St. Petersburg; (813) 823–3767. This museum features the world's most comprehensive collection of works by this Spanish master. Kids who are bored by the mere mention of fine arts will be captivated by Dalí's paintings, which they may label "bizarre" or "awesome." Don't miss the extensive gift shop with everything from Dalí "softwatches" to frisbees.

Allow up to two hours at the Dali Museum before heading to **Great Explorations**, 1120 Fourth Street, St. Petersburg; (813) 821–8992. This hands-on museum for all ages features five permanent pavilions with exhibits on art, science, and health. Best bets include the hundred-foot-long Touch Tunnel, a dark maze of curves and slopes; sound sculptures where visitors activate high-tech art with their bodies; and the Body Shop, an interactive group of computers that teach health education by providing such data as nutritional analysis of your lunch.

The **Suncoast Seabird Sanctuary**, 18328 Gulf Boulevard, Indian Shores (813–391–6211), is just off the west coast of Tampa. Here a wide variety of injured native birds, including pelicans, herons, egrets, owls, and hawks are rehabilitated and then released. Families with a budding naturalist will find this humanistic refuge offering guided tours a must-see stop. A springtime favorite for children are the bouncing baby pelicans that nest here yearly. Come watch these playful brown birds in their pelican pen as they toss and bat at tennis balls with their bills or play "steal from your neighbor," a "game" in which they take something from another pelican and initiate a chase and a tug-of-war.

Sarasota

Sarasota, approximately 100 miles to Tampa's south, features the **John and Mable Ringling Museum of Art**, 5401 Bay Shore Road; (813) 355–5101. At this combination history-and-art museum created by the famous circus brothers, older children will appreciate the Circus Gallery filled with authentic circus posters, costumes, clown props, and calliopes. But there's more than the big-top hoopla: The museum is renowned for its fine collection of baroque art, including masterworks by Rubens. It's all housed in the Ringling mansion Ca'd'Zan, a thirty-room Venetian Renaissance palace of marble arches, ballrooms, and balconies built with a 1920s flair.

FOR MORE INFORMATION

Visitor Information Centers

The Tampa/Hillsborough Convention and Visitors Association, 111 Madison Street, Suite 1010 (800–44–TAMPA or 813–223–1111, ext. 44), has brochures on attractions, hotels, and restaurants. Other visitor centers are located at Ybor Square, at the Tampa Convention Center, and at the Shops on Harbour Island.

Other Useful Information and Numbers

Traveler's Aid: (813) 955–8771.

The public transit system, HARTline Information for Hearing Impaired: (813) 626–9158.

TDD Florida Relay Station: (800) 955–8771.

North Tampa Chamber of Commerce: (813) 980–6966.

Ybor City Chamber of Commerce: (813) 248–3712.

Greater Tampa Chamber of Commerce: (813) 228–7777.

Check out *Creative Loafing,* a weekly entertainment magazine, for current events.

Emergency Numbers

Ambulance, fire, and police: 911

Tampa General Hospital Emergency Room: (813) 251–7100

Poison Hotline: (813) 253–4444

Free medical information twenty-four hours a day: Ask-a-Nurse; (813) 870–4444

Twenty-four-hour pharmacy: Eckerd Drugs, 3714 Henderson Boulevard; (813) 876–2485

36
COLONIAL WILLIAMSBURG AND JAMESTOWN
Virginia

Colonial Williamsburg may be America's most well-known living-history museum. The area served as the capital of Virginia, England's oldest, largest, most populous, and richest colony from 1699 to 1776. Williamsburg's leading citizens were at the forefront of the struggle toward independence. Colonial Williamsburg and the historic Virginia triangle of Jamestown and Yorktown offer hands-on history that makes learning about Colonial life fun.

GETTING THERE

Williamsburg is midway between Richmond and Norfolk, Virginia. I-64 leads into town, which is easily accessible via car, plane, train, and bus.

Three airports will get you to the city of Williamsburg, which contains more than just Colonial Williamsburg, the historic area. The Newport News–Williamsburg International Airport (804–877–0221) offers only limited service. The Richmond airport, about 40 miles east of Williamsburg, and the Norfolk airport, 55 miles south of Williamsburg, offer frequent domestic and international service and also have car rental facilities.

Amtrak trains (800–USA–RAIL) stop in Williamsburg, 468 North Boundary Street, on northeast routes that also stop in Boston, New York, Philadelphia, Baltimore, Washington, and other major East Coast cities. Greyhound/Trailways, 468 North Boundary Street (804–229–1460), offers direct service to Williamsburg. For Colonial Williamsburg travel assistance and information, call 1–800–HISTORY.

GETTING AROUND

Once you reach Colonial Williamsburg, the best way to experience the
ambience is to travel around town the way most colonists did—on foot!
As cars are not allowed on historic site streets, visitors should park at the
visitor's center. From here a free shuttle bus service takes ticket holders
to the historic area. To travel to Jamestown and other attractions in the
area, a car is a necessity.

WHAT TO SEE AND DO

Colonial Williamsburg

This living-history community recreates eighteenth-century life in
Virginia's capital as it existed in the 1770s just before the Revolutionary
War. Stroll the streets and imagine the atmosphere and independent poli-
tics that drew Revolutionaries such as Thomas Jefferson and Patrick
Henry.

Tickets. What you see depends on what you pay, and your plans.
Williamsburg, once the political and cultural center of the New World,
has more than 500 buildings on its 173 acres, including eighty-eight
original homes, shops, public buildings, and taverns. To see it all—the
ninety acres of gardens, the exceptional museums (the DeWitt Wallace
Decorative Arts Gallery and the Abby Aldrich Rockefeller Folk Art Center), plus the nearby Carter's Grove plantation—a multiday stay is recommended. A basic admission gains you entrance to the historic area
buildings, plus a half-hour guided tour, but it doesn't admit you to some
highlights such as the Governor's Palace, the two museums, and the
plantation listed above. The Royal Governor's Pass, good for three consecutive days, adds entrance to the DeWitt Wallace Gallery, the Folk Art
Center, and Carter's Grove, all very much worth a visit.

If you plan to return to Williamsburg within a year, then consider the
slightly more expensive Patriot's Pass which gives you unlimited admission to all major exhibits, homes, and museums for one year. All types of
tickets are available at children's prices. Tickets are sold at the visitor's
center and at the courthouse in the historic area. Although you may
roam the historic district for free, you need a ticket to enter any of the
buildings and to use the public shuttles.

Visitor's Center. Colonial Williamsburg is big and can be overwhelm-
ing, so take some time to plan. Start off early at the visitor's center. First
make reservations for lunch and dinner if you have not already booked
them before your arrival, especially if you plan to dine at one of the historic taverns. Then get oriented by viewing the introductory thirty-five-
minute movie, *Williamsburg—The Story of a Patriot*. Pick up a copy of

the *Visitor's Companion*, a weekly newsletter, for a listing of specific events that may interest your family.

Special Interests: Family Life and Black History

The visitor's center or the **Family Resource Service** in the historic area (at the Robert Carter North Quarters, near the Governor's Palace) can direct you to specific exhibits about Colonial life. Do you live with kids who complain about loading the dishwasher or setting the table? Show them the chores their Colonial peers did every day by visiting the places that portray families with children. Depending on the season, these include the **James Geddy House,** home to a family of silversmiths, where you might encounter the children assisting in the shop. At the **Benjamin Powell House,** you may come upon the teenage daughters weeding the garden, practicing their cross-stitch with their mother, or doing their lessons with their music teacher. You may also meet Benjamin and Sarah, children of Mrs. Powell's personal slave, Rose. Listen to the boys speak in dialect as they help with the house laundry. At **Wetherburn's Tavern** meet Clarissa the laundress, Billy the waiter, and children Tom, Rachel, and Judy, who daily made beds, fetched water and firewood, and ran errands.

Colonial Williamsburg is also a good place to talk to your kids about slavery. After downplaying or downright ignoring the issue, Colonial Williamsburg began a Black History program in 1979, with events and activities steadily increasing since then. For a guide to places that tell the story of the "other half" (throughout the eighteenth-century half the town's population was black), obtain the brochure *African-American Interpretation and Presentations*. A two-hour walking tour, **The Other Half Tour,** highlights sites important to blacks and talks about their lives. In February, Black History Month, Colonial Williamsburg hosts additional lectures, storytellers, and activities. Ask about the **Brush-Everard House,** a home which at times is presented from the point of view of the slaves who worked there.

For another side of family life, a relatively new program explores the lives of another often forgotten group—women. The **Widows of Williamsburg Tour** discusses the ironic benefits of eighteenth-century widowhood and is told from the perspective of five widows of the era who represent different social classes. Listen to the slave Charlotte; Jane Vobe, proprietor of the King's Arms Tavern, and others talk of their lives. In March, in celebration of Women's History Month, the historic area offers more programs. Check for tickets and admission policies to these tours and special programs. Generally, there is an additional fee.

More tour highlights

Stroll the main road, the **Duke of Gloucester Street,** which extends from the Wren Building to the Capitol. Side streets lead to museums, private homes, shops, and to the Governor's Palace. While walking throughout the historic area, children often have the most fun engaging in spirited conversations with costumed interpreters on their way to the wig maker, the apothecary, or the tavern. Encourage your kids to talk to these "characters" who speak as if they are living in the eighteenth century. They'll tell you about running low on candles, and how their children play quoits (the Colonial version of horseshoes), but not about electricity or Nintendo. Touring the **Capitol** conveys a sense of English government, while a visit to the bakery, basket maker, apothecary, and wig maker shops presents the everyday necessities of eighteenth-century life. Kids find out who a cooper is and what a milliner does, and they witness a shoemaker and blacksmith at work. On an evening "Lanthorn Tour," find out about life before electricity and how craftspeople continued their work after the sun went down.

At the **Governor's Palace**, once home to Virginian governor Thomas Jefferson, view Colonial artifacts including some 800 guns and swords. Touring this gracious mansion instills a sense of English power, and a stroll by the Palace Green might get your kids to join in a game of quoits, hoop rolling, lawn bowling, or stilt walking. At the **courthouse**, from March through December, take the family to participate as plaintiffs, defendants, witnesses, and judges in eighteenth-century court cases.

In summer, a prime time for family visits, join a military encampment, a favorite attraction, which makes army folk out of tenderfoot visitors, kids included. After signing up with the Second Virginia Regiment, the new recruits practice drills, learn the bayonet lunge, present arms (using sticks instead of loaded muskets), and assist with cleaning and firing a cannon.

In winter, a less popular but extremely pretty time for a family visit, enjoy the festivities and natural decorations. Yes, Virginia, there is a holiday beyond neon, flashing red and green lights, and glad-handing Santas. Dance the minuet at a candlelight ball (great for teens who have learned their rhythms with hard rock), enjoy the carolers, visit tastefully decorated homes, and gaze at the moonlight reflecting on the icicles.

Don't miss the **Abby Aldrich Rockefeller Folk Art Center**, 307 South England Street. Kids are intrigued by the folk art with its unusual perspective; they comment on the lack of proportion and like the easily recognizable figures. Reopened in 1992 after extensive renovations, the collection is the first in the country devoted solely to folk art. With more than 400 paintings and objects, including old-fashioned toys, plus a schedule of temporary exhibits, the center is definitely worth a stop. You will be surprised at how much your kids like the tour.

The **DeWitt Wallace Decorative Arts Gallery**, 325 Francis Street, in the Public Hospital, is home to Colonial Williamsburg's art masterworks.

More than 8,000 seventeenth- through early nineteenth-century decorative delights, from silver and ceramics to linen and lace, are presented here. While the gallery may cater more to older children, don't avoid the place; instead find something to catch your child's interest. Go on a treasure hunt here; let your kids follow their fancies through a door and see what they find. These exceptional galleries unfold like boxes within boxes from the central masterworks gallery, which features exquisite Colonial furnishings, including tall case clocks, silk quilts, and a Chinese Chippendale mirror aflutter with gilded birds. Does your child take music lessons? Then find the case of eighteenth-century instruments. Is your fifth grader learning about geography? Browse the gallery of hand-colored Colonial maps where the pink for Virginia bleeds all the way past the Mississippi River, and Indian names mark the territories of Michigan.

Carter's Grove Plantation, U.S. 60 (804–220–7649), included in some ticket packages, is about 8 miles from the Colonial area. Take in the fourteen-minute slide presentation, *A Thing Called Time*, which provides a general overview of the 400 years of history at Carter's Grove. Then tour the mansion, dependencies, and grounds. The mansion, built by Carter Burwell in the 1750s, has been restored to its 1930s appearance. Take a guided tour of what architectural historian Samuel Chamberlain called the "most beautiful house in America."

The **Slave Quarter**, however, reveals a darker side of the plantation history. These reconstructed quarters, complete with corn crib, garden plots, and chicken coops, give a glimpse of the lives of 1770s farm slaves. Adjacent to the buildings are representative fields of wheat and corn.

Also on the plantation you'll find the **Winthrop Rockefeller** archeological museum, where artifacts discovered on the property reveal a seventeenth-century village, **Wolstenholme Towne**, which was destroyed by Indians in 1622, just three years after its founding. Some of partially recreated buildings are nearby. The plantation is closed in January and February.

Colonial National Historical Park: Jamestown and Yorktown

Colonial history continues at Jamestown, just 8 miles from Colonial Williamsburg, and at Yorktown. The National Park Service maintains the historic ruins here as part of the Colonial National Historical Park, which encompasses 9,000 acres of land on the peninsula between the York and James rivers, and includes the Jamestown Island, the Colonial Parkway, the Yorktown Battlefield, and the Cape Henry Memorial.

Jamestown Island, the westernmost point of Colonial Parkway (804–229–1733), is the original site of the Jamestown settlement, the first permanent English settlement, established in 1607, thirteen years before the pilgrims landed in Massachusetts. The colonists suffered se-

Trying out navigation equipment aboard Jamestown Settlement's Susan Constant.
(Courtesy Jamestown Settlement)

vere hardships. Two years after the settlement was founded, 440 of the
original 500 inhabitants had died from starvation and disease. Today the
only remaining structure among the ruins is the Old Church Tower.

Begin your tour at the visitor's center by watching an audiovisual presentation of the colony's tragic story. Then take the mile-long self-guided
tour of the ruins of New Towne, imagining the colonists life here nearly
four hundred years ago. For a more extensive exploration of the island,
take the 5-mile loop drive to witness the wilderness that these first
colonists encountered. Before you leave be sure to stop by the reconstructed Glasshouse of 1608 where a seventeenth-century craftsman
demonstrates glassblowing.

Jamestown Settlement, next to Jamestown Island (804–229–1607),
recreates the story of the colonists' struggle and eventual success, as well
as the life-style of the Native Americans whom the settlers encountered.
An indoor museum features three permanent galleries, and the history
continues outdoors in three recreated settings: a Powhatan Indian village,
James Fort, and full-scale replicas of the three ships that landed in 1607.

Begin your tour with a dramatic twenty-minute film, *Jamestown: The
Beginning,* for an overview. The English Gallery outlines the events in
England that led to the colonization of Jamestown and includes an exam-

ination of ship designs, navigational tools and maps. In the Powhatan Gallery contrast the British way of life with the Powhatan Indians, whose 10,000-year-old civilization is described through displays about their food, shelter, religion, and government. The Jamestown Gallery traces the development of the Jamestown Colony from the colonists' landing to the 1699 movement of the Virginia capital from Jamestown to Williamsburg.

Informed, families are ready to be transported to the seventeenth-century in the outdoor exhibits. At the Powhatan Indian Village, families can watch, and even help, the Native Americans grow and prepare food, tan animal hides, and make pottery or tools from antlers and bones. Follow a path from the Indian Village and arrive at a pier on the James River, where full-size replicas of the three ships that sailed to Jamestown are docked. Board one of the ships, climb the ladders, and experiment with the navigational tools and equipment. Costumed performers recount the four-and-a-half-month voyage, demonstrate piloting and navigation, and even set the sails. At Fort James help build and defend Jamestown, a recreated colony of homes, a church, a storehouse, and a guardhouse built in seventeenth-century style. Children can tend the gardens, play in games with the costumed colonists, and even be called to duty as part of the colony's militia.

Take the Colonial Parkway from Williamsburg to Yorktown, best known for the **Yorktown Battlefield** (804–898–3400), site of the finale of the American Revolution, October 1781. Stand on the ground where the Revolutionary War was finally considered over. This National Park Service site includes a museum and film as well as battlefield sites, Washington's Headquarters and Surrender Field, and the Yorktown Victory Monument.

Yorktown Victory Center (804–887–1776) leads you from the Boston Tea Party to the Yorktown victory in a short film, *The Road to Yorktown*. Outside in an encampment, history comes to life with costumed actors demonstrating war-time activities from musketry and field medicine to farming and cooking.

Other Area Attractions

In Williamsburg several other attractions are worth a browse. **The Old Dominion Opry**, 3012 Richmond Road, Williamsburg (804–564–0200), brings a little bit of Nashville to Williamsburg. Sing along to country music or laugh aloud at the featured comic. The nightly entertainment here is for the whole family. At the **Williamsburg Doll Factory**, 7441 Richmond Road (804–564–9703), old-fashioned dolls are alive and well. Visitors watch porcelain Lady Anne dolls being made and also can shop for dollhouse furnishings and stuffed animals.

Kids who are curious about how things are made will enjoy the movie about soap and candle making at the **Williamsburg Soap and Candle**

Factory, Route 60 West; (804) 564–3354. Then watch production first-hand from the factory's observation booth.

Water Country U.S.A., P.O. Box 3008, Williamsburg, Virginia 23187 (804–229–5665), is a water theme park located 3 miles (ten minutes) east of Busch Gardens and Colonial Williamsburg. Partner-up with your older kids and try the new Malibu Pipeline, a slippery chute that forms an enclosed tube for three-quarters of the ride. Tiny holes allow in just enough light for a wild strobe light effect. Young children like Kids Kingdom for inner tubing, tunnel crawling, and general splashing. Afterward, see the shows at Lillipad Landing.

In **Newport News,** visit the Mariners' Museum (804–595–0368) with its extensive collection of ship and maritime artifacts, and the **Virginia Living Museum** (804–595–1900), which features such native wildlife as otters and bobcats. (See the chapter on Virginia Beach/Hampton Roads.)

Special Tours

For a broad overview or a higher perspective on the area's geographical layout, try **Historic Air Tours;** (804) 253–8185. They'll fly you over Colonial Williamsburg, the Jamestown and Yorktown settlements, and the James River plantations.

SPECIAL EVENTS

For more information on Colonial Williamsburg, call (800) HISTORY.

February: In Williamsburg, activities take place over Washington's Birthday Weekend to celebrate Washington's life, from his youth through his service as a statesman and burgess in Williamsburg.

March: In honor of Women's History Month, Colonial Williamsburg focuses on the contributions of eighteenth-century women to the shaping of our nation. Military Through the Ages, Jamestown, is a reenactment of camp life, tactics, weaponry, and military encounters throughout history.

April: Garden Day in Williamsburg, tour local homes and gardens in celebration of Virginia's Garden Week.

May: Relive the dramatic events leading to the American Revolution in Colonial Williamsburg. Celebrate the 1607 landing of the Jamestown Settlers with the fanfare on Jamestown Landing Day.

June: Families participate in the colorful festivities of the Virginia Indian Heritage Festival, Jamestown, which include storytelling, dance, demonstrations, and sales of Indian crafts and foods.

July: Experience the British occupation of Williamsburg.

August: Experience the excitement of the seventeenth-century militia during the Muster of Seventeenth-Century Military Arts, Jamestown.

September: Don't miss the Publick Times celebration, Colonial Williamsburg. Kids and parents alike enjoy the dances, games, auctions, horse races, barbecues, magic shows, and military events.

November: Cast your vote in the election of the new mayor during the St. Andrew's Day and Mayoral Election, Colonial Williamsburg. Meet the candidates and learn about the political issues of the day and the electoral process. Enjoy the feasts in Seventeenth-Century Virginia, Jamestown, which features the foods of the English settlers and the Powhatan Indians.

December: Christmas season officially opens with the Grand Illumination of the City, Colonial Williamsburg. Celebrate Christmas the old-fashioned way, the seventeenth-century way.

WHERE TO STAY

Colonial Williamsburg offers a number of hotels within the historical area or nearby. The hotels vary in elegance and price, but the one most suited for families, and one of the least expensive, is the **Williamsburg Woodlands**, located right behind the visitor's center. This lodging offers babysitting services, bike rentals, and, in summer, the Young Colonials Club, available to kids ages five to twelve from noon to 3:00 P.M. and 5:30 to 9:30 P.M. daily. The Woodlands Grill offers Family Night with an all-you-can-eat menu.

Both the **Williamsburg Lodge** and the **Williamsburg Inn**, which is an upscale property, offer activity programs in summer for kids. In addition to arts and crafts, Little Patriots takes kids five to seven on animal tours, and the Capitol Kids' club offers ages eight to twelve fitness classes, miniature golf, and other activities.

The Governor's Inn is a motel-type property within walking distance of the historic area. Guests here have access to the recreational activities at the Williamsburg Woodlands, including Young Colonials Club activities. Guests at any of the Official Colonial Williamsburg Hotels receive specially priced Hotel Guest admission tickets and complimentary guided walking tours. Call 1–800–HISTORY for reservations at any hotel.

Kingsmill Resort, 1010 Kingsmill Road, Williamsburg; (804) 253–1703 or (800) 832–5665. Situated on the banks of the James River, this conveniently located, upscale property offers a respite for kids and adults. Besides an eighteen-hole golf course, tennis courts, outdoor and indoor swimming pools, racquetball, and a fitness center, in summer the property offers a supervised, half-day or full-day children's program, the Kingsmill Kampers, for ages five to twelve. Ask about off-season packages including a Family Times package which includes such benefits as one free night's stay for every two nights purchased.

Many **bed and breakfasts** welcome families. **The War Hill Inn**, 4 miles from Colonial Williamsburg, is decorated with comfortable country furnishings and offers thirty-two acres of fields to roam and black Angus cattle to watch. The property offers a separate, two-bedroom cottage that works well for families. The **Williamsburg Cottage**, a 1,300-square-foot house less than a mile from the historic area, has a bedroom, parlor with pull-out sofa, and kitchenette for snacks. Contact Bensonhouse, 2036 Monument Avenue, Richmond (804–353–6900), for more information on both of these.

A Virginia historian hosts guests at the **Newport House** (804–229–1775), five minutes by foot from Colonial Williamsburg. **The Legacy of Williamsburg Bed and Breakfast** (804–220–0524 or 800–962–4722) is just six blocks from Colonial Williamsburg and offers billiards or eighteenth-century games to families.

The following campgrounds offer discounts: **Jamestown Beach Campsites** (804–229–7609 or 804–229–3300) and **Williamsburg KOA Kampground** (804–565–2907 or 800–635–2717), which also has a complimentary shuttle service to Colonial Williamsburg.

Call the Williamsburg Area Convention and Visitor's Bureau (804–253–0192) for a free brochure on accommodation packages. The Williamsburg Hotel and Motel Association (800–446–9244) offers a complimentary reservation service.

WHERE TO EAT

In Colonial Williamsburg try the four local taverns. With waiters and waitresses in period costumes and balladeers strolling through, dining is fun, and the food is okay. As these places are popular, book your meal reservations when you make your room reservations. Each tavern serves a different cuisine, with some Colonial dishes. **Campbell's Tavern**, 120 Waller Street, offers seafood. Campbell's most noteworthy plates include clam chowder, jambalaya, and lobster. Try the spoon bread here. **Chowning's Tavern**, 100 East Duke of Gloucester Street, serves up meat: pork chops, prime rib, pork rib, and steak; and is known for its Brunswick stew. The **King's Tavern**, 409 East Duke of Gloucester Street, has southern dishes such as Virginia Baked Ham, fried chicken, and peanut soup. **Shield's Tavern**, 417 East Duke of Gloucester Street, is a fowl place—in the sense of winged fare—and also serves a modest seafood menu, including crayfish soup. At Shield's try such Colonial desserts as Indian pudding or syllabub—a whipping cream and lemon juice dessert. Call (804) 229–1000 to make reservations for all the Williamsburg taverns.

Nearby Route 60 (Richmond Road) offers a string of restaurants from fast-food to fine dining. Here's a listing of a few reliable, family-friendly restaurants: **La Tolteca**, 2227 Richmond Road (804–253–2939), offers Mexican cuisine; **Nick's Pewter Plate**, 1329 Richmond Road (804–229–4309), is open for breakfast and lunch and serves a variety of pancake and breakfast dishes; **Calabash Seafood**, 6528 Richmond Road (804–565–1074), serves fresh seafood for lunch and dinner.

DAY TRIPS

Busch Gardens, Williamsburg; (804) 253–3350. Take a break from history at an all-fun park where you get twirled, tossed, drenched with torrents of water, scared by monsters—and still come away giggling for more. Busch Gardens combines high-speed "loopy" roller coasters, such as Drachen fire, with live entertainment, and throws in a bit of culture with German, French, and Italian villages. Be sure to experience one of the park's newest attractions, Haunts of the Olde Country, a ghoulish film in four dimensions; this 3-D movie includes unexpected gusts of cold air, mist, and rain. Totally Television, another production, pays homage to the sport of couch potatoes with a combination of live action and TV clips. Little kids find pint-size entertainment at Grimm's Hollow where they can hop on a ride or join in as Mother Goose leads in song singing and story telling.

Paramount's **King's Dominion**, Doswell (804–876–5000), yet another family theme park, has recently added the razzle dazzle of movies to the thrills of roller coasters, water rides, and a wild animal park. The new Days of Thunder ride puts you in the driver's seat for a simulated stock-car race. Calm down by watching the new Paramount on Ice skating show, where performers glide along to movie hit songs, satirize scenes from *Naked Gun Two and a Half*, and create "Star Trek" aliens on ice skates. Who knows, you may even spot some Klingons or Romulans in the crowd.

The **plantations along the James River** give a glimpse into the pomp and pleasures of prosperous life in the New World. From the drawing rooms of Shirley and Berkeley Plantations, the lawns sweep to the river, and the antiques trace an ancestry that dates to Queen Elizabeth.

Some of the lesser-known plantations offer a more personal view of history, fewer crowds, and more space to enjoy the sweeping views of the James River. **Shirley Plantation**, 35 miles west of Williamsburg on Route 5, Charles City (804–829–5121), is Virginia's oldest. This imposing brick, Queen Anne, manor house built in 1723, sits like a crown jewel, flanked by its dependencies. Shirley exudes a genteel hospitality and a lived-in practicality; it is still a working plantation and home to the ninth generation of Hill Carters, whose scion may often be seen out the windows overseeing farm chores in his blue jeans.

At **Berkeley**, two miles down the road, Route 5, Charles City (804–829–6018), you'll discover a site of unusual historic firsts. Birthplace of Benjamin Harrison, a signer of the Declaration of Independence, and William Henry Harrison, ninth President of the United States, this Georgian, brick manor house was built in 1726. It was the site of the first "Thanksgiving" in 1619 and witnessed the composition of "Taps" during a Civil War encampment.

If children don't appreciate the Virginian antiques and landscaped terraces, their curiosity will be piqued by the story of the plantation's thirty-year restoration from its 1907 condition when sheep inhabited the manure-covered basement and pigs ate out of the dining room windows. For more information contact the **James River Plantations**, Petersburg Visitor Center, Old Market Square, Petersburg (804–733–2400), or Hopewell Visitor Center, 201-D Randolph Square, Route 10, Hopewell (804–541–2206).

FOR MORE INFORMATION

For more tourist information concerning Colonial Williamsburg, contact (800) HISTORY. For information about Williamsburg, Jamestown, and Yorktown, call the **Williamsburg Area Convention and Visitors Bureau**, P.O. Box GB, Williamsburg, Virginia 23187; (804) 253–0192 or (800) 368–6511.

Emergency Numbers
Ambulance, fire, and police: 911
Poison Control: (800) 552–6337
There are no twenty-four-hour pharmacies in the Williamsburg area. In the event of a pharmaceutical emergency, try contacting Williamsburg Community Hospital's emergency room. For normal pharmaceutical service, try the Williamsburg Drug Company, Duke of Gloucester Street in Merchants Square, Williamsburg, Virginia; (804) 229–1041.
Williamsburg Community Hospital Emergency Room, 1238 Mount Vernon Avenue, Williamsburg, Virginia; (804) 253–6000

37
CHICAGO
Illinois

Chicago, one of the Midwest's most popular destinations, serves up great architecture and art, world-class museums, a top-notch aquarium, and miles of lakefront and bicycle paths. Stroll the parks and the zoo, pedal by the lake, take a boat ride, and play ball on the beach. In this exciting city you and your kids won't be bored. Take your family on weekends when hotels are discounted, or be sure to bring the kids along on a business trip so all of you can savor this dynamic city.

GETTING THERE

O'Hare International Airport (312–686–2200), 17 miles from the Loop, is served by most major airlines. The Chicago Transit Authority (CTA—312–686–7000) offers train transportation between Chicago and O'Hare. Train service originates at O'Hare Terminal #4 and in Chicago at the Dearborn Subway station. Midway Airport (312–767–0500), 15 minutes from the Loop at 5700 South Cicero Avenue, is the second most traveled airport in Chicago. Merril C. Meigs Field (312–744–4787) sits on Chicago's lakeshore at Fifteenth Street and caters mostly to private aircraft.

Amtrak (800–USA–RAIL) stops at Chicago's Union Station, 210 South Canal Street; (312) 558–1075. Continental Bus Airport Service (312–454–7800) shuttles to and from Chicago's main airports. Greyhound/Trailways buses (312–781–2900) stop at Chicago station, 630 West Harrison Street.

The main highways to Chicago are I–90, which cuts across Chicago's northwest axis and becomes the Chicago Skyway south of the Loop; I–94 (the Dan Ryan Expressway), which runs north-south. From the south, take I–55 (Stevenson Expressway) and I–57. From the west, take I–294 west of Chicago and I–88.

GETTING AROUND

The key to Chicago's streets is to know where you are in relation to Lake Michigan, due east of the city, which looms like an inland ocean. Chicago's north-south axis is Madison Avenue, and its east-west axis is State Street. As you move away from these streets, addresses increase 100 for each block.

Chicago's elevated train system, fondly called the "El," operates six routes throughout the city and suburbs. For information contact RTA Travel Information Center at (312) 836–7000 or (800) 972–7000, or the CTA office on the 7th floor of the Merchandise Mart. El routes have "A" and "B" trains which, during rush hours, each make different stops. Fares can be paid in cash or in tokens, which are offered, among other places, at Jewel and Dominick's grocery stores.

CTA buses (312–836–7000) travel along Chicago's major streets. For both bus and the El, senior citizens, the physically challenged, and children seven to eleven receive discounted fares and transfers. Kids under seven ride for free. For a **PACE** bus (312–836–7000), which provides additional service, wait at the blue-and-white PACE signs. PACE transfer tickets are valid for El trains.

METRA offers train service from the suburbs into the city, with eleven commuter routes transporting riders from 225 outlying stations to four Chicago stations. Call (312) 322–6777 weekdays from 8:00 A.M. to 5:00 P.M., (312) 836–7000 evenings and weekends.

Sometimes the easiest and quickest way to get somewhere is by boat. **Wendella Commuter Boats,** Michigan Avenue Bridge at the Wrigley Building (312–337–1446), offers boat taxi service on the Chicago River at prices competitive with CTA transit. Boats leave every ten minutes from a commuter dock north of Madison Avenue, or from the Wendella dock south of Michigan Avenue below the Wrigley Building. Besides its seven-minute Madison-Wrigley Building route, the company offers extended trips into Lake Michigan, as well as two-hour, ninety-minute, and one-hour guided tours. Senior citizens and kids under eleven receive discounted tickets.

WHAT TO SEE AND DO

Must-See Museums

At the **Museum of Science and Industry**, Fifty-seventh Street and Lake Shore Drive (312–684–1414, TT/TDD 312–684–DEAF), the diverse exhibits take you on a fun tour of fact and fantasy. A walk through a U-505 German submarine captured in 1944 makes the hard-to-envision world of undersea gauges, gizmos, and cramped quarters real. Browse silent screen star Colleen Moore's elaborate Fantasy Castle. With its tapestries, and over 1,000 miniature pieces, this dollhouse delights the child within and the one by your side. Explore the human body by walking through a 16-foot pulsating heart and by looking at fetuses floating in bottles.

Train buffs won't want to leave the model train exhibit with its eight railroads that run through reconstructed sets of the Midwest, the Great Plains, the Grand Canyon, and California. Two more top picks are the OMNIMAX theater, with its 5-story-high screen, and, for kids ages seven to twelve, the "Kids Stairway, A Path to Self-Discovery." This interactive exhibit is designed to build children's self-esteem, help them discover feelings, and teach them about alcohol and substance abuse. A visit here serves as a start to important discussions you and your children continue later.

For another, less intense take-home "item," visit the gift shop where your kids can bring home a bit of science fun with a physics game, a rocket model kit, an anatomical coloring book, stickers, and puzzles.

Marine science is the thing at the **John G. Shedd Aquarium,** 1200 South Lake Shore Drive; (312) 939–2438. Billed as one of the world's largest indoor marine mammal habitats, kids fall in love with this undersea world of brightly colored fish, coral reefs, turtles, sea otters, dolphins, and whales.

Time your visit for 11:00 A.M. or 2:00 P.M., and watch the action in the 900,000-gallon Coral Reef tank as divers feed the sharks, sea turtles, and scores of tropical fish. Each of several galleries serves up tankfuls of colorful critters. In the Indo-Pacific gallery, admire such brightly marked wrigglers as the yellow longsnout butterfly fish or the white-and-brown spotted clown triggerfish. Other galleries feature anemones swaying gently in the water, neon-colored starfish, and purple sea urchins.

The spectacular **Oceanarium,** with its sweeping view of Lake Michigan, recreates a Pacific Northwest coastal environment. The view alone is worth the admission, but the wildlife is great, too. Follow the "trails" through a mini–rain forest accompanied by chirping birds and crickets, and the rush of a waterfall, then admire the sea otters in tidal pools, the beluga whale, and the colony of penguins.

But the big attraction is the dolphin show, held five times daily in the ampitheatre. Learn why these graceful behemoths lobtail (slap their tails on the water), breach, porpoise (leap out of the water and enter again), and tail walk (move backwards on their tails). These are just some of the animal behaviors explained and delightfully demonstrated.

Across the street from the Shedd Aquarium, the **Field Museum of Natural History,** Roosevelt Road, Lake Shore Drive (312–922–9410), is an amazing place of a different sort. It's housed in a large, 1921 marble building claiming to be the largest marble structure in the United States. Although

The interactive exhibits at Chicago's Field Museum of Science will intrigue adults and kids alike. (Photo by Ron Schramm/courtesy Chicago Tourism Council)

the collection celebrates its centennial in 1993–1994, the exhibits are anything but old-fashioned and stodgy. Interactive, visually exciting, and interesting, these exhibits intrigue kids. There's too much here even for one visit. So let your kids hit the highlights, pausing at what intrigues them.

Don't miss Inside Ancient Egypt, a well-done exhibit which demystifies and explains the ancient burial rites. Walk into a recreated Egyptian tomb with its passageways and learn about mummies, hieroglyphics, and embalming. See your face transformed with "Egyptian" features, and find out the symbolism of the pyramid.

Traveling the Pacific brings you to a world of outrigger canoes, intricately carved masks, and a recreated Tahitian market. Into the Wild takes you through habitats as diverse as prairies, wetlands, lakes, and cliffs to learn about birds and other critters.

If you liked this place during the day, try it out on a special family overnight. Ever wonder what it would be like to roam through a museum after-hours when the crowds have left, and it's only you, the elephant bones, and the sound of your footsteps echoing on the linoleum? This Chicago museum gives you the chance to sleep with the dinosaurs, the Polynesian spear throwers, or the gigantic mounted elephants. On overnights, families select two workshops from possibilities as diverse as how to read Egyptian hieroglyphics, recognize dinosaur footprints, or identify owl calls. After a snack the evening offers such fun as a storyteller who relates Eskimo or African legends, or an educational scavenger hunt. When the lights go out, join a group of adventurers for a flashlight tour of the Egyptian tomb, or walk into the prairies, oceans, and forests of Into the Wild, alive with birdcalls and insect noises. Then, cuddle up in your sleeping bag, maybe next to a bushman, the gorilla, or among the thousands of mounted birds. This is a night you'll remember. A family overnight occurs each month. Fees are charged, and book well in advance. Call (312) 322–8854.

Explore the skies at the **Adler Planetarium**, 300 South Lake Shore Drive; (312) 322–0304. The planetarium's multimedia Sky Show shuttles visitors through our solar system and off into distant galaxies. Before Sky Show ends it transports you back in time fifteen million years to revisit the origins of the universe. As part of the Evening Sky Shows, which occur each Friday night, the planetarium gives close-up looks at the moon, planets, and galaxies via the planetarium's 20-inch telescope, which is hooked up with a large-screen closed-circuit monitor. For children under six, who are not admitted to the regular sky show, reserve a spot in the Children's Sky Show, Saturdays and Sundays. Allow time to browse the exhibits on the solar system, the stars, telescopes, and astronomy.

Heavenly is what you're likely to call the art at the **Art Institute of Chicago**, Michigan Avenue at Adams Street; (312) 433–3600. Spanning more than forty centuries from Mayan to modern, this place is a visual treat.

Among the highlights are the prized collection of French Impressionist and Postimpressionist paintings by Degas, Monet, and Renoir; the collection of American and European painting 1900–1950; the sixty-eight Thorne Miniature Rooms, and Marc Chagall's stained-glass work "America Windows."

Drop by the Kraft General Foods Education Center, a just-for-kids-and-families place that has changing exhibitions, a computer, storytelling, and often hands-on workshops. Tuesdays are free admission days at the **Art Institute**.

The city's history comes alive at the **Chicago Historical Society**, Clark Street at North Avenue; (312) 642–4600. Learn about pioneer life in the Land of Lincoln—often crafts demonstrations are held—climb aboard the *Pioneer*, the first twelve-ton locomotive to steam through this railroad town, and find out what Mrs. O'Leary's cow did or didn't do in the Great Chicago Fire, October 1870.

Visiting with a child ages five to nine? Then check out Kidstory, every Saturday at 2:00 P.M. Kids paint, listen to tales, make crafts, and do a variety of other projects. At the Hands-on History Gallery little fingers touch some real city legends by feeling a beaver skin, perusing old Sears' Catalogues, and listening to tapes of "Fibber McGee and Molly."

More Attractions and Views

Watch the art of the deal at Chicago's big three exchanges. From visitor's galleries look at the bustling floor frenzy at the **Chicago Board of Trade**, 141 West Jackson Boulevard (312–435–3590) open 8:00 A.M.–2:00 P.M. It's the oldest and the largest futures exchange. The **Chicago Mercantile Exchange**, 30 South Wacker Drive (312–930–8249), is open 7:30 A.M. to 3:15 P.M.; and you can visit the **Chicago Board Options Exchange** at 400 South LaSalle Street (312–786–5600) from 8:30 A.M. to 3:15 P.M.

A Chicago institution of another sort is Frank Lloyd Wright. At the **Frank Lloyd Wright Historic District Visitors Center**, 158 North Forest Avenue, Oak Park, Illinois 60301 (708–848–1500), take a guided tour of this architect's home and studio, and see the birthplace of the Prairie School of architecture. Wright's vision and others made this midwest city famous for its buildings.

From the **Sears Tower Skydeck**, Jackson Boulevard between Franklin Street and Wacker Drive (312–875–9696); or from the **John Hancock Center Observatory**, 875 North Michigan Avenue (312–751–3681), enjoy a panoramic view of Chicago, which on a clear day can include a glimpse of Michigan, Indiana, and maybe even Wisconsin.

For some great skyline views, visit **Navy Pier**, 600 East Grand Avenue (312–791–7437), and **North Pier**, 435 East Illinois Street (312–836–4300). In summer Navy Pier hosts many free public programs both indoors and outdoors. North Pier also has a shopping mall, the **Chicago Children's Museum**, and the **Chicago Maritime Museum**. Relatively small, the

Chicago Children's Museum is at 435 East Illinois Street on the top floor of the North Pier (312–527–1000). It offers a playful place where kids can dress up as a CTA driver, slip into a body bubble, pretend in a log cabin, and crawl through a tunnel of textures. A separate walled-in area for toddlers and tots eighteen months and younger has boxes of safe goodies, balls, and mirrors. Find out when crafts workshops are held so your kids can create their own special Chicago souvenir.

Before you leave North Pier, take a peek at the Chicago Maritime Museum, 465 East Illinois (312–836–4343), which includes a gallery of model schooners, cargo vessels, and other boats that helped build Chicago's business.

Chicago also boasts world-class street art that's worth a look. Among the best is the Picasso Sculpture, Washington and Dearborn streets at the Daley Center. The artist dedicated this 50-foot-tall structure to the people of Chicago.

Another city staple is Wrigley Field, 1060 West Addison; (312) 404–CUBS. One of the oldest baseball stadiums, it has ivy-covered fences and home runs that catch the wind and fly out of the park onto Waveland Avenue. Check the schedule for Cubs' games.

Green Spaces and Lakefront

Parks along the lakefront were part of Chicago's design. These include Lincoln Park, Grant Park, Burnham Park, Jackson Park, and Washington Park. All have playing fields and usually host a festival or two throughout the year. A 20-mile bike path cuts through these parks and offers scenic views of both the lake and Chicago's skyline; for more information on the park's bike path call (312) 744–8092.

Gardens and Zoos

Brookfield Zoo, First Avenue and Thirty-first Street, Brookfield, Illinois 60513; (708) 485–0263. Located 14 miles west of downtown, this naturalistic habitat zoo covers 204 acres and displays more than 2,000 animals. Visit Tropic World and The Fragile Kingdom for Brookfield Zoo's most extravagant attempts at recreating nature. Tropic World portrays life in the three great rainforests: Africa, Asia, and South America. The exhibit features a mixture of fauna, free-roaming small animals, exotic birds, and three daily thunderstorms. The Fragile Kingdom highlights desert, rainforest, and mountainous regions. The Seven Seas Panorama displays Bottle-nose Dolphins, and the Children's Zoo has tame creatures to pet. And don't miss the zoo's newest exhibit, Habitat Africa! Save your feet and take a Motor Safari tour. During winter, the tram offers heated tours of the zoo aboard the Snowball Express. The zoo can be accessed by I–55 and I–290 (Stevenson and Eisenhower expressways) as well as I–294 (Tri-State Tollway).

Chicago Botanic Garden, Lake Cook Road, a half-mile east of I–90–94 (Edens Expressway), Glencoe, Illinois; (708) 835–5440. This blooming, three-hundred-acre wonder contains a sensory garden for the visually impaired, a nine-acre prairie and nature trail, and a three-island authentic Japanese Garden. Be sure to visit the greenhouses, gift shop, and the Museum of Floral Arts.

Minutes north of downtown, the **Lincoln Park Zoo**, 2200 North Cannon Drive (312–294–4662), is the place to bring your kids for a city safari. Take a close look at a swimming polar bear, elephants, rhinos, giraffes, gorillas, orangutans, and chimpanzees. To entertain wee ones, head for the petting zoo at the Pritzker Children's Zoo.

Tours

For **Architecture/Walking** tours of the city contact the following: **ArchiCenter**, 224 South Michigan Avenue (312–922–3432); **Chicago Architecture Foundation**, 1800 South Prairie Avenue (312–922–3432); **Oak Park Tour Center/Frank Lloyd Wright Tour**, 951 Chicago Avenue, Oak Park, Illinois (708–848–1500); and **Pullman Historic District**, 11111 South Forrestville Avenue (312–785–8181).

Boat Tours. **Chicago's First Lady**, southwest corner and lower level of the Michigan Avenue bridge and Wacker Drive (708–358–1330), offers lunch, brunch, and dinner tours of Chicago sailing aboard the *Chicago's First Lady* 1920s-style luxury cruiser. **Mercury, Chicago's Skyline Cruiseline**, southwest corner and lower level of the Michigan Avenue Bridge (312–332–1353), offers daily one-hour, ninety-minute, or two-hour cruises and skyline tours during the morning, afternoon, and evening from May 1 through October 1 (ask about the Pirate Cruise for Kids). **Chicago From the Lake**, North Pier Terminal, 455 East Illinois Street (312–527–1977 and 527–2002), offers a ninety-minute tour of the Chicago River or the Chicago skyline; both tours are led by a member of the Chicago Architecture Foundation.

Bus Tours. **Gray Line of Chicago Sightseeing Tours**, originating at the Palmer House, 33 East Monroe Street (312–346–9506), offers daily comprehensive tours. **London Motor Coach** departs from Pearson and Michigan Avenue (312–226–2870) on its one-hour narrated double-decker bus tour of the city. Day Long Transfer passes are available for getting on and off the bus at designated points of interest, including the Wrigley Building, Art Institute, Sears Tower, Shedd Aquarium, the Field Museum, Adler Planetarium, Water Tower, and the Magnificent Mile.

Other Tours. **Untouchable Tour's Chicago's Original Gangster Tour** takes you back to Chicago's gangster days. Visit Al Capone's, John Dillinger's, and Bugs Moran's notorious hangouts and hit spots. For reservations call (312) 881–1195.

For a slow-paced, sweet, horse-drawn tour in a buggy, see the

Chicago Horse and Carriage Company, southeast corner of Pearson Street and Michigan Avenue (312–94–HORSE); or try the Noble Horse, available at the southwest corner of Pearson and Michigan (312–266–7878).

Shopping

Hit the Magnificent Mile's shops along Michigan Avenue, from the Chicago River north to Oak Street. If you have time for just one stop, you might visit Water Tower Place, 835 North Michigan Avenue (312–440–3165), which has department stores Marshall Field's and Lord and Taylor, as well as specialty shops such as Benetton, Laura Ashley, a Disney Store, Beauty and the Beast, F.A.O. Schwarz, and, for snacks, Aunt Diana's Old Fashioned Fudge, Mrs. Field's Cookies, and California Pizza Kitchen.

Performing Arts

Chicago offers cutting-edge theater, good comedy, and well-done plays. Home to some of the best are the Steppenwolf Theatre, 2851 North Halstead (312–472–4141); Second City, 1616 North Wells (312–337–3992); and Second City Children's Theater. Around Christmas, the Goodman Theater, 125 East Monroe Avenue (312–855–1524), puts on *A Christmas Carol;* and the Arie Crown Theater, McCormick Place (312–791–6000), hosts *The Nutcracker* ballet.

Some children's theaters include the Animart Puppet Theater, 3901 North Kedzie Avenue (312–267–1209); The Children's Theatre Fantasy Orchard (Chicago Historical Society), 1629 North Clark Street (312–539–4211); DePaul Merle Reskin Theatre, 60 East Balbo Drive (312–362–8455); Funstuff at the Improv, 504 North Wells Street (312–527–2500), which hosts a musical variety show for kids on Saturdays at 2:00 P.M. Arrive by 1:30 P.M. for the cartoons and the magician. Hystopolis Puppet Theatre, 441 West North Avenue (312–787–7387) offers sophisticated puppet play, and the Stage Left Theater, 3244 North Clark Street (312–883–8830), offers plays about social issues but aimed at kids. Check local listings or call the Theatre Information Line at (312) 977–1755.

The Chicago Symphony Orchestra, as well as other orchestras and singers, perform at the Civic Opera House (312–346–0270) and the Lyric Opera House (312–332–2244), both located at 20 North Wacker Drive.

Looking for art galleries? Head to Chicago's "Su-Hu" district, located aptly enough at the intersection of Superior and Huron streets.

More Useful Numbers. Hot Tix booths are at 24 South State Street, Chicago; 1020 Lake, Oak Park, Illinois; and 1616 Sherman Avenue, Evanston, Illinois. They offer half-price day-of-performance and full-price advance tickets for theater, music, dance, and all Ticketmaster events. Call (312) 977–1755 for hours and additional booth locations. Ticketmaster (312–559–8989 or 559–1212) offers full-price tickets for theater, dance, and musical events.

SPECIAL EVENTS

Sporting Events

Chicago Bears Football, Soldiers Field Stadium, 425 East Mcfetridge Drive: (312) 663–5100.

Chicago Blackhawks Hockey, Chicago Stadium, 1800 West Madison Street: (312) 733–5300.

Chicago Bulls Basketball, Chicago Stadium, 1800 West Madison Street: (312) 559–1212.

Chicago Cubs Baseball, Wrigley Field, 1060 West Addison: (312) 404–CUBS.

Chicago White Sox Baseball, Comiskey Park, 333 West Thirty-fifth Street: (312) 924–1000.

Festivals

The big crowds come to Grant Park in May, usually Memorial Day weekend, for **Chicago's Blues Festival** and in June for the annual **Gospel Festival. Ravinia Festival** in north suburban Highland Park, Illinois, draws large crowds during the summer months for its schedule of outdoor jazz, blues, classical, and folk concerts.

January: University of Chicago Folk Festival.

February: African-American History Month.

March: St. Patrick's Day Festival, where parents can drink green beer and see the Chicago River dyed green.

April: Chicago Cubs and White Sox Baseball season opens. Chicago Park District Public Golf Courses open. Spring Festival of Dance. Spring Flower Show (free). International Kennel Club Spring Dog Show Weekend.

May: Chicago Blues Festival. Chicago Day.

June: Chicago Neighborhood Festivals (free). Chicago Gospel Festival (free). International Children's Festival. Lincoln Central Association Dickens Street Summerfest. Taste of Chicago begins (free admission).

July: Taste of Chicago continues. Independence Eve Concert and Fireworks Show (free). Chicago Park District Air and Water Show (free), Chicago Neighborhood Festivals (free). Grant Park Music Festival (free).

All summer long: Ravinia Outdoor Music Festival. Swimming at Chicago Park District lakefront beaches and outdoor pools (free). Grant Park Music Festival (free).

September: Chicago Jazz Festival (free). "Viva! Chicago" Latin Music

Festival (free). Chicago Bears Football season begins. Chicago Symphony Orchestra season begins. Chicago Neighborhood Festivals (free).

October: Columbus Day Parade (free). Chicago International Film Festival. Children's Film Festival. Chicago Blackhawks Hockey season begins. Lincoln Park Zoo's Spooky Zoo Spectacular. International Kennel Club Fall Dog Show.

November: American Indian Center Powow. Chrysanthemum Show. *A Christmas Carol* at the Goodman Theatre. City of Chicago Christmas Tree Lighting Ceremony (free). Christmas Around the World Festival at Museum of Science and Industry, Christmas Parade (free). Chicago Bulls Basketball season begins. Holiday Lights Festival (free). Skate on State (free outdoor ice skating).

December: *The Nutcracker* ballet at Arie Crown Theater. Caroling to the Animals at Lincoln Park Zoo. Christmas Eve Flower Show (free). Holiday Lights Festival (free).

WHERE TO STAY

Embassy Suites Hotel, 600 North State Street (312–943–7629), offers suites and a hot breakfast, as does the **Guest Quarters Suite Hotel,** 198 East Delaware Place (312–664–1100 or 800–424–2900). **The Hyatt Regency Chicago,** 151 East Wacker Drive (312–565–1234 or 800–233–1234), offers big-hotel amenities, plus the Camp Hyatt kid's menus, and a 50 percent discount on a second room for the kids. They do not usually offer children's activities.

The Four Seasons Hotel, 120 East Delaware Place (312–280–8800) comes with large rooms and special turn down of milk and cookies for the kids (ask). The **Holiday Inn-Mart Plaza,** 350 North Orleans Street (312–836–5000); the **Sheraton Plaza,** 160 East Huron Street (312–787–2900 or 800–325–3535); and the **Days Inn-Lake Shore Drive,** Lake Michigan and the Navy Pier (312–943–9200), are less costly options.

Mariott's Lincolnshire Resort, 10 Marriott Drive; (800) 228–9290 or (708) 634–0100, is located forty-five minutes from downtown. The Children's Activity House has plenty of activities that will amuse kids including swimming, relay races, crafts, movies, and outdoor games. Since the summer of 1993, the resort has sponsored these supervised activities in one-hour blocks on Saturdays. Different age groups participate at different times: ages four to six from 9:00 to 10:00 A.M. and from 2:00 to 3:00 P.M.; ages seven to ten from 10:00 to 11:00 A.M. and from 2:00 to 3:00 P.M. Be sure to confirm these times as they may be extended. There is a theater on the premises that features occasional children's productions as well as standard movie fare.

WHERE TO EAT

The **Berghoff,** 17 West Adams Street (312–427–3170) is famous for its
bratwurst, sausage, schnitzel, and strawberry short cake. **Carson's For
Ribs,** 612 North Wells Street (312–280–9200) offers barbequed ribs,
chicken, and children's menus. **Claim Company,** 900 North Michigan
Avenue (312–787–5757) serves chicken, ribs, burgers, and has kid's
menus and crayons for paper-covered tabletops. **Ed Debevic's Short Or-
ders Deluxe,** 640 North Wells Street (312–664–1707), open for lunch
and dinner, is a fifties-style diner with prizes for kids and a nostalgic atmosphere and inexpensive diner fare for parents, including five-way
chili, roast turkey, chicken fried steak, burgers and fries, meatloaf, cherry
cokes, and chocolate shakes.

You can't visit Chicago without sampling the deep dish pizza. **Gior-
dano's,** 747 North Rush (312–951–0747), serves up the traditional thick,
Chicago-style pizza. **Pizzeria Uno,** 29 East Ohio (312–321–1000), is the
birthplace of Chicago-style/deep dish pizza. Uno also serves generous
portions of soup, sandwiches, salads, and gourmet appetizers. **Pizzeria
Due,** 619 North Wabash (312–943–2400), Uno's sister restaurant, serves
the same, tasty, Chicago-style deep dish pizza. **Redmak's New Buffalo
Chicago,** 2263 North Lincoln (312–787–4522), has burgers and such for
lunch, and dinner.

If your kids are basketball fans, they might like dining at **Michael
Jordan's Restaurant,** 500 North La Salle (312–644–DUNK). This mid-
priced place offers Jordan's pre-game meal of steak and potatoes and
other Jordan favorites such as pasta, macaroni and cheese, filet of sole,
and peach pie.

DAY TRIPS

More amusements are not too far away at **Six Flags Great America,** in
Gurnee, Illlinois, I–94 at Route 132; (708) 249–1776. This amusement
park has rides for kids and adults as well as an IMAX theater.

Head to Indiana for the **Indiana Dunes National Lakeshore**
(219–926–7561) and **Indiana Dunes State Park** (219–936–1952). Only a
ninety-minute drive south of the city lies Mt. Baldy, the park's tallest
dune, along with miles of hiking trails and actual sand beaches.

Make a trip south into Illinois to **Starved Rock National Park** for
beautiful woods, trails, rivers, waterfalls, and the famed Starved Rock
cliff. The **Wisconsin Dells** also attract lots of Chicagoans. (See the chapter on Wisconsin Dells.)

FOR MORE INFORMATION

Contact the Chicago Tourism Office, Historic Water Tower, 806 North Michigan Avenue, Chicago, Illinois 60611; (312) 280–5740 or (800) ITS–CHGO. At press time the tourism office was preparing a booklet *Chicago For Families, a Guide to Family Fun.* Ask if this is available.

Emergency Numbers

Ambulance, fire, and police: 911

Children's Memorial Hospital, Children's Plaza at Fullerton and Lincoln avenues; (312) 880–4000

Poison Control: the Northwestern Memorial Hospital emergency room; (312) 908–2000

Twenty-four-hour pharmacy: Walgreen's, 757 North Michigan Avenue; (312) 664–8686

38
COLUMBUS
Ohio

Columbus will surprise you. The largest U.S. place named for the explorer, Columbus offers families a friendly and affordable urban destination within easy reach of the countryside. Among the finds are an impressive arts center, a high-technology, interactive children's science museum, and easy day trips that let you discover heartland history.

GETTING THERE

American, Continental, Delta, Midway, Trans World Airlines, and USAir, offer international and domestic flights via Port Columbus International Airport; (614) 293–4000. Contact individual airlines for more information. A-Ultimate Transportation Network, 3115 East Seventeenth Avenue (614–478–3000 or 800–443–3519), transports visitors between Port Columbus International Airport and downtown Columbus.

Two major highways intersect in Columbus, making this city easy to reach. I–70 links the city with areas to the east and west. I–71 links Columbus with Cleveland to the north and Cincinnati and other areas to the south. I–270 combines with I–670 to circle Columbus and its surrounding areas. The nearest Amtrak train (800–USA–RAIL) arrives in Cleveland. Greyhound, 111 East Town Street (614–221–5311 or 294–5100), provides bus service from Cleveland to Columbus.

GETTING AROUND

COTA (Central Ohio Transit Authority), 177 North High Street (614–228–1776), provides public bus transportation for the city. COTA offers normal and express fares, plus transfers for a minimal fee. Call ahead for information on routes, schedules, and hours of operation. Several companies offer taxicab service, including the **Independent Taxicab Association of Columbus** (614–235–5551) and the **Yellow Cab Company** (614–221–3800).

WHAT TO SEE AND DO

Museums

Ohio's Center of Science & Industry, 280 East Broad Street; (614) 228–COSI. Called COSI for short, this first-rate, hands-on science museum is the place to take your young explorers. The adventure starts outdoors with the High Wire Cycle. When you ride this bicycle along wire suspended 20 feet above the ground, you not only feel like a circus performer, but you get a lesson in mass and balance.

The exhibit Toys and Games relates playthings to scientific principles. With the Kids Construction Company, learn how cranes and pulleys help lift objects. At Catch The Wind test different sails for navigation, and at Roller Coaster find out why you experience the thrills without tumbling out. More not-to-miss highlights include Kidspace, a play area for preschoolers that features a computer whose touch-screen lets kids "fingerprint" puppets, and a water area where the point is to get wet and wild with different toys.

At Familiespace the whole gang gets into the fun. Become an anchor and tape your own news show, make a music video, operate the toy trains, or simply be silly by trying on the dress-up costumes. Walk through the Old Time Street of Yesteryear, with its mock cobblestones, dry goods stores, and craftspeople, and be sure to browse the Cracker Jack Collection of more than 10,000 prizes. Yes, the prizes were really better then; it wasn't just that you were a wide-eyed kid happy at the thought of a plastic dinosaur, metal whistle, wooden top, or mini storybook.

Another nice touch: You can opt for valet parking. Instead of carrying tired kids back to the car, let the polite attendants bring your car to you, a welcome, small pleasure at the end of a busy touring day.

The Columbus Museum of Art, 480 East Broad Street; (614) 221–6801. The Sirak Collection, among the more recently acquired collections, is valued at $80 million. It includes works of nineteenth- and twentieth-century European masters.

The museum is also known for its seventeenth-century Dutch and nineteenth-century French paintings, and its collection of American art from 1850 through 1945. Don't miss the outdoor sculpture garden, an oasis with enough room for running. Kids like such works as *Streams,* a postmodern stainless steel waterfall sculpture.

Allow time for the gift shop, which has the usual notecards and niceties, but also an interesting collection of jewelry by some local craftspeople.

The Center of Science and Industry is a must-see when you visit Columbus.
(Courtesy Columbus Convention and Visitors Bureau)

Attractions

Columbus combines interestingly ethnic and all-American attractions. Columbus has The German Village—a restored area originally settled by German immigrants in the nineteenth century; it also has a major university and one of the largest state fairs in the country, held every August.

The German Village is a restored area of approximatley 233 acres. It features brick homes built by German immigrants between 1840 and 1880 and offers cobblestone streets, boutiques, historic walks, and lots of bratwurst and beer. The sturdy, but small houses, built by workers, often feature hand-carved lintels, clay chimney pots, wrought iron fences, and small yards. Interestingly, the area is the largest privately funded restoration of its kind in the United States. Stop by the **Meeting Haus** of the German Village Society, 588 South Third Street (614–221–8888), for brochures on restaurants and bed and breakfast lodgings, and to sign up for a guided bus tour (614–221–1064), which begins with a short, historic film.

Another option is to buy a **Brick Tick** for $5.00, which details a self-guided neighborhood tour that takes you by blocks of restored brick houses. If it's fall plan on checking out the German Village's annual **Okto-berfest** (September), at Christmas there are tours of homes, June brings a **Haus Und Garten** tour, and August features a **Backyard Candelight Tour.**

For a time-out romp, stop by **Schiller Park**, bounded by Reinhard, City Park, Deshler, and Jaeger streets. It's a great green space in the heart of the village, perfect for the kids. In summer, come here for theater under the stars, usually two Shakespearean productions and one musical. Donations are requested.

In the **brewery district**, adjacent to the German Village, the former breweries are now beer gardens, offices, or shops. The **William Graystone Winery**, 544 South Front Street (614–228–2332), is housed in an 1875 brewery that's open for tastings, tours, and breakfast in the vault—a cozy space of limestone arched walls and wooden chairs. Even though your kids can't taste the wine, they'll like this winery. For a unique souvenir, take home the William Graystone wines; each bottle is graced with a scene or symbol of Columbus. For more information on the Brewery District, call (614) 241–2070.

Wexner Center for the Arts, the Ohio State University, North High Street at Fifteenth Avenue; (614) 292–0330 (building, offices, galleries) or 292–2354 (tickets). Part of the Ohio State University, the Wexner Center has four galleries, a film and video theater, two auditoriums, plus a smaller theater and fine arts library. Wexner's most active months are October through June. The center opens its galleries, performances, and screenings to the public. Traditionally, the galleries are closed on Mondays, call for operating hours and upcoming events. The center also features a good bookshop and a café.

The Ohio State University, 30 West Fifteenth Avenue; (614) 292–0418, offers a free two-hour tour, which begins on the third floor of the Lincoln Tower, Monday–Friday 8:00 A.M.–5:00 P.M. Reservations are required for five or more.

Parks and Zoos

Battelle Riverfront Park and the Santa Maria. The Battelle Riverfront Park on the Scioto River waterfront near City Hall offers a pleasant bit of greenery. Its fountain, created especially for children, offers a rim of stone slabs that are the perfect size for skipping along. This is a good place to bring a picnic lunch, rest, and enjoy the river view.

The area's main attraction is the *Santa Maria*, one of the more authentic, full-size replicas of Columbus's flagship. This one was built for the city's 1992 Quincentennial celebration. On board you hear tales of a typical day at sea, find out why hot meals were rare (fear of fire) and where the crew slept (on deck), get a chance to ogle the signal cannons and touch the huge tiller, and find out why navigation was a shared responsibility (because there wasn't any way to see ahead and maneuver the tiller at the same time). Call (614) 645–8760.

Franklin Park Conservatory, in Franklin Park, 1777 East Broad Street. At this indoor conservatory, stroll through acres of indoor gardens and several climate zones. Originally built in 1859, this facility was significantly enlarged for Ameriflora 92, the city's tribute to the Columbus quincentennial. The tiny and intricate bonsai plants, the tropical rain forest, and desert areas are kid favorites. Avoid strolling through the park as this area has seen some crime.

The Columbus Zoo, 9990 Riverside Drive (614–645–3400), is actually located northwest of Columbus in Powell; it's off I–270 and Sawmill Road, exit 20. If your family loves animals, this is a worthwhile trip, especially in good weather. Consider combining this outing with a visit to Wyandot Lake Amusement Park. (See below.)

The Columbus Zoo, while offering a variety of animals plus a petting zoo for little ones, is a beautifully landscaped park known for its gorillas and cheetahs. Four generations of gorillas climb through the ropes of two adjacent yards. Sunshine, a muscular silverback gorilla, is a special crowd pleaser, especially when he shoves a head or two of lettuce into his mouth for lunch.

The walkway at the cheetah habitat literally gives you a unique perspective on these special cats. Peering down on them allows even preschoolers to get a good look at these sinewy animals stretched out on the grass. A new exhibit, the Discovery Reef, will eventually contain 300 to 400 species of fish, and include a wave machine to simulate the ocean's movements.

Hungry? Eat at Wendy's, one of the on-site restaurants. Columbus, after-all, was the birthplace of this fast-food chain. One caution: The tram takes you around for an overview, but doesn't let you get out to view the animals. For that, be prepared to walk. Strollers are available for rental.

The gift shop offers kids a good place to spend their allowance. Kids like the animal cards, T-shirts, books, and puzzles.

Wyandot Lake Amusement Park, 10101 Riverside Drive, is next to the Columbus Zoo; (614) 889–9283. Open May–September, your kids can cool off here with such wet thrills as a wave pool, water slides, and an inner-tube adventure that will take them through such "backcountry" scenery as a misty canyon, waterfall, and a mill camp. Dry fun includes go-carts and miniature golf. There are locker and shower facilities.

Often coupons are available for discounted, combined admission to Wyandot Lake and the Columbus Zoo. Check the *Columbus Official Visitors Guide* brochure, available from the Convention and Visitors Bureau.

Performing Arts

BalletMet, 322 Mt. Vernon Avenue (614–229–4860), performs a variety of classical to contemporary works, including a holiday favorite, *The Nutcracker.* CAPA (Columbus Association of the Performing Arts), 55 East State Street (614–469–0939), owns and operates the Ohio Theatre,

55 East State Street, and the Palace Theatre, 34 West Broad Street, which traditionally attracts international jazz, pop, comedy, children's, folk, and classical entertainers. CAPA also offers a classic film series. Call for information. **CATCO (Contemporary American Theater Company)**, 512 North Park Street (614–461–0010), is a semiprofessional theater performing off-Broadway productions in an intimate 176-seat theater. The **Columbus Symphony Orchestra**, 55 East State Street, 5th Floor, (614–224–3291 for tickets or 224–5281), performs symphonic and pops concerts and has a series for children. **Opera/Columbus**, 50 West Broad Street (614–461–0022), is Columbus's opera company. Dress rehearsals, held on Tuesdays before opening night performances, are open to students and senior citizens at discounted admission. **The Wexner Center For the Arts**, Fifteenth and High streets (614–292–2354), presents a variety of contemporary groups and traditional concerts.

Ohio State, Capital, Otterbein, and Ohio Wesleyan Universities frequently hold theatrical, dance, and concert events. For information call OSU (614–292–2787), Capital (614–236–6801), Otterbein (614–898–1600), and Ohio Wesleyan (614–369–4431).

Ticketmaster (614–431–3600) has full-price tickets to theater, dance, concerts, and sporting events. Call for booth locations and hours of operation. For more information on the arts, contact the **Greater Columbus Arts Council** at (614) 224–2606.

SPECIAL EVENTS

Sports

Columbus Baseball Team, Inc., Columbus Clippers, 1155 West Mound Street; (614) 462–5250. The Clippers, the top farm club of the New York Yankees, play AAA ball at Cooper Stadium, I–70 and Mound Street, from April through mid-September. **Columbus's Chill Hockey Team**, 1460 West Lane Road (614–488–4455), skates at the Fairgrounds Coliseum from November to March. **Columbus Horizon**, the city's professional basketball team, plays in the Convention Center, 400 North High Street, from December through March; (614) 224–3865.

For golf enthusiasts, there's the **Memorial Tournament at Muirfield**, 5750 Memorial Drive, Dublin; (614) 889–6700. This Jack Nicklaus–designed course hosts the PGA for one stop of the tour during June. For college sports call the **Ohio State University Athletic Department**, 410 Woody Hayes Drive (614–292–2624), for information on all Buckeye sporting events.

Scioto Downs, 6000 High Street (614–491–2525), 2½ miles south of I–270, offers harness racing from May to September.

Festivals

Columbus's biggest festival is in August when the city goes "whole hog" for the **Ohio State Fair**, one of the city's biggest attractions and a tradition since 1848. This is a special treat for city kids, who may get their first chance to pet a cow, cheer at the pig races, ogle the huge butter sculptures, watch a tractor pull, and browse through buildings of agricultural exhibits. The midway with its rides and games of chance and skill may be unavoidable; to avoid nagging, set a limit ahead of time on how much money the kids can spend here.

The two-week fair also features nightly entertainment, free music concerts held twice a day, a free Kiddie Park, a quilt show, baking contests, crafts, a daily parade, and a petting zoo. For more information call the administrative offices; (614) 644–4000 or (800) BUCKEYE.

Additional festivals. **June:** The five-day Columbus Arts Festival features performances by the ballet and jazz groups, and the symphony. There's also a street fair with crafts and food. Especially for Kids offers two days of mime, music, puppets, and poets.

July: The Motorists Riverfest along the Scioto River has powerboat races, free pontoon and paddleboat rides, and entertainment.

September: The German Village hosts its own Oktoberfest festival, which includes the Kinderplatz (Children's Place) with free kiddie rides and family entertainment. The **KidSpeak KidsFest**, Bicentennial Park, Civic Center Drive along the river, is a full day of free street performances, music, and games.

October: On **Columbus Day** the whole city takes to the streets with a weekend full of festivities. Besides parades and fireworks enjoy arts and crafts, street performers, a chili and salsa challenge, music, boat rides, plus a fun run just for ages five to eight.

November: The Columbus International Festival, generally held at the Veteran's Memorial Hall, 300 West Broad Street, features the song, dance, arts, and food of more than fifty cultures, and usually special activities just for kids.

For more information, call (800) BUCKEYE.

WHERE TO STAY

Columbus offers a variety of lodging options in town and nearby. In town is **The Great Southern Hotel**, 310 South High Street (614–228–3800 or 800–328–2073), with a turn-of-the-century lobby and comfortable rooms. The **Hyatt on Capital Square**, 75 East State Street (614–228–1234 or 800–233–1234), is connected to the City Center and Ohio Theatre, and located across from the State Capitol. **Guest Quarters Suite Hotel**, 50 South Front Street (614–228–4600), offers families extra space, and in-room refrigerators. The **Holiday Inn Crowne Plaza**, 33 Nationwide Boulevard (614–461–4100), is another family- friendly alternative.

Embassy Suites is near town at 2700 Corporate Exchange Drive (614–890–8600), located at I–270 and Cleveland Avenue. It offers suites, and indoor and outdoor pools. The **Worthington Inn**, 649 High Street, in nearby Worthington, began as a stagecoach stop in 1831 and now features twenty-six rooms decorated with Victorian furnishings, small inn hospitality, and full-service convenience. Not the least of the amenities at this four-star lodging is the regional American cuisine. The seared salmon wins acclaim as among the best in the city, as does the duck sausage. Try the sour apple tart for dessert. Rooms, which are oversized, include a continental breakfast. Children are welcome. Kids twelve and under stay for free; (614) 885–2600.

WHERE TO EAT

Head for these restaurants in the German Village and in the Brewery District. **Schmidt's Sausage Haus und Restaurant**, 240 Kossuth Street; (614) 444–6808. Among the more famous eateries, this restaurant, open since 1886, offers steins of brew and an array of sausages. The place is noted for the Bahama Mama—a spicy sausage—plus good German potato salad, sauerkraut, and applesauce. If you're still hungry, try the huge cream puffs for dessert. Kids will like the accordion music and the festive air. Children, accompanied by adults of course, are welcome at **Diebel's Bier Stube**, 263 East Whittier Street (614–444–1139), a beer garden with sing-along sheet music and enough space to polka. **Juergen's**, 525 South Fourth Street (614–224–6858), is a German restaurant known for its excellent pastry and unusual varieties of pretzels. **The Engine House #5**, 121 East Thurman Avenue (614–443–4877), offers traditional seafood, pastas, and steaks. Your kids will like the ambience of the renovated firehouse. Come here to celebrate a birthday and watch the waiters slide down the firepole with a cake. **B.G. Salvi's Italian Eatery**, 450 South Front Street (614–224–2002), housed in a former nineteenth-century brewery, features fresh pasta; veal, chicken, and seafood specialties; and a great Sunday brunch. More expensive, but worth a visit if you have older children and teens, is **Handke's**, 520 South Front Street; (614) 621–2500. Noted chef Hartmut Handke offers such pleasing dishes as onion cream soup, grilled duck breast, and seared sea scallops.

Other Columbus eateries: **The Spaghetti Warehouse**, 397 West Broad Street (614–464–0143), serves pastas. **Morton's of Chicago**, 2 Nationwide Plaza, corner of Chestnut and High streets (614–464–4442), is more expensive but offers fine steaks and seafood; share your plate with the kids as portions are large.

DAY TRIPS

Olentangy Indian Caverns and Ohio Frontier Land, 1779 Home Road, Delaware; (614) 548–7917. Only about one-half hour away, these caverns and a cave house museum are filled with Indian artifacts and geological displays. Open 9:30 A.M.–5:00 P.M. from April to October. Kids under seven are admitted for free.

Roscoe Village, 381 Hill Street, Coshocton; (614) 622–9310 or (800) 877–1830. The drive to Roscoe Village, about 90 miles from Columbus, takes you through Coshocton County past farmland and fields. At the village, six restored nineteenth-century buildings are strung along two blocks and interspersed with nineteen shops, creating a sense of life circa 1830–1860 when the Ohio & Erie Canal brought goods, people, and prosperity to the area. Watch a blacksmith and a broom maker, tour the schoolhouse and the fashionable physician's residence, and browse the shops. Best bets include the duck carver, the basket maker, and the Johnson-Humrickhouse Museum, known for its collections of Oriental and Native American art.

Be sure to visit the **canal**, 2 miles away. From Memorial Day to Labor Day, barges pulled by draft horses take you along the canal as guides tell you anecdotes about the people and animals that made the trip. But in fall, allow time to walk the towpath. The brilliant foliage is a gift to the eye, and the soft peacefulness a welcome respite during any city tour.

Roscoe Village hosts a Gingerbread House Contest on the Fourth of July, a Gay 1890s Celebration in September, with banjo playing and barbershop quartets; and an Apple Butter Stirrin' Festival in October with demonstrations of rope making and chair caning, as well as hog-calling contests.

Roscoe Village has several bed and breakfasts, none of which welcome children, but the **Roscoe Village Inn** (614–622–2222 or 800–237–7397) welcomes children and has comfortable rooms and good food.

Hocking Valley Canoe Livery and Family Fun Center, 31251 Chieftain Drive, Logan; (614) 385–8685 or (800) 686–0386. Located about an hour outside of Columbus off U.S. 33 at Enterprise exit, this center offers canoe, kayak, raft, and go-cart rentals, miniature golf and a driving range, plus canoeing packages and tours of points of interest. Open April to October, reservations are required.

Sea World of Ohio, 1100 Sea World Drive, Aurora; (800) 63–SHAMU. It's two hours northeast of Columbus on Route 43, near I–271 and I–480 (Ohio Turnpike exit 13). Open mid-May–September, the center features ninety acres of marine life, entertainment, and a well-designed kids' play area—Shamu's Happy Harbor (named after one of Sea World's killer whales).

FOR MORE INFORMATION

Ask for a copy of the Kidspeak! Calendar, published by *Kids Connection* magazine, 572 City Park Avenue (614–224–3003), which lists items of interest to families. The calendar highlights hundreds of family-oriented programs. While some are geared to city residents, many are also of interest to visiting kids.

Have politically aware children who want to give a city official a piece of their mind or offer a suggestion? Let your kids call the KidSpeak telephone line (614–645–KIDS) and leave a message for any city official.

Ohio Council for International Visitors (614–231–9610) offers translation services. City of Columbus Construction Hotline; (614) 645–PAVE. For tourist information, contact the Greater Columbus Convention and Visitors Bureau, Monday–Friday 8:00 A.M.–5:00 P.M.; (614) 221–6623 or (800) BUCKEYE. When in town, stop by their visitor's office on the third floor of the City Center shopping mall, 111 South Third Street. The hours are Monday–Saturday 10:00 A.M.–9:00 P.M., and Sunday noon–6:00 P.M.; (800) 645–3472.

Emergency Numbers
Ambulance, fire, and police: 911
Children's Hospital, 700 Children's Drive; (614) 461–2244
Poison Control Center: (614) 228–1323
Police (nonemergency): (614) 645–4545
Twenty-four-hour pharmacy: Super X, 7660 Sawmill Road; (614) 889–5104

39
DEARBORN
Michigan

Dearborn, Michigan, (about 12 miles west of Detroit) was founded by auto pioneer Henry Ford and welcomes two million tourists a year. They invariably head straight to the Henry Ford Museum and Greenfield Village, the most visited indoor/outdoor historical complex in North America. The museum alone is worth the trip, but you'll find other interesting and fun things to do with your family in this city of 90,000 and the surrounding area. You may want to avoid downtown Detroit, which can be rather bleak and frenetic, particularly in the extremely hot and humid summers.

GETTING THERE

Detroit Metropolitan Airport, about fifteen minutes west of the museum and village, is served by major commercial airlines (call individual carriers for information). Car rentals are available at the airport. Commuter Transportation Company (313–946–1000/800–351–5466) provides hourly coach service from the airport to major hotels in Dearborn from 6:45 A.M. to midnight. Taxis are plentiful. Detroit's City Airport (313–267–6400) is 30 miles east and serves commuter airlines.

Amtrak (800–USA–RAIL) runs trains to Dearborn's station, near Michigan Avenue and Greenfield. Greyhound/Trailways bus line serves Detroit's downtown terminal at 1000 West Lafayette Street. Call (313) 963–9840 for information about fares and schedules. Interstate highway systems provide easy access to Dearborn; take I–94 from the northeast and west, I–75 from the south.

GETTING AROUND

From May to late September, Classic Trolley (313–945–6100) provides inexpensive, convenient shuttle service that kids will especially like. The

Learning about cars is just one of the many activities you can participate in at the Henry Ford Museum and Greenfield Village complex. (Courtesy Henry Ford Museum and Greenfield Museum, Dearborn, Michigan)

red trolley buses run from 9:30 A.M. to 5:30 P.M. (5:00 P.M. on Sunday). Their ten stops include hotels, restaurants, shopping, and tourist attractions. They also offer express service to the Henry Ford Museum and Greenfield Village every day except Sunday. Taxis are available at hotels and on call. SMART (Southeast Michigan Area Rapid Transit) buses (313–256–8600) serve Dearborn's major arteries and also operate between Detroit and the Henry Ford Museum and Greenfield Village.

WHAT TO SEE AND DO

Museums

Henry Ford Museum and Greenfield Village, 20900 Oakwood; (313) 271–1620/ (800) 343–1929. Visitors arriving at the museum expecting to see endless displays of cars are pleasantly surprised to find there's so much more. One thing is for sure: You'll never hear the word "bor...ing" uttered by your kids while you're on the premises.

Be sure everyone wears very comfortable shoes; you will cover a lot of ground. (Although strollers are rented in Greenfield Village for a nominal fee, they aren't allowed in all the buildings.) The museum has twelve acres of exhibits; the adjacent outdoor Greenfield Village spreads out over eighty-one acres. Ideally, you should spend two days here, allowing one day per attraction. Admission is separate, but combination and two-day tickets are available.

At the entrance, there's a replica of Philadelphia's Independence Hall. Inside, fascinating exhibits show how technology changed life in America. Both kids and parents will enjoy the Automobile in American Life exhibit which includes original landmarks such as an entire 1946 diner, 1940s Texaco service station, 1950s drive-in movie theater, and a 1960s Holiday Inn room, along with one hundred historically significant cars. All kids love trains, and yours will revel in the museum's enormous 600–ton Allegheny locomotive, used to haul huge coal trains. It's part of a transportation exhibit that also includes aircraft, horse-drawn vehicles, streetcars, and firefighting apparatus. Other museum highlights include the limousine in which President John F. Kennedy was shot and Robert Byrd's 1925 plane, the first to fly over the North Pole.

A must-see (and must-do) is the new Innovation Station, a 3,200-square-foot interactive learning game on the main concourse that offers all ages a chance to find creative, fun ways to solve problems. About thirty players team up at various activity stations to provide the manpower (pedaling bicycles, turning hand cranks, etc.) and brainpower (sorting balls by color, etc.) to propel thousands of brightly colored balls through a network of tubes and sorting devices into bins. If a problem develops, everyone "brainstorms" to provide a solution. The game takes from twenty to thirty minutes.

The colorful Made in America multimedia exhibit uses hands-on activities, video and film presentations—even a troupe of cartoon characters—to show visitors of all ages how industry affects their lives. Kids will be fascinated by the overhead conveyor that carries a continuous flow of American-made products—including a kitchen sink. There's also a giant light bulb–making machine, a step-inside hydroelectric generator, and a touch-screen computer that lets visitors feel what it's like to run an electrical power plant.

The adjacent **Greenfield Village** features more than eighty homes, work places, and community buildings from different periods and locations, each displaying the day-to-day processes that helped build this nation. Some are homes of famous people: the Wright Brother's model Ohio home (their Cycle Shop is elsewhere in the Village); the city home of Noah Webster, author of America's first dictionary; the farm where Henry Ford was born and raised; and tire magnate Harvey S. Firestone's 1880s farm, where costumed interpreters perform daily tasks. Other residences reveal the struggles and adversities faced by less famous people: the 1850 slave homes from a Georgia plantation, for instance, and the wilderness home of an eighteenth-century Connecticut family.

Thomas Edison's Menlo Park Laboratory was recently restored to its 1880 state and includes over 400 inventions created here, including the phonograph and incandescent light. (Who knows how many future inventors will be inspired by what they see?) Nearby, the Sarah Jordan Boarding House, one of the first residences wired for electric light, housed several of Edison's assistants.

Your kids can take part in the day's lessons at **Scotch Settlement School**, which Henry Ford attended, or enjoy hands-on activities and old-fashioned games on The Green. Demonstrations in glassblowing, pottery, and other crafts are also fascinating for kids, and you can buy many of the products created in the museum gift shop.

Suwanee Park will delight the entire family with 1913 carousel rides and a zoo with lions, tigers, and other creatures. Stop for a soda at the old-fashioned 1870 ice cream parlor. For an extra fee you can ride a paddle-wheel boat or steam-powered locomotive around the village perimeter. Narrated carriage tours (sleigh tours in the winter, weather permitting) and 1931 bus rides are also available for an additional charge.

From early January to mid-March, there is a single admission fee to both museums, although visitors to Greenfield Village may view building exteriors only.

Henry Ford Estate, Fair Lane, the campus of University of Michigan Dearborn, off Evergreen and U.S. 12; (313) 593–5590. If your museum visit whets your family's interest in Henry Ford, stop by his mansion, one mile away. You can tour the house with its self-contained power plant, which is connected to the mansion by a tunnel, or stroll along the gardens and trails on the grounds. In the summer, follow a self-guided forty-five-minute walking tour that includes a treehouse, bathhouse, boathouse, and scenic views. Christmastime brings Santa's Workshop, breakfast with Santa, a floral tour of the estate, and special holiday luncheons and events.

For those interested in Arab Culture, the **Arab Folk Museum**, 2651 Saulino Court (313–842–7010), has exhibits on Arab cultures and archives on Michigan's Arab community.

Parks and Zoos

Belle Isle is reached via a toll-free bridge at East Jefferson Avenue and East Grand Boulevard, Detroit; (313) 267–7115. About 15 miles from Dearborn, it's the nation's largest urban island park, with 1,000 acres of wooded paths and drives, including one that goes along the shore. Recreational possibilities abound here: golf, tennis, and swimming (at a sandy beach with lifeguards). Signs point the way to the various attractions.

Younger kids will love the terrific playground where they can climb up
and down nets and over wooden structures, crawl through tunnels, and
slide down poles. **The Nature Center** (313–267–7157) has wooded trails
where you can view plants, animals, and changing exhibits (donations
requested). Allow about an hour for the thirteen-acre zoo where, for a
fee, you can stroll the winding elevated walkway and view uncaged animals in natural settings. **Dossin Great Lakes Museum** (313–267–6440)
is worth a visit with older kids who may appreciate the restored smoking
lounge taken from the 1912 steamer *City of Detroit III,* complete with
tons of hand-carved oak work. There's also a 40-foot hydroplane (*The
Miss Pepsi*), observation deck, periscope, and ship-to-shore radio messages (donations). If your family is lucky enough to be around during
one of the six seasonal flower shows at the **Whitcomb Conservatory**
(313–267–7134), you're in for a fragrant visual treat. There are permanent displays of palms, ferns, and cactuses, as well as one of the country's
largest orchid collections, and it's all free. Another no-cost attraction is
the **Aquarium,** one of the country's oldest, where you can see various
freshwater fish from the Great Lakes and beyond.

The Detroit area has another zoo. The **Detroit Zoological Park,**
Woodward Avenue and Ten Mile Road (I–696), Royal Oak (a northern
suburb of Detroit, about 12 miles from Dearborn); (313) 398–0900. This
zoo is one of the country's largest and most modern. It has 125 acres of
landscaped grounds with cageless exhibits grouped according to continent, simulating the animals' natural habitats. Don't miss the four-acre
chimpanzee exhibit. There's also a miniature railroad ride around the
park. You can buy food, or bring your own and picnic. Allow about four
hours for a visit here.

Performing Arts

The **Greenfield Village Theatre Company** performs time-honored
plays (*Father of the Bride* was a recent selection) suitable for family viewing at the Henry Ford Museum Theater throughout the year. Although
season subscriptions are sold, individual tickets and dinner/theater tickets also are available. Call (313) 271–1620 for information.

Shopping

Fairlane Town Center, between Hubbard Drive, Evergreen Road,
Southfield Expressway (M–39) and Michigan Avenue (U.S. 12), is one of
the state's largest indoor malls with The Disney Store and two toy stores
of special interest to kids. The information center on the lower level is
the place to stop for bus schedules, tips on lodging, and the answers to
other questions. The mall is open every day; call (313) 593–3330 for
more information.

SPECIAL EVENTS

Sporting events

Sports enthusiasts may want to take in a Detroit Tigers baseball game at Tiger Stadium or Lions football at Pontiac Silverdome. The Detroit Pistons play basketball at the Palace of Auburn Hills, while Red Wings hockey games are played in the Joe Louis Sports arena, part of the city's downtown riverfront Civic Center. Games are frequently sold out; you can order tickets in advance of your visit from Ticketmaster (313) 645–6666, or call the Detroit Visitor's Hotline (see FOR MORE INFORMATION) for specifics.

Fairs and Festivals

Call the Detroit Visitor's Hotline for more information on sporting events as well as other goings-on. The Dearborn Chamber of Commerce also publishes a calendar of events. There are three notable area fairs and festivals.

March: Maple Syrup Festival, Cranbrook Institute of Science, Bloomfield Hills, first three weekends.

Late June–early July: International Freedom Festival, a celebration shared by Detroit and Windsor, Ontario, with fireworks, parades, craft shows, and entertainment.

Late August–early September: Ten-day Michigan State Fair, Michigan Exposition and State Fairgrounds, Detroit.

WHERE TO STAY

Sixteen Dearborn hotels offer packages that include tickets to the Henry Ford Museum and Greenfield Village. Request a list from the Dearborn Chamber of Commerce (see FOR MORE INFORMATION). Four of these are also on the Classic Trolley circuit, making them especially convenient.

The Dearborn Inn, 20301 Oakwood Boulevard, a Marriott hotel, is a recently renovated landmark building with three separate wings: Main Inn, Colonial Lodge, or Famous Americans Colonial Homes suites. It's a good choice for families. Call (313) 371–2700/(800) 228–2900.

Hyatt Regency Dearborn, Fairlane Town Center, offers a shopping mall at your doorstep, plus an indoor pool, restaurants, fitness center, and more. Your family won't have to worry about how to pass the time here. Call (313) 593–1234/(800) 233–1234.

Holiday Inn—Dearborn, 22900 Michigan Avenue, has no surprises. It's just what you would expect from this chain: indoor and outdoor pools, restaurants, and nearby shopping. Call (313) 278–4800/(800)

465–4329. There's another Holiday Inn in the Fairlane area that's not on the trolley circuit.

Quality Inn—Fairlane, 21430 Michigan Avenue, is one-half mile from the Henry Ford Museum and Greenfield Village and features an outdoor pool, on-site picnic grounds, complimentary breakfast, VCRs, movie rentals, and refrigerators. Call (313) 565–0800/(800) 228–5151. Also on the site is the Dearborn Historical Museum, which you might not bother visiting unless you're a guest at the inn or an avid history buff. Exhibits show the development of Dearborn in two historical buildings: one, part of an original arsenal; the other, the original powder magazine, which stored ammunition as early as 1839. Call (313) 565–3000 for museum information.

Also worthy of note: For the big splurge, there's the **Ritz-Carlton Dearborn,** Fairlane Plaza; (313) 441–2000/(800) 241–3333.

WHERE TO EAT

The Dearborn Chamber of Commerce offers a helpful restaurant guide that includes maps and general price ranges. East Dearborn is home to the largest Middle Eastern population in the United States, and if you like that style of cooking, locals say you can't go wrong at any of their restaurants. **LaShish,** 12918 Michigan, is a casual family restaurant serving authentic Middle Eastern dishes and fresh juices. Call (313) 584–4477. Some other styles of cooking: **Bill Knapp's of Dearborn,** 3500 Greenfield, serves affordable American food and has a children's menu; (313) 271–7166. No matter when your family's appetite kicks in, **Andoni's Family Dining,** 1620 North Telegraph, open twenty-four hours, can whip up a satisfying meal; (313) 582–2024.

DAY TRIPS

If your kids have never been to Canada, you can take a quick trip some 15 miles south of the border to the pleasant town of **Windsor, Ontario.** That's right—south. Look at a map, and you'll see that Dearborn and Detroit are actually north of Windsor, Ontario, where you can grab a bite to eat and stroll around town. Access is via bridge or tunnel. If you're in town during the **International Freedom Festival** (see Special Events), you'll find plenty to do during the week-long celebration of Canada Day and Independence Day.

Cranbrook is the former estate of George Booth, publisher of *The Detroit News.* It's now a well-known cultural and educational center 18 miles away from Dearborn, in Bloomfield Hills. Surrounding Booth's home are forty acres of public gardens, woods, pine walks, and two lakes. Also on the property: an art museum, which exhibits both contemporary art and artwork by students at Cranbrook schools; a natural history museum with a large mineral collection; a planetarium with weekend shows; and a nature center. Call (313) 645–3000 for information.

FOR MORE INFORMATION

Dearborn Chamber of Commerce, 15544 Michigan Avenue, has helpful pamphlets and brochures; (313) 584–6100. Detroit Visitor's Hotline: (313) 567–1170,

Emergency Numbers
Police and fire: 911
Henry Ford Hospital at Fairlane Center: (313) 593–8100
Oakwood Hospital, 18101 Oakwood Boulevard; (313) 593–7000
Poison Control: (313) 745–5711
Twenty-four-hour pharmacy: Perry Drugs, Shaefer at Ford Road; (313) 581–3280

40
GRAND TRAVERSE AREA
Michigan

Along with being the "Cherry Capital of the World," the Traverse City, Michigan, area is known as a "Great Lakes Paradise." This city of 15,000—the largest in Northwest Lower Michigan—is blessed by a superb location at the head of Grand Traverse Bay on Lake Michigan's northern shore. (The bay is separated into east and west sections by the scenic Old Mission Peninsula.) Situated on the 45th parallel, halfway between the equator and the North Pole, the area has four distinct seasons. Summers offer miles of beaches, fabulous freshwater fishing, and countless recreational possibilities. Winter's bountiful snows bring cross-country and downhill skiing, snowmobiling, sledding, and skating. Add fall's spectacular foliage and abundant fruit harvests and spring's white and pink cherry blossoms, and you'll see why families come back season after season, year after year.

GETTING THERE

The area is easily accessible by car via state highways. Traverse City's Cherry Capital Airport (616–947–2250) is serviced by several national and regional carriers. Hertz and Avis car rental agencies are at the airport; others are in town.

Taxis and BATA (Bay Area Transportation Authority) bus service (616–941–2324) are also available. Greyhound buses (616–946–5180) link Traverse City to the Upper Peninsula and southern Michigan. There's no train service to this area.

GETTING AROUND

Although there are buses, taxicabs, and limousine services, it is quickest and easiest to have a car.

WHAT TO SEE AND DO

Museums and Zoos

Dennos Museum Center, 1701 East Front Street, Traverse City; (616) 922–1055. Located at the campus entrance of Northwestern Michigan College, this spacious museum's motto is Come Alive Inside. The Discovery Gallery's hands-on exhibits will tickle the fancy of any age. Among them: an antigravity mirror that gives you the illusion of floating, and Recollections II, a video experience that transforms a child's movements into delayed motion, multicolored images. Unique to the museum is Weiss Wall I (named after its creator, Detroit area artist and musician Ed Weiss), with multicolored wood panels that produce different sounds when touched: percussion, synthesizer, and even "rap." Older kids will have a ball playing the wall. They'll also like the museum's extensive collection of Inuit Art, considered one of the country's most complete. The graceful *Dancing Bear* sculpture at the entrance is a charmer, and the *Enchanted Owl* print by a master artisan appeared on a Canadian postage stamp. There's also a sculpture court and galleries with traveling exhibitions. Open daily to 5:00 P.M. plus summer evenings.

The Music House, 7377 U.S. 31 North, Acme (about 6 miles east of Traverse City); (616) 938–9300. Automated instruments, including music boxes, nickelodeons, and a vintage hand-carved Belgian dance organ, are displayed in a nineteenth-century farm complex. Guided tours last about ninety minutes.

Clinch Park Zoo, Grandview Parkway at Cass, Traverse City; (616) 922–4906. Northern Michigan wildlife such as bear, otters, bison, and beavers; an aquarium with native game fish, including trout and perch; a beach; and a miniature steam-train ride make this stop a hit with kids.

More Attractions

Amon Orchards and Farm Market, U.S. 31 North, Acme; (616) 938–9160/(800) 937–1644: Educational and entertaining orchard tours include a See It Made Kitchen where goodies such as cherry butter are concocted. There's even cherry mustard! Pick your own fruit, if you like. There's a petting farm, too. Kids love it here! Closed November–April.

Candle Factory, Grandview Parkway, Traverse City; (616) 946–2280. This leading retailer features candle-making demonstrations at various times daily.

Pirates Cove/Adventure Golf, U.S. 31 North, Traverse City; (616) 938–2333. Sunken treasure and challenging minigolf.

River Country Funland, U.S. 31 North, Traverse City; (616) 946–6663. A kids' paradise, with miniature golf, go-karts, bumper boats, a water slide, and more.

Beaches and Parks

With 250 miles of Lake Michigan shoreline, beaches are the big summer attraction here. All have free public access, and the following particularly appeal to families. Take the kids beachcombing for Petroskey stones—grey hexagonal-patterned petrified coral. (If you don't find any, they're sold in local gift shops.)

East Bay: The majority of hotels and motels are located here, on a strip of beach called the Miracle Mile, or across the street.

West Bay: Bryant Park, at the foot of Garfield, is the area's best for families with young children; kids can safely wade in the shallow water. There's also a picnic area, large playground, and rest rooms. Clinch Park, on Grandview Parkway at Cass, (see previous zoo listing) is also popular, with more than 1,500 feet of sandy beach plus rest rooms and concessions. Because of the boats in the area, however, this is best for families with teens. Elmwood Township Park, off M–22, a mile north of the M–72 junction, is another family favorite, with playground and rest rooms.

Sleeping Bear Dunes National Lakeshore: If you only have a short time in this area, start out early and spend the day at Sleeping Bear Dunes National Lakeshore, about 30 miles west, which includes 33 miles of Lake Michigan shoreline dotted with beaches. The one at North Bear Lake, central park area, reportedly has the warmest water. According to the Chippewa Indian legend that gave the park its name, a mother bear and her cubs swam across Lake Michigan to escape a forest fire. The mother waited on shore for her cubs, who lagged behind. It's said she still keeps watch in the form of a large, dark hill of sand, while her cubs became the North and South Manitou Islands.

The park boasts incredible dunes, deposits left by melting glaciers some 11,000 years ago, that rise over 400 feet above Lake Michigan. If your kids are old—and adventurous—enough, you can try the Dune Climb, 5 miles north of Empire on M–109. The Platte River, on the southern end, and Crystal River, on the north—with adjacent lakes—provide ideal fishing and canoeing. Rentals are available from Crystal River Canoes; (616) 334–3090. Thirty-five miles of marked trails are set aside for hiking and cross-country skiing. At the Coast Guard's Historic Maritime Museum, one mile west of Glen Haven, displays unfold the area's maritime history. The 7.1-mile Pierce Stocking Scenic Drive (open mid-May through early November) offers scenic views of the dunes, Lake Michigan, and the offshore Manitou Islands. (See DAY TRIPS.) There are two campgrounds: one in Glen Arbor (616–334–4634), without showers; the other in Honor (616–325–5881), with them. The park is open in winter for cross-country skiing and snowshoeing. Stop at Philip Hart Visitor Center in Empire, at the center of the park, for brochures and slide shows; (616) 326–5134.

Ski Areas

These destination resorts close to Traverse City entice families with a variety of children's programs, affordable packages, and après-ski fun. Since most are open year-round, these resorts also make great warm weather destinations offering mountain biking, golf, tennis, and other summer recreation. Always inquire about packages when you call. In addition, the Traverse City Convention and Visitors Bureau lists public downhill and cross-country trails.

Crystal Mountain, M–115, Thompsonville; (616) 378–2000/(800) 968–7686. This year-round resort, 28 miles southwest of Traverse City, offers summer and winter kids' programs, 23 slopes, and more than 16 miles of cross-country ski trails; plus mountain biking, tennis, golf, indoor/outdoor pools, and a fitness center. Stay in motel units, condos, or resort homes. During the winter there's a nursery for newborns to age three; nursery and skiing for potty-trained toddlers through age five; and a ski program for ages five to ten. Summers bring programs for ages three to ten or twelve, three days and evenings weekly, plus three weekly overnight camps for ages seven or eight through teens.

The Homestead, Wood Ridge Road, Glen Arbor; (616) 334–5000. In a scenic setting 25 miles west of Traverse City, this resort is open winter weekends and all summer. It offers downhill skiing from high above Lake Michigan, cross-country skiing into Sleeping Bear National Lakeshore, skating, and snowshoeing. You'll also find a game room, shops, and kids' programs, including child-care for ages three to eight and ski instruction for ages three to five and five to twelve. Munchin' Movies are held Saturday evenings and holidays for ages three to twelve. They offer a wide variety of price ranges and packages for lodge rooms, suites, and condos.

Shanty Creek/Schuss Mountain Resorts, Bellaire; (616) 533–8621/(800) 678–4111: These two separate ski areas, 38 miles from Traverse City and 3½ miles apart, are connected by a free shuttle. Shanty Creek is primarily for beginners and intermediates; Schuss Mountain, with a greater vertical drop, has terrain for beginner to expert. Snow Stars (ages three to five) and Kids Academy (ages five to eleven) teach youngsters the joy of skiing. Lodging at this all-season resort is in 600 rooms, suites, and condos. Ice skating, horse-drawn sleigh rides, indoor/outdoor pools, tennis, and a beach club round out the fun.

Sugar Loaf, Cedar Loaf; (616) 228–5461/(800) 968–0574. This resort, 18 miles northwest of Traverse City, has slopes ranging from gentle beginners to steep terrain. Ski schools teach children age three and ages four to twelve. Look for midweek packages and special weeks where kids sleep, ski, and eat free. Slopeside lodging in hotel rooms, town houses, or condos. The resort opens in the summer when golf is the big attraction.

Performing Arts

The Traverse City Players perform year-round at the **Old Town Playhouse** (616–947–2210), including kids-only productions. The **Michigan Ensemble Theatre** appears summers at Dennos Museum Center in Broadway productions such as *Chorus Line*. The Center's winter series includes performances by the local jazz society, folk singers, and musicians. Classical music lovers can attend concerts by **The Traverse City Symphony** (616–947–2210) between October and April. The internationally known **Interlochen Center for the Arts**, 17 miles south of Traverse City on Route 137 (616–276–6230), presents free or nominally priced year-round concerts by the faculty, students, and renowned international performers.

Shopping

Several shops in downtown Traverse City cater to kids. **Children's World** offers toys, games, and dolls; **Storyland** stocks books, educational supplies, toys, and more; **Old Town Kid Stuff** has clothing and other items; **Hocus Pocus** is a magic and novelty shop; and there's **Grand Bay Kite**.

Popular malls include **Cherryland Mall**, South Airport Road (across the street from **Skateworld** roller rink), where there's a hobby shop, **Trains & Things**, and a video game arcade, plus **Grand Traverse Mall**, U.S. 31 and South Airport Road, with a carousel, food court, multiplex theater, and game arcade.

Bargains abound at **Manufacturer's Marketplace**, 3639 Marketplace Circle, an outdoor outlet mall with more than thirty stores, including Levi/Dockers and Eddie Bauer.

SPECIAL EVENTS

These calendar highlights include a sampling of area events.

January: Discover Michigan Skiing, special rates offered by all Traverse City area resorts.

February: Michigan Special Olympics at Sugar Loaf, winter sports competitions for handicapped children and adults. North America Cross-Country Ski Race in Traverse City.

March: Spring Carnivals at Crystal Mountain and Shanty Creek-Schuss Mountain resorts.

July: July Fourth Fireworks Display. National Cherry Festival, eight days of fireworks, parades, concerts, competitions, ferris wheels, and lots of cherries! Traverse Bay Outdoor Art Fair.

August: Northwestern Michigan Fair.

Labor Day Weekend: Northport's Famous Fish Boil includes arts fair, entertainment, and tons of fish! Northport, on the tip of the Leelanau Peninsula, is about forty-five minutes from Traverse City.

Late September/Early October: Fall color season and winery tours.

Thanksgiving–Christmas: Hometown Holiday features a host of special gala activities and events plus affordable packages.

WHERE TO STAY

The area offers more than 4,500 hotel rooms in every price range. The Traverse City Convention and Visitors Bureau publishes lodging brochures. Always inquire about special packages. In addition to the ski and summer resorts already mentioned, the following places in Traverse City have special family appeal.

In the East Bay Area

These lodgings are on or near the "Miracle Mile" beaches. **The Beach Condominiums,** 1995 U.S. 31 North, on East Bay, gives families a chance to stretch out in thirty units that sleep four and feature sundecks, whirlpool baths, kitchens, and cable TV. Outside there's a beach, heated pool, and hot tub. Call (616) 938–2228. **Blue Water Beach Resort,** 1819 U.S. 31 North, rents fourteen cottage-style units on East Bay by the week. All have kitchenettes and cable TV. Special rates are offered in June and September. Call (616) 938–1370. **Driftwood Motel,** 1861 U.S. 31 North, on East Bay, boasts a beachfront and large indoor pool and recreation area with game room and whirlpool. Choose from poolside or economy rooms; most have refrigerators and cable TV. Free lift tickets at Mt. Holiday for each registered guest in your party. Call (616) 938–1600. **On A Bay Motel/ Resort,** 1773 U.S. 31 North, on East Bay, has one- and two-bedroom cottages and condos perfect for large families. Motel rooms and kitchenettes are also available. There are weekly or daily rates. Call (616) 938–2680.

Other Area Lodging

Grand Traverse Resort, 6300 U.S. 31 North, Acme, contains 750 luxury rooms, suites, and condos, some with refrigerator, fireplace, and whirlpool; ten restaurants and lounges; shopping gallery; indoor-outdoor tennis; pools and whirlpools; weight room; aerobic studio; cross-country skiing; championship golf; and seasonal activities for kids. Call (616) 938–2100/(800) 748–0303/(800) 678–1308—in Canada.

Hampton Inn, 1000 U.S. 31 North, is across from State Park Beach, 3 miles from downtown, and adjacent to River Country Funland. The 127 units include complimentary continental breakfast, local phone calls, and airport transportation. There's also an indoor pool, whirlpool, and exercise room. Call (616) 946–8900/(800) HAMPTON.

There is always something special happening just for kids at Grand Traverse Resort.
(Courtesy Grand Traverse Resort)

Ranch Rudolph, 6841 Brown Bridge Road, a four-season resort, is comprised of sixteen motel units and twenty-five campsites in Pere Marquette State Forest. Located on the Boardman River, 12 miles southeast of Traverse City, the ranch features horseback riding, canoeing, and cross-country skiing. Call (616) 947–9529.

WHERE TO EAT

The Traverse City guide includes restaurant listings featuring everything from burgers to fresh seafood, such as Lake Michigan whitefish and rainbow trout. Morel mushrooms are a popular delicacy hunted in the local woods each spring. (Only do this if you know exactly what to look for.)

For in-between nibbles, try the famous cherry pecan muffins at **The Muffin Tin**, 115 Wellington at Front (616–929–7915), a country-style store that also sells other regional products; and the Traverse City Cherry Vanilla Fudge at **Kilwin's Chocolates**, 129 East Front Street; (616) 946–2403/(800) 433–0596. (Fudge is very big in this area!)

For the main course there are equally good options. On Sunday afternoons at **Dills Olde Town Saloon**, 423 South Union Street, kids (and adults) can sing karaoke on stage to favorite tunes—including "Twinkle, Twinkle Little Star" for tots. Souvenir videos are available; ribs, steaks, seafood, and salads are on the menu; (616) 947–7534. At **Geppettos On the Bay**, 13641 West Bayshore Drive, dine on pasta specialties while enjoying the magnificent view; (616) 947–7079. **Cousin Jenny's Cornish Pasties**, 129 West Union Street, serves seven varieties, including the Breakfast Bobby; (616) 941–7821. **Mabel's**, 472 Munson Avenue, U.S. 31 North (two doors down from Days Inn), serves breakfast, lunch, or dinner anytime. Specialties include seven pastas, fresh steamed vegetables, Mabel's Original Vegetarian Nutburger, and "Just Enough Menus." Call (616) 947–0252.

DAY TRIPS

There are five wineries in the area; some open seasonally, others year-round. The closest is **Chateau Grand Traverse** on Old Mission Peninsula on M–37; (616) 223–7355.

Seaworthy older kids and teens might enjoy afternoon or sunset sailing adventures aboard the **Tall Ship Malabar**, on West Grand Traverse Bay. Picnic lunch or dinner is included. Call (616) 941–2000/(800) 968–8800.

The 8-square-mile **South Manitou Island** is worth a trip. It's part of the Sleeping Bear Dunes National Lakeshore (listed on page 380) and several miles offshore. Drive along the coast on scenic M–22 to the picturesque fishing village of Leland, where ferries (no cars allowed) leave daily; (616) 256–9061. Sights include The Valley of the Giants, consisting of 500 year-old light cedar trees, scenic dunes, a historic lighthouse, and a late 1800s cemetery. Kids can stand on the shoreline and see a real shipwreck (the Liberian freighter *Francisco Morazan*)! There are guided jeep tours and overnight camping—but no food for sale and no visible bathrooms! The "wilder" North Manitou Island isn't recommended for families.

FOR MORE INFORMATION

Brochures and guides to the area are available from **Traverse Convention and Visitors Bureau**, 415 Munson Avenue, Suite 200, Traverse City; 496–1120/800–TRAVERS. Ask for their excellent *Traverse City* magazine, published seasonally.

Emergency Numbers

In Grand Traverse, Kalaska, and Leelanau counties for ambulance, fire, police, and medical emergencies: 911

Emergency number in Antrim County: 533–8627

Emergency number in Benzie County: 882–4484

Grand Traverse Community Hospital, 550 Munson Avenue (922–8400), has a physician referral and health information service, 1:00 P.M. to 9:00 P.M. (946–INFO). The hospital's Med-Care Walk-In Clinic is open twenty-four hours, seven days a week (922–8686). From the eastern part of town, this is most accessible in an emergency.

From the western part, head to the Munson Medical Center, 1105 Sixth Street (935–5000), for their Walk-In Emergency Service (935–8507, also the number for their physician referral service).

For the disabled, bus service within Traverse City is available from Specialized On-Call Service (SOS); (616) 947–0796.

Poison Control: (800) 632–2727.

There is no twenty-four-hour pharmacy. The pharmacy at Meijer, 3955 U.S. 31 South (616–941–2727), is open 8:00 A.M.–10:00 P.M. Monday through Satuday, and 9:00 A.M.–7:00 P.M. Sunday. After closing time, either of the above hospitals can provide enough medicine to last until its pharmacy opens.

41
INDIANAPOLIS
Indiana

The movers and shakers of this heartland USA town made a concerted effort to establish Indianapolis as a sports center. After they built the arenas and stadiums, numerous athletic organizations came, bringing with them top sporting events. The results are great facilities—many of which are available for public use—and a city known as the Sports Capital of the United States.

Besides watching world-class competitions, visitors to Indianapolis enjoy two surprises: the world's largest children's museum and, nearby, Conner Prairie, a recreated pioneer town.

GETTING THERE

Indianapolis International Airport (317–487–9594) is 8 miles, about fifteen minutes, from downtown. The airport services American, American Trans Air, Canadian Partner, Continental, Delta, Northwest, Skyway, Southwest, TWA, USAir, and United Airlines. Call the individual airlines for flight information and reservations. Shuttlexpress (317–247–7301 or 800–439–3021) and AAA Airport Limousine (317–247–7301) offer van service to downtown.

Amtrak pulls into Union Station, 350 South Illinois Street (800–USA–RAIL), and buses arrive at the Greyhound/Trailways station, 127 North Capitol Avenue (317–635–4501).

Three major U.S. highways—I–69, I–70, and I–65—lead directly to Indianapolis, and I–74 leads traffic into the bypass route, I–465.

GETTING AROUND

The public bus system, the METRO (317–632–3000), is equipped to serve physically challenged riders. The METRO Trolleys (317–635–3344) have two downtown routes and operate Monday through Friday only. There are several cab companies, including Yellow Cab (317–637–5421).

Car rental companies include Budget Rent A Car, 7050 West Washington Street (317–248–1100); Dollar Rent A Car, 6175 West Minnesota Street (317–241–0829); Hertz Rent A Car, 2621 South High School Road (317–243–9321); and National Car Rental, 7111 West Washington Street (317–243–1177).

WHAT TO SEE AND DO

Museums

The Children's Museum of Indianapolis, 3000 North Meridian Street (317–924–5431), is the world's largest. As its motto indicates, it "is a place where children grow up, and adults don't have to." This museum appeals to kids of all ages. The "What If" gallery aims at ages six–ten by presenting three exhibits requested by more than 1,000 children: a dinosaur den, an underwater coral reef, and an Egyptian mummy. Kids dig for fossils, peer at a coral reef, and put together a mummy puzzle. Playscape lets preschoolers ages two and up experiment with water, shapes, and sand. Teens aren't forgotten either. At the Center for Exploration, visitors get to vote on such controversial issues as capital punishment and gun control.

This is the place to give in to the child within. Be sure to ride the Victorian carousel, browse the antique doll collection, and view the extensive array of model trains, among the largest train exhibits anywhere. For special kid's events, call the Kidsline at (317) 924–KIDS.

Eiteljorg Museum of American Indian and Western Art, 500 West Washington Street; (317) 636–WEST. The Eiteljorg holds one of the most extensive collections of American Western art and Native American art and artifacts. Situated next to an old grain elevator, the Eiteljorg looks both incongruous and intriguing. Cleverly designed to resemble the adobe architecture of the Taos Pueblo, the museum houses a first-rate collection of western paintings, including one by Georgia O'Keeffe, as well as Native American art and artifacts. The first-floor galleries capture the faces and forms of the West, from the dignity and power of Indian chiefs and warriors painted in the nineteenth and early twentieth century to contemporary and whimsical mixed-media works that depict cowboys with hip slouches, and toy guns.

Upstairs, Spirited Hands: Continuing Traditions in Native American Art displays an eye-catching array of everyday artifacts decorated with beadwork. Ask your kids to compare the varying cradle boards (carriers used to transport infants) fashioned by the different tribes.

Before you leave the museum, be sure to browse the gift shop. Kids will love spending their allowance on drums, posters, cards, charms, and some great T-shirts.

The Children's Museum of Indianapolis is, as its motto professes, "a place where children grow up and adults don't have to." (Courtesy The Indianapolis Project)

Indianapolis Museum of Art, 1200 West Thirty-eighth Street (317–923–1331), is not only an art museum with European, American, contemporary, Asian, and African art on permanent display; but the facility also features a 152-acre park, a botanical garden, a theater, a concert terrace, and a restaurant. In this museum, the seventh largest art museum in the United States, be sure to see the Eiteljorg Collection of African Art. The masks, carvings, and jewelry appeal to kids. A special touch: The videos near the displays show the masks in motion being worn in ceremonial dances. Other highlights include the largest collection of J. W. M. Turner works outside the United Kingdom, a comprehensive collection of Oriental art, and the famous Love sculpture by Robert Indiana (remember the Love stamp?) out on the lawn. Allow time to stroll the botanical gardens and browse the gift shop.

Sports Museums

Serious about sports, Indianapolis boasts several museums dedicated to the subject.

Indianapolis Motor Speedway Hall of Fame Museum, 4790 West Sixteenth Street; (317) 241–2500. If your kids collect model racing cars and root for their favorite speed demon, they will love it here. Crammed into the two large galleries of this hall are the sleek, shiny, and select cars—more than thirty of them—from the world of racing. Admire the 1914 Duesenberg driven by Eddie Rickenbacker (the first car to reach the amazing speed of 79 miles per hour), A.J. Foyt's four winning cars, and recent Indy champions. The walls feature photographs of racing's Hall of Fame.

Do your kids want to brag they rode the Indy? Then, board the bus for a narrated trip around the track and a close-up view of the stands, work pits, and famous finish line.

National Art Museum of Sport, Bank One Center/Tower, Second Floor; (317) 687–1715. Although small, consisting of several galleries and a second-floor office hallway, this museum is the only one in the United States devoted exclusively to sporting art. The general collections and special exhibitions rotate. You might see oils, prints, and sculpture on boxing, baseball, basketball, horse racing, or hockey. A visit here could be a good way to interest your sports enthusiast in art. The gift shop has some great puzzles and T-shirts, especially a baseball shirt with famous faces in the stadium à la "Where's Waldo?"

Several other sports museums are worth a browse. The **Hoosier Dome and National Track and Field Hall of Fame Museum,** One Hoosier Dome; (317) 261–0483 or (317) 262–3410. Go inside the stadium for a look at the VIP suites and the locker rooms. The **National Track and Field Hall of Fame Museum,** inside the Hoosier Dome, showcases the medals and uniforms of such track greats as Jim Thorpe, Jesse Owens, and Bruce Jenner. Located in New Castle, the **Indiana Basketball**

Hall of Fame, One Hall of Fame Court, New Castle (317–529–1891), pays homage to Indiana's love of hoops. Interactive exhibits take you onto the playing floor, and into the locker rooms.

ADDITIONAL ATTRACTIONS

President Benjamin Harrison Home, 1230 North Delaware Street (317–631–1898), is a National Historic Landmark. This Victorian home features many original family pieces plus rotating exhibits about the twenty-third President of the United States. **Hook's 1890 Drug Store,** 1202 East Thirty-eighth Street (317–924–1503), is outfitted like a Victorian soda parlor; grab an ice cream cone along with turn-of-the-century ambience. **The Indiana War Memorial,** 431 North Meridian Street (317–232–7615), is dedicated to soldiers killed in the two world wars and the Korean and Vietnam wars. It displays military weapons, uniforms, a jeep, and a helicopter. **The Murat Temple,** 510 North New Jersey Street (317–635–2433), modeled after an Islamic mosque, is the largest shrine temple in the world. Check out its stained-glass windows, theater, mosaic mural, and the Egyptian room constructed like Tutankhamen's burial chamber. **Holocomb Observatory and Planetarium at Butler University,** 4600 Sunset Avenue (317–283–9333), operates a 38-inch reflecting telescope that is available to the public. Call ahead for hours.

Sports Facilities Open to the Public

As the Sports Capital of the United States, the city offers visitors world-class facilities not just for watching, but for doing. Simply show your hotel room key to take advantage of the inexpensive entry fees and the top-rated facilities, which are open to the public when not hosting major events. Always call first to check availability and to find out about any age restrictions.

Indiana University Natatorium, 901 West New York Street; (317) 274–3517. Bring your own towel and a lock for the lockers, and swim, swim, swim in this first-class pool. Doing laps here your teens will feel like Matt Biondi, Summer Sanders, or Rowdy Gains. Work out at the aerobics classes and in the weight room.

Indiana University Track & Field Stadium, 901 West New York Street; (317) 374–6780. Located in the same complex as the natatorium, the check-in for the track-and-field facility is at the east entrance of the natatorium. Jog on the 400-meter, outdoor, rubber lanes or join in the free fun runs every Wednesday at 6:00 P.M. Registration is at 5:30 P.M.

Practice your tennis at the indoor and outdoor courts at the **Indianapolis Sports Center,** 815 West New York Street, (317) 278–2100.

While it's better to bring your own racquet, a limited number are available for use at no charge. Lessons are available too.

National Institute for Fitness and Sport, 250 North University Boulevard; (317) 274–3432. Parents and teens especially appreciate working out on the Olympic-quality training equipment and running on the 200-meter indoor track. Admission is just $7.00 per day when a hotel key is presented.

Your clan can cut quite a figure when skating together at the indoor **Indiana World Skating Academy,** Pan American Plaza, 201 South Capitol Avenue; (317) 237–5565. For more skating October through April, try the **Perry Ice Rink,** 451 East Stop 11 Road; (317) 888–0070.

Cyclists aren't forgotten either. Pedal around the top-notch track at the **Major Taylor Velodrome & BMX Tracks,** 3649 Cold Spring Road (317–926–8356), the site of many national competitions. Riders must be at least eight years old and wear helmets. Next door the BMX Track offers more training possibilities. Enjoy rowing and paddling at the **Regatta Course at Eagle Creek,** 7840 West Fifty-sixth Street; (317) 327–7110.

Parks and Zoos

Indianapolis Zoo, 1200 West Washington Street (317–630–2001), close to downtown Indianapolis, is worth a trip. Known for its large whale and dolphin pavilions (check the times for the daily shows), this sixty-four-acre "cageless" zoo exhibits animals in waters, deserts, forests, and plains. The Waters building, always a favorite, features penguins, reef fish, turtles, and seals. Living Deserts of the World, an enclosed conservatory filled with cacti and other desert plants, takes you by free-roaming lizards, turtles, and hummingbirds.

In addition, young kids covet the camel, pony, and elephant rides, as well as a stint on the free trolley—a good way to get around and avoid aching feet. A stroll through this beautiful zoo is a delight, especially in spring when beds of black-eyed Susans, day lilies, and lilacs bloom.

In May, attend the "Zoopolis 500," a humorous take-off on the famed Indy race. In this race two tortoises—A.J. and J.R.—vie for the championship. On Thursday nights in summer, stay after hours for "Animals and All that Jazz" performances by local groups.

Eagle Creek Park, 7840 West Fifty-sixth Street (317–293–4827), is run by the Indianapolis Department of Parks and Recreation and stretches for more than 3,000 acres. One of the largest municipal parks in the country, the fun here includes swimming, sailing, and canoeing in the 1,300-acre reservoir.

White River State Park, 801 West Washington Street (317–634–4567), is located on 250 acres downtown. It includes the Indianapolis Zoo, the National Institute for Fitness and Sport, and The Eiteljorg Museum of American Indian and Western Art.

Thunder Island Water and Recreation Park, 19830 U.S. 31 North, Westfield (317–896–5172), has water slides, kiddie and adult pools, miniature golf, go-carts, tubing, bumper boats, and softball batting cages.

Special Tours

If your young children get cranky during the early evening hours, take a soothing horse-drawn carriage ride around the city. Stately Percherons pull the carriages of the Metropolitan Carriage Company, 1311 South Drover Street (317–631–4169), which picks people up in front of the Holiday Inn, Union Station. On this half-hour tour, you can sit back and enjoy Indianapolis lit up at night. The horses take you around the landmark Soldiers and Sailors Monument, in the center of Monument Circle, past the State Capitol Building, Capitol Avenue and Washington Street (317–232–8687), by the famed Hoosier Dome, 100 South Capitol (317–262–3452), and to Union Station, Georgia Street between Meridian Street and Capitol Avenue. Besides falling in love with the horses, your kids will enjoy the leisurely pace and the Cinderella ambience.

Carriage tours are available year-round, weather permitting, Monday through Friday from 6:30 P.M. to midnight, and Saturday and Sunday from 3:30 P.M. to 1:00 A.M. While you can hail a coach most evenings, reservations are strongly suggested for Saturday night.

Performing Arts

Deer Creek Music Center, 12880 East 146th Street; (317) 776–3337 (box office), (317) 841–8900 (main office). This outdoor covered amphitheater seats 18,000 and hosts musical performances in summer, including a multiday June festival. The Indiana Repertory Theatre, 140 West Washington Street (317–635–5277), has three stages and a variety of performances. Indianapolis Ballet Theatre, 411 East Michigan Street (317–637–8979), performs full-length and contemporary ballets. Indianapolis Civic Theatre, 1200 West Thirty-eighth Street, Indianapolis Museum of Art (box office 317–923–4597, main office 317–924–6770), uses volunteers and professionals. This is the home of the Kid Connection, an adult acting group that tours Midwestern elementary schools. Indianapolis Opera, 250 East Thirty-eighth Street (box office 317–283–9696, main office 317–283–3531), performs at Clowes Memorial Hall, Butler University. Indianapolis Symphony Orchestra, 45 Monument Circle (box office 317–639–4300, main office 317–262–1100), performs classical and popular music each season at the Circle Theatre. In summer there are performances under the stars at Conner Prairie (See DAY TRIPS). The Phoenix Theatre, 749 North Park Avenue (317–635–PLAY), performs off-Broadway and contemporary plays. Starlight Musicals, Forty-ninth and Boulevard (box office 317–239–1000, main office 317–631–5700). Nationally known stars lead this resident professional company as they perform musicals in the summer at Hilton University's Brown Theatre. **Beef and Boards Dinner Theatre**, 9301 North Michigan Road (317–872–9664), is an equity troupe that serves up Broadway shows in dinner-theater format.

For performing arts schedules at local universities, contact **Clowes Memorial Hall**, Butler University, 4600 Sunset Avenue; (317) 283–9696.

For tickets, call the individual box offices listed above, or try these agencies: **Oasis Tickets and Tours**, 5224 Keystone Court, (317) 255–4493; **TicketMaster**, (317) 239–5151; and **Tickets Up Front and Travel**, 1099 North Meridian Street, Suite 150, (317) 633–6400.

Sports

The **Indiana Pacers**, a National Basketball Association team, play at the Market Square Arena, 300 East Market Street (main office 317–263–2100, tickets 317–239–5151). Catch the **Indianapolis Colts**, a National Football League team, at the Hoosier Dome, 100 South Capitol Avenue, P.O. Box 535000; (317) 297–7000. The **Indianapolis Indians**, the farm-league team of the Montreal Expos baseball team, plays from April to November at Bush Stadium, 1501 West Sixteenth Street; (317) 269–3545.

The **Little League Baseball Central Region Headquarters**, 4360 North Mitthoeffer Road (317–897–6127), hosts the Central Region Little League Baseball Championship each August, the winner goes on to the World Series. Find out about the summer camps held at this thirty-acre facility.

SPECIAL EVENTS

Festivals and Sporting Events

March: Biennial National Beethoven Fellowship Auditions and Finals. Midwestern Collegiate Conference (MCC) Men's Basketball Championship. NCAA Men's and Women's Division I Indoor Track Championships. NCAA Men's Division I Basketball Championship, First and Second Rounds. Indiana High School Athletic Association (IHSAA) Boy's Basketball Finals.

April: 500 Festival of the Arts at the Children's Museum.

May: The Indianapolis 500 is held Memorial Day weekend each year. The city celebrates with a month of events that include a minimarathon, parade, and the 500 Festival Kids' Day—the largest festival for children in the city. The fun includes splashing paint on old cars, racing Big Wheel bikes, and creating arts and crafts. The fair is generally held around Monument Circle.

June: Savor more than six tons of Indiana strawberries in shortcakes and cheesecakes at the Strawberry Festival, Monument Circle. The Deer Creek Fair, Deer Creek Music Center, has arts and crafts, and concerts.

Watch the U.S. Rowing National Championships, Eagle Creek Park, and the National Track Cycling Championships, Major Taylor Velodrome.

Late June–July: Indiana Black Expo, Indiana Convention Center and Hoosier Dome, is the nation's largest minority health, historical, and musical festival.

July–August: At Festival of Emerging American Theater (FEAT), Phoenix Theatre, plays that won in a national contest are performed.

August: Indiana State Fair, RCA U.S. Men's Hardcourt Tennis Championships, and the Indiana Avenue Jazz Festival.

September: National Hot Rod Association (NHRA) U.S. Nationals, Indiana Raceway Park.

October: Wordstruck: The Indiana Festival of Books. Halloween Zoobilee, special Halloween events at the zoo. Greater Indianapolis CROP Walk For the Hungry, a 10-K walk to raise funds to fight worldwide hunger.

November: Butcherin', Stuffin', and Smokin' demonstrations at Conner Prairie. The Winter Festival at the Children's Museum begins.

December: Conner Prairie by Candlelight, a holiday candlelight tour. Christmas at the Zoo. Winter Festival at the Children's Museum continues through the beginning of January.

WHERE TO STAY

Embassy Suites Hotel—Downtown, 110 West Washington Street; (317) 236–1800 or (800) EMBASSY. Situated just blocks from the Indiana Convention Center and Hoosier Dome, this all-suite hotel offers families extra space and the conveniences of a microwave, refrigerator, coffee maker, and fold-out sofa bed. The property also has an indoor pool.

Holiday Inn Union Station, 123 West Louisiana Street; (317) 631–2221 or (800) HOLIDAY. Located across from the Hoosier Dome, this hotel has 276 rooms, twenty-six of which are authentic Pullman car suites permanently parked on tracks off the hotel's main floors. Named for famous personalities of the twenties and thirties such as Diamond Jim Brady and Greta Garbo, these cars are furnished with period pieces and reproductions; many have pull-out sofas and all add fun to an overnight stay. Lurking near the trains are white fiberglass statues of soldiers, sailors, and people of the era. Called the "ghosts" of Union Station, they add charm. The hotel also has an indoor pool. Be sure when requesting rooms you are not near the pool or central atrium, which can be noisy.

Hyatt Regency Indianapolis, One South Capitol Avenue; (317) 632–1234 or (800) 233–1234. Located directly across from the Indiana Convention Center and Hoosier Dome, this hotel features a 20-story atrium, and a 20-foot waterfall in the lobby, and an indoor pool.

The Westin Hotel Indianapolis, 50 South Capitol Avenue; (317)

262–8100/(800) 228–3000. Located in downtown's business district, the hotel has a restaurant and lounge, indoor pool, and exercise facilities. For less pricey lodging try the **Comfort Inn** at 5040 South East Street (317–783–6711 or 800–221–2222), located ten minutes from downtown.

WHERE TO EAT

Paramount Music Palace, 7560 Old Trails Road (317–352–0144), is a pizza restaurant that features a Wurlitzer pipe organ, silent movies, and sing-alongs. Kids love the excitement as much as the food. **Capitol Food Court,** 25 West Market Street (317–634–4148), houses Ed and Marge's Cafeteria and a variety of fast-food restaurants: Long John Silver's, Wendy's, Arby's, Pizza Hut. **Charlie and Barney's Bar and Grill,** Merchants Plaza (317–636–3101) and 225 East Ohio Street (317–637–5851), serves award-winning chili, gourmet burgers, fresh soups and salads, and specialty sandwiches. **Noble Roman's Pizza,** 136 North Delaware Street (317–637–9997), offers four styles of pizza: pan, deep-dish Sicilian, hand-tossed round, and super thin; sandwiches and salads are also on the menu. **Union Station,** 39 West Jackson Place (317–267–0701), is a century-old, refurbished station which now includes shops and restaurants (including inexpensive eateries), as well as trains. Kids like the "ghosts," those white statues of Victorian-era train riders.

The Indianapolis Convention and Visitors Association offers a visitor's guide that lists many family-friendly restaurants throughout the city.

DAY TRIPS

Conner Prairie, 13400 Allisonville Road, Noblesville; (317) 776–6000. This 250-acre living-history museum with about forty buildings is definitely worth a trip. Just fifty minutes from Indianapolis, the facility transports you to 1836. History is anything but boring here. Kids will be intrigued by the costumed interpreters who make the frontier come alive. The doctor's wife tells you how her piano had an easier trip from the East than she did, and the carpenter shows you how to fashion a chair leg. At the Golden Eagle Tavern, Martha Zimmermann bakes cookies and warns you about the dangers of women traveling alone. It's hands-on fun at the Pioneer Adventure area, where kids try their skill at weaving, grinding corn, and walking on stilts, a popular pioneer pastime.

The seasonal events are fun as well. In June be a guest at a wedding. On July 4th kick up your heels at a traditional village celebration. During August the Indianapolis Symphony Orchestra performs evening concerts in the museum's outdoor amphitheater. Bring a picnic supper and blanket for the lawn. Special fall events include demonstrations of hog butchering—the real thing—and smoking meats pioneer style.

Zionsville, a northern suburb of Indianapolis, features nineteenth-century architecture. Lincoln stopped here in 1861 to speak while en route to Washington, D.C., for his inauguration. A monument dedicated to the speech stands near the train station. Guided walking tours are available. Annual events include Country Market Arts Fair in May and a Fall Festival in September. For a brochure write to Zionsville Chamber of Commerce, 125 South Elm Street, or phone (317) 873–3836 from Tuesday to Friday, 10:00 A.M. to 4:30 P.M.

Indiana Dunes National Lakeshore. The lakeshore, in Indiana's northwestern corner, covers 13,000 acres along the southern shores of Lake Michigan. In season enjoy swimming, fishing, hiking, and cross-country skiing. Dunes, of course, are big here. See the view from the top of Mount Baldy, the lakeshore's tallest dune. As the area is located on a north-south migratory route, seasonal bird watching is great here. The visitor's center at Kermil Road and U.S. 12 has information, pamphlets, and maps. Call or write to Indiana Dunes National Lakeshore, 1100 North Mineral Springs Road, Porter, Indianapolis 46304; (219) 926–7561.

The French Lick Springs Resort, 8670 State Road 56, French Lick, Indiana 46432; (800–457–4042 or 812–936–9300), caters to children by offering summertime family programs including Mysterious Monday, for amateur detectives; the Pluto Club, for ages five through twelve; and Chuckwagon Cookouts every night of the week. Ask about reduced rates for children.

FOR MORE INFORMATION

Begin your visit with a stop at the visitor's center in the **Indianapolis City Center,** 201 South Capitol Avenue; (800) 468–INDY or (317) 237–5206. Browse the more than 300 brochures, examine the model of the city, and watch the eight-minute slide show, a fast-paced pastiche of city images. The hours are Monday to Friday, 10:00 A.M.– 5:30 P.M., and Saturday 10:00 A.M.–4:00 P.M. Call for information about weekend packages and special events.

Emergency Numbers
Ambulance, fire, and police: 911
Poison Control: (317) 929–2323
Riley Hospital for Children, at the Indiana University Medical Center, 702 Barnhill Drive; (317) 274–5000
Twenty-four-hour pharmacy: Hook's Drugstore, 1744 North Illinois; (317) 923–1491

42
NORTHWOODS AREA
Wisconsin

The vast Northwoods area of Wisconsin offers families an unspoiled, natural setting for a vacation of down-to-earth pleasures. Most northern Wisconsin communities were once lumbering centers, and the lore and legends of those days live on, although the logging industry declined by the early 1900s. Today the Northwoods is a sporting paradise and summer vacation retreat. Families come here for the scenic woodlands and lakes.

While there are no official boundaries for the Northwoods, the region is considered to be the north central (north of Wausau), and northeastern (north of Green Bay) part of the state. Oneida County, where Minocqua and Rhinelander are situated, and Vilas County, home to Lac du Flambeau, are its tourist centers. Minocqua, called the "Island City," is one of the area's popular summer resorts, thanks to the lake that surrounds it and its proximity to more than 3,000 lakes and ponds, the largest concentration of freshwater lakes in the world. Pine-scented forests offer hiking and biking trails, and day trips lead to man-made and natural wonders. In winter this area (Minocqua and surrounding towns are referred to as the Lakeland area) is a top snowmobile destination.

GETTING THERE

The Rhinelander–Oneida County Airport (715–362–3641), 25 miles from Minocqua, is served by major commercial carriers. Taxi service is available at the airport. Greyhound (715–362–2737) also goes to Rhinelander. There are no nearby Amtrak stations.

GETTING AROUND

Cars, boats, and bikes are the popular transportation modes around these parts. There's no public transportation.

WHAT TO SEE AND DO

Parks

Torpy Park, downtown Minocqua, has a beach with approximately 340 feet of frontage on Lake Minocqua. The beach is safe for kids as it has a roped area, a lifeguard, and no boats are allowed. Swimming lessons are offered, and there's a diving area. You'll also find tennis courts and picnic tables, plus a band shell where a number of local events take place. In winter dress warmly and come here for ice skating.

Bearskin State Park Trail is a wilderness trail that extends for 18 miles, from just north of the Lincoln and Oneida county line north to Minocqua. The trail, which you enter from behind the Minocqua Post Office, is a former railroad grade that's been surfaced for hiking and biking. Deer, raccoon, otter, beaver, and other native wildlife scamper about. You cross the scenic Beaver Creek several times via rustic trestles. In winter, snowmobiles are allowed to use the trails, although no other motorized vehicles are permitted. Midpoint on the shore of South Blue Lake, there's a rest area with toilets, picnic tables, grills, and drinking water. Bikers need an admission card, which costs $2.00 daily and can be purchased at the Minocqua Chamber of Commerce, as can a guidebook detailing the history and points of interest on the trail.

Minocqua is within striking distance of two forests, both offering wilderness recreational opportunities. Chequamegon National Forest, Headquarters, 1170 Fourth Street, Park Falls; (715) 762–2461. It's about 13 miles from downtown Minocqua to the eastern part of this vast forest, which features nearly 850,000 acres of lakes, rivers, streams, northern hardwoods, pines, and meadowlands. There are twenty-four campsites: the Chippewa Campground in the Medford District is the only one with warm water showers and flush toilets. It has a swimming beach and play area. For camping reservations call (800) 283–CAMP. The forest publishes a number of helpful brochures on different aspects of the park, including cross-country ski and hiking trails, scenic overlooks, wetland wildlife viewing areas, historic sites, and fishing and boating areas. Contact the forest headquarters for more information.

Northern Highland–American Legion State Forest, Woodruff, is the other forest. It's about 5 miles north from Minocqua to the southwest fringe of the forest near the Woodruff area headquarters. This forest offers 222,000 acres with 900 lakes, plus woodland, and nature and hiking trails. Families also enjoy picnicking, swimming, and canoeing.

There are nine unsupervised beach and picnic areas throughout the park. The closest to Minocqua is Clear Lake, which also has a rustic campground (no flush toilets or running water) and a swimming area. For more information, stop by or contact Woodruff Area Forest Headquarters, 8770 Highway J, Woodruff 54568; (715) 356–5211.

In winter **Minocqua Winter Park**, Squirrel Lake Road off Highway 70 West, offers visitors 60 kilometers of groomed cross-country trails, a certified ski school, and special trails groomed for small children. The day lodge provides child-care for all ages on Tuesdays, weekends, and holidays. Call (715) 356–3309.

Museums

Dr. Kate Pelham Newcomb Museum, 923 Second Avenue, Woodruff; (715) 356–6896. This museum pays tribute to an extraordinary local woman who reached the sick in a special car outfitted with skis on the front wheels and tractor treads on the rear. To access more remote areas, she used snowshoes. Dr. Newcomb practiced until she died in 1956 at age seventy, and her story, told in this museum, is really an inspiration.

Jim Peck's Wildwood, 2 miles west on Highway 70; (715) 356–5588. This is primarily a petting zoo, where kids feed tame deer, pet a porcupine, and cuddle a llama. There's a bear, too, just to admire. Kids will also like the adventure boat rides and nature walk on this thirty-acre property.

Journey Into the Wild Museum, 8 miles south on Highway 51, Hazelhurst; (715) 356–4496. Now for something completely different. Some kids like this, and others are appalled. Here you'll find more than 880 life-size, mounted animals, including wild jungle creatures, all displayed in natural habitat settings. There's a sandwich shop on the premises and—not that you'll need it—a taxidermy service, too.

Lac du Flambeau Chippewa Museum & Cultural Center, Peace Pipe Road just south of the Indian Bowl, in Lac du Flambeau; (715) 588–3133. The nearby village of Lac du Flambeau lies in the center of the 144-square-mile Lac du Flambeau Chippewa Indian Reservation. The Museum and Cultural Center, which is open late June through mid-August, appeals to kids. The French name, meaning "Lake of the Flaming Torches," was given by fur traders who saw Chippewas fishing in their canoes by torchlight. Exhibits include an authentic Indian dugout canoe, birchbark canoes, crafts and traditional clothing, ceremonial drums, artifacts, and an exhibit displaying Chippewa activities and clothing. Demonstrations take place regularly.

The **Lac du Flambeau Indian Pow Wow**, Indian Bowl, takes place Tuesday evenings at 7:00 P.M. from late June through mid-August; (715) 588–3346. Kids love the ceremonial dance presented by authentic Chippewa performers.

At the **Lac du Flambeau Fish Hatchery**, on the Chippewa Reservation, Highway 47, there's a fishing pond open from May through August where you and the kids can fish without a license and pay only for the trout you catch. Call (715) 588–3303.

Scheer's Lumberjack Show, Highway 47, Woodruff. This town, which adjoins Minocqua, used to be a boisterous logging settlement, and

Kids love the ceremonial dances presented at the Lac du Flambeau Indian Pow Wow.
(Photo by Chris Driers/courtesy Wisconsin Division of Tourism)

this show, offered mid-June through August, brings back some of those colorful days. The kids love the chopping and sawing, canoe jousting, speed climbing, clown acts, and log rolling. It's great fun. Call (715) 356–4050.

Attractions

Circle M Corral, 2½ miles west of U.S. 51 on SR 70; (715) 356–4441. This amusement and theme park is guaranteed to keep everyone happy for the greater part of the day. There's a water slide, kid's rides and splash area, bumper boats, go-carts, train and pony rides, miniature golf, horseback riding, batting cages, a shooting gallery, and video games.

The Min-Aqua Bats, one of the oldest amateur water ski shows in the United States, presents a show at Minocqua's downtown Aqua Bowl every Wednesday, Friday, and Sunday night from mid-June to mid-August, at 7:00 P.M. The show is free, though donations are requested. Call (715) 356–5266.

Rhinelander Logging Museum, Pioneer Park; (715) 369–5004. Rhinelander began as a supply center for the logging camps when logging was in its heyday. Today the museum, open from mid-May through mid-September, boasts a replica of an 1870s lumber camp, complete with bunkhouse, cook shanty, and blacksmith shop constructed of Norway pine logs. Logging artifacts on display include tools and equipment and fascinating photographs. On the grounds are early logging equipment, such as a narrow-gauge locomotive and a rare steam-powered snow snake used to haul sleds of logs over icy highways. There's also a cage containing a black "hodag" (see Shopping for a description of this local mythical creature) and a miniature electric sawmill. Stop by the gift shop for a hodag souvenir or other northwoods item. Most of these are crafted by senior citizens who work at the museum.

Special Tours

Wilderness Cruises, from mid-May to mid-October, offers narrated tours aboard the *Wilderness Queen*. This boat cruises the unspoiled shoreline of the Willow Flowage, a man-made lake built as a reservoir for regulating the Wisconsin River. The boat has an enclosed, heated lower level and an open upper level. Sights along the way include wildlife (osprey nests, eagles, loons, and sometimes deer), plus islands and coves. Lunch, dinner, and Sunday brunch cruises are available. Wilderness Cruises is in a rural area about 15 miles from Minocqua. Call (715) 453–3310/(800) 472–1516 for directions and reservations.

Performing Arts

Northern Lights Playhouse, 5611 Highway 51, Hazelhurst, 5 miles south of Minocqua, presents different shows weekly, including Broadway smashes. There's a children's matinee on Wednesday morning; (715) 356–7173.

Shopping

There are lots of antique and craft shops in the area. Don't miss the famous Wisconsin fudge at **Dan's Minocqua Fudge Shop**, 521 Oneida Street, downtown; (715) 356–2662. Loons—the symbol of the northwoods—are the theme of the **Loon Land Trading Co. Twisted Root Emporium**, 207 Front Street, downtown; (715) 356–5179. Buy a loon souvenir, then take a look at the solid wood accessories and log furniture.

If you're in Rhinelander, stop by any gift shop for a souvenir "hodag," a dragon-like creature with white claws and white horns along its back. This mythical creature was "photographed" in 1896 by a local lumberman who claimed to have led a party of loggers to capture the monster in a cave. Later, of course, it was revealed as a harmless hoax— done "to get people talking." Today, the hodag is the name of every athletic team at the local high school, as well as the name of a park, a weekly shopping guide, and numerous area events. (See SPECIAL EVENTS for one example!)

SPECIAL EVENTS

Check with the Minocqua Chamber of Commerce for special doings in the area. The Lakeland *Times*, published twice weekly, also includes local events. Some highlights:

July: The Fourth Celebration, featuring giant parade, special water ski show and fireworks, downtown Minocqua. Hodag Country Festival, Rhinelander. This three-day celebration—the largest in the Northwoods—features an outdoor amphitheater with top country-music entertainment, camping on grounds, food, souvenirs (hodags, anyone?), and family fun.

August: Oneida County Fair, Rhinelander.

WHERE TO STAY

There are a variety of accommodations in the area, ranging from motel rooms to housekeeping cottages to luxury suites. The Minocqua Chamber of Commerce has a guide that lists lodgings. Here are a few selections for families.

Just-N-Trails Bed and Breakfast, Route 1, Box 263, Sparta, WI 54656; (608) 269–4522, is the place where families experience farm life first-hand. Visitors can do everything from milking cows to helping with chores.

Minocqua Shores, Island City Point. One mile from town, this resort offers three- and four-bedroom lakeside condos with dishwashers and microwaves, one- to three-bedroom cottages. There's a beach area, pontoon, and paddleboat rentals; (715) 356–5101.

New Concord Inn, Highway 51, has fifty-four rooms, an indoor pool, and game room. It's across the street from Torpy Park Beach, one block from the Bearskin Trail, and within walking distance of the water ski show. Call (715) 356–1800.

Pine Hill Resort, 8544 Hower Road, 2 miles west on Highway 70 on Lake Kawaguesaga, one of the Minocqua Chain of Lakes. Plain but comfortable two- and three-bedroom lakefront housekeeping cottages have refrigerators and gas stoves. There's a rec room and safe sandy beach. Call (715) 356–3418.

WHERE TO EAT

Hearty meals are the norm in the northwoods. The Minocqua Chamber of Commerce guide lists a number of area restaurants. Here are several families will like.

Paul Bunyan Famous Lumberjack Meals, 8653 Highway 51 North, has an 1890s logging camp feel and specializes in hearty camp breakfasts—lunch and dinner served, too. Stop by for the Friday Fish Blast. (Note: Just about every restaurant in town has fish fries on Friday.) Call (715) 356–6270 for information.

Mama's Supper Club, overlooking Curtis Lake, has kid's menus and serves delicious Sicilian fare, including homemade pizza; (715) 356–5070. **Four Seasons Supper Club & Resort,** Big Arbor Vitae Lake, Woodruff, is a meat-and-potatoes place—ribs, chicken, steaks, and chops. This is also a cottage resort, with year-round rentals available. Call (715) 356–5095.

DAY TRIPS

Take an excursion aboard the Laona and Northern Railway's steam train, the **Lumberjack Special.** The train departs from the historic depot in Laona, which is about 1½ hours east of Minocqua. The train goes to the Camp Five Museum Complex. The train operates from mid-June to late August, except Sundays, and leaves at 11:00 A.M., noon, 1:00 P.M., and 2:00 P.M. Check ahead for times, and don't miss the train. Unless you arrive at boarding time, there's not much else to do in this rural area. Return trains leave at 11:20 A.M., 12:20, 1:20, and 4:00 P.M. Buy your tickets at the depot, about ⅓ mile out of Laona toward Rhinelander on Highway 8.

The complex, accessible only by train, is about 2½ miles from the depot. Here you'll find a logging museum with artifacts, active blacksmith and harness shops, a lumber company money collection, a thirty-minute video on how the steam engine gets going in the morning, and much more.

There's also an old-fashioned country store, an animal corral, an ecology walk, and a nature center. A half-hour forest tour by surrey is included in the admission fee, or take a hayrack/pontoon boat ride through a bird refuge and along banks of wild rice for a slight additional charge. Call (715) 674–3414 in summer and (715) 845–5544 in winter.

FOR MORE INFORMATION

Contact the Greater Minocqua Chamber of Commerce, P.O. Box 1006, Minocqua 54548, for literature on the area, or call (800) 44–NORTH. For Rhinelander information, call the Rhinelander Chamber of Commerce at (800) 236–4FUN. For free Wisconsin travel literature, including the excellent *Wisconsin Auto Tours Guide* featuring the Northwoods and Minocqua, call (800) 432–TRIP.

Emergency Numbers

Ambulance, fire, and police: 911

Twenty-four-hour physician-staffed emergency service: Howard Young Medical Center, 240 Maple Street, Woodruff; (715) 356–8000

Poison Control: (608) 262–3702 (Madison)

There's no twenty-four-hour pharmacy; the hospital will dispense an overnight supply of medicine after pharmacy hours. Joe's Lakeland Pharmacy, Save-More Plaza, Route 51N, downtown Minocqua (715–356–3303), is open from 9:00 A.M. to 6:00 P.M. weekdays and 9:00 A.M. to 4:00 P.M. Saturday. Closed Sunday.

43
SANDUSKY, OHIO, AND THE LAKE ERIE ISLANDS

Often dubbed "Ohio's summer playground," Sandusky and the Lake Erie Islands offer lots of family finds. Sandusky has miles of lake shoreline for boating and bathing plus an old-fashioned amusement park with up-to-speed roller coasters. For island fun Great Lakes–style, visit the Lake Erie islands, especially Kelleys Island, and South Bass Island famed for Put-in-Bay. These islands gained significance in 1813 as the site of Commodore Perry's victory over the British in the War of 1812. But now the islands offer much more placid pleasures such as sunning, swimming, fishing, and bicycling, all at affordable prices.

GETTING THERE

The Cleveland-Hopkins International Airport (216–267–8282), about 65 miles from Sandusky, is the closest major airport to the area. Car rentals are available at the airport. Amtrak (800–USA–RAIL) arrives at Cleveland's main terminal, Ninth Street and Cleveland Memorial Shoreway. Greyhound/Trailways (216–781–1400) offers daily bus service between Sandusky, 6513 Milan Road, and Cleveland, East Fifteenth Street and Chester Avenue.

To reach the Sandusky area by car, take the Ohio Turnpike, I–80, to exit 7 and follow U.S. 250 north to the Sandusky area. If you're heading to Port Clinton, take U.S. 250 to Route 2 west and follow signs to Port Clinton; Marblehead is off 269 east; and Catawba lies off 163 east. Each of these towns has ferry service to the Lake Erie Islands. Catawba and Port Clinton have ferry service to South Bass Island. Marblehead serves Kelleys Island. (See GETTING AROUND.)

GETTING AROUND

There are two things to remember when visiting the Lake Erie Islands: one, island hopping means living by the ferry schedule; two, don't think twice about leaving your car on the mainland. Getting around without an auto is easy and fun. Most of the islands offer bicycle and golf-cart rentals, and guided island tours. Walking is also great fun in good weather. Kelleys Island and Put-in-Bay also offer narrated tram services. If you're adamant about bringing your car, call ahead to reserve ferry space.

Miller Boat Line (419–285–2421) serves south Bass Island from Catawba Point. Jet Express (800–245–1JET) shuttles between South Bass (Put-In-Bay) and Port Clinton. Sonny-S Ferry (419–285–8774) serves Middle Bass from downtown Put-In-Bay with ferries departing on the hour. Neuman Boat Line (419–626–5557) and Kelleys Island Ferry Boat Lines, Inc. (419–746–2605) both run boats between Kelleys Island and Marblehead.

If you're only in the Lake Erie Islands area for a day, take an island-hopping cruise aboard the *M/V City of Sandusky* (419–627–0198), which originates at the Jackson Street Pier in downtown Sandusky and stops at the Casino Docks in Kelleys Island, Put-In-Bay, Lonz Winery, and Middle Bass Island.

WHAT TO SEE AND DO

Sandusky Area
Combine two days in the Sandusky area with several days of island hopping for a sure-to-please, moderately priced family vacation that couples amusement park thrills with plenty of beach attractions.

Life's little ups and downs are lots of fun at Cedar Point Amusement Park, P.O. Box 5006, Sandusky (419–627–2223), situated on the 364-acre Lake Erie Peninsula. This 124-year-old amusement park, which debuted its first roller coaster in 1892, offers up-to-date excitement. Best known for its ten roller coasters, the park bills itself as the largest ride park in the country, with 54 rides. (*Rides*, the promoters say, not *attractions* as in Disney World). Whether or not this phrase is a bit of hyperbole, the fact remains that there's lots to do here, and your kids won't be bored.

Thrill-seeker favorites include the Magnum XL200, one of the tallest and fastest coasters in the world, reaching heights of 205 feet and speeds of up to 72 miles-per-hour. The Mean Streak, a 161-foot-tall wooden wonder, has dips and drops calculated to make you shriek with delight. Snake River Falls, a log flume ride, rivals Disney World's Splash Moun-

The whole family can take a spin on the Cadillac Cars at Cedar Point amusement park in Sandusky, Ohio. (Photo by Dan Feicht/courtesy Cedar Point Image Library)

tain, hurtling passengers down a 50-degree 80-foot slide at speeds close to 40 miles-per-hour.

At Jungle Larry's Safari your kids eye alligators, exotic birds, and performing leopards. For more animal moments, drop by the Oceana Aquarium for dolphin and sea lion shows.

Importantly, this park also pleases preschoolers, especially tykes who love to listen to Berenstain Bears stories and tapes. This special bear family "lives" at Cedar Point's Berenstain Bear Country. Kids delight in sets taken from their favorite tales. Come inside the Bear Family Tree House, meet Papa, Mama, Sister, and Brother bear, play at the Berry Bush Island clubhouse, and sit at the desks the bears use in "Berenstain Bears Go To School." All this and a water play area too. Your little ones will be charmed. Other pint-size attractions at the park include Kid Arthur's Court, Kiddieland, and the Gemini Children's area with its junior-size roller coaster. Obtain a copy of *The Official Kid's Guide to Cedar Point*, which tells about the attractions in storybook format.

After exploring the park, take some time to cool off and relax at the IMAX screen movies at the Cedar Point Cinema. For more sedate fun, try the steam train or a carousel. Admission to Cedar Point goes by height. Those over 4 feet tall pay adult fares, those under 4 feet pay children's fees.

You're not finished yet. The adjacent Challenge Park keeps kids busy with go-carts, miniature golf, and Soak City's ten water slides. Cedar Point's accommodations include the Hotel Breakers, a turn-of-the-century landmark property, as well as campsites. (See WHERE TO STAY.)

If you can get your kids out of the water, and off the roller coasters, take them to **African Safari Wildlife Park**, 267 Lightner Road, Port Clinton; (419) 732–3606 or (800) 521–2660. At this drive-through safari, you see tropical birds, camels, and a white tiger outside your window. Kids get close to the animals with camel and pony rides, and a Turtle Taxi service (bring the cameras). At the pig races, root for your favorite porker. Let the wee ones work off some energy at the Jungle Junction playground.

Were carousels a part of your childhood, and did calliope music always signal a good time? Share the pleasures with your kids at the **Merry-Go-Round Museum**, corner of Jackson and Washington streets, Sandusky; (419) 626–6111. Take a spin on a merry-go-round and browse the carved animals, some caught in midprance. Check the schedule for carving demonstrations and hours.

The **Inland Seas Maritime Museum**, 480 Main Street, Vermillion (216–967–3467), details the nautical history of the Great Lakes. Step into the pilot house of a simulated 400-foot bulk-carrier ship, and view models, paintings, and photographs. Find out about some of the 10,000 vessels that were lost on the Great Lakes waters, from Sieur de la Salle's *Griffin*, which set sail in 1679 in search of furs, to the *Edmund Fitzgerald*, which sank nearly 300 years later.

The **Milan Historical Museum**, 210 Edison Drive, Milan; (419) 499–2968. This complex of six buildings takes you back to the nineteenth century. In the 1843 dwelling, once owned by Robert Sayles, see pressed glass, china, and doll collections. Other buildings to browse include a country store and blacksmith shop. It's open April through October.

Historic Lyme Village, Route 113, Bellevue (419–483–6052 or 419–483–4949), offers more nineteenth-century history. Tour restored homes, barns, shops, a post office, an 1880's mansion that serves as the village museum, a schoolhouse, and a general store. Call ahead for a listing of seasonal events, activities, and festivals. Guided tours of the village are available Tuesdays through Sundays June through August; and Sundays only May and September. The rest of the year tours are by appointment only.

LAKE ERIE ISLANDS

For top walleye fishing and hours of sailing, visit **Kelleys Island** and **South Bass Island,** two of the most popular Lake Erie Islands.

Kelleys Island

Less than 5 miles from Ohio's Lake Erie shore, **Kelleys Island** offers beaches, natural areas, and interesting archeological sites. Busy in summer, but not bustling, the island's year-round (winter) population hovers at about 200. To find out what's happening, pick up a copy of the *Kelleys Island Funfinder* when you arrive.

Summer vacationers began arriving at this 2,800-acre island, the largest American island in Lake Erie, by steamer in the 1830s, and guests have been coming ever since. On Kelleys combine a beach vacation with a bit of archeological history. Take your kids to the prehistoric Indian mounds and petroglyphs, some of which date back to 12,000 B.C. while others portray Native American cultures. **Inscription Rock**, a large boulder on the south shore, is famous as having the most extensive and best-preserved prehistoric Indian pictographs in the United States. The animals, birds, and men that appear on **Inscription Rock** were created by Erie Indians between 300 and 400 years ago. After your kids peer at these, have them create an Indian story about life on the island back then.

The **Glacial Grooves State Memorial**, on the north shore, offers another not-to-miss archeological site. Among the finest glacial markings in the United States, this 400-foot-long trough with its fossilized marine life was pressed into Kelleys' limestone during the Pleistocene Ice Age. **Kelleys Island State Park**, 661 acres, offers miles of hiking trails, relatively uncrowded beaches, campsites, and nature programs.

What else can you do? Fish for your dinner, and for fun, as this island and Put-In-Bay catches the title "Walleye Capital of the World." Fishing charters are available for those without boats. Be sure to walk around town to admire the buildings which date from the 1830s through the turn-of-the-century.

South Bass Island–Put-in-Bay

More developed than Kelleys Island, **Put-In-Bay**, on South Bass Island, features beaches, wineries, fish hatcheries, shopping, restaurants, and pubs. A bustling beach area, Put-In-Bay is famed for its tactical role in the Battle of Lake Erie, the War of 1812. On September 10, 1813, Commodore Oliver Hazard Perry and his troops sought much-needed shelter in Put-In-Bay. Here they rested before successfully battling the British. After winning, Perry sent his now famous message to General William Harrison: "We have met the enemy and they are ours." Today, the 352-foot **Perry's Victory and International Peace Memorial** stands in Put-In-Bay as a reminder of this historic event. The view from the top of the monument is one of the best in the area.

Near Perry's Memorial is a popular beach, called simply **Bathing Beach**. **Stone Beach**, part of **South Bass Island State Park** (419–285–2112), on the island's northwest, may be less crowded.

For some off-the-beach fun tour the **Heineman's Winery**, Catawba Avenue; (419) 285–2811. Afterwards, taste the wine or sample nonalcoholic grape juice. Even if your kids aren't excited by looking at crushers and storage tanks, they'll probably like the tour of **Crystal Cave**, included with admission to the winery. Inside, you see a giant geode discovered in 1897, whose largest crystal weighs about 300 pounds, and measures 2 feet in length and 1½ feet in width. The cave is open from mid-May through late September. For more cave sites go underground at **Perry's Cave**, 979 Catawba Avenue (419–285–2405), to see stalactites and stalagmites.

For above-ground tours little kids especially like a ride on the **Put-In-Bay Tour Train** (419–285–4855), whose one-hour narrated tour gives an island overview. What's also nice for families: for the same price, you can get on and off at different stops, which include all the island highlights—Heineman's Winery, Crystal Cave, Perry's Cave, and Perry's Memorial. Beginning in late May, the tram runs all week during the summer months from 10:00 A.M. to 5:00 P.M. From September through October the tram will run on weekends only, 10:00–5:00. Children under six are free.

Another special ride is a spin on **Kimberly's Carousel**, Delaware Avenue, adjacent to the Carriage House, a children's clothing store. This restored 1917 carousel has thirty-six menagerie animals and a Wurlitzer organ. George Stoiber, a local businessman, bought the carousel in 1976, named it for his daughter, and spent eight years restoring this gem.

Shopping

On the mainland, near Sandusky, stop at the **Lake Erie Factory Outlet Center**, U.S. 250, ½ mile north of Ohio Turnpike exit 7 (419–499–2528). Scores of shops here advertise savings of 30–70 percent. As always with factory outlets, the quality and the price vary, but with a quick eye and some luck you could come away with bargains on clothing, housewares, and toys. Shops include **Corning Revere, Farberware, Mikasa, Bass Shoes, Gitano, Izod, Bugle Boy, Van Heusen,** and **Toy Liquidators**.

Performing Arts

On the Marblehead peninsula **Lakeside Associations**, 236 Walnut, Lakeside (419–798–4461), each summer organizes a series of summer performances in the well-preserved Victorian town of Lakeside. In the past these have included ballet, folk music, international puppetry groups, acrobats, the Lakeside Symphony, and Shakespearean productions.

The **Huron Playhouse**, Ohio Street, Huron; (419) 433–4744. Ohio's oldest summer-stock theater, offers performances Tuesdays through Thursdays during July. Huron is a few miles east of Sandusky off of U.S. 6. The **State Theatre**, 107 Columbus Avenue, Sandusky (419–626–3945), hosts concert pianists, ballet groups, drama, and popular musical groups.

SPECIAL EVENTS

From May throughout September **Port Clinton** hosts the Summer Jazz program every Sunday at the Mon Ami Restaurant and Winery. Call (800) 441–1271 to find out who will be performing.

April: Arts Festival, Sandusky Mall. Kelleys Island hosts a "Welcome Back" fish fry.

May: Bed and Breakfast Tour of Kelleys Island. Port Clinton hosts its Walleye Festival at the Water Works Park.

June: Marblehead Lighthouse Tour, Marblehead. Tour of Homes and Bicycle Rally, Kelleys Island.

July: Fireworks at Lakeside, Port Clinton and Put-In-Bay. Also at Put-In-Bay is the Amish Quilt Festival.

August: Clam Bake at Kelleys Island.

September: Celebrate the Battle of Lake Erie during Put-In-Bay's historical weekend.

October: Oktoberfest, Put-In-Bay.

WHERE TO STAY

Sandusky Area

Adjacent to the Cedar Point Amusement Park are two lodgings. The **Sandcastle Suites Hotel,** Cedar Point, P.O. Box 5006 (419–627–2106), offers two-room suites. Take a breather from the park to play tennis or lounge on Sandcastle's beach on the shores of Lake Erie. Sandcastle Suites offers shuttle service between the park and the hotel. For those who like historic properties and grande dame hotels, there's the **Hotel Breakers,** Cedar Point, P.O. Box 5006 (419–627–2106). This landmark property has 400 rooms, some stained glass windows, lots of wicker, and dates to 1905. Impress your kids by telling them that former guests included Annie Oakley, Abbott and Costello, and John Phillip Sousa. "Who?," they'll ask, but then you have something to talk about over lunch. The hotel has an ice cream parlor, a swimming pool, and a beach, three kid-pleasing places.

Other possibilities include the **Holiday Inn, Sandusky,** 5513 Milan Road (419–626–6671 or 800–465–4329), which features an indoor pool and miniature golf. **The Econo Lodge,** U.S. 6, 1904 Cleveland Road (419–627–8000 or 800–424–4777), is a less-costly alternative and is across from the entrance to Cedar Point. **Camper Village,** also part of the Cedar Point complex, Cedar Point (419–627–2106), is a recreational vehicle campground with more than 400 sites. Each area has picnic tables, grills, electricity, water, showers, laundromat, and supply store.

Sawmill Creek Resort, off of Route 13 North, Huron

(419–433–3800), offers resort amenities within a reasonable drive of Cedar Point. With an eighteen-hole golf course, indoor and outdoor swimming pools, saunas, three restaurants, whirlpool, exercise room, tennis courts, gift shop, and marina docks, Sawmill has plenty to offer the family traveling with kids.

Kelleys Island

Kelleys Island has a number of bed and breakfast inns that more often than not prefer couples or families with older children. If you want to stay at a bed and breakfast, look in the *Kelleys Island Funfinder* for a list. Be candid about the ages of your children to be certain that your kids will feel comfortable at these properties.

More suitable family-friendly accommodations include **Sunrise Point**, P.O. Box 431; (419) 746–2543 or (419) 433–6368. They offer one-bedroom units and lakefront efficiencies, plus a play area for kids. **Chalet East Apartments**, P.O. Box 512 (419–746–2335 in summer or 813–624–3811) offers one- and two-bedroom suites with kitchens. A number of private homes are for rent as well. **Lake-Woods Edge** is on the lakefront. Contact the owner at 1036 Jeff Ryan Drive, Herndon, Virginia 22070; (703) 435–6635. For the most up-to-date listings, obtain a copy of *Kelleys Island Funfinder.*

Put-In Bay

Accommodations in the Put-In-Bay area include motels, resorts, hotels, and cottages. **Saunder's Resort**, Catawba Avenue (419–285–3917), offers fully furnished cottages a mile from downtown. The complex includes a pool as well as tennis, badminton, and shuffleboard courts. The **Perry Holiday**, 99 Concord Avenue (419–285–2107), has 33 rooms, each with a private bathroom, air conditioning, and color television. One block from downtown, their facilities include a pool, laundry, picnic tables, and grills. **East Point Cottages**, Massie Lane (419–285–2204) offers eight, furnished cottages from May though October for rental. Each cottage has its own kitchen. Fishing licenses, tackle, and bait are available at the cottages.

For more accommodations information, contact the **Ottawa County Visitors Bureau**, 109 Madison, Port Clinton, Ohio 43452; (419) 734–4FUN or (800) 441–1271. Also contact the **Sandusky/Erie County Visitors & Convention Bureau**, P.O. Box 1639, Sandusky, Ohio; (410) 625–2984 or (800) 255–ERIE.

WHERE TO EAT

Your kids may even come away from a vacation at Sandusky and the islands liking fish. At least have them taste the local specialties of Lake Erie perch and walleye.

The Sandusky Area

In Port Clinton try **Mon Ami Restaurant and Historic Winery,** 2845 East Wine Cellar Road; (419) 797–4445 or (800) 777–4266. Mon Ami serves perch, walleye, and Italian specialties. Just outside the Cedar Point Amusement Park, the **Breakwater Cafe,** Cedar Point, Sandusky (419–626–0830), is a casual restaurant serving up a range of good eats from walleye to fajitas. **Bay Gulls Bagels and Deli,** 134 Shoreline Drive and 137 East Water Street, Sandusky (419–625–0550), serves up fresh bagels, deli sandwiches, and soups. Take your older children, especially preteen girls, to the **Tea Rose Tearoom,** 218 East Washington Street (419–627–2773), for afternoon tea and a reading of the tea leaves.

Kelleys Island

Head to the **Village Pump,** Water Street; (419) 746–2281. Here, the locals recommend the roast beef sandwiches, the hand-dipped onion rings, and the Lake Erie perch. The **Casino,** on the lakeshore off Lakeshore Drive (419–746–2773), has weekend entertainment and is known for its barbecued ribs, perch, and clam chowder. Go to **David's,** Village Plaza, Division Street, for home-baked desserts, sandwiches, and ice cream.

Put-In-Bay

The **Boardwalk,** downtown Put-In-Bay (419–285–3695), is the island's only waterfront restaurant. The food ranges from seafood to tacos to pizza. **The Village Bakery and Sandwich Shoppe,** at the Depot (419–285–5351), offers a variety of inexpensive choices and light meals. The **Bay Burger,** Village Center (419–285–6192), charms kids with its burgers and milk shakes. Try to get the tykes to try the walleye sandwiches. **The Snack House,** Delaware Avenue (419–285–4595), features home-made ice cream.

DAY TRIPS

For an interesting trip while visiting the Lake Erie Area, consider **Maumee Bay State Park,** 1750 Park Road #2, off I–280, 10 miles east of downtown Toledo in Oregon, Ohio, a great spot for fishing on Lake Erie. Aside from fishing the park offers golf, swimming, hunting, cross-county skiing (seasonally), a nature center, and lodging. Call (419) 836–1466.

Also try **Sea World of Ohio,** 1100 Sea World Drive, Aurora, Ohio (216–562–8101), which is thirty minutes southeast of Cleveland. See Shamu the killer whale in **Shamu's Happy Harbor,** a three-acre Caribbean-theme area, and thirteen "sea monsters and dinosaurs" at **Monster Marsh,** plus twenty geographically themed aquariums featuring a variety of sea life.

Combine a visit to Sandusky and the Lake Erie Islands with a stay in **Columbus**, about 105 miles away (see the Columbus chapter) or Indianapolis, about 245 miles away (see the Indianapolis chapter).

FOR MORE INFORMATION

Contact the **Ottawa County Visitors Bureau** for information concerning the Port Clinton/Put-In-Bay area, 109 Madison Street, Suite E, Port Clinton, Ohio; (800) 441–1271. If you're looking for more information on the Sandusky/Kelleys Lake/Bass Islands area, contact, **Erie County Convention and Visitors Bureau**, 231 West Washington Row, Sandusky, Ohio; (419) 625–2984, (800) 255–ERIE. Sandusky County Convention and Visitors Bureau, 1510 East State Street, Freemont; (419) 332–4470 or (800) 255–8070.

Emergency Numbers
Ambulance, fire, and police: 911

There are no hospitals on Kelleys or South Bass Islands. For hospitals with emergency facilities, try Firelands Community Hospital, 1101 Decatur Street, Sandusky; (419) 626–7400; or Providence Hospital, 1912 Hayes Avenue, Sandusky; (419) 621–7000. Port Clinton does have a hospital, the Magruder Hospital, 615 Fulton Street, Port Clinton; (419) 734–3131.

Poison Control: (419) 626–7423

Twenty-four-hour pharmacy: refer to the hospital emergency room facilities listed above. Rite Aid Discount Pharmacy has stores in Port Clinton and the Sandusky area, including the one located at 220 Columbus Avenue, Sandusky; (419) 625–3801. Also located in Sandusky: Discount Drug Mart, 124 East Perkins Avenue; (419) 625–0733.

44
WISCONSIN DELLS

Wisconsin Dells, 55 miles northwest of Madison, Wisconsin, is an area of more than 18 square miles with two distinct personalities. If you're looking for natural beauty, the area (which includes the city of Wisconsin Dells and the village of Lake Delton) offers miles of spectacular dells—unusually shaped sandstone formations rising 100 feet above the tree-lined Wisconsin River. If it's fun, games, and a little glitz you want, the area offers a mind-boggling assortment of man-made wonders including a circus, the nation's largest water park, amusements, 360 holes of miniature golf, and more. Obviously, families find it a winning vacation combination: Wisconsin Dells is the midwest's largest tourist attraction, visited by some 3 million people a year.

GETTING THERE

The airport closest to the Dells area is Dane County Airport in Madison (608–246–3300), which is served by a number of major commercial airlines. Car rentals are available at the airport.

Greyhound Bus tickets and schedule information are available at Bork & Kane Rexall Drug Store, 214 Broadway; (608) 254–2081. Greyhound also stops at Burger King, Highway 13 off I–90/94, exit 87.

Amtrak (800 USA–RAIL stops at the downtwon Wisconsin Dell train station on Eddy Street (608–254–7700), which is only open when a train is due.

Wisconsin Dells, directly off I–90/94, is easily accessible by car.

GETTING AROUND

While there are some shuttles that run between attractions, there is no public transportation, so a car is a must.

WHAT TO SEE AND DO

Museums

Some of the attractions listed here aren't conventional four-walled museums, but come now—would you really expect to find a stuffy museum in Wisconsin Dells? All of the following offer enjoyable learning experiences.

Circus World, 426 Water Street, Baraboo; (608) 356–0800. The Ringling Bros. Circus actually began in 1884 in this town fifteen minutes from the Dells, the original winter headquarters. This is circus heaven! The exhibit hall is open year-round and contains fascinating memorabilia, including old circus posters and the world's largest collection of colorful vintage circus wagons. But the big attractions during the summer are the live performances under a 2,000-seat big-top tent, including the circus and magic shows.

Mid-Continent Railway Museum, Walnut Street, North Freedom; (608) 522–1261. Located in a tiny town fifteen minutes south of the Dells, the museum provides a nice change of pace from the area's many purely amusement attractions. Steam passenger trains leave a turn-of-the-century depot for fifty-minute rides through the countryside, giving kids a chance to experience the Golden Age of Railways. On exhibit back at the train yard are steam and diesel engines, passenger cars, wooden freight cars, and other vintage railway equipment. It's open daily mid-May through Labor Day; and on weekends until mid-October, when autumn train rides are especially colorful. A winter Snowtrain runs the third weekend in February. You can visit another steam-powered train ride closer to town—a miniature fifteen-inch-gauge version—at **Riverside and Great Northern Railway**, a mile north on Stand Rock Road; (608) 254–6367.

Museum of Norman Rockwell Art, 227 South Park Street, Highway 23, Reedsburg; (608) 524–2123. Located fifteen minutes south of the Dells, this museum has the world's largest collection of the popular artist's work—some 4,000 examples—including original magazine covers, ads, posters, books, calendars, and Boy Scout memorabilia. Rockwell's art has universal appeal; even younger children can relate to its warmhearted humor. Combine this stop with a visit to Pioneer Log Village and Museum, highways 23 and 33 (608–524–2123), operated by the Reedsburg Historical Society. The eleven-building complex includes a school, church, blacksmith shop, and country store dating from 1850–65.

Tommy Bartlett Robot World & Exploratory, 560 Wisconsin Dells Parkway, Highway 12; (608) 254–2525. This commercial operation is not technically a museum, but the numerous hands-on experiences offered are on par with those you'll find at many children's exhibits at science museums. Children of all ages learn about electric energy, gravity, air currents, robotics, sound, and more by "doing." They can make their hair stand on end, turn upside down in a gyro ride, interact with a robot (who leads a guided tour), and more. Next door, Tommy Bartlett's Ski, Sky, and Stage Show (same phone as Robot World) has been packing them in for over forty years, offering three shows a day, rain or shine, including an evening laser spectacular.

Animal Attractions

International Crane Foundation, E11376 Shady Lane Road, Baraboo; (608) 356–9462. If you're going to Circus World, it is definitely worth a stop at this nearby attraction to see the world's most complete collection of cranes. The foundation works with other nations, including China, India, and Australia, to save seven endangered species of the fifteen in existence. A pair of each of the fifteen are housed in an exhibition pod. Take a self-guided tour to a restored prairie and marsh to get an up-close view of the graceful birds, or take a guided tour to see the cute crane chicks and adult birds.

Wisconsin Deer Park, 583 Highway 12; (608) 253–2041. Nearly 150 deer roam over this twenty-eight-acre facility—step right in and interact. If your kids have never been around animals, they may be intimidated at first, but once they get up the nerve to pet and feed black deer, white tails, and rare white deer, they'll be completely won over. A big hit: the tiny spotted fawns in the baby nursery. Other wildlife to view include elk and buffalo.

Tours of the Dells

A Winnebago Indian legend attributes the spectacular formations of the dells to the path of a giant serpent; geologists say the dells (from the French word *dalle*, meaning "slab-like or tile rock") were caused by the erosion of Cambrian sandstone by thousands of years of glacial water. A downtown power dam separates the Upper and Lower Dells; both are worth seeing, although most of the rock formations appear on the lower end. To get the most out of this gift of nature, you really have to take some sort of a tour. A variety of choices exist.

School-age kids, teens, and adults will get the biggest kick out of taking one of the "ducks," World War II amphibious vehicles used in the invasion of Normandy and other famous battles. The vehicles, retired in 1958, now have a new mission: transporting tourists over miles of land and water and back again. They venture through fields of wild flowers, along breathtaking trails such as Black Hawk Gorge with its steep canyon walls, and through pristine water past the sculpted cliffs. As you might expect, the land part of the voyage can be bouncy; if anyone in your group has a delicate constitution, opt for a more traditional boat cruise down the river. One-hour 7½-mile duck tours are available from Original

A ride aboard a "duck," one of the amphibious vehicles used during World War II, is an exciting way to tour the Wisconsin Dells. (Courtesy Wisconsin Dells Visitor and Convention Bureau)

Wisconsin Ducks, one mile south of Wisconsin Dells on Highway 12 (608–254–8751); and from Dells Duck Tours, the Main Duck Dock on Highway 12 (608–254–6080). The latter also runs boat tours. A one-hour Lower Dells cruise features colorful local stories of the logging era, plus Indian history and legends; a 2½-hour Upper Dells tour stops at Witches Gulch and Stand Rock, where you can walk along nature trails and hidden canyons.

Other options: a one-mile canyon tour via horse-drawn carriage with Lost Canyon Tours, 720 Canyon Road; (608) 253–2781. Badger Helicopter Rides, on Highway 13 next to the Holiday Inn (608–254–4880), has three different rides over the Dells in three different price ranges, mid-May through mid-October. At Holiday Shores Boat Rentals along the east bank of the Upper Dells (608–254–2878), the choice includes pontoons, canoes, paddleboats, and wave runners. Lake Delton Water Sports, Highway 12, Lake Delton (608–254–8702), offers the same selection of boats and also runs Lower Dells Raft Trips. Ride tall in the saddle over one hundred acres of trail on a horse from the OK Corral, a mile south on Highway 16; (608) 243–2811. Kids ride free with parents, and there's a free petting zoo and pony rides for the younger set back at the corral.

Parks

When you need a break from the nonstop amusements, head to **Mirror Lake State Park**, 8 miles west of Baraboo off Highway 12; (608) 254–2333. The park, partially surrounded by sandstone bluffs, is a haven for fishing, camping, swimming at a sandy beach, and canoeing. It's open year-round and in the winter has cross-country skiing, including candlelight evenings in January and February when they provide lit cooking grills and a warming fire.

There's also a small public beach on the south shores of **Lake Delton**, off Hiawatha Drive.

Other Attractions

Water park fans (aren't all kids?) will love the three massive water parks in Wisconsin Dells. **Noah's Ark**, U.S. 12 and SR 23 (608–254–6351), the country's largest; **Family Land**, a mile south on U.S. 12 (608–254–7766), boasting mid-America's largest wave pool; and **Riverview Park**, ¼ mile south on U.S. 12; (608) 254–2608. Those with young kids might opt for Family Land, with Tiny Tots' Water Slides and a complete kiddie playground; or Riverview Park, with four children's activity pools and kiddie go-carts. Each park has wave pools (Family Land boasts the largest), picnic areas, food, shopping, midway rides, bumper boats, and much more.

Big Chief Go Kart World has two parks near each other (one on Highway 12, the other on County Highway A) that comprise the nation's largest complex. There's a track to suit all ages and levels, including Little Chief tracks for young drivers. Tickets are good at either location; call (608) 254–2490 for information.

Storybook Gardens, 1500 Wisconsin Dells Parkway, is a very low key attraction for the very young. There is a petting zoo and miniature train ride tours of the gardens, plus life-size storybook characters; (608) 253–2391.

Xanadu, downtown on U.S. 12 (608–254–6096), is a futuristic house created from sprayed foam. It features solar heating and high-tech furnishings and equipment that you can explore at your leisure; (608) 254–6096.

Anyone for fishing? There's no license required at these attractions. Try **B & H Tour Fishing**, 7 miles north on Highway 13 (608–254–7280), where there's no limit to the number of rainbow trout you can catch. They furnish poles and bait, clean the fish, and freeze and store them until you go home; so does **Beaver Springs Fishing Park**, 600 Trout Road (608–254–2735/800–236–7288). Seven spring-fed ponds on thirteen acres are stocked with trout, catfish, bass, pike, and more.

SPECIAL EVENTS

All the following annual events have special appeal for families. The Wisconsin Dells Visitor and Convention Bureau (800–22–DELLS, ext. R) can provide exact dates and locations.

January: Child's Play Doll & Toy Show & Sale at Holiday Inn.

February: Flake Out Festival snow-sculpting competition, includes children's events, snow softball, food, and more. Mid-Continent Railway Museum's Steam Snow Train, third weekend.

May: Putter's Cup National Mini-Golf Championship. Auto Show, downtown. Mid-Continent Railway Museum Railfest, two days of steam train rides, steam wrecker demonstrations, and a flea market. Hot Air Balloon Rally.

June: Heritage Day Celebration, Bowman Park, features arts and crafts exhibits, ice cream social, quilters show, and more.

July: Ultra Light Fly-In at Yukon Trails Campground is a glider and ultra-light aircraft competition. Country Carvers show, Parson's Indian Trading Post.

August: All-Ford show of collectible cars, downtown.

September: Polish Fest, Riverview Park and Waterworld, features ethnic food, colorful costumes, dance music, and art exhibit. Wo-Zha-Wa Days Fall Festival, downtown, with arts and crafts, antique flea market, street carnival, and parade finale.

October: Mid-Continent Steam Train Autumn Color Tours, selected weekends.

Shopping

Over sixty shops of all descriptions are in downtown Wisconsin Dells, just a short walk from most hotels and motels. (If you drive, there's plenty of free parking.) But if you think you'll get away with a few dollars in purchases, guess again. In addition to the shops and some twenty restaurants, you'll find approximately twenty "glitzy" attractions, such as Ripley's Believe It or Not!, Bull Nehring's Dungeon of Horrors (with a choice of "subtle and funny" scares for kids), The Skreeemer space shuttle simulator ride, Count Wolff Von Baldasar's Haunted Mansion, Waxy World of the Stars, and Dells Auto Museum, to name but a few. While many of the attractions are fun, this type of razzmatazz is not for everybody, and it can get expensive. Of course, most kids eat it right up, and the attractions can be a welcome refuge on a rainy day. You might want to save a visit here for your last night in town. That way the kids can't beg you to return the next day.

Don't leave the state without Wisconsin cheese! You'll find a good selection at Market Square Cheese and Gifts, 1150 Dells Parkway South,

Lake Delton; (608) 254–8388. Genuine Native American handicrafts and art are for sale at Parson's Indian Trading Post and Museum, 2½ miles south on Highway 12; (608) 254–8533. You'll also see artifacts on display.

Performing Arts

As you might imagine, the performing arts in Wisconsin Dells don't consist of symphonies and Shakespeare—just good, old American fun.

Molly's "Music America!" Stage Show and Restaurant, 1541 Wisconsin Dells Parkway (608–254–6222), is a lively nightly musical revue of song, dance, and comedy, suitable for the whole family. Opt for the show only or dinner/show packages. They also serve a family breakfast and dinner buffet. At **The Dickinson Family's Wisconsin Opry**, E10964 Moon Road, Highway 12, Baraboo (608–254–7951), everybody will have a knee-slapping, hand-clapping, toe-tapping good time. They're open nightly from mid-May to mid-September and Sunday afternoon. A flea market takes place here on the weekends.

Stand Rock Indian Ceremonial, 4 miles north on Stand Rock Road (608–253–7444), is a fascinating, colorful presentation by Native American musicians and ceremonial dancers (including young children). It's held at Stand Rock, the pillar that has become the symbol of the Dells. You can drive here or take a boat (608–254–8555), departing the Upper Dells Landing nightly, mid-June to Labor Day.

WHERE TO STAY

This area offers a huge assortment of accommodations in all price ranges. A complete listing, including a map that pinpoints locations, can be found in the Convention and Visitor Bureau's *Travel and Attractions Guide*. Most Wisconsin Dells' hotels and motels are located along two commercial strips: Highway 13 and Highway 12. These merge into Lake Delton, where you can also find some quieter, lakeside accommodations, including cabins (some with their own sandy beaches). Families with kids are the mainstay of the tourist economy, so most lodgings are extremely family friendly and are constantly adding amenities for children. Here are a few of the many possibilities.

Wisconsin Dells

Chula Vista Resort, Scenic River Road, has family suites, including new Fantasy Dream Suites. Fantasy settings include a Caribbean Pirate Ship, Space, and the Wild Wild West, where the beds resemble covered wagons. Facilities include indoor/outdoor pools, an athletic club, tennis courts, golf, hiking trails, a kiddie playground, and a full-service restaurant. Ask about summer packages. Call (608) 254–8366/(800) 38–VISTA.

Polynesian Suite Resort, Highway 13 north, equips some of its 118 suites with microwaves, refrigerators, and separate living areas. Along with an indoor pool, sauna, whirlpools, and tanning booth are outdoor activity pools, rock waterfalls, a water slide, and a kiddie activity area, featuring geysers, swings, a waterfall, and a toddler water slide. Call (608) 254–2883/(800) 272–5842.

River Inn, 1015 River Road, two blocks from downtown, boasts a riverfront location and great views of the Dells from the restaurant and most of the rooms, which include family units and economy rooms. There are indoor and outdoor pools, a playground, and a fitness room. Call (608) 253–1231.

The Copa Cabana Resort Hotel and Suites, 611 Wisconsin Dells Parkway, Wisconsin Dells, WI 53965; (800) 364–2672 or (608) 253–1511, features its own water park called **Lost Lagoon.** Kids delight in the geysers, shark slide, octopus swing, and children's play area.

Meet Yogi Bear himself and have fun during the special three-day weekend programs offered at **Yogi Bear's Camp–Resort,** located off I–90 at S1915 Ishnala Road, P.O. Box 510, Wisconsin Dells, WI 53965; (800) GO–2–YOGI or (608) 254–2568.

Lake Delton

Sandy Beach Resort, 55 Dam Road, with its own beach directly on the lake, has one- and two-bedroom kitchen cottages and one-room kitchenettes. One week is the minimum stay during the peak summer season. Call (608) 254–8553.

Lighthouse Cove, directly on Lake Delton, offers tastefully furnished one- and two-bedroom shore-side condominiums with fully equipped kitchens. Indoor and outdoor pools, tennis and basketball courts, a beach, and boat docks add to the appeal; (800) 447–5946.

WHERE TO EAT

Name your family's favorite food, and you'll find it in this area. Along with the tried-and-true burger, fried chicken, and pizza places, are these restaurants popular with the locals:

Jimmy's Del-Bar, Highway 12, Lake Delton, designed by Frank Lloyd Wright protege James Dresser, offers three casual, family-style meals daily, including a summer buffet dinner. A kiddie menu is available. Call (608) 253–1511/(800) 444–0332. **Isnala Supper Club,** overlooking Mirror Lake, serves steaks, seafood, and more in a lovely natural setting. There are even giant Norway pines growing through the dining area! Call (608) 253–1771. Heaps of hearty ethnic food are served at **Dick's Polish American Smorgasbord,** 400 County Trunk A and Highway 12; (608) 253–4451.

DAY TRIPS

All ages will be fascinated by **LaReau's World of Miniature Buildings**, south of Pardeeville on Highway 22, under an hour's drive east of the Dells. This is a Lilliputian collection of scale model buildings constructed of wood, styrofoam, metal, and concrete. Recreations include the White House, Independence Hall, Washington Monument, and the Statue of Liberty. Call (608) 429–2848. Wisconsin Auto Tours (see below) offers an interesting car tour of the area.

FOR MORE INFORMATION

Wisconsin Dells Visitor and Convention Bureau, 701 Superior Street, P.O. Box 390, Wisconsin Dells 53065–0390 (608–254–8088/800–22–DELLS), has a helpful *Travel & Attraction Guide,* plus other useful information.

Free Wisconsin Travel literature is available from Wisconsin Tourism Development, 123 West Washington Avenue, P.O. Box 7606. Call (608) 266–2161 in Wisconsin and neighboring states; (800) 432–TRIP elsewhere). Send for the excellent *Wisconsin Auto Tours,* featuring 23 road adventures, including one that details the Wisconsin Dells area. The guide notes which attractions are handicapped-accessible.

Emergency Numbers
Ambulance, fire, and police (Adams, Columbia, and Sauk counties): 911
Poison Control: (608) 253–1171
Two hospitals with twenty-four-hour emergency services are approximately 10 miles from Wisconsin Dells: St. Clare Hospital, 707 Fourteenth Street, Baraboo (608–356–5561); Reedsburg Area Medical Center, 200 North Dewey, Reedsburg (608–524–6487). The Dells Clinic, 1310 Broadway, Wisconsin Dells (608–253–1171), provides general health services from 8:00 A.M. to 6:00 P.M.
There are no twenty-four-hour pharmacies in the area. Bork & Kane Rexall Drugstore, 214 Broadway (608–254–2081), is open in the summer from 8:00 A.M. to 10:00 P.M. For an emergency after hours, call the Wisconsin Dells police, and they will contact a pharmacist.

CANADA

45
MONTREAL
Quebec

Montreal, an island city on the St. Lawrence River, is exciting and dynamic, with a distinctively Continental flavor. French is the official language, though you'll find English widely spoken, especially in the western half of the city. If your kids have never been to Europe, a visit here will definitely make an impression; they'll certainly notice the cultural differences and may even pick up some French. Indeed, in Montreal there is so much to see and do that your family will pronounce it "magnifique!"

GETTING THERE

Montreal International Airport in Dorval (514–842–2281), services approximately forty major American and Canadian airlines. The airport, twenty-to-thirty minutes from downtown, can be reached by taxi or regular bus lines. Call Autobus Aero Plus (514–633–1100) for information. Car rentals are available at the airport.

Voyageur, which provides bus service from other Canadian cities, has a terminal at 505 boulevard de Maisonneuve East (514–842–2281). Other bus service: Greyhound from New York and Vermont Transit from Boston.

Train service from the United States is provided by Amtrak (800–426–8725) and from Canadian destinations by VIA Rail (514–871–1331/800–361–5390—Quebec/800–561–8630—Canada). Both arrive and depart from Central Station, 935 de La Gauchetiere Street West (under the Queen Elizabeth Hotel).

The major artery leading to Montreal from Toronto and Ottawa is Highway 401; from Quebec you can take Highway 20 or 40. Most U.S.

interstates connect with Highway 10, which runs through the Eastern
Townships area.

GETTING AROUND

Montreal has a quiet, clean, and efficient Metro subway—an experience
not to be missed. Save money by buying a strip of six tickets. Four color-
coded interconnecting lines service sixty-five station stops. In addition,
there are over 150 bus routes. Call (514) 288–6287 for transportation information. The Metro connects a huge underground city network of
shops, restaurants, banks, hotels, theaters, and railway and bus terminals.

The city is divided into east-west streets by boulevard St. Laurent (The
Main) which runs north-south. Montreal is a compact city and highly
walkable. Old Montreal (*Vieux Montréal*), where you'll find the Old Port
(*Vieux-Port*), is a great place to stroll. In the summer, water shuttles operate
between the Old Port and the city's two islands, Île Notre-Dame and Île
Sainte-Hélenè (see Parks section) as well as to Cité du Havre Park, where
there are outdoor children's activities, picnic tables, and bicycle paths.

WHAT TO SEE AND DO

Museums
     This sophisticated city has a rich assortment of fine museums. Unless
your kids are avid museum goers, however, they may find some too sophisticated or esoteric. Actually, many of the most stimulating exhibits
and experiences in Montreal are not in traditional museums. The following are surely worth a visit.

     Canadian Railway Museum, 122–A Saint-Pierre Street West, Saint-
Constant; (514) 283–4602/4623. If your kids love trains, it's worth going
out of your way for this collection of railway, tramway, and steam-
locomotive equipment. It's in suburban Monteregie, so you'll have to
drive or take the Longueuil or Angrignon metro to a Monette bus
(514–632–2020) to the museum. Stop by on Sunday when visitors are
treated to a train ride. During the week there are tram rides.

     Dow Planetarium, 1,000 Saint-Jacques Street West; (514) 872–4530.
A lecturer provides live commentary for original star shows presented
under the theater dome. Shows alternate in English and French.

     The International Museum of Humour, 2111 St. Laurent Street;
(514) 845–4000, opened its doors on April Fool's Day, 1993. You won't
find a museum like this anywhere else. The fun exhibits here exude
laughs and treasured memories of days past. Two favorites are the Birth
of the Couch Potato, which commemorates the American sitcom, and a

replica of a city street from the 1920s, where the audience watches Charlie Chaplin on the big screen as they are served refreshments by Keystone Cops. Stop by the Humour Hall of Fame, where your kids can watch Mickey Mouse cartoons as they relax in huge, cushy chairs.

Montreal Museum of Fine Arts, 1379 and 1380 Sherbrooke Street West; (514) 285–1600. Head to Canada's oldest art museum on Sunday when family activities, such as films and workshops, are included with the admission. The impressive collections of paintings, furniture, sculptures, and other art may not capture a younger child's interest without some parental guidance.

Redpath Museum, 859 Sherbrooke Street West; (514) 398–4086. Kids are captivated by the old fossils, rocks, crystals, and gems, and by the fascinating antiquities of ancient Egypt.

Parks

You'll find superb parks throughout the city. Here are the best for families.

MacDonald Campus of McGill University, 21–111 Lakeshore Road, Sainte-Anne-de Bellevue (Route 40). Located on Montreal's southwest tip, this vast area features three attractions with family appeal. **The Morgan Arboretum** (514–398–7812) has nature and wooded trails and cross-country skiing. **The Ecomuseum** (514–457–9449), devoted to the St. Lawrence Valley, features sixteen exhibits in outdoor settings that include turtles, bears, and a walk through a waterfowl aviary. **The Farm** (514–398–7701) welcomes families to view its animals and use the picnic and play area.

Mont Royal Park, the lush green stretch of land that sweeps up the highest peak of Mont Royal (from which the city took its name), is the finest in town. The 83-foot cross at the top of the mountain, lit at night and visible for miles, was installed in 1924 and paid for mostly with children's donations. It commemorates the cross that Maisonneuve, founder of Montreal, carried to the mountaintop in 1643 after the colony was spared from a flood.

Approach this must-see park from Camillien-Houde Parkway from the east or from Remembrance Road from the west. Frederick Olmsted, who also planned New York's Central Park, designed this oasis. Picnic, stroll, bike, jog, and enjoy spectacular vistas of downtown and the Appalachian Mountains from Mountain Chalet and Parkway lookouts. Winters bring cross-country skiing, skating, and sledding.

The Centre de la Montagne (514–872–3911), a nature appreciation center, offers interpretive programs and information. The kids will enjoy seeing the only Mounted Police in Montreal patrolling the park. Their horse stables are open to visitors from 9:00 A.M. to 5:00 P.M.

To get to Île Notre-Dame (514–872–6093), take the Metro or the water shuttle. This man-made island, constructed for Expo '67, now serves as a recreational haven with a beach, boat rentals, winter ice skating, and lovely floral park.

The Metro or water shuttle will also get you to Île Sainte-Helene (514–872–6093). Island attractions include swimming pools, picnic tables, and, in the winter, skiing and snowshoeing. Families usually head straight to **La Ronde** (514–872–6222), an amusement park that has the highest wooden double-track roller coaster in the world. A simulation ride, Hydroid 94, and kiddie rides round out the fun. If this hasn't exhausted you, grab your suits and head to **Aqua-Parc**; (514) 872–7326. In addition to twenty-one water slides, there's a kiddie area and large heated pool. La Ronde/Aqua-Parc combination tickets are available.

If you can, stop by the **David M. Stewart Museum** (also known as the Old Fort or *Le Vieux Fort*) with its interesting collections of kitchen and fireplace utensils, firearms, ancient maps, and other displays (mostly military) of colonial Canada. The real attraction in the summer is the outdoor demonstrations of eighteenth-century military maneuvers held several times daily. Call (514) 861–6701 for information. The island, site of the spectacular annual fireworks competition (see SPECIAL EVENTS), has two restaurants and a theater for concerts and shows.

Lafontaine Park is centrally located (bordered by Sherbrooke, Rachel, Papineau, and Parc Lafontaine streets). Stroll through this park and see a slice of Montreal life, including street musicians and, on weekends, families out to have fun. There are wading pools, pedal boats, tennis courts, and a puppet theater. In winter, cross-country skiing and illuminated skating rinks make this a popular retreat. Call (514) 872–2644 for information.

More Attractions

The Old Port, 333 de la Commune Street West, between McGill and Berri streets; (514) 496–7678. This lively developed riverfront area in Old Montreal offers families the chance to watch street performers, rent a bicycle (or quadricycle), have a picnic (or eat at a restaurant), and stop by noteworthy attractions.

Expotec, Saint Laurent Boulevard and de la Commune Street; (514) 496–4629. An interactive scientific exhibit and game for all ages, the theme display changes yearly. **The Lockkeepers Hut** (514–496–7678), at the entrance to the Lachine Canal, is a tourist information and interpretation center dispensing facts on the Canal locks. **S.O.S. Labyrinthe**, King Edward Pier; (514) 496–7678. Here visitors wander through twisting paths and conquer challenges such as a net ladder, secret passsage, and tunnel. Guides assist those who need it, and the course changes weekly. **Images du Futur**, 15 de la Commune Street West; (514) 849–1612. This fascinating multimedia exhibition changes its theme every year, but whenever you visit, you'll be treated to a huge panorama

Steeped in history, the Old Port section of Montreal offers an exciting array of cultural, historic, and scientific attractions. (Courtesy Greater Montreal Convention and Visitors Bureau)

showing how technology is applied to art and communications. Laser images, holographic pictures and sculptures, computer-drawn pictures and videos, and electronic music combine to create a fascinating exhibit that includes interactive participation. **Imax Cinema** (514–496–4629) shows breathtaking films on a 7-story-high screen.

Olympic Park, 4141 Pierre-De-Coubertin Avenue; (514) 252–8687.

There's much to do around this site of the 1976 Summer Olympic Games. Start with a tram ride up the world's tallest inclined tower for great views of the surrounding city. The stadium, with its retractable roof (the site of Expo baseball), is open to the public, as are the complex's swimming pools. Summer shuttles connect the park to the not-to-be-missed **Botanical Gardens** (*Jardin Botanique*). This indoor/outdoor treat for the senses delights all with the largest Chinese garden outside Asia, a huge bonsai collection, serene Japanese garden, spectacular displays of orchids and chrysanthemums, and more. There are frequent shows and special events. Call (514) 872–1400 for information.

Admission includes entry into a real kid-pleaser—the **Insectarium**, with thousands of living and mounted insects. Watch butterflies flutter about in their own aviary while bees buzz around a working hive. Hands-on games and activities help kids learn about the variety, function—and, yes, (sometimes) beauty—of these little creatures. For more information call (514) 872–8753.

The Biodome, at 4777 Pierre-De-Coubertin, is an environmental museum located in the former Olympic Velodrome. It's not a zoo, though four complete reconstructed ecosystems are inhabited by birds, mammals, and fish. The Polar World, Tropical Forest, Laurentian Forest, and Saint-Laurent ecosystems include waterfalls, towering trees, and an interactive discovery room that kids will like. Call (514) 872–3034 for special program information.

Special Tours

Call **Lachine Rapid Tours** and shoot the only rapids on the St. Lawrence River in a jet boat. It's definitely not for younger kids or the faint of heart: You wear slickers and get wet. The trip lasts about ninety minutes. Call (514) 284–9607. More sedate river tours include the glass-roofed **River Boat**, which leaves from the Old Port for the restored section of the Canal, then heads into the Port of Montreal, around Île Sainte-Hélenè Island and Île Notre-Dame. Call (514) 849–9952.

Shopping

Because of Montreal's extreme temperatures—frigid winters and hot summers—many of the city's shops and services are part of a vast **Underground City** network. It's connected throughout by the Metro, so you can enter from any stop or from the **Place Bonaventure**, which houses the Viaduc shopping center and its delightfully diverse shops.

Performing Arts

Montreal offers a wide variety of cultural activities, including some of special interest to kids. The **Theatre Biscuit** (514–845–7306) is the only permanent puppet theater in the city, and has weekend performances. All of the plays at **Maison-Théâtre** (Salle Tritorium) are geared to children; call (514) 288–7211. If you're in town when the **Cirque du Soleil** is performing at the Old Port, run—do not walk—to see this incredibly original theatrical performance. This is not a conventional circus (there are no animals), but it is a truly unique experience. Performances are generally from late April to June. Call (514) 522–2324.

SPECIAL EVENTS

Montreal's **Expos** play eighty-one home games during baseball season (April to October) at the stadium in Olympic Park. For more information call (514) 253–3434/3595/(800) 361–6807. **Montreal Canadien Hockey Club** plays forty home games at the Montreal Forum from October to March. Tickets frequently sell out early, so call (514) 932–2582.

Admission Network (514–522–1245/800–361–4595) sells tickets for sporting events, concerts, and a number of seasonal festivals, including the popular fireworks festival listed next.

Fairs and Festivals

They don't call Montreal "Festival City" for nothing. It seems that no matter when you come, there's something special—and fun—going on. The Greater Montreal Convention and Tourism Bureau (GMCTB) has a complete calendar of events.

June–July: Benson & Hedges International Fireworks Competition, weekends.

July: International Jazz Festival features more than ninety indoor and 200 outdoor shows and events. Just For Laughs, the world's largest comedy festival, includes outdoor performances. Player's International Tennis Tournament.

WHERE TO STAY

The Tourist Guide from the GMCTB has listings that classify some (but not all) lodgings by type and quality and include details on accessibility for persons with reduced mobility. **Reservation Center** provides a free service for all major hotels of Greater Montreal, including special packages: (514) 932–9121/(800) 567–8687. There are also several bed and breakfast services; contact the GMCTB for more information.

There are so many hotels in Montreal in so many price ranges that deciding on one can be an arduous task. You'll find many familiar, reliable names such as Best Western, Holiday Inn, Hilton, Le Meridien, Intercontinental, Journey's End, and Ritz Carlton. This small selection—all conveniently located downtown —indicates the variety available for families:

Delta Montreal, 450 Sherbrooke Street, offers both rooms and suites, two pools, and a game room. The supervised Children's Creative and Activity Center is open weekends year-round for ages two to twelve (small fee) who may stay for up to three hours. Call (800) 877–1133/(800) 268–3777—Canada/(800) 877–1133—United States.

Hotel Novotel, 1180 Rue de la Montagne, lets kids up to sixteen stay free and enjoy a free breakfast when sharing with parents (maximum 2 kids). There's indoor parking. Call (514) 861–6000/(800) 221–4542.

Le Quatre Saisons, 1050 Sherbrooke Street West, lives up to the Four Seasons standard of luxury, with 300 rooms with sitting areas, 26 suites, an indoor pool, and elegant restaurant. Call (514) 284–1110/(800) 268–6282—Canada or (800) 332–3442.

Gray Rocks, P.O. Box 1000, St. Jovite, Quebec, JOT 2HO (819–425–2771; (800) 567–6767) about 75 miles northwest of Montreal, is sprawled on 2,000 acres in Mont Tremblant. Before or after a city tour, this mid-price resort offers a friendly respite for families. In winter, Gray Rocks features ski programs for kids along with other outdoor activities. In summer there are supervised children's programs for ages three to twelve. Warm weather fun includes boating on the lake plus perfecting your tennis game at the intensive camp.

WHERE TO EAT

The *Montreal Restaurant Guide* from the GMCTB contains tips on a number of fine dining experiences, including elegant French-Canadian restaurants for special nights out. But, honestly, you don't have to spend a fortune to eat well in this city. In the summer, residents and tourists take to the streets to eat at outdoor cafes and bistros. Your kids will want to try poutine, a mixture of cheese, gravy, and *frites* (French fries) served at establishments around town, including McDonalds. Do give Montreal's ethnic restaurants a try. The Jewish area north of downtown, for instance, has superb bakeries and great delis. Montreal's bagels are said to rival, even surpass, New York's—taste for yourself. Those from the brick oven at **La Maison de Original Fairmount Bagel**, 74 West Fairmount Street (514–272–0667), are reputedly the best in town.

DAY TRIPS

Where do Montreal families go for a nearby getaway? The **Laurentian Mountains** and **Eastern Townships** are each about an hour's drive from the city and present a wealth of recreational opportunities, from skiing and skating in the winter to summer activities. A one-hour drive east on Highway 3 is the **Granby Zoo**, where the kids can take an elephant ride and delight in seeing more than 750 animals, including wildlife species from all continents. Call (514) 372–0113 for information. South of the city in Hemmingford, **Safari Park** combines a drive-through animal reserve, petting area, deer trail, water play area, and amusement park. For information call (514) 247–2727/(800) 465–8724—Ontario and Quebec. Quebec City, the provincial capital, is about two-and-one-half hours east while two hours to the west lie the pleasures of Ottawa.

FOR MORE INFORMATION

To request Montreal information by mail, write to Greater Montreal Convention and Tourism Bureau, *Les Cours Mont-Royal*, 1555 Pell Street, Suite 600, Montreal H3A 1X6, or call (514) 873–2015/(800) 363–7777. In person, visit INFOTOURISTE, 1001 Square-Dorchester, for tourist information, services, and brochures on Montreal and Quebec province. They have branches at Place Jacques-Cartier in Old Montreal and at Montreal International Airport. Tourism Quebec also operates several seasonal bureaus at major highways throughout the province.

Montreal has several associations and referral centers for the handicapped, including *Association regionale pour le loisir des personnes handicapées de l'Île de Montréal* (514–933–2739), which offers ways for both residents and nonresidents to participate in recreational activities. Canadian National Institute for the Blind (514–284–2040) supplies volunteer escorts, if needed. Reserve in advance. Keroul (514–252–3104) gives assistance and pertinent information to those with impaired mobility.

Emergency Numbers
Ambulance, fire, and police: 911
Sainte-Justine Hospital, 3175 Cote-Sainte-Catherine Road; (514) 345–4931
Montreal Children's Hospital, 2300 Tupper Street (514) 934–4400
Poison Hotline: (800) 463–5060
Twenty-four-hour pharmacy: Pharmaphix at 901 Sainte-Catherine Street
    East (514–842–4915) and 5122 Cote-des-Neiges Road (514–738–8464).

46
NEW BRUNSWICK
Canada

New Brunswick, an Atlantic province, shares a common border with Maine, but once you enter the area you know you're not in New England any more. For one thing the Union Jack still flies on front lawns in some southern and western parts of the province. Of the approximately 34,000 Loyal Americans who fled the Thirteen Colonies for Nova Scotia at the end of the American Revolution, more than 14,000 settled in present-day New Brunswick. This Loyalist fervor is alive and well in some quarters, although American tourists are graciously welcomed (bygones are indeed bygones). There's a French influence as well in the eastern and northern sections, where descendants of the Acadians, French settlers, still reside.

New Brunswick is a beautiful province bordered on the east by the Gulf of St. Lawrence and on the south by the Bay of Fundy. It offers rocky coasts, lush green countryside, and several interesting cities. The Fundy Coast and the St. John River Valley are of special interest because of their proximity to the United States and their many offerings for families. If you have time to explore more, however, we urge you to sample all of New Brunswick's delightfully diverse districts.

GETTING THERE

The main commercial airports, in Fredericton, Moncton, and Saint John, are served by major Canadian airlines and Northwest Airlines, which operates to and from Boston.

VIA Rail serves much of this area. For information and reservations, call (506) 642–2916.

SMT Eastern Limited is a regional bus service which has links to bus routes in other provinces and in the United States. Call (506) 648–3500.

Coastal Transport Limited ferry to Grand Manan leaves from Blacks Harbour, just off Route 1. Call (506) 662–3606. Marine Atlantic's ferry to

Digby, Nova Scotia, leaves from Saint John. For general information call (506) 636–3606; for central reservations call (902) 794–5700.

New Brunswick can be reached from Maine via I–95, which turns into the Trans-Canada Highway, Route 2, in New Brunswick.

GETTING AROUND

Public buses are available in the larger cities. Fredericton issues tourist parking passes for all visitors, permitting free parking at all municipal parking meters and parking lots for three days. Obtain them from the Information Centre at City Hall or during the summer at the Legislative Assembly and the highway information center.

WHAT TO SEE AND DO

Fundy Tidal Coast

This beautiful stretch of coast boasts the highest tides in the world, due to the shape and dimensions of the bay. Approximately every twelve hours and thirty minutes, one hundred billion tons of ocean pour in from the open Atlantic, a quiet-but-steady swirl. Note: Bay waters are cool, so be prepared for a brisk dip. East of Moncton the waters are warmer.

If you're entering the area from Maine, the coastal city of **St. Stephen** will be your first stop. Downtown is usually bumper to bumper, but stop at the Information Center for maps, literature, and advice. Next, head to the **Ganong Chocolatier Shop**, 73 Milltown Boulevard; (506) 466–6437. There you can watch chocolate-dipping demonstrations and see the world's tallest jelly bean display. The world's first candy bar was supposedly created at the Ganong candy factory in 1910. You can tour the factory, on the outskirts of town, during the annual Chocolate Festival in August. Nearby, Oak Bay is one of the province's seven supervised saltwater beaches.

Your next stop, **St. Andrews-by-the-Sea**, is where you will want to stay awhile. At the tourist information center near the wharf, get maps and walking-tour brochures. Many of the gracious homes date to the 1880s, and some to the 1700s. Some Loyalist settlers who came here during the American Revolution dismantled their homes and brought them over in barges to reassemble here. In this charming town on the shores of Passamaquoddy Bay, whale-watching tours leave from the town wharf. Some additional local sights your family will like follow.

Atlantic Salmon Information Center, Route 127; (506) 529–4581. True, it doesn't sound fascinating, but you'll be surprised how much you and the kids will learn. Walk along the nature trail by the stream that shows the fish in their natural environment. A coloring book detailing the salmon's life cycle is for sale.

Huntsman Marine Science Centre and Aquarium, Branch Cove; (506) 529–4285. This aquarium is a must-see, with a "Please Touch" Tank, harbor seals, and interpretive displays.

Nearby, high over the bay in a lovely setting, sits the historic **Blockhouse,** once used to keep watch in case of invasions by sea. You can go inside to have a look around; a guide will answer questions.

Heading east, you arrive at **Saint John,** on the Bay of Fundy at the mouth of the Saint John River. This is Canada's oldest city and New Brunswick's largest. If you're driving here in the morning, watch out for the thick fog that is a trademark of this area. Saint John (it's not abbreviated in order to avoid confusion with St. John's, Newfoundland) is full of surprises and family pleasures. An industrial city and international seaport, Saint John has undergone major restoration in recent years. Today the **Market Square Waterfront** complex, with its hundred-year-old brick facade, is a charming area of shops, boutiques, and restaurants. Historic walking tours are guided by costumed leaders daily in July and August. Tours leave from Barbour's General Store, Market Slip, restored and stocked with goods from the years 1840 to 1940.

Another family-friendly highlight is **Saint John City Market,** 47 Charlotte Street; it is believed to be the oldest building of its kind in use in Canada. Stop at a café or buy snacks of fresh cheese, baked goods, produce, maple syrup, and other goodies. Often Indians sell hand-woven baskets here.

Let your kids try dulse, the local sea-vegetable specialty gathered from rocks along the Bay of Fundy and dried in the sun. While an acquired taste, the locals love it, and some prefer it to popcorn. The Market is closed Sundays.

Reversing Falls is a natural phenomenon occurring where the St. John River empties into the Bay of Fundy. The falls are really below the water: Explain this to the kids first, or else they might be disappointed. During low tide, tidal waters drop 14½ feet below river levels, causing the full force of the 450-mile river to crash through a narrow gorge into the harbor. As the tides rise in the bay, the river waters gradually calm and actually reverse in direction as the bay waters rise above them. To get the most out of this sight, try to observe the falls twice on the same day: at or near high and low tides. For a short interpretive film explaining, but not actually showing, the phenomenon, go to the rooftop theater at the Reversing Falls Tourist Information Center; (506) 658–2937. It's at the west end of the Route 100 bridge that crosses the river.

Rockwood Park, in the middle of the city, covers 2,200 acres, so plan to spend some time here. The freshwater lakes offer supervised swimming, canoeing, and paddle boating. Visit the zoo and children's petting farm, enjoy the hiking and jogging trails, and try the bumper boats and miniature golf. The park also has camping and trailer facilities.

Canada Games Aquatic Centre, 50 Union Street, just across from Market Square, is a find. This modern facility features two huge warm water, shallow leisure pools, separated by an island with a double looping water slide. There's also a competition pool and two exercise rooms. Visitors pay a small fee. Call (506) 634–7946.

Aitken Bicentennial Exhibition Center (ABEC), 20 Hazen Avenue, is a colorful and lively arts-and-sciences museum. It features ScienceScape, a permanent children's gallery. Call (506) 633–4870.

Fort Howe Lookout, Main Street (North End), is a blockhouse that once protected the harbor. Though you can't go inside, the grounds offer a great view of the city and port.

Saint John Valley: Fredericton

Northwest of Saint John is **Fredericton**, the provincial capital. Called the "City of Stately Elms," it is situated along the picturesque Saint John River. Fredericton is small, very walkable, and a pleasant place to spend some time before or after you visit the Fundy Coast. Once an important military center, much of its historic past remains. The *Fredericton Guide* has a suggested walking tour, and some sites may pique your kids' interest. Your best bet: Take the walking tours led by historically costumed guides who offer dramatic commentary. Call City Hall information at (506) 452–9500. Another option, especially with younger children, is to take a Victorian-style horse-and-carriage tour of downtown. Even if they don't absorb the history, kids love the ride. Call (506) 444–1044 for prices and reservations.

A riverfront pathway ideal for strolling stretches along the green starting at the Sheraton Inn and extending to the Princess Margaret Bridge. Stop in at the **Fredericton Lighthouse Museum**. As you walk to the top level, a variety of interactive exhibits describe the history of the region. The view is lovely on a clear day. Call (506) 459–2515 for information.

Fredericton has lots of inviting, green spaces, including **Odell Park**, where landscaped paths lead to geese, ducks, and deer, and a lovely arboretum. **The Mactaquac Provincial Park**, just outside of town on Route 105, is the largest recreation park in the province, with more than 1,400 acres of open land and forest. The two supervised beaches are a draw for families, as are the self-guided nature trails, an eighteen-hole golf course, camping facilities, and a restaurant. In winter, the park is popular for its skating, sledding, snowmobiling, cross-country skiing, and horse-drawn sleigh rides. Call (506) 363–1011 for information.

Your kids will enjoy the **Changing of the Guard** which takes place July and August in Officers' Square and at City Hall, Tuesday through

Saturday. The Sentry changes every hour on the hour. The Guard was formed in 1793. Call City Hall information for details. **The Guard House,** Carleton Street, appears as it was in 1866 when the Fifteenth Regiment was in residence. In summer, guards wearing the regiment's red-coated uniforms give tours.

The Legislative Assembly Building, Queen Street, is very British and quite majestic. Even young kids will say "wow!" when they see the throne (Speaker's Chair) set on a dais in the Assembly Chamber under a canopy bearing a carved Royal Coat of Arms. You can visit the Chamber while the Legislature is in session, although chances are your kids will appreciate it more when it's empty. Call (506) 453–2527 for information.

On Saturday mornings visit the **Boyce Farmers Market,** just behind the Old York County Jail, between Regent and Saint John Street. Farmers and their wares, artisans, and craftspeople make this a colorful place to linger, browse, and buy; (506) 451–1815.

Don't miss **King's Landing Historical Settlement,** 23 miles west of Fredericton, off the Trans-Canada Highway (Route 2) at exit 259; (506) 363–5805/(800) 561–0123. A visit to this nearly 300-acre recreated Loyalist settlement circa 1790–1870 will be a high point of your family's stay in the area. The setting, high above the Saint John River, is stunning: green and lush, with winding dirt roads, open expanses of farmland, and woods. You can—and should—hitch a ride aboard a horse-drawn wagon; there's much to cover here and lots of walking. The village buildings, which were brought from nearby, include houses varying from plain and simple to utterly grand, a church, a one-room schoolhouse, a general store, a tavern and inn, blacksmith shop, and a bakery. The smell of baking, the sights of men tilling the fields and women weaving, the sounds of children playing are all part of this wonderful experience. Costumed interpreters include children age nine and older who take part in a five-day live-in Visiting Cousins program, which transforms them into children of the 1800s. After a visit, your kids may want to come back and participate. Special theme weekends, such as the Scottish and Harvest festivals and the agricultural fair, add zest to this well-done settlement. There's a self-service restaurant as well as the full-service King's Head Inn.

Combine this with a visit to nearby **Woolastook Park,** 15 miles west of Fredericton on Route 2, the Trans-Canada Highway. Your kids will like the giant water slides, wading pool, beach, minigolf, and nature trails along which animals ranging from raccoons to bobcats are housed. Call (506) 363–5410.

Performing Arts

Fredericton Outdoor Summer Theatre, downtown on the lawn of Officers' Square, features theater-in-the-square seven days a week from July 1st to September 6th. The Square is also the setting for the July and

August Summer Music Concerts held weekly at 7:30 P.M. Call (506) 452–9500 for information on both programs. In Saint John, the **Classical Music Summer Sounds Concerts** at Centenary Queen Square, United Church, Princess Street, are held Tuesdays at 8:00 P.M. Call (506) 634–8123. The city also has free **Outdoor Concerts**, mid-June to late July, at King's Square, featuring a variety of performers; (506) 658–2893.

Shopping

New Brunswick is well known for its crafts—from folk art to dolls to pottery and metal. The Department of Economic Development and Tourism publishes a *New Brunswick Craft Directory* listing studios, boutiques, and outlets. Fredericton, with the highest concentration of craftspeople, is known as the pewter-smithing capital of Canada.

SPECIAL EVENTS

Fairs and Festivals

Contact the individual tourist associations for information on the following festivities.

Late June or early July: Festival Moncton is a nine-day celebration with music, sporting events, street entertainment, concerts, children's and teen events, and fireworks.

July: Loyalist Days, Saint John, includes a street parade. Family day at Rockwood Park features strolling costumed Loyalist soldiers.

July/August: Buskers on the Boardwalk, Saint John's Market Square and adjacent boardwalk, features entertainers from around the world.

August: Festival-by-the-Sea, Saint John, is a multicultural arts and entertainment event featuring hundreds of performers from across Canada. Chocolate Fest, St. Stephen, is part of the St. Stephen-Calais (Maine) International Festival. Chocolate teas, meals, tours, and chocolate-eating contests are included.

Late August–early September: Grand Ole Atlantic National Exhibition, Saint John Exhibition Park, features stage shows, livestock judging, harness racing, and a large midway.

September: Fredericton Exhibition hosts six days of agricultural shows with a midway.

WHERE TO STAY

New Brunswick has a free, in-province reservation system, Dial-A-Nite, available at provincial tourist information centers (shown at major entry points on the New Brunswick Highway map). The system enables travel-

ers to make advance reservations directly with hotels, motels, inns, outfitters, farm vacations, and many privately owned campgrounds. Here are
some picks for families.

Fredericton

Lord Beaverbrook Hotel, 659 Queen Street, is conveniently located.
It has been here for years and is still perfectly comfortable. There's a nice
family restaurant, and the kids will like the indoor pool. Call (506)
455–3371.

Sheraton Inn Fredericton, 225 Woodstock Road, is the city's newest.
Located on the banks of the Saint John River, the hotel has 223 rooms,
with fourteen suites. Indoor and outdoor pools, tennis courts, a family
restaurant, and free parking are some of the offerings. Call (506)
457–7000/(800) 325–3535.

Near King's Landing, in Prince William, the **Chickadee Lodge** is a
cozy, log, bed and breakfast by the river, set back from the Trans-Canada
Highway. You have to share a bath, but the rooms are clean and comfort-
able. This is a good place to stay if you're en route or spending the day at
King's Landing: otherwise, you're basically in the middle of nowhere.
Call (506) 363–2759.

The Carriage House Bed and Breakfast, a three-story Victorian home
in downtown, welcomes children even though it is decorated with antiques. Call (506) 452–9924.

St. Andrews-by-the-Sea

The **Algonquin**, 184 Adolphus, is a large and luxurious Canadian Pacific resort with a pool, golf, tennis, biking, and more. In July and August, there's a supervised program for a fee for ages five to twelve from
10:00 A.M. to 4:00 P.M. Call (506) 529–8823/(800) 268–9411—Canada/
(800) 828–7447—United States.

Pansy Patch, 59 Carleton, is a charming, beautifully furnished lodging.
All rooms have private baths. Breakfast is served in a cozy nook off the
kitchen. There's a large antique shop downstairs. Call (506) 529–1351.

Saint John

Delta Brunswick, 39 King Street, has a great downtown location, indoor pool, and family restaurant with kid's menu. An unsupervised Children's Creative Centre is open from 6:00 A.M. to 11:00 P.M. with games,
movies, and toys. Call (506) 648–1981/(800) 268–1133.

Parkerhouse Inn at 71 Sydney Street, housed in a red Victorian building, doesn't look special from the outside. Once inside, however, you enter
the Victorian era. Each room is decorated differently. There's a small suite
with antique toys for families. The private baths are completely modernized, and the breakfast room is large and sunny. Call (506) 652–5054.

WHERE TO EAT

In Fredericton, stop by the Tourist Information Centres to look through their menu binders. In-the-know locals in Saint John congregate at **Reggie's Restaurant**, 26 Germain Street, famous for its bagels and smoked meat from Montreal, hearty breakfasts, and inexpensive lunches that include clam and fish chowders, lobster rolls, and bagel burgers; (506) 657–6270. Indeed, lobster is everywhere: in the summer, even McDonald's serves McLobster sandwiches, although this isn't the best way to sample this seafood delight. **Keystone Kelly's**, in Saint John's Market Square Complex, has a menu to please all, with Italian, Mexican, and Canadian cuisine. Call (506) 634–0616.

DAY TRIPS

There's lots to explore east of Saint John. On your way to **Moncton**, detour on Route 111 to **St. Martin's** and explore the long stretch of beach and sea caves (but note the tide schedules first). There are twin covered bridges at the harbor, and a tourist information center. As you drive east you're entering the Southern Shores District, home of **Fundy National Park**, on Highway 114 between Saint John and Moncton. Hike, fish, boat, beachcomb, or take part in nature interpretation programs. Kiosks in the park have information about special activities for kids age six to twelve, campfire programs, and entertainment, which takes place at a natural amphitheatre. Salt water is piped in from the Bay of Fundy and heated for the swimming pool. Lodging is available in the park's hostel or in nearby Alma. Call (506) 887–2000.

The lively city of **Moncton** has great family appeal. At **Magnetic Hill**, Mountain Road just off the Trans-Canada Highway on the northwest outskirts of town, cars appear to coast uphill and water seems to flow upwards. Set your car in neutral and feel it coast uphill backwards; trained staff is there to help you experience this optical illusion.

Magnetic Hill's Wharf Village has enough attractions to encourage families to stay the day: **Mountain Magic Water Park** (open mid-May to mid-October), **Magnetic Hill Zoo**, an outdoor concert center, mini–steam engine rides that transport visitors around the complex, crafts and souvenir shops, and **Wharf Village Family Restaurant**. Across from the complex, the **boardwalk** has go-karts, miniature golf, batting cages, fishing, and other attractions. For information on Magnetic Hill attractions, call (506) 853–3516.

In downtown Moncton's **Bore Park**, just off Main Street, twice daily Bay of Fundy tides rise up to 30 feet in little over an hour, creating a

The sea caves at St. Martin's, a short drive from New Brunswick, are great places to explore. (Courtesy New Brunswick Department of Tourism)

wave known as the Tidal Bore. The town of **Dieppe**, which adjoins Moncton's eastern borders, boasts the **Crystal Palace**, 499 rue Paul Street, a huge indoor amusement park with roller coaster, carousel, playground areas, games of skill, a science center with twenty-nine interactive exhibits, and lots more. The complex also includes four cinemas, a food court, McGinnis Landing Restaurant, and a Best Western hotel (506–858–8584 or 800–528–1234). Call (506) 859–4FUN for Crystal Palace Information. For complete information on the area, contact the Convention and Visitor Services, 774 Main Street, Moncton, NB E1C 1E8; (506) 853–4352.

FOR MORE INFORMATION

Fredericton has two Tourist Information Centres: Trans-Canada Highway near Hanwell Road, exit 289 (506–458–8331/8332) and City Hall, corner of Queen and York (506–452–9500). Saint John has several Tourist Information Centres around town. For information, contact their Visitor and Convention Bureau, P.O. Box 1971, Saint John E2L 4L1; (506) 658–2990. Tourism New Brunswick can be reached at (800) 561–0123.

The province maintains Tourist Information Centres at major entry points.

Emergency Numbers

Ambulance, fire, police, and poison control in Fredericton: 911. Police, fire, and rescue squad in Saint John: 911

Poison control in Saint John: (506) 648–7111. Elsewhere, consult the front of the phone book.

Twenty-four-hour emergency room in Fredericton: Dr. Everett Chalmers Hospital, Priestman Street; (506) 452–5400

Twenty-four-hour emergency room in Saint John: Saint John Regional Hospital, Tucker Road; (506) 648–6366

Shopper's Drug Mart is a provincewide chain of pharmacies open late and on Sundays. In Saint John, the store at 57 Landsdowne Place is open from 8:00 A.M. to midnight, seven days a week.

47
NOVA SCOTIA

Nova Scotia's beautiful, diverse landscape, which consists of the Atlantic Coastal Region and the interior woodlands of the Acadian National Forests, has long attracted tourists. This peninsula province is 350 miles from end to end with a coastline that stretches for 4,625 miles. Visitors are never far from rugged shores dotted with sandy beaches, picturesque fishing villages, and scenic coves. **Halifax**, the capital (and its sister city Dartmouth, across the harbor), sits about midway along the Atlantic coast, making these areas an ideal base from which to explore the province. Perhaps your family will eventually wend its way east to Cape Breton Island to the spectacular Cabot Trail that winds around Cape Breton Highlands National Park. Or you may choose to follow one of the province's other ten scenic trailways that reflect its rich ethnic and geographic diversity. But don't rush off from Halifax: the area has some pleasures in store for families who linger.

GETTING THERE

Air Canada has daily flights to Nova Scotia from New York, Boston, Toronto, Montreal, and St. John's, Newfoundland. An affiliate offers connections within Atlantic Canada. Limousine service and car and motor home rentals are available at Halifax International, Sydney, and Yarmouth airports; call (800) 565–0000 for information. Halifax Airport, Highway 102, is 24 miles from downtown. Aerocoach shuttle buses (902–468–1258) travel to major downtown hotels. Share-A-Cab (902–429–4444) services the airport from any part of Halifax, but the service suggests a three-hour notice.

Acadian Lines (902–454–9321) operates buses throughout the province. Greyhound from New York, and Voyageur from Quebec City and Montreal, connect in New Brunswick with SMT Bus Lines, which in turn connects with Acadian Lines. The Halifax bus terminal is at 6040 Almon Street; (902) 454–9321.

VIA Rail travels throughout Canada. Amtrak passengers from Montreal or Toronto can connect with VIA Rail to reach the Halifax station, 1161 Hollis Street, in the south end; (902–429–8421).

Car ferry service to Yarmouth, Nova Scotia, about 328 miles from Halifax, is a comfortable transportation option. Reserve the following in advance: Bluenose from Bar Harbor, Maine (902–794–5700); Scotia Queen from Portland, Maine (800–341–7540—United States/ 800–482–0955—Maine/800–565–7900—Nova Scotia, New Brunswick, or Prince Edward Island). Other ferry service includes Newfoundland to North Sydney, Nova Scotia; Prince Edward Island to Caribou, Nova Scotia; and Saint John, New Brunswick, to Digby, Nova Scotia. Cruise ships dock at ocean terminals in the south end of Halifax.

Highways from all points in the United States and Canada join the Trans-Canada Highway from New Brunswick into Nova Scotia.

GETTING AROUND

Halifax is a compact city. You can walk to most of the major sights (though it is hilly walking from the harbor to the Citadel). Barrington is the city's main street. Metro Transit (902–421–6600) has buses that run regularly throughout the city. Maps are available at any information center. Darmouth-Halifax ferry operates daily from the foot of George Street, Halifax, to the harbor side of Dartmouth's City Hall. The inexpensive fifteen-minute trip offers a good view of the harbor.

WHAT TO SEE AND DO

Museums and Historic Sites

Combine museum visits with sight-seeing tours of different areas of Halifax. First, head to the **harborfront**, a lively place where your family can stroll through the shops of the nineteenth-century waterfront **Historic Properties** buildings, grab a bite to eat, see (or sail on) the *Bluenose II* schooner, and board the *HMCS Sackville*, a World War II convoy escort, now a Naval memorial with an interpretive center and multimedia presentation. The **Halcyon Playground**, near the Ferry Terminal, is designed like a tugboat and appeals to younger kids.

Maritime Museum of the Atlantic, Lower Water Street; (902) 424–7490/7491. This pleasant, airy museum houses some interesting objects, including relics from the *Titanic* (a number of the dead were brought to Halifax, where they were buried), and other vintage Cunard steamship memorabilia. Downstairs is a permanent exhibit of photos and memorabilia devoted to the Halifax Explosion, which older school-age children and teens should find absorbing. Sit down to watch the short video that describes the 1917 disaster, which occurred when two ships—one carrying explosives—collided. The result was the biggest man-made explosion before the nuclear age. Over 1,900 people were killed immediately; 9,000 were injured, and almost the entire north end of Halifax was destroyed.

The museum also has a number of small boats, including one that belonged to Queen Victoria, and a full-size replica of a coastal schooner. The *CSS Academia,* Canada's first hydrographic vessel, is permanently moored outside of the museum.

Next door, at the small **Halifax Touch Tank** Aquarium, roll up your sleeves and carefully handle the marine animals in the pool. Young kids love this.

The next day, visit the star-shaped **Citadel Hill National Historic Park** (902–426–5080), which has dominated the city since 1759. At the foot of Citadel Hill, the Old Town Clock, a city landmark, was given to the city as a gift in 1803 by Prince Edward. Though the fort was never attacked by the French (or anyone else), it was considered the bastion of the British defense of North America. You can go inside the fortress, actually the fourth built on the site by British soldiers, and have a look around the barracks. Walk along the fortress walls for good views of the city and harbor.

A fifty-minute *Tides of History* audiovisual presentation on Halifax and its defenses may be a trifle too long for some kids. But their attention will be riveted by the college students who, playing members of the 78th Highlanders and Royal Artillery, reenact life within the fort. Activities (summer only) include artillery and infantry drills and firing the noonday cannon. Guided tours and food service are available.

Just behind the hill is **Nova Scotia Museum,** 1747 Summer Street; (902) 424–7453. This facility, headquarters of the provincial museum system, presents the human and natural history of the province in an appealing way. Kids will especially enjoy the huge whale, which they can help measure; the stuffed black bear and moose; and—everyone's favorites—lifelike dinosaurs. Artifacts belonging to the province's original inhabitants, the Micmac Indians, are on display, including a 121-pound beaded Indian costume. Changing exhibits frequently reveal the history and contributions of a particular ethnic group: a recent display, for instance, highlighted the Jewish heritage of Canada. Call ahead to find out about regularly scheduled activities.

The Discovery Centre, on the upper level of Scotia Square Mall, Barrington and Duke streets (902–492–4422), offers changing interactive exhibits. Call to ask about their Science Workshops.

Parks and Beaches

How many cities can boast a formal English garden right in the middle of downtown? **Halifax Public Gardens,** across from the Citadel, is a wonderful place for a family stroll. Enjoy seventeen acres of formal Victorian gardens—the oldest in North America—including colorful and fragrant roses, hibiscus, magnolias, and formal floral displays. Sundays are especially festive, with afternoon musical performances on the bandstand. If you haven't brought a picnic, bring some bread crumbs to feed the ducks and pigeons.

Halifax Commons, just outside the city center, is Canada's oldest park. It boasts a large playground where your kids are sure to find lots of open spaces and playmates.

Point Pleasant Park, Point Pleasant Drive, at the south end of Halifax, has 186 acres with walking paths that lead along the Atlantic coast (where you can watch ships come in) and through forests. Motor vehicles are prohibited; park in the lots at the entrances. (A city bus comes here from Barrington Street.) The western entrance, at Tower Road and Point Pleasant Drive, features a large map indicating walkways and interesting points, including the remains of several fortresses. Besides picnic facilities, this park features supervised saltwater bathing at Black Rock Beach, which also has canteen facilities. Because of the frequent "red tide," this beach is not always swimmable. (See DAY TRIPS for nearby beaches.) Kids can play in the sand, however, and there are playgrounds nearby.

The heather at the southern tip of the park was brought to Halifax when the Scottish Highland Regiment shook out their mattresses and bedrolls after landing here—and heather seeds came falling out.

Have a look at the **Prince of Wales Martello Tower,** built in the late 1790s by Queen Victoria's father. This round, thick-walled structure, intended as protection against a French attack, was the first in North America of what was later known as a Martello tower. Exhibits portray the tower's history, and staff is on hand to answer questions.

Shopping

Many shops at **Historic Properties** and **Granville Mall** feature locally made products such as hand-knit blankets and sweaters, Nova Scotia tartan kilts, and pewter. Downtown **Barrington Street** has the more conventional shopping complexes of **Scotia Square, Barrington Place,** and **Maritime Mall.** At **Spring Garden Road,** another popular shopping area, **Clearwater Lobster** packs this local specialty for travel (at the airport, Atlantic Seafoods does this, too). **Jennifer's of Nova Scotia** features local crafts and maple syrup recipe books. The **Rose Bowl** deli across the street sells the maple products, including syrup, butter, cream, and sugar. Don't miss the Farmer's Market on Saturdays at the historic **Brewery Center,** where arts, crafts, and foods are sold. An antique, flea, and produce market takes place on Sundays at **Halifax Forum.**

Performing Arts

Unfortunately for tourists the **Neptune Theater**, the city's leading professional company, and the **Symphony Nova Scotia** don't perform in the summer. It's possible, however, that **Halifax Metro Centre** may host a musical performance during your visit. Call their recording: (902) 451–2602. The **Grafton Street Dinner Theatre** features music, comedy, drama, food—and fun for all. Call (902) 425–1961 to see what's on the entertainment menu. Summer theater is available in the town of Chester (see DAY TRIPS).

SPECIAL EVENTS

Contact provincial or Halifax tourist information for more details on these exciting events.

Late June–early July: Nova Scotia International Tattoo, Halifax, military bands from around the world, gymnasts, dancers, choirs, and more.

July: Festival of Light, Halifax and Dartmouth waterfronts and harbors, includes fireworks and other festivities.

July–August: Tea with the Mayor, weekdays from 3:30 to 4:30 P.M. Casual tea, cookies, and chat with Halifax's mayor.

August: BuskerFest features street performers from around the world who converge on downtown Halifax to juggle, clown, and ride unicycles.

September: Shearwater Air Show, Dartmouth, features daring stunts by air force planes.

WHERE TO STAY

Check In Nova Scotia, the province's free reservation system, has a minireservation center in Halifax, but it's best to reserve as far ahead as possible. Their phone numbers are the same as the provincial travel information numbers listed under FOR MORE INFORMATION. *The Greater Halifax Visitor's Guide* features a comprehensive chart of area lodgings. Here are a few choices for families.

Chateau Halifax, 1990 Barrington Street, is one of the luxurious Canadian Pacific hotels. You can't miss with their convenient location, indoor pool and parking, and lovely rooms and suites. Call (902) 425–6700/(800) 268–9411/(800) 828–7447—United States.

Delta Barrington, 1875 Barrington Street, is also in a terrific location, only a block from the waterfront. Tastefully decorated rooms include triples and suites. A supervised Creative Children's Centre for ages two to twelve is open weekends. There's a pool and health club, and the hotel is connected to two shopping malls. Call (902) 420–6524/(800) 268–1133—Canada/(800) 877–1133—United States.

Summer brings BuskerFest to Halifax, where street performers from all over the world converge here to demonstrate their skills. (Courtesy Nova Scotia Department of Tourism and Culture)

Keddy's Halifax Hotel, on Chocolate Lake, St. Margaret's Bay Road, has 135 rooms, including suites, a recreation pool area, and lake swimming. At the family restaurant, kids eat for under $1.00. Call (902) 477–5611/(800) 561–7666.

WHERE TO EAT

The Greater Halifax Visitor's Guide has a listing of restaurants, categorized by type of food. Here are some of the entries for families.

How could you resist a restaurant called **Alfredo, Weinstein and Ho?** Make everyone happy with inexpensive Italian, Jewish, or Chinese food at this delightfully named Grafton Avenue restaurant; (902) 421–1977. Or dine aboard a historic ferry at **Lobsters Ahoy,** anchored next to the Halifax Ferry Terminal; (902) 422–CLAW. There's a kid's menu, open-air and enclosed dining, and a selection that includes lobster, steak, chicken, and mussels.

DAY TRIPS

Head southwest along the shore toward **Yarmouth**, following **The Lighthouse Route**. Some of the lighthouses along the way are still working and accessible by roads; others can only be reached by boats. Although it's 328 miles to Yarmouth, you need not venture that far. The charming fishing village of **Peggy's Cove** is about thirty minutes away. Set atop spectacular granite rocks, it's one of the most photographed spots in Canada. In the summer, a post office opens in the town's lighthouse. (Be prepared for summer crowds.) Another must-see: a colossal monument to Canadian fishermen, carved into a 100-foot rock face over a ten-year period.

Continue south to **Queensland,** where there are three stretches of sandy beaches. Though it's not large, the Queensland Beach Provincial Park is one of the South Shore's most popular. Arrive early to find a parking space. Further on, the popular summer retreat of **Chester** sits on a peninsula at the head of Mahone Bay, overlooking some of the bay's 365 islands. A passenger ferry runs to the island of **Big Tanook,** where you can sample a local specialty—sauerkraut. August brings Chester's large sailing regatta and professional Theatre Festival, which starts in mid-July. Cafés and restaurants are plentiful. Stroll to the old railway station, where local artists exhibit their work.

In addition to the Lighthouse Route and Cabot Trail, Nova Scotia tourism information can provide information about other distinctively different scenic provincial trailways to explore after leaving Halifax. These include Evangeline Trail, the land settled by the French in 1605; Glooscap Trail, with high Bay of Fundy tides, ancient fossils, and cliffs studded with semiprecious stones; and the Sunrise Trail area, where the Scottish influence is strong. This coastal trail skirts the Northumberland Strait, boasting the warmest waters north of the Carolinas and about one dozen beach parks.

FOR MORE INFORMATION

For information on Nova Scotia, including the reservation service, call (902) 424–4247/(800) 565–0000—Canada/(800) 341–6096—United States/(800) 492–0643—Maine. Ask about the Nova Scotia Host program, where your family can meet a compatible local family. Provincial Information Centres are located at Halifax Airport arrival area (902–426–1223) and in Red Store building, Historic Properties, Lower Water Street, Box 130, Halifax B3J 2M7; (902) 424–4247. Tourism Halifax is in City Hall, corner of Duke and Barrington streets; (902) 421–8736.

The *Greater Halifax Visitor's Guide* lists wheelchair accessibility for lodgings and restaurants. **Lewis Lake**, a provincial park 12 miles west of Halifax, offers disabled persons outdoor recreation, including wheelchair-accessible nature trails and lookouts, and two specially designed fishing piers.

Emergency Numbers

Ambulance and medical emergencies: Izaak Walton Killam Hospital for Children, 5830 University Avenue; (902) 428–8050

Fire: 4103

Poison Control Centre: (902) 428–8161

Police: 4105

Shopper's Drug Mart, Fenwick Medical Center, 5595 Fenwick Street, is open Monday through Saturday from 7:00 A.M. to 11:00 P.M.; Sunday and holidays from 9:00 A.M. to 11:00 P.M.

48
OTTAWA
Ontario

When Queen Victoria selected Ottawa as Canada's capital in 1857, she made a shrewd—albeit unlikely—choice. Although it was then a small wilderness community called Bytown, Ottawa had a central location and was politically acceptable to both East and West Canada. Ottawa has come a long way since then. An attractive, down-to-earth, accessible city, it has great museums, natural beauty, and bountiful year-round recreation—much of it centering around the Rideau Canal, which divides the city in two. What's more, Ottawa is the only capital city in the world with an operating farm within its downtown! No matter what time of year your family comes, you'll find a variety of activities to keep everybody happy. Some are in Hull, just over the bridge, which is in Quebec Province (and has a different area code). Note: In Ottawa, where there's a 40 percent French population, everyone is bilingual, although English is the predominant language.

GETTING THERE

Ottawa International Airport, a twenty-minute ride south of the city (613–998–3151), is served by major carriers. Para Transpo express buses (613–523–8880) run regularly between the airport and a number of Ottawa hotels; pickup can also be arranged from other hotels not on their route. Taxi service is available. Car rentals are at the airport and in town.

VIA Rail, Canada's national railway, runs several daily trains from Montreal and Toronto to Ottawa's VIA Rail Station, 200 Tremblay Road; (613) 244–8289. Connections with Amtrak (800–USA–RAIL) can be made in Montreal or Toronto.

Voyageur Bus, 265 Catherine Street (613–238–5900), has service throughout Canada. Connections to the United States can be made via Montreal or Toronto through Greyhound.

Cars enter Ottawa by following the red maple leaf signs from Highway 417 or by approaching downtown along a commercial truck route.

U.S. citizens and legal residents don't need passports or visas to enter Canada, though they are preferred. Native-born U.S. citizens should have a birth certificate or voter's registration which shows citizenship, plus a picture I.D. Naturalized citizens need naturalization certificates or other proof of citizenship. Permanent residents who are not citizens need alien registration receipts.

GETTING AROUND

OC Transpo is the city's excellent bus system. Call (613) 741–4390 for route information. All downtown routes meet at the Rideau Centre (Rideau Street between Nicholas and Sussex and the Mackenzie King Bridge). You may purchase tickets at OC Transpo offices and many convenience stores. Get transit maps weekdays from the OC Transpo downtown public office at 294 Albert Street. They're also included in the official visitor's map, which is free at all information centers.

You'll be able to drive to a number of attractions not in the downtown area, where there's restricted street parking. Along the **Rideau Canal**, which divides the city, are pedestrian walkways and bike paths. In the winter you'll see people skating to work on the Canal, which is considered the world's longest skating rink.

Recreational boaters arrive via the Rideau Canal or the Ottawa River.

WHAT TO SEE AND DO

Ottawa has a surprising number of museums. Though we've selected only those of special interest to families, see the complete museum listing in the *Visitor Guide* from Ottawa Tourism and Convention Authority.

Museums

Canada Museum of Civilization, 100 Laurier Street, Hull; (819) 776–7000. While the name may not sound exciting, don't miss a visit to this architecturally splendid, large, and interesting attraction. Your kids will love this place as soon as they enter the Grand Hall and see the towering totem poles and six longhouses, tributes to Canada's Northwest Coast. At the stage area here, regularly scheduled performances by a variety of colorful entertainers are often geared to kids. The adjoining History Hall presents Canada's past through life-size reconstructions, such as a sixteenth-century sailing vessel, that include simulated sounds. Kids will love this experience. The Children's Museum area is extremely popu-

The Canada Museum of Civilization, in Ottawa, is host to an assortment of kid-oriented exhibits and special programs. (Courtesy Ottawa Tourism and Convention Bureau)

lar with visitors as well as school groups. Though it's geared for toddlers to about age eight, changing, hands-on exhibits may pique the interest of an older child. Inside, younger kids play at the circular post office where they can rubber stamp and "mail" letters, try on clothes, and play in an outdoor area. An adjoining room full of art supplies is the site of various projects and programs. Get a schedule when you enter.

The **CINEPLUS theater** (admission extra) projects either IMAX or OMNIMAX films, so plan to spend the day. Call (819) 776–7010 for show times.

Canadian Museum of Nature, McLeod Street at Metcalfe; (613) 996–3102. The "castle" that houses this museum was briefly the governmental seat after the Parliament buildings burned down in 1916. On display are all the things that school-age kids like: huge dinosaurs, gems and minerals, birds, mammals, plants, and assorted creatures, plus a Discovery Den, with nature-related kid's activities and exhibits.

National Gallery of Canada, 380 Sussex Drive; (613) 990–1985. Yes, this museum houses the world's most comprehensive collection of Canadian art and European, Asian, and American works; chances are that won't impress the kids. What will is the physical appearance of this contemporary glass and granite building which, as the museum puts it, "rises like a giant candelabrum." Inside, in the Great Hall, enjoy sweeping views of the city. No, there's nothing "just for kids," but if yours haven't been to a strictly-art museum before, this is the place to start.

Most will find something of interest in the Contemporary galleries, flooded with light from the skylights overhead. There are two restaurants, on-site parking, and an excellent bookstore with kid's books. For a visual treat drive or walk by at night, when this illuminated glass treasure house is a sight to behold.

National Aviation Museum, Rockcliffe Airport (follow biplane signs on Rockcliffe Parkway); (613) 993–2010. True, non-Canadians might not find this collection of Canadian aircraft quite as fascinating as Canadians do. Still, if your kids are turned on by vintage aircraft, they'll love it here. The collection is one of the world's largest. It spans aeronautical history and includes a reproduction of the *Silver Dart* (which Alexander Graham Bell helped to design) and the vintage Stearman biplane, which "passengers" are allowed to board. Family Sundays are held monthly; frequent weekday activities are designed for various ages.

National Museum of Science and Technology, 18678 St. Laurent Boulevard; (613) 991–3044. This informal museum, while not as sophisticated as some big-city counterparts, prides itself on being user friendly. A push of a button, turn of a dial, or pull of a lever activates such exhibits as printing presses and water pumps. Plus, take a lopsided walk through the Crazy Kitchen where nothing is as it seems. Bring a picnic or get something from the cafeteria to eat in the shady adjacent parkland, where there's a real lighthouse, steam train, observatory, and rocket ship. When weather permits, evening astronomy programs are held at the museum and the Helen Sawyer Hogg Observatory; reservations are required. While you're there, discover the natural earth at "The Living Earth" exhibit where kids can wiggle into a damp cave and stretch their necks as they wander through a rain forest and get showered by the spray of a tall waterfall.

Historical Sites

Parliament Hill's Centre Block is home to the Senate and the House of Commons, where Canada's laws are created. When Parliament is in session, you can get tickets to sit in the public galleries and listen to debates in either of the two chambers. Older kids may find this interesting. Call (613) 992–4793 for information about the days and times.

The Changing of the Ceremonial Guard is the best show in town—and it's free! It takes place daily at 10:00 A.M. from late June to late August (weather permitting) on the Hill. The Ceremonial Guard is made up of two regiments: the Governor General's Foot Guards (with the red plumes) and Canadian Grenadier Guards (white plumes). The parade forms at Cartier Square Drill Hall (at Laurier Avenue, by the canal) at 9:30 A.M. and marches up Elgin Street to reach the Hill at 10:00 A.M. Don't miss it!

Same-day reservations for free **Parliament Hill Tours** must be made in the Infotent, east of the Centre Block on Parliament Hill, from mid-May to early September.

Parks and Farms

Central Experimental Farm, Queen Elizabeth Driveway; (613) 995–5222. Located on the edge of downtown Ottawa, this beautiful 1,200-acre working farm makes for a delightful family excursion. Set up by the government in 1886 to improve techniques and offer farmers technical help, the complex attracts some half million visitors a year. Start with a free, fifteen-minute wagon ride, drawn by two Clydesdales (weekdays; just east of the Agriculture Museum). The dairy barn (where the museum and vintage farm machinery display is located) houses 50 cows of various breeds. The kids won't want to miss the calves in the southeast wing. Nearby are sheep, lambs, and piglets. Pack a picnic: there are lots of green spaces, including an arboretum along the canal with panoramic vistas. Take in a tropical plant show in the main greenhouse on Maple Drive or stop by the old observatory which, though no longer in use, has a rotunda displaying instruments used to measure earthquakes and tides. The Ottawa Convention and Tourism Authority has a map of the farm that includes a self-guided walking tour.

Dows Lake, Queen Elizabeth Driveway; (613) 232–1001. There's lots going on in and around this man-made lake no matter when you visit. In the summer, rent pedal boats and canoes, cycle, stroll, or just relax. In May, come to see the colorful tulips—the pride and joy of this area. During the February Winterlude festival, centered on the Rideau Canal, skaters come to Dows Lake Pavilion (where skate rentals are available) to warm up, use the bathrooms, or to have a bite to eat at one of three restaurants.

Gatineau Park, with a gateway minutes north of Hull, is a huge recreational paradise. The Gatineau Park Visitor Center, Meech Lake Road, Old Chelsea (819–827–2020), has maps and information year-round. Lac Phillippe (Highway 5 then Highway 366 west), forty-five minutes from Ottawa, is the most popular summer area. It offers two beaches with lifeguards (fee), camping sites, picnic facilities, hiking trails, and boat rentals. There's a snack bar and a swimming pier for visitors of impaired mobility. The Lac Phillippe Visitor Center is open weekends in the summer.

In all, the Park has 115 miles of hiking and cross-country skiing trails, rolling hills, and scenic lookouts. If you have time, visit the 568-acre MacKenzie King Estate, summer retreat of Canada's tenth prime minister. Take a stroll through the restored cottages and along walking trails and formal gardens that feature interesting ruins collected by King.

Log Farm, 670 Cedarview Road, Western Greenbelt; (613) 825–4352. Yes, another farm—but with a difference. At this restored 1870s rural homestead, interpreters do daily tasks and invite visitors—particularly kids—to join in. Special fall and winter holiday programs include sleigh rides.

Special Tours

Paul's Boat Lines offers seventy-five-minute cruises of Ottawa's attractions on the Rideau Canal from the Conference Center. Call their office at (613) 225–6781, or summer dock at (613) 235–8409.

Performing Arts

National Arts Centre, 51 Elgin Street, showcases a variety of performing arts from pop to classical music, theater, dance, and other entertainment. Call the box office at (613) 996–5051, or TicketMaster at (613) 755–1111. For specific entertainment information check the *Ottawa Citizen*, the official daily tourism newspaper, *WHERE Ottawa-Hull* magazine's monthly events listing, and the *Ottawa Sun* English-language newspaper, Sunday through Friday.

Landsdowne Park, Bank Street at the Rideau Canal, hosts programs throughout the year that include stage shows, concerts, craft exhibitions, and other family fare. It's also the home to several sports teams. (See SPECIAL EVENTS.) *The Capital Calendar*, available from the Ottawa Tourism and Convention Bureau, has listings, or call (613) 564–1485.

On Parliament Hill, free sound-and-light shows (separate English and French performances) take place daily from early June to early September and four nights a week in May. Kids will like the carillon concerts held year-round on most weekdays from 12:30 to 12:45 P.M. On Tuesday and Thursday summer evenings, one-hour concerts are played on the bells in the Peace Tower, with special concerts on other occasions. Call (613) 992–4793 for information.

Shopping

The street stalls of the By Ward Market, Lower Town, have been selling seasonal produce, ranging from maple syrup to flowers to honey, since 1840. This lively market successfully blends the old with the new: specialty food shops (some over a hundred years old), art galleries, cafés, restaurants, and, in the old Market building, arts and crafts stalls. For more conventional shopping, the downtown Rideau Centre is the city's main shopping mall.

SPECIAL EVENTS

Sports

Landsdowne Park is home to professional football and National Hockey League teams. For tickets to the Ottawa Football Club Rough

Riders' game, call (613) 563–4551; for Ottawa Senators hockey tickets, call (613) 721–0115.

Fairs and Festivals

Be sure to get a calendar of events from the Ottawa Tourist and Convention Authority; there's lots going on. Here are some highlights.

February: Winterlude, a ten-day family celebration at various sites centers on the Rideau Canal, includes shows, skating, ice sculptures, kid's snow playground, entertainers, food, fireworks, and more.

May: Tulip Festival, with entertainment, crafts, food.

Late June–July: National Capital Art Show.

July: Ottawa International Jazz Festival includes Children's Day.

August: Superex, the Central Canada Exhibition with midway and exhibits. Hull's International Cycling Festival with family events.

Labor Day Weekend: Gatineau Hot Air Balloon Festival.

November: Chrysanthemum Show, Central Experiment Farm in the main greenhouse.

December: Christmas Lights Across Canada.

WHERE TO STAY

Ottawa has a wide choice of accommodations in every price range. The Visitor Information Center, 65 Elgin Street, offers a free summer booking service with participating hotels, motels, or bed and breakfast inns. Call (613) 233–3035. Their visitor guide has a handy grid chart of hotels and bed and breakfasts that include locations and features. Yes, you can save money by staying on the outskirts of town. But the following lodgings in Central Ottawa frequently have summer packages for families, so check with them first.

Chateau Laurier, 1 Rideau Street, is in a convenient location, overlooking the Canal and next to Parliament Hill. This elegant grand dame has hosted an endless assortment of notables, including Queen Elizabeth. Their vintage indoor pool is delightful. Though the rates can be on the steep side, summer family packages, which include Children's Play Centre activities, can make this an affordable option. Call (613) 232–6411/ (800) 268–9411.

Delta Ottawa, 361 Queen, part of the family-friendly Delta hotel chain, has a large indoor pool and children's play area. Kids under six eat free. Call (613) 238–6000/(800) 268–1133.

Minto Place Suite Hotel, 433 Laurier Avenue, West, offers various size suites with fully equipped kitchens. Located close to Parliament, the high-rise hotel has an indoor pool, restaurants, shops, and indoor parking. For the past few summers, they've had a summer Kids' Club, with supervised activities and outings for ages four to fourteen; ask if it's in operation when you call: (613) 782–2350/(800) 267–3377—Ontario and Quebec/(800) 267–3377.

WHERE TO EAT

The visitor guide groups restaurants by specialty and includes price ranges and other features. For a special treat, take your tykes to **The Tea Party**, 119 York Street, near Byward Market, for English afternoon tea, complete with scones and cream. The atmosphere is charming, and the shelves of teapots and collectibles are all for sale; (613) 562–0352. **Bako Bakery**, in the By Ward Market, is popular with locals for its tasty breakfasts and light lunches; (613) 230–1417.

DAY TRIPS

Following the Ottawa River west of the capital region, you'll find scenic farm country, nature trails, beaches, and riverside parks. At **Pinto Valley Ranch**, near Fitzroy Harbour, there's horseback riding or wagon rides, nature trails, pony rides, and a petting zoo; (613) 623–3439. In Lanark County, **Fulton's Pancake House and Sugarbush**, near Pakenham, has cross-country skiing, sleigh rides, maple sugaring, a playground, nature trails, and guided tours; it's open winter weekends and daily in the spring; (613) 256–3867. **Storyland**, 50 miles west of Ottawa, just west of Renfrew, is a theme park, plus minigolf, pedal boats, nature trails, and more; (613) 432–5275. Or head to **Logos Land Resort**, further west near Cobden, an amusement park with water slides, horseback riding, minigolf, and pedal boats. Call (613) 646–2313/(800) 267–5885—Canada. In the winter, skiers head to Mont Cascades, twenty minutes north of town.

FOR MORE INFORMATION

Ottawa Tourism and Convention Authority, Visitor Information Centre, National Arts Centre, 65 Elgin Street, offers visitors free half-hour underground parking. Call (613) 237–5158, or for automated, up-to-date tourist information, (613) 692–7000. You'll see Ottawa Citizen Tourist Info Trikes at downtown tourist spots and at special events and festivals during the summer. Canada's Capital Information Centre is opposite the Parliament Buildings at 14 Metcalfe Street. Call (613) 239–5000/ (800) 465–1867—Canada. For information on the entire Ontario province, call 800–ONTARIO.

Special Needs

Door-to-door wheelchair accessible service is available to qualified disabled visitors in Ottawa-Carleton. Call Para Transpo at (613) 244–4636 before arrival. Welcoming Services (819–996–9238) provides special needs information and assistance during the ten-day Winterlude festival. All national museums and attractions in Ottawa and Hull are universally accessible. Wheelchair accessible codes are listed in the visitor guide.

Emergency Numbers

Ambulance, fire, and police: 911
Ontario Provincial Police: (800) 267–2677
Poison Control: (613) 737–1100
Twenty-four-hour emergency service: Children's Hospital, 401 Smythe Road (located between Ottawa General Hospital and National Defense Medical Center); (613) 737–7600
Twenty-four-hour pharmacy: Shoppers Drug Mart, 1460 Merivale Road: (613) 224–7270. A list of pharmacies open until midnight appears in the Sunday edition of the *Ottawa Citizen*.

49
QUEBEC CITY
Quebec

Quebec City offers families a distinctly different vacation experience. Perched atop the rocky Cap Diamant (Cape Diamond) and overlooking the St. Lawrence River, this provincial capital is the only fortified city in North America. Indeed, from the seventeenth through the nineteenth centuries, Quebec was vital in the ultimate defense of all of northeastern America. The historic district, Old Quebec (*Vieux Quebec*), has been proclaimed a "world heritage treasure" by UNESCO. Wherever you venture in this district, you'll be immersed in history. The French influence dominates in culture, cuisine, and language: at least 95 percent of the population is French-speaking. It helps to speak the language, though it's possible to get by without it. Just minutes from the city, your family will find unlimited outdoor activities in stunning natural settings.

GETTING THERE

Quebec City Airport in Sainte-Foy, 10 miles outside of town, is served by Air Canada and affiliates and by Northwest Airlink. Daily shuttles from the airport to major city hotels are run by Maple Leaf Sightseeing Tours; (418) 649–9226. Car rentals are available at the airport.

VIA Rail Canada arrives and departs from *Gare du Palais* and Sainte-Foy station. For information and reservations, call (418) 692–3940. It's possible to connect with Amtrak trains in Montreal or Toronto.

Orleans Express bus lines, whose main station is at 225, boulevard Charest est (418–524–4692), serves this area. You can make connections with Greyhound in Montreal. A number of highways connect to Quebec City, which is approximately six hours from Boston and eight-and-one-quarter hours from New York City.

GETTING AROUND

CTCUQ (Commission de transport de la Communauté Urbaine de Quebec) buses run regularly. Call (418) 627–2511 for routes and schedules. During ski season the daily Skibus leaves from six downtown hotels to Monte Sainte-Anne and Stoneham, and also offers sight-seeing tours from all hotels. Call (418) 653–9722.

A ferry leaves opposite Place Royale to Lévis on the south shore. The scenic ten- to fifteen-minute ride affords panoramic views of Old Quebec from the St. Lawrence River. Call (418) 644–3704.

WHAT TO SEE AND DO

Museums and Historical Sites

Wherever you go in and outside the walls of Old Quebec, you'll be near a monument, museum, or historical site. If your kids are school age, prepare them with a brief historical summary: it will make their visit much more meaningful. The city's history in a nutshell: Quebec served as the base for early French explorers and missionaries in North America. In 1608, Samuel de Champlain built its first dwelling; the town ultimately grew into a fortified city. In 1759, British troops defeated the French and, in 1763, Canada was ceded to Great Britain. The British, in turn, threatened by the patriot army during the American Revolution, rebuilt many of the French fortifications and constructed structures of their own. The last battle was fought in Quebec City in 1776, when the British repulsed an American patriot army invasion led by Benedict Arnold.

There's lots to see in Old Quebec, but be selective. Balance museum and historical sites with parks and café stops. You can take a tour of **Old Quebec,** but it's more fun to explore it yourself. Make sure you have a good map (available from the Convention and Visitors Bureau), cluster the sights you want to see, and take your time. Here are some highlights.

The Citadel and Parc des Champs-de-Bataille

At the Promenade des Gouverneurs, a stairway and scenic boardwalk with river views lead uphill to the star-shaped **Citadel,** dramatically set atop Cap Diamant, the eastern flank of Quebec's fortifications. The entrance is on rue St. Louis; (418) 648–3563. The facility is comprised of twenty-five buildings, including the officers' mess and Governor General's residence. Guided tours are available. Some kids may enjoy the **Royal 22e Regiment Museum,** an old military prison, with a collection of uniforms, documents, firearms, and other memorabilia from the seventeenth century to the present. The regiment still guards the citadel. A must-see: the Changing of the Guard, held at 10:00 A.M. daily from mid-June to Labor Day (weather permitting); it lasts forty minutes. The noon and 9:30 P.M. cannon is another military tradition, as is the Beating of Retreat, four nights a week in July and August.

Next to the citadel is the **Parc des Champs-de-Bataille** (Battlefields Park), located between Grande Allée and Champlain Boulevard. The park is the site of the Plains of Abraham, where the 1759 battle between British and French forces took place. Besides viewing the numerous military artifacts and monuments, come here for the 250 acres of gardens and woodlands. Picnic and hike, or, in winter, cross-country ski and skate.

A summer shuttle takes passengers to a number of the park's main sites including the *Musée du Quebec* (418–643–4103), which spans generations of Quebec art. Two museums that will be of more interest to kids, however, are listed in the following section.

Museums and Parliament

Take the Promenade des Gouverneurs downhill to Terrasse Dufferin promenade. At the bottom of this popular promenade rises the huge, baroque **Château Frontenac** (418–692–3861), built in 1893 by Canadian Pacific Company and now a luxury hotel. If you're not staying here, stop in for a peek at its grand hall. Nearby, the Place d'Armes has fountains and horse-drawn buggies (calèches). While not inexpensive, the rides provide a picturesque mode of transportation.

Next to the Place d'Armes, you may want to stop in for a look at the interior of the ornately decorated **Notre Dame Basilica**, 16 Rue Buade, (418) 692–2533. Nearby are two museums of interest to families.

Musée du fort, 10 rue Sainte-Anne; (418) 692–2175. This is a good way to introduce the kids to the city's history. There's a model of the city as it looked in 1750. A sound and light show reenacts the six sieges fought to control Quebec.

Musée historique de cire (wax museum), 22 rue Sainte-Anne; (418) 692–2289. Kids (and adults) may not recognize many of the eighty figures represented here, such as Montcalm and Réné Levesque. But most kids like wax museums. Christopher Columbus and his shipmates are included.

Many sidewalk cafés and restaurants line rue Sainte-Anne, where these museums are located. In the summer, musicians and street entertainers make this a lively place to linger.

From here it would be convenient to walk east down the **casse cou** (breakneck) stairways—not really that bad—or to the funicular, to go down to the Lower City, the oldest part of Quebec.

If you're interested in seeing **Parliament Hill**, however, head southwest to avenue Dufferin and the tree-lined Grand Armée Est, considered the

Champs Elysées of Quebec. Stop for a bite at one of the many restaurants along the way. You can take a guided tour of Parliament including the National Assembly Chamber, where Quebec's elected representatives meet, although the experience may be lost on the very young. Call (418) 643–7239.

Lower City

In Place Royale, one of the oldest districts on the continent, stroll through narrow streets, past historic homes, boutiques, and workshops. The parks of Place Royale host a number of events with family appeal, including plays and variety shows. Stop by the Information Centre, 215 rue du Marché-Finlay, for schedules of activities. In the Quartier du Petit Champlain, at times, the quaint, narrow streets sport musicians, clowns, and jugglers. **Explore**, 63 rue Dalhousie (418–692–2175), is a sound-and-light show that retells the discovery of America and the voyages of early French explorers up the St. Lawrence River. The lively Old Port includes a farmer's produce market and a cinema—**Imax-Maison de l'Image**, 60 St.-Andre; (418) 692–IMAX.

Parks

In addition to thirty-six green spaces within the city, The Greater Quebec Area, with its St. Lawrence River location, has a number of parks and wildlife reserves where families can enjoy the great outdoors. Going east along the Côte de Beaupré, you'll find these attractions.

Cap-Tourmente National Wildlife Area, Saint-Joachim; (418) 827–4591 from April to October and (418) 683–2432 from November to April. About thirty-five minutes east of Quebec, this striking preserve on the St. Lawrence River's north shore was created especially to protect the natural habitat of the Greater Snow Geese. During migration periods, the area attracts some 300,000 geese. The preserve is made up of four separate environments: marsh, plain, cliff, and mountain. Footpaths reveal a wide variety of plants, trees, nesting and migratory birds, and mammals. Some trails lead to the summit of Cap Tourmente, or you can opt for the views from an observation tower. The welcome and interpretation centers have exhibitions and films. In season, naturalists offer activities and guided tours.

North of the city: Parc de la Jacques-Cartier, Route 175 north; (418) 848–3169. Summer canoeing, rock climbing, mountain biking, and hiking are the big attractions at this beautiful provincial park on the Jacques-Cartier River. You can rent equipment. During mid-May to October, activities include canoe excursions, outings, and a moose observation safari in September.

West of the city: **Lac-Saint-Joseph**, in Sainte-Catherine-de-la-Jacques-Cartier, has a beach that is popular with local families. It adjoins the *Station forestière de Duchesnay* (Forest Educational Centre), which is open to the public for nature walks. Call (418) 875–2711.

Attractions

Aquarium du Quebec, 1675 avenue du Parc, Sainte-Foy (Quebec); (418) 659–5264. Located in a wooded area southwest of Old Quebec, with nice views of the St. Lawrence River, the aquarium is home to some 2,000 sea creatures. The ever-popular seals perform twice daily. You might combine a trip here with another Sainte-Foy attraction: **Musée de geologic**, pavillon Adrien-Pouillot (fourth floor), avenue de la Médecine; (418) 656–2193. Most kids like fossils and minerals, and you'll find hundreds of them here from all around the world.

Centre récréatif des Galeries de la Capitale, 5401 boulevard des Galeries; (418) 627–5800. This enormous recreation center, part of a shopping mall, sports a ferris wheel and roller coaster among its rides and, for more fun, there's a skating rink and minigolf.

Jardin Zoologique du Quebec, 8191 avenue du Zoo, Charlesbourg (Quebec); (418) 622–0312. Along with the usual bears, chimps, and wild cats, kids enjoy the sea lion show and the farm. A river linked by waterfalls crosses through the zoo and, in winter, the surrounding trails are open for cross-country skiing and snowshoeing.

Village des Sports, 1860 boulevard Valcartier, Saint-Gabriel-de-Valcartier (Quebec); (418) 844–3725/(800) 463–2111—Canada. Bring your bathing suits: This place boasts a huge wave pool, water games, water slides, and acrobatic diving shows. When you dry off, choose from roller skating trails, Maxi-Golf, and a racing car circuit. Winters, this enormous recreation center north of the city has sledding on inner tubes or carpets, skating paths with music, and cross-country skiing.

Ski Areas

The ski season can last almost six months in Greater Quebec. Two of the province's best downhill ski areas are within a half-hour's drive of the city. **Parc du Mont-Sainte-Anne**, Route 360, Beaupré; (418) 827–4561. This enormous park, thirty minutes east of downtown Quebec, includes Mont-Sainte-Anne, a popular winter downhill ski area, the largest in Quebec. Day care and a kinderski program are available for ages two to six. In summer, the park becomes a recreational mecca, with golf, mountain biking, picnicking, and cable car rides to the mountain summit of Monte Sainte-Anne. Ski area reservations: (418) 827–3121/(800) 463–1568.

Stoneham, 1429 avenue du Hibou, Stoneham (Quebec); (418) 848–2411/(800) 463–6888—Canada. Twenty-five minutes north of town, Stoneham offers a network of twenty-five runs on four mountains. The nursery takes kids two years and up, and teens meet at the Coketail Bar. Lodging includes 600 hotel or condo rooms, either slopeside or at the mountain base.

Special Tours

Try a scenic boat ride with **Quebec City Cruises,** Quai Chouinard at 10 rue Dalhousie. From mid-June through Labor Day choose from one-hour harbor tours, ninety-minute excursions to **Île d'Orleans** (418) 692–1295. (See DAY TRIPS.)

Performing Arts

Among the city's cultural attractions are the **Quebec Symphony Orchestra,** which performs at the Grand Théâtre de Quebec, the **Trident** theatre troupe; the **Danse-Partout Dance** company; and the **Quebec Opera,** with spring and fall productions. In addition, the Greater Quebec area has excellent summer theater performances. Listings of area cultural events are published every Wednesday in English in the Quebec *Chronicle Telegraph.*

Shopping

In Quebec's Lower City, stroll and browse along rue Saint-Paul's antique shops, boutiques, and art galleries. Across from the Château Frontenac, sketches and watercolors are sold on the narrow rue du Trésor. At **La Cabane,** 94, Petit Champlain in Old Quebec, sample (and buy) maple sugar products; (418) 692–2817.

SPECIAL EVENTS

Sports

The Quebec Nordiques National Hockey League Club is exceedingly popular, and they play mid-September through mid-April at the Colisee de Quebec; (418) 523–3333/(800) 463–3333—Quebec Province.

Fairs and Festivals

The Greater Quebec area abounds in year-round fairs and festivals. *The Greater Quebec Area Tourist Guide* has an exhaustive listing of events. Some highlights include the following.

February: Winter Carnival, the world's largest, features eleven days of parades, ice sculpture contests, and numerous other activities and events.

July: Quebec International Summer Festival, French-speaking cultural events held in the streets and parks of Old Quebec.

August: Expo Quebec, Parc de l'Exposition, is a huge agricultural exhibition with fair, rides, and entertainment.

September: Festival of Colors includes sports, outdoor activities, and cultural events to herald the start of the fall and winter season, Parc Du Monte Sainte Anne.

If you visit Quebec during February, be sure to participate in the Winter Festival happenings. (Courtesy of Quebec Tourism)

WHERE TO STAY

The Greater Quebec Area Tourist Guide features listings of hotels. If you're on a budget, consider one of the convenient lodgings outside of the city. To reach the reservation service for Quebec province, call (800) 363–RESA. For lodging in Parc du Mont-Sainte-Anne area, call (800) 463–1568. Here's a family-friendly selection that includes a variety of locations and price ranges.

Downtown
Hotel Classique, 640 St.-Jean Street, offers large rooms with kitchenettes, indoor pool, and parking. Call (418) 629–0227/(800) 463–5753—Canada.

Old City (outside walls)
Holiday Inn, 395 de la Coutonne, is within walking distance of Old Quebec's walled city. The 18-story high rise features 232 rooms, with seven suites. The kids will love the pool—the largest in town. Call (418) 647–4317/(800) HOLIDAY.

Old City (inside walls)

L'Hôtel Du Vieux Quebec, 1190 rue Saint-Jean, is housed in a historic building. Twenty-seven comfortable rooms feature kitchenettes; (418) 692–1850.

Côte-de-Beaupré

Chalets Montmorency et Motels, 1768 avenue Royale, Saint-Ferreol-les-Neiges. In a quiet setting near Mont-Sainte-Anne, this Swiss-style apartment lodge features spacious one- to four-bedroom suites, an indoor pool, and golf packages. Call (418) 826–2600/(800) 463–2612.

WHERE TO EAT

A dining guide is available from the Tourism and Convention Bureau. The local cuisine has lots for kids to like: try *croque monsieur*, an open ham sandwich covered with melted cheese, and crepes. Depending on the filling, this serves as either a main course or a dessert. For inexpensive *crepes*, try **Casse Crepe Breton**, 1136 rue St. Jean, where you can also get sandwiches, salads, soups, and a hearty breakfast; (418) 692–0438.

Fondue is fun: dip right in at **Au Café Suisse**, 32 rue Sainte-Anne (418–694–1320), where seafood, steaks, and *raclette* are also on the menu. Two-hour free parking at city hall is included. The location is good, too, right near the Musée du fort and the Musée historique de cire.

Kids love the pink pig statue outside of **Le Cochon Dingue**, 46, boulevard Champlain, across from the Lévis ferry. The house specialty: steaks and fries. Call (418) 523–2013. For a big-splurge meal with a twist, head to **L'Astral**, at Loews Le Concorde, 1225 Place Montcalm. The restaurant slowly revolves to reveal fabulous vistas below; (418) 647–2222.

DAY TRIPS

Î'le d'Orléans, about 6 miles downstream from downtown and accessible by car, is a pleasant excursion for those who like simple charms. This sparsely populated island (about 7,000 people) offers historic homes, churches, mills, and chapels. In season, roadside stands have fresh produce, and some producers allow the public to pick their own strawberries, apples, and corn. Call (418) 828–9411 for information. In the village of Saint-Laurent, where shipbuilding was once the largest industry, there's a maritime museum and riverfront views. An arts-and-crafts center sells handmade traditional handicrafts, such as pottery, wood carvings, knitted garments, and porcelain jewelry. During July and August weekends, local artists offer demonstrations.

From the Île d'Orléans, head east to Route 138 to the lower section of **Chute Montmorency**, in Beauport-Boischatel (bus 50 or 53). The upper section is accessible via Route 360. This is a breathtaking waterfall, one-and-half times as high as Niagara Falls. The site, divided into upper and lower sections, features lookout points, trails, picnic tables, and a tourist information center, which is open from mid-May to late October. Upstream, Manor Montmorency, now a hotel surrounded by lovely gardens, offers a terrific lookout. In the winter, an unusual phenomenon occurs. The crystallized water vapor forms an enormous ice cone that locals call *pain de sucre* or sugar loaf.

Continue east about 13 miles to **Sainte-Anne-de-Beaupré Basilica**. It's long been believed that Sainte-Anne, mother of the Virgin Mary, has saved shipwreck victims off cap Tourmente. Many still believe she works miracles: every year, more than 1,500,000 pilgrims come to pray to this saint.

Farther east, near **Parc du Mont-Sainte-Anne**, the Grand Canyon des chutes Sainte-Anne is a waterfall with breathtaking chasms and streams. Shuttle service in open sight-seeing cars is included in the admission fee (open May to October). There's also a cafeteria and picnic area. Call (418) 827–4057.

FOR MORE INFORMATION

For booklets and maps of the area: Maison du Tourisme de Quebec, 12 rue Sainte-Anne (across from Château Frontenac) is open seven days a week; or write to Tourisme Quebec, Case postale 20,000, Quebec, Canada G1K 7X2. In the summer in Old Quebec's historic area, motorized tourist information agents ride green mopeds with a "?" sign. Information on Quebec's nineteen tourist regions is available by calling (800) 363–7777 from Quebec, Canada, and the United States.

Emergency Numbers
Fire and police in Quebec: (418) 691–6911
Pharmacie Brunet, Les Galeries Charlesbourg, 4266, 1ère (Première) Avenue, Charlesbourg, is open until midnight seven days a week, opening at 8:00 A.M. Monday through Saturday and 10:00 A.M. on Sunday: (418) 623–1571.
Poison Control: (418) 656–8090 or (800) 463–5060
Twenty-four-hour emergency room: L'Hôtel Dieu, 11, Côte du Palais, Old Quebec; (418) 691–5151. A hospital specializing in children's health: CHUL (Laval University Hospital Center), 2705 boulevard Laurier, Sainte-Foy (a western suburb); (418) 656–4141

50
TORONTO
Ontario

If you shy away from city vacations because of the hassles associated with large metropolitan areas, take a trip to Toronto, Ontario, Canada's largest city and top visitor destination. This spanking clean city offers families everything a major metropolitan area should—without the hassles. Your family will find all the things you might expect: interesting sights, kid-friendly museums, arts and entertainment, shopping, great restaurants, and a wide selection of accommodations. You'll also find some things you might not expect: a sparkling, lively waterfront, safe, clean streets; and a friendly, ethnically diverse population that adds much to Toronto's character and charm.

Note: Effective October 4, 1993, several hundred phone exchanges in outlying areas will have their area codes changed to 905, so you may get a recording of the new area code when you dial certain attractions listed below, including the Pearson International Airport.

GETTING THERE

U.S. citizens and legal residents don't need passports or visas to enter Canada, though they are preferred. Native-born U.S. citizens should have a birth certificate or voter's registration card that shows citizenship, plus a picture I.D. Naturalized citizens need naturalization certificates or other proof of citizenship. Permanent residents who are not citizens need alien registration receipts.

Metropolitan Toronto is a major transportation center. Some thirty-five major airlines offer regular service through three terminals at Pearson International Airport (416–612–5100), in the northwest corner of metropolitan Toronto. Car rentals are available at the airport. Gray Coach Lines (416–351–3300) has scheduled service every twenty minutes between most major downtown hotels and the airport. Only taxis with TIA on their license plates are authorized to pick up passengers. Toronto Island Airport; (416) 868–6942, services a number of commuter airlines, including flights originating in the United States. The airport can be accessed via a brief public ferry ride that leaves from the foot of Bathurst Street.

Amtrak (800–USA–RAIL) runs trains from New York and Chicago to Toronto, where passengers can link up to the VIA Rail Canada, Inc. (416–868–7277), which provides rail service throughout Canada. Union Station is downtown on Front Street, directly on Toronto's subway line.

Greyhound, Voyageur, and regional bus lines serve Metro Toronto, arriving and departing from the bus terminal at 610 Bay Street. Fares and schedules for all bus companies may be obtained by calling (416) 393–7911.

Those coming by car can reach Toronto by one of several major routes that parallel Lake Ontario's shores: Highway 401 and Highway 2 from the west and east; Queen Elizabeth Way from the west only; and Highway 400, which connects with Highway 401, from the north.

Note: While you're at Pearson airport, check out the boutique complex at the new terminal, where there's the only Harrod's in North America.

GETTING AROUND

Metro Toronto is made up of six municipalities: the City of Toronto, the Borough of East York and the Cities of York, North York, Scarborough, and Etobicoke. Shared transit service via Toronto Transit Commission (TTC) includes 818 miles of subway, bus, trolley and streetcar, and ferry routes. Riders must have exact change or purchase TTC tickets and tokens at subway stations or from stores displaying the EXACT FARE sign. For information about routes, schedules, and fares, call (416) 393–4636 or pick up a *Ride Guide* at subway entrances.

Toronto has so many diverse, decentralized neighborhoods that you may sometimes prefer your car to public transportation. The Metropolitan Toronto Convention and Visitors Association (MTCVA) has free maps that include area highways. Avoid heavy rush hour traffic. Street parking, when you can find it, is usually limited to one hour; although you may park overnight until 7:00 A.M. Day parking is also free at outlying subway stations. The city streets are arranged in a grid pattern, running north–south and east–west.

Ferries operated by the Metro Parks Department (416–392–8193) leave from the foot of Bay Street to the three Toronto Islands on a regular schedule. Taxis cruise throughout the city.

WHAT TO SEE AND DO

Museums

Toronto's museums are inspired and innovative places where even the fussiest kid will find something to tickle his or her fancy.

Bata Shoe Museum, 131 Bloor Street West (416–924–7463), proves that museums can be fun. Although the kids may be skeptical at first ("We're going to a shoe museum?"), this fascinating collection will soon win them over. Astronaut Buzz Aldrin's moon boot and tiny two-inch slippers worn by Chinese women with bound feet are part of the exhibit. There's a special rate for families.

Ontario Science Center, 770 Don Mills Road, Toronto; (416) 696–2127. Plan on spending the better part of the day here: you'll enjoy it as much as your kids. Located in a pleasant setting about a half hour from downtown, the museum is famous throughout North America for its innovative exhibits. There are over 800 exhibits, including The Space Hall, popular with older school-age children, teens, and adults. Interactive options include experiencing weightlessness by riding in a rocket chair and the Challenger Learning Centre, a hands-on space shuttle mission.

SPORT started as a temporary exhibit but was so well received it's now permanent. The hands-on, bodies-on exhibit includes a radar-clocked baseball pitch, climbing rock wall, bobsled video run, and the chance to judge sports performances, comparing scores with a replay of reactions from real experts.

Although especially relevant for high school students, even younger kids will be fascinated by some of the exhibits at the Chemistry Hall, called Matter, Energy, Change. Inside the Hall an ultraviolet light makes visitors' clothes glow. Kids can leave their shadow behind "trapped" by a strobe light on a phosphorescent vinyl wall and witness the melting and reforming of crystals on a large screen.

Inquire about OSCOTT weekend and vacation discovery classes for ages three to thirteen. There's a fee for parking and special family admission.

Royal Ontario Museum (ROM), 100 Queen's Park, Bloor Street at Avenue Road (416–586–4414), is Canada's largest museum and a real gem. The dinosaur exhibit is the biggest attraction for the younger set; the armor display and the Ancient Egypt gallery, especially the mummies, score with kids of school age and older. There are also artifacts from other civilizations—such as a complete Ming tomb—that everyone will find fascinating. The life sciences exhibit, complete with stuffed animals and live insects, is educational and fun. Be sure to inquire about Family Sundays, workshops for adults and kids. The McLaughlin Planetarium at the museum features star shows on astronomy and laser concerts. Both are closed on Monday.

"Please Touch" is the policy at the Ontario Science Center, which features more than 800 hair-raising exhibits. (Courtesy Metropolitan Toronto Convention and Visitors Association)

Historical Attractions

These next two sites are fun ways for all ages to learn more about this area's fascinating past.

Fort York, Garrison Road off Fleet Street; (416) 392–6907. "Toronto," a Huron Indian word for "meeting place," was established as a French fur trading post in 1750 and colonized by the British in 1793 on this site. This is also where The Battle of York was fought in the War of 1812. The American raid of York, resulting in the burning of the parliament building, led to retribution by the British, who invaded Washington and tried to burn down the president's residence. Although the building wasn't destroyed, the scorched walls outside had to be whitewashed resulting in what was thereafter known as The White House. All has been forgiven, of course, and today costumed soldiers and their wives give tours and are delighted to answer any questions you and the kids have.

Black Creek Pioneer Village, 1000 Murray Ross Parkway, Downsview, northwest Toronto (416–736–1733), is an authentic mid-nineteenth-century village that recreates life of that period in a most interesting way. Costumed interpreters are there to answer questions and demonstrate crafts of the day, such as broom making, weaving, baking, and tinsmithing. Over forty restored homes and shops plus a cafeteria

and restaurant are on the premises. Be sure to ask about their special
weekends throughout the year, which include an apple pie baking contest (where visitors can buy what's left after the judging) and fall fair.
Open mid-March–December 31.

PARKS AND ZOOS

High Park, west of downtown, south of Bloor Street and north of
Queensway, is accessible by streetcar or subway. It's a good place to toss a
frisbee or take a stroll. Considered Toronto's "Central Park" there's a
menagerie, hiking trails, sports fields, pond, and restaurant on the premises.
  Kortright Centre for Conservation is south of Major MacKenzie on
Pine Valley Drive in suburban Kleinburg, about a thirty-minute drive
(416–661–6600). Here kids and adults can commune with nature. Daily
1:00 P.M. programs vary according to the season, weather, and specialty of
the naturalist leader; reserve in advance. The scenic hiking trails are popular with families, and there's a marsh habitat on the premises. Ask about
special seasonal events: the fall honey festival (there's a beehouse here),
for instance, or the popular maple syrup demonstrations in spring.
  Metro Toronto Zoo, in Scarborough on Highway 401 at Meadowvale
Road (416–392–5900), is rated as one of the world's best. There are more
than 4,000 animals, eight tropical pavilions, and Monorail and Zoomobile
rides for viewing outdoor exhibits. Look for a schedule of the daily demonstrations and zookeeper talks. This is the only zoo to match prospective
mates of endangered species by computer. You can see the result of a successful match: the first Great Indian rhinoceros ever born in Canada.

Attractions

  CN Tower, 301 Front Street West (416–360–8500) the tallest free-
standing structure in the world, has a glass elevator that leads to three
observation decks, with spectacular views of the city, Toronto Islands,
and Lake Ontario. There's a revolving restaurant on top. But the most fun
for kids won't be the view: take them to the Tower base for the "awesome" Tour of the Universe simulator ride; (416) 363–TOUR.
  SkyDome is adjacent to the Tower (416–341–3663). The stadium has
a fully retractable roof and is home to the Toronto Blue Jays, Toronto
Argonauts, and other events (see SPECIAL EVENTS). Even if there's
nothing going on, sports nuts will enjoy the guided tour.
  Canada's Wonderland, Rutherford Road exit from Highway 400
(416–832–2205), a thirty-minute drive north of Toronto, is a full-service
amusement park. This enormous attraction is divided into seven theme
areas, including Hanna Barbera Land, Smurf Forest, and White Water
Canyon. The fifty-four rides include eight roller coasters. While your

teen might want to try Vortex, Canada's only suspended coaster, lead younger kids to their own ride area. A theme water park, strolling entertainers, dolphin shows, cliff divers, restaurants, shops, free summer concerts, and more make this an all-day commitment: arrive early.

Centreville, on Toronto's Centre Island, is accessible via a five-minute city ferry; (416) 363–1112. This theme park is comprised of a scaled-down version of a nineteenth-century Ontario village. School-age kids and younger tots will have a blast: There's a fire hall, with red fire engines to ride, model 1890s steam engine rides, paddleboats shaped like swans, minigolf, a cable car, and a farm with cows, geese, and pigs. Don't forget the Centre Island attractions: a public beach, park, picnic areas, maze, gardens, roller blade and bike rentals, and more. A free tram transports passengers around the island.

Harbourfront, on the south side of Queens Quay West, including York, John, and Maple Leaf Quays (415–973–3000), is a nonprofit cultural organization that produces events year-round, many of them free. The HarbourKid programs vary from month to month and might include free family concerts and family workshops. Call to ask if there's a Day Camp in session. Ages five to sixteen (divided into age groups) can register for one day or more. In the winter, there's free ice skating at York Quay, the world's largest artificial skating rink.

The **Hockey Hall of Fame,** inside BCE Palace at Front and Yonge streets; (416) 360–7735, opened in spring of 1993. Inside the $25 million, 51,000-square-foot building, you will find museum-style exhibits, theaters that show hockey's best plays, trivia games, and a plastic ice rink that the aspiring player can glide across. Walk through a recreation of the Montreal Canadiens' dressing room and feel the spirit that surges through Canadian hockey fans. The Hall of Fame's Bell Great Hall is expected to become the home of the precious Stanley Cup and is dedicated to Canadian hockey greats including Woody Dumart, Lanny McDonald, and Marcel Dionne.

The Hole, 257 Adelaide Street West (416–348–0519), is an artist-created indoor miniature golf course that stands out because it features a unique experience: candlelight golf on weekends. (Tell that to the folks back home!)

Ontario Place, 955 Lake Shore Boulevard West (416–965–7917), stretches out over three man-made islands into Lake Ontario. This is the place to be in the summer (open mid-May to Labor Day), particularly when the sun is shining and the lake seems to sparkle. Here you'll find strolling mimes and musicians, minigolf, and a water-play area with water slide, bumper boats, pedal boats, and Wilderness Adventure ride. The Children's Village is terrific, with a LEGO creative play center, award-winning playground, and more. Evenings are lively, with IMAX movies shown in the Six-Storey Cinesphere and frequent concerts, bands, and fireworks.

In addition to an admission charge, you'll pay extra for some things (such as bumper boats). There are lots of cafés, pubs, and restaurants.

Performing Arts

No matter when you visit, you're sure to find something exciting going on in the performing arts. Get the monthly events calendar, *About Town,* and the *Where Toronto* publication put out by the MTCVA, available at most hotels. Toronto has three daily papers with listings of events, including the "What's On" section in Thursday's *Toronto Star.*

The **Toronto Symphony** frequently performs young people's and special family concerts at Roy Thomson Hall (416) 593–4828. The Canadian Opera Company and National Ballet of Canada performances take place at O'Keefe Center; (416) 393–7474. In the summer the **Canadian Stage Company** stars in the outdoor Shakespearean festival "The Dream in High Park," which older kids may enjoy, particularly because of the setting. Call (416) 367–8243 for schedules.

Toronto has a large theater industry, with plays being performed in forty-odd theaters. These include the **Pantages Theater,** where the long-running *Phantom of the Opera* was playing at press time, and the **Elgin and Winter Garden** complex, with theatrical, musical, and dance performances. If you don't mind standing in line (arrive before the noon opening), Five Star Tickets (415–596–8211) sells half-price tickets to all arts events on the day of performance from their booth in front of the Eaton Centre on Dundas and Yonge streets, which they share with the MTCVA.

SPECIAL EVENTS

Sporting Events

The Toronto Maple Leafs, in the National Hockey League, play in Maple Leaf Gardens, Carlton and Church streets; (416) 977–1641. The big summer attraction is the Toronto Blue Jays, in the American League, winners of the 1992 World Series, who play in the SkyDome. Although games sometimes sell out, you can often get tickets at the box office (416–341–1000). The Toronto Argonauts football team also plays in the Skydome; call (416) 872–5000 for tickets. Get tickets for the Player's International Tennis Tournament, held in late July, by calling (416) 665–9777 or from Ticketmaster (416–870–8000), which also can provide tickets to some (but not all) sporting, theatrical, and other events.

Fairs, Festivals and Special Events

Call the Convention and Visitors Association for more information on the following events.

June: Benson & Hedges Symphony of Fire, fireworks competition at Ontario Place. Dragon Boat Race Festival on Toronto Islands, with traditional Chinese dragon-shaped boat races and concession stands.

August: Player's International Tennis Championship; Canadian National Exhibition, the world's largest annual fair. See Canadian arts, agriculture, architecture, and more at the Canadian National Exhibition.

Labor Day: Canadian National Air Show, over the harbor, can be watched from Ontario Place, Harbourfront, or Toronto Islands.

WHERE TO STAY

Toronto has two free reservations services: Accommodation Toronto (416–415–3800) is operated by the Hotel Association of Metropolitan Toronto and features more than one hundred luxury, moderate, and economy properties; Econo-Lodging Services (416–494–0541) offers hotels in all price ranges as well as short-term furnished apartments. There are also a number of bed and breakfast reservation services listed in the *Metropolitan Toronto* publication, free from the MTCVA, which sponsors seasonal package deals. Here are some choices for families.

Downtown

The **Delta Chelsea Inn,** 33 Gerrard Street West; (416) 595–1975/(800) 877–1133—Canada, New York, Ohio, Pennsylvania, or Michigan/(800) 877–1133—elsewhere in the United States. Family area with pool, separate adult pool, whirlpool, and games rooms, plus Children's Creative Centre with supervised activities, make this inn special. It houses 1,600 rooms and several restaurants.

Royal York Hotel, 100 Front Street West; (415) 368–2511/(800) 268–9411—Canada/(800) 828–7447—United States. Newly renovated, with 1,408 rooms, this hotel has a health club with pool and whirlpool plus a wading pool. The seven restaurants here include a coffee shop.

Midtown

Town Inn Hotel, 620 Church Street; (416) 964–3311/(800) 387–2755. This 200-suite hotel is a conveniently located, economical alternative to some of the area's pricier hotels. All suites have kitchen facilities: they're really small, but comfortable apartments. There's a heated pool in the basement that, while not fancy, keeps young kids happy, and tennis courts outdoors. Breakfast and underground parking available.

East/Parklands

Four Seasons Inn on the Park, 1100 Eglinton Avenue East; (416) 444–2561/(800) 268–6282—Canada/(800) 332–3442—United States.

There's also a Four Seasons in midtown Toronto (21 Avenue Road), but this is less pricey. Though not in the thick of things, it's close to attractions, such as the zoo and Science Center, and across from 600 acres of parkland where you can picnic, stroll, or jog. Inn Kids, an activity program for ages five to twelve, takes place seven days a week during the summer, and weekends year-round (free, except for lunch charge). Other features: indoor/outdoor pool, health club, squash and tennis, free parking, weekend packages, and dining room.

Scarborough

University of Toronto, Scarborough Campus, 1265 Military Trail; (416) 287–7369. Families on a budget love these eighty-one furnished town houses located in a beautiful, park-like Student Village, thirty minutes from downtown Toronto. Available from mid-May through the third week in August, units have equipped kitchens and sleep four to six in rooms with one or two twin beds (minimum stay two nights). There's a recreation center, free parking, and dining hall—but no TV, air conditioning, or room phones.

WHERE TO EAT

Toronto is packed with 5,000 restaurants, many reflecting the city's diverse ethnic population, including Greek, Italian, and Chinese. If you're exploring some of the various ethnic neighborhoods on foot, watch and ask where the locals eat. (While these explorations can be fascinating for adults who enjoy local color, kids might be bored since there's not much "action" in these neighborhoods, some of them thirty to forty minutes from downtown.)

The MTCVA has several guides listing restaurants, including *Toronto Day and Night,* which lists both eateries and shopping by neighborhood and category. Downtown has its share of fine dining spots, including these with family appeal: **Hard Rock Café-SkyDome,** 300 Brenner Boulevard, has great burgers and Canada's largest rock 'n roll collection; (416) 341–2388. Eat in style and watch your favorite team play at **Cafe on the Green,** Skydome Hotel, 45 Peter Street South, where the sports-theme dining room provides a great view of the SkyDome playing field; (416) 341–5045. **The Old Spaghetti Factory,** 54 The Esplanade, is economical, casual, and fun—and there's a children's menu; (416) 864–9761. **Mr. Greenjeans Galleria** has an entertainment theme that kids love and menus bigger than your table. It's located in the downtown's Eaton Centre, an enormous shopping mall; (416) 979–1212. (Cross the street to show the kids the World's Biggest Bookstore on Eaton Street.)

DAY TRIPS

Niagara Falls, 90 miles from Toronto, is one of the great natural wonders of the world. En route, stop by **Royal Botanical Gardens**, Hamilton, (30 minutes from downtown Toronto) to stroll among vibrant flowers. If you're headed to Montreal, stop in **Whitby**, a forty-minute drive from downtown, where **Cullen Gardens and Miniature Village** features flowers (there's a tulip festival every April), 140 miniature buildings (built to $\frac{1}{12}$ scale), puppet shows, and more. About an hour west of Toronto, near the town of Cambridge, is **African Lion Safari** (open until early October), where you can drive through game reserves in your own car or take a guided bus tour. Call (519) 623–2620.

FOR MORE INFORMATION

Metropolitan Toronto Convention and Visitors Association has multilingual information counselors and helpful publications. Call (416) 203–2500/(800) 363–1990, or write to MTCVA, Queen's Quay Terminal at Harbourfront Centre, 207 Queens Quay West, Box 126, Toronto, Ontario, Canada M51 1A7. You may visit their office in the Queen's Quay Terminal on weekdays or their Information kiosk at the Eaton Centre (corner Yonge and Dundas streets) seven days from 9:30 A.M. to 5:30 P.M. Call about additional kiosk locations during the summer. On Highway 401, at Winston Churchill Boulevard exit 333 off the eastbound lanes, stop by the Shell Info Centre, which has year-round, twenty-four-hour interactive computer facilities and a video on the area.

For visitor's information on the Province of Ontario, visit the Ontario Ministry of Tourism and Recreation's Travel Centre in the Eaton Centre, 220 Yonge Street, or call (416) 965–4008/(800) 268–3736.

Kids' Toronto, free at many locations, is an excellent monthly source for family-oriented events. Single issues are mailed for $2.50. Call (416) 481–5696, or write to them at 540 Mt. Pleasant Road, Suite 201, Toronto, Ontario M4S 2M6. Community Information Centre of Metro Toronto, (416) 392–0505, offers complete information on services for the disabled, twenty-four hours a day.

Emergency Numbers
Ambulance, fire, and police: 911
Poison Information Center: (416) 598–5900
Twenty-four-hour emergency service: Hospital for Sick Children, 555 University Avenue; (416) 597–1500
Twenty-four-hour pharmacy: Shopper's Drug Mart, 700 Bay Street at Gerrard (downtown); (416) 979–2424

INDEX

ABOUT THE AUTHOR

(Photo by Matthew Gillis)

Candyce H. Stapen is an expert on family travel. A member of the Society of American Travel Writers as well as the Travel Journalists Guild, she writes several family travel columns on a regular basis including a column for *Vacations* magazine and *The Washington Times*.

Her articles about family travel appear in a variety of newspapers and magazines including *Ladies' Home Journal, Family Circle, Parents, Family-Fun, USA Weekend, Better Homes and Gardens, Rocky Mountain News, The Boston Globe, Family Travel Times, The Miami Herald, Caribbean Travel and Life,* and *Cruises and Tours.*

She lives in Washington, D.C., and travels whenever she can with her husband and two children.